PSYCHOLOGY OF EMOTIONS, MOTIVATIONS AND ACTIONS

HANDBOOK ON PSYCHOLOGY OF MOTIVATION

NEW RESEARCH

PSYCHOLOGY OF EMOTIONS, MOTIVATIONS AND ACTIONS

Additional books in this series can be found on Nova's website under the Series tab.

Additional e-books in this series can be found on Nova's website under the e-books tab.

PSYCHOLOGY OF EMOTIONS, MOTIVATIONS AND ACTIONS

HANDBOOK ON PSYCHOLOGY OF MOTIVATION

NEW RESEARCH

JASON N. FRANCO
AND
ALEXANDER E. SVENSGAARD
EDITORS

Copyright © 2012 by Nova Science Publishers, Inc.

All rights reserved. No part of this book may be reproduced, stored in a retrieval system or transmitted in any form or by any means: electronic, electrostatic, magnetic, tape, mechanical photocopying, recording or otherwise without the written permission of the Publisher.

For permission to use material from this book please contact us:
Telephone 631-231-7269; Fax 631-231-8175
Web Site: http://www.novapublishers.com

NOTICE TO THE READER

The Publisher has taken reasonable care in the preparation of this book, but makes no expressed or implied warranty of any kind and assumes no responsibility for any errors or omissions. No liability is assumed for incidental or consequential damages in connection with or arising out of information contained in this book. The Publisher shall not be liable for any special, consequential, or exemplary damages resulting, in whole or in part, from the readers' use of, or reliance upon, this material. Any parts of this book based on government reports are so indicated and copyright is claimed for those parts to the extent applicable to compilations of such works.

Independent verification should be sought for any data, advice or recommendations contained in this book. In addition, no responsibility is assumed by the publisher for any injury and/or damage to persons or property arising from any methods, products, instructions, ideas or otherwise contained in this publication.

This publication is designed to provide accurate and authoritative information with regard to the subject matter covered herein. It is sold with the clear understanding that the Publisher is not engaged in rendering legal or any other professional services. If legal or any other expert assistance is required, the services of a competent person should be sought. FROM A DECLARATION OF PARTICIPANTS JOINTLY ADOPTED BY A COMMITTEE OF THE AMERICAN BAR ASSOCIATION AND A COMMITTEE OF PUBLISHERS.

Additional color graphics may be available in the e-book version of this book.

LIBRARY OF CONGRESS CATALOGING-IN-PUBLICATION DATA

Handbook on psychology of motivation : new research / editors, Jason N. Franco and Alexander E. Svensgaard.
 p. cm.
Includes index.
ISBN 978-1-62100-755-5 (hbk.)
1. Motivation (Psychology) I. Franco, Jason N. II. Svensgaard, Alexander E.
BF503.H364 2011
153.8--dc23
 2011038508

Published by Nova Science Publishers, Inc. † New York

CONTENTS

Preface vii

Chapter 1 Motivation in the Field of Tourism: An Analysis of Its Influence on Consumer Decisions and Its Implications for the Planning of Tourist Services 1
María Devesa Fernández, Marta Laguna García and Andrés Palacios Picos

Chapter 2 Motivation to Donate: New Perspectives from Psychology, Economics and Marketing 35
Jennifer Wiggins Johnson and Pamela E. Grimm

Chapter 3 Building the Future for Remote Indigenous Students in Australia: An Examination of Future Goals, Motivation, Learning and Achievement in Cultural Context 61
Dennis M. McInerney, Lyn Fasoli, Peter Stephenson and Jeannie Herbert

Chapter 4 Dietary Intake and Physical Activity Behavior in Commercial Weight-Loss Program Users: An Application of Organismic Integration Theory 85
Philip M. Wilson, Kimberly P. Grattan, Diane E. Mack, Chris M. Blanchard and Jenna D. Gilchrist

Chapter 5 Motivation for Creativity in Design: Its Nature, Assessment and Promotion 107
S. Kreitler and H. Casakin

Chapter 6 Influences of Motivational Factors on Educational Outcomes: Cultural and Gender Issues 125
Alexander Seeshing Yeung and Gurvinder Kaur

Chapter 7 Behavioral Consequences of Counterfactual Thinking: A Self-Evaluation Model 147
Maurissa P. Tyser and Sean M. McCrea

Chapter 8	A Trans-Contextual Model of Motivation in Physical Education *Vassilis Barkoukis and Martin S. Hagger*	**169**
Chapter 9	Cognitive and Motivational Factors for Reading: The Need for a domain Specific Approach to Motivation *Emma Medford and Sarah P McGeown*	**187**
Chapter 10	Motivation to Learn, Self-regulation and Academic Achievement: How Effective Are Study Skills Programmes? *Marcus Henning and Emmanuel Manalo*	**209**
Chapter 11	Theoretical Content of Physical Activity Websites for Persons with Depression *Paul D. Saville, Jennifer R. Tomasone, Desmond McEwan and Kathleen A. Martin Ginis*	**227**
Chapter 12	Intrinsic and Extrinsic Motivation among Japanese Elementary School Students *Junko Matsuzaki Carreira*	**245**
Chapter 13	Incentive Design Utilizing Intrinsic Motivation *Ryohei Matsumura and Norimasa Kobayashi*	**257**
Chapter 14	Secondary Students' Motivation and Learning Strategies Profiles: The Importance of an Autonomy-Supportive Classroom Structure *Kee Ying Hwa, Wang C. K. John, Lim B. S. Coral and Liu Woon Chia*	**271**
Chapter 15	Implicit Theories of Intelligence, Effort Beliefs, and Achievement Goals as Antecedents of Learning Motivation and Engagement *Dirk T. Tempelaar, Bart Rienties, Bas Giesber and Sybrand Schim van der Loeff*	**283**
Chapter 16	Motivation: Implications for Intervening with Adolescent Substance Abusers *Ashley Austi and Brett Engle*	**295**
Chapter 17	Motivation for Learning EFL among Japanese University Students *Junko Matsuzaki Carreira*	**307**
Chapter 18	The Association between Deceptive Motivations and Personality Disorders in Male Offenders *Alicia Spidel, Hugues Hervé and John C. Yuille*	**311**
Index		**341**

PREFACE

This book presents topical research in the study of the psychology of motivation. Topics discussed include motivation in the field of tourism; new perspectives in the psychology and economics of donating; commercial weight-loss programs and motivation; motivation for creativity in design and architecture; cognitive and motivational factors for reading; motivation to learn, self-regulation and academic achievement and the implicit theories of intelligence, effort beliefs, and achievement goals as antecedents of learning motivation and engagement.

Chapter 1 - In one of its many aspects, tourism may be considered a socio-psychological experience. Although factors such as socio-demographic characteristics affect tourism behavior, other factors related to subjective customer experience are emerging strongly to explain this complex process. This study summarizes the latest insights into one such complex process; individual motivation from the standpoint of consumption. Specifically, the authors review and discuss the concept as well as the factors that shape tourist motivation. Interest therein is justified by the key implications that motivation has on visitor decisions. Such consequences not only impact the initial stage –where product/destination is chosen– but go further, affecting perception and experience during the visit. The authors also explore the link between motivation and perceived image, visitor satisfaction and loyalty. In the tourist sector, motivation has become a meta-concept triggering traveler behavior and shaping various facets of tourist activities. Motivation thus provides an answer to three key questions in the tourist cycle: (i) reasons for traveling, or why; (ii) specific choice, or where; and (iii) outcome, or post-visit satisfaction. In order to answer these questions, the authors establish various motivational typologies and posit several proposals based on dimensionality, many linked to specific tourist sectors (convention attendees, senior visitors, rural tourists). The most recent studies to explore the topic have focused on analyzing the impact of motivation on individual behavior, positing models, and describing the impact on decision-making. In this line, academic papers addressing the positive relation which certain motivational factors have on consumer satisfaction and loyalty have shed much light on the issue. These works also point to a number of major differences in the assessment that individuals make of certain aspects of the visit/destination. This has enabled a series of factors to be established, describing the satisfaction indicators impacted by visit motivation (specific factors) as well as others that are independent thereof (general factors). Such findings have important implications for the planning and management of tourist products and destinations. The first concerns the need to understand visitor motivation as a prior requirement in an effort to ensure satisfaction and loyalty. The second refers to the need to identify different types of individuals based on their travel motivations, since these may shape expectations and valuation of the experience. This will enable efforts and resources to focus on the areas which prove most interesting to organizations and institutions charged with designing tourism offer, or will allow them to adapt to a greater or lesser extent to their strengths and comparative advantages.

Chapter 2 - Individual donations of money, time, blood, and organs, and the motivations that underlie the decision to donate, have long been of interest to researchers in psychology, economics, and marketing. While the early research in each of these fields was largely separate, the three fields have converged in the past ten years around a core question: *why* do individuals donate? This chapter reviews the current literature on motivations to donate from all three fields, examining the commonalities in theory and findings as well as the unique contributions of each of the fields to the authors overall understanding of donor motivations. The authors conclude with suggestions for future research that will continue to bring the three fields together and provide valuable information for charities and nonprofit organizations as they continue to seek donations from individuals.

Chapter 3 - Education is the corner stone of social justice because it is the basis of opportunity, but education as currently provided is failing Indigenous students in the Northern Territory (NT) of Australia. Ramsey estimated that 20 per cent of NT Indigenous students did not attend school, and, although those who were enrolled comprised 32 per cent of the NT secondary cohort, the number who achieved a Northern Territory Certificate of Education in 2000 amounted to only 6 per cent of the total school cohort. In 2009, 'educational outcomes in the bush remain abysmal'. Over half of the NT's Indigenous students leave school without completing secondary education. Many of them are, therefore, condemned to a life in which their potential is unrealised, and the fortunes of their families severely circumscribed. Little is known of what motivates or should motivate these young people to achieve successful school outcomes. This chapter reports on an Australian Research Council (ARC) funded research project, 'Building the future for Indigenous students', which asked 733 remote and very remote students what their hopes and dreams for the future were, what motivated them at school, and how they studied. Statistical analyses are used to establish the construct validity and reliability of psychological scales and to examine similarities and differences between very remote and remote Indigenous students, and a comparator group of 300 non-Indigenous students. The findings provide critical hard data on the Indigenous students' future visions and aspirations, motivation, and approaches to study.

Chapter 4 - Current estimates indicate the prevalence of excess body weight in adults inhabiting westernized countries is increasing. Many adults use dieting strategies and leisure-time physical activity (LTPA) in an attempt to mitigate the negative health effects of excess body weight, yet long-term adherence to these lifestyle behaviors central to weight management is poor. Motivation has been identified as a critical variable underpinning the decision to engage in, and maintain, healthy lifestyle habits in people seeking to lose fat mass or control body weight.

Chapter 5 - The chapter presents a new approach to motivation for creativity based on the cognitive orientation theory. The major theoretical constructs of this approach are motivational disposition, themes, four belief types, and behavioral program. The basic tool for assessment of motivation for creativity – the cognitive orientation questionnaire of creativity (COQ-CR) - is described as well as several studies carried out about the motivation of creativity of design students in architecture and engineering. The COQ-CR provides information not only about the level of motivation but also about the structural and thematic composition of motivation for creativity. It thus enables to characterize differences in motivation in different individuals and domains of creativity. Implications for design education include the need and possibility of embedding motivation for creativity training in the regular teaching and practice of design.

Chapter 6 - Motivation research has shown significant relations of self-concept and value of schooling to educational outcomes, but has not simultaneously scrutinized the relative influences of different constructs on various educational outcomes. In the present investigation, a sample of Australian students from 6 primary schools in Western Sydney (N = 730) completed a multidimensional self-concept scale that measured components of self-concept (competence and affect) for each scale and a motivational construct (value of schooling). They were also asked to rate their sense of identity. Their achievement scores were obtained by conducting both a reading and a numeracy test. Structural equation modeling (SEM) was applied to relate the motivational constructs (competence, affect, and value) to the outcomes (achievement and identity). Multivariate analysis of variance was also conducted to test cultural and gender differences in the motivational constructs. Results showed that students' sense of competence was the strongest predictor of achievement whereas value of schooling, was a strong predictor of both achievement and sense of identity. Australian students with an Asian ethnicity tended to be higher in their self-concepts (both competence and affect) compared to their Anglo peers. Girls were also slightly higher than boys in affect to learning. There were small ethnicity x gender interaction effects showing that the difference between the Asian and Anglo Australian students in self-concept (both competence and affect) was predominant for boys. Given that a sense of competence was found to be a strong predictor of achievement, it seems that educators should pay more attention to enhancing Anglo students' development of their sense of competence so as to maximize their potential. In addition, as value of schooling was also a strong predictor of both outcomes (achievement and identity), it is important to maintain the students' high level of value of school so that they can enjoy both short-term and long-term benefits of education.

Chapter 7 - Upward counterfactual thoughts identify how a prior performance could have been better. For example, after receiving a low grade on an important test, a student might think to him or herself "I should have studied more for the test." Such thoughts have been linked to increased intentions to improve in the future and better subsequent performance. One would therefore expect the student in this example to increase his or her study effort in the future. Of course, people do not always act out of such conscientious motives. Individuals often attempt to shift the blame for their failure elsewhere rather than seek to improve, and in other cases persist only out of a reluctance to admit failure. The authors propose a new theoretical model integrating theories of self-regulation and self-evaluation to explain the consequences of counterfactual thinking for motivation and performance. The authors suggest the effects of upward counterfactual thoughts crucially depend upon their implications for self-evaluation. Currently active self-evaluation motives determine whether upward counterfactuals are used to excuse poor performance, motivate additional effort, or justify prior decisions. Moreover, counterfactuals that suggest personal responsibility for prior outcomes appear to accentuate the behavioral consequences of these thoughts.

Chapter 8 - The trans-contextual model of motivation has been developed to describe and explain the motivational processes by which motivation from one context can be transferred to another. The model comprises an integration of self-determination theory, the hierarchical model of intrinsic and extrinsic motivation, and the theory of planned behaviour. This chapter reviews the rationale for integrating these theories into the trans-contextual model and outlines recent developments in research using the model. Empirical data from the application of the trans-contextual model in the context of physical education are presented. These data provide support for the model's assumptions and highlight the efficacy of the model to describe the mechanisms by which support for autonomous motivation and motivational regulations in educational contexts (e.g., physical education) can lead to motivation in other contexts (e.g., leisure time physical activity). Finally, avenues for future research on the conceptual and methodological aspects of the model are outlined.

Chapter 9 - This study examined the importance of both cognitive and motivational factors for children's reading attainment. Furthermore, the nature of motivation that contributes to children's reading attainment was examined: whether domain specific (reading motivation) or general (school motivation). One hundred and five children (44 boys, aged 8 - 9) completed assessments of reading skill, cognitive ability (verbal IQ, phonological decoding and memory) and questionnaires examining their motivation and competency beliefs for reading (domain specific) and school (general). It was found that both cognitive and motivational factors contributed unique variance to children's reading attainment; however only children's intrinsic reading motivation and reading competency beliefs explained variance in their reading skills; extrinsic reading motivation, school motivations and school competency beliefs did not. The importance of considering both cognitive and specific motivational factors for reading instruction and intervention are discussed.

Chapter 10 - *Background:* There is an established body of research that links various forms of motivation to academic achievement. It has further been documented that students' engagement in educational activities is moderated by motivation and self-regulatory processes, and levels of the latter processes have been shown to be associated with outcome measures of effort, persistence, choice, and achievement. Because of these apparent connections, study skills courses are often provided in universities and other tertiary institutions to ameliorate student problems in motivation, self-regulation, and achievement. However, the effectiveness of such courses, as well as the mechanisms by which they may work, have not been sufficiently examined in research. *Purpose:* The purpose of this study was to assess the impact of a study skills course on students' levels of motivation and self regulation, and ultimately their academic achievement. The main research questions were: (1) Do students who attend study skills courses differ from those who do not in their levels of motivation and self regulation? (2) Do students who participate in such courses evidence change in their levels of motivation and self regulation? (3) Does completion of study skills courses contribute to better academic outcomes? *Method:* Three hundred and seventeen students (241 female, 76 male), predominantly from social science and education disciplines, volunteered to participate in this study. The students were asked to complete a demographic survey and the Learning and Study Skills Strategies Inventory (LASSI) at the beginning and at the end of an academic semester. A study skills course was offered to all these students, and comparisons were subsequently made between those who participated in the course and those who did not. In addition, with their permission, academic grades were obtained for all the students. *Results:* Statistical analyses incorporating a hierarchical regression procedure revealed a number of significant findings. With regard to attendance of the study skills course, significant correlations were found with the students' scores on the LASSI attitude

(ATT) scale and their age. With regard to the academic grades obtained by the students, significant correlations were found with attendance of the course, the students' age, and changes in the LASSI ATT and motivation (MOT) scales. Older students who attended the course evidenced improvements in the LASSI information processing (INP), selecting main ideas (SMI), and use of study aids (STA) scales. A comparison of the students according to their attendance of the course also revealed that those who did not attend subsequently evidenced increases in their scores on the LASSI anxiety (ANX) scale and decreases in their scores on the STA and self testing (SFT) scales. *Discussion and Conclusion:* The findings indicate that students who possessed better attitudes and interest in academic success, and those who were older, were more likely to attend the study skills course. In turn, students who attended the course, and those who were older, achieved better grades. Better grade achievement could therefore be partly explained by the better attitudes that attendees bring to their studies, as well as possibly the experience and maturity in outlook of the older students leading them to apply more of the study techniques advised in the course. Finally, indications of some deterioration in anxiety and application of study techniques among those who did not attend the study skills course – not observed among those who attended the course – suggest a more stable management of the demands of tertiary education among the latter group. In conclusion therefore, the findings of this research suggest that both the attitude and maturity that students bring to their studies, as well as input from study skills courses, have significant impact on grade achievement.

Chapter 11 - Because physical activity (PA) messages based on behavior change theories have been found to enhance intentions, motivation, and PA behavior, efforts need to be directed toward making such information available to sedentary individuals. Previous research has identified a lack of theory-based information in PA websites aimed at increasing PA among the general population; however, with the exception of the spinal cord injury population, the content of PA websites directed toward populations with chronic health conditions remain largely unexplored. Because research has identified PA as an effective means for preventing and treating depression, this study was designed to extend scientific knowledge by evaluating the theoretical content of PA websites specifically designed for people with depression. Findings indicated that approximately two-thirds of messages on PA websites targeting people with depression were theory-based. The majority of messages concerned individuals' outcome expectations, while relatively few messages were devoted to self-regulation or self-efficacy messages. This is disconcerting because both self-efficacy and self-regulation are important theoreical constructs that can enhance the influence of PA information on readers' PA beliefs and behavior. Moreover, messages based on self-efficacy and self-regulation have been shown to be particularly useful for influencing behavior in people with depression. Therefore, PA websites aimed at people with depression would benefit from including additional theory-based messages that embody an equal distribution of all the theoretical constructs. Because the Internet has become a primary source of health-related information for many individuals looking to get physically active, the current study identifies a specific need to improve the content of websites designed to increase PA among individuals with depression. Therefore, future investigations should be directed toward analyzing the content of PA websites intended for other populations with chronic health conditions that may also be seeking to increase their PA levels for both mental and physical health benefits.

Chapter 12 - To elucidate development and gender differences in motivation between 20 years ago and now in Japanese elementary school, this study investigated intrinsic and extrinsic motivation using a questionnaire developed by Sakurai and Takano (1985). Third, fourth, fifth, and sixth graders in two elementary schools, located in a suburb of Tokyo, were selected to participate in the present study. The total number of participants in this research was 485. This study revealed that there is more of a developmental decline in intrinsic motivation among elementary school pupils, compared to those 20 years ago; gender differences are almost similar to 20 years ago.

Chapter 13 - : In this article, the authors introduce a mathematical model in economics called principal agent model. The authors then present the authors work that extends a standard principal agent model by referring to the literature in psychology. Principal agent model is used for the design of a contract regarding a two-person relationship called agency relationship. In an agency relationship, the principal hires the agent to work for her. Due to the private information the agent possesses, it is impossible for the principal to specify the work in detail. Instead, the model suggests the contract that controls the effort level of the agent indirectly by providing adequate outcome-based incentives. Standard principal agent models in economics consider only extrinsic incentives. However, the literature in psychology shows that intrinsic motivation is also important. The authors thus extended the standard model by introducing intrinsic motivation.

Chapter 14 - The aim of this research is to profile secondary school students' motivated strategies for learning using Pintrich and De Groot's Motivated Strategies for Learning Questionnaire (MSLQ). The sample of the study consisted of 382 secondary students from Singapore. The students completed the MSLQ, Learning Climate Questionnaire, and Academic Self-Regulation Questionnaires. The results of the cluster analysis found four unique clusters with differing MSLQ profiles. Students with either high or average MSLQ, regardless of anxiety levels, seems to perform better in their academic performance. However, students with very low MSLQ scores performed badly for their tests. Having an autonomy-supportive learning climate and more autonomous regulations may be the keys to enhance students' motivation and learning strategies.

Chapter 15 - This empirical chapter focuses on the analysis of the Motivation and Engagement Wheel, a framework for learning motivation designed to integrate several theoretical perspectives, whilst at the same time offering a use-inspired approach suitable for practitioners. The framework encompasses aspects of cognitive views on motivation as developed by Pintrich, attributions and expectancy and valuing dimensions, self-regulation, planning and task management, and self-efficacy. The architecture of the framework consists of four higher order dimensions, being the adaptive cognitive, the adaptive behavioral, maladaptive cognitive or impeding, and maladaptive behavioral dimensions, shaped by 11 first-order dimensions. The suitability of this integrative motivation theory for practical purposes is based on the presumption of changeability of these dimensions: motivation is learnable. Using a sample of first year university students (N=2587) in a collaborative learning context based on problem-based learning, the authors investigate this aspect of malleability of motivations by developing a model that explains motivational factors from stable, individual difference antecedents. Implicit theories of intelligence and associated conceptions such as beliefs about the role of effort in learning and goal setting behavior serve the role of these stable antecedents. Implicit theories of intelligence refer to beliefs people develop about the nature of their intelligence, and contrast two opposite beliefs: that of the 'entity theorists', who view intelligence as being a fixed internal characteristic, and the 'incremental theorists', who believe that intelligence is fluid and can be cultivated by learning. Students endorsing an entity view are hypothesized to see effort as a negative characteristic, signaling lack of intelligence, whereas those with an incremental view develop a positive effort belief: exerting effort is the key to cultivating intelligence. In turn, implicit theories and effort views determine students' goal setting behavior, especially whether students are stronger mastery or performance goal oriented. Relationships between these antecedents implicit theories, effort beliefs, and goal setting behavior, and the dimensions of the Motivation and Engagement Wheel, are investigated with structural equation models. Results indicate that implicit theories of intelligence are only indirectly impacting motivational factors, but that effort views play a crucial role in explaining both goal setting behavior and motivation and engagement.

Chapter 16 - Client motivation has emerged as an increasingly important topic for substance abuse treatment providers and researchers and has been implicated as one of the most important predictors of successful treatment engagement and outcome. There is a growing interest in identifying and understanding the specific factors that both enhance and inhibit motivation for substance use change among clients, particularly among specific subgroups of substance use clients including adolescent substance users. Because it is widely recognized that motivation for change plays a critical role in treatment response, it is increasingly expected that substance abuse treatment providers take an active role in enhancing client motivation for change. As adolescent substance users present with unique needs and challenges particular to their developmental stage (i.e., striving toward autonomy and individuation), substance use patterns (i.e., binge use vs. dependency) and reasons for entering treatment (i.e., mandated by parents, schools or courts), motivational interventions may be particularly appropriate. Motivational interviewing (MI) is a person-centered and increasingly evidence-based approach for addressing substance abuse among adolescents. Fundamental components that comprise the "spirit" of MI will be discussed particularly as they apply to work with high-risk adolescents. Evidence-based interventions targeting client motivation, such as MI, espouse a very different view of motivation as it relates to substance use and recovery. These interventions do not view motivation as an explanation for treatment failure and continued substance use problems but rather as the key to engaging clients in the behavior change process.

Chapter 17 - In second language (L2) learning, the authors should pay attention to motivation, referring to "the process whereby goal-directed activity is instigated and sustained" because "motivation can predict important academic outcomes like performance and persistence". For several decades, motivation has long been considered one of the key factors that determine L2 achievement and attainment . "Due to its great importance, L2 motivation has been the subject of a considerable amount of research in recent decades, exploring the nature of this complex construct and how it affects the L2 learning process".

Chapter 18 - The detection of deception is an integral part of any forensic assessment. Unfortunately, the motives underlying the use of deceptive strategies by offenders and how these may differ between different types of personality-disordered offenders are not well established. The aim of the present study was to identify different deception-related motivations in a sample of offenders and to examine the relationship between these motivations and personality pathology. Archived file and videotaped information for 103 Canadian federal offenders were reviewed in order to identify personality disorder pathology, as well as patterns of deceptive motivations (compulsive, secretive, avoiding punishment, avoiding negative evaluation, protective, to obtain a reward, to heighten self-presentation, altruistic, and careless). In general, as expected within a forensic context, offenders lied to avoid punishment. With respect to the other motivational categories investigated, personality pathology was found to significantly mediate the motivational patterns leading to offender-perpetrated deception. The relevance of these findings to credibility assessment and personality pathology is discussed.

In: Handbook on Psychology of Motivation
Editors: J. N. Franco and A. E. Svensgaard
ISBN: 978-1-62100-755-5
© 2012 Nova Science Publishers, Inc.

Chapter 1

MOTIVATION IN THE FIELD OF TOURISM: AN ANALYSIS OF ITS INFLUENCE ON CONSUMER DECISIONS AND ITS IMPLICATIONS FOR THE PLANNING OF TOURIST SERVICES

María Devesa Fernández[1]*, Marta Laguna García[1] and Andrés Palacios Picos[2]

[1]Fac. CC. Sociales, Jurídicas y de la Comunicación, Universidad de Valladolid, Plaza de la Tierra, Segovia, Spain
[2]Escuela de Magisterio, Universidad de Valladolid, Plaza de Colmenares s/n, Segovia, Spain

ABSTRACT

In one of its many aspects, tourism may be considered a socio-psychological experience. Although factors such as socio-demographic characteristics affect tourism behavior, other factors related to subjective customer experience are emerging strongly to explain this complex process.

This study summarizes the latest insights into one such complex process; individual motivation from the standpoint of consumption. Specifically, we review and discuss the concept as well as the factors that shape tourist motivation. Interest therein is justified by the key implications that motivation has on visitor decisions. Such consequences not only impact the initial stage –where product/destination is chosen– but go further, affecting perception and experience during the visit. We also explore the link between motivation and perceived image, visitor satisfaction and loyalty.

In the tourist sector, motivation has become a meta-concept triggering traveler behavior and shaping various facets of tourist activities. Motivation thus provides an answer to three key questions in the tourist cycle: (i) reasons for traveling, or why; (ii) specific choice, or where; and (iii) outcome, or post-visit satisfaction.

---

* Tel. +34 921 112122; Fax: +34 921 112101, Email: mdevesa@eco.uva.es

In order to answer these questions, we establish various motivational typologies and posit several proposals based on dimensionality, many linked to specific tourist sectors (convention attendees, senior visitors, rural tourists).

The most recent studies to explore the topic have focused on analyzing the impact of motivation on individual behavior, positing models, and describing the impact on decision-making. In this line, academic papers addressing the positive relation which certain motivational factors have on consumer satisfaction and loyalty have shed much light on the issue. These works also point to a number of major differences in the assessment that individuals make of certain aspects of the visit/destination. This has enabled a series of factors to be established, describing the satisfaction indicators impacted by visit motivation (specific factors) as well as others that are independent thereof (general factors).

Such findings have important implications for the planning and management of tourist products and destinations. The first concerns the need to understand visitor motivation as a prior requirement in an effort to ensure satisfaction and loyalty. The second refers to the need to identify different types of individuals based on their travel motivations, since these may shape expectations and valuation of the experience. This will enable efforts and resources to focus on the areas which prove most interesting to organizations and institutions charged with designing tourism offer, or will allow them to adapt to a greater or lesser extent to their strengths and comparative advantages.

1. INTRODUCTION

In a classic Psychological report, Morgan (1961) relates the case of a three year old child who, after undergoing a medical examination, was admitted to hospital as he presented disturbances in his growth. After seven days of a normal nutritional diet, the child died. It was discovered at autopsy that the child had suffered serious problems in the adrenal glands. It is well known that these glands control the concentration of saline in the blood. When subjected to the hospital diet, the child lost salt without the capacity to compensate for it, which led to his being struck down. The parents then reported that the child had never eaten in a normal manner: he detested sweet things but loved the salty. He liked to eat the salt instead of the potato chips; lick it off the salted cod; and the parents realised that they needed to put three times as much of this condiment in his foods than for the rest of their children. They very often gave him a teaspoonful of this condiment as an aperitif. According to the parents, which came as no great surprise, that when he was about to turn two, he took a salt shaker and ate the entire contents.

As we have seen, it is not always easy to understand the causes of behaviour. Nevertheless, on other occasions our actions are easily understood by others. In both cases, we are referring to motivation as a theoretical construct that explains and gives sense to our actions, strange as they may seem to us. Motivation makes the causes of behaviour understandable and, therefore, seems closely linked to the action.

Thus, it is understood, from an already classic study of the subject, that motivation refers to the many conditions that prompt behaviour (in our example, a salt deficiency), as the motivating behaviour for this condition (the quest for saline homeostasis) or for the aims, goals and objectives of such behaviour (theft of the saltshaker, for instance). These processes can be studied from the *motivational cycles* that explain the greater part of human behaviour (Figure 1).

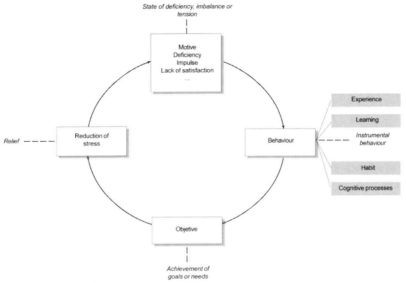

Source: Authors' own material.

Figure 1. The Motivational Cycle.

The motive, which may also be referred to as the impulse, deficiency or need, is the element that initiates the cycle. Motive relates to the state that activates and directs the individual's behaviour. Etymologically, the word is derived from the Latin *motio*, which means movement. A motive, therefore, is that which moves act or provokes action.

In the field of tourism, Gnoth (1997) distinguishes between motives and motivations. The motives tend to be more global and less related to a specific situation, while motivations are cognitive in nature and would relate more to a specific product or destination. While motivations reflect observable aspects, which can be measured objectively, motives bring a more profound understanding of what leads tourists to undertake certain activities.

Motives can have different causes and, like external stimuli, can initiate many internal feelings. In the first instance, we spoke of the physiological needs, or primary needs, serving tissular homeostasis. Hunger, thirst or sleepiness would be other very simple examples of this type of motive. Other more complex motives have their basis in hormonal processes and their objective is the internal regulation of the organism, as we stated in the introduction to this chapter.

However, other natural psychosocial motivations exist (designated as secondary needs), which have their origin in the world around us, such as friendship, prestige, the motivation to achieve and self-actualisation. These are a product of learning and the environment and, therefore, they are greatly influenced by social values and historical and cultural contexts. They usually reflect the aspirations, life goals and deepest anxieties of the individual and, thus, are fully subjective in character as each person may experience different needs and varying degrees of intensity.

We can, then, distinguish between *primary motives*, linked to the maintenance of our biological systems and vital to our survival, and *secondary motives* which are the product of learning and social interaction.

A second component of the motivational cycle is instrumental behaviour which is triggered by a lack or an impulse. It is, therefore, the visible (observable) part of the motivational cycle. Its nature is purposeful as it has but one objective: the reduction of initial tension. It depends, to a great extent, on learning, cognitive processes, experience and habit.

Achieving the goal is the third element of the process. In the case of the primary motives, it concerns the re-establishment of lost equilibrium and, therefore, is easy to observe and study. Not so with the secondary motives which, in certain cases, remain hidden even for the subject himself. This stage, owing to the influence of certain theories which will be analysed later, is usually referred to as 'incentive'.

Logically, if we achieve the reduction of a drive, a new process is initiated (a new cycle) with other needs and with new instrumental behaviours. If the intended objective is not attained, the original impulse is abandoned and new strategies and instrumental behaviours are set to work or the exiting impulse persists.

2. GENERAL THEORIES OF MOTIVATION

The approach that has just been presented adequately fits the *reactive explanations* that characterise human motivation. Under this approach, human beings are seen as responsive subjects (reactive beings), who act in a way that changes both internal and external states. Motivation is initiated at the point that an emotion, a biological or psychosocial need, or an external stimulus causes an imbalance in the individual. In either case, the goal of motivational behaviour always involves satisfying a lack and reducing a state of tension.

Nevertheless, since the end of the 19th century and throughout the 20th century, different theoretical models of the nature of human motivation have developed within Psychology, though not all fit the reactive model. They are general theories of human personality, which, indirectly, explain the nature of motivation. Hence, explanations of motivation can be categorised as psychoanalytical, behaviourist, humanistic or cognitive (Table 1).

Although Freud certainly never intended to devise an explanation of human motivation, it is beyond question that his theory explicitly presumes a frame of reference of great significance to human motivation. For this author, human drives form part of one's biological architecture and are responsible for regulating actions. But, since these drives are of an unconscious nature, the behaviour is, to a great extent, outside of the conscious control of the individual. Given that these impulses are libidinous in nature and that life is a constant quest for pleasure (the more the better; and better now than tomorrow), this theory can be considered as hedonic and homeostatic: the pleasure, when found, re-establishes the lost equilibrium and momentarily calms our internal drives.

With the pinnacle of behaviourism and the standing of Skinner, drives and impulses gave way to the *incentive* (reinforced behaviour) as the motivational explanation for behaviour. Although it remains a hedonic theory, since the incentives are pleasure seeking, well-being and the avoidance of pain, it is the environment and its consequences that explain the conduct instrumental to behaviour. From this perspective, the behaviours that are reinforced will be maintained, by reason of their consequences; the evidence being that these behaviours are sustained over time. A person will be motivated by doing something to the extent that, through his personal history, if he perceives that, by it, pleasant consequences are going to be obtained.

Table 1. Theories of motivacion

Sense of motivation	Most significant representatives	Explanation of the nature of motivation
Motivation as an individual's own impulse	Psychoanalysis (Freud)	The true nature of human motivation is unconscious and, therefore, arises from within and from the depths of the human psyche: the core human motivations must be sought deep within the unconscious mind.
	Humanistic (Maslow)	Human needs are distributed according to a hierarchy of the most urgent and basic to the most valued such as self-actualisation.
Motivation as an attraction derived from an object.	Behaviourist (Skinner)	Overt behaviour is the result of contingent consequences which flow from it. It is, therefore, the environment and its stimuli that explain human behaviour.
Motivation as a combination of the impulse of the subject and/or of the attraction of the object.	Cognitive Behaviour Theory (Beck)	The emotions and behaviour of an individual are determined by the way such individuals perceive the world.

Source: Adapted from Mesurado (2008) by the authors.

We can say that the incentive *pulls* the behaviour unlike the drives and impulses that *push* the behaviour. Both aspects are of enormous interest for tourist motivation since they have given rise to theories of great significance for the topic at hand.

Maslow's hierarchy theory had a great impact on the explanation of human motivations and, today, it remains one of the most cited in the field of motivation in general and of tourist motivation in particular. Set within the positions that came to be designated as reactive, it considers motivation as the tendency to reduce or eliminate the tension produced by a deficient state, which arises from needs that are both biological and psychosocial in nature. However, its true significance stems from the idea of establishing an order in which importance is attributed to each motive or impulse in what is known as the Hierarchy of Needs model or the Pyramid of Human Needs (Table 2).

This idea is based on a series of concepts. One of the most relevant, perhaps central, is to establish large groups of impulses, such as those closest to biological needs or to those more complex in nature relating to belonging, knowledge or self-actualisation. Moreover, another of the ideas advanced by Maslow's theory is that for a need to lead to an action, the lower order needs must first be resolved. When a need has been fulfilled it stops being a motive for behaviour.

This approach supposes that, necessarily, one has to climb the steps of the pyramid sequentially: it is neither possible to consider self-actualisation when one does not have the assurance of daily sustenance nor to seek aesthetic contemplation of the world on an empty stomach. However, today, it is deemed that individuals do not always fulfil the requirements of the hierarchical structure. That is to say, save for those of physiological character which determine survival, it is possible to satisfy needs located on higher levels without having to totally fulfil those of a lower order. For example, a person may first decide to fulfil their needs for esteem before those of security or belonging.

Table 2. Maslow's Hierarchy of Needs: adapted for the field of Tourism

General Motivations		Tourist Motivations
Rest, cleanliness, hunger, thirst, sex…	Physiological Needs	Escape from monotony, rest, relief of tension…
Stability in work, physical health, mental health …	Security	Health tourism, keep fit, cures for stress, bathing in seawater, etc.
Love, family unity, feeling loved and accepted, sense of belonging…	Belonging	Family togetherness, social relations, ancestry and ethnicity tourism…
Obtaining status, improving self-esteem, achieving something, being competent at something, social recognition…	Respect	Prestige, professional recognition, social status…
Knowledge of self and of the world, exploration…	Know and Understand	Interest in other cultures and other peoples, tourism studies …
Appreciation of beauty	Aesthetics	Expressions of culture and art, cultural tourism and monuments…
Personal development, self-exploration, realisation of own potential…	Self-actualisation	Internal satisfaction, self-discovery…

Source: Author's own material.

The cognitive view of motivation is based on the theoretical assumption that the emotions and conduct of an individual are determined to a large extent by the way in which the said individual has structured the world. The influence of this theory arose after the so-called *cognitive revolution* of the 1960s. One of its most notable characteristics is that it directs attention towards complex aspects of psychological processes, such as experience, expectations and beliefs: processes that are all encompassed within the sphere of the conscious and voluntary control of the individual. There are good examples of this school's studies that focus on achievement motivation, target planning, or theories based on expectancy/valency models. Many models exist within this cognitive paradigm, though all of them share the idea that the central point of the motivational process is the search for consistency in our thinking. Examples of this approach are: the dissonance theory (Festinger, 1957), psychological reactance (Brehm, 1966), the self-perception model (Bem, 1972) and equity theory (Adams, 1965; Homans, 1961). The theories, which have had particular relevance, are those which have focused their interest on the role of expectations and valency – as anticipatory processes for action – in determining behaviour, as in the development models of Atkinson (1957), Feather (1959) and Vroom (1964).

3. TOURIST MOTIVATION

In the field of tourism, motivation – the study of which has its origin in the aforementioned works of Maslow (1943, 1954) – has become a meta-concept that acts as a trigger for travellers' conduct and an explanatory factor of almost all aspects related to tourist activity.

Thus, motivation allows us to answer three essential questions about the tourist cycle: (i) the reasons for the trip, or *why*; (ii) the specific choice, or *where*; and (iii) the results achieved, or *satisfaction* of the visit (Castaño, Moreno, García and Crego, 2003). Though motives are only one of multiple variables that explain behaviour, they are the point from which the decision making process emanates (Crompton and McKay, 1997).

As is evident from the literature review, motivation is a multidimensional, dynamic and complex construct. *Multidimensional* because, usually, the people who travel do so not just for one motive but through the convergence of a more or less varied set of them. *Dynamic* because the motivation of individuals in general, and of tourists in particular, may vary over time.

Additionally, the reasons that lead to travel may vary from one person to another, from one market sector to another, from one destination to another and can even be modified in the next decision process (Kozak, 2002). Finally, motivation is *complex* by its emotional and cognitive nature because it is conditional on multiple factors of a diverse nature such as personal characteristics (age, state of health, life-style, prior experience), social (family influences, reference groups), economic (income, personal finance), or cultural (pride, patriotism) (Gnoth, 1997).

3.1. Types of Tourist Motivation

The importance and significance that motivation has for the behaviour of individuals has meant that this has been studied by various disciplines including psychology, sociology, marketing and communications. This factor has caused it to be classified from different perspectives. Table 3 depicts some of the most common typologies of motivation and their application to the field of tourism.

In addition to these typologies of a general nature, there are others, such as those proposed by the United Nations World Tourism Organisation. This international body in its *Recommendations for Tourism Statistics* (UNWTO, 1994), formulated with the aim of promoting the international comparison of tourism data, established a distinction between two classes of motivation.

The principal motive for the visit, which is defined as that *without which the journey would not have been undertaken*; and secondary motives that may imply an additional attraction which reinforces the decision to travel or to choose a particular destination (Table 4).

More recently, this institution has extended this classification in response to a dynamic and growing boom in the tourist sector. Starting from the idea, presented above, that individuals always have a primary motive, but may also perform other kinds of activities of a secondary nature during their travels, they established a new taxonomy. In it, *professional* or *business motives* acquire their own identity, constituting a distinct typology. The rest of the motivations established in the 1994 classification are included within *personal motives* and are extended with new ones such as motives of education, shopping or the movement of passengers (Table 4).

Table 3. Types of tourist motivation

Types of motivation	Definition	Situation
Positives	These are those that stimulate or reinforce a behaviour or acquisition of a service.	A person who likes to get in touch with nature and appreciates the wealth of nature will be positively motivated towards ecologically rich destinations.
Negatives	These determine rejection, non-performance or non- utilization of tourist services.	This type of motivation is what makes some people avoid travelling to certain destinations due to their fear of flying or from visiting a theme park because they have an aversion to the speed or height involved in certain attractions.
Primary	These cause people buy a particular class or category of product.	There are visitors who enjoy cultural contact and they want to augment it but without any preference for a particular destination, such as Italy.
Secondary	These guide the consumer to purchase a particular brand, service format or use of tourist accommodation.	This kind of motivation makes the visitor choose a destination by displaying a marked predisposition. It would be exhibited were, for example, a tourist to only want a sun and beach holiday in Spain. In such a situation, the individual would not consider opting for another holiday destination with a similar climate.
Rational	These are based on objective factors and specific, logical considerations that are easily identifiable and measurable. They are usually associated with the objective characteristics of the product.	A visitor goes to a tourist district to spend a public holiday because it is the closest to their place of residence.
Emotional	These involve a choice or behaviour which is based on feelings and personal, subjective criteria such as affection for, bonding with, pride in the product and the pleasure associated with it.	To celebrate their 25th (silver) wedding anniversary, a couple decides to return to the same destination and stay in the same hotel as they did on their honeymoon.
Intrinsic	An individual engages in certain activities for the pleasure experienced while performing them (exploring, learning and trying to understand something new).	These are the motives that induced/ pushed the great travellers of past centuries. Their desire to know and explore led them to travel to unknown places for the pleasure it involved for them, the adventure of travel.
Extrinsic	These are associated with activities or decisions which are actually a means of achieving a goal sought by the individual.	A visitor may go to a spa tourist destination, not because he wishes to, but to seek the reputed health benefits characteristic of its waters.
Conscious	These are those reasons that are perceived and accepted by the individual which influence his decisions. They are usually linked to rational motives.	A visitor chooses to go by plane because it is the fastest method of getting to the place he wants to visit.
Unconscious	These refer to factors that have an important bearing on consumers' decisions, but which are not usually consciously accepted. They are usually associated with emotional motives.	Compulsive buying behaviour as a symptom of emotional disorders.

Source: Author's own material.

**Table 4. Classification of motives for visits or journeys proposed
by the World Tourism Organisation (UNWTO)**

Types of tourist motivation 1994	Types of tourist motivation 2008

1. Leisure, recreation and holidays
2. Visits to family and friends
3. Business and professional reasons
4. Health Treatment
5. Religion / pilgrimages
6. Other reasons
	1. Personal reasons
	   1.1. Holidays, recreation and leisure
	   1.2. Visits to family and friends
	   1.3. Education and training
	   1.4. Health and medical care
	   1.5. Religion / pilgrimages
	   1.6. Shopping
	   1.7 Transit
	   1.8. Other reasons
	2. Business and professional reasons

Source: UNTWO (1994, 2010).

3.2. Principal Theories of Tourist Motivation

The importance of motivation as a trigger for tourist behaviour has generated a series of theoretical developments and applied studies whose zenith occurred in the 1980s, though some earlier studies existed but were developed later. Some of the lines of argument come from the general theories already discussed, especially mentioning Maslow, but they advanced in different directions.

Although differences exist between the said theories, the researchers do not perceive these approaches as competing, but as elements that contribute to the understanding of tourist behaviour in different ways. It is, thus, difficult for them to agree on a single theory to explain tourist behaviour (Hung and Petrick, 2011). Below are listed some of the most important theories that have had a great impact on tourist motivation. From them, we can highlight some of particular interest, inter alia Crompton's theoretical model and Iso-Ahola and Pearce's seeking-escaping dichotomy model.

a) The Push-Pull Model

One of the theories most used in the study of tourist motivation is the model of push-pull factors. This theory was applied to tourism in the 1970s and 80s, primarily by two authors, Dann and Crompton. Later, it became the frame of reference for numerous studies on motivation in the field of tourism.

Dann (1977, 1981) states that tourist motivation has two fundamental dimensions: on the one hand, the need to escape (stress, the pattern of daily life, the work environment) that are referred to as push factors. On the other hand, the pull factors are constituted from the need to seek out historical sites or fine art museums in certain settings. In turn, in the primary factors include *anomie* and *ego-enhancement*: *anomie* being people's desire to escape from everyday life, which may be accomplished through travel, while *ego-enhancement* signifies a person's need to be recognised by others. It is precisely the former motives that are the tourists' own, while the latter represents destination-specific attractions that lead the traveller to go there once they have taken the decision to travel (Dann, 1981). This author points out the sequential nature of these factors which indicate that the push factors precede the pull factors.

From these two factors, Crompton (1979) establishes a dual classification of tourist motivations. On the one hand, the psychological motives are formed from seven push factors which include the following: escape from a perceived mundane environment; exploration and evaluation of self; relaxation; prestige; regression; enhancement of kinship relationships; facilitation of social interaction. On the other hand, the cultural motives comprise two factors two pull factors: novelty and education (Table 5).

Table 5. Crompton's tourist motivation model

Socio-Psicological Motivations	
Escape from a perceived mundane environment	A temporary change of environment both physically and socially. Escape is sought not only from the general residential locale but also from specific home and job environment.
Exploration and evaluation of self	Vacations may be viewed as an opportunity for re-evaluating and discovering more about oneself or for acting out self-images and in so doing refining or modifying oneself.
Relaxation	Relaxation means taking time to pursue activities of interest and hobbies that have no space during the normal routine.
Prestige	Travel can be a symbol of higher life stile, but as travel has become more frequent it is perceived to be less prestigious. Prestige potential disappears with frequency of exposure.
Regression	Pleasure vacation provide an opportunity to do things which are inconceivable within the context of their usual life styles, which could be considered as puerile, irrational and more reminiscent of adolescent or child behavior. Also, tourists search for the life style of a previous era; they desire to regress to a less complex, less changeable, less technologically advanced environment.
Enhancement of kinship relationships	Vacation is perceived as a time when family members are brought close together and it serve as a medium through which family relationships could be enhanced or enriched.
Facilitation of social interaction	A motive for traveling may be to meet new people in different locations. These trips are people rather than place oriented. Some dimensions emerge: an opportunity for transitory meetings with others from outside familiar reference groups to exchange views; seeking more permanent relationships that would serve to extend the range of social contacts; the interaction with non-familiar people.
Cultural Motivations	
Novelty	It is defined as curiosity, adventure, new and different. Novel means new experience but not necessarily entirely new knowledge, since often tourists know a lot about the place. The novelty results from actually seeing something rather than simply knowing of it vicariously.
Education	Traveling is a way to satisfy educational needs and it is perceived as a mean of developing a rounded individual. It is perceived as almost a moral obligation to take the opportunity to visit a distinctive phenomenon, particularly if it is reasonably accessible.

Source: Author's own material after Crompton (1979).

Although the original model has been modified and expanded by Crompton himself (Crompton and McKay, 1997) it is still recognised that, in tourism research, it may be fundamentally classified into two basic forces that suggest that people are pushed or pulled by various factors (Yoon and Uysal, 2005). On the one hand, individuals are pushed by motivational variables to make travel decisions, i.e. push factors that are related to the desires of the tourist (internal or emotional factors). On the other hand, individuals are drawn or attracted to the attributes of the destination or pull factors that are connected to external, situational or cognitive aspects. However, the destination attributes can stimulate and strengthen the pull motivation (Yoon and Uysal, 2005).

This model has had a great impact on the field of heuristic research having been applied – with nuances and differences – in numerous papers and empirical studies. Many have attempted to find push-pull motivational factors at different venues and tourist destinations (Hanquin and Lam, 1999; Jang and Cai, 2002; Kozak, 2002). Some authors have analysed the influence that these factors can have on variables, such as the nationality of tourists in their determination (Cha, McCleary and Uysal, 1995; Kim and Lee, 2000; Kim and Prideaux, 2005). Others have applied them to areas such as 'seniors' tourism (Hsu, Cai and Wong, 2007; Jang and Wu, 2006); 'volunteer' tourism (Chen and Chen, 2011); the tourism of cruises (Hung and Perick, 2011), 'rural' tourism (Devesa, Laguna and Palacios, 2010; Molera and Albadalejo, 2007; Park and Yoon, 2009) and that of events and festivals (Kim, Borges and Chon, 2006; Lee, Lee and Wicks, 2004).

b) The Escaping-Seeking Dichotomy

Iso-Ahola's motivational model is based on two motivational forces: seeking and escaping. So while the quest is for the desire to obtain a psychological reward (intrinsic) by journeying through a different environment, whether new or already known, escaping is the desire is to leave behind the everyday environment (Iso-Ahola, 1982; Ross and Iso-Ahola, 1991). These concepts are related, in turn, to the push-pull factors proposed by Dann and Crompton. The push factors would correspond to the reasons for escape, while the pull factors would be related to search factors.

However, Iso-Ahola goes further in his dichotomy of motivation and distinguishes, in turn, between a personal dimension and an interpersonal dimension. The author notes that when deciding on the importance of seeking and escaping, the individual takes into account both personal and interpersonal dimensions of their motives (Iso-Ahola, 1982; Mannel and Iso-Ahola, 1987). In this sense, the individual can escape their personal world (personal concerns, problems, difficulties and failures) and/or the interpersonal world (co-workers, friends, relatives, neighbours). Likewise, personal rewards may be found (sense of mastery, feelings of mastery, learning about other cultures, rest, relaxation, etc.) and/or interpersonal rewards (social interactions, wider and more varied, interaction with old friends in new places or new friends in familiar places, etc.). All this is summarised in Figure 2.

A visitor may be in one of these boxes under certain conditions at a given time. Likewise, groups of tourists can travel to the same destination for different reasons. And some tourists can even move from one box to another. In short, motivation is dynamic in character (Iso-Ahola, 1982).

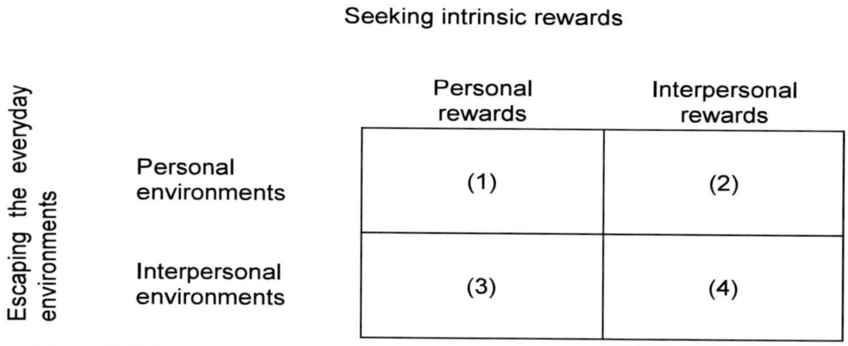

Seeking intrinsic rewards

	Personal rewards	Interpersonal rewards
Personal environments	(1)	(2)
Interpersonal environments	(3)	(4)

Escaping the everyday environments

Source: Iso-Ahola (1982).

Figure 2. A Social Psycological Model of Tourism Motivation.

Although this model has had a major impact and influence on numerous empirical studies, some authors miss the biological dimension to motivation, which may be crucial to some tourists, like *seniors*, and so they do include other motivational theories. Furthermore, they stress the idea that seeking and removing, or escaping, concepts emphasise more the *what* than the *why* of actions (Hsu et al., 2007).

c) Pearce's Theoretical Model

Pearce's (1988, 1993) theoretical model of tourist motivation incorporates a new element to the motivational factors previously cited: the tourist experience. For Pearce tourist motivation is not a static process, but an evolving and dynamic one that stimulates the individual to change his experience and holiday preferences as a function of age, status, experience etc.

In this respect, Pearce concludes that motivations differ depending on whether the experience was positive or negative in character. In positive experiences, the lower level needs of the Maslow scale are found to be inactive, while they are active in the negative experiences. The more experienced and mature the tourist the greater the concern with higher needs of the scale (Pearce and Caltabiano, 1983). As a consequence of these results, Pearce (1988) subsequently made an adaption to Maslow's hierarchy of needs (Figure 3), which permits the rigidity of this model to be overcome. In that regard, Pearce suggests that each individual, the level of need in each category may be satisfied in an incomplete way and so permit progression to the next level of the hierarchy (Holden, 1999).

d) The Motivation of Leisure Scale

Beard and Ragheb's (1983) Leisure Motivation Scale is based on the work of Maslow and states that leisure is related to recreation and self-discovery. It is argued that there are four motives that determine the satisfaction that comes from leisure activities (Ryan and Glendon, 1998). First, an intellectual motive that determines the extent of the individuals' motivation to do leisure activities (mental activities such as learning, exploration, discovery, thought, and imagination). Second, a social component that determines to what extent individuals carry out leisure activities for social reasons (seeking friendship, interpersonal relations and needing to be appreciated by others). Third, a competency/expertise component by which individuals seeks achievement, challenges, skills, etc. Finally, a stimulus-escape motive that evaluates the strength of escape and flight from over-stimulating life situations.

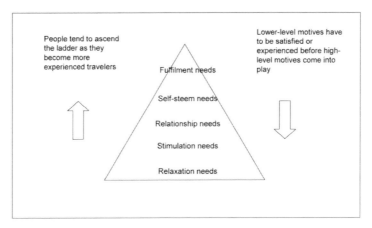

Source: Adapted from Pearce (1982).

Figure 3. Application of Pearce to Maslow's Scale of Motivation.

These four motivations are close to the motives analysed in earlier sections, with both Iso-Ahola's need to escape and to seek and Dann and Crompton's push-pull factors. In fact, it has been applied to the study of tourism in the work of Kleiven (2005), Lounbury and Polik (1992) and Yusof and Shah (2009).

Ryan and Glendon (1998) carried out a study in the United Kingdom, where four main motivational factors were identified: a social dimension, related to establishing and maintaining relationships while on holiday; a relaxation dimension, which combines aspects of escape and search; an intellectual dimension, linked to knowledge, discovery, and imagination; and, finally, a competence/expertise dimension, related to the challenge of skills and the use of them.

e) Goossen's Hedonic Tourism Motivation Model

Based on Crompton's (1979) model and the push-pull factors of tourist motivation, Goossens (2000) constructed a new conceptual model *disposition-stimulus-response* taking the emotional aspects of destination choice behaviour as the starting point. This author argues that it is necessary to analyse the relationship between the push-pull factors. In this regard, he points out that both are two sides of the same motivational coin, which are connected by a psychological factor: emotion. From this perspective, consumers, and especially tourists, are pushed by their (emotional) needs and pulled by the (emotional) benefits of the leisure services of the destinations.

Consequently, the emotional needs and experience are relevant to them in their pursuit of pleasure and in consumer behaviour. Hence, if marketers want to understand the motivation mechanisms that determine the selection process for the destination, they will have to incorporate these kinds of factors in their analysis and planning (Figure 4).

The model considers the feelings of pleasure, relaxation, excitement (push factor - consumer disposition) and some environmental variables such as marketing stimuli, including the supply of tourism services, tourism attractions – such as sunshine, culture, friendly people or brand and advertising (pull factors) – that are important sources of information. Goosens (2000) suggests that a combination of these and hedonic responses is what will motivate tourists to plan a trip.

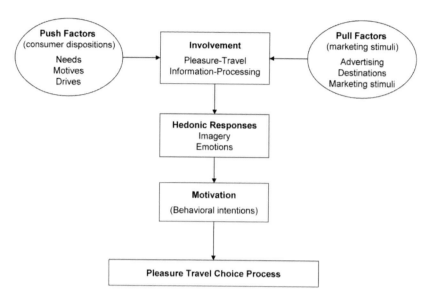

Source: Adapted from Goossens (2000).

Figure 4. A Hedonic Tourism Motivational Model.

Thus, as can be seen in the earlier outline, the push motives (internally generated drivers) and the pull motives (knowledge about goal attributes) merge in the consumer's brain, and this is what will motivate them – or not – to take advantage of what the market offers.

The integration of these two forces plays a fundamental role in the concept of commitment (involvement) which is defined as an unobservable motivational state, arousal or interest. It has the nature of a driving force and its consequences are *types of searching, information processing and decision making*. In the context of tourism, commitment is characterised by the perception of *importance, pleasure value, sign value, risk probability and risk consequences* (Goossens, 2000).

Hedonic responses specifically occur during consumption, but also during the acquisition phase and the processing of information, when tourists are involved with promotional information materials. These hedonic responses are manifested as emotions and images of the consumer or tourist, thereby reflecting the individual's reaction when the push-pull factors interact with each other.

Although the model is not empirically verified, from a management perspective, it could be a very useful tool for tourism managers and policymakers, in helping them to better understand the individual's response (target group) to marketing and communication policies and to learn the effect that these strategies have.

f) Hsu, Cai and Wong's Motivational Model

The growing interest in the study of the motivation and distinctive characteristics of certain tourists has favoured the development of motivational models centred on specific sectors. This is the case for the conceptual model proposed by Hsu, Cai and Wong (2007) for 'seniors' tourism.

By undertaking a qualitative study, conducted through a series of in-depth interviews and based on a review of the motivation literature, these authors distinguish two main components: external conditions and internal desires. The first group includes societal progress, health, personal finances and time, the last two elements being mediated by family support and responsibility. Inner desires include improving well-being, escaping routines, the concept of opportunity, socialising, seeking knowledge, pride and patriotism, personal reward and nostalgia. These first four desires are influenced by the life continuity concept while the search for knowledge, pride and patriotism are conditioned by the respect concept.

The innovation and most striking contribution of this model is that of integrating external conditions of motivation in the explanation of this variable. However, its validity has not yet been confirmed on an empirical level. Moreover, the identification of certain factors associated with the inner desires have a strong cultural component, so some rearrangement of factors may be required to extend it to tourists of other nationalities.

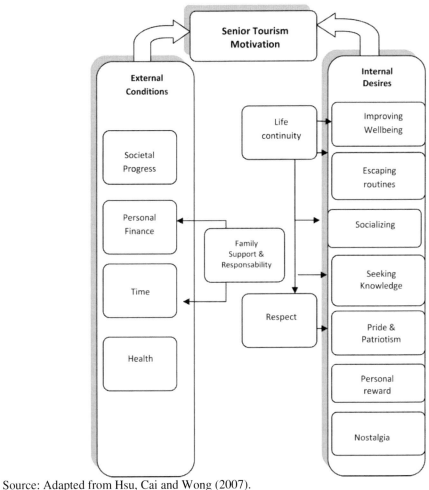

Source: Adapted from Hsu, Cai and Wong (2007).

Figure 5. Hsu, Cai and Wong's motivational model.

4. THE IMPORTANCE OF TOURIST MOTIVATION

Research into the reasons or into the motives for a trip that we have been analysing contribute to the understanding of tourism as a social and psychological phenomenon and allows us to offer some practical input from the point of view of tourism management.

These studies show that motivation is a complex, multidimensional and dynamic construct which can vary from person to person, from one sector of the market to another, from one destination to a different one and from one process decision to the next.

Interest in the study of tourist motivation stems from not just the importance of this aspect on tourist behaviour, but also that motives can form the basis of market segmentation, each sector responding with different strategies that allow supply to adequately satisfy tourists' wishes and demands.

Similarly, knowledge about motivation can be used for product and/or tourist destination development; for the evaluation of the quality of service; for the development of the destination's image; or for the development of promotional activities and positioning (Fodness, 1994). Furthermore, the influence of motivation on individual behaviour is not confined to this preliminary phase of consumption or experience of the tourism product but transcends beyond the subjective perception of the said experience, the perceived image itself, the post-consumption assessment – or satisfaction – and loyalty to the product or destination. All these issues will be developed in the sections that follow.

4.1. Segmentation of the Tourism Market and Motivation as a Segmentation Variable

4.1.1. The Notion of Segmentation in Tourism

The tourism market of today is characterised by a high level of heterogeneity. This, coupled with its increasing globalisation and a widespread tendency to search for a distinct offer, is causing an ever more diverse and fragmented demand. Thus, we are finding ourselves facing a traveller that is ever more experienced, independent and demanding, who is calling for more individualised forms of tourism.

In this scenario, it is obvious that by trying to satisfy all individuals with a single offer it will be difficult to achieve their satisfaction, since their needs, resources, attitudes and purchasing behaviour can be very diverse. These circumstances oblige businesses and institutions responsible for the design and planning of tourism products to put into practice targeting policies. This has meant that in recent decades, a massive consideration of a different, much more selective and fragmented market has taken place.

Segmentation assumes the division of the market into relatively homogenous groups of consumers on the basis of some criterion or characteristic. This line of investigation is especially relevant to the marketing of tourism since it allows more efficient use company resources by selecting those strategic groups that are most significant; determining the policy of the product or service; the price, the distribution and the most suitable communication (Witt and Moutinho, 1994).

It also presents obvious advantages to destinations and/or businesses as well as to the tourists themselves. For the former, it allows them to detect and analyse the opportunities presented by the market and assess to what extent they fulfil the needs of the consumer. At the same time, it supports the prioritisation of resources and capacities and the possibility of a more effective business planning through knowing its characteristics and needs better. On the other hand, and from the perspective of the consumer, the most exhaustive market knowledge enables more effective satisfaction of their wishes through the adaptation of products, as well as the rest of the marketing stimuli and activities, to their needs and expectations.

In the segmentation process, one key aspect is the identification and selection of the criteria to use. These criteria will permit us to characterise the profiles of the sectors obtained so as to later determine their appeal and then select that, or those, which are most interesting. These homogenous groups are the foundation on which the competitive positioning of the product or destination will be based.

In the literature, the criteria used to carry out the segmentation are many and varied. Kotler, Bowe and Maken (1999) classify them by differentiating between geographical criteria (region, climate, etc.), demographic criteria (education, profession, race, etc.), psychographic (social class, personality, etc.) and specific purchase criteria (purchase frequency, loyalty, availability to make purchase, etc.).

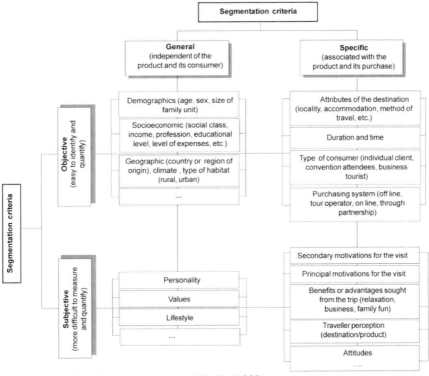

Source: Adapted from González, Cervantes and Muñiz (1999).

Figure 6. Segmentation criteria for the tourism market.

Other authors prefer to differentiate between objective and subjective – depending on whether the factors are directly observable or not and the ease or difficulty of quantification – and general variables or specific – in terms of their relationship or not to the product and to the purchasing process and/or consumption – (Frank, Massey and Wind, 1972). The combination of these criteria permits the establishment of four basic types of segmentation variables (general-objective, general-subjective, specific-objective, specific-subjective) in which are framed a variety of factors such as socioeconomic, demographic, geographic, personality, lifestyle, purchase intentions, product use, the place of purchase, preferences, perceptions and the benefits sought from the product, amongst others (Figure 6).

4.1.2. Segmentation of the Tourist Market by Lifestyle

Of the different tourism market segmentation criteria, we are especially interested in the psychology of those labelled *subjective*, both of a general and a specific nature (Figure 6). This segmentation may be included in the current psychographic lifestyles instigated by Lazer (1963). From this point of view, the habits and purchasing patterns are induced from the individuals' internal aspects rather than objective characteristics. In introducing these criteria, a more human portrayal of the purchaser/tourist is obtained, one in which aspects related to, his values, beliefs and motivations are considered.

The segmentation methods by lifestyle supposes that the individual adopts a way of life in accordance with the dominant traits of the social groups to which he belongs or of which he desires to be a member (Baudrillard, 1970). For the construction of the different lifestyle profiles, aspects have been included such as lifestyle and work, type of leisure, beliefs, opinions, and attitudes toward life, consumption patterns and worldview. All this is within a dynamic perspective since it has to take into account, not only the present moment, but also evolution and personal development (new experiences, environmental influences, changes in lifestyle, etc.).

Therefore, it is frequent that, when working with the concept of lifestyle, aspects related to activities, interests and opinions are analysed, which is why it is also known as the AIO model (*Activities, Interests, Opinions*). When we talk about *Activities*, we refer to the way in which we occupy ourselves in our free time. By *Interests* we mean all those aspects of the world around us that attract our attention by their importance or by the significance we give them. We talk of *Opinions* when referring to the knowledge we have about that environment and the assessment we make of these events.

The research that has utilised these criteria of tourism market segmentation is copious and, hence, we will pause only to examine one line of investigation; specifically the work of González (2005) and of González and Bello (2002).

González (2005) establishes a direct relationship between the lifestyle variables of the AIO constructs and tourist consumer behaviour on both short trips and those of a longer duration. In both cases, the relationship is strengthened when the sample is segmented for lifestyle criteria beforehand. Specifically, 5 tourist segments by lifestyle (*Home-loving, Idealistic, Autonomous, Hedonistic y Conservative*) are obtained, which were developed in an earlier investigation by González and Bello (2002).

The first of the segments identified by these authors is composed of people that work at home, with a high level of satisfaction with this job; conservative in ideology; who like to enjoy a quiet life as a family with the children; who put quality before price; reasons that led to the sector being given the name *Home-loving*. The second in importance is designated

Idealistic; worth mentioning from among its features are personal value, social involvement, the search for a better world and the fight against injustices. Its character is flexible, loving of tolerance and of innovations. The most frequent motives for travel among the subjects of this segment are being amused, a break from daily life, engaging in activities, attending sports events and meeting and interacting with other people.

The *Autonomous* are the third segment. They are people who greatly value their independence and personal liberty and consider it fundamental to the enjoyment of life. They are liberal-minded and optimistic about the future. Their main motives for travel are fun, entertainment and discovery of new places. Among their principal interests would be the nightlife.

The fourth segment, designated *Hedonistic*, would comprise people who accept life as it comes, love personal relationships and success at work. They are politically tolerant and have a special appetite for the latest novelties on the market. Logically, their main motives for travel are centred on the search for pleasure and the joyful aspects of life. The fifth and final segment, designated *Conservative*, considers family well-being very important and adaptation to daily life, a thing that is not always achieved (it is a fairly dissatisfied group). They are naturally pessimistic about the future and of society. Among their main motives for travel are visiting friends and family, relaxing and enjoying the weather.

4.1.3. Segmentation of the Tourist Market by Motives for Travel

As we have noted above, motivation has been another of the possible criteria for segmenting the tourism market. As a consequence of its importance in the consumer decision-making process, in recent years the number of studies relating to tourist motivation and the segmentation of the market has increased (Table 6).

However, a significant portion of these investigations have used segmentation based on the motivation variables of the visit more as a means to an end in itself; several of these, which are outlined below, will be developed with a greater degree of detail in later sections.

Such is the case of the work of Devesa et al. (2010) who discovered four homogenous groups of cultural visitors using motivational variables as a criterion of allocation. Thus, the first group would be formed of visitors who are seeking rest and relaxation as well as contact with nature. For this reason, the sector is called *Tourism as an alternative to the big city*. The second cluster, labelled *Cultural Visitor*, would seek, as their main motives for travel, visits to museums and monuments as well as discovering new places. The third cluster would comprise all those visitors who have made gastronomy and contact with nature their main motives for travel; hence, they are referred to as *Gastronomic and Nature Visitors*. The fourth and last cluster, the *Return Tourist* has visiting friends and family as its crucial motive for travel.

Recently, the same authors (Devesa, Laguna and Palacios, 2011), working with a sample of visitors to a domestic tourist destination, have found five sectors based on motivational variables for the visit (Table 7). The motivational scale used to carry out the identification of the groups includes 17 principal reasons for travel and conforms to the *pull* and *push* motives developed by Crompton (1979).

The first of these clusters presents significant values in the motivational variables of enjoying gastronomy and the natural environment, as well as visiting monuments and heritage sites; likewise it is the segment that scored most highly on attending Holy Week processions and celebrations, for which they are designated *Seasonal gastronomic and cultural visitors*.

The second of the clusters has been labelled *Visitors who seek new relationships and escape from routine,* as their principal motivations for travel are to foster new relationships and escape from stress.

Table 6. Segmentation based motivational variables

Authors	Field of investigation	Segmentation variables (Factors /dimensions)	Segments identified based on motivation
Frochot (2005)	Rural Tourism	Benefits sought	Actives Relaxers Gazers Rurals
Lee, Lee and Wicks (2004)	Festival motivation (2002 World Culture Expo)	Cultural exploration Family togetherness Novelty Escape (equilibrium recovery) Event attractions Socialization	Culture and family seekers Multi-purpose seekers Escape seekers Event seekers
Devesa and Palacios (2005)	Cultural Tourism	Monumental and gastronomic motivation Search for tranquillity Contact with nature Visiting friends Employment purposes	Alternative to the big city Monumental and gastronomic motivation Specialised long distance tourism Circumstantial visitor
Devesa, Laguna and Palacios (2010)	Rural Tourism	Hedonists and rest Relational and social motives Monumental and gastronomic motivation	Visitor looking for tranquillity, rest and contact with nature. Cultural visitor Proximity, gastronomic and nature visitor Return tourist
Devesa, Laguna and Palacios (2011)	Cultural Tourism	Hedonists and rest Relational and social motives Monumental and gastronomic motivation	Seasonal gastronomic and cultural visitor Visitor seeking new relationships and escape from routines Visitors to nearby monuments Hedonist and rest visitor
Loker-Murphy (1996)	Backpackers in national parks	Excitement/adventure Meeting local people	Achievers Self-developers Socialising/excitement seekers Escapers/relaxers
Kastenholz, Davis and Paul (1999)	Rural tourism		Want-it-all ruralist Independent ruralist Traditional ruralist Environmental ruralist
Molera and Albadalejo (2007)	Rural Areas	(Benefits sought) Nature and peacefulness Physical and cultural activities Family Trip features Rural life	Family rural tourist Relax rural tourist Active rural tourist Tourist of rural accommodation

Authors	Field of investigation	Segmentation variables (Factors /dimensions)	Segments identified based on motivation
Park and Yoon (2009)	Rural Areas	Relaxation Socialisation Learning Family togetherness Novelty Excitement	Family Passive Want it all Learning and excitement
Beh and Bruyere (2007)	National reserves	Escape Culture Personal Grow Mega-fauna Adventure Learning Nature General viewing	Escapists Learners Spiritualist

Source: Author's own material.

The third cluster, the most numerous, have visiting monuments and heritage sites as their priority interests; also, they travel few kilometres to the tourist destination; for these reasons naming the cluster as *Visitors to nearby monuments* is justified. Finally, the fourth cluster is characterised as being a social and holiday visitor who makes the trip fundamentally to rest; enjoy the holiday as a break from routine; making good use of the visit to be with family/friends; and to increase their level of culture. It is designated *Hedonistic and rest visitor*.

Table 7. Characterisation of clusters according to motivational variables

Name of cluster	Motivational variables relating to each cluster
Seasonal gastronomic and cultural visitor	Attends Holy Week processions and ceremonies Enjoys gastronomy Visits monuments and Heritage Sites Fosters new relationships Enjoys the natural environment
Visitors who seek new relationships and escape from routine	Fosters new relationships Escape from stress
Visitors to nearby monuments	Visits monuments and Heritage Sites Close to their place of residence
Hedonistic and rest visitors	Augment culture and education Travel with family and friends New experiences and places Do nothing but rest Escape stress Enjoys the holidays and free time Enjoys the natural environment For the good weather The option of cheap travel

Source: Devesa, Laguna and Palacios (2011).

Molera and Albaladejo (2007) found five segments operating in the rural tourism sector. The first of these, the largest since it represents 30% of the sample, is designated *Family Rural Tourist*. Their main motivations are to share time and space with family and travelling a reasonable distance as they are travelling with children. The second cluster is designated *Relaxation Rural Tourist*; as is logical to suppose, they value the possibility of rest, independence and flexibility as their motivation to travel. The third segment, *Active Rural Tourist*, is characterised by the pursuit of open air cultural activities; furthermore, they want to take in visits to monuments so as to appreciate the architecture typical of the chosen place. The fourth segment, *Rural Life Tourist*, seek places that are uncrowded; food and popular traditions; relationships with the local people; and agricultural activities. The last segment, identified as *Rural Accommodation Tourist*, wants to spend most of their time together with friends, which happens to be the main, and almost only, motivation for the trip.

In a different context from above, Beh and Bruyere (2007), using motivational variables, investigated the existence of different segments among tourists visiting Kenya's three natural parks. The questionnaire used for segmentation is composed of 49 motivational indicators (viewing elephants, learning about Samboru culture, etc.) from which three key segments were identified. The first, *The Escapist*, is mainly composed of young Europeans, who seek from their trip aspects such as getting out of the monotony of everyday life and its daily routines or physical relaxation as the main reasons for the visit.

The second of these segments is called *The Learners*. This is the largest group and they score highly on motivational indicators relating to knowing and learning about specific aspects of the ecosystems of the African reserves and natural parks. Cultural motivations are important to them as is the mere contemplation of the fauna, since they possess a higher cultural level within the sample. The third and final segment, which was the smallest identified, the authors called *Spiritualist*. The reason for this lies in the high scores obtained from the personal growth section (*Think about who you are, grow and develop spiritually, think about personal values...*). The quest for adventure appears to be another important motivation for this segment.

4.2. The Influence of Motivation on Consumer Decisions

Understanding what makes a person/tourist behave in a certain way or make a specific choice is, undoubtedly, a question of enormous interest to both researchers and tourism managers. When explaining the dynamic of individuals' purchasing, the behavioural models of the consumer have pointed to the existence of factors of a very diverse nature (social, cultural, economic, psychological, etc.) that determine it. The individuals' final choice, in fact, is derived from the complex interaction of these factors, among which, as we have noted, is found motivation.

The importance and significance of this variable in the individuals' decision-making process is reflected in the numerous papers that can be found in the tourism literature. These studies, in general terms, are marked by two great lines of research. In the first, the studies have centred on the identification of motivational factors that trigger and determine the decision to travel and where to go. Many have allowed the identification of the motivational dimensions and the design of scales which have made it possible to operationalise and measure visitors' motivation.

The second, more recently developed, is more ambitious in that it has analysed the role of motivation in the individual's post-purchase decisions. This latter line has focused its interest on analysing the influence of two key aspects of motivation connected to the decision-making process. These are, on the one hand, the evaluation that the individual makes during the stay, which determines his level of satisfaction; and on the other hand, the influence that motivation could have on his behaviour and future intentions/decisions (loyalty) and, more specifically, on his intention to make a return visit to the destination; also, the probability that his satisfaction is translated into a positive message that he can use to recommend the destination to other people in his milieu. In turn, this area of investigation has been extended to other concepts of great significance like perceived image, which also influences the tourists' process of choice in the assessment that they make of their stay and their future intentions.

4.2.1. The Relationship between Motivation and Satisfaction

Motivation and satisfaction are, as we have already noted, two key aspects to explain and understand individuals' behaviour. In recent years, there has been a growing interest in understanding the link between these two concepts in both the professional and academic fields.

Although the existing definitions of the concept of satisfaction are many and varied, nowadays, there is a general agreement that considers it a post-purchase evaluation judgement, which incorporates cognitive and affective elements that the consumer makes about his experience. To this end, there are numerous authors who stress satisfaction as an emotional component.

Rust and Oliver (1994) understand satisfaction as the emotional response of the consumer at the realisation of their objectives. These objectives, which explain the consumer's purchase process, act as motives, tendencies or impulses that we desire to satisfy; an idea that has already been suggested by the aforementioned Crompton (1979), for whom the attributes of the tourist offer do not adequately explain the final satisfaction with the trip.

Satisfaction is a psychological outcome derived from the visitor's experience (Lee, Petrick and Crompton, 2009). Much of the research into this concept is conceived as an emotional response that follows a cognitive one of the service experienced (Zabkar, Makowec and Dmitrovic, 2009).

Papers from different fields of tourism have revealed the intimate relationship between satisfaction and motivation. Gnoth (1997) notes, for example, that once the needs and values have been set in motion and applied to a holiday scenario, motivation constitutes a fundamental parameter in the formation of expectations, and these in turn determine the perception of products and experiences.

In the sphere of rural tourism, Martín and Recio (2006) consider that the enduring relationships with clients, based on the concept of satisfaction, have not only to do with the concept of perceived quality of service but also and, above all, with the knowledge of their preferences. In turn, this knowledge must in the first place start from the study of their motivations for choosing a tourist experience before all other possible alternatives.

The study of this relationship between motivation and satisfaction has been approached from different perspectives and using diverse working methods. The multiplicity and specificity of the existing tourist destinations and products has meant that specific studies focusing on tourist destinations and products, in particular, have been carried out. In this context, the work of Ross and Iso-Ahola (1991) on *sightseeing tourism* is outstanding; Qu and Ping (1999) on the *tourism of cruises*; Lee et al. (2004) on the *tourism of festivals*; Yoon and Uysal (2005) on *a particular destination*; García and Gil (2005) on the *hospitality sector*; Rodríguez del Bosque, San Martín and Collado (2006) on the case of *rural tourism*; Lopes (2006) on *thermal tourism*; and Severt, Wang, Chen and Breiter (2007) on *convention tourism*.

In the same vein, Devesa, Laguna and Palacios (2008, 2010) analysed the relationship that exists between both constructs. Their study is centred on the impact of motivation – the trigger factor for the trip and, therefore, an antecedent of traveller behaviour – over the satisfaction obtained by the visitor in the chosen destination. These authors start from the hypothesis that individuals, who visit a given destination or resort, will gain a greater or lesser overall satisfaction depending on the evaluation they make of those aspects of their visit most related to their motivation for the trip. From this perspective, motivation would act as a determinant of satisfaction through the assessment of those *satisfaction indicators* linked to motivation.

Their study is grounded in the identification of the motivations that most determine the choice of destination for rural tourists, and based on these they establish four segment typologies, which have already been outlined above (Table 7). According to these visitor typologies, they establish a collection of elements offered to the tourist, which maintain a close link to the motivational variables that characterise them, and whose positive valuation could determine, a priori, further satisfaction.

In this way, they suggest the existence of an expected relationship between the dimensions or motivational factors and the aspects of the destination most linked to the visitors' motivations. Thus, for example, they consider it logical to think that for cluster A – consisting of visitors who have tranquillity, rest, inexpensive leisure and contact with nature as their principal motive for travel – their satisfaction will be determined by aspects or attributes linked to the peacefulness, conservation of natural heritage, the satisfactoriness of price and the quality of access. This last aspect is related to the flight from the big city and the great value that this visitor has for convenient, rapid access, without traffic jams.

In the same vein, they presume that the individuals in cluster B (cultural visitors), who have made Culture, History and monuments the principal objective of their trip and have had to travel a long distance to get to their chosen destination, value aspects relating to road signage, monument opening hours, guided tours and the conservation of cultural heritage as a premium.

After dividing the cluster in accordance with the degree of satisfaction expressed: satisfied – above average overall satisfaction – and not satisfied – below average satisfaction –; the results obtained to compare the evaluations of the attributes of the offer best linked to each motivational typology confirmed the existence of significant differences in some of them. So, for example, the *relaxation visitors* valued more the aspects of peace and quiet, the conservation of natural heritage and the access; the long distance *cultural visitor* who expressed a high level of satisfaction tended to score better, with a statistically significant difference, on aspects of the tourist offer related to his motivations: visiting hours of monuments and museums, guided tours, conservation of architectural heritage, as well as road signage and parking.

This allows us to conclude the existence of a relationship between the visitor typologies identified based on the motivation and assessment that these have made of the elements that constitute the tourist offer of the destination.

These results are consistent with the similarity established by Ross and Iso-Ahola (1991) between the motivation and satisfaction dimensions but, additionally, pose a step forward as they demonstrated that the individuals make a different evaluation of some aspects, activities and attributes of the destination, according to whether they are more or less related to the reasons that motivated and determined the trip.

Thus, for example, the cultural visitor, who presents high levels of satisfaction, registers more elevated evaluations, significant in statistical terms, on those items related to his cultural motivation: inter alia, the opening hours of monuments and museums, guided tours, and the conservation of architectural heritage. This fact indicates the existence of certain *specific satisfaction* elements directly linked to the motivation for the trip and which relate to satisfaction with the visit.

But on the other side, these authors established the existence of certain elements that have an impact in a definite way on global satisfaction and which are independent from the reasons that justify the trip. Within this group, that they designate as *general satisfiers*, are included aspects such as the treatment received, the quality of the cuisine, the availability of time and services, and the tourist information, which impact on the visitors' satisfaction in all the segments identified, though, at the same time, for some of them – as happens with the quality of cuisine – they can have a specific character that is linked to the motivation of a particular type of visitor.

Studies by these same authors (Devesa et al., 2008) have delved into the correlation between motivational factors and satisfaction criteria confirming causal relationships between the two. Their findings allow us to affirm that:

- There is a direct relationship between the motivations for the visit and satisfaction with aspects of the tourist offer relating to the said motivations.
- There are indicators that determine tourist satisfaction but do not necessarily relate to the motivations for the trip.
- The satisfier indicators related to the motivations for the trip, along with indicators of satisfaction not related to the motivations, determine the general satisfaction of what was accomplished on the tourist visit.

Through the development of a structural equations model (SEM), these authors established cause and effect relationships between the motivational factors and the indicators of the offer linked to these motivations. According to this model, the motivations for the trip determine the aspects pertinent to the tourist offer which are going to be used in the evaluation of satisfaction. To the extent that these motivations are delivered, or perceived to be delivered, the satisfaction linked to the motivation increases. By contrast, the satisfaction diminishes to the same extent in which it is perceived as not confirmed.

There exists, then, a relationship between visitors' motivation and their satisfaction, since that satisfaction depends on the fulfilment of the expectations that the individual has formed, and these expectations are the product, among other aspects, of the motives that have given place to the trip. At the same time, these same visitors assess aspects of the offer, which by their importance and nature, are not necessarily related to motivations. That is to say, satisfaction is a result of the partial experiences of satisfaction, linked to aspects relating to the motivations for the trip, and of the satisfaction with other aspects of the tourist offer that may be independent of the motive for the visit.

However, other studies like those of Yoon and Uysal (2005) open up certain questions in relation to the influence of motivation on satisfaction and extend their field of study to include loyalty. These authors propose a model that examines the causal relationship between push and pull factors, satisfaction and loyalty. Their results, surprisingly, indicate that the *pull motivations* influence tourist satisfaction in a negative manner, though it is not possible to confirm the effect that *travel push motivation* has on it. Instead, these latter factors do affect the destination loyalty in a positive way. For these authors this fact suggests that satisfaction is determined to be a mediating construct between travel motivation and destination loyalty.

In this same line of study, using structural equation models, Barroso, Martín and Martín (2007) empirically contrasted the influence of a particular motivational factor, the need to seek new things, against the intensity of the relationship between service quality and satisfaction and the link between satisfaction and the tourist's future behaviour; all these variables being of enormous importance to the success and profitability of the tourist destinations and products. Indeed, we will deal with the link between motivation and loyalty more broadly in the next section.

4.2.2. The Relationship between Motivation and Loyalty

Getting customers to have a distinctive, memorable and highly satisfactory experience is, without doubt, one of the priority objectives that tourism managers currently have. In this field, visitor satisfaction may translate into a repetition of the visit and a favourable report about the destination.

Nowadays, loyalty is considered as the major predictor of consumer behaviour and is a fundamental element in marketing strategies. The studies on consumer loyalty and tourism, usually distinguish between two types of loyalty: a *behavioural* loyalty, linked to the repetition of the purchase, and an *attitudinal* loyalty, linked to a favourable attitude towards the product or destination. From a tourism perspective, the former determines the number of times that a destination is visited, and the latter usually is measured through the visitor's intention to return to the destination and/or to recommend it to people in his milieu.

Some authors have differentiated within the attitudinal loyalty a cognitive loyalty that is linked to the beliefs and perception of the attributes of product/destination; an affective loyalty linked with the sentiments and emotions derived from the experience of satisfaction; and a conative loyalty specific to the future intentions and behaviour, which is linked to the repetition of the stay (Oliver, 1997, 1999; San Martín, Collado and Rodríguez del Bosque, 2009).

As has been amply contrasted, satisfaction is an antecedent of loyalty. The positive relationship existing between satisfaction and the intention to revisit has been widely established in the literature. The influence that motivation has on satisfaction has made some studies analyse the role or influence of motivation in relation to satisfaction-loyalty.

Research by Severt et al. (2007) examined this relationship of motivation, the perceived performance and the behavioural intentions for convention attendees. These authors identified five motivational factors in this type of tourist. Their results indicate a positive effect for educational activities on overall satisfaction, on word of mouth satisfaction and intention to return. This suggests that motivation for this type of visitor, though not having a direct impact on behavioural intention, does influence it in an indirect way through satisfaction.

The work of Devesa et al. (2011) establishes the existence of different levels of loyalty for different tourist segments identified on the basis of their motivations: gastronomic and cultural visitors; visitors seeking new relationships; visitors to nearby monuments; and hedonistic and rest visitors. The visitors that show a greater behavioural and attitudinal loyalty are those who seek travel to foster new relationships and escape from stress. The hedonistic visitors – whose main motivations are to gain new experiences, get to know new places, relaxation and enjoy the holiday with family and friends – are, however, the segment with greater attitudinal loyalty.

The importance that time has on the individuals' decisions, which can make their intentions change as time passes, has led to an analysis of its impact on tourists' intentions. Jang and Feng (2007) studied the effect that it has on a specific motivation: novelty seeking on the revisit intention for a temporary destination.

In this regard, the search for new things is a central component of motivation and has been defined as the degree of contrast between present perception and past experience (Pearson, 1970). In the field of tourism, it has been associated with new experience, adventure, surprise, thrill, a curiosity drive, boredom alleviation and an exploratory drive. The search for novelty plays an important role in tourists' decisions in experience seeking travel as the attitude of tourists towards the destination can be conditioned by its degree of novelty.

Jang and Feng (2007) confirmed that the search for novelty has a discrete effect on the intention to revisit as a function of the timeframe being considered. Thus, novelty seeking does not affect the intention to return to visit the destination in the short-term (short-term revisit intention) but it does have a direct effect on the mid-term revisit intention and is an indirect antecedent of long-term revisit intention.

Other work, such as that of Bigné, Hernández, Ruiz and Andreu (2010), has also analysed the importance of motivation as an explanatory factor of repatronage intentions through the application of the MOA model (motivation, opportunity and ability). This model, initially proposed by MacInnis and Jaworsky (1989) suggests that motivation combined with opportunity (factors and conditions that permit and facilitate an action or behaviour that usually are measured through travel constraints indicators) and the ability (the skills and competences of the individual to accomplish a given behaviour or action) are antecedents of consumer behaviour. These authors identify as motivational elements of the on-line purchase of airline tickets, the convenience, financial advantages, the variety and enjoyment. The results of their analysis indicate the importance of motivation to explain ticket purchasing intentions as its impact is greater than the other two variables (ability and opportunity) involved in the model.

4.2.3. The Influence of Motivation on Destination Image

The changes that are taking place in the tourist markets make it necessary for destinations to be increasingly managed from a strategic perspective. Based on this approach, one of the key elements that tourism managers have to control is the destination's brand image.

Image plays a fundamental role in the success of tourist sites and exerts a vital influence on the behaviour of those who visit. On one side, the destinations with a better image have more likelihood of being selected by visitors and, on the other, the perceived image influences satisfaction and the probability of a repeat visit.

Image is a complex, multiple, subjective and dynamic concept, that has been increasingly studied and form many different angles. One of the precursors to its study in the field of tourism was Hunt (1971), who defined it as the impression that a person has of a place in which they do not reside. Other authors agree in seeing it as resulting from a subjective interpretation, a representation or *mental picture* that the tourist forms from his experience in the destination and in which configuration as many cognitive factors (perception of the attribute of the destination) are involved as affective (emotions and sentiments about a place). Hence, Crompton (1979) defines it as the sum of beliefs, ideas and impressions that a person holds of a place that he visits.

Although the methodologies used for the measurement of image are diverse, from a cognitive viewpoint, the Tourism Destination Image (TDI) has frequently been measured on the basis of an exhaustive list of destination attributes that usually correspond to the most distinctive assets that characterise the destination. These attributes usually are those which allure the visitors to travel to the chosen location (places to see, activities to do, etc.) and, therefore, are constituted as elements that motivate and exert the magnetism necessary to persuade the individual so that he visits a particular place (Alhemoud and Armstrong, 1996; Lew, 1987; Stabler, 1988). Hence, the elements comprising the destination's image have a close link and accords with the *pull factors*.

The influence of motivation on image has been studied by distinguished researchers. However, despite the work accomplished in this area, as there has not yet been sufficient analysis of how the motives for travel are influenced in the formation and structure of the TDI, there exists a certain fragmentation in the investigations.

Some studies such as those of Gartner (1993), Dann (1996) and Baloglu (1997) have pointed out the direct influence that motivation exerts on the affective component of image. Others such as those of Baloglu and McCleary (1999), although they have attempted to test the incidence of socio-psychological and emotional motivations on the overall image, they have only confirmed the direct and significant relationship of one of the five factors analysed in their emotional scale. More recent studies such as those of Beerli and Martín (2004) also evince this relationship and suggest that when there is congruence between motivations, tourists and the nature of the destination, the affective image is positively conditioned by the reasons that motivated the trip.

Based on the consideration of motivation as the benefits sought by tourists, these authors identify four motivational factors for visitors to an island (sun and sand tourism): knowledge, relaxation, entertainment and prestige. These authors established two differential visitor typologies: the first-time tourist and the repeat tourist. Their results point to the existence of a statistically significant relationship between motives linked to relaxation and knowledge and the affective image for individuals who travel to the destination for the first time. Instead, the factors linked to entertainment and prestige do not have a significant impact on it. For the second segment, the repeat stay tourists, only motivation associated with knowledge influences the emotional dimension, but in a negative form.

Other work like that of Barroso et al. (2007) expands the area of study, analysing the influence of motivation in relation to image with other variables of tourist behaviour. Based on the hypothesis that perceived image is an antecedent of quality of service and satisfaction (perceived image - service quality - customer satisfaction), they analysed the effect that specific psychographic variable has on perceived image and on tourists' decisions and behaviour. These authors identify four clusters, according to the degree of intensity in which the visitors have this motivation. Their results establish the capacity of motivational factors to condition tourist perception as well as their behaviour. In particular, they confirm, among other things, the moderating effect that the need for variety or the search for new sensations has on: the intensity of the relationship between image and destination quality of service; the intensity of the relationship between destination satisfaction; and the intensity between the destination image and the tourist's future behaviour.

Thus, for example, for those individuals with a very intense need for change and to seek out new things, the perceived image influences future behaviour through satisfaction but only in respect of positive word of mouth communication. That is to say, this type of tourist has no intention of revisiting the resort but, in lieu, they give good references when they are satisfied. However, the influence of image on future intentions for the segment that has an *average desire for novelty* is measured through the quality of service and satisfaction.

CONCLUSION

Motivation is a key variable for the tourism sector. Its importance and capacity to determine, along with other factors, the decisions of individuals, has meant that interest in this variable is mounting. Motivation is the force that propels and makes people act. In the field of tourism, this variable allows knowledge of why people travel and what makes them choose a particular destination. Its importance as a trigger for the behaviour of tourists has resulted in the implementation of research that has permitted the formulation of different theories about tourist motivation, in which, factors and variables that explain and help us better to understand the travel choice process are specified.

The fact that visitors have very different motivations at the time of travel, and they are increasingly more heterogeneous, makes setting this variable an effective criterion to segment the tourism market. The literature review shows a notable number of works that utilise this subjective criterion and specifically to establish tourist typologies. Doubtless, this is an indispensible prerequisite that allows the design of different strategies suited to the wishes and demands of each type of visitor.

But, additionally, to determine their needs and expectations, motivation shows a close link to satisfaction. The results obtained in some studies demonstrate the correspondence between the motivational dimensions and those attributes with the capacity to determine satisfaction. In this regard, it has been established that satisfaction is determined by the evaluation made by the visitors of certain aspects or characteristics of the destination, associated with the reasons that motivated their trip (specific satisfiers) and others, that are independent of them (general satisfiers as, for example, the treatment received or the times that the service is available).

These results further contribute to the understanding of tourism as a social and psychological phenomenon, permitting us to offer some practical input from the point of view of tourism management. Those charged with the design of the offer, should devote their attention as a priority to the resources and efforts required to assure the correct provision of those attributes that determine general satisfaction, which are shared by all visitors irrespective of their motivation and/or their socio-demographic characteristics. But at the same time, the existing diversity of the tourism market requires not neglecting the identification and promotion of those attributes that are set as "specific satisfiers" for those segments, whose attraction and size result in priorities for the destination, given that its relationship with motivation makes that have the capacity to determine the evaluations of certain visitors.

On the other hand, the impact that motivation has on the formation of image, and more specifically on its emotional dimension, has important implications for destinations' strategic planning. The managers and planners of the tourist sites, based on a thorough analysis of the market, have to target those types of visitors whose motivations are linked more to the characteristics, resources and attractions of the place they manage. Likewise, they should design products and activities according to their visitors' motivations and expectations with the goal of efficiently satisfying their needs. It is recommended that the projected image of the destination is promoted through various communication means and media (advertising, publicity, brochures, internet etc.) highlighting those distinctive aspects that are most representative or characteristic of the destination and which best correspond with the motivations of their priority targets.

Finally, the effect – which may have certain motivational factors – on the tourist's loyalty and on their future behaviour, makes the identification of tourists by their motivational profile necessary, in order to be able to design effective measures that permit the assurance of a positive report and to influence, in a favourable way, the tourist's intention to revisit the destination.

REFERENCES

Adams, J. S. (1965). Inequity in social exchanges. In L. Berkowitz (Ed.), *Advances in experimental social psychology* (pp. 14-46). New York: Academic Press.

Alhemoud, A. M., and Armstrong, E. G. (1996). Image of tourism Attractions in Kuwait. *Journal of Travel Research*, 34(4), 76-80.

Atkinson, J. W. (1957). Motivational determinants of risk taking behavior, *Psychological Review*, 64, 359-372.

Baloglu, S. (1997). The relationship between destination images and socio-demographic and trip characteristics of international travellers. *Journal of Vacation Marketing*, 3, 221-233.

Baloglu, S., and McCleary, K. (1999). A model of destination image formation. *Annals of Tourism Research*, 26(4), 868-897.

Barroso, C., Martín, E., and Martín, D. (2007). The influence of market heterogeneity on the relationship between a destination's image and tourists' future behaviour. *Tourism Management*, 28, 175-187.

Baudrillard, J. (1970). *La Société de consommation*. Paris: Gallimard.

Beard, J. G., and Ragheb, M. G. (1983). Measuring Leisure Motivation. *Journal of Leisure Research*, 15, 219-228.

Beerli, A., and Martin, J. D. (2004). Tourists' characteristics and the perceived image of tourist destinations: a quantitative analysis–a case study of Lanzarote, Spain. *Tourism Management*, 25, 623-636.

Beh, A., and Bruyere, B. L. (2007). Segmentation by visitor motivation in three Kenyan national reserves. *Tourism Management, 28*, 1464-1471.

Bem, D. J. (1972). Self-perception theory. In L. Berkowitz (Ed.), *Advances in experimental social psychology* (pp.128-143). New York: Academic Press.

Bigné, E., Hernández, B., Ruiz, C., and Andreu, L. (2010). How motivation, opportunity and ability can drive online airline ticket purchases. *Journal of Air Transport Management*, 16, 346-349.

Brehm, J. W. (1966). *A theory of psychological reactance*. New York: Academic Press.

Castaño, J. M., Moreno, A., García, S., and Crego, A. (2003). Aproximación psicosocial a la motivación turística: variables implicadas en la elección de Madrid como destino. *Estudios Turísticos*, 158, 5-41.

Cha, S., McCleary, K., and Uysal, M. (1995). Travel motivations of Japanese overseas travelers: a factor-cluster segmentation approach. *Journal of Travel Research*, 34(1), 33-39.

Chen, L. J., and Chen, J. S. (2011). The motivations and expectations of international volunteer tourists: A case study of "Chinese Village Traditions". *Tourism Management*, 32, 435-442.

Crompton, J. L. (1979). Motivations for pleasure vacation. *Annals of Tourism Research*, 6(4), 408-424.

Crompton, J. L., and McKay, S. L. (1997). Motives of visitors attending festival events. *Annals of Tourism Research*, 24(2), 425-439.

Dann, G. M. S. (1977). Anomie, ego-enhancement and tourism. *Annals of Tourism Research*, 4(4), 184-194.

Dann, G. M. S. (1981). Tourism motivation: an appraisal. *Annals of Tourism Research*, 8(2), 187-219.

Dann, G. M. S. (1996). Tourists' image of a Destination-An alternative analysis. *Journal of Travel and Tourism Marketing*, 5(1-2), 41-55.

Devesa, M., and Palacios, A. (2005). Predicciones en el nivel de satisfacción percibida por los turistas a partir de variables motivacionales y de valoración de la visita. *Información Comercial Española*, 821, 241-255.

Devesa, M., Laguna, M., and Palacios, A. (2008). Un modelo estructural sobre la influencia de las motivaciones de ocio en la satisfacción de la visita turística. *Revista de Psicología del Trabajo y de las Organizaciones*, 24(2), 253-268.

Devesa, M., Laguna, M., and Palacios, A. (2010). The role of motivation in visitor satisfaction: Empirical evidence in rural tourism. *Tourism Management*, 31, 547-552.

Devesa, M., Laguna, M., and Palacios, A. (2011). Motivación, satisfacción y lealtad en el turismo: el caso de un destino de interior. *Revista Electrónica de Motivación y Emoción*, Vol. XIII (35-36), 169-189.

Feather, N. T. (1959). Subjective probability and decision under uncertainty. *Psychological Review*, 66, 150-164.

Festinger, L. (1957). *A theory of cognitive dissonance*. Stanford: Stanford University Press.

Fodness, D. (1994). Measuring Tourist Motivation. *Annals of Tourism Research*, 21, 555-581.

Frank, R. E., Massy, W., and Wind, Y. (1972). *Marketing segmentation*. Englewood Cliffs: Prentice-Hall.

Frochot, I. (2005). A benefit segmentation of tourists in rural areas: a Scottish perspective. *Tourism Management*, 26, 335-346.

García, M., and Gil, I. (2005). Expectativas, satisfacción y lealtad en los servicios hoteleros. Un enfoque desde la cultura nacional. *Papers de Turisme*, 37-38, 7-25.

Gartner, W. C. (1993). Image formation process. *Journal of Travel and Tourism Marketing*, 2(2), 191-215.

Gnoth, J. (1997). Tourism motivation and expectation formation. *Annals of Tourism Research*, 24(2), 283-304.

González Fernández, A. M. (2005). La segmentación del mercado turístico por estilos de vida: una estrategia empresarial en auge. *Investigación y Marketing*, 87, 18-24.

González, A. M., and Bello, L. (2002). The construct lifestyle in market segmentation. The behaviour of tourist consumer. *European Journal of Marketing*. 36(2), 51-85.

González, A., Cervantes, M., and Muñiz, N. (1999). La incidencia de los estilos de vida en la segmentación del mercado turístico: aplicación a la población urbana de Castilla y León. *Revista de Investigación Económica y Social de Castilla y León*, 2, 41-56.

Goossens, G. (2000). Tourism information and pleasure motivation. *Annals of Tourism Research*, 27(2), 301-321.

Hanquin, Z. Q., and Lam, T. (1999). An analysis of Mainland Chinese visitors' motivations to visit Hong Kong. *Tourism Management*, 20, 587-594.

Holden, A. (1999). Understanding Skiers' Motivation using Pearce's Travel Career' Construct. *Annals of Tourism Research*, 26(2), 435-438.

Homans, G. C. (1961). *Social behavior: Its elementary forms*. New York: Harcourt, Brace, and World.

Hsu, C. H. C., Cai, L. A., and Wong, K. K. F. (2007). A model of senior tourism motivations. Anecdotes from Beijing and Shanghai. *Tourism Management*, 28, 1262-1273.

Hung, K., and Perick, J. F. (2011). Why do you cruise? Exploring the motivations for taking cruise holidays, and the construction of a cruising motivation scale. *Tourism Management*, 32, 386-393.

Hunt, J. D. (1971). Image: A factor in tourism. Unpublished Ph.D. dissertation, Fort Collins: Colorado State University.

Iso-Ahola, S. E. (1982). Toward a Social Psychological Theory of Tourism Motivation: A Rejoinder. *Annals of Tourism Research*, 9(2), 256-262.

Jang, S. C., and Wu, C. M. E. (2006). Seniors' travel motivation and the influential factors: An examination of Taiwanese seniors. *Tourism Management*, 27, 306-316.

Jang, S., and Cai, L. (2002). Travel motivations and destination choice: a study of British outbound market. *Journal of Travel and Tourism Marketing*, 13(3), 111-133.

Jang, S., and Feng, R. (2007). Temporal destination revisit intention: The effects of novelty seeking and satisfaction. *Tourism Management*, 28, 580-590.

Kastenholz, E., Davis, D., and Paul, G. (1999). Segmenting Tourism in Rural Areas: the Case of North and Central Portugal. *Journal of Travel Research*, 37(4), 353-363.

Kim, C., and Lee, S. (2000). Understanding the cultural differences in tourist motivation between Anglo-American and Japanese tourists. *Journal of Travel and Tourism Marketing*, 9(1/2), 153–170.

Kim, H., Borges, M. C., and Chon, J. (2006). Impacts of environmental values on tourism motivation: The case of FICA, Brazil. *Tourism Management*, 27, 957-967.

Kim, S. S., and Prideaux, B. (2005). Marketing implications arising from a comparative study of international pleasure tourist motivations and other travel-related characteristics of visitors to Korea. *Tourism Management*, 26, 347-357.

Kleiven, J. (2005). Measuring leisure and travel motives in Norway: replicating and supplementing the Leisure Motivation Scales. *Tourism Analysis*, 10, 109-122.

Kotler, P., Bowe, J., and Maken, J. (1999). *Marketing for Hospitality and Tourism*. London: Prentice-Hall.

Kozak, M. (2002). Comparative analysis of tourist motivations by nationality and destinations. *Tourism Management*, 23(3), 221-232.

Lazer, W, (1963). *Life-Style Concepts and Marketing*. Conference of the American Marketing Association: Toward Scientific Marketing, Fall, 130-139.

Lee, C. K., Lee, Y. K., and Wicks, B. (2004). Segmentation of festival motivation by nationality and satisfaction. *Tourism Management*, 25, 61-70.

Lee, H. Y., Petrick, J. F., and Crompton, J. (2007). The roles of quality and intermediary constructs in determining festival attendees' behavioural intention. *Journal of Travel Research*, 45(4), 402-412.

Lew, A. A. (1987). A Framework of Tourist Attraction Research. *Annals of Tourism Research*, 14(4), 553-575.

Loker-Murphy, L. (1996). Backpackers in Australia: a motivation-based segmentation study. *Journal of Travel and Tourism Marketing*, 5(4), 23-45.

Lopes, E. (2006). La motivación turística: el caso de la región de las aguas termales de Goiás, Brasil. *Boletín de la AGE*, 42, 303-314.

Lounbury, J. W., and Polik, J. R. (1992). Leisure needs and vacation satisfaction. *Leisure Science*, 14, 105-119.

MacInnis, D. J., and Jaworsky, B. J. (1989). Information processing from advertisements: Toward an integrative framework. *Journal of Marketing*, 53, 1-23.

Mannel, R. C., and Iso-Ahola, S. E. (1987). Psychological Nature of Leisure and Tourism Experience. *Annals of Tourism Research*, 14, 314-331.

Martín, M. T., and Recio, M. (2006). *Análisis de la calidad percibida y motivación del turismo rural*. Madrid: Servicio de Publicaciones de la Universidad Rey Juan Carlos.

Maslow, A. H. (1943). A Theory of Human Motivation. *Psychological Review*, 50, 370-396.

Maslow, A. H. (1954). *Motivation and Personality*. New York: Harper and Brothers.

Mesurado, B. (2008). Explicaciones psicológicas sobre la motivación y el sustrato neurobiológico que posibilita la misma. *Psicología y Psicopedagogía,* 7(19), 1-14.

Molera, L., and Albadalejo, I. P. (2007). Profiling segments of tourists in rural areas of South-Eastern Spain. *Tourism Management*, 28(3), 757-767.

Morgan, C. L. T. (1961). *Introduction of Psychology*. New York: McGraw Hill.

Oliver, R. L. (1997). *Satisfaction. A behavioral perspective on the consumer*. New York: McGraw-Hill.

Oliver, R. L. (1999). Whence consumer loyalty? *Journal of Marketing*, 63, 33-44.

Park, D. B., and Yoon, Y. S. (2009). Segmentation by motivation in rural tourism: A Korean case study. *Tourism Management*, 30(1), 99-106.

Pearce, P.L. (1982). *The social psychology of tourism behaviour*. Oxford: Pergamon Press.

Pearce, P. (1988). *The Ulysses Factor: Evaluating Visitors in Tourist Settings*. New York: Springer Verlag.

Pearce, P. (1993). Fundamentals of tourist motivation. In D. Pearce and R. Butler (Eds.), *Tourism Research: Critiques and Challenges* (pp. 113-134). London: Routledge.

Pearce, P. L., and Caltabiano, M. L. (1983). Inferring Travel Motivation from Travelers' Experiences. *Journal of Travel Research*, 22(2), 16-20.

Pearson, P. H. (1970). Relationship between global and specified measures of novelty seeking. *Journal of Consulting and Clinical Psychology*, 34, 199-304.

Qu, H., and Ping, E. W. Y. (1999). A service performance model of Hong Kong cruise travelers' motivation factors and satisfaction. *Tourism Management*, 20, 237-244.

Rodríguez del Bosque, I. A., San Martín, H., and Collado, J. (2006). The role of expectation in the consumer satisfaction formation process: Empirical evidence in the travel agency sector. *Tourism Management*, 27, 410-419.

Ross, E. L., and Iso-Ahola, S. E. (1991). Sightseeing tourists' motivation and satisfaction. *Annals of Tourism Research*, 18(2), 226-237.

Rust, R. T., and Oliver, R. L. (1994). Service Quality. Insights and Managerial Implications from the frontier. In R. T. Rust, and R. L. Oliver (Eds.), Service Quality: New Directions in Theory and Practice (pp. 1-19). California: SAGE.

Ryan C., and Glendon, I. (1998). Application of Leisure Motivation Scale to Tourism. *Annals of Tourism Research*, 25, 169-184.

San Martín, H., Collado, J., and Rodríguez del Bosque, I. (2009). Análisis de los efectos moderadores y la involucración sobre la relación satisfacción-lealtad en turismo. *XXI Congreso Nacional de Marketing*. Madrid: ESIC.

Severt, D., Wang, Y., Chen, P., and Breiter, D. (2007). Examining the motivation, perceived performance, and behavioural intentions of convention attendees: Evidence from a regional conference. *Tourism Management*, 28, 399-408.

Stabler, M. J. (1988). The image of destination region: Theoretical and empirical aspects. In B. Goodall and G. Ashworth (Eds.), Marketing and tourism industry: The promotion of destination regions (pp. 133-159). London: Croom Helm.

UNWTO (1994). *Recomendaciones sobre Estadísticas de Turismo*. Madrid. España.

UNWTO (2010). *Recomendaciones internacionales para estadísticas de turismo 2008*. http://unstats.un.org/unsd/publication/SeriesM/ Seriesm_83rev1s.pdf [Accessed July 12, 2011].

Vroom, V. H. (1964). *Work and motivation*. New York: Wiley and sons.

Witt, S. F., and Moutinho, L. (1994). *Tourism Marketing and Management Handbook*. London: Prentice Hall.

Yoon, Y., and Uysal, M. (2005). An examination of the effects of motivation and satisfaction on destination loyalty: a structural model. *Tourism Management*, 26(1), 45-56.

Yusof, A., and Shah, P. M. (2009). Application of Leisure Motivation Scale to Sport Tourism. *International Journal of the Humanities*, 6(1), 105-114.

Zabkar, V., Makowec, M., and Dmitrovic, T. (2009). Modelling perceived quality, visitor satisfaction and behavioural intentions at the destination level. *Tourism Management*, 31, 274-284.

In: Handbook on Psychology of Motivation
Editors: J. N. Franco and A. E. Svensgaard
ISBN: 978-1-62100-755-5
© 2012 Nova Science Publishers, Inc.

Chapter 2

MOTIVATION TO DONATE: NEW PERSPECTIVES FROM PSYCHOLOGY, ECONOMICS AND MARKETING

Jennifer Wiggins Johnson and Pamela E. Grimm*
Kent State University, Kent, OH, US

ABSTRACT

Individual donations of money, time, blood, and organs, and the motivations that underlie the decision to donate, have long been of interest to researchers in psychology, economics, and marketing. While the early research in each of these fields was largely separate, the three fields have converged in the past ten years around a core question: *why do individuals donate?* This chapter reviews the current literature on motivations to donate from all three fields, examining the commonalities in theory and findings as well as the unique contributions of each of the fields to our overall understanding of donor motivations. We conclude with suggestions for future research that will continue to bring the three fields together and provide valuable information for charities and nonprofit organizations as they continue to seek donations from individuals.

INTRODUCTION

For as long as individual behavior has been studied by psychologists, economists, and marketers, researchers in all three fields have been interested in behaviors that benefit others more than they benefit the actor, alternately referred to as helping behaviors, altruistic behaviors, and prosocial behaviors. Discussions of helping behavior are often traced back to the early economics literature, primarily to Adam Smith's observation in his 1759 book *The Theory of the Moral Sentiments* that, "How selfish soever man may be supposed, there are evidently some principles in his nature, which interest him in the fortune of others, and render their happiness necessary to him, though he derives nothing from it except the pleasure of seeing it" (Smith 1759, p. 7). This early view seems to imply that individuals sometimes

---

* Phone 330-672-1259, Fax 330-672-5006, E-mail: jwiggin2@kent.edu

engage in behavior that is performed solely for the benefit of another, with no benefit to the helper other than the pleasure of knowing that he or she has helped.

Sociobiologists offered similarly extreme definitions of helping behavior such as, "enhancing the net fitness of another individual at some net cost to one's own fitness" (Krebs and Miller 1985, p. 11), and, "self-destructive behavior performed for the benefit of others" (Wilson 1975, p. 578). While these definitions fit with the philosophical concept of "pure altruism," more recent research in economics, sociobiology, and psychology questions the realism of such a concept, and offers less extreme definitions of helping behavior. Economists have primarily studied helping behavior in the context of games such as the prisoner's dilemma, and define helping behavior as acting in a manner that takes into consideration the preferences or needs of others, rather than acting solely in self interest (Andreoni 1990, Rabin 1993). Contemporary sociobiologists consider a behavior to be altruistic if it benefits the actor less than it benefits the recipient, and many psychologists now define behavior as altruistic or helping behavior if the act is motivated primarily by concern for another's needs (Piliavin and Charng 1990). Finally, marketing researchers focus on the consequences of the behavior and define an act as altruistic when the intent of the act is to provide a greater benefit to the recipient of the help than to the actor, and when the act enhances the recipient's welfare (Bendapudi, Singh, and Bendapudi 1996). While there are nuanced differences in emphasis and terminology, the definitions put forth in these fields are largely in agreement about the fundamental nature of helping behavior.

Methods for studying altruistic or helping behavior have varied across these three fields; however, they have all frequently focused their research on the same behavioral acts, specifically donations of money, blood, organs, or time in the form of volunteerism. While the psychology literature has also examined instances of individuals helping individuals who are in need, the common ground across all three of these disciplines appears to be the more institutional forms of helping that Penner and colleagues (2005) refer to as macro-level helping, in which individuals engage in prosocial behavior within the context of an organization or group. This is a form of mediated helping behavior, in which an agent, such as a charity or nonprofit organization, acts as an intermediary to facilitate the relationship between the individual who acts as the helper and the individual who receives and benefits from the help (Bendapudi et al. 1996). Donation behaviors such as charitable giving and many forms of volunteerism fall into this category, as the helper is giving money or time to an organization that subsequently uses it to help others who are in need.

Early research on this form of donation behavior focused on understanding who engages in these behaviors, under what circumstances they engage in these behaviors, and what external influences, such as offering incentives or varying the request for help, can increase their likelihood of making a donation. Much of the research from the latter half of the 20th century appears to have been influenced by the underlying assumptions and theoretical lenses of the different fields, with the psychologists examining psychological traits and processes, the economists studying incentives and reciprocity, and the marketing researchers testing the effectiveness of different requests for help. However, as the 1990's came to a close, the research in all three fields began to converge around a common question: *why* are individuals donating? Interest in motivations to donate began to appear in all three literature streams, and the resulting research revealed intriguing new findings about donor motivations that were replicated across all three fields.

This chapter will review and analyze the current literature on motivations to donate in psychology, economics, and marketing to help researchers better understand what motivates individuals to engage in donation behaviors. This review is based on a search of leading academic journals in all three fields from 2000-2011, with an emphasis on articles that examine motivations in the context of charitable donations, volunteerism, and donations of blood or organs. Research on individuals helping other individuals, general socially responsible behaviors such as political activism or environmentally conscious behaviors, and the considerable research on the influence of role identity on donation behavior were considered beyond the scope of this review.

We will begin with a brief overview of the early literature from each of the three fields leading up to the focus on motivations to donate. The remainder of the chapter is organized into several common themes that are evident in the current literature across psychology, economics, and marketing, including gaining an understanding of individuals' motivations to donate, the relationship between altruistic and egoistic motivations to donate, the influence of social motivations to donate, and efforts to influence motivations to donate. We conclude with a set of future research directions that will continue to connect the three fields and build on their common understanding of donor motivations.

EARLY RESEARCH ON DONATION BEHAVIOR

Individual Differences in Donation Behavior

Understanding who donates and who does not donate was at the core of the early research in both psychology and marketing. Much of the focus of psychological research on donation behavior was in the form of an ongoing debate about the existence of an altruistic personality (see Piliavin and Charng 1990 for a review). Psychology researchers attempted to link altruistic or donation behavior to personality characteristics such as self-esteem, competence, locus of control, need for approval, and moral development (Staub 1978, Aronoff and Wilson 1984, Piliavin et al. 1981, Rushton 1981). Individuals who had and had not engaged in altruistic behaviors were compared on demographic variables (Oliner and Oliner 1988, Piliavin and Unger 1985), personality differences as measured by the MMPI (Simmons, Klein, and Simmons 1977), specific personality traits (Reddy 1980), moral or personal norms (Oliner and Oliner 1988, Schwartz 1970, Zuckerman, Siegelbaum, and Williams 1977, Piliavin and Libby 1986), and beliefs such as trust (Simmons et al. 1977) and risk-taking (Farnill and Ball 1982). While some significant correlations were found, the existence of altruism as a personality trait remains an ongoing debate (Piliavin and Charng 1990).

The early marketing literature on donations similarly focused on identifying differences between those who donated and those who did not donate. Many of these studies followed segmentation principles, differentiating between donor groups and non-donor groups on demographic variables (Pessemier, Beamon and Hanssen 1977, Burnett 1981, Danko and Stanley 1986, Harvey 1990, Cernak, File and Prince 1994, Broadbridge and Horne 1994), psychographic variables (Pessemier et al. 1977, Harvey 1990, Cernak et al. 1994), and attitudinal or behavioral variables (Burnett 1981, Riecken and Yavas 1986). Early marketing researchers also identified some individual differences in motives or reasons for donating

(Dawson 1988, Guy and Patton 1989, Broadbridge and Horne 1994), but these studies were largely limited to identifying rather than explaining these differences.

Situational Influences on Donation Behavior

In addition to individual differences, donation behavior was also linked to different circumstances or situational variables in all three literature streams. Experimental economics researchers studied cooperative or altruistic behavior in the context of economic games, and identified specific situations in which individuals were likely to strategically engage in altruistic behaviors, as opposed to self-interest seeking behaviors, in order to achieve a desired outcome (Axelrod 1984, Rabin 1993). Individuals were also found to be more likely to act altruistically when they were personally endowed with a higher level of resources (Rapoport 1988) and when there were fewer resources to be shared among the participants (Poppe and Utens 1986). Extensive research in economics also established the traditional public goods model, in which individuals contribute to a public good because, as part of the public who benefits from the good, they would benefit from its existence (see Andreoni 1989 for a discussion).

Psychologists also examined a number of situational variables, such as the well-known bystander effect, in which the likelihood of helping is dependent on the number of other available helpers (Latane, Nida, and Wilson 1981), the urgency of the situation (Shotland and Stebbins 1983), the cost of helping (Piliavin et al. 1981, Shotland and Stebbins 1983), and whether they are directly asked for help (Oliner and Oliner 1988). Psychology researchers also identified aspects of the help recipient that would influence the likelihood of helping, such as gender (Eagly and Crowly 1986), perceived need (Batson 1987), dependence or inability to help oneself (Berkowitz 1972), the recipient's need being due to circumstances beyond his or her control (Schopler and Matthews 1965), and the ability to inspire empathy in the potential donor (Batson 1987, Batson et al. 1995). Marketing researchers similarly found that individuals are more likely to donate to familiar charities with positive images (Harvey 1990), charities whose needs are perceived to be higher (Fisher and Ackerman 1988), and charities that meet Berkowitz's (1972) definition of being dependent on the donor for help (Moore, Bearden and Teel 1985).

Researchers in psychology and marketing have also examined characteristics of the relationship between the potential helper and the potential recipient. Clark and Mills (1979, 1993) have repeatedly demonstrated that individuals have different expectations for when help is to be given, and what benefits should be received in exchange for helping, depending on the nature of the relationship between the helper and the recipient. Individuals who perceive an exchange relationship with the recipient are less likely to help and expect to receive comparable benefits in exchange for their help, while individuals who perceive a communal relationship with the recipient are more likely to help and do not expect to receive benefits in return (Clark and Mills 1993). These results have recently been replicated in relationships between individuals and organizations (Aggarwal 2004, Johnson, Peck, and Thomas 2009, Johnson and Grimm 2010). The closeness of the relationship has also been found to influence helping behavior. Individuals have been found to be more likely to help relatives than strangers (Campbell 1983), as well as causes or charities with which they feel a personal connection (Supphellen and Nelson 2001) or identify strongly (Bhattacharya and

Sen 2003). Taken together, this research suggests that it is not only characteristics of the individual, but also characteristics of the recipient, the situation, and the relationship between the donor and the recipient that influence willingness to donate.

External Influences on Donation Behavior

Not surprisingly, the majority of the research on external influences can be found in the economics and marketing literatures. The economics literature has largely focused on the effectiveness of incentives in soliciting donation behavior, dating back to Titmuss' (1971) seminal work on the use of incentives in blood donation requests. Much of this extensive research has revolved around the idea of incentives having a negative (crowding-out) effect or a positive (crowding-in) effect on individual donations (Frey 1994, 1997). This work is theoretically grounded in Deci and Ryan's (1985) self-determination theory of intrinsic and extrinsic motivations, and suggests that when the individual perceives an incentive to be controlling, he or she is less likely to donate, but when the incentive is perceived to be supportive, the likelihood of donation increases (Frey 1997).

Marketing researchers have also found that incentives can increase helping behavior, particularly in the area of volunteering to participate in market research. In studies of responses to mail surveys, both monetary and nonmonetary incentives offered in exchange for responses increased response rates significantly (Armstrong 1975, Hansen 1980, Yu and Cooper 1983). Monetary incentives have also been shown to increase cooperation rates in interviews and willingness to participate in research a second time (Wiseman, Schafer, and Schafer 1983). Offering to donate money to a charity of the respondent's choice resulted in increased response rates that were comparable to offering a direct monetary incentive to the respondent (Furse and Stewart 1982, Robertson and Bellenger 1978).

Economists have also considered reciprocity as an incentive for helping behavior. For example, Axelrod (1984; Axelrod and Hamilton 1981) examined the strategies of cooperation and competition that individuals will use in a Prisoner's Dilemma experiment, and found that the most beneficial strategy is Tit-for-Tat, a strategy in which individuals cooperate when their partner cooperates and defect when their partner defects. This type of reciprocal interaction, in which cooperation, or helping, by the partner is rewarded with cooperation by the individual, was found to result in the maximum benefit for both partners in the interaction. A great deal of research in economics has considered the possibility that the individual will still donate in the absence of a tangible external reward in order to receive an intangible or psychological benefit usually described as "warm glow" (Andreoni 1989, 1990). This "impure" altruism is contrasted with the traditional public goods model and suggests that the individual may donate in order to feel good about their behavior, thus receiving psychological benefits that reciprocate for the donation behavior (Andreoni 1989, Margolis 1982, Ribar and Wilhelm 2002).

Reciprocal behavior has also been found in psychology studies where subjects engage in helping behaviors. Thomas and Batson (1981) found that subjects were more willing to help a fellow student with a research project when they were told that the student in question had earlier provided them with help. Lee, Piliavin, and Call (1999) found a comparable effect among blood donors, noting that individuals who had previously received blood or were related to someone who had received blood were significantly more likely to become blood donors than individuals who had not received blood.

Finally, marketing researchers have also examined the effectiveness of different types of requests for donations, including the size of the request (Reingen 1978, Blockner et al. 1984, Fern, Monroe and Avila 1986, Fraser, Hite and Sauer 1988, Schibrowsky and Peltier 1995), the type of advertising or medium used to communicate the request (Moore, Bearden and Teel 1985, Horton 1991), the type of message delivered in the request (Burnkrant and Page 1982, LaTour and Manrai 1989, Meyers-Levy and Maheswaran 1992, Bagozzi and Moore 1994), and the method of collecting the donations (Schlegelmilch and Tannin 1989). Bendapudi, Singh, and Bendapudi (1996) summarize these findings into an overall framework designed to help charitable organizations develop effective promotion plans to solicit donations.

By the close of the 20th century, psychologists, economists, and marketing researchers had learned a great deal about who donates, when they donate, and what can make them more likely to donate. Researchers had identified individual characteristics and situational variables that made an individual more likely to donate, but had not answered the question of why the individual was donating in the first place. Towards the end of the 1990's and beginning of the 2000's, researchers in all three fields began to shift their focus to understanding what motivates individuals to donate their money, time, blood, and organs to help others.

UNDERSTANDING MOTIVATIONS TO DONATE

Individual Differences in Motivations to Donate

As attention in the literature turned to motivations to donate, researchers from psychology and marketing began by conducting survey-based research of charitable donors and volunteers to catalog reported motivations to donate. Several taxonomies of donor motivations were developed, with somewhat similar results. Dawson (1988) measured motivations to donate money to charities that support medical research and identified four motivations: reciprocity (individuals had benefitted from the charity before and felt an obligation to give back), self-esteem (a desire to improve one's image or social worth), career motives (a desire to gain political advantages or career advancement), and income or tax motives (a desire to gain the tax benefits associated with charitable giving). Drawing on Clary, Snyder and Ridge's (1992) functional theory of volunteering, Omoto and Snyder (1995) examined motivations among AIDS volunteers and found five motivations: values (a desire to express prosocial or altruistic values), understanding (a desire to gain new knowledge or skills that help the volunteer to understand the world), personal development (a desire to grow socially and individually), community concern (a sense of obligation to or concern about the community), and esteem enhancement (to feel better about oneself). Individuals in both Dawson's (1988) and Omoto and Snyder's (1995) studies reported experiencing one or more of these motivations in their decisions to donate money or time.

Clary and colleagues (1998) subsequently validated a measure of six motivations based on the functions that are potentially served by volunteerism: values (expressing altruistic values), understanding (gaining new knowledge and skills), social (cultivating or maintaining social relationships), career (gaining career-related benefits), protective (reducing guilt over being more fortunate than others), and self-enhancement (experiencing emotional growth or positive affect). Individuals were found to differ across these functional motivations, and individuals who received functional benefits that were consistent with their motivations exhibited higher satisfaction with their volunteer experience and greater intentions to volunteer in the future.

Rioux and Penner (2001) and Finkelstein and Penner (2004) expanded the taxonomy approach to organizational citizenship behaviors, prosocial behaviors directed at an organization by its employees. Rioux and Penner (2001) developed and validated a multidimensional scale, with this research resulting in three motivations: organizational concern, prosocial values, and impression management. Rioux and Penner (2001) found that only the prosocial values motive significantly and strongly predicts organizational citizenship behaviors, while Finkelstein and Penner (2004) found effects of both prosocial values and impression management. Finkelstein (2006) extended this research to incorporate motive fulfillment, and found that organizational citizenship behaviors are positively correlated with prosocial values and impression management motives as well as the fulfillment of these motives. Finkelstein further found that impression management motives were related to organizational citizenship behaviors that are directed toward coworkers but not to those that are directed toward the organization itself.

Supphellen and Nelson (2001) took a slightly different approach, creating a taxonomy of givers who rely on different criteria to make their decision to donate. They identify three categories of donors: analysts, who are highly involved in the decision and carefully analyze both the organization making the request and the cause behind it; relationists, who are loyal to specific organizations and consider only the organization making the request; and internalists, who have internalized donation norms and values and respond positively to a request without considering either the cause or the organization making the request. Though Supphellen and Nelson (2001) do not specifically test motivational differences between these groups, they observe parallels between the internalists' behavior and traditional altruistic motives, and between the relationists' behavior and motives related to social ties and relationships. One can also see a connection between the internalists' behavior and the value-expressive motives discussed by Omoto and Snyder (1995) and Clary and colleagues (1998), and perhaps between the analysts' behavior and Omoto and Snyder's (1995) community concern motives. This would suggest that individual differences in motivation may influence donors' decision making processes and what information they consider in making the decision to donate.

Altruistic and Egoistic Motivations to Donate

Much of the discussion of individual differences in motivations to donate revolves around two general classes of motivations, referred to either as intrinsic and extrinsic motivations or as altruistic and egoistic motivations. Deci and Ryan (1985, Ryan and Deci 2000) define intrinsic motivation as, "doing something because it is inherently interesting or enjoyable," and extrinsic motivation as, "doing something because it leads to a separable outcome" (Ryan and Deci 2000, p. 55). These definitions are most commonly operationalized through the offering of an extrinsic reward for the individual's behavior, which is assumed to activate an extrinsic motivation to behave. Individuals who freely choose to engage in a behavior in the absence of an extrinsic reward are assumed to be intrinsically motivated to behave. In fact, the most frequently used measure of intrinsic motivation involves measuring the amount of time that an individual engages in a behavior in the absence of an extrinsic reward (Ryan and Deci 2000).

In the context of donation behavior, an extrinsically motivated individual would be making a donation in order to receive an extrinsic benefit or reward for his or her donation. This is frequently referred to as an egoistic motivation, in which the individual is acting in their own self-interest in order to receive a benefit or incentive in return for their donation (Bendapudi et al. 1996, Penner et al. 2005). Donating in the absence of an extrinsic reward, on the other hand, is frequently seen as an altruistically motivated act (Piliavin and Charng 1990, Bendapudi et al. 1996, Penner et al. 2005), in which the individual acts with no expectation of receiving a benefit other than the positive feelings derived from the actual act of donating, such as "warm glow" (Andreoni 1989, 1990). This is consistent with Ryan and Deci's (2000) view of intrinsic motivation as driven by a positive emotional response to the behavior itself.

In the economics literature, intrinsic and extrinsic motivations are frequently discussed in terms of extrinsic rewards for donations crowding out intrinsic motivation to donate (Frey 1994, 1997), a variation on Deci and Ryan's (1985) overjustification effect. This effect has been frequently replicated in both the psychology and economics literature, and involves a decrease in intrinsic motivation to behave following the receipt of extrinsic rewards for behavior. This negative effect of extrinsic rewards is moderated by the individual's perceptions of the purpose of the reward or, in alternate terms, their perceived causality of their behavior. If the reward is perceived as controlling (Frey 1997), the individual perceives an external locus of control for their behavior (Ryan and Deci 2000), and attributes their behavior to the extrinsic reward, thus decreasing their intrinsic motivation. However, if the reward is perceived as supportive (Frey 1997), allowing the individual to maintain a sense of autonomy (Ryan and Deci 2000), the individual perceives an internal locus of control for their behavior and their intrinsic motivation is not diminished by the reward.

This effect has been replicated a number of times in the context of donation behavior. Frey and Oberholzer-Gee (1997) tested the crowding in and out of donation behavior in the context of a "Not in My Backyard" study, in which individuals were asked to allow an undesirable entity such as a nuclear power plant to be placed near their homes, donating either their own land or the proximity to their homes to benefit the community. The authors found that civic-minded individuals were prepared to bear the cost of living near the undesirable entity in order to benefit the larger community, but this willingness diminished dramatically when financial compensation was offered. Gneezy and Rustichini (2000) similarly found that volunteers who were offered payment for their time exhibited a drop in volunteer behavior over those who were not offered compensation. Janssen and Mendys (2001) demonstrated theoretical support for this crowding out effect of extrinsic rewards in the context of blood donation, and suggested that the individual's response to receiving a reward may depend on whether their initial motivation to donate is egoistically or altruistically motivated. Lacetera and Macis (2010) conducted an empirical test of blood donors' responses to being offered extrinsic rewards, and found evidence to support the crowding out of intrinsic motivation and decrease in future willingness to donate when donors are offered cash incentives, but not when they are offered non-cash incentives with the same monetary value.

Researchers have also noted positive effects of extrinsic rewards or incentives under conditions when intrinsic motivation is likely to be low. Holmes, Miller and Lerner (2002) framed requests for charitable donations as either an exchange transaction (purchasing a decorative candle with some of the proceeds going to charity) or an altruistic donation. In a context in which donation amounts were very small (on average less than $1.00), suggesting that intrinsic motivation to donate was low, they found that offering the exchange transaction as an incentive increased both the mean donation amount and the proportion of participants who made a donation. Goette and Stutzer (2008) found similar results when they offered incentives to individuals who had varying levels of intrinsic motivation to donate blood. Participants whose intrinsic motivation to donate blood was low experienced an increase in motivation to donate when they were offered incentives, while participants who were frequent blood donors responded negatively to incentives. Bertacchini, Santagata and Signorello (2011) found similar results in a field study of individuals' willingness to donate to cultural institutions. They initially measured participants' willingness to donate without any form of incentive, then offered them a variety of financial and social incentives. The incentives converted between 5.8% and 36.4% of the participants who had previously declined to donate into donors, depending on the type of incentive.

Across the economics, psychology, and marketing literatures, the fundamental notion of two sets of motivations, one more self-focused and one more other-focused, has been repeatedly supported, and these motivations have been found to differentially impact individuals' willingness to donate. Several studies have supported a negative or crowding out effect between the two, in which the presence of extrinsic rewards diminishes intrinsic or altruistic motivations to donate. However, there is theoretical support for the idea that the relationship between altruistic and egoistic motivations may be more complex, suggesting that an expanded view of motivation may be a more accurate representation of donation behavior.

Social Motivations to Donate

While the psychology literature on motivations has traditionally focused on intrinsic and extrinsic motivations, the economics literature has examined a third category of motivations, alternately called prestige motivations (e.g. Harbaugh, 1998a), image motivations (e.g. Ariely, Bracha, and Meier, 2009), status-based motivations (e.g. Wichardt, 2008), or social motivations (e.g. Rege and Telle, 2004). The common phenomenon described in all of these studies is an individual who is motivated to donate in order to gain a reward that is social in nature or avoid a social punishment for not donating (Fehr and Falk 2002). Social rewards can include opportunities to gain social acceptance, social status, or social approval, while social punishments can include social disapproval, "loss of face," or even exclusion from a social group. In the specific case of volunteerism, social rewards can also include career-oriented motives, such as gaining knowledge and skills that would increase the individual's career prospects, or gaining access to a network of contacts that can help the individual to succeed in his or her career (Ziemek 2006).

Glazer and Konrad (1996) and Harbaugh (1998a, 1998b) were among the first economics researchers to suggest that donors can be motivated by the opportunity to have their donations made known to others. For example, Harbaugh (1998b) finds that individuals frequently donate the minimum amount needed to be included in a category of donors (e.g. $250-$599), and attributes this to their desire to be seen as a member of a social group that donates or to gain prestige from others who donate at the same or lower levels. Glazer and Konrad (1996) similarly introduce the concept of conspicuous giving, analogous to conspicuous consumption (Veblen 1899) as the desire to gain social status through others knowing your actions. Fehr and Fischbarcher (2003) further suggest that individuals can use altruistic behavior such as donations as a means to signal favorable but unobservable personality traits to other individuals in order to be perceived as a good potential friend or partner, or even a good potential mate.

Evidence from experimental economics supports this desire to have others be aware of the individual's donation behavior. Andreoni and Petrie (2004) varied the anonymity of donors in a public goods experiment, alternately making the individual's identity, the amount he or she donated, or both pieces of information public to the other participants in the experiment. They found that participants who knew that their identity and the amount they donated to the public good would be made public donated the highest amount to the public good. They further found evidence of leaders and followers among participants, and found that making the leaders' donation amounts known to the other participants increased the donation amounts of the followers.

Several researchers replicated this effect in different contexts. Rege and Telle (2004) conducted a similar public goods experiment in which some participants had their identity and contribution amount publicly revealed, while others received instructions that were framed to prime social norms of cooperation, and found that the public revealing of the individual's behavior had a stronger influence on donation amounts than even priming social norms of cooperation. Soetevent (2005) conducted a field experiment in which offerings at a church were collected in either an open basket (publicly revealed) or a closed bag (kept private), and found that the open baskets increased offerings when the recipient of the donation was an outside charity, but not when the recipient was the church itself. While the difference between the two collection basket conditions was significant at first, the effect was found to diminish over time, as the open basket with its publicly revealed donations became the new norm for individuals in that condition.

Economics researchers have also examined the interplay between intrinsic, extrinsic, and social motivations to donate. Janssen and Mendys-Kamphorst (2004) presented a theoretical model that suggested that financial incentives are likely to diminish or crowd out social motivation as well as intrinsic motivation, suggesting that social motivation behaves more similarly to intrinsic motivation than extrinsic motivation despite the receipt of an external social reward. Ariely, Bracha and Meier (2009) further found that extrinsic incentives can interact with social motivations in influencing the individual's donation behavior. Across two experiments in which participants were exerting effort to support a charity (for example, participating in a "bike for charity" event in which the total donation received depended on the distance the participant biked), they found that individuals who were given an extrinsic incentive increased their effort when the incentive was given in private, but decreased their effort when the incentive was given in front of others. The authors' explanation for this effect was a potential social punishment if others saw the individual accept the incentive and assumed that his or her donation behavior was motivated by the extrinsic reward.

DellaVigna, List and Malmendier (2009) also found evidence of social motivations as an extrinsic motivator. They conducted two identical door-to-door donation drives, but in one they informed participants ahead of time what day and time they would be coming to collect the donations. This information essentially enabled individuals to opt out of the donation drive by avoiding the donation collectors. The authors found that giving individuals the opportunity to opt-out of the donation drive reduced participation by between 10% and 30%, and ultimately resulted in lower donation amounts for the charity. Their explanation is that the same percentage of individuals in both drives were intrinsically motivated to donate, but for those individuals who were not given the opportunity to avoid the donation collectors, the perceived social pressure to donate was strong enough to overcome their lack of intrinsic motivation and convert them into donors.

The economics literature has clearly identified an additional form of motivation that can drive individual donation behavior. The desire for social approval or to avoid social punishment has been found to influence individuals' willingness to donate in multiple contexts. Evidence seems to suggest that social rewards can behave similarly to extrinsic rewards and have negative effects on intrinsic motivation to donate. However, research on multiple motivations in psychology and marketing suggests that this may not be as simple as it seems.

Multiple Motivations to Donate

Several researchers have examined the co-existence of both altruistic and egoistic motivations within the same individual's decision to donate. This research on multiple motivations to donate parallels similar research streams in areas such as achievement motivation in psychology, in which both intrinsic and extrinsic motivations have been found to co-exist and jointly motivate individuals (Barron and Harackiewicz 2000, Hayenga and Corpus 2010), and incentives research in economics, in which extrinsic rewards have sometimes been found to enhance or crowd in intrinsic motivation (Frey and Jegen 2001, Nyborg and Rege 2003). Both of these research streams suggest that an individual may be simultaneously motivated by both intrinsic and extrinsic motives. Donation behaviors such as blood donation (Ferguson, Farrell and Lawrence 2008) and volunteerism (Bierhoff 2001, Schroeder et al. 1995) have similarly been found to be motivated by a combination of self-serving or egoistic motives and other-oriented or altruistic motives. Batson, Ahmad and Tsang (2002) apply this concept of multiple motivations to community involvement, developing a taxonomy of motives that includes both egoistic and altruistic motives and concluding that an individual may be motivated by both forms of motivation and that these motives may either complement or conflict with each other. In a cross-national study of volunteer behavior, Van de Vliert, Huang and Levine (2004) find that national income levels can help to explain when egoistic and altruistic motives for volunteering are complementary or conflicting. Using data from 33 countries, they find evidence of conflicting motivations in lower income countries, in which volunteers face more of a trade-off between helping others and ensuring their own survival, and complementary motivations in higher income countries, were the standard of living is higher and individuals have to sacrifice less in order to help others.

Kiviniemi, Snyder and Omoto (2002) go a step further, directly measuring single versus multiple motivations among volunteers to determine the outcomes of being singly or multiply motivated. Using Omoto and Snyder's (1995) multidimensional measure of volunteer motivations, the authors classified volunteers who were beginning their service as multiply motivated if their scores on their highest motivation dimension were within a single scale point of their scores on any of the other motivation dimensions. Six months after the volunteers had reported their motivations, multiply motivated volunteers were found to perceive significantly more stress, higher costs, less fulfillment of their personally relevant motives, and lower satisfaction with their volunteer experience than their singly motivated counterparts. These negative effects of multiple motivations were found in spite of the multiply motivated volunteers reporting a higher overall level of motivation than the singly motivated volunteers.

Johnson and Grimm (2010) further explore this issue and find that while tangible extrinsic rewards tend to conflict with intrinsic motivations to donate, social rewards can complement both intrinsic and extrinsic motivations to donate. In a study of charitable donations, donors were found to exhibit a combination of intrinsic, extrinsic, and social motivations to donate, depending on the type of relationship they perceived with the charitable organization. Social motivations were found to be consistent with both an exchange relationship, which was also related to extrinsic motivations to donate, and a communal relationship, which led to intrinsic motivations to donate. Thus, social motivations were able to successfully co-exist with both intrinsic and extrinsic motivations, despite intrinsic and extrinsic motivations being negatively related to each other. It is clear that intrinsic or altruistic motivations and extrinsic or egoistic motivations are not simply opposing forces that crowd each other out. Individuals may instead be driven by a mix of motivations that can combine to have positive or negative outcomes for the individual, depending on how the motivations complement or conflict with each other.

ANTECEDENTS AND CONSEQUENCES OF MOTIVATIONS TO DONATE

Antecedents of Differences in Motivations to Donate

As researchers' understanding of different motivations to donate grew, taxonomies of motivations were linked to a series of individual difference variables to explain why individuals had different motives for engaging in the same donation behavior. Several studies found evidence to suggest that motivations to donate may change depending on where the individual is in his or her life course. Omoto, Snyder and Martino (2000) examined motives among volunteers of different ages and found that younger volunteers were more likely to be motivated by outcomes related to interpersonal relationships, while older volunteers were more likely to be motivated by a desire to serve or a sense of obligation to their community. Mathur (1996) examined charitable donations among older adults and found that motivations related to social interactions and perceived influence over how the funds would be used were positively related to donation behavior, while esteem enhancement motives were negatively related to donation behavior. Mowen and Sujan (2005) also examined volunteers who were older adults, measuring Clary and colleagues' (1998) six functional motivations, and found that among an older population, self-enhancement was negatively related to volunteer behavior, while the other five functional motivations positively predicted volunteer behavior.

A number of researchers have also attempted to link motivations to differences in personality traits. Carlo and colleagues (2005) linked having a prosocial values motivation to donate to the Big Five personality traits among a sample of volunteers, and found that individuals' agreeableness and extraversion positively predicted volunteer behavior, partially mediated by their prosocial values motivation. Finkelstein and Brannick (2007) found similar connections between volunteer motivations, perceived role identity as a volunteer, and having a prosocial personality, and found that all three significantly and positively predicted informal volunteer behavior among a student sample.

Omoto, Snyder and Hackett (2010) also linked volunteer motivations to the Big Five personality traits, along with measures of interpersonal orientations, among a sample of volunteers who engaged in activist and civic engagement behaviors. They combined the five motivations in Omoto and Snyder's (1995) scale into two underlying dimensions of self-focused motivations and other-focused motivations. Activism and civic engagement behaviors were found to be significantly correlated with both forms of motivation, but more strongly with other-focused motivations, and only other-focused motivations significantly predicted these volunteer behaviors. Activism behaviors were also found to be predicted by the Big Five traits of extraversion and emotional stability, and by the individual having a communal orientation, a universal orientation, or having experienced personal distress. Civic engagement behaviors, however, were only predicted by empathic concern for others, and were not predicted by any of the Big Five personality traits.

Several researchers have also examined individual differences between individuals who exhibited altruistic and egoistic motivations to donate. De Groot and Steg (2010) examine motivations to donate alongside individuals' value orientations, including egoistic (concerned with benefitting the self), altruistic (concerned with benefitting others), and biospheric (concerned with benefitting the environment in general) orientations, and found that differences in these underlying orientations explained more of the variance in donations to an environmental cause than specific motivations to donate. Harbaugh, Mayr and Burghart (2007) take individual differences a step further, placing individuals in an MRI machine while they were playing an experimental economics game in which they were given a choice to give money to others or take it for themselves. They found that individuals who were more likely to give money to themselves, who they termed egoists, exhibited different brain patterns while playing the game from individuals who were more likely to give money to others, who they termed altruists.

Finally, several researchers have also found that the donor's relationships can influence his or her motivations to donate. Maner and Gailliot (2007) found that a kinship relationship with the donation recipient led individuals to have a more altruistic motivation, while a stranger relationship led individuals to have a more egoistic motivation. Johnson and Grimm (2010) found that a perceived communal relationship with a charitable organization leads individuals to be intrinsically motivated to donate, while a perceived exchange relationship leads individuals to be extrinsically motivated to donate, and that social motivations to donate are found within both communal and exchange relationships. Small and Simonsohn (2008) found that motivations to donate can also be influenced by other relationships in the individual's life besides the recipient of the donation. Individuals who had a relationship with someone who had been through a hardship (e.g. fighting breast cancer) were found to experience greater sympathy and have a higher likelihood of donating to organizations that worked to reduce the hardship that the acquaintance had experienced (e.g. a charity raising funds for breast cancer research). The authors further found that closer relationships with the person who had been through the hardship led to increased sympathy and increased motivation to donate.

Taken together, this research suggests that there is a link between underlying personality traits, orientations, and relationships and individuals' motivations to donate, but motivations are typically the more immediate predictor of donation behaviors. Mowen and Sujan (2005) describe this as a hierarchical model in which motivations reside at the surface level, directly influencing behavior, but are influenced themselves by underlying traits. In their study of volunteerism, Clary and colleagues' (1998) functional motives were found to be immediate predictors of volunteer behavior, but the functional motives were themselves predicted by the individual having a volunteer orientation, which was in turn predicted by personality traits such as altruism, need for activity, and need for learning. This suggests that there are individual difference variables that act as antecedents of motivations to donate, influencing the nature and intensity of the individual's motivations to donate, which subsequently influence donation behavior.

Consequences of Differences in Motivations to Donate

Motivations to donate have also been found to influence outcomes beyond willingness to donate or donation behavior. Davis, Hall and Meyer (2003) conducted a year-long longitudinal study of volunteers across several different organizations and found that volunteers whose specific motives were fulfilled by their volunteer work were more satisfied with their volunteer experience than volunteers whose work did not fulfill their specific motives for volunteering, regardless of whether their specific motives were altruistic or self-oriented. However, several similar studies have found evidence that overall, individuals who are motivated by intrinsic or altruistic motives experience greater satisfaction with their donation or volunteer experience than individuals who are motivated by extrinsic or egoistic motives. Millette and Gagné (2008) examined the influence of volunteer job characteristics on volunteer motivation, and found that job characteristics that led volunteers to be intrinsically motivated led to greater satisfaction and better volunteer performance than job characteristics that led volunteers to be extrinsically motivated. Moreno-Jiménez, Pilar and Villodres (2010) also found that volunteers who were intrinsically motivated were less likely to experience volunteer burnout than those who were extrinsically motivated to volunteer.

The positive outcomes associated with intrinsic or altruistic motivations extend beyond donor or volunteer satisfaction. Grant (2008) examined intrinsic and extrinsic motivations to engage in organizational citizenship behaviors and found that individuals who were intrinsically motivated to engage in these behaviors also experienced greater job performance and productivity, and continued to persist in engaging in organizational citizenship behaviors, when compared to individuals who were extrinsically motivated. Piferi, Jobe and Jones (2006) examined charitable donations in New York in the wake of the 9/11 tragedy and also found that donation behavior persisted longer when it was motivated by altruistic motives rather than egoistic motives. Finally, Weinstein and Ryan (2010, Weinstein, De Haan and Ryan 2010) found that even the recipient benefits more when the donor is intrinsically motivated. When recipients perceived their donor's motivations to be autonomous, rather than controlled by extrinsic rewards, donation recipients experienced more gratitude, more positive attitudes, greater felt closeness with the donor, and higher overall well-being.

INFLUENCING MOTIVATIONS TO DONATE

If individuals can have different motivations for engaging in donation behavior, and some of these motivations have consequences that are more beneficial for the donor and the recipient, it is a logical next step to determine whether organizations can influence what motivates an individual to donate. Researchers have found evidence of marketing strategies that can increase altruistic motivation to donate. Ellen, Mohr and Webb (2000) conducted a field study in which two retailers, a grocery store and a hardware store, offered to collect donated goods to be given to charity. The nature of the goods was altered to be either congruent with the store (food and cleaning supplies with the grocery store, building supplies with the hardware store), or incongruent with the store (food and cleaning supplies with the hardware store, building supplies with the grocery store). The authors found that for the hardware store, individuals were less altruistically motivated to donate when the goods being collected were congruent with the store. The explanation offered is that the individuals perceived the congruent goods to be a way for the store to profit from the charitable act, while the collection of incongruent goods was perceived to be altruistically motivated, thus increasing the individual's altruistic motivation to donate.

Popkowski Leszczyc and Rothkopf (2010) conducted two real-world auctions in a field experiment, one a standard retailer auction and one a retailer auction with a percentage of the proceeds being given to charity. The items in the two auctions were identical, suggesting that participants should value them equally whether they are purchases or extrinsic rewards for donating. However, participants in the charity auction were found to consistently pay higher prices for identical items when compared to participants in the standard auction, and the higher the percentage of the proceeds that went to the charity, the higher the prices the participants in the charity auction were willing to pay. Offering a high percentage of the proceeds to the charity was so successful in creating altruistic motivation to donate above and beyond the price of the good, that the percent increase in the prices paid ultimately exceeded the percent increase in the amount being donated to the charity, meaning that when the retailer offered a higher percentage to the charity, they actually made more profit than when they offered a lower percentage.

Several researchers have also found that individuals are likely to be more persuaded to donate when the message that they receive from the organization requesting the donation matches their motivations for donating. Julka and Marsh (2005) examined knowledge and value-expressive motivations for donating and found that individuals who received messages that emphasized their underlying motivations were more persuaded to make a donation. Pham and Avnet (2004) found a similar outcome with promotion-focused and prevention-focused motivations. Persuasive messages that emphasized affective information were found to activate a promotion-focused motivational state, and were therefore more persuasive to individuals who were motivated by promotion goals. In contrast, persuasive messages that emphasized more substantive arguments were found to activate a prevention-focused motivational state, and were therefore more persuasive to individuals who were motivated by prevention goals.

Messages have also been found to directly influence the individual's intrinsic, extrinsic, or social motivations to donate. Goldstein, Cialdini and Griskevicius (2008) conducted a field study in which individuals staying at a hotel were asked to reuse their bathroom towels in order to conserve energy. The messages requesting this help were framed either as a simple "help save the environment" appeal or a more socially focused message that invited the individual to join his or her fellow guests in helping to save the environment. In some conditions, the messages even specified the percentage of guests that reuse their towels, further emphasizing the social normative aspect of the decision. The socially framed messages, which presumably increased the individuals' social motivation to donate, resulted in a significantly higher reuse rate than the messages that simply appealed to the individual's intrinsic motivation to save the environment.

Johnson, Grimm and Ellis (2010) manipulated a canned food drive conducted across groups of students at two different universities, delivering intrinsically focused messages to one group and extrinsically focused messages to the other group. They found that the intrinsically focused messages decreased participants' extrinsic motivations to donate when compared to the extrinsically focused messages group. In addition, when both groups were given an extrinsic reward for their donations, the group that had received intrinsically focused messages experienced less of a decrease in intrinsic motivation, suggesting that the messages had at least partially mitigated the crowding out effect of the extrinsic reward.

Johnson and Ellis (2011) found that messages can influence attributed motivations even when they are received after a donation has been made. The authors surveyed donors from a set of charitable organizations, measuring their attributed motivations for the last donation they had made. These attributed motivations were compared across donors who had received intrinsically-focused, extrinsically-focused, or mixed messages from the organizations to which they had donated, as well as across donors who had received different levels of incentives for their donations. The authors found that donors who had received more extrinsically-focused messages and more incentives were more likely to attribute their past donation behavior to extrinsic motivations, while donors who had received more intrinsically-focused messages and fewer incentives were more likely to attribute their past donation behavior to intrinsic motivations.

CONCLUSION

Interest in donation behavior has linked the fields of psychology, economics, and marketing throughout the development of these fields. Early research on this topic was largely in keeping with the focus of each of the fields, focusing on personality traits in psychology, incentives in economics, and requests for donations in marketing. This enabled researchers to develop a fairly comprehensive understanding of who was more likely to donate, when they were more likely to donate, and what conditions were likely to increase their donation behavior. The three fields ultimately converged around a common question around the turn of the 21st century: what are the underlying motivations driving donation behavior?

Research on motivations to donate has progressed from simple taxonomies of motives through individual differences in motivations to a complex understanding of multiple motivations influencing the individual's decision to donate. Much of the recent research in all three fields has focused on the nuances of intrinsic/extrinsic or altruistic/egoistic motivations, with the addition of social motivations to donate from the economics literature. These motivations have been found at times to act in concert to influence donation behavior, and at times to conflict with each other or even to drive each other out of the individual's decision. These different motivations have also been found to have different consequences for both the donor and to influence the response of the recipient of the donation, emphasizing their importance to our understanding of donor motivations.

Finally, recent research has considered the possibility that organizations may be able to influence not only an individual's overall level of motivation to donate, but also the type of motivation that the individual perceives. The findings that message framing and marketing strategies can influence motivation type have intriguing possibilities for future research. The limited work in this area needs to be expanded to develop a better understanding of how messages can and should be used to target individuals with different motivations or to influence individuals' motivations to donate.

Future research should also continue to explore the differential effects of intrinsic or altruistic motivations and extrinsic or egoistic motivations on donation behavior. Many charities and nonprofit organizations rely on extrinsic incentives and rewards to encourage individuals to make donations. While psychologists, economists, and marketers all demonstrate a clear understanding of the risks of this strategy for intrinsic or altruistic motivations to donate, recent findings seem to suggest that this dynamic may be more nuanced than originally thought. A richer understanding of the interplay of these motivations can help researchers to provide charities and nonprofit organizations with better advice on the use of incentives.

In particular, the influence of social rewards has been understudied in both psychology and marketing. The economics literature suggests that the effects of social rewards may be more complex than more tangible extrinsic rewards and incentives, and even that social rewards may sometimes be supportive of intrinsic or altruistic motivation rather than detrimental. Social rewards have begun to be examined in the marketing literature, but further examination of social motivations to donate and the effectiveness of social rewards is clearly needed. Researchers have also only scratched the surface of understanding the influence of relationships with the charity or organization on motivations to donate. With the increased focus on fundraising through social networks and cultivating relationships with potential donors, researchers in all three fields would benefit from a better understanding of social influences and effects.

Further exploring these avenues of research will be valuable to researchers in all three fields. Gaining an improved understanding of the organization's ability to influence individuals' motivations to donate, along with better usage of current knowledge from psychology, economics and marketing, may be a necessary step in securing the funds needed to keep nonprofit and charitable organizations successful in the future.

REFERENCES

Aggarwal, P. (2004). The Effects of Brand Relationship Norms on Consumer Attitudes and Behavior. *Journal of Consumer Research, 31*, 87-101.

Andreoni, J. (1989). Giving with Impure Altruism: Applications to Charity and Ricardian Equivalence. *Journal of Political Economy, 97*, 1447-58.

---- (1990). Impure Altruism and Donations to Public Goods: A Theory of Warm-Glow Giving. *The Economic Journal, 100*, 464-77.

Andreoni, J., and Petrie, R. (2004). Public Goods Experiments Without Confidentiality: A Glimpse Into Fund-Raising. *Journal of Public Economics, 88*, 1605-1623.

Aranoff, J., and Wilson, J. P. (1984). *Personality in the Social Process*. Hillsdale, NY: Erlbaum.

Ariely, D., Bracha, A., and Meier, S. (2009). Doing Good or Doing Well? Image Motivation and Monetary Incentives in Behaving Prosocially. *American Economic Review, 99*, 544-555.

Armstrong, J. S. (1975). Monetary Incentives in Mail Surveys. *Public Opinion Quarterly, 39*, 111-16.

Axelrod, R. (1984). *The Evolution of Cooperation*. New York: Basic Books, Inc.

Axelrod, R., and Hamilton, W. D. (1981). The Evolution of Cooperation. *Science, 211*, 1390-96.

Bagozzi, R. P., and Moore, D. J. (1994). Public Service Advertisements: Emotions and Empathy Guide Prosocial Behavior. *Journal of Marketing, 58*, 56-70.

Barron, K. E., and Harackiewicz, J. M. (2000). Achievement Goals and Optimal Motivation: A Multiple Goals Approach. In C. Sansone and J. M. Harackiewicz (Eds.), *Intrinsic and Extrinsic Motivation: The Search for Optimal Motivation and Performance*. San Diego: Academic.

Batson, C. D. (1987). Prosocial Motivation: Is It Ever Truly Altruistic? *Advances in Experimental Social Psychology, 20*, 65-122.

Batson, C. D., Ahmad, N., and Tsang, J. (2002). Four Motives for Community Involvement. *Journal of Social Issues*, 58, 429-445.

Batson, C. D., Batson, J. G., Todd, R. M., Brummett, B. H., Shaw, L. L., and Aldeguer, C. M. R. (1995). Empathy and the Collective Good: Caring for One of the Others in a Social Dilemma. *Journal of Personality and Social Psychology, 68*, 619-631.

Bendapudi, N., Singh, S. N., and Bendapudi, V. (1996). Enhancing Helping Behavior: An Integrative Framework for Promotion Planning. *Journal of Marketing, 60*, 33-49.

Berkowitz, L. (1972). Social Norms, Feelings, and Other Factors Affecting Helping and Altruism. In L. Berkowitz (Ed.), *Advances in Experimental Social Psychology, Vol. 6*. New York: Academic Press.

Bertacchini, E., Santagata, W., and Signorello, G. (2011). Individual Giving to Support Cultural Heritage. *International Journal of Arts Management, 13*, 41-55.

Bhattacharya, C.B., and Sen, S. (2003). Consumer-Company Identification: A Framework for Understanding Consumers' Relationships with Companies. *Journal of Consumer Research, 67*, 76-88.

Bierhoff, H. W. (2001). Responsibility and Altruism: The Role of Volunteerism. In A. E. Auhagen and H. w. Bierhoff (Eds.), *Responsibility–The Many Faces of a Phenomenon*. London: Routledge.

Blockner, J., Guzzi, B., Kane, J., Levine, E., and Shaplen, K. (1984). Organizational Fundraising: Further Evidence on the Effect of Legitimizing Small Donations. *Journal of Consumer Research, 11,* 611-614.

Broadbridge, A., and Horne, S. (1994). Who Volunteers for Charity Retailing and Why? *Service Industries Journal, 14,* 421-437.

Burnett, J. J. (1981). Psychographic and Demographic Characteristics of Blood Donors. *Journal of Consumer Research, 8,* 62-66.

Burnkrant, R. E., and Page, Jr., T. J. (1982). An Examination of the Convergent, Discriminant, and Predictive Validity of Fishbein's Behavioral Intention Model. *Journal of Marketing Research, 19,* 550-561.

Campbell, D. T. (1983). The Two Distinct Routes Beyond Kin Selection to Ultrasociality: Implications for the Humanities and Social Sciences. In D. L. Bridgeman (Ed.), *The Nature of Prosocial Behavior*. New York: Academic Press.

Carlo, G., Okun, M. A., Knight, G. P., and de Guzman, M. R. T. (2005). The Interplay of Traits and Motives on Volunteering: Agreeableness, Extraversion and Prosocial Value Motivation. *Personality and Individual Differences, 38,* 1293-1305.

Cernak, D. S. P., File, K. M., and Prince, R. A. (1994). A Benefit Segmentation of the Major Donor Market. *Journal of Business Research, 29,* 121-134.

Clark, M. S., and Mills, J. (1979). Interpersonal Attraction in Exchange and Communal Relationships. *Journal of Personality and Social Psychology, 37,* 12-24.

---- (1993). The Difference Between Communal and Exchange Relationships: What It Is and Is Not. *Personality and Social Psychology Bulletin, 19,* 684-91.

Clary, E. G., Snyder, M., and Ridge, R. D. (1992). Volunteers' Motivations: A Functional Strategy for the Recruitment, Placement, and Retention of Volunteers. *Nonprofit Management and Leadership, 2,* 333-350.

Clary, E. G., Snyder, M., Ridge, R. D., Copeland, J., Stukas, A. A., Haugen, J., and Miene, P. (1998). Understanding and Assessing the Motivations of Volunteers: A Functional Approach. *Journal of Personality and Social Psychology, 74,* 1516-1530.

Danko, W. D., and Stanley, T. J. (1986). Identifying and Reaching the Donation-Prone Individual: A Nationwide Assessment. *Journal of Professional Services Marketing, 2,* 117-122.

Davis, M. H., Hall, J. A., and Meyer, M. (2003). The First Year: Influences on the Satisfaction, Involvement, and Persistence of New Community Volunteers. *Personality and Social Psychology Bulletin, 29,* 248-260.

Dawson, S. (1988). Four Motivations for Charitable Giving: Implications for Marketing Strategy to Attract Monetary Donations for Medical Research. *Journal of Health Care Marketing, 8,* 31-37.

Deci, E. L., and Ryan, R. M. (1985). *Intrinsic Motivation and Self-Determination in Human Behavior.* New York: Plenum Press.

de Groot, J. I.M., and Steg, L. (2010). Relationships Between Value Orientations, Self-Determined Motivational Types and Pro-Environmental Behavioural Intentions. *Journal of Environmental Psychology, 30,* 368-378.

DellaVigna, S., List, J. A., and Malmendier, U. (2009). Testing for Altruism and Social Pressure in Charitable Giving. National Bureau of Economic Research Working Paper No. 15629.

Eagly, A. H., and Crowly, M. (1986). Gender and Helping Behavior: A Meta-Analysis Review of the Social Psychological Literature. *Psychological Bulletin, 100,* 283-308.

Ellen, P. S., Mohr, L. A., and Webb, D. J. (2000). Charitable Progams and the Retailer: Do They Mix? *Journal of Retailing, 76,* 393-406.

Farnill, D., and Ball, I. K. (1982). Sensation Seeking and Intention to Donate Blood. *Psychological Reports, 51,* 126.

Fehr, E., and Falk, A. (2002). Psychological Foundations of Incentives. *European Economic Review, 46,* 687-724.

Fehr, E., and Fischbacher, U. (2003). The Nature of Human Altruism. *Nature, 425,* 785-791.

Ferguson, E., Farrell, K., and Lawrence, C. (2008). Blood Donation is an Act of Benevolence Rather Than Altruism. *Health Psychology, 27,* 327-336.

Fern, E. F., Monroe, K. B., and Avila, R. A. (1986). Effectiveness of Multiple Request Strategies: A Synthesis of Research Results. *Journal of Marketing Research, 23,* 144-152.

Finkelstein, M. A. (2006). Dispositional Predictors of Organizational Citizenship Behavior: Motives, Motive Fulfillment, and Role Identity. *Social Behavior and Personality, 34,* 603-616.

Finkelstein, M. A., and Brannick, M. T. (2007). Applying Theories of Institutional Helping to Informal Volunteering: Motives, Role Identity, and Prosocial Personality. *Social Behavior and Personality, 35,* 101-114.

Finkelstein, M. A., and Penner, L. A. (2004). Predicting Organizational Citizenship Behavior: Integrating the Functional and Role Identity Approaches. *Social Behavior and Personality, 32,* 383-398.

Fisher, R. J., and Ackerman, D. (1988). The Effects of Recognition and Group Need on Volunteerism: A Social Norm Perspective. *Journal of Consumer Research, 25,* 262-75.

Fraser, C., Hite, R. E., and Sauer, P. L. (1988). Increasing Contributions in Solicitation Campaigns: The Use of Large and Small Anchor Points. *Journal of Consumer Research, 14,* 284-287.

Frey, B. S. (1994). How Intrinsic Motivation is Crowded Out and In. *Rationality and Society, 6,* 334-352.

Frey, B S. (1997). *Not Just for the Money: An Economic Theory of Personal Motivation.* Cheltenham, UK: Edward Elgar Publishing.

Frey, B. S., and Jegen, R. (2001). Motivation Crowding Theory. *Journal of Economic Surveys, 15,* 589-612.

Frey, B. S., and Oberholzer-Gee, F. (1997). The Cost of Price Incentives: An Empirical Analysis of Motivation Crowding-Out. *American Economic Review, 87,* 746-755.

Furse, D. H., and Stewart, D. W. (1982). Monetary Incentives Versus Promised Contribution to Charity: New Evidence on Mail Survey Response. *Journal of Marketing Research, 19,* 375-80.

Glazer, A., and Konrad, K. A. (1996). A Signaling Explanation for Charity. *American Economic Review, 86,* 1019-1028.

Gneezy, U., and Rustichini, A. (2000). Pay Enough or Don't Pay at All. *The Quarterly Journal of Economics, August,* 791-810.

Goette, L., and Stutzer, A. (2008). Blood Donations and Incentives: Evidence from a Field Experiment. Working Paper: Federal Reserve Bank of Boston No. 08-3.

Goldstein, N. J., Cialdini, R. B., and Griskevicius, V. (2008). A Room with a Viewpoint: Using Social Norms to Motivate Environmental Conservation in Hotels. *Journal of Consumer Research, 35,* 472-482.

Grant, A. M. (2008). Does Intrinsic Motivation Fuel the Prosocial Fire? Motivational Synergy in Predicting Persistence, Performance, and Productivity. *Journal of Applied Psychology, 93,* 48-58.

Guy, B. S., and Patton, W. E. (1989). The Marketing of Altruistic Causes: Understanding Why People Help. *Journal of Consumer Marketing, 6,* 19-30.

Hansen, R. A. (1980). A Self-Perception Interpretation of the Effect of Monetary and Nonmonetary Incentives on Mail Survey Respondent Behavior. *Journal of Marketing Research, 17,* 77-83.

Harbaugh, W. T. (1998a). What Do Donations Buy? A Model of Philanthropy Based on Prestige and Warm Glow. *Journal of Public Economics, 67,* 269-284.

Harbaugh, W. T. (1998b). The Prestige Motive for Making Charitable Transfers. *American Economic Review, 88,* 277-282.

Harbaugh, W. T., Mayr, U., and Burghart, D. R. (2007). Neural Responses to Taxation and Volunary Giving Reveal Motives for Charitable Donations. *Science, 316,* 1622-1625.

Harvey, J. (1990). Benefit Segmentation for Fundraisers. *Journal of the Academy of Marketing Science, 18,* 77-86.

Hayenga, A. O., and Corpus, J. H. (2010). Profiles of Intrinsic and Extrinsic Motivations: A Person-Centered Approach to Motivation and Achievement in Middle School. *Motivation and Emotion, 34,* 371-383.

Holmes, J. G., Miller, D. T., and Lerner, M. J. (2002). Committing Altruism under the Cloak of Self-Interest: The Exchange Fiction. *Journal of Experimental Social Psychology, 38,* 144-151.

Horton, R. L. (1991). Marketing the Concept of Becoming a Potential Organ Donor. *Journal of Health Care Marketing, 11,* 36-45.

Janssen, M. C. W., and Mendys, E. (2001). The Price of a Price: On the Crowding Out of Social Norms. Tinbergen Institute Discussion Paper TI 2001-065/1.

Janssen, M. C. W., and Mendys-Kamphorst, E. (2004). The Price of a Price: On the Crowding Out and In of Social Norms. *Journal of Economic Behavior and Organization, 55,* 377-395.

Johnson, J. W., and Ellis, B. (2011). The Influence of Messages and Benefits on Donors' Attributed Motivations: Findings of a Study With 14 American Performing Arts Presenters. *International Journal of Arts Management, 13,* 4-15.

Johnson, J. W., and Grimm, P. E. (2010). Communal and Exchange Relationship Perceptions as Separate Constructs and Their Role in Motivations to Donate. *Journal of Consumer Psychology, 20,* 282-294.

Johnson, J. W., Grimm, P. E., and Ellis, B. (2010). The Influence of Intrinsic and Extrinsic Messages and Benefits on Motivations to Donate. In M. C. Campbell, J. Inman, and R. Pieters (Eds.), *Advances in Consumer Research,* Vol. 37. Duluth, MN: Association for Consumer Research.

Johnson, J. W., Peck, J., and Thomas, V. (2009). Individual Social Responsibility Versus Relational Norms in Consumer Helping Behavior. *Proceedings of the American Marketing Association Winter Educators' Conference, 20*, 228-236.

Julka, D. L., and Marsh, K. L. (2005). An Attitude Functions Approach to Increasing Organ-Donation Participation. *Journal of Applied Social Psychology, 35*, 821-849.

Kiviniemi, M. T., Snyder, M., and Omoto, A. M. (2002). Too Many of a Good Thing? The Effects of Multiple Motivations on Stress, Cost, Fulfillment, and Satisfaction. *Personality and Social Psychology Bulletin, 28*, 732-743.

Krebs, D. L., and Miller, D. T. (1985). Altruism and Aggression. In G. Lindzey and E. Aronson (Eds.), *Handbook of Social Psychology*, Vol. 2. New York: Random House.

Lacetera, N., and Macis, M. (2010). Do All Material Incentives for Pro-Social Activities Backfire? The Response to Cash and Non-Cash Incentives for Blood Donations. *Journal of Economic Psychology, 31*, 738-748.

Latane, B., Nida, S., and Wilson, D. (1981). The Effect of Group Size on Helping Behavior. In *Altruism and Helping Behavior*, ed. J. P. Rushton, R. M. Sorrentino, 287-317, Hillsdale, NJ: Erlbaum.

LaTour, S. A., and Manrai, A. K. (1989). Interactive Impact of Informational and Normative Influence on Donations. *Journal of Marketing Research, 26*, 327-335.

Lee, L., Piliavin, J. A., and Call, V. R. A. (1999). Giving Time, Money, and Blood: Similarities and Differences. *Social Psychology Quarterly, 62*, 276-90.

Maner, J. K., and Gailliot, M. T. (2007). Altruism and Egoism: Prosocial Motivations for Helping Depend on Relationship Context. *European Journal of Social Psychology, 37*, 347-358.

Margolis, H. (1982). *Selfishness, Altruism, and Rationality: A Theory of Social Choice*. Chicago: University of Chicago Press.

Mathur, A. (1996). Older Adults' Motivations for Gift Giving to Charitable Organizations: An Exchange Theory Perspective. *Psychology and Marketing, 13*, 107-123.

Meyers-Levy, J., and Maheswaran, D. (1992). When Timing Matters: The Influence of Temporal Distance on Consumers' Affective and Persuasive Responses. *Journal of Consumer Research, 19*, 424-433.

Millette, V., and Gagné, M. (2008). Designing Volunteers' Tasks to Maximize Motivation, Satisfaction and Performance: The Impact of Job Characteristics on Volunteer Engagement. *Motivation and Emotion, 32*, 11-22.

Moore, E. M., Bearden, W. O., and Teel, J. E. (1985). Use of Labeling and Assertions of Dependency in Appeals for Consumer Support. *Journal of Consumer Research, 12*, 90-96.

Moreno-Jiménez, M. P., and Villodres, M. C. H. (2010). Prediction of Burnout in Volunteers. *Journal of Applied Social Psychology, 40*, 1798-1818.

Mowen, J. C., and Sujan, H. (2005). Volunteer Behavior: A Hierarchical Model Approach for Investigating Its Trait and Functional Motive Antecedents. *Journal of Consumer Psychology, 15*, 170-182.

Nyborg, K., and Rege, M. (2003). Does Public Policy Crowd Out Private Contributions to Public Goods? *Public Choice, 115*, 397-418.

Oliner, S. P., and Oliner, P. M. (1988). *The Altruistic Personality: Rescuers of Jews in Nazi Europe*. New York: Free Press.

Omoto, A. M., and Snyder, M. (1995). Sustained Helping Without Obligation: Motivation, Longevity of Service, and Perceived Attitude Change Among AIDS Volunteers. *Journal of Personality and Social Psychology, 68,* 671-686.

Omoto, A. M., Snyder, M., and Hackett, J. D. (2010). Personality and Motivational Antecedents of Activism and Civic Engagement. *Journal of Personality, 78,* 1703-1734.

Omoto, A. M., Snyder, M., and Martino, S. C. (2000). Volunteerism and the Life Course: Investigating Age-Related Agendas for Action. *Basic and Applied Social Psychology, 22,* 181-197.

Penner, L. A., Dovidio, J. F., Piliavin, J. A., and Schroeder, D. A. (2005). Prosocial Behavior: Multilevel Perspectives. *Annual Review of Psychology, 56,* 365-392.

Pessemier, E. A., Beamon, A. C., and Hanssen, D. M. (1977). Willingness to Supply Human Body Parts: Some Empirical Results. *Journal of Consumer Research, 4,* 131-140.

Pham, M. T., and Avnet, T. (2004). Ideals and Oughts and the Reliance on Affect versus Substance in Persuasion. *Journal of Consumer Research, 30,* 503-518.

Piferi, R. L., Jobe, R. L., and Jones, W. H. (2006). Giving to Others During National Tragedy: The Effects of Altruistic and Egoistic Motivations on Long-Term Giving. *Journal of Social and Personal Relationships, 23,* 171-184.

Piliavin, J. A., and Charng, H. W. (1990). Altruism: A Review of Recent Theory and Research. *Annual Review of Sociology, 16,* 27-65.

Piliavin, J. A., and Libby, D. (1986). Perceived Social Norms, Personal Norms, and Blood Donation: Aggregate and Individual Level Analyses. *Humboldt Journal of Social Relations, 13,* 159-194.

Piliavin, J. A., Dovidio, J. F., Gaertner, S. L., and Clark III, R. D. (1981). *Emergency Intervention.* New York: Academic Press.

Piliavin, J. A., and Unger, R. K. (1985). The Helpful but Helpless Female: Myth or Reality? In *Women, Gender, and Social Psychology,* ed. V. O'Leary, R. K. Under, B. S. Wallston, 149-190, Hillsdale, NJ: Erlbaum.

Popkowski Leszczyc, P. T. L., and Rothkopf, M. H. (2010). Charitable Motives and Bidding in Charity Auctions. *Management Science, 56,* 399-413.

Poppe, M., and Utens, L. (1986). Effects of Greed and Fear of Being Gypped in a Social Dilemma Situation with Changing Pool Size. *Journal of Economic Psychology, 7,* 61-73.

Rabin, M. (1993). Incorporating Fairness into Game Theory and Economics. *The American Economic Review, 83,* 1281-302.

Rapoport, A. (1988). Provision of Step-Level Public Goods: Effect of Inequality in Resources. *Journal of Personality and Social Psychology, 54,* 432-440.

Reddy, R. D. (1980). Individual Philanthropy and Giving Behavior. In *Participation in Social and Political Activities Annual,* ed. S. Long, Vol. 1, Boulder, CO: Westview.

Rege, M., and Telle, K. (2004). The Impact of Social Approval and Framing on Cooperation in Public Good Situations. *Journal of Public Economics, 88,* 1625-1644.

Reingen, P. H. (1978). On Inducing Compliance with Requests. *Journal of Consumer Research, 5,* 96-102.

Ribar, D. C., and Wilhelm, M. O. (2002). Altruistic and Joy-of-Giving Motivations in Charitable Behavior. *Journal of Political Economy, 110,* 425-457.

Riecken, G., and Yavas, U. (1986). Seeking Donors Via Opinion Leadership. *Journal of Professional Services Marketing, 2,* 109-116.

Rioux, S. M., and Penner, L. A. (2001). The Causes of Organizational Citizenship Behavior: A Motivational Analysis. *Journal of Applied Psychology, 86,* 1306-1314.

Robertson, D. H., and Bellenger, D. N. (1978). A New Method of Increasing Mail Survey Responses: Contributions to Charity. *Journal of Marketing Research, 15,* 632-33.

Rushton, J. P. (1981). The Altruistic Personality. In J. P. Rushton, and R. M. Sorrentino (Eds.), *Altruism and Helping Behavior: Social, Personality, and Developmental Perspectives.* Hillsdale, New Jersey: Lawrence Erlbaum Associates.

Ryan, R. M., and Deci, E. L. (2000) Intrinsic and Extrinsic Motivations: Classic Definitions and New Directions. *Contemporary Educational Psychology, 25,* 54-67.

Schibrowsky, J. A., and Peltier, J. W. (1995). Decision Frames and Direct Marketing Offers: A Field Study in a Fundraising Context. *Journal of Direct Marketing, 9,* 8-16.

Schlegelmilch, B. B., and Tannin, A. C. (1989). Market Segment-Oriented Fund-Raising Strategies: An Empirical Analysis. *Marketing Intelligence and Planning, 7,* 16-24.

Schopler, J., and Matthews, M. W. (1965). The Influence of the Perceived Causal Locus of Partner's Dependence on the Use of Interpersonal Power. *Journal of Personality and Social Psychology, 2,* 609-12.

Schroeder, D. A., Penner, L. A., Dovidio, J. F., and Piliavin, J. A. (1995). *The Psychology of Helping and Altruism: Problems and Puzzles.* New York: McGraw-Hill.

Schwartz, S. H. (1970). Elicitation of Moral Obligation and Self-Sacrificing Behavior: An Experimental Study of Volunteering to Be a Bone Marrow Donor. *Journal of Personality and Social Psychology, 37,* 283-293.

Shotland, R. L., and Stebbins, C. A. (1983). Emergency and Cost as Determinants of Helping Behavior and the Slow Accumulation of Social Psychological Knowledge. *Social Psychology Quarterly, 46,* 35-46.

Simmons, R. G., Klein, S. D., and Simmons, R. L. (1977). *The Gift of Life: The Social and Psychological Impact of Organ Transplantation.* New York: Wiley.

Small, D. A., and Simonsohn, U. (2008). Friends of Victims: Personal Experience and Prosocial Behavior. *Journal of Consumer Research, 35,* 532-542.

Smith, A. (1759). *The Theory of Moral Sentiments.* London: A. Millar, A. Kincaid, and J. Bell.

Soetevent, A. R. (2005). Anonymity in Giving in a Natural Context – A Field Experiment in 30 Churches. *Journal of Public Economics, 89,* 2301-2323.

Staub, E. (1979). *Positive Social Behavior and Morality: Socialization and Development,* Vol. 2. New York: Academic Press.

Supphellen, M., and Nelson, M. R. (2001). Developing, Exploring, and Validating a Typology of Private Philanthropic Decision Making. *Journal of Economic Psychology, 22,* 573-603.

Thomas, G., and Batson, C. D. (1981). Effect of Helping Under Normative Pressure on Self-Perceived Altruism. *Social Psychology Quarterly, 44,* 127-131.

Titmuss, R. (1971). *The Gift Relationship: From Human Blood to Social Policy.* New York: Random House.

Van de Vliert, E., Huang, X., and Levine, R. V. (2004). National Wealth and Thermal Climate as Predictors of Motives for Volunteer Work. *Journal of Cross-Cultural Psychology, 35,* 62-73.

Veblen, T. (1899). *The Theory of the Leisure Class.* New York: Penguin.

Weinstein, N., DeHaan, C. R., and Ryan, R. M. (2010). Attributing Autonomous versus Introjected Motivation to Helpers and the Recipient Experience: Effects on Gratitude, Attitudes, and Well-Being. *Motivation and Emotion*, *34*, 418-431.

Weinstein, N., and Ryan, R. M. (2010). When Helping Helps: Autonomous Motivation for Prosocial Behavior and Its Influence on Well-Being for the Helper and Recipient. *Journal of Personality and Social Psychology*, *98*, 222-244.

Wichardt, P. C. (2008). A Status-Based Motivation for Behavioural Altruism. *International Journal of Social Economics*, *36*, 869-887.

Wilson, E. O. (1975). *Sociobiology: The New Synthesis*. Cambridge, MA: Harvard University Press.

Wiseman, F., Schafer, M., and Schafer, R. (1983). An Experimental Test of the Effects of a Monetary Incentive on Cooperation Rates and Data Collection Costs in Central-Location Interviewing. *Journal of Marketing Research, 20*, 439-42.

Yu, J., and Cooper, H. (1983). A Quantitative Review of Research Design Effects on Response Rates to Questionnaires. *Journal of Marketing Research, 20*, 36-44.

Ziemek, S. (2006). Economic Analysis of Volunteers' Motivations – A Cross-Country Study. *Journal of Socio-Economics, 35,* 532-555.

Zuckerman, M., Siegelbaum, H., and Williams, R. (1977). Predicting Helping Behavior: Willingness and Ascription of Responsibility. *Journal of Applied Social Psychology, 7,* 295-299.

In: Handbook on Psychology of Motivation
Editors: J. N. Franco and A. E. Svensgaard
ISBN: 978-1-62100-755-5
© 2012 Nova Science Publishers, Inc.

Chapter 3

BUILDING THE FUTURE FOR REMOTE INDIGENOUS STUDENTS IN AUSTRALIA: AN EXAMINATION OF FUTURE GOALS, MOTIVATION, LEARNING AND ACHIEVEMENT IN CULTURAL CONTEXT[*]

Dennis M. McInerney[1], Lyn Fasoli[2], Peter Stephenson[2] and Jeannie Herbert[3]

[1]The Hong Kong Institute of Education, Hong Kong
[2]Batchelor Institute of Indigenous Tertiary Education, Australia
[3]Charles Sturt University, Australia

ABSTRACT

Education is the corner stone of social justice because it is the basis of opportunity (Burney, 2003), but education as currently provided is failing Indigenous students in the Northern Territory (NT) of Australia. Ramsey (2003) estimated that 20 per cent of NT Indigenous students did not attend school, and, although those who were enrolled comprised 32 per cent of the NT secondary cohort, the number who achieved a Northern Territory Certificate of Education in 2000 amounted to only 6 per cent of the total school cohort. In 2009, 'educational outcomes in the bush remain abysmal' (Rothwell, 2009). Over half of the NT's Indigenous students leave school without completing secondary education. Many of them are, therefore, condemned to a life in which their potential is unrealised, and the fortunes of their families severely circumscribed. Little is known of what motivates or should motivate these young people to achieve successful school outcomes. This chapter reports on an Australian Research Council (ARC) funded research project, 'Building the future for Indigenous students', which asked 733 remote and very remote students what their hopes and dreams for the future were, what motivated them at school, and how they studied. Statistical analyses are used to establish the construct validity and reliability of psychological scales and to examine similarities and differences between very remote and remote Indigenous students, and a comparator

---

[*] This research was supported by an *Australian Research Council Linkage Grant LP0561651* in collaboration with the Northern Territory Department of Education and Training.

group of 300 non-Indigenous students. The findings provide critical hard data on the Indigenous students' future visions and aspirations, motivation, and approaches to study.

INTRODUCTION

Children from many Indigenous cultural backgrounds, such as Aboriginal Australians, are particularly disadvantaged with regard to academic achievement and school retention (Bradley, Draca, Green, and Leeves, 2006; Hunter and Schwab, 2003; Mellor and Corrigan, 2004; Penman, 2006). Many demographic studies indicate that retention rates and school achievement for Indigenous groups, and most particularly for remote Indigenous groups, lag far behind mainstream groups, and in some cases, retention rates appear to be worsening (Hossain, Gorman, Williams-Mozley, and Garvey, 2008; Rothwell, 2009; Shah and Widin, 2010). Many factors have been related to this situation. Socio-economic factors such as ill health, poverty, high unemployment, poor job prospects and racial prejudice are no doubt involved. Geographic and locale factors such as the placement of poorly prepared and inexperienced teachers in remote areas, high teacher turnover, isolation from mainstream experiences and lack of resources are also likely to have severe impact on the quality of education provided for these children (Leigh and Gong, 2009; Malin and Maidment, 2003; New South Wales Department of Community Services, 2009). Home background factors such as the relatively recent introduction of compulsory education for Indigenous people, particularly in remote areas of Australia, level of parental understanding of the importance and function of education, and level of parental encouragement and support for children to continue schooling, are potentially important influencing factors on children's motivation to attend school. Substandard housing and overcrowding giving poor facilities for home study and relatively few Aboriginal models of success in a school environment are also likely to be implicated (Bradley et al., 2006; Dowson and McInerney, 2005; Gray and Beresford, 2002; Hewitt, 2000; Steering Committee for the Review of Government Service Provision, 2009). Other influences posited from time to time include sociocultural factors such as: language (English is a second or third language for many remote Indigenous communities), discipline and academic achievement motivation, cognitive, motivational and learning style differences, socialization practices at variance to mainstream culture, peer group influences antipathetic to formal schooling, shyness, and poor attendance (Boulton-Lewis, Marton, Lewis, and Wilss, 2004; 2000; Dockery, 2010; Johns, 2008; Sonn, Bishop, and Humphries, 2000).

It is also thought by some that a cultural conflict exists between the values and goals of a Westernised schooling and the values and goals of Indigenous communities predisposing children from these communities to drop-out (see, for example, Fogarty and White, 1994; Berry, Poortinga, Segall, and Dasen, 2002; James, Chavez, Beauvais, Edwards, and Oetting, 1995; Ledlow, 1992; Triandis, 2001). Authors discussing this issue suggest that while mainstream schools and teachers value mastery, future time orientation, competition and success, individuality and aggression, their Indigenous pupils, in contrast, value harmony, present time orientation, maintenance of the status quo, anonymity, submissiveness, group orientation and non competitiveness (Lee, 2002; McInerney and Swisher, 1995; Triandis, 2004; Tucker and Herman, 2002). As a result, remote Indigenous Australian children are often stereotyped as lacking the motivation to achieve and the cognitive and learning approaches needed to achieve in Western school settings. It is also proposed that they come from homes that lack the socialization practices needed to inculcate Western oriented achievement values in children (Dowson and McInerney, 2005; McInerney, 2003; 2000; McInerney, Yeung, and McInerney, 2000).

While the above factors may have an impact on the motivation and achievement of Indigenous students in mainstream school settings, and on their desire to complete schooling, there are inadequate research data available on many of these variables, and in particular on the psychological variables implicated. Indeed, many of these beliefs about the lack of achievement of Indigenous children in school settings are based upon little more than folkloric tradition passed on from teacher to teacher, or academic to academic. Little hard data exist to guide communities, schools and teachers in the development of programs to improve this situation. Furthermore, many of these posited influences, such as socio-economic factors, lie outside the influence of the school and so remain intractable unless more effective social equality policies are introduced at a national level. Nevertheless, some of the above factors, particularly those dealing with motivational and learning factors, lie within the influence of schools.

In this study we concentrate on motivational and learning variables. We examine, through a large scale psychometric study in thirteen remote and very remote Australian schools in the Northern Territory, the goals Indigenous students have for their future and compare this with a non-Indigenous group. We also examine the nature of the motivational values held by remote and very remote Indigenous children between the ages of 12 and 17 in school settings and compare these to a non-Indigenous group at the same remote schools. We finally examine the approaches to learning endorsed by these children and compare them to those endorsed by the non-Indigenous students.

The research addressed the following questions:

- Are psychological scales drawn from Western research valid and reliable for Indigenous, non-Western students?

If valid and reliable:

- What *future goals* are endorsed by remote and very remote Indigenous students and are they any different from the non-Indigenous students?
- What *achievement goals* are endorsed by remote and very remote Indigenous students and is their endorsement of achievement goals different from those endorsed by non-Indigenous students?
- What *cognitive and learning strategies* are endorsed by remote and very remote Indigenous students and are they different from those endorsed by non-Indigenous students?

METHOD

This study was conducted among students attending grades 7 to 10 located in remote and very remote Indigenous communities in the Northern Territory of Australia where English is spoken largely as a second language, and where attendance at school is, for many of the participants, relatively infrequent. A survey instrument was used to tap student attitudes towards future goals, motivational goals, and cognitive and learning strategies. In the first instance items were drawn from established questionnaires (described below), which were then carefully scrutinized by key Indigenous informants as to the likely validity of the items in terms of constructs and language usage. The survey instrument went through a number of minor revisions before a final form was decided upon. The research, while clearly embedded within a Western tradition of research, sought to explore the validity and heuristic value of these psychological variables within a non-Western Indigenous community while taking account of cultural issues that might moderate the relevance and applicability of such psychological variables within a non-Western context.

Considerable logistics were involved in setting up the survey at each of the schools. Informed consent was obtained from the parents of the participants through negotiation with the participating schools, and informed consent was obtained from all students participating. Researchers visited each school at least once before the survey to ensure that the schools were prepared for the research and had allocated a suitable time for the survey to be conducted. The questionnaire was read aloud to maximize, as much as possible, completion rates in the available time, and to help alleviate problems participants may have had reading and completing the form on their own. At each presentation of the survey one or more Indigenous helpers were available to assist students who were having difficulty completing the form. Students that did not have permission or did not want to participate were provided with other activities to do.

Instruments

Items were drawn from six pre-existing instruments. (1) the Inventory of School Motivation (McInerney and Ali, 2006), (2) the General Achievement Goal Orientation Scale (GAGOS) (McInerney, Marsh, and Yeung, 2003) (3) the PISA Learning Scale (OECD, 2007), (4) the revised Learning Process Questionnaire (R-LPQ-2F; Kember, Biggs, and Leung, 2004), (5) the Future Goals Questionnaire (McInerney, Liem, Ortiga, Lee, and Mazano, 2008; Lee, McInerney, Liem, and Ortiga, 2010), and (6) the Goals-S (Dowson and McInerney, 2004) which has two parts, cognitive strategies (SRCS) and metacognitive strategies (SRMC). The survey form consisted of a total of five sections. The first section collected demographic data. The second section of 49 items asked the student "what motivates you at school?" The third section of 65 questions asked the student "how you like to study and learn at school". The fourth section of 36 questions asked students how they regulated their learning. The fifth section of 8 questions asked students about their future goals. All questions apart from those in the fifth section (which included forced ranking questions) were answered using a Likert-type scale anchored with (1) strongly disagree and (5) strongly agree. Although schooling at even the very remote schools is conducted largely in English and questionnaires are commonly used within the school context the response format was carefully explained to the participants. Terms such as "motivation", "goals and aspirations" were explained out loud to the students, with visual examples and each section had a descriptive introduction explaining the purposes of the questions. Students were encouraged to complete the form with the questions being read out aloud, and told to answer truthfully as the survey was not a test, there were no right or wrong answers, and that no-one other than the researchers would see their answers.

Table 1. Number of Participants in Different Schools

School	N	Indigenous	Type
1	39	39	Very Remote
2	60	60	Very Remote
3	40	40	Very Remote
4	26	25	Very Remote
5	71	70	Very Remote
6	38	38	Very Remote
7	97	21	Remote
8	103	83	Remote
9	119	119	Remote
10	159	82	Remote
11	218	108	Remote
12	51	29	Urban
13	23	23	Urban
Total	1044	737	

Total very remote Indigenous students surveyed = 272.
Total remote Indigenous students surveyed = 413.
Total urban Indigenous students surveyed = 52.
Total non-Indigenous students surveyed in very remote and remote schools = 285.
Total urban non-Indigenous students surveyed = 22.

There was some skepticism expressed by school personnel that the remote and very remote Indigenous students would be able to complete the survey owing to three major factors: limited English reading, writing and aural listening skills; limited concentration span; and the limited cultural and applied relevance of the questions (constructs) to the participants. It was essential, therefore, to test the reliability and construct validity of the measurement instruments as a major element of the research design.

Participants

School sites were selected in collaboration with the Northern Territory Department of Employment, Education and Training (now named Northern Territory Department of Education and Training). A major criterion was to sample a wide range of both Central Australian desert, Arnhem Land and northern communities. Each school site had to have a sufficient number of Indigenous students enrolled and attending school on a regular basis to make a visit to the site practicable in terms of the amount of data collected relative to cost. Ultimately a good spread of sites was obtained which is listed in Table 1 below.

Thirteen school sites and 1044 participants contributed to the study. 66% of the participants were Aboriginal, 1.6% Torres Strait Islander, 2.8 % Aboriginal and Torres Strait Islander, and 30% (N=307) non-Indigenous. Most of the non-Indigenous students were drawn from four high schools in remote areas. 59% of the participants were male. The average age of the participants was 13.9 years, and they were drawn from Years 7 to 10, with a small number being drawn from combined classes in some of the smaller schools. Of the Indigenous respondents 45.6% were male and 53.9% were female. Of these 50.9% nominated that English was the predominant language spoken at home. 38.9% nominated that an Indigenous language was predominantly spoken at home. 8% nominated that both English and an Indigenous language was spoken at home equally. 13% indicated that they were raised by one parent, and 87% by two parents.

RESULTS AND DISCUSSION

The research set out to examine four questions:

- Are psychological scales drawn from Western research valid and reliable for Indigenous, non-Western students?

If valid and reliable:

- What *future goals* are endorsed by remote and very remote Indigenous students and are they any different from the non-Indigenous students?
- What *achievement goals* are endorsed by remote and very remote Indigenous students and is their endorsement of achievement goals different from those endorsed by non-Indigenous students?
- What *cognitive and learning strategies* are endorsed by remote and very remote Indigenous students and are they different from those endorsed by non-Indigenous students?

In the following sections of the Chapter we explore each of these questions.

Reliability. In line with the first objective of the study to test the reliability and construct validity of the survey scales for remote and very remote Indigenous students, reliability tests were conducted on scales comprising the survey using Cronbach's alpha. It was anticipated that there would be lower reliabilities among the Indigenous students than typically obtained for these scales among non-Indigenous students and, also variation from less to more remote Indigenous groups in the study with the very remote being less reliable than the remote and urban Indigenous students.

Reliabilities for pooled data for all participants across the full set of scales were very good with the lowest reliability coefficient being .52, but typically most reliabilities were over .70. However, when the reliabilities were decomposed into three major groupings, very remote Indigenous, remote Indigenous and non-Indigenous, it was apparent that there was variability in reliability across these groups. In all cases the very remote Indigenous students' reliabilities were lower than those for both the remote Indigenous students and the non-Indigenous students. However, in contrast to expectations, the remote Indigenous students' reliabilities were very similar to the non-Indigenous students and in many cases higher. Nevertheless, the reliabilities for the very remote Indigenous students were, in most cases and somewhat surprisingly, acceptable apart from the social scales in the Inventory of School Motivation (affiliation and social concern) where the reliabilities were unacceptably low. Refer to Tables 2a, 2b, and 2c below.

Table 2a. Reliabilities of Motivation Scale among Four Groups

Scale Reliabilities Motivation Scale	TOTAL	Very Remote	Remote	Urban	Non Indigenous
Task R	.52	.46	.54	.61	.57
Effort R	.74	.61	.78	.73	.77
Competition R	.78	.59	.79	.63	.71
Social Power R	.80	.67	.80	.75	.79
Affiliation R	.61	.30	.59	.48	.76
Social Concern R	.68	.52	.71	.77	.71
Praise R	.76	.65	.79	.68	.75
Token R	.80	.68	.83	.68	.78

Table 2b. Reliabilities of General Achievement Goal Orientation Scale (GAGOS) Scale among Four Groups

Scale Reliabilities GAGOS Scale	TOTAL	Very Remote	Remote	Urban	Non Indigenous
General mastery R	.67	.55	.71	.68	.73
General performance R	.72	.59	.75	.48	.71
General social R	.71	.52	.71	.64	.80
Global motivation R	.79	.61	.74	.81	.86

Table 2c. Reliabilities of Learning Styles Scale among Four Groups

Scale Reliabilities Learning Styles	TOTAL	Very Remote	Remote	Urban	Non Indigenous
Control Strategies R	.67	.55	.69	.40	.75
Memorization R	.74	.67	.77	.51	.72
Elaboration1 R	.71	.57	.74	.70	.75
Effort and Perseverance R	.71	.56	.72	.63	.77
Deep R	.73	.59	.76	.68	.71
Surface R	.64	.61	.62	.65	.61

Table 2c. (Continued)

Scale Reliabilities Learning Styles	TOTAL	Very Remote	Remote	Urban	Non Indigenous
Elaboration2					
R	.82	.67	.82	.79	.87
Organization					
R	.79	.69	.79	.77	.82
Rehearsal					
R	.81	.67	.83	.73	.80
Monitoring					
R	.71	.60	.73	.60	.78
Planning					
R	.78	.72	.78	.62	.79
Regulating					
R	.72	.61	.72	.78	.78

Table 3a. The Goodness of Fit Statistics for the ISM

	χ^2	df	χ^2/df	CFI	GFI	NNFI	RMSEA	SRMR
Overall sample (N=968)	1267.59	499	2.54	.98	.92	.97	.044	.048
Very remote Indigenous (N=272)	703.01	499	1.41	.96	.84	.95	.040	.058
Remote Indigenous (N=413)	944.15	499	1.89	.97	.87	.97	.050	.056
Remote non-Indigenous (N=283)	919.98	499	1.84	.94	.84	.93	.053	.067

Note:

χ^2/df Chi square/degrees of freedom
Comparative Fit Index (CFI)
Goodness of Fit Index (GFI)
Non-Normed Fit Index (NNFI)
Root Mean Square Error of Approximation (RMSEA)
Standardized Root Mean Square Residual (SRMR)

In summary, the reliability analyses confirmed the expectation that the very remote Indigenous reliabilities would be lower than the non-Indigenous. The remote Indigenous students' reliabilities and those of the non-Indigenous students were very similar and quite high across most scales. The reliabilities for the very remote group were, however, adequate.

Confirmatory Factor Analysis. A more thorough check on construct validity and whether the survey questions were being responded to in a systematic manner was conducted through confirmatory factor analysis (CFA). Each of the scales within each section of the survey was subjected to CFA. Four groups were examined: whole sample, very remote Indigenous, remote Indigenous, remote non-Indigenous. The urban samples (Indigenous and non-Indigenous) were not included in the CFA's owing to small sample size (N=52, N=22 respectively). The preliminary results without any post-hoc adjustments were promising with the RMSEA and SRMR across most scales for all groups in general approaching or meeting the threshold of <.05 (an exception being the Learning Process Questionnaire which was uniformly poorly fitted across all groups on these two indices).

Table 3b. The Goodness of Fit Statistics for the GAGOS

	χ^2	df	χ^2/df	CFI	GFI	NNFI	RMSEA	SRMR
Overall sample (N=968)	177.73	84	2.12	.99	.97	.98	.036	.034
Very remote Indigenous (N=272)	132.31	84	1.58	.95	.93	.94	.049	.056
Remote Indigenous (N=413)	148.11	84	1.76	.98	.95	.98	.045	.042
Remote non-Indigenous (N=283)	117.38	84	1.40	.99	.95	.98	.038	.046

Table 3c. The Goodness of Fit Statistics for the PISA Learning Scale

	χ^2	df	χ^2/df	CFI	GFI	NNFI	RMSEA	SRMR
Overall sample (N=968)	250.90	113	2.22	.99	.96	.99	.041	.034
Very remote Indigenous (N=272)	137.29	113	1.21	.98	.93	.98	.036	.050
Remote Indigenous (N=413)	160.52	113	1.42	.99	.95	.99	.034	.040
Remote non-Indigenous (N=283)	275.68	113	2.44	.97	.89	.96	.074	.062

Table 3d. The Goodness of Fit Statistics for the LPQ

	χ^2	df	χ^2/df	CFI	GFI	NNFI	RMSEA	SRMR
Overall sample (N=968)	244.97	53	4.88	.93	.95	.91	.071	.059
Very remote Indigenous (N=272)	76.24	53	1.40	.95	.94	.94	.045	.057
Remote Indigenous (N=413)	147.49	53	2.84	.93	.92	.91	.080	.065
Remote non-Indigenous (N=283)	157.83	53	2.98	.86	.91	.82	.086	.094

Table 3e. The Goodness of Fit Statistics for the Goals-S(SRCS)

	χ^2	df	χ^2/df	CFI	GFI	NNFI	RMSEA	SRMR
Overall sample (N=968)	321.71	132	2.44	.99	.96	.99	.044	.032
Very remote Indigenous (N=272)	223.56	132	1.69	.95	.89	.94	.058	.061
Remote Indigenous (N=413)	236.52	132	1.79	.98	.92	.98	.050	.041
Remote non-Indigenous (N=283)	238.28	132	1.81	.98	.91	.98	.056	.047

Other typical goodness of fit indices such as NNFI, CFI, and GFI were, in general, strong across the groups, typically greater than .85 with most exceeding the .9 threshold. Of particular note here is that the goodness of fit for the very remote Indigenous group met the threshold for almost all scales indicating that the measurement validity was quite strong for this group. Refer to Tables 3a to 3f for fit statistics.

Future goals. Our second question addressed the level of endorsement of future goals that remote and very remote Indigenous students held, and whether they were different from non-Indigenous students.

Future goals are self-relevant, self-defining goals that provide incentive for action. They are self-determined and may reflect such things as pursuing an education, work or career, establishing a family, and making a contribution to society. Holding valued future goals is important to students because these future goals help give meaning to school tasks. In this study we asked students to indicate how important the following future goals were to them: becoming an important person, getting a good job, making a lot of money, supporting a family, contributing to their community, leaving the community to work, becoming a community elder, and getting a valued job in the community.

Two styles of questions assessed the importance of eight future goals to the students. The first was a forced ranking from 1 to 8 of each of the goals, in which students had to number their most important future goal (1), their second most important future goal (2), through to their least important future goal (8). The results for this are presented in Tables 4 and 5 below. The second type of question asked students to agree or disagree on a five point Likert-type scale to each of the future goals separately (see Table 6 below). Let us first examine the future goals to which very remote Indigenous, remote Indigenous, urban Indigenous, and non-Indigenous students aspired as a group.

Keeping in mind that these results are for the full sample, the most frequently endorsed first choice future goal was 'want to get a good job' (36.8%) and the second "want to support a family' (29.8%). The least frequently endorsed future goal was 'want to make a contribution to my community' (1.3%) and 'want to become a community elder' (1.6%). The three most popular second choices were 'get a good job', 'make a lot of money' and 'support a family'. In effect, over 60% of the students listed 'I want to get a good job' as their first or second choice, while approximately 52% listed 'I want to support a family' as their first or second choices. The importance of money begins to emerge from the second and third choices. Less popular choices were ones related to community orientation such as 'want to become a community elder', 'make a contribution to my community', 'becoming an important person' and 'get a job in my community'. However, this lack of community orientation should be considered alongside responses to the question relating to whether students wanted to leave their community to get a job which was also ranked lowly as a goal. It is important to note here that these responses were from the pooled data across all schools and included both Indigenous and non-Indigenous results.

When the rankings were disaggregated by very remote Indigenous, remote Indigenous and remote non-Indigenous interesting patterns emerged, as illustrated in Table 5. Considering the total percentages given for the first three ranks across the three groups on getting a good job, making a lot of money, and supporting a family the remote non-Indigenous group was higher on each future goal, followed by the remote Indigenous and then the very remote Indigenous group. Although 68.7% of very remote students ranked getting a good job in their top three, this was considerably lower than the remote Indigenous

(85.6%) and the remote non-Indigenous (95.9%). And while 47.2% of the very remote Indigenous participants ranked making money and 59.3% supporting a family in the top three, the relative percentages for the remote Indigenous group were 69.0% and 75.9% respectively, and the non-Indigenous group 82.8% and 85.0% respectively. Particularly noteworthy here is the lower overall ranking of getting a good job by the very remote Indigenous students. This is underlined by the consistent pattern of lower ranking by this group of two other job related goals, making money, and supporting a family.

In interesting contrast to these findings, the very remote Indigenous group ranked becoming an important person in the community more highly as a first choice than either of the other two groups, and when aggregated across the first three rankings 44.6% of the very remote participants ranked this in their first three choices in contrast to 27.0% of the remote Indigenous and 14.3% of very remote non-Indigenous students. Two other features are worth drawing attention to, namely the future goals of wanting to leave the community to work where 24.6% of the very remote Indigenous students listed this in their first three choices in contrast to 13.1% and 8.6% for the remote Indigenous and non-Indigenous students respectively, and wanting to get a job as a teacher, police or nurse where 34.4% of the very remote Indigenous students listed this in their first three choices, in contrast to 15.7% and 7.1% of the remote Indigenous and non-Indigenous respectively.

Two other future goals, making a contribution to my community and becoming a community elder were similarly endorsed as 4th, 5th 6th and 7th choices across the three groups.

It appears from the forced ranking of eight future goals that while there was a striking similarity in the relative rankings within each group, that is, that getting a good job, making money, and supporting a family were pre-eminently endorsed in the first three ranks across the groups, there were considerable differences between the groups with a smaller percentage of the very remote group listing these as first ranked goals. In contrast, leaving community and getting a professional job in the community were more often mentioned in the first three choices by the very remote group.

MANOVA tests based on the Likert-scale format for future goals (see Table 6 below) indicated that there were a number of significant differences between the groups. For these analyses we included the urban Indigenous group. Remote students were significantly higher on *important person* than very remote Indigenous and non-Indigenous groups. The very remote students were significantly lower on *job value* than the remote and non-Indigenous groups and significantly lower on *make money* than any of the other three groups which is in line with the forced ranking results reported above. The non-Indigenous group was significantly lower than the very remote and remote groups on *make money*. There were no significant differences between the three Indigenous groups on *support family*. However, the non-Indigenous group was significantly lower on this dimension than the very remote and remote groups, in contrast to the forced ranking results above. This pattern was repeated for the *contribute to community* dimension.

There were no significant differences between the Indigenous groups on the *leave community to work* dimension although in the forced ranking approach the very remote Indigenous students ranked this more highly as their 3rd choice. The non-Indigenous group was significantly lower on the *become an elder* dimension than the very remote and remote groups, but was not different to the urban group on this dimension. Finally, there were no significant differences between groups on the *become a professional (teacher, police, nurse)* dimension.

Table 3f. The Goodness of Fit Statistics for the Goals-S (SRMC)

	χ^2	df	χ^2/df	CFI	GFI	NNFI	RMSEA	SRMR
Overall sample (N=968)	518.87	132	3.93	.96	.92	.96	.067	.051
Very remote Indigenous (N=272)	211.33	132	1.60	.94	.90	.93	.051	.062
Remote Indigenous (N=413)	291.83	132	2.21	.96	.90	.96	.068	.057
Remote non-Indigenous (N=283)	267.03	132	2.02	.97	.90	.97	.067	.056

Table 4. Rank Ordering of Future Goals (Full group) percentages

Future Goals	1st	2nd	3rd	4th	5th	6th	7th	8th
I want to become an important person in my community	9.8	5.9	10.0	20.8	20.2	13.4	11.2	8.8
I want to get a good job	36.8	34.5	14.5	4.9	3.1	2.9	1.5	1.8
I want to make a lot of money	13.5	24.5	30.9	11.4	4.9	4.7	4.1	6.0
I want to support a family	29.8	22.0	23.8	11.9	5.1	3.1	2.4	1.8
I want to make a contribution to my community	1.3	3.4	5.4	16.4	27.1	22.6	15.1	8.8
I want to leave my community to work	2.7	4.0	7.4	19.3	15.3	19.0	16.0	16.3
I want to become a community elder	1.6	2.7	3.2	6.5	11.1	20.1	26.3	28.4
I want to get a job in my community such as a teacher, police, or nurse	6.7	4.8	5.6	9.4	13.2	12.8	21.2	26.5

Table 5. Rank Ordering of Future Goals in Very Remote Indigenous, Remote Indigenous, and Remote Non-Indigenous NT High School students in percentages

Future Goals	Groups	1st	2nd	3rd	4th	5th	6th	7th	8th
I want to become an important person in my community	Very Remote Indigenous	23.6	7.2	13.8	7.2	13.8	10.3	15.9	8.2
	Remote Indigenous	10.1	7.9	9.0	21.2	18.0	14.0	7.1	12.7
	Remote non-Indigenous	1.8	3.7	8.8	27.5	26.4	15.0	13.2	3.7
I want to get a good job	Very Remote Indigenous	27.9	26.9	13.9	10.4	7.0	5.5	3.0	5.5
	Remote Indigenous	35.4	34.6	15.6	5.0	3.2	4.0	1.6	0.8
	Remote non-Indigenous	46.5	36.6	12.8	1.5	0.4	0.4	0.7	1.1

I want to make a lot of money	Very Remote Indigenous	7.7	16.4	23.1	9.7	9.2	10.8	9.2	13.8
	Remote Indigenous	13.6	26.1	29.3	12.3	4.8	4.0	4.0	5.9
	Remote non-Indigenous	16.5	28.6	37.7	9.5	1.8	2.2	1.5	2.2
I want to support a family	Very Remote Indigenous	22.3	21.8	15.2	17.8	7.1	7.1	5.6	3.0
	Remote Indigenous	31.0	18.6	26.3	9.8	6.4	3.4	2.4	2.1
	Remote non-Indigenous	30.4	26.4	28.2	11.0	3.3	0.4	0.0	0.4
I want to make a contribution to my community	Very Remote Indigenous	4.1	9.3	8.3	17.1	21.8	17.1	14.0	8.3
	Remote Indigenous	1.1	2.7	5.1	16.9	23.3	22.5	16.9	11.5
	Remote non-Indigenous	0.0	1.1	2.6	14.9	35.7	25.3	14.5	5.9
I want to leave my community to work	Very Remote Indigenous	2.6	7.3	14.7	16.8	11.0	17.3	12.6	17.8
	Remote Indigenous	3.7	4.3	5.1	18.1	18.7	17.3	16.0	16.8
	Remote non-Indigenous	1.5	1.5	5.6	25.6	13.0	21.9	18.1	13.0
I want to become a community elder	Very Remote Indigenous	3.1	7.8	7.3	9.8	15.0	15.5	21.2	20.2
	Remote Indigenous	1.1	2.1	3.8	7.5	13.9	24.9	28.4	18.2
	Remote non-Indigenous	1.5	0.4	0.4	4.1	5.2	16.2	24.4	48.0
I want to get a job in my community such as a teacher, police, or nurse	Very Remote Indigenous	17.7	10.6	6.1	10.6	13.1	11.1	13.1	17.7
	Remote Indigenous	5.3	4.3	6.1	9.9	12.0	8.8	21.6	32.0
	Remote non-Indigenous	1.5	1.9	3.7	7.0	15.6	18.9	27.0	24.4

Table 6. Future Goals and differences between Very Remote (VR), Remote (R), and Urban (U) Indigenous, and Non-Indigenous (NI) NT High School students

	Groups Mean				Standard Deviation			
	VR	R	U	NI	VR	R	U	NI
Important Person	3.98[a]	4.25[b]	3.96[ab]	3.88[a]	1.34	0.97	1.07	1.11
Job Value	4.21[a]	4.60[b]	4.54[ab]	4.49[b]	1.17	0.68	0.80	0.88
Make Money	3.78[a]	4.36[b]	4.33[bc]	4.11[c]	1.26	0.90	0.96	1.08
Support Family	4.34[a]	4.50[a]	4.42[ab]	4.10[b]	1.01	0.77	0.70	1.06
Contribute to Community	3.91[a]	4.01[a]	3.69[ab]	3.35[b]	1.19	1.04	1.01	1.11
Leave Community to Work	3.60[ab]	3.86[a]	3.44[ab]	3.56[b]	1.45	1.15	1.07	1.14
Become Elder	3.57[a]	3.68[a]	3.19[ab]	2.82[b]	1.41	1.23	1.10	1.23
Become Professional	4.00[a]	3.98[a]	3.71[a]	3.75[a]	1.30	1.31	1.36	1.37

Note. means with different superscripts in a row are significantly different from each other.
VR very remote Indigenous.
R remote Indigenous.
U Urban Indigenous.
NI non-Indigenous.

Achievement goals. Our second question addressed the level of endorsement of achievement goals by remote and very remote Indigenous students and whether there were significant differences across groups including urban Indigenous, and non- Indigenous students.

Achievement goals are the motivational purposes students adopt for their learning in achievement situations. Two goals commonly researched are mastery approach and performance approach goals. Students who hold mastery approach goals focus on improving or developing understanding, competence and skills, according to self-set standards. In contrast, students who hold performance approach goals focus on demonstrating competence or ability relative to others. In this research two constructs represent a mastery goal orientation, namely, task and effort, and two constructs represent a performance goal orientation, namely competition and power. Two goals, social goal orientation and an extrinsic goal orientation are less well researched. Students who hold social goals value building or maintaining inter-personal relationships and helping others in their learning. Students with extrinsic goals are motivated by praise and rewards as a form of recognition of their work. In this research two constructs represent a social goal orientation, namely, social concern and affiliation, and two constructs represent an extrinsic goal orientation, namely, praise and token (Ames, 1992; Anderman and Dawson, 2011; Covington, 2000; Dowson and McInerney, 2003; Kaplan and Maehr, 2007; McInerney, 2008; McInerney and Ali, 2006; Meece, Anderman, and Anderman, 2006; Schunk, Pintrich, and Meece, 2008).

The eight motivation goal orientations described above were drawn from the Inventory of School Motivation (ISM) (McInerney and Ali, 2006). Students' achievement goals have been shown to affect the way students process learning materials, how much they are involved or motivated in academic activities, and eventually their achievement outcomes. Mastery approach goals such as task involvement and effort, have been consistently associated with deep-level processing of information and self-regulated learning as well as higher academic achievement and hence are considered adaptive goal orientations. Performance approach goals, such as social power and competitiveness, in contrast, tend to be associated with surface, rote-level processing of information and in general, lower academic performance. While extrinsic goals such as token rewards may be important to motivate and engage lower achieving students they are often negatively related to achievement at school, and so should be used sparingly. Praise, while an extrinsic reinforcer, may be beneficially used to enhance learning engagement. Students who are achieving well are usually not dependent on extrinsic rewards and praise must be used strategically and appropriately to have a positive effect. For this reason performance goal orientations are considered to be less adaptive than mastery goal orientations. It is still unclear how social goals such as affiliation and social concern orientations affect learning and achievement outcomes. However, there is some evidence that high achieving students, who are socially concerned also like to assist their peers to do well. On the other hand those who are affiliation oriented (for example, wanting to be at school primarily to socialize with friends) achieve at lower levels than those who are mastery or performance oriented.

Four general motivation goals (mastery general, performance general, social general and global motivation) drawn from the General Achievement Goal Orientation Scale (GAGOS) (McInerney, Marsh, and Yeung, 2003) were also used in the study.

Inventory of School Motivation (ISM). Table 7 presents the results for the ISM analyses. There were no significant differences in the task variable between the four groups. The very remote and remote Indigenous students were significantly more effort oriented than either the urban Indigenous students or the non-Indigenous students. There was no difference between the urban Indigenous students and the non-Indigenous students on this scale. The very remote Indigenous students were significantly more competitive and social power oriented than either of the other groups. The remote Indigenous students were significantly more competitive and social power oriented than the urban Indigenous and non-Indigenous students. There was no difference between the urban Indigenous and non-Indigenous students. The very remote Indigenous students were significantly more social concern oriented than any of the other three groups. The urban Indigenous group was significantly less social concern oriented than the remote Indigenous and non-Indigenous students. There was no difference between the remote Indigenous and non-Indigenous students on this dimension. The very remote Indigenous and remote Indigenous students were significantly more affiliation oriented than the non-Indigenous group, however, there was no difference between the urban Indigenous students and the non-Indigenous students. The very remote Indigenous students were significantly higher on praise and token than the other three groups, and the remote Indigenous group was significantly higher than the non-Indigenous students. There was no difference between the remote group and urban Indigenous group in praise, but the remote Indigenous group was significantly higher than the urban Indigenous group on token. However, there was no difference between the urban Indigenous and non-Indigenous students on these two variables.

In summary, there were significant differences across the groups. In general, the very remote Indigenous group was significantly higher than the other groups on most of the eight motivational variables. This might indicate a response bias. The pattern across the other three groups was more variable although there were very few significant differences between the urban Indigenous students and the non-Indigenous students. Probably the most salient points to come out of these MANOVA results are 1). that the very remote Indigenous students were significantly high on four of the dimensions relative to the other groups (competition, social power, social concern and praise) which is counter to what might have been expected; 2). there was only one significant difference between the urban Indigenous group and the remote non-Indigenous group (social concern); 3). On six dimensions there was a significant difference between the remote Indigenous and the non-Indigenous participants with the remote Indigenous being significantly higher on each of these dimensions (the exceptions being task and social concern).

General Achievement Goal Orientation Scale (GAGOS). Table 8 presents the results for the GAGOS analyses. There were no significant differences between groups on the general mastery scale. The very remote Indigenous group was significantly higher than the other three groups on general performance orientation. The remote Indigenous group was significantly higher than the non-Indigenous group. There was no significant difference between the urban Indigenous and non-Indigenous groups. The very remote Indigenous group was significantly higher on the general social scale than the non-Indigenous group. There were no other significant differences on this scale. The very remote Indigenous group was significantly higher on the global motivation scale than the other three groups. The remote Indigenous group was significantly higher than the urban Indigenous and non-Indigenous groups. There were no significant differences between these latter two groups.

In summary, while it appears that there may be a positive response bias for the very remote Indigenous students, these findings shed important light on the motivation goal orientations of Indigenous students, namely, 1). There were no differences in mastery orientation, which is one of the key predictors of academic engagement and success at school; 2). The Indigenous groups appear to be more performance oriented than the non-Indigenous group, 3). There was little difference between groups on social motivation, and 4). The very remote and remote Indigenous groups were higher on global motivation than the other two groups. Finally, it is important to note that general mastery, in keeping with much international research, was the most highly endorsed motivational orientation across all groups.

Learning strategies. Our last question examined the cognitive and learning strategies endorsed by remote and very remote Indigenous students and similarities and differences across groups. Learning strategies are the approaches that students use in learning. Such strategies include establishing connections between new topics and existing knowledge, memorizing, and making sure of their understanding of what they learn. Research has shown that the learning strategies a student adopts for learning an academic task influence the quality of learning outcomes achieved (Heikkilä and Lonka, 2006; Liem, Lau, and Nie, 2008; Pugh and Bergin, 2006; Zimmerman, 2008). Students who adopt deep learning strategies—organizing new information, relating ideas, and monitoring their understanding of learning materials—perform better on academic tasks. Surface learning strategies (e.g. memorization) are often associated with boredom, fear of failure, and assessment methods that reward low-quality learning (Nesbit and Adesope, 2006; Pugh and Bergin, 2006; Watkins, McInerney, Akande, and Lee, 2003; Watkins, McInerney, Lee, Akande, and Regmi, 2002; Wolters, 2004). Table 9 presents the results for the learning strategies analyses.

Table 7. Level of Motivational (ISM) and differences in Very Remote, Remote, and Urban Indigenous, and Non-Indigenous NT High School students

	Groups							
	Mean				*Standard Deviation*			
	Very remote	Remote	Urban	Non-Indigenous	Very remote	Remote	Urban	Non-Indigenous
Task	3.90[a]	4.03[a]	4.00[a]	4.05[a]	0.78	0.62	0.68	0.59
Effort	3.92[a]	3.93[a]	3.55[b]	3.68[b]	0.77	0.73	0.73	0.74
Competition	3.91[a]	3.23[b]	2.58[c]	2.64[c]	0.79	1.01	0.84	0.89
Social Power	3.54[a]	2.94[b]	2.48[c]	2.51[c]	0.90	0.95	0.82	0.85
Social Concern	3.89[a]	3.70[b]	3.20[c]	3.60[b]	0.71	0.75	0.79	0.68
Affiliation	3.94[a]	3.92[a]	3.94[ab]	3.69[b]	0.78	0.83	0.72	0.95
Praise	3.99[a]	3.81[b]	3.49[bc]	3.46[c]	0.79	0.79	0.72	0.79
Token	3.96[a]	3.63[b]	3.11[c]	3.11[c]	0.86	1.01	0.84	0.96

Note. means with different superscripts in a row are significantly different from each other.

Table 8. Level of GAGOS and differences in Very Remote, Remote, and Urban Indigenous, and Non-Indigenous NT High School students

	Groups							
	Mean				*Standard Deviation*			
	Very remote	Remote	Urban	Non-Indigenous	Very remote	Remote	Urban	Non-Indigenous
General Mastery	4.05[a]	4.11[a]	3.97[a]	3.99[a]	0.72	0.64	0.53	0.64
General Performance	3.84[a]	3.45[b]	3.18[bc]	3.08[c]	0.81	0.91	0.74	0.86
General Social	3.86[a]	3.78[ab]	3.74[ab]	3.63[b]	0.87	0.90	0.84	0.98
Global Motivation	3.98[a]	3.72[b]	3.36[c]	3.28[c]	0.82	0.76	0.81	0.91

Note. means with different superscripts in a row are significantly different from each other.

Self-regulation refers to students' self-generated thoughts, feelings, and actions towards attaining an academic goal. It includes processes such as planning and managing time, attending to and concentrating on instruction, organizing information, establishing a productive work environment, and seeking help effectively.

In this study we examined 12 learning and self-regulation strategies. Four learning strategies, viz, control strategies, memorization, elaboration(1), and effort and persistence are drawn from the Program for International Student Assessment (PISA) inventory. Two learning strategies, deep and surface learning are drawn from the Learning Process Questionnaire (Kember, Biggs, and Leung, 2004). Six self-regulation strategies, viz., elaboration(2), organization, rehearsal, monitoring, planning and regulating are drawn from the GOAL-S inventory (Dowson and McInerney, 2004) with the first three dimensions (elaboration(2), organization and rehearsal) being cognitive strategies (SRCS) and the latter three dimensions (monitoring, planning and regulating) being metacognitive strategies (SRMC). Refer to Table 9 and Table 10 for the means and standard deviations for each of these variables.

With regard to the PISA dimension, the non-Indigenous students were significantly lower on control strategies than either the very remote Indigenous or remote Indigenous students. There was no difference with the urban Indigenous students. The very remote Indigenous group was significantly higher on memorization than any of the other groups, and the remote Indigenous group was significantly higher than either the urban Indigenous or non-Indigenous groups, with no significant differences between the latter two groups. The very remote Indigenous and remote Indigenous groups were significantly higher on elaboration(1) than the urban Indigenous and non-Indigenous groups, but not significantly different from each other. There was no significant difference between the urban Indigenous and non-Indigenous students on this dimension. This pattern was repeated for the effort and perseverance dimension. The very remote Indigenous group was significantly higher than each of the other groups on deep and surface learning. The remote group was significantly higher on deep and surface than the urban and non-Indigenous groups, but there was no significant difference between these latter two groups. This pattern was repeated for elaboration(2), organization and rehearsal dimensions (taken from the GOALS-S). The very remote Indigenous and remote Indigenous groups were not significantly different from each other on the monitoring and planning dimensions, but were significantly higher than either the urban Indigenous and non-Indigenous groups on both of these dimensions. The latter two groups were not significantly different to each other. Finally the remote Indigenous group was significantly higher on regulating than any of the other groups, between which there were no significant differences.

In summary, the patterns of responses suggest no significant differences between the urban Indigenous and non-Indigenous group on any of the learning strategy dimensions taken from three different sources (PISA, LPQ and GOAL-S). In general the very remote Indigenous and remote Indigenous group were significantly higher than the urban Indigenous and non-Indigenous groups on most dimensions, with the very remote group being significantly higher than the remote groups on seven of these dimensions. Although there are significant differences these are relatively minor. The level of endorsement of each of the 12 learning strategies is similar across the four groups with the higher mean scores of the very remote Indigenous group perhaps suggesting a response bias, as noted earlier. Substantially, the results provide evidence that the scales used have meaning for the very remote and remote Indigenous students in the study.

Table 9. Level of Learning Strategies and differences in Very Remote, Remote, and Urban Indigenous, and Non-Indigenous NT High School students (PISA & LPQ)

	Groups Mean				Standard Deviation			
PISA	Very remote	Remote	Urban	Non-Indigenous	Very remote	Remote	Urban	Non-Indigenous
Control Strategies	3.73^a	3.71^a	3.49^{ab}	3.50^b	0.76	0.72	0.59	0.74
Memorization	3.81^a	3.58^b	3.12^c	3.09^c	0.88	0.92	0.74	0.85
Elaboration1	3.73^a	3.57^a	3.16^b	3.37^b	0.83	0.79	0.73	0.81
Effort and Perseverance	3.86^a	3.79^a	3.38^b	3.47^b	0.80	0.79	0.76	0.86
LPQ								
Deep	3.64^a	3.42^b	3.00^c	3.04^c	0.73	0.78	0.63	0.71
Surface	3.68^a	3.50^b	3.11^c	3.20^c	0.73	0.66	0.65	0.67

Note. means with different superscripts in a row are significantly different from each other.

Table 10. Level of Learning Strategies and differences in Very Remote, Remote, and Urban Indigenous, and Non-Indigenous NT High School students (GOAL-S)

	Groups Mean				Standard Deviation			
GOAL-S (SRCS)	Very remote	Remote	Urban	Non-Indigenous	Very remote	Remote	Urban	Non-Indigenous
Elaboration2	3.77^a	3.58^b	3.08^c	3.26^c	0.78	0.80	0.72	0.82
Organization	3.80^a	3.53^b	3.17^c	3.24^c	0.76	0.77	0.76	0.81
Rehearsal	3.86^a	3.56^b	3.04^c	3.21^c	0.74	0.82	0.70	0.79
GOAL-S (SRMC)								
Monitoring	3.68^a	3.74^a	3.37^b	3.49^b	0.75	0.68	0.56	0.71
Planning	3.77^a	3.65^a	3.08^b	3.29^b	0.84	0.79	0.64	0.78
Regulating	3.71^a	3.89^b	3.57^a	3.66^a	0.76	0.66	0.71	0.75

Note. means with different superscripts in a row are significantly different from each other.

DISCUSSION AND CONCLUSION

This research set out to examine four questions: Are psychological scales drawn from Western research valid and reliable for Indigenous, non-Western students, and if valid and reliable, what future goals, achievement goals, cognitive and learning strategies are endorsed by the participants in this study, and does level of endorsement vary by group? The results of the reliability and construct validation tests on the various instruments used give evidence that both the constructs and methodology used were appropriate to the remote Indigenous and very remote Indigenous students participating in the survey.

Based on this validity evidence the research explored the relevance and importance of eight future goals; the salience of a range of motivational goal orientations, and the salience of cognitive and learning strategies used by very remote Indigenous, remote Indigenous, and urban Indigenous students. The data provide interesting insights into the future goals, motivational orientations, and cognitive and learning strategies of very remote and remote Indigenous students and which confirm that Indigenous students perceive their learning in ways similar to a comparison non-Indigenous group.

While there were significant differences between groups on particular dimensions the similarities of the profiles are quite strong in the context that the very remote Indigenous and remote Indigenous students are indeed *remote* on many levels from the cultural contexts in which these dimensions may be thought to be most culturally salient. Significant differences demonstrated through the MANOVA analyses indicate differences of degree rather than kind.

This research provides strong evidence that there is a corpus of future goals, motivational values, cognitive and learning strategies that have relevance and heuristic value to educators working with Indigenous communities.

In a series of Australian Research Council (ARC) funded studies with Aboriginal, Navajo, Betsiamite and Yavapai school students, McInerney (2000; McInerney, Hinkley, Dowson, and Van Etten, 1998; McInerney, Roche, McInerney, and Marsh, 1997) explored the nature of the achievement goals for these groups and made comparisons with a number of Western cultural groups. The findings from these studies suggested that the motivational profiles of the diverse groups are more similar than different; and that key variables used to distinguish Western and Indigenous groups do not appear to be salient in the school contexts studied. These results, replicated on a number of occasions with diverse groups, suggest two paradoxes. First, if the motivational profiles of the different groups are so similar why is there a difference in educational outcomes? Second, within any of the Indigenous groups participating there are invariably always some students who achieve well, despite the relatively poor achievement levels of the group as a whole. What is it that the successful Indigenous students 'have' or 'do' that distinguishes them from their unsuccessful peers? These paradoxes suggest that at least five elements need to be considered in order to further our understanding of the motivational dynamics that influence achievement for these disadvantaged groups. *First*, there is a need to more closely examine the nature of the future goals that students' hold; their development over time, and their relationship to day-to-day achievement goals and learning processes. It is plausible that Indigenous students do not do well academically because they have a different perspective on their future and do not perceive the instrumental value of education in the same way as other students. *Second*, the motivational goals examined in earlier studies may have failed to uncover goals that are more salient to Indigenous students; goals that, if reflected in educational settings, might better facilitate learning. *Third*, although Indigenous students endorse learning and self-regulatory strategies in similar ways to the non-Indigenous group they may, nevertheless, have different learning and self-regulatory modes of behaviour or may lack, or fail to use, learning and self-regulatory strategies effectively. *Fourth*, the historical experiences of Indigenous people within assimilationist and often-racist educational institutions may moderate the future goals, achievement goals and perceived utility of education for Indigenous students. *Fifth*, the quality of education Indigenous students receive may be inferior for a variety of reasons (e.g., isolation, poor teachers, poor facilities, perceived irrelevance of the curriculum) predisposing these students to achieve poorly relative to more advantaged groups.

We addressed the first three of these elements directly in this research. The future goals held by the Indigenous students participating in this study appear to align closely with those held by the non-Indigenous students, although there are some interesting differences in levels of endorsement and rankings. This finding begs the question as to whether there are other future goals that might be more salient to the remote and very remote Indigenous students. Nevertheless, in a qualitative component of this research there were no future goals suggested as more relevant than the eight proposed in our study. A clear understanding, therefore, of the role and utility value of schooling in achieving future goals might be lacking for the Indigenous students.

The set of motivational goals presented to the Indigenous students in this study were based upon Western theorizing, and the levels with which they are endorsed by the Indigenous students, albeit with some differences in emphases, are similar to the non-Indigenous students. This is particularly strongly demonstrated in their endorsement of the GAGOS scales. Again, our qualitative research failed to uncover any motivational goals that may have been more relevant salient to Indigenous students.

While it was speculated that Indigenous students may have different learning and self-regulatory modes of behaviour it is clearly the case from our data that Indigenous students espouse the same set of learning and self-regulatory strategies as the non-Indigenous students. Indeed, there were very few significant differences between the Indigenous and non-Indigenous groups on these important dimensions. A possible explanation for the poor achievement levels of remote Indigenous students may be their failure to use the learning and self-regulatory strategies needed to coordinate their learning effectively.

The fourth possibility, that the historical experiences of Indigenous people within assimilationist and often-racist educational institutions of the past, and communicated to today's children through continuing community disengagement with education, may both moderate the future goals, achievement goals and perceived utility of education for remote Indigenous students, and the fifth possibility, that the quality of education remote Indigenous students receive may be inferior for a variety of reasons predisposing these students to achieve poorly are issues that, in light of the data we have presented above addressing the first four issues, need very close examination.

It is clear from our research that the very remote Indigenous and remote Indigenous students participating in our study, albeit some with limited educational experiences, have the psychological pre-requisites to function very well within educational environments that are structured to provide them with effective educational opportunities. But issues of the historical context for the importance of education to these communities, as well as a close scrutiny of the quality of educational provision made available, need to be addressed before education will be the path to optimising the future for very remote and remote Indigenous students.

REFERENCES

Ames, C. (1992). Classrooms: Goals, structures, and student motivation. *Journal of Educational Psychology, 84*, 261-71.

Anderman, E. M., and Dawson, H. (2011). Learning with motivation. In Mayer, R. E., and Alexander, P. A. (Eds.), *Handbook of Research on Learning and Instruction* (pp. 219-241). NY: Routledge.

Berry, J. W., Poortinga, Y. H., Segall, M. H., and Dasen, P. R. (2002). *Cross-cultural psychology: Research and applications (2nd ed.).* New York: Cambridge University Press.

Boulton-Lewis, G. M., Marton, F., Lewis, D. C., and Wilss, L. A. (2000). Learning in formal and informal contexts: Conceptions and strategies of Aboriginal and Torres Strait Islander university students. *Learning and Instruction, 10 (5),* 393-414.

Boulton-Lewis, G. M., Marton, F., Lewis, D. C., and Wilss, L. A. (2004). A longitudinal study of learning for a group of Indigenous Australian university students: Dissonant conceptions and strategies. *Higher Education, 47 (1),* 91-111.

Bradley, S., Draca, M., Green, C., Leeves, G. (2006). The magnitude of educational disadvantage of Indigenous minority groups in Australia. *Journal of Population Economics, 20 (3),* 547-569.

Burney, L (2003). *Inaugural speeches 06/05/2003.* NSW Legislative Assembly Hansard. Article No.36 of 06/05/2003 (37). Retrieved 11.5.11 from: http://www.parliament.nsw.gov.au/prod/parlment/hansart.nsf/V3Key/LA20030506036

Covington, M. V. (2000). Goal theory, motivation, and school achievement: An integrative review. *Annual Review of Psychology, 51,* 171-200.

Dockery, A. M. (2010). Culture and well-being: The case of Indigenous Australians. *Social Indicators Research, 99 (2),* 315-332.

Dowson, M., and McInerney, D. M. (2003). What do students say about their motivational goals?: Towards a more complex and dynamic perspective on student motivation. *Contemporary Educational Psychology, 28,* 91-113.

Dowson, M., and McInerney, D. M. (2004). The development and validation of the Goal Orientation and Learning Strategies Survey (GOALS-S). *Educational and Psychological Measurement, 64,* 290-310.

Dowson, M., and McInerney, D. M. (2005). Motivation for school and beyond: Continuing the search for cultural differences. Paper presented at the Annual Meeting of the American Educational Research Association, Montreal, April 11-15.

Fogarty, G. J., and White, C. (1994). Differences between values of Australian Aboriginal and non-Aboriginal students. *Journal of Cross-Cultural Psychology. 25(3),* 394-408.

Gray, J., and Beresford, Q. (2002). Aboriginal non-attendance at school: Revisiting the debate. *The Australian Educational Researcher, 29,* 27-42.

Heikkilä, A., and Lonka, K. (2006). Studying in higher education: students' approaches to learning, self-regulation, and cognitive strategies. *Studies in Higher Education, 31 (1),* 99-117.

Hewitt, D. (2000). A clash of worldviews: Experiences from teaching Aboriginal students. *Theory into Practice, 39,* 111-18.

Hossain, D., Gorman, D., Williams-Mozley, J., and Garvey, D. (2008). Bridging the gap: Identifying needs and aspirations of Indigenous students to facilitate their entry into university. *The Australian Journal of Indigenous Education, 37,* 9-17.

Hunter, B. H., and Schwab, R. G. (2003). Practical reconciliation and continuing disadvantage in Indigenous education. *The Drawing Board: An Australian Review of Public Affairs, 4 (2),* 83-98.

James, K., Chavez, E., Beauvais, F., Edwards, R., and Oetting, G. (1995). School achievement and dropout among Anglo and Indian females and males: A comparative examination. *American Indian Culture and Research Journal, 19,* 181-206.

Johns, G. (2008). The Northern Territory intervention in Aboriginal affairs: Wicked problem or wicked policy? *Agenda, 15 (2),* 65-84.

Kaplan, A., and Maehr, M. L. (2007). The contribution and prospects of goal orientation theory. *Educational Psychology Review, 19,* 141-184.

Kember, D., Biggs, J., and Leung, D. Y. P. (2004). Examining the multidimensionality of approaches to learning through the development of a revised version of the Learning Process Questionnaire. *The British Psychological Society, 74,* 261-280.

Ledlow, S. (1992). Is cultural discontinuity an adequate excuse for dropping out? *Journal of American Indian Education, 31(3),* 21-36.

Lee, J. (2002). Racial and ethnic achievement gap trends: Reversing the progress toward enquiry. *Educational Review, 31,* 3-12.

Lee, J. Q., McInerney, D.M., Liem, G. A. D., and Ortiga, Y. Y. (2010). The relationship between future goals and achievement goal orientations: An intrinsic-extrinsic motivation perspective. *Contemporary Educational Psychology, 35,* 264-279.

Leigh, A., and Gong, X. (2009). Estimating cognitive gaps between Indigenous and non-Indigenous Australians. *Education Economics, 17 (2),* 239-261.

Liem, A. D., Lau, S., and Nie, Y. (2008). The role of self-efficacy, task value, and achievement goals in predicting learning strategies, task disengagement, peer relationship, and achievement outcome. *Contemporary Educational Psychology, 33 (4),* 486-512.

Malin, M., and Maidment, D. (2003). Education, Indigenous survival and well-being: Emerging ideas and programs. *The Australian Journal of Indigenous Education, 32,* 85-100.

McInerney, D. M. (2000). Relationships between motivational goals, sense of self, self-concept and academic achievement for aboriginal students. Paper presented at the Aboriginal Studies Association Annual Conference, Sydney, July 12th-14th.

McInerney, D. M. (2000). Multidimensional aspects of motivation in cross-cultural settings and ways of researching this. Paper presented at the SELF Conference, Medlow Bath, Australia, October.

McInerney, D. M. (2003). What do Indigenous students think about school and is it any different from the Anglos? Paper presented at the combined AARE and NZARE Conference, Auckland, 29 Nov – 3 Dec.

McInerney, D. M. (2008). Personal investment, culture and learning: Insights into school achievement across Anglo, Indigenous, Asian and Lebanese students in Australia. *International Journal of Psychology, 43,* 870-9.

McInerney, D. M., and Ali, J. (2006). Multidimensional and hierarchical assessment of school motivation: Cross-cultural validation. *Educational Psychology: An International Journal of Experimental Educational Psychology, 26*, 717-734.

McInerney, D. M., and Swisher, K. (1995). Exploring Navajo motivation in school settings. *Journal of American Indian Education, 34*, 28-51.

McInerney, D. M., Hinkley, J., Dowson, M., and Van Etten, S. (1998). Aboriginal, Anglo, and Immigrant Australian Students' motivational beliefs about personal academic success: Are there cultural differences? *Journal of Educational Psychology, 90*, 621-629

McInerney, D. M., Marsh, H. W., and Yeung, A. S. (2003). Toward a hierarchical model of school motivation. *Journal of Applied Measurement, 4(4)*, 335-357.

McInerney, D. M., Roche, L., McInerney, V., and Marsh, H. W. (1997). Cultural perspectives on school motivation: The relevance and application of goal theory. *American Educational Research Journal 34*, 207-236.

McInerney, D. M., Yeung, A. S., and McInerney, V. (2000). The meaning of school motivation: Multidimensional and hierarchical perspectives and impacts on schooling. Paper presented at the annual meeting of the American Educational Research Association, New Orleans, April 24-29.

McInerney, D.M., Liem, A. D., Ortiga, Y. P. Y., Lee, J. Q., and Manzano, A. S. (2008). Future goals and self-regulated learning among Singaporean Chinese students: The mediating role of utility values of schooling, perceived competence, academic self-concept and academic motivation. In O. S. Tan, D. M. McInerney, A. D. Liem, and A-G. Tan (Eds.), *What the West can learn from the East: Asian perspectives on the psychology of learning and motivation, Research on Multicultural Education and International Perspectives Series (Vol. 7)*. Charlotte, NC: Information Age Publishing.

Meece, J. L., Anderman, E. M., Anderman, L. H. (2006). Classroom goal structure, student motivation, and academic achievement. *Annual Review Psychology, 57*, 487-503.

Mellor, S. and Corrigan, M. (2004). *Case for Change: A Review of Contemporary Research on Indigenous Education Outcomes*. Camberwell, Vic.: ACER Press.

Nesbit, J. C., and Adesope, O. O. (2006). Learning with concept and knowledge maps: A meta-analysis. *Review of Educational Research, 76 (3)*, 413-448.

New South Wales Department of Community Services (2009). *Working with Aboriginal People and Communities: A Practice Resource*, Retrieved 11.5.11 from http://www.community.nsw.gov.au/docswr/_assets/main/documents/working_with_aboriginal.pdf

OECD. (2007). *PISA, 2006. Science Competencies for Tomorrow's World. Volume 1 and 2*. Paris: OECD.

Penman, R. A. (2006). The "growing up" of Aboriginal and Torres Strait Islander children: a literature review. Occasional Paper No. 15, Commonwealth of Australia.

Pugh, K. J., and Bergin, D. (2006). Motivational influences on transfer. *Educational Psychologist, 41*, 147-60.

Ramsey, G. (2003). *Future Directions for Secondary Education in the Northern Territory: Report of the Secondary education*. Retrieved 13.5.11 from: www.det.nt.gov.au/__data/assets/pdf_file/0016/425ReportFullVersion.pdf

Rothwell, N. (2009). Education failure in any language. *The Weekend Australian*, pp.5.

Schunk, D. H., Pintrich, P. R., and Meece, J. (2008). *Motivation in Education: Theory, Research, and Application*. Prentice Hall: New Jersey.

Shah, M, and Widin, J. (2010). Indigenous students' voices: Monitoring Indigenous student satisfaction and retention in a large Australian University. *Journal of Institutional Research, 15 (1),* 28-41.

Sonn, C., Bishop, B., and Humphries, R. (2000). Encounters with the dominant culture: Voices of Indigenous students in mainstream higher education. *Australian Psychologist, 35 (2),* 128-135.

Steering Committee for the Review of Government Service Provision (2009). *Overcoming Indigenous Disadvantage: Key Indicators 2009.* Canberra: Productivity Commission.

Triandis, H. C. (2001). Individualism-collectivism and personality. *Journal of Personality,* 69(6), 907-924.

Triandis, H. C. (2004). The many dimensions of culture. *Academy of Management Executive, 18(1),* 88-93.

Tucker, C. M., and Herman, K. C. (2002). Using culturally sensitive theories and research to meet the academic needs of low-income African American children. *American Psychologist, 57,* 762-73.

Watkins, D., McInerney, D. M., Akande, A. and Lee, C. (2003). An investigation of ethnic differences in the motivation strategies for learning of students in desegregated South African schools. *Journal of Cross-cultural Psychology, 34,* 189-94.

Watkins, D., McInerney, D. M., Lee, C., Akande, A., and Regmi, M. (2002). Motivation and learning strategies: A cross-cultural perspective. In D. M. McInerney and S. Van Etten (eds), *Research on Sociocultural Influences on Motivation and Learning (Volume 2).* Greenwich, CT: Information Age.

Wolters, C. A. (2004). Advanced achievement goal theory: Using goal structures and goal orientations to predict students' motivation, cognition, and achievement. *Journal of Educational Psychology, 96,* 236-50.

Zimmerman, B. J. (2008). Investigating self-regulation and motivation: Historical background, methodological developments, and future prospects. *American Educational Research Journal, 45 (1),* 166-183.

In: Handbook on Psychology of Motivation
Editors: J. N. Franco and A. E. Svensgaard

ISBN: 978-1-62100-755-5
© 2012 Nova Science Publishers, Inc.

Chapter 4

DIETARY INTAKE AND PHYSICAL ACTIVITY BEHAVIOR IN COMMERCIAL WEIGHT-LOSS PROGRAM USERS: AN APPLICATION OF ORGANISMIC INTEGRATION THEORY

Philip M. Wilson[1]*, Kimberly P. Grattan[2], Diane E. Mack[1], Chris M. Blanchard[3] and Jenna D. Gilchrist[1]

[1] Behavioral Health Sciences Research Lab, Department of Kinesiology, Faculty of Applied Health Sciences, Brock University, Canada

[2] Healthy Active Living and Obesity Research, Children's Hospital of Eastern Ontario, Canada

[3] Canada Research Chair, Department of Medicine, Dalhousie University, Centre for Clinical Research, Dalhousie University, Nova Scotia, Canada

ABSTRACT

Background

Current estimates indicate the prevalence of excess body weight in adults inhabiting westernized countries is increasing (Shields, Gorber, & Tremblay, 2009). Many adults use dieting strategies and leisure-time physical activity (LTPA) in an attempt to mitigate the negative health effects of excess body weight (Franz et al., 2007), yet long-term adherence to these lifestyle behaviors central to weight management is poor (French, Jeffery, & Murray, 1999). Motivation has been identified as a critical variable underpinning the decision to engage in, and maintain, healthy lifestyle habits in people seeking to lose fat mass or control body weight (Mihalko et al., 2004).

---

* Correspondence concerning this article should be addressed to: Philip M. Wilson, PhD, Behavioural Health Sciences Research Lab, Department of Kinesiology, Faculty of Applied Health Sciences, Brock University,500 Glenridge Ave, St. Catharines, Ontario Canada, L2S3A1. E-mail: pwilson4@brocku.ca. Tel: 1 905 688 5550 Ext 4997

Study Purpose

The purpose of this study was to examine the motivational basis for LTPA and healthy eating behaviors within a sample of commercial weight-loss program users.

Methods

Participants ($N = 37$; 83.80 percent female; $M_{age} = 32.45$ years; $SD_{age} = 10.86$ years) enrolled in commercial weight-loss programs ($M_{Duration} = 0.74$ years; $SD_{Duration} = 1.18$ years) completed a self-report survey on a single occasion via a secure internet location.

Results

Descriptive statistics indicated that participants endorsed more autonomous than controlled motives for LTPA and healthy eating. Autonomous motives were positively correlated with more frequent daily fruit and vegetable intake, engagement in more strenuous types of LTPA, and greater frequency of typical LTPA per week. Both amotivation and external regulation were negatively correlated with LTPA, yet were unrelated to daily fruit and vegetable intake. Introjected regulation was unrelated to daily fruit and vegetable intake but positively associated with more frequent engagement in LTPA during a typical week.

Summary

Overall, the results of this investigation support the importance of understanding the motivational basis for healthy eating and LTPA amongst users of commercial weight-loss programs, and provide additional evidence supporting the positive link between motives centered on the personal values, congruent beliefs, and interest or enjoyment with adaptive health behaviors integral to weight control.

Key Words: Health Behaviors, Construct Validity, Self-Determination Theory, Human Autonomy, Intrinsic/Extrinsic Motivation, Amotivation

INTRODUCTION

Population health studies indicate the prevalence of excess body weight is alarmingly high and escalating in many countries worldwide (Katzmarzyk & Janssen, 2004; Shields & Tjepkema, 2006; Tjepkema, 2006). Epidemiological data (see Lemieux, Mongeau, Paquette, Laberge, & Lachance, 2004) indicate that at least 36 percent of Canadian adults (≥ 18 years old) are overweight (Body Mass Index [BMI] = 25.00 to 29.99 kg/m^2) while 23 percent are obese (BMI ≥ 30.0 kg/m^2). The total estimated cost of obesity to the Canadian health care system is $4.30 billion per annum (Katzmarzyk & Janssen, 2004) with predicted life expectancy reduced by up to 3 years in overweight Canadians (Le Petit & Berthelot, 2004). These alarming trends have led health professionals to proclaim the fight against excess body weight to be one of the most vexing public health challenges facing the modern world (Deci,

2007) and calls to identify effective and sustainable approaches to reduce and control excess body weight have been forthcoming (DiRuggerio, Frank, & Molughney, 2004; Katzmarzyk & Janssen, 2004; Sheilds & Tjepkema, 2004).

Risk factors associated with body weight regulation have been well documented for some time and include uncontrollable factors such as metabolic susceptibility, age and gender (Bouchard, Blair, & Haskell, 2007). In contrast, controllable factors such as participation in leisure-time physical activity (LTPA) and healthy eating represent key lifestyle behaviors amenable to modification that can optimize body weight and offset weight-related ailments (Silva et al., 2008). Nevertheless, public health data indicate that 47.80 percent of Canadians (aged > 12 years) were inactive during their leisure-time in 2005 (Gilmour, 2007). Additional research indicates that one-quarter of Canadian adults (aged 31 to 50 years) get more than 35.00 percent of their daily calories from fat while at least 50.00 percent do not eat the minimum serving of fruits and vegetables per day recommended by health professionals (Garriguet, 2006). Collectively, these data suggest that a greater understanding of the mechanisms contributing to the regulation of LTPA and healthy eating represents an important research agenda embedded in the prevention and management of health complications related to excess body weight in Canada.

Commercial weight-loss programs (e.g., Jenny Craig, Weight Watchers) designed to foster greater self-control of modifiable lifestyle behaviors (such as LTPA and healthy eating) represent a plausible intervention for addressing the growing crisis pertaining to excess body weight (Franz et al., 2007; Wing & Hill, 2001). Although commercial weight loss programs are readily available, there is a paucity of scientific evidence from which to evaluate their efficacy (Tsai & Wadden, 2005). Recent evidence from a large-scale randomized controlled trial (unblinded) conducted in the United Kingdom illustrates the potential for commercial weight-loss programs to facilitate loss of excess body weight in adult cohorts (Truby et al., 2006).[1] Adults classified at study outset as overweight or obese (BMI's ranged from 27.00 to 40.00 kg/m^2) were provided with one of four commercially available weight-loss programs and monitored across six consecutive months. On average, adults who adhered to using a commercial weight-loss program lost approximately 5.90 kg of body weight and 4.40 kg of body-fat across the duration of the 6-month study (Truby et al., 2006).

Despite the utility of commercial weight-loss programs for promoting loss of excess body weight it is clear that adherence issues remain a pervasive challenge (Mihalko et al., 2004; Truby et al., 2006). Prospective studies indicate that few individuals (i.e., ~20 percent) sustain reduced body weight over time as a function of using lifestyle-based interventions (e.g., commercial weight-loss programs; Franz et al., 2007; Silva et al., 2008; Wing & Hill, 2001). Substantial attrition rates have been reported in weight-loss studies (see Wing & Hill, 2001, for a review). For example, Truby et al. (2006) report a 28 percent attrition rate within the first 6-months of initiating a commercial weight-loss program in conjunction with treatment compliance rates that ranged between 47 and 57 percent across this period of the study. Overall, this evidence supports previous literature reviews focused on clinical trials and lifestyle-based interventions centered around weight control that implicate motivation to comply with treatment regimens as a key factor determining intervention effectiveness (Franz et al., 2007; Mihalko et al., 2004; Silva et al., 2008).

ORGANISMIC INTEGRATION THEORY: A BRIEF OVERVIEW

One framework that is proving useful for understanding the motivational issues influencing adherence to various health behaviors including LTPA and healthy eating is Self-Determination Theory (SDT; Deci & Ryan, 2002). SDT is a macro-level theory of motivation comprised of five mini-theories (or sub-theories) that provide an omnibus account of human functioning, integration, development, and assimilation with the social world. One sub-theory central to the approach taken by Deci and Ryan (2002) within SDT is Organismic Integration Theory (OIT) that is concerned with the quality (and quantity) of human motivation initiating and sustaining behavior within and across life domains. According to the OIT framework, motivation is conceptualized as a continuum of regulations that range from highly coercive to more autonomous (or self-determined) reasons posited to underpin behavior (Deci & Ryan, 2002). Conceptually, the motivational continuum housed within OIT represents the degree to which different reasons that regulate target behaviors (e.g., LTPA, healthy eating) have been internalized by the individual and/or integrated with the person's sense of self (Deci & Ryan, 2002; Ryan, 1995).

Amotivation and intrinsic regulation anchor the distal ends of the motivational continuum within OIT (Deci & Ryan, 2002). According to Deci and Ryan (2002), amotivation is a state akin to learned helplessness defined by a lack of intention to act within a given domain that likely results from an inability to see value in a particular behavior or a lack of perceived competence (Deci & Ryan, 2002; Vallerand, 2007). At the opposite end of the motivational continuum resides the concept of intrinsic motivation, the most autonomous or self-determined form of regulation housed within OIT (Deci & Ryan, 2002), which is defined as "doing an activity for its own sake" (Ryan & Deci, 2007, p.2). Separating the distal anchors of the OIT continuum sit four types of extrinsic motivation that conceptually represent the extent to which the reasons that regulate the behavior have been internalized by the person and/or integrated with their sense of self (Deci & Ryan, 2002; Ryan & Deci 2007). The least self-determined forms of extrinsic motivation outlined within OIT (Deci & Ryan, 2002) function in a controlling fashion to regulate behavior via a desire to appease the demands imposed by others (external regulation) or a sense of intrapersonal pressure based on negative emotions (e.g., guilt, shame) and/or to support contingent self-worth (introjected regulation). On the contrary, the most self-determined types of extrinsic motivation regulate behavior in an autonomous manner (c.f., Deci & Ryan, 2002) based on the personal value or importance ascribed to the behavior itself (identified regulation) or the degree to which engaging in the behavior is congruent with other values that symbolize the person's sense of identity (integrated regulation).

The practical appeal of OIT's motivational continuum is the facilitation of a more refined understanding of the motivational basis for participatory behaviors such as LTPA and healthy eating. Initial theorizing and evidence provided support for role of intrinsic motivation as the most adaptive type of regulation underpinning sustained behavior and well-being with limited support for the long-term effectiveness of either external or introjected regulations (see Deci & Ryan, 2002 for a review). Ryan (1995) was the first to query the utility of intrinsic regulation within domains of life where the target behavior can be perceived as inherently uninteresting (e.g., voting). In such domains, Ryan (1995) contended that more self-determined forms of extrinsic motivation (namely identified and integrated regulations) may play a more central role in motivating behavior. Emerging support for Ryan's (1995) assertions and the central tenets of OIT has been forthcoming in health behavior research. For example, Wilson and colleagues demonstrated that identified regulation (as opposed to intrinsic motivation) was a key factor shaping more frequent LTPA behavior in young, healthy adults (Wilson, Rodgers, Fraser, & Murray, 2004). Additional research has supported the positive association between regulation of dietary intake for integrated reasons with more healthy eating behaviors in comparison to either identified regulation or intrinsic motivation per se (Pelletier, Dion, Slovenic-D'Angelo, & Reid, 2006). Joint consideration of these studies implicates the level of perceived self-determination rather than the intrinsic-extrinsic orientation of the motivation per se as the key factor regulating LTPA and healthy eating. It remains unclear at present if the observations extrapolated from these investigations generalize to users of commercial weight-loss program.

AIMS AND JUSTIFICATION FOR THE PRESENT STUDY

The overall goal of this study was to test the feasibility of OIT (Deci & Ryan, 2002) as a framework for understanding patterns of LTPA and healthy eating behaviors linked with weight control in users of commercial weight-loss programs. To address this goal, the primary aim of this study was to determine the link between motives that vary in perceived self-determination along the OIT-continuum with LTPA behavior and consumption of healthy foods within a cohort of commercial weight-loss program users. The secondary aim of this study was to further explicate the role played by two distinct forms of self-determined motivation, namely identified regulation and intrinsic motivation, in relation to weight-control behaviors.

Careful examination of the literature applying OIT (Deci & Ryan, 2002) to the study of weight-control behaviors provided the impetus for the present study. First, it is clear that most investigations concerned with lifestyle behaviors linked with weight-control have restricted their focus to motives for healthy eating (e.g., Pelletier et al., 2006) or LTPA (e.g., Wilson et al., 2004) rather than assessing the motivational basis of both behaviors within the a given cohort. Isolated studies have been forthcoming to suggest the potential for cross-contextual (Hagger & Chatzisarantis, 2007) or cross-behavioral effects (Matta et al., 2009) whereby motivation for one behavior (e.g., healthy eating) can also energize participation in other behaviors (e.g., LTPA). Given that caloric restriction (via dietary intake) and caloric expenditure (via increased LTPA) both play an integral role in optimizing the control of body weight, it would appear prudent to consider the motivational foundations of each behavior within the same cohort.

A second line of reasoning providing the impetus for this study is concerned with the diversity of populations evident in the published literature applying OIT to the study of weight-control behaviors. External validity is concerned with "generalizability of findings *to* or *across* target populations, settings, times, and the like" (Pedhazur & Pedhazur-Schmelkin, 1991, p. 229). The central issue of concern with external validity is the degree to which a given sample 'represents' a target population (or any population) such that the data may be generalized either 'to' a population of interest or 'across' populations that share equivalent characteristics (see Pedhazur & Pedhazur-Schmelkin, 1991, for a review of this issue). Close inspection of the OIT literature concerned with LTPA and/or health eating behaviors indicates a range of cohorts have been the focus of study including asymptomatic, young adults (e.g., Wilson et al., 2004; Pelletier et al., 2006 - Studies 1 & 2), people living with cardiac disease (D'Angelo et al., 2007), and patients enrolled in behavioral change programs as a function of physician referral (Edmunds, Ntoumanis, & Duda, 2007). A series of recent studies from Europe report data in cohorts of obese and/or overweight women (see Silva et al., 2008, for a review) yet it remains unclear to what extent these findings can be 'generalized' with confidence to any population of commercial weight-loss program users.

A final line of reasoning supporting the rationale for this study concerns the lack of sustained attention dedicated to unraveling the important consequences associated with distinct types of autonomous motivation in relation to weight-control behaviors. Ryan (1995) contended that in domains where the target behavior lacks personal interest to the individual that identified regulation rather than intrinsic motivation could play a more salient role in the uptake and maintenance of behavior. A series of investigations by Burton and colleagues lends partial support to Ryan's (1995) contentions given that intrinsic motivation was central to understanding individual well-being whereas identified regulation was linked more strongly with performance behavior (Burton, Lydon, D'Alessandro, & Koestner, 2006). It is worthy of note that Burton et al. (2006) caution against the external validity of their observations given that the focus of their multi-study investigation was centered exclusively within the context of education. Consequently, it remains unclear if the observations generalize to other contexts (e.g., health behaviors) where motivational issues remain pivotal for understanding the dynamics of human behavior.

The hypotheses for this investigation were drawn from arguments central to OIT (Deci & Ryan, 2002) combined with previous research germane to the focal issues under scrutiny in this study (e.g., Burton et al., 2006; Pelletier et al., 2007; Wilson et al., 2004). First, it was hypothesized that more self-determined motives would be positively associated with greater LTPA and more frequent consumption of healthy foods. Stated differently, it was hypothesized that autonomous motives (identified, integrated, and intrinsic regulations) would be associated with greater frequency of engagement in LTPA and the consumption of more healthy foods in the diet on a regular basis compared with either controlled motives (i.e., external and introjected regulations) or amotivation. Second, it was hypothesized that identified regulation would be more strongly linked with both LTPA participation and healthy eating behavior in comparison to intrinsic motivation.

METHODS

Participants

The sample providing data for this study ($N = 37$; 83.80 percent female) were recruited from three commercial weight-loss programs. Six participants (16.20 percent) did not provide their gender. The sample ranged in age from 18 to 65 years old at the time of data collection ($M_{age} = 32.45$ years; $SD_{age} = 10.86$ years). Most of the sample indicated that they were Caucasian/White ($n = 28$; 75.68 percent) in ethnic origin with a small portion of the sample recording their ethnicity as 'Other' ($n = 3$; 8.11 percent). The bulk of the sample indicated they were currently employed full-time (n = 19; 51.35 percent), held a university or college degree (n = 20; 54.05 percent), and at the time of data collection were either married or in a common law relationship (n = 23; 62.16 percent). Most of the sample (75.00 percent) did not self-report living with any chronic disease. Asthma, hypothyroidism, and polycystic ovarian disease (n = 2; 5.60 percent) were the most prevalent chronic diseases reported in this sample with cardiovascular disease (n = 1), lower back pain (n = 1), arthritis (n = 1), and degenerative disc disease (n = 1) observed at a reduced frequency (2.70 percent per chronic disease).

Considerable variability was evident in terms of the duration of enrollment in each commercial weight-loss program used by this sample (M = 0.74 years; SD = 1.18 years; $Range$ = 0.00 to 6.00 years). Self-reported height and weight data were converted to metric units then combined using this formula to provide estimated Body Mass Index (BMI): Weight (kg)/Height (m)^2. BMI scores for the total sample (M_{BMI} = 30.55 kg/m^2; SD_{BMI} = 7.96 kg/m^2; $Range$ = 22.31 to 49.49 kg/m^2) were, on average, consistent with previous studies of overweight/obese adults enrolled in commercial weight-loss programs (Truby et al., 2006). Using the classification system developed by Health Canada (2003) to designate BMI cut-scores into health risk strata, the following distributions were noted in this sample per subgroup: (a) Underweight (BMI < 18.50 kg/m^2) = 0.00 percent; (b) Normal Weight (BMI = 18.50-24.99 kg/m^2) = 23.30 percent (c) Overweight (BMI = 25.00-29.99 kg/m^2) = 43.33 percent; (d) Obese Class I (BMI = 30.00-34.99 kg/m^2) = 10.00 percent; (e) Obese Class II (BMI = 35.00-39.99 kg/m^2) = 10.00 percent; and (f) Obese Class III (BMI ≥ 40.00 kg/m^2) = 13.30 percent.

Instruments

Demographics

Participants responded to a series of items that queried personal factors (e.g., age, marital status), anthropometric factors (e.g., height, weight), and program-specific factors pertinent to commercial weight-loss ventures (e.g., program name, length of enrollment).

Eating Motives

Participants completed the 24-item Reasons for Eating Behavior Scale (REBS; Pelletier et al., 2004) designed to assess the differentiated approach to motivation with specific reference to eating in line with OIT (Deci & Ryan, 2002). The REBS is comprised of the following six subscales each containing 4 items per subscale: (a) Amotivation (Sample item: "I don't know why I bother"); (b) External Regulation (Sample item: "It is expected of me"); (c) Introjected regulation (Sample item: "I would be ashamed of myself if I was not eating healthy"); (d) Identified Regulation (Sample item: "I believe it will eventually allow me to feel better"); (e) Integrated Regulation (Sample item: "Eating healthy is an integral part of my life"); and (f) Intrinsic Regulation (Sample item: "I take pleasure in fixing healthy meals"). Participants responded to each item on a 7-point Likert-scale (1 = Does not correspond at all,…, 7 = Corresponds exactly). The full set of REBS items was preceded by the following stem: "There are a variety of reasons why people regulate their eating. The following questions outline different reasons why you currently do or would regulate your eating in your life. Please indicate the extent to which each reason is true for you on the scale provided". Previous studies have provided evidence supporting the reliability and construct validity of REBS scores including issues of structural and predictive validity in samples of asymptomatic, young adults (Pelletier et al, 2004, Study 1 and 2; Pelletier & Dion, 2007) and patients seeking medical assistance from clinicians (Pelletier et al, 2004, Study 3). Scores for each REBS subscale were created by computing the mean value for the scored items per subscale within the instrument (Morris, 1979).

Physical Activity Motives

Participants completed the Behavioural Regulation in Exercise Questionnaire-2 (BREQ-2; Markland & Tobin, 2004), a 19-item self-report instrument designed to measure a range of motives that regulate LTPA central to continuum proposed by Deci and Ryan (2002) within OIT. The BREQ-2 contains five subscales that assess controlled (external and introjected regulations) and autonomous (identified and intrinsic regulations) motives for LTPA in addition to amotivation. Sample items that exemplify the content represented within each subscale were as follows: (a) Amotivation (4 items; "I don't see the point in exercising"); (b) External Regulation (4 items; "I exercise because other people say I should"); (c) Introjected Regulation (3 items; "I feel guilty when I don't exercise"); (d) Identified Regulation (4 items; "I value the benefits of exercise"); and (e) Intrinsic Regulation (4 items; "I enjoy my exercise sessions"). Following the stem (i.e., "The following list identifies reasons why people engage in physical activity. Please indicate on the scale provided how true each statement is for you"), participants responded to each BREQ-2 item on a 5-point Likert scale (0 = Not true for me,..., 4 = Very true for me). Previous research has provided evidence supporting the reliability and construct validity of scores derived from the BREQ-2 in samples of asymptomatic, young adults (Wilson et al., 2004) and patients enrolled in exercise programs supervised by clinical health professionals or medical practitioners (Markland & Tobin, 2004). Scores for each BREQ-2 subscale were created by computing the mean value for the scored items per subscale within the instrument (Morris, 1979).

Physical Activity

Participants completed the Godin Leisure Time Exercise Questionnaire (GLTEQ; Godin & Shephard, 1985) to assess LTPA during a typical week. Participants used an open-ended response format to identify the frequency of mild, moderate, and strenuous exercise undertaken for a minimum of 15 minutes per occasion over a typical week. A total physical activity score (GLTEQ-METS) was calculated using this formula: $\sum([\text{mild} \times 3] + [\text{moderate} \times 5] + [\text{strenuous} \times 9])$. The GLTEQ also contains a second item that queries the frequency of regular physical activities that induce sweating during a typical week (GLTEQ-SWEAT Item: "During a typical 7-day period (a week), in your leisure time, how often do you engage in any regular activity long enough to work up a sweat [heart beats rapidly]?"). Participants respond to the GLTEQ-SWEAT item using a 3-point scale (1 = Often,..., 3 = Never). The GLTEQ-SWEAT item was reverse coded prior to all data analyses in this study. Previous research indicates the GLTEQ items seem understandable to various populations, scores from these items respond to changes in exercise behavior, and correlate in the expected direction with physical fitness indices (Jacobs, Ainsworth, Hartman, & Leon, 1993).

Dietary Intake

Participants completed two self-report questions designed to measure healthy eating based on the frequency of daily fruit and vegetable intake (DFVI; Prochaska & Sallis, 2004). Both questions were preceded by a stem that focused participants' responses on daily intake (i.e., "In a typical day,...") of fruits ("...how many servings of fruit do you eat?") and vegetables ("...how many servings of vegetables do you eat?"). Participants were also provided with examples of serving sizes to aid the interpretability of each item. One serving of fruit was defined as follows: "A serving of fruit is equal to any of the following: (a) 1 medium piece of fresh fruit, (b) ½ cup of fruit salad, (c) ¼ cup of raisins, (d) 6oz. of 100% orange, apple, or grapefruit juice (Do not count fruit punch, lemonade, Gatorade, Sunny Delight, or fruit drink)". One serving of vegetables was defined as follows: "A serving of vegetables is equal to any of the following: (a) 1 medium carrot or other fresh vegetable, (b) 1 small bowl of green salad, (c) ½ cup of fresh cooked vegetables, (d) ¾ cup of vegetable soup (Do not count French Fries, Onion rings, Potato Chips, or Fried Okra)". Responses to each item were made on a 5 point closed-option scale (0 = None, ..., 4 = 4 or more). Previous research has demonstrated modest stability of scores derived from these items along with concurrent and predictive validity using 3-day food record data as the criterion (Prochaska & Sallis, 2004).

Data Collection Procedures and Data Analyses

Data were collected via an electronic interface hosted on a secure internet site. Eligible participants were sent a Letter of Information (LOI) that included a Uniform Resource Locator (URL) via e-mail. Those choosing to participate selected the URL which directed the participant to a secure website containing an informed consent form and the study questionnaire. Participants were informed about the nature of the study in the LOI and encouraged to ask questions of the investigators via e-mail or telephone prior to consenting to participate in the study. Informed consent was secured from each participant before permitting access to the survey by having each participant select a box indicating they had read the LOI and were consenting to participate. Participants choosing not to provide informed consent were thanked for their interest and redirected away from the survey page to a random URL. Standard instructions were given in the LOI to minimize the likelihood of between-groups effects introduced on the basis of test administration. All aspects of this study received clearance from a university-based Research Ethics Boards prior to any participant contact or data collection.

Participant recruitment used a multi-focal strategy to advertise and recruit a heterogeneous sample of commercial weight-loss program users. Participant recruitment occurred using a rolling inclusion format across four consecutive months at the outset of the calendar year (January 30th, 2009 to May 28th, 2009). Generalized recruitment strategies to advertise the study were adapted on the basis of Dillman's (2007) Tailored Design Method. First, a series of advertisements in poster format were placed in prominent locations throughout the community (e.g., grocery stores, commercial weight-loss clinics, fitness centers, etc). Second, presentations were made at locally-based fitness centers and commercial weight-loss clinics. Third, a series of postings were made to advertise the study at different social networking sites (e.g. Facebook) and using select listservs derived from an internet-based search. Finally, the study was advertised through a dialogue broadcast on a local television station that updates the public with relevant events occurring throughout the community on a daily basis. Snowball sampling was also employed to maximize recruitment efforts within this study. Participants who provided data upon request to a single question (i.e., 'How were you directed to complete our survey?') indicated that advertising via the internet/worldwide web (n = 17; 45.90 percent) was more successful than e-mail strategies (n = 5; 13.50 percent) or in-person clinic presentations (n = 2; 5.40 percent).

Data analyses followed a sequential protocol. First, data were screened for outliers, missing values, and conformity to assumptions of relevant statistical tests. Second, the presence of missing values was scrutinized within the data to detect any systematic patterns of non-response that could adversely impact subsequent analyses. Third, a multiple imputation procedure using an expectation maximization algorithm was utilized to replace all missing values. Fourth, internal consistency estimates of score reliability were calculated followed by descriptive statistics. Fifth, correlations (Pearson r and Spearman's Rho) were computed to examine patterns of bivariate association between each motive spanning the OIT-based continuum and both weight-control behaviors. Finally, a series of simultaneous multiple regression analyses (SMRA) were computed to further explicate the role of identified regulation and intrinsic motivation in relation to LTPA and healthy eating as behavioral markers of weight-control. Structure coefficients (r_s; Courville & Thompson, 2001)[2] and unique variance estimates ($r_{Y,Xn}$; Hair Black, Babin, Anderson, & Tatham, 2006)[3] along with effect size estimates (f^2; Cohen, 1992)[4] were calculated to aid the interpretability of each regression model.

RESULTS

Preliminary Analyses and Replacement of Missing Data

No out-of-range responses were observed for any manifest BREQ-2, REBS, GLTEQ, or DFVI item. Missing values were evident amongst a portion of the data provided by this sample (percent missing values ranged from 0.00 to 29.70 percent across manifest survey items used in this study). It was evident that the bulk of the missing values were in response to the items assessing mild (27.00 percent), moderate (24.30 percent), and strenuous (29.70 percent) LTPA with the GLTEQ (missing values across manifest BREQ-2 and REBS items ranged from 0.00 to 10.80 percent in this sample). No evidence of missing data was noted for responses to the DFVI items. Interpretation of Little's (1988) test suggested that the missing values could be considered missing at random in this sample (χ^2 = 236.71, df = 307, p = 0.99). All missing values were replaced with an imputed score derived from an expectation maximization algorithm that used data provided within this sample to estimate scores for each missing data point.

Internal Consistency Score Reliability Estimates

Estimates of score reliability using Cronbach's α (Cronbach, 1951) for responses to REBS and BREQ-2 items are presented in Tables 1 and 2. Considerable variability was evident in Cronbach α-values noted in this sample for both REBS scores ($M_α$ = 0.85; $SD_α$ =

0.09) and BREQ-2 scores ($M_\alpha = 0.76$; $SD_\alpha = 0.15$). Amotivation items within both the REBS and BREQ-2 exhibited the largest amount of error variance in item scores whereas identified regulation items exhibited the least error variance.

Descriptive Statistics and Bivariate Correlations

Descriptive statistics for all study variables are presented in Tables 1 and 2. Inspection of the data indicates that this sample of commercial weight-loss program users provided greater endorsement of autonomous motives for healthy eating and physical activity behavior in contrast to controlled motives. Identified regulation was the most strongly endorsed motives for healthy eating and LTPA with amotivation being the least endorsed form of regulation noted in this sample. Considerable variability was evident in DFVI consumption and typical LTPA behaviors. On average, the pattern of daily fruit and vegetable consumption behavior did not conform to levels recommended by health agencies for adults (Health Canada, 2007). Self-reported patterns of LTPA revealed minimal engagement in strenuous LTPA behaviors on a regular basis (Median$_{\text{GLTEQ-SWEAT}}$ = 2.00; Mode$_{\text{GLTEQ-SWEAT}}$ =2.00) although a small portion of the sample (21.60 percent) indicated they undertook this form of LTPA 'often' during a typical week.[5] Observations of LTPA frequency derived from the GLTEQ-METS responses indicated, on average (see Table 2), this sample engaged in low levels of LTPA during a typical week.

Patterns of bivariate association between motives and both weight-control behaviors revealed several interesting patterns in the data (see Tables 3 and 4). Amotivation was negatively correlated with LTPA, but largely unrelated to DFVI. Controlled motives were, in general, uncorrelated with DFVI and negatively correlated with LTPA. The exception to this pattern was introjected regulation that was positively correlated with GLTEQ-METS but not more strenuous activities captured by GLTEQ-SWEAT. More self-determined motives were positively correlated with both DFVI and LTPA. Identified regulation was the dominant correlate of LTPA compared with other forms of autonomous motivation yet this pattern was not replicated with regards to healthy eating. In contrast, intrinsic motivation was the strongest correlate of DFVI followed closely by identified then integrated regulations.

Simultaneous Multiple Regression Analyses Predicting Healthy Eating and LTPA Behaviors

Separate models were calculated using a SMRA-approach to variable entry to test the contributions of identified regulation and intrinsic motivation to distinct weight-control behavior characterizing LTPA and healthy eating. Visual examination of the scatterplots depicting the distribution of standardized residuals implied linearity and homscedasticity were tenable assumptions in each regression model depicted in Table 5. Variance inflation factor values (Range = 0.36 to 0.82) and Tolerance values (Range = 1.22 to 2.81) implied potential for collinear effects amongst the predictor scores in each regression model. Closer inspection of the Variance Proportion Values (VV; Pedhazur, 1997) when the Condition Index (CI) exceeded ten indicated no grave multicollinearity issues in the regression model concerning DFVI (no two VPV's ≥ 0.50).

Table 1. Descriptive statistics and estimates of internal consistency reliability for eating motives and fruit/vegetable intake

Variables	M	SD	Skew.	Kurt.	Range	α
1. REBS-Amotivation	1.33	0.60	1.96	3.13	1.00-3.25	0.67
2. REBS-External Regulation	2.09	1.09	0.61	-1.08	1.00-4.00	0.88
3. REBS-Introjected Regulation	4.06	1.71	-0.29	-0.74	1.00-7.00	0.87
4. REBS-Identified Regulation	6.45	0.67	-1.02	0.07	4.75-7.00	0.92
5. REBS-Integrated Regulation	5.80	0.99	-1.01	2.04	2.50-7.00	0.84
6. REBS-Intrinsic Regulation	5.35	1.50	-1.16	1.22	1.00-7.00	0.92
7. Daily Fruit/Vegetable Intake	5.03	2.99	0.71	4.29	0.00-16.00	-

Note: REBS = Regulation of Eating Behaviors Scale (Pelletier et al., 2004). *M* = Mean. *SD* = Standard Deviation. *Skew.* = Univariate Skewness. *Kurt.* = Univariate Kurtosis. *Range* = Observed range of scores per REBS subscale score measured in this study. α = Cronbach's (1951) coefficient alpha estimate of internal consistency reliability.

Table 2. Descriptive statistics and estimates of internal consistency reliability for physical activity motives and LTPA

Variables	M	SD	Skew.	Kurt.	Range	α
1. BREQ-2 Amotivation	0.24	0.44	1.93	2.74	0.00-1.50	0.60
2. BREQ-2 External Regulation	0.84	0.82	1.02	-0.04	0.00-2.75	0.78
3. BREQ-2 Introjected Regulation	1.47	0.85	0.25	-0.31	0.00-3.33	0.62
4. BREQ-2 Identified Regulation	2.74	0.93	-0.52	-0.06	0.25-4.00	0.91
5. BREQ-2 Intrinsic Regulation	2.52	1.02	-0.65	-0.13	0.00-4.00	0.89
6. GLTEQ-METS	38.49	22.64	0.26	0.69	0.00-87.00	-
7. GLTEQ-SWEAT	1.86	0.75	0.23	-1.15	1.00-3.00	-

Note: BREQ-2 = Behavioural Regulation in Exercise Questionnaire-2 (Markland & Tobin, 2004). *M* = Mean. *SD* = Standard Deviation. *Skew.* = Univariate Skewness. *Kurt.* = Univariate Kurtosis. *Range* = Observed range of scores per BREQ-2 subscale score measured in this study. α = Cronbach's (1951) coefficient alpha estimate of internal consistency reliability. Responses to the GLTEQ-SWEAT item included the following options: (a) 1 = Never/Rarely, (b) 2 = Sometimes, and (c) 3 = Often.

Table 3. Bivariate correlations between motives for healthy eating and daily fruit/vegetable intake

Variables	1	2	3	4	5	6	7
1. REBS-Amotivation	-						
2. REBS-External Regulation	0.34	-					
3. REBS-Introjected Regulation	-0.01	0.39	-				
4. REBS-Identified Regulation	-.030	-0.15	0.13	-			
5. REBS-Integrated Regulation	-0.33	-0.02	0.09	0.54	-		
6. REBS-Intrinsic Regulation	-0.31	0.14	-0.13	0.44	0.72	-	
7. Daily Fruit/Vegetable Intake	-0.08	0.06	0.06	0.27	0.23	0.30	-

Note: REBS = Regulation of Eating Behaviors Scale (Pelletier et al., 2004). Pearson correlations are presented in the lower diagonal of the matrix based. Sample size is consistent across each pairwise comparison presented in the lower diagonal of the matrix ($N = 37$). All *r*-values presented in the lower diagonal of the matrix > |0.27| were statistically significant in this sample at $p < 0.05$ (one-tailed significance).

Table 4. Bivariate correlations between motives for physical activity behavior and LTPA

Variables	1	2	3	4	5	6	7
1. REBS-Amotivation	-						
2. REBS-External Regulation	0.12	-					
3. REBS-Introjected Regulation	-0.14	0.27	-				
4. REBS-Identified Regulation	-0.46	-0.21	0.48	-			
5. REBS-Intrinsic Regulation	-0.28	-0.08	0.48	0.80	-		
6. GLTEQ-METS	-0.33	-0.20	0.35	0.44	0.33	-	
7. GLTEQ-SWEAT	-0.46	-0.21	0.08	0.51	0.32	0.41	-

Note. BREQ-2 = Behavioural Regulation in Exercise Questionnaire-2 (Markland & Tobin, 2004). Pearson correlations are presented in the lower diagonal of the matrix based for all variable pairs except GLTEQ-SWEAT which are Spearman's Rho correlations. Sample size is consistent across each pairwise comparison presented in the lower diagonal of the matrix ($N = 37$). All *r*-values presented in the lower diagonal of the matrix > |0.27| were statistically significant in this sample at $p < 0.05$ (one-tailed significance) in this sample.

Table 5. Regression models illustrating the role of identified and intrinsic regulations in LTPA and healthy eating

Predictor Variables	F	df	p	Adj. R^2	B	SE B	β	t-value	p-value	r_s	$r_{Y.X_n}$
LTPA Model 1: GLTEQ-METS	4.12	2, 34	< 0.05	0.15							
BREQ-2 Identified Regulation					12.17	6.27	0.50	1.94	0.06	0.99	0.09
BREQ-2 Intrinsic Regulation					-1.70	5.73	-0.08	-0.30	0.77	0.74	<0.01
LTPA Model 2: GLTEQ-SWEAT	6.83	2, 34	< 0.01	0.25							
BREQ-2 Identified Regulation					0.58	0.20	0.72	2.96	0.06	0.96	0.18
BREQ-2 Intrinsic Regulation					-0.19	0.18	-0.26	-1.05	0.30	0.60	0.02
Healthy Eating Model: DFVI	2.23	2, 34	0.12	0.06							
REBS Identified Regulation					0.77	0.80	0.17	0.96	0.34	0.80	0.02
REBS Intrinsic Regulation					0.45	0.36	0.23	1.27	0.21	0.89	0.04

Note: BREQ-2 = Behavioural Regulation in Exercise Questionnaire-2 (Markland & Tobin, 2004), REBS = Regulation of Eating Behaviors Scales (Pelletier et al., 2004). F = Univariate F-statistic per regression model. df = Degrees of freedom within each regression model. p = probability values associated with each F-statistic per regression model. Adj. R^2 = Adjusted R-squared value per criterion score. B = Unstandardized beta coefficient per predictor variables. SE B = Standard error per unstandardized beta coefficients. $B_{95\% CI}$ = Ninety-five percent confidence interval around the point estimate for the unstandardized beta coefficients. β = Standardized beta coefficient per predictor variable. t-value = t-values per predictor in each regression model. p-value = probability value for each predictor variable per regression model. r_s = Structure coefficients (Courville & Thompson, 2001). $r_{Y.X_n}$ = Unique variance estimate accounted for in each criterion score per predictor variables based on the observed R^2 value in each regression model (Hair et al., 2006).

However, it was noteworthy that when the CI was high (CI = 11.38) in each regression model concerning LTPA (see Table 5) that the VPV's for identified regulation (VPV = 0.97) and intrinsic motivation (VPV = 0.80) exceeded the threshold (i.e., 0.50) recommended by Pedhazur (1997). On the basis of this observation, it is recommended that caution should be used when interpreting the results of the regression models concerning LTPA.

Results of the SMRA provided mixed support for the tenability of each model using GLTEQ-METS, GLTEQ-SWEAT, and DFVI as separate criterion (see Table 5). Comparison of the structure coefficients depicting the strength and direction of the predictive relationship between identified regulation and intrinsic motivation with LTPA and DFVI behaviors revealed several noteworthy patterns in the data. First, identified regulation made a stronger contributor to each regression model compared with intrinsic regulation when LTPA served as the criterion of interest. Second, identified regulation accounted for the largest portion of unique variance explained in terms of LTPA frequency and sweat-inducing forms of LTPA undertaken on a regular basis. Finally, the pattern of relationships characterizing the motivation-behavior relationship using LTPA as the criterion of interest was not substantiated in the regression model concerning DFVI where intrinsic motivation was a stronger predictor (albeit marginally so) of healthy eating than identified regulation. Overall, it is worthy of note that effect sizes (f^2; Cohen, 1992) ranged from moderate-to-large across each regression model ($f^2_{DFVI} = 0.18$; $f^2_{GLTEQ-METS} = 0.24$; $f^2_{GLTEQ-SWEAT} = 0.40$).

DISCUSSION

The present study explored the motivational basis for LTPA and healthy eating in a sample of commercial weight-loss program users. In brief, the primary aim of this study was to examine the association between motives varying in perceived self-determination with behaviors central to weight-control. Additionally, the secondary aim of this study was to determine if identified regulation and intrinsic motivation played a differential role in terms of predicting engagement in two important health behaviors integral to the control of body weight. Overall, the results of this investigation provide mixed support for the a priori hypotheses given that (a) more self-determined motives were positively linked with greater frequency of healthy eating and LTPA, and (b) identified regulation was a more potent motivational resource linked with regular LTPA compared to intrinsic motivation in this cohort. Inconsistencies between the observations noted within the data and the investigation's a priori hypotheses were also evident. Introjected regulation was positively linked with more frequent LTPA per week, and intrinsic motivation appears pivotal to the regulation of healthy eating in the form of daily fruit and vegetable intake compared with identified regulation. Overall, it would appear reasonable to contend that more self-determined than controlled motives represent fundamental resources integral to the regulation of weight-control behaviors in users of commercial weight-loss programs. Yet the motivation-behavior link may be sensitized to type of weight-control behavior under scrutiny, namely caloric expenditure based on variations in LTPA versus caloric restriction dictated by food intake. In sum, these observations provide support for the tenability of OIT (Deci & Ryan, 2002) as a framework for understanding the nature and function of motivation for two important health behaviors linked to weight-control in a unique sample of commercial weight-loss program users.

Consistent with our first hypothesis, it seems apparent from this study that the primary source of behavioral regulation linked with adaptive patterns of LTPA and healthy eating in users of commercial weight-loss programs focuses on self-determined, not controlled, forms of motivation. Proponents of OIT (Deci & Ryan, 2002; Ryan & Deci 2007) have long extolled the importance of motives that reflect higher levels of perceived self-determination as a fundamental source of adaptive behavioral regulation. The central issue concerned with this facet of OIT is the focus on identifying motivational resources that underpin enduring patterns of adaptive behavior without concomitantly impairing a person's well-being. Combining the results of this preliminary study with the broader tenets of OIT (Deci & Ryan, 2002), it seems clear that controlling strategies that impose action-behavior contingencies on the person seem unlikely to yield adaptive benefits with reference to weight-control behaviors. On the contrary, and in line with proponents of OIT (Deci & Ryan, 2002; Ryan & Deci, 2007), it would appear that health professionals working with cohorts who use commercial weight-loss programs may wish to encourage the development of autonomous motives irrespective of their intrinsic or extrinsic origin to promote investment in weight-control behaviors.

In contrast to our initial hypotheses, closer inspection of the data presented in Table 4 makes it apparent that stronger endorsement of introjected regulation was associated with more frequent LTPA per week amongst commercial weight-loss program users. Such observations are not wholly inconsistent with OIT given that introjection motivates behavior via coercive intrapersonal pressure to avoid negative emotions (e.g., guilt, shame) or maintain conditional self-worth (Deci & Ryan, 2002; Ryan & Deci, 2007). At least one previous study has reported similar findings concerning the salience of introjected regulation as a motivational resource for weekly LTPA behavior in a sample of young, university-based women but not men (Wilson et al., 2004). Given the large percentage of females comprising the sample for this investigation, it seems reasonable to assert that introjected regulation is an important source motivating LTPA but not healthy eating behavior within various cohorts of women. Notwithstanding these observations, it remains clear from studies in domains beyond physical activity that introjected regulation is associated predominantly with short-term persistence behavior that is often accompanied by a diminished sense of well-being (c.f., Deci & Ryan, 2002; Ryan & Deci, 2007). Overall, it seems reasonable to assert that health professionals avoid the use of strategies designed to foster introjected regulation as a vehicle to motivate LTPA behavior amongst cohorts using commercial weight-loss programs.

Of additional interest in this study was the second hypothesis that conducted a preliminary assessment of the differential contributions made by two self-determined yet conceptually distinct forms of behavioral regulation to adaptive weight-control behaviors. Building upon the seminal contentions set forth by Ryan (1995) and the empirical work conducted by Burton et al. (2006), the observations noted in this study offer mixed support for the a priori hypothesis that identified regulation would play a more central role in the regulation of functional weight-control behaviors compared to intrinsic motivation. Closer inspection of the data reported in Table 5 clearly indicate that, in this sample of commercial weight-loss program users, identified regulation is the motivational source linked with more frequent and vigorous LTPA yet intrinsic motivation is more likely to regulate healthy eating on a daily basis. Several factors may account for the discrepancy between the hypothesized relationships anticipated on the basis of Ryan's (1995) assertions and previous research (Burton et al., 2006) and the empirical findings noted in this study of weight-control behaviors. One plausible account for these observations concerns the ample statistical overlap between identified regulation and intrinsic motivation that renders it challenging to disentangle any unique contributions made by either form of self-determined motivation. Such observations have been forthcoming in other studies using the BREQ-2 across diverse cohorts (Markland & Tobin, 2004; Wilson et al., 2004) and imply further construct validation research using this instrument may be worthwhile.

At least two additional explanations for the observations pertaining to the second hypothesis investigated in this study seem plausible and worthy of consideration. First, it is conceivable that links between distinct forms of self-determined motivation with adaptive weight-control behaviors represent a function of sample idiosyncrasies or, more broadly, to unique characteristics that define users of commercial weight-loss programs. To date, only a limited number of studies have examined the motivational basis for weight-loss behaviors using OIT as a guiding framework (Silva et al., 2008) with no clear indication that these investigations sampled from populations that represent users of commercial weight-loss programs. Given the paucity of motivational research conducted with cohorts of this nature it seems prudent to augment the present findings with additional research using OIT to further understand the basis of functional and sustainable weight-control behaviors. A second plausible explanation for these findings concerns potential differences in the distinct set of behaviors that define successful weight-control, namely LTPA and health eating. Joint consideration of Ryan's (1995) contentions with the findings noted in this study lend partial credence to the belief that users of commercial weight-loss programs simply perceive managing the challenges integral to dietary behaviors as more auto-telic compared with the repertoire of behaviors warranted to be physically active. While this account is intuitively appealing it remains speculative based on the findings of a solitary investigation yet worthy of consideration and further inquiry.

While the results of this study hold appeal for OIT and health professionals with a vested interest in counteracting the ravages of excess body weight, a number of limitations seem worthy of note in conjunction with future directions to advance our understanding of the motivational basis of weight-control behaviors. First, the design of this study was cross-sectional in nature relying on a small sample of participants recruited using purposive sampling techniques. Research designs of this nature confer limited evidence for causality whilst the use of a non-probability based sampling approach constrains the external validity of these findings (Pedhazur & Pedhazur-Schmelkin, 1991). Future studies could extrapolate from these initial findings to embrace more sophisticated longitudinal designs that provide greater insight into the dynamics of causal flow including temporal precedence combined with probability-based sampling techniques that confer greater confidence in the generalizability of any study observations. Second, this study relied exclusively on self-report methods for data collection that can be susceptible to confounds such as monomethod bias and social desirability response bias (Streiner & Norman, 2008). Additional investigations employing indices of LTPA and healthy eating that do not require self-report mechanisms would be useful to rule out potential biases in data interpretation. Third, this study assessed only daily fruit and vegetable intake as the index of healthy eating. Public health agencies (e.g., Canada's Food Guide) often include other food groups as a component of healthy eating so the assessment used in the present study may under-represent this important behavioral criterion. Future studies would do well to expand on the present investigation to use instrumentation to assess healthy eating that focuses on multiple food groups or provides more open-ended response options (e.g., food diaries).

In summary, the purpose of this study was to examine the feasibility of OIT (Deci & Ryan, 2002) as a framework to understand the motivational basis of healthy eating and LTPA behaviors amongst users of commercial weight-loss programs. The findings reported in this preliminary study provide clear support for two major propositions set forth within OIT by Deci and Ryan (2002), namely that motivation is a complex set of reasons for behavior that is best understood as a continuum and more self-determined (than controlled) motives appear to be linked with positive consequences exemplified in this study by two distinct yet adaptive weight-control behaviors. Additional support for the important distinction between identified regulation and intrinsic motivation was also forthcoming in this study that is worthy of further consideration in the next generation of OIT-based research concerning behavioral issues within and across domains. Overall, this study provides ongoing support for the tenability of OIT as a framework for understanding motivated behavior in a unique cohort of commercial weight-loss program users.

ACKNOWLEDGMENTS

This research was supported by a grant from the Social Sciences and Humanities Research Council of Canada (SSHRC) awarded to Drs. Wilson, Mack, and Blanchard. Thanks are extended to the participants who gave freely of their time and effort in this research study. The results of the investigation reported in this manuscript represent a portion of the graduate thesis requirements completed by the second author under the supervision of the first author at Brock University.

REFERENCES

Bouchard, C., Blair, S. N., & Haskell, W. L. (2007). *Physical activity and health*. Champaign, IL: Human Kinetics.

Burton, K. D., Lydon, J. E., D'Alessandro, D. U., & Koestner, R. (2006). The differential effects of intrinsic and identified motivation on well-being and performance: Prospective, experimental and implicit approaches to self-determination theory. *Journal of Personality & Social Psychology, 91*, 750-762.

Cohen, J. (1992). A power primer. *Psychological Bulletin, 112*, 155-159.

Cronbach, L. J. (1951). Coefficient alpha and the internal structure of tests. *Psychometrika, 16*, 297-234.

Deci, E. L. (2007). *Motivation in Canada 1: Self-determination in life contexts*. Paper presented at the annual meeting of the Canadian Psychology Association, Ottawa, ON.

Deci, E. L., & Ryan, R. M. (2002). *Handbook of self-determination research*. Rochester NY: University of Rochester Press.

Dillman, D. A. (2007). *Mail and internet surveys: The tailored design* (2nd Edition). Hoboken, NJ: Wiley.

DiRuggiero, E., Frank, J., & Moloughney, B. (2004). Strengthen Canada's public health system now. *Canadian Journal of Public Health, 95,* 5-11.

Edmunds, J., Ntoumanis, N., & Duda, J. L. (2007). Adherence and well-being in overweight and obese patients referred to an exercise on prescription scheme: A self-determination theory perspective. *Psychology of Sport & Exercise, 8,* 722-740.

Franz, M. J., VanWormer, J. J., Crain, A. L., Boucher, J. L., Histon, T., Caplan, W., Bowman, J. D., & Pronk, N. P. (2007). Weight-loss outcomes: A systematic review and meta-analysis of weight-loss clinical trials with a minimum 1 year follow-up. *Journal of American Dietetic Association, 107,* 1755-1767.

French, S. A., Jeffery, R. W., Murray, D. (1999) Is dieting good for you?: prevalence, duration and associated weight and behaviour changes for specific weight loss strategies over four years in US adults. *International Journal of Obesity Related Metabolic Disorders, 23,* 320-327.

Garriguet, D. (2006). Canadians' eating habits. *Health Reports, 18,* 17-32.

Gilmour, H. (2007). Physically active Canadians. *Health Reports, 18,* 45-66.

Godin, G., & Shepherd, R. (1985). A simple method to assess exercise behavior in the community. *Canadian Journal of Applied Sport Science, 10,* 141-146.

Hagger, M. S., & Chatzisarantis, N. L. D. (2007). The trans-contextual model of motivation. In M. S. Hagger & N. L. D. Chatzisarantis (Eds.), Intrinsic motivation and self-determination in exercise and sport (pp. 53-70). Champaign, IL: Human Kinetics.

Hair, J. F., Black, W. C., Babin, B. J., Anderson, R. E., & Tatham, R. L. (2006). *Multivariate data analysis* (6th Edition). Upper Saddle River, NJ: Prentice Hall.

Health Canada. (2003). *Canadian guidelines for body weight classification in adults.* Ottawa: Health Canada. Retrieved July 20th, 2011, from http://www.hc-sc.gc.ca/hpfb-dgpsa/onapp-bppn/cg_bwc_introduction_e.html

Health Canada/. (2007). *Canada's Food Guide.* Ottawa; Health Canada. Retrieved July 20th, 2011, from http://www.hc-sc.gc.ca/fn-an/food-guide-aliment/index-eng.php

Jacobs, D. R., Jr., Ainsworth, B. E., Hartman, T. J., & Leon, A. S. (1993). A simultaneous evaluation of 10 commonly used physical activity questionnaires. *Medicine & Science in Sports & Exercise, 25,* 81-91.

Katzmarzyk, P. T., & Janssen, I. (2004). The economic costs associated with physical inactivity and obesity in Canada: An update. *Canadian Journal of Applied Physiology, 29,* 90-115.

Lemieux, S., Mongeau, L., Paquette, M. C., Laberge, S., & Lachance, B. (2004). Health Canada's new guidelines for body weight classification in adults: Challenges and concerns. *Canadian Medical Association Journal. 23,* 171-182.

Le Petit, C. & Berthelot, J. M. (2006). Obesity-a growing issue. *Health Reports, 17,* 43-52.

Markland, D., & Tobin, V. (2004). A modification of the Behavioral Regulation in Exercise Questionnaire to include an assessment of amotivation. *Journal of Sport & Exercise Psychology, 26,* 191-196

Little, R. J. A. (1988). A test of missing completely at random for multivariate data with missing values. *Journal of the American Statistical Association, 83,* 1198-1202.

Mata, J., Silva, M. N., Vieira, Pn. N., Carraca, E. V., Andrade, A. M., Coutinho, S. R., Sardinha, L. B., & Teixeira, P. J. (2009). Motivational "spill-over" during weight control: Increased self-determination and exercise intrinsic motivation predict eating self-regulation. *Health Psychology, 28,* 709-716.

McArdle, W. D., Katch, F. I., & Katch, V. L. (2009). *Exercise physiology: Nutrition, energy, and human performance.* Philadelphia, PA: Lippincott, Williams, & Wilkins.

Mihalko, S. L., Brenes, G. A., Farmer, D. F., Katula, J. A., Blakrishman, R., & Bowen, D. J. (2004). Challenges and innovations in enhancing adherence. *Controlled Clinical Trials, 25,* 447-457.

Morris, J. D. (1979). A comparison of regression prediction accuracy on several types of factor scores. *American Educational Research Journal, 16,* 17-24.

Pedhazur, E. J. (1997). *Multiple regression in behavioral research* (3rd ed.). Orlando, FL: Harcourt Brace.

Pedhauzer, E., & Pedhazur Schmelkin, L. (1991). *Measurement, Design, & Analysis.* Hillsdale, NJ: Lawrence Erlbaum Associates.

Pelletier, L. G., & Dion, S. C. (2007). An examination of general and specific motivational mechanisms for the relations between body dissatisfaction and eating behaviors. *Journal of Social & Clinical Psychology, 3,* 303-333.

Pelletier, L. G., Dion, S. C., Slovenic-D'Angelo, M., & Reid, R. (2004). Why do you regulate what you eat? Relationship between forms of regulation, eating behaviors, sustained dietary behavior change, and psychological adjustment. Motivation & Emotion, 28, 245-277.

Prochaska, J., & Sallis, J. (2004). Reliability and validity of a fruit and vegetable screening measure for adolescents. *Journal of Adolescent Health, 34,* 163-165.

Ryan, R. M. (1995). Psychological needs and the facilitation of integrative processes. Journal of Personality, 63, 397-427.

Ryan, R. M., & Deci, E. L. (2007). Active human nature: Self-determination theory and the promotion and maintenance of sport, exercise, and health. In M. S. Hagger & N. L. D. Chatzisarantis (Eds.), Intrinsic motivation and self-determination in exercise and sport (pp. 1-19). Champaign, IL: Human Kinetics.

Shields, M. & Tjepkema, M. (2006). Trends in adult obesity. *Health Reports, 17,* 53-60.

Shields, M. N., Gorber, S. C., & Tremblay, M. S. (2009). Estimates of obesity base don self-report versus direct measures. *Health Reports, 19,* 61-76.

Silva, M. N., Markland, D., Minderico, C. S., Viera, P. N., Castro, M. M., Coutinho, S. R., Santos, T. C., Matos, M. G., Sardinha, L. B., & Teixeira, P. J. (2008). A randomized controlled trial to evaluate self-determination theory for exercise adherence and weight control: Rationale and intervention description. *BMC Public Health, 8,* 234-247.

Streiner, D. L., & Norman, G. R. (2004). *Health measurement scales: A practical guide to their development and use* (4th ed.). Toronto, ON: Oxford University Press.

Tjepkema, M. (2006). Adult obesity. *Health Reports, 17,* 9-26.

Truby, H., Baic, S., deLooy, A., Fox, K. R., Livingstone, M. B. E., Logan, C. M., Macdonald, I. A., Morgan, L. M., Taylor, M. A., & Millward, D. J. (2006). Randomized controlled trial of four commercial weight-loss programmes in the UK: Initial findings from the BBC "diet trials". *British Medical Journal, 332*: 1309.

Vallerand, R. J. (2007). Intrinsic and extrinsic motivation in sport and physical activity: A review and a look at the future. In G. Tennenbaum & R. C. Eklund (Eds.), *Handbook of Sport Psychology* (3rd Edition, p. 59-83). New York, NY: Wiley.

Wilson, P. M., Rodgers, W. R., Fraser, S. N., & Murray, T. C. (2004). The relationship between exercise regulations and motivational consequences. *Research Quarterly for Exercise & Sport, 75*, 81-91.

Wing, R., & Hill, J. (2001). Successful weight loss maintenance. *Annual Review of Nutrition, 21*, 323-341.

Endnotes

[1] Participants (*N* = 293 randomized at study outset; seventy-three percent female) in this study (British Broadcasting Corporation [BBC] Diet Trials; Truby et al., 2006) were enrolled as a function of their consent to be in the study whereby they received access to one of four commercial weight-loss programs. The programs were as follows: (a) Rosemary Clooney (Eat Yourself Slim & Fitness Plan; *n* = 59); (b) Slim-Fast (Plan; *n* = 58); (c) Dr. Atkin's (New Revolution Diet; *n* = 57); or (d) Weight Watchers (Pure Points Program; *n* = 58). A weight-list control condition (*n* = 61) was also included in the investigation for comparison purposes.

[2] Structure coefficients were calculated using the formula presented by Courville and Thompson (2001) as follows: r / R where r is he bivariate correlation between predictor and criterion variable and R is the multiple correlation from each regression model calibrated in this sample.

[3] Unique variance estimates were calculated for each predictor variables in the regression models using the formula advocated by Hair et al. (2006) where $r_{Y.Xn}$ is the square of the part-correlation between each predictor and criterion variable per regression model.

[4] Estimates of effect size were calculated using the following formula: $f^2 = R^2/1 - R^2$ where R^2 represents the squared multiple correlation per regression model analyzed in this sample of commercial weight-loss program users.

[5] This observation was based on the frequency of participants reporting 'often' as a response to the GLTEQ-SWEAT question.

In: Handbook on Psychology of Motivation
Editors: J. N. Franco and A. E. Svensgaard

ISBN: 978-1-62100-755-5
© 2012 Nova Science Publishers, Inc.

Chapter 5

MOTIVATION FOR CREATIVITY IN DESIGN: ITS NATURE, ASSESSMENT AND PROMOTION

S. Kreitler[1] and H. Casakin[2]

[1]Tel Aviv University, Department of Psychology, Israel
[2]Ariel University Center of Samaria, School of Architecture, Ariel, Israel

ABSTRACT

The chapter presents a new approach to motivation for creativity based on the cognitive orientation theory. The major theoretical constructs of this approach are motivational disposition, themes, four belief types, and behavioral program. The basic tool for assessment of motivation for creativity – the cognitive orientation questionnaire of creativity (COQ-CR) - is described as well as several studies carried out about the motivation of creativity of design students in architecture and engineering. The COQ-CR provides information not only about the level of motivation but also about the structural and thematic composition of motivation for creativity. It thus enables to characterize differences in motivation in different individuals and domains of creativity. Implications for design education include the need and possibility of embedding motivation for creativity training in the regular teaching and practice of design.

Keywords: Cognitive orientation, motivation, creativity, design

1. CREATIVITY IN DESIGN

Design is informally referred to as "the act of working out the form of something (as by making a sketch or outline a plan)", or producing "an arrangement scheme" (Cambridge Dictionaries Online, 2011). Design is also concerned with making drawings or plans for the construction of an object or a system, such as a building or a bridge. Design enables to guide and plan actions, and to anticipate how an intended outcome will look and perform, and get along. According to Ralph and Wand (2009) to design implies using a set of primitive components to create an object in a certain environment that should satisfy goal specifications and a set of requirements. While design embraces a number of areas such as industrial, graphic, and textile design, in this paper we focus on architectural and engineering design. Although both domains are concerned primarily with the creative manipulation of form, function, space, material, and light, it needs barely to be mentioned that at least architectural design places a particular emphasis on aesthetic aspects.

It is well known that creativity plays an important role in design practice and design education (Casakin and Kreitler, 2008a; Kreitler and Casakin, 2009a). In all design areas, acts of design are expected to lead not only to useful and functional products, but also to original and valuable ones (Christiaans, 2002). Due to its ill-defined nature of being complex, ambiguous, and unique (e.g. Goel, 1995; Simon, 1981), a design problem cannot be tackled by means of routine problem-solving procedures (Gero, 1996). Dealing with design problems involves often taking recourse to creative thinking abilities needed to produce unpredictable and novel solutions (Suwa, Gero and Purcell, 1999).

Most research on design problem solving has centered on aspects leading to the promotion of creativity, such as the development and application of models, methods and strategies for enhancing, supporting, or enabling the generation of creative design outcomes (e.g., Akin and Akin, 1998; Gero, 1996; Goldschmidt et al., 1996; Golschmidt and Smolkov, 2006; Lawson, 2005; Schmitt, 1993). However only few studies explored the personal motivations leading to the generation of creative acts (Casakin and Kreitler, 2008b). As a consequence, attention has focused mainly on the mechanics of creativity without dwelling on the driving force that directs such creative acts.

2. MOTIVATION FOR CREATIVITY

In the last two decades, research on creativity acknowledged the critical role played by motivation. It became increasingly evident that motivation may be one of the principal components affecting creativity (Collins and Amabile, 1999; Runco, 2004, 2005). Therefore, motivation came to be considered as a key concept for understanding the creative process (Amabile, 1996; Kaufman, 2002)

Studies carried out on motivation for creativity can be grouped into three major trends. They will be presented in this context because they have inspired also most of the work on creativity in design (see Approaches to motivation for creativity in design). The first one is concerned with intrinsic motivation, namely, motivation that is based on interest or enjoyment in the task itself. An intrinsically motivated person performs an activity mainly for its own sake, e.g., because it is pleasant or enjoyable (Amabile, 1983; Eisenberg and Thompson, 2003; Kaufman, 2002). The second one refers to extrinsic motivation, namely, motivation that is based on striving to get a goal or reward external to the activity itself; e.g., earning a lot of money, becoming famous, or wining a prize (Baer, 1997; Lepper et al., 1973).

The third group is concerned with unconscious motivation, which is based on the psychodynamic approach. Its major claim is that creative activity represents an attempt to solve a personal problem that is mostly unconscious, like for example fulfilling a dream, or satisfying a repressed need (Freud, 1957; Kreitler and Kreitler, 1972; Stokes, 1963).

These three basic approaches accommodate most of different theses concerning motivation for creativity that have been presented or discussed. The claim that creativity is basically reactive, namely, an attempt to respond to some external need (Finke, 1990) represents a variation on extrinsic motivation. The thesis that creativity is a result of a certain character structure or personality traits (Feist and Barron, 2003) can be considered as reflecting both the intrinsic motivation approach and the psychodynamic one. The interrelations between intrinsic and extrinsic components of motivation for creativity have intrigued several investigators (Rubenson and Runco, 1992; Runco, 2004). Thus, Csikszentmihalyi (1990) argued that a low extrinsic motivation coupled with high intrinsic motivation can be an ideal recipe for enhancing creative performance. Others, on the other hand, (Amabile, Hennessey, and Grossman, 1986; Amabile, Hill, Hennessey, and Tighe, 1994) supported the claim that in regard to creative tasks, intrinsic motivation has a stronger effect than extrinsic motivation.

2.1. Approaches to Motivation for Creativity in Design

In recent years it has become increasingly evident that learning and performance in the domain of design are affected not only by teaching procedures and task characteristics, and context but also by motivation and a host of factors shaping motivation, such as attitudes to success and failure (Kimbell et al, 1991; Naughton, 1986). Thus, Atkinson (1999) found that those pupils who were motivated achieved high mean scores for their drawing, writing and designing in comparison with those whose motivation was low. Vattam et al. (2010) studied the reasons which motivated students to use an interactive knowledge-based design environment – DANE – to help interdisciplinary teams develop biologically inspired designs. Krippendorf (2004), who investigated intrinsic and extrinsic motivation with regard to human-centered and object-centered design, reported a strong relation between intrinsic motivation and the design of human-centered artifacts. Verner and Maor (2001) examined the effect that integrating structure design problems into the calculus curriculum would have on students' achievements and motivation. They found that increasing motivation encourages students to use mathematical methods in their design activities. Gambatese et al. (2005) showed that motivation is a fundamental factor that impacts the consideration of designing for construction safety, and suggested key motivational aspects needed for the promotion and practical implementation of design-for-safety.

Some attempts have also been done to study motivation in relation to design creativity. In different design creativity models that included key elements, such as flexibility and knowledge (Chakrabarti, 2006), cognitive abilities, culture, history, experience, and resources (Lindemann, 2010), motivation was shown to be a common highly influential factor, shared by many of the basic key elements. Chakrabarti (2010) argued that motivation and knowledge have synergistic relationships in regard to creativity. While motivation helps in developing and updating creative design products and processing knowledge, knowledge contributes to developing and updating motivation. According to Chakrabarti (2010), these factors exert a major influence on ability and effort, but nevertheless not much has been done to investigate the nature of knowledge, motivation and their synergistic interactions in design creativity.

In another study, Kroper et al. (2010) explored how motivation for creativity is affected by the different phases of the design thinking process. They found a differential impact on the motivation of the design team members as a function of the specific design phase considered. Motivation was significantly higher when executing creative tasks assumed to be dominant in the phases of 'understanding', 'observing', and 'ideating', and lower when doing administrative tasks. Waks and Merdler (2003) found in students of engineering design and architecture that lack of collaboration of teachers can restrain students' motivation to perform creatively, mainly if they manifest high creativity while forming the idea for the project. Positive motivation factors were shown to play an important role in initializing projects based on creative ideas, helping the students attain higher levels of flexibility and originality.

Intrinsic motivation is often considered as a particularly critical factor for enhancing creativity in design problem solving (Perkins, 1884). However, Nagai and Taura (2010) noted the difficulty in studying intrinsic motivation in real time design processes, when designers are immersed in the intricate processes of shaping their idea. The problem of analyzing design thinking from an inner perspective is that when engaged in their own design tasks, designers enter into a mental state of "flow" (Csizentmihalyi, 1990) that is largely influenced by their intrinsic motivations. In order to handle this problem, Nagai et al. (2010) developed a methodology for the internal observation of design thinking through the creative self-formation process that enables to identify the novel motifs responsible for stimulating the designer's intrinsic motivation in the course of creative thinking.

The described studies show that despite increasing consensus about the importance of motivation for creativity in design, there has been relatively little progress in unraveling the major aspects and processes of motivation for creativity in general and in trying to explore insofar motivation for creativity in design is unique to this domain (Casakin and Kreitler, 2010). Information of this kind is crucial both for designers involved in the actual acts of designing and for teachers of design preparing the designers of the future. There may be several reasons why motivation for creativity in design has not been sufficiently studied. A major set of obstacles consists of various prevalent largely unfounded conceptions about creativity, such as that creativity appears mostly on high levels, affiliated to geniality, that it is implanted in the human being and cannot be changed or trained, or that creativity cannot be assessed. Also the study of motivation has been hindered by inadequate conceptions, such as that motivation is akin to decision making and is concerned with the rational weighing of pros and cons in regard to the considered act. Further factors that may have damped the investigation of motivation for creativity are the mistaken assumption that motivation is a conscious process that needs to be assessed in the course of the act of designing.

The approach to motivation for creativity in design that will be presented in this chapter circumvents the mentioned difficulties by being grounded in a better founded conceptual foundation and by being provided with better tools for assessing motivation for creativity.

3. THE COGNITIVE ORIENTATION APPROACH TO MOTIVATION FOR CREATIVITY

The present chapter presents a new approach to the issue of motivation for creativity which enables assessment of motivation for creativity in design and exploration of the issue to which extent the motivation for design resembles or differs from motivation for creativity in other domains. It would also contribute to integrating the training of motivation for creativity into the frameworks of education for design.

The motivational approach introduced in this chapter is based on the Cognitive Orientation (CO) theory (Kreitler and Kreitler, 1982; Kreitler, 2004) which is a cognitively-based wide-ranging theory of motivation with a solid conceptual structure, and an assessment method with a firm empirical basis (Kreitler and Kreitler, 1987a; 1987b; 1988a; 1988b; 1990a; 1990b; 1994). The CO theory is a cognitive-motivational approach aimed for the understanding, prediction, and changing of behaviors in a diversity of domains, such as cognitive, motor, and emotional (Kreitler and Kreitler, 1976; Kreitler and Kreitler, 1987a). The CO shares with other cognitive models of motivation the assumption that cognitive contents, viz. beliefs, meanings, or attitudes guide behavior, but in contrast to these models it does not assume that motivation needs to be shaped by beliefs which are rational, veridical, reasonable or that motivation is a decision making process that may be voluntarily controlled (Kreitler, 2004). Rather, it centers on the main construct of meaning, and indicates the manner in which behavior proceeds from meanings and clustered orientative beliefs. Moreover, the theory focuses on real, observable explicit behaviors or outputs differing from intentions, self-reported behaviors and commitments, or decisions to act.

A major tenet of the CO theory is that behavior in all domains – including design and creativity – is the function of motivation and performance. In other words, in order to understand or predict or change behavior it is necessary to consider the motivational disposition for that behavior, and the implementation of that disposition in the real world. The disposition provides the directionality of the behavior and responds, as it were, to the questions of 'what' or 'where to', while the enactment is the practical manifestation of the directionality and responds, as it were, to the questions of 'in which manner' or 'with which means'. Cognition plays a role both in regard to the motivational disposition and the performance, but in a different form and through the involvement of different processes.

3.1. Belief Types and Themes

The cognitive orientation (CO) theory defines motivational disposition for creativity as a function of the combined product of beliefs of four types, namely, about goals, norms, oneself and reality, referring to themes identified as relevant for creative acts. Beliefs about goals refer to actions or states either desired or undesired by the individual (e.g., 'I want to earn money through my work as a designer'). Beliefs about rules and norms, express ethical, esthetic, social and other rules and standards (e.g., 'An architect should respect the physical and cultural context'). Beliefs about self express information about oneself, such as one's habits, actions or feelings (e.g., 'I cannot stop designing before attaining perfection'). Finally, general beliefs refer to information concerning others and the environment (e.g., 'The city is a complex and intriguing place').

The beliefs refer to particular themes representing meanings of the behavior under consideration, which were identified by in-depth stepwise interviewing, and validated by prior empirical testing (Kreitler and Kreitler, 1982). The major characteristics of the motivational disposition are directionality – which defines the activity towards which the motivational disposition is directed, and strength – which can be measured by the number of belief types directed toward the activity under consideration. Thus, the more beliefs there are supporting or orienting towards the direction of a particular activity, the stronger is the motivational disposition for such activity.

3.2. The CO Questionnaire

The motivational disposition is assessed by means of a special standardized procedure generated in the framework of the CO theory (Kreitler and Kreitler, 1982). It consists in assessing the motivational disposition for the behavior by means of a CO questionnaire, which includes items related to the themes of the four belief types. The questionnaire assesses the extent to which the respondent agrees or rejects the relevant beliefs orienting toward the behavior under consideration. A 4-point scale is used to assess the degree to which each belief is endorsed by the respondent.

Essentially, a CO instrument is based on a prediction matrix, where the columns represent the four beliefs, and the rows represent the themes or groupings of themes. The four belief types stay fixed across different behaviors but the themes change in line with the particular behavior dealt with and represent the underlying meanings of that behavior. For example, themes that refer to creativity are focusing on internal experiences, or doing things one chooses even if they are not functional.

Thus, each CO questionnaire includes different beliefs or items. In practice, the questionnaire is organized into four sections concerned with one of the four types of beliefs, which are presented in arbitrary order. Each section includes beliefs representing the different themes. As noted, the themes represent the underlying meanings of the behavior, but do not refer to or mention that behavior in any direct way. Therefore, assessing the directionality and strength of the motivational disposition is not related by any means to the conscious considerations of the respondents.

The validity of CO measures of motivational tendencies was demonstrated in previous studies assessing CO motivations that embraced a large number of different behaviors and domains of application (Kreitler et al., 1994; Kreitler and Kreitler, 1987a, b, 1988a, 1994), including planning and problem solving (Kreitler and Kreitler, 1987a, 1987b, 1988b).

The scores produced by the CO questionnaire of the motivation for creativity (COQ-CR) consist of one score for each of the four belief types, and 79 scores for the themes which have undergone grouping into 11 clusters by means of cluster analysis and confirmatory factor analyses (Kreitler and Casakin, 2009a). The groupings refer to the following clusters: 1. Self development [investing, promoting and guarding oneself]; 2. Emphasis on the inner world [identifying, knowing, developing and expressing one's thinking, feeling and imagination]; 3. Inner-directedness [emphasis on one's desires, will and decision, self confidence in one's ability to succeed]; 4. Contribution to society [concern with contributing something meaningful to the community or society even if it does not involve personal advancement]; 5. Awareness of one's own uniqueness as an individual [emphasis on oneself as an individual unique in one's talents and way of perceiving, behaving and being, not necessarily due to nonconformity]; 6. Freedom in acting [need to act at least in specific domains in line with rules and regulations set by oneself rather than by others]; 7. Restricted openness to the environment [readiness and need to absorb from the environment knowledge and inspiration coupled with resistance to being overwhelmed and harmed by too much openness]; 8. Acting under conditions of uncertainty [readiness to act under conditions of uncertainty concerning the results, with no control over the circumstances, a tendency which may resemble risk-taking]; 9. Demanding from oneself [demanding from oneself effort, perseverance, giving up comfort coupled with readiness for total investment, despite difficulties and even failures]; 10. Self expression [concern with using one's talents and expressing oneself with authenticity and characteristically]; 11. Non-functionality [readiness to act even if functionality is not clearly evident from the start].

The COQ-CR as a measure of the motivation for creativity was developed and applied in different samples and tested in regard to a variety of creative tasks, for example, solving architectural problems (Kreitler and Casakin, 2009a), engineering problems (Giessen and Kreitler, 2009), or devising innovative uses for energy (Margaliot, 2005).

Some of the particular advantages of using the CO measure of the motivation for creativity are: (a) it was conceived and developed within the framework of a well-established and evidence-based theory of cognitive motivation; (b) the contents of the items have been identified by a theoretically-driven procedure, which increases the probability that the assessed themes are relevant to creativity; (c) it has been tested and validated empirically; (d) it provides a profile of themes that allows for flexibility in defining and studying creativity across different types of creativity, different contexts and samples, and different individuals; (e) it is independent of rational and conscious considerations of the participants; and (f) it has a great number of applications for creativity outcomes.

4. STUDIES OF THE CO MOTIVATION FOR DESIGN CREATIVITY

The present section describes several studies that were carried out about motivation for design creativity in the context of the CO theory.

One study focused on the structure of the motivational tendency for creativity in design (Kreitler and Casakin, 2009b). In a sample of design students, a factor analysis of the 11 groupings of the themes of the COQ-CR yielded two factors which account together for 63.72% of the variance. The first and main factor referred to the self—its uniqueness, development and expression, whereas the emphasis of the second factor was on maintaining openness to the environment but without compromising inner directedness. The 11 groupings of the themes of the COQ-CR and the factors based on them provide important insights into the dynamics of the motivation for creativity in design. They reveal the double complementary emphases on the self and the environment, the inner and outer directedness that make up the special combination of motivational determinants necessary for design creativity.

Another study on CO motivation for creativity in design students (Casakin and Kreitler, 2008b) had two goals: first, to investigate what are the themes identified in motivation for creativity that differentiate between more creative and less creative students; and second, to find out whether such differences are independent of whether the assessment of creativity is carried out by architects, teachers, or students. It was expected to find differences in the scores of the themes between more creative and less creative students, as assessed by the different evaluators. Creativity was defined in terms of overall assessment of design creativity by design students, four expert architects, as well as by the mean score obtained by each student in the design studio in the course of his/her academic studies from the design instructors. The student groups differing in creativity scores were compared in the scores of the themes and beliefs based on the COQ-CR. Comparisons were carried out between the high-creativity and low-creativity groups for each creativity variable as assessed by each group of referees. Significant differences in regard to several motivational themes were found between more creative and less creative students in the three analyses based on the assessments by architects, students, and teachers. Findings relating to the assessment by architects yielded significant differences between students high and low in creativity in the following themes: (i) feeling it is incumbent upon them to activate and use their talents and unique abilities, (ii) interest and no discomfort in regard to views which differ or contradict their own, and (iii) daydreaming a lot. In the second analysis, based on the assessments of creativity by the students themselves, there were significant differences between students high and low in creativity in the following themes: (i) demanding a lot from themselves, (ii) not in need of firm framework or strict regulations, (iii) tendency to do original things, and (iv) tendency to delve deeply into what one deals with and examine it from all points of view. The third analysis, based on comparing students differing in the assessment by design studio teachers indicated that students high and low in creativity differed significantly in the following themes: (i) thinking about things in one's own way, and not necessarily as one has been taught, (ii) thinking and doing one's own thing even with no support from others, (iii) concern with the functionality of what one does, and (iv) ability and tendency to invest a lot of effort.

As expected, differences in scores of motivational themes were observed between more creative and less creative students. The more creative students scored higher in beliefs of the four types and the themes reflecting their motivations to achieve creative designs, as compared to the less creative ones. This finding recurred irrespective of who was the evaluator of creativity, i.e., an architect, a design studio teacher, or a student, and independently of the design environment where the assessment was carried out, i.e., inside or outside the design studio.

Comparing the results of the three independent comparisons shows common tendencies shared by the high creativity students. These are the need to have freedom to apply individual criteria, the tendency to delve into the unknown, the readiness to make efforts and invest in the design task, and willingness to use talent to achieve originality. These motivational themes may be considered as intrinsic to the essence of design problem solving. Thus, the results supported the validity of the COQ-CR for assessing motivation for creativity, and of the cognitive motivational approach to creativity.

In a further study, Kreitler and Casakin (2009b) investigated motivational disposition for creativity in design students, based on self-reported evaluations and on evaluations by architects. The self-reported evaluations focused on the design outcomes as well as on the different aspects of the design process. The idea was to include a variety of key aspects concerned with the assessment of creativity in general (Andersson and Sahlin, 1997; Gruber and Wallace, 2000), and design creativity in particular. It was expected that the four belief types would predict the scores of the respondents on the different measures of creativity considered in the study and that the themes would provide further insights into the specific personal dynamics of the motivation for creativity. Further, it was expected that the creativity manifested in the design outcome would be predicted by COQ-CR better than the variables referring to the design processes, such as preparing sketches or using additional materials. The rationale for this was the assumption that processes involved in producing creative outputs depend to a greater extent than the output itself on determinants that are not purely motivational, such as cognitive abilities. The motivational variables considered in this study were the scores of the four belief types and the 11 belief groupings based on the COQ-CR (See Section 3.2). The compared groups were defined in terms of the evaluation of the creativity of the designs by four expert architects (one variable, averaged across the four evaluators that were highly similar), and the following two sets of variables based on self-evaluation of the students: the first set included 8 variables characterizing the design output that had been validated in previous studies for evaluating architectural designs (Casakin and Kreitler, 2005a, 2005b): fluency, flexibility, elaboration, usefulness and functionality, innovation, fulfilling requirements, considering the context, mastery of skills concerning the aesthetics of the design. Factor analysis of the latter variables yielded the following three factors, labelled as fulfilling requirements of the task design; functionality; and innovation. The second set included 7 variables characterizing the designing process: having a central idea, difficulties in designing, use of additional materials, value, meaningfulness of the task, involvement of feelings in designing, and handling constraints.

Regression analyses were used for testing the major hypothesis of the study concerning the relation of the four belief types and each of the variables characterizing creativity (n=19). The findings supported the validity of the COQ-CR for assessing motivation for design creativity, and of the cognitive motivational approach to creativity. The major results were that the four CO belief types (about self, goals, norms and general) predicted the majority of the variables assessing different aspects of design creativity. Accordingly, the four belief types provided a significant prediction in regard to the creativity evaluations by the architects and the majority (5 out of 8) of the variables of the variables assessing the creativity of the design outcome: fluency, flexibility, elaboration, fulfilling requirements, and considering the context, as well as two of the three factors based on this set of variables: Factor 1 labelled "fulfilling requirements of the task design" and Factor 3 labelled "innovative elaboration". Furthermore, the four belief types predicted significantly also four out of seven variables that dealt with the design process: coping with constraints, having a central idea, meaningfulness of the task and involvement of feelings in addition to reason in the design process.

The creativity variables predicted by the CO of motivation for creativity included both the more objective assessment of creativity by experts and those carried out by the students themselves. As expected, the four belief types predicted more of the variables relating to the design outcome, than of the variables referring to the design processes. Of the four belief types involved in the predictions of creativity variables, beliefs about norms and beliefs about goals were the two belief types with the largest contributions (i.e., they had a significant contribution in 10 of the 12 variables with significant results). In contrast, general beliefs had a significant contribution in regard to 7 variables, and beliefs about self in regard to 2 variables only. This means that the motivation for creativity in design was affected mainly by beliefs about how things should be, that is, beliefs about the values and conceptions the designer is supposed to consider, supported by the designer's personal goals. From the perspective of contents, the CO measure indicates that motivation for creativity is a complex and variegated construct that enables multiple combinations of themes reflecting motivation for creativity in different individuals.

Correlation analysis between the 11 groupings of themes in the COQ-CR and the creativity variables (based on the responses of the students) were carried out in order to gain a deeper understanding into the relations between the cognitive motivational variables and the assessments of creativity. It was found that each of the 11 groupings was related significantly to one or more of the creativity variables. Elaboration was related to a broad set of groupings including self development, inner world, inner directedness, awareness of one's own uniqueness, demanding from oneself and self expression, in sum, most of the groupings loaded on the first CO factor labeled "the self—its uniqueness, development, and expression". Additional findings showed that fulfilling requirements was also related to several groupings, notably emphasis on the inner world, inner directedness, freedom in acting, and acting under conditions of uncertainty. Also Factor 3 "elaborative innovation" was found to be related to four groupings (i.e., self development, freedom in acting, demanding from oneself, and self expression). These findings show that the largest number of significant correlations of creativity characteristics was with groupings of themes emphasizing one's inner world followed by self development and demanding from oneself. The results highlight clearly the important role played by the self in the motivation for design creativity.

A recent focused on comparing motivation for creativity in architectural design and engineering design students (Casakin and Kreitler, 2010). The research hypothesis was that there would be differences in motivation for design creativity between architectural and engineering students. Further, it was expected that these differences would be manifested in the structure of the motivation— consisting in the belief types and themes of the motivation—rather than in the overall creativity.

The 11 groupings based on the themes of the COQ-CR were factor analyzed in order to compare the findings in the present sample of students of architecture and engineering with the results in samples of design students in previous studies (e.g., Giessen and Kreitler, 2009). The comparison was designed to assess the stability of the conceptual structure of the CO questionnaire across samples, and to look for similarities and differences between the groups of participants. Similar factors were observed in the two groups of students, confirming the validity of the structure of the COQ-CR. In both groups the first factor was mainly related to the self—its uniqueness, development and expression (accounting for 48.4% of the variance in the group of architectural students, and for 39.11% of the variance in the group of engineering students), whereas the second factor was concerned with the openness to the environment without jeopardizing inner directness (accounting for 15.4% of the variance in the group of architectural students, and for 11,69 % of the variance in the group of engineering students). Altogether, the two factors accounted for 50.80% of the variance of the engineering students, in contrast to the two factors of the architectural design students which accounted for 63.7%. Notably, the two factors in the two groups of students were quite similar to those obtained in earlier research with students of engineering (Giessen and Kreitler 2009). The findings confirmed the hypothesis that the structure of the motivation for creativity would not be radically different in the two groups of students. The replication of the findings concerning factorial structure in a sample of engineering students provides evidence for the stability of the factors across samples of students in affiliated domains. Further studies are needed to test the generality of the findings in other samples and other kinds of creativity.

In addition, also the mean scores of the motivational variables of the COQ-CR (i.e., the four belief types, the 79 themes, and the 11 groupings) were compared in the groups of architectural and engineering design students. The results indicated that architects scored significantly higher than engineers in beliefs about goals and beliefs about self, but did not differ in general beliefs, and in beliefs about norms. Further, significant differences were observed between students of architecture and of engineering in the scores of the 11 groupings of themes. Architectural students scored higher than engineering students in the following seven groupings: self development [investing in oneself, promoting oneself, guarding oneself]; emphasis on the inner world [identifying, knowing, developing and expressing thinking, feeling and imagination]; inner-directedness [emphasis on one's desires, will and decision, self confidence in one's ability to succeed]; underscoring one's uniqueness [emphasis on oneself as an individual unique in one's talents and one's way of perceiving, behaving and being, not necessarily accompanied by nonconformity]; functioning under conditions of uncertainty [readiness to act under conditions of uncertainty concerning the results, with no control over the circumstances, which may resemble risk-taking]; self expression [concern with using one's talents and expressing oneself and one's feelings with authenticity]; non-functionality [readiness to act even if functionality is not clearly evident from the start]. On the other hand, engineering students scored higher than the architectural students in the following three groupings: freedom in functioning [need to act in line with rules and regulations set by oneself rather than by others]; being receptive to the environment, absorbing from the environment; and demanding from oneself [demands from oneself effort, perseverance, giving up comfort coupled with and readiness for total investment, despite difficulties and even failures].

The findings from Casakin and Kreitler (2010) suggest that despite differences between the architectural and engineering students, a similar pattern of motivation for creativity centered on the axis defined by the poles of self versus environment was common to both disciplines.

On the whole, motivation for creativity consisted of fewer elements in the engineering group than in the architectural one, which indicates that motivation for creativity in the engineering group is narrower or possibly more focused. Further, while in the engineering students, motivation for creativity was characterized by being pro-functionality (i.e., in favor of functional concerns as an important goal in the design activity), in the architectural group motivation for creativity was characterized by a non-functional approach (i.e., not caring about functional concerns as a major goal for the design activity).

Additionally, the fact that architectural students scored higher than engineering students in goal beliefs and beliefs about self suggests that the motivation for creativity in the architectural group was chiefly based on beliefs focused on the self, in contrast to beliefs that concern mainly the external world (i.e., norms and general beliefs).

The differences between the groups in the thematic groupings of the COQ-CR indicate that the profile of creativity motivation in the group of architectural students is focused mainly on one's inner world, inner-directedness, development of the self, promotion of self expression and awareness of one's talent and uniqueness, the main motivational components in the engineering group were being receptive to the environment, absorbing from the environment, in addition to demanding from oneself, despite potential difficulties.

In sum, the different studies of motivation for creativity in design students in different domains demonstrated the usefulness of the conceptualization of motivation for creativity provided by the CO theory and supported the validity of the CO approach to the assessment of motivation for creativity.

5. FUNCTIONS OF ASSESSMENT OF MOTIVATION FOR CREATIVITY IN DESIGN

Assessing motivation for creativity has several theoretical as well as practical advantages. On the theoretical level, the assessment of motivation for creativity by means of the COQ-CR opens new vistas for the conceptualization and applications of motivation for creativity in design. First, it provides a framework for integrating information about different determinants of motivation for creativity that have been identified. Cultural values and conceptions form one set of determinants that is likely to affect motivation for creativity. For example, the cultural tendencies of individualism and collectivism were shown to affect creativity whereby the individualistic values promote creativity more than the collectivistic ones (e.g., Zha et al., 2006). In order to explain how cultural values affect motivation it has been suggested that culture operates by means of rewards, punishments or taboos (Adams, 2001) concerning creativity. The CO approach offers a more ready explanation by indicating that cultural values shape the thematic contents of the motivation for creativity endorsed by the individual. Thus, the values of individualism are reflected for example in the themes focused on the self, in particular the theme of "Awareness of one's uniqueness as an individual". The acquisition of themes by the individual proceeds in culturally sanctioned frameworks of learning (e.g., schools, the media) and through the families.

Another set of determinants of the motivation for creativity are personality tendencies and traits. A great number of personality traits have been identified as related to creativity, for example, self-control (Dacey, Lennon and Fiore,1998), playfulness (Berg, 1995) and tolerance of ambiguity (Tegano, 1990). It is likely that the trait of self-control is affiliated with the theme "Demanding from oneself", that playfulness is affiliated with the theme "Non-functionality" and that tolerance of ambiguity is affiliated with the theme "Acting under conditions of uncertainty". There is at present no basis for claiming that personality traits affect the themes of motivation or the other way round. Be it as it may, the correspondence between the traits and the themes suggests that they interact with the result that they enhance each other in creative individuals.

A further theoretically important implication of COQ-CR is that it provides insight into the components that make up motivation for creativity. The major components are the four belief types and the thematic contents. Hence, COQ-CR enables comparing the components of motivation for creativity in different settings, i.e., cultures, societies, families, individuals and domains of creativity. Information of this kind may reveal that motivation for creativity in the setting of one culture may differ in its components from that motivation in another culture. For example, in a culture that is characterized by individualism the motivation for creativity may be based on themes such as "awareness of one's uniqueness as an individual", while in a collectivistic culture it may be based on other themes, e.g., "contribution to society". Again, also the salience of the four belief types may vary in the motivation for creativity in different cultures. For example, beliefs about norms may play a more prominent role in the motivation for creativity in a normative and authoritarian culture than in a more democratic culture which fosters to a greater extent personal goals and beliefs about oneself. These examples indicate that there may be motivation for creativity in highly different cultures. Moreover, it is evident that two similar levels of motivation for creativity may consist of motivations that are differentially composed.

Similar reasoning and conclusions apply in regard to individuals. Different individuals may have the same or similar levels of motivation for creativity but the composition of that motivation may differ. For example, in one case the motivation for creativity may be based primarily on the self-promoting themes whereas in another case it may be based primarily on the externally-oriented themes of openness to the environment and contribution to society. Similarly, motivation for creativity in the case of some individuals may depend more on general beliefs or beliefs about norms while in the case of others it may depend more on beliefs about self.

Again, similar assumptions and conclusions may apply in regard to different domains of creativity. Motivation for creativity in regard to different domains may be expected to differ. It is likely that motivation for creativity in the technological domains may include a strong thematic component of contribution to society and of general beliefs about reality but only a weak thematic component of non-functionality. Similarly, motivation for creativity in the arts is likely to include strong thematic components of inner-directedness and self expression, as well as beliefs about oneself but a relatively weak component of contribution to society. Notably, all the mentioned differences in the thematic composition of the motivation for creativity need not be attended by differences in the level of motivation per se. Moreover, the different thematic composition of motivation for creativity in regard to different domains is functional and adequate for promoting creativity in the different domains.

There are also practical implications to a precise assessment of motivation for creativity that provides not only an overall estimate of the level or degree but also information about thematic composition and the relative salience of the four belief types. Information about the thematic and structural composition of the motivation for creativity may facilitate arousing in individuals or particular settings the motivation for creativity by applying the adequate cues for the different themes or beliefs. Failing to use the adequate cues may result in failing to arouse motivation for creativity in individuals or settings when it actually exists. Furthermore, the precise assessment of the thematic and structural composition of the motivation provides clues as to the training of motivation in individuals who have only a weak motivation for creativity (See 7. Promoting motivation for creativity in design students).

6. MOTIVATION FOR CREATIVITY IN THE CONTEXT OF THE STUDY OF CREATIVITY

An important theoretical advantage of studying the motivation for creativity in the framework of the CO theory is that it enables placing motivation for creativity within the broader context of the study of creativity. From the perspective of the CO theory, motivation is an important factor but it is not the only determinant of action, in regard to creativity or any other act, for that matter. The basic tenet of the CO theory is that any act is a function of a motivational disposition and a behavioral program that controls the implementation of the motivational disposition in reality. In regard to creativity, the behavioral program consists of a variety of learned action schemes that differ in line with the domain in which creativity is manifested. In the domain of design these action schemes would include diverse skills of designing and planning that would involve also cognitive processes and would be based on learning and practice.

In addition, however, creativity would require a trigger, that is, an input that evokes the need or possibility for creativity, such as a problem, a situation that requires creative problem-solving, a teacher that evokes interest, or some other stimulus with a similar effect. There is however in the very least still a fourth element that needs to be considered in this context: the circumstances and setup in which the act of creativity will be enacted. The circumstances are important insofar as they provide the space and time required for performing something in a creative manner.

Thus, if an act of creativity takes place, it is possible to conclude that the four major elements cited above were present, at least to some extent. However, if creativity fails to show up, it is not always possible to conclude which element or elements were missing. The cause of the failure may be weak motivation for creativity but it could also be inadequate circumstances of operation or simply the absence of a problem interesting or challenging enough for the evocation of creativity.

7. PROMOTING MOTIVATION FOR CREATIVITY IN DESIGN STUDENTS

The findings from the studies based on the CO theory about motivation for creativity in design suggest important implications for improving design education. It seems that design teachers are aware of the importance of creativity in design and would like to promote it. However, they may not be aware of the importance of motivation for creativity or of the fact that it is impossible to promote creativity without promoting the motivation for creativity if it is not strong enough. Teaching the skills of designing, even on a high level of expertise, may help in promoting the production of creative designs if the students or practitioners already have a strong motivation for creativity, which may often be the case. Otherwise, the teaching of skills per se may not result in the desired production of creative outputs.

As has been clarified by the CO theory and the studies of motivation for creativity based on it, the motivation for creativity is not manifested necessarily in the conscious declaration of the kind "I would like to be creative in design". Actually, it has nothing to do with the conscious awareness of motivation for creativity. Individuals who are completely unaware of the motivation for creativity and may even not be personally interested in creativity may turn out to be highly motivated for creativity. As was shown, the motivation for creativity in design or other domains is a function of specific themes structured in terms of four belief types.

Motivation for creativity may be trained. The application of the findings of the different studies carried out in the framework of the CO theory can be a first step for developing intervention programs of design education for the promotion of creativity in the architectural and engineering disciplines. Intervention programs can be put into practice in design studio sessions by reinforcing or systematically increasing the number of beliefs supporting a desired behavioral manifestation. The increase can be carried out by promoting the meanings the students assign to the different themes that constitute the motivation for creativity. The procedure of increasing the number of adequate beliefs orienting toward creativity needs to be performed in considering the four belief types for a any theme that is being promoted (for a detailed description of the method see Kreitler and Kreitler, 1990b).

The enhancement of themes and beliefs can be performed on the individual level, considering the particular strengths and weaknesses of the individual in regard to the motivation for creativity. But it can also be implemented on the group level, referring to all themes and all belief types without taking into account the individual characteristics. In this manner, the training of motivation for creativity could be embedded within the regular curriculum of studies in design education frameworks.

REFERENCES

Adams, J. L. (2001). *Conceptual blockbusting*. New York: Perseus Publishing.

Akin, O. and Akin, C. (1998). On the process of creativity in puzzles, inventions, and designs. *Automation in Construction*, 7(2-3), 123-138.

Andersson, A. E., and Sahlin, N. E. (1997). *The complexity of creativity*. New York: Kluwer Academic Publishers (Synthese Library,Vol. 258).

Amabile, T. M. (1983). The social psychology of creativity. New York: Springer-Verlag.

Amabile, T. M. (1996). *Creativity in context*. Boulder, CO: Westview Press, Inc.

Amabile, T. M., Hennessey, B. A., and Grossman, B. S. (1986). Social influences on creativity: The effects of contracted-for reward. *Journal of Personality and Social Psychology, 50,* 14–23.

Amabile, T. M., Hill, K. G., Hennessey, B. A., and Tighe, E. M (1994). The Work Preference Inventory: Assessing intrinsic and extrinsic motivational orientations. *Journal of Personality and Social Psychology, 66,* 950–967.

Atkinson, E. S. (1999). Key factors influencing pupil motivation in design and technology . *Journal of Technology Education, 10,* 2,4-26.

Baer, J. (1997). Gender differences in the effects of anticipated evaluation on creativity. *Creativity Research Journal, 10,* 1, 25-31.

Berg, D. H. (1995). The power of playful spirit at work. *Journal of Quality and Participation, 18,* 32-39.

Casakin, H. and Kreitler, S. (2005a). The determinants of creativity: flexibility in design. *3rd Engineering and Product Design Education International Conference*. Napier University, Edinburgh, Scotland.

Casakin, H. and Kreitler, S. (2005b). The nature of creativity in design: factors for assessing individual creativity. *Studying Designers International Conference*. Provence University, Aix-en-Provence, France.

Casakin, H. and Kreitler, S. (2008a). Correspondences and divergences in creativity. evaluations between architects and students. *Environment and Planning B: Planning and Design, 35,* 666-678.

Casakin, H. and Kreitler, S. (2008b). Identifying motivation for creativity in design education. *EandPDE08 10th International Conference on Engineering and Product Design Education: New Perspectives in Design Education*, Escola Tècnica Superior d'Enginyeria Industrial de Barcelona (ETSEIB), Universitat Politècnica de Catalunya (UPC), Barcelona, Spain, pp. 49-54.

Casakin, H. and Kreitler, S. (2010). Motivation for creativity in architectural design: differences between architects and engineers. *International Journal of Technology and Design Education, 20,* 477-493.

Chakrabarti, A. (2006). Defining and supporting design creativity. *International Design Conference – DESIGN 2006*. Dubrovnik, Croatia, pp. 479-486.

Chakrabarti, A. (2010). Motivation as a major direction for design creativity research. *The First International Conference on Design Creativity ICDC2010*. Taura T. and Nagai Y. (eds.), Kobe, pp. 49-56.

Christiaans, H. (2002). Creativity as a design criterion. *Creativity Research Journal, 14*, 41–54.

Collins, M. A., and Amabile, T. M. (1999). Motivation and creativity. In R. J. Sternberg (Ed.), *Handbook of creativity*. New York: Cambridge University Press, pp. 297–312..

Csikszentmihalyi, M. (1990). *Flow: The psychology of optimal experience*. New York: Harper and Row.

Dacey, J. C., Lennon, K., and Fiore, L. (1998). *Understanding creativity: the interplay of biological, psychological and social factors*. San Francisco: Jossey-Bass.

Eisenberg, J., and Thompson, W. F. (2003). A matter of taste: evaluating improvised music. *Creativity Research Journal*, 2003, *15*, 2-3, 287-296.

Finke, R. (1990). Creative imagery: Discoveries and inventions in visualization. Hillsdale, New Jersey: Erlbaum.

Feist, G. J., and Barron, F. X. (2003). Predicting creativity from early to late adulthood: intellect, potential and personality. *Journal of Research in Personality, 37*, 62-88.

Freud, S. (1957). The unconscious. In J. Strachey (Ed. and Trans.).*The standard edition of the complete psychological works of Sigmund Freud*. London: Hogarth (original work published 1915), Vol. 14, pp. 166-204.

Gambatese, J.A., Behm, M., and Hinze, J. W. (2005). Viability of designing for construction worker safety. *Journal of Construction Engineering and Management, 131*, 9, 1029-1036.

Gero, J. S. (1996). Creativity, emergence and evolution in design. *Knowledge based systems, 9*, 7, 435-448.

Giessen, E., and Kreitler, S. (2009). Creativity and inventiveness in engineering students. *Creativity Research Journal* (Submitted).

Goel, V. (1995). *Sketches of thought*. Cambridge, MA: MIT Press.

Goldschmidt, G. Ben-Zeev, A., and Levi, S. (1996). Design problem solving: the effect of problem formulation on the solution space. In R. Trappl (Ed.), *Cybernetics and systems '96*, (pp. 388-393). Vienna: University of Vienna Press.

Golschmidt, G., and Smolkov, M. (2006). Variances in the impact of visual stimuli on design problem solving performance. *Design Studies, 27*, 5, 549-569.

Gruber, H. E., and Wallace, D. B. (2000). The case study method and evolving systems approach for understanding unique creative people at work. In R. J. Sternberg (Ed.), *Handbook of creativity*. Cambridge, UK: Cambridge University Press, pp. 93-115. .

Kaufman, J. (2002). Dissecting the golden goose: components of studying creative writers. *Creativity Research Journal, 14*, 1, 27-40.

Kimbell, R., Stables, K., Wheeler, T., Wosniak, A., and Kelly, V. (1991). *The assessment of performance in design and technology - The Final Report of the APU Design and Technology Project 1985-91,* London: School Examinations and Assessment Council/Evaluation and Monitoring Unit.

Kreitler, S. (2004). The cognitive guidance of behavior. In J.T.Jost, M. R. Banaji, and D. A. Prentice (Eds.), *Perspectivism in Social Psychology: The Yin and Yang of scientific progress*. Washington, DC: American Psychological Association, pp. 113-126.

Kreitler, S. and Casakin, H. (2009a). Self-perceived creativity: the perspective of design. *European Journal of Psychological Assessment, 25*, 3, pp. 194-203.

Kreitler, S. and Casakin, H. (2009b). Motivation for creativity in design students. *Creativity Research Journal,* 21, 2, 282 – 293.

Kreitler, S., Chaitchik, S., Kreitler, H., and Weissler, K. (1994). Who will attend tests for the early detection of breast cancer. *Psychology and Health*, 9, 463–483.

Kreitler, H., and Kreitler, S. (1972). *Psychology of the arts*. Durham, NC: Duke University Press.

Kreitler, H. and Kreitler, S. (1976). *Cognitive Orientation and Behavior*. New York: Springer Publishing.

Kreitler, H., and Kreitler, S. (1982). The theory of cognitive orientation: Widening the scope of behavior prediction. *Progress in Experimental Personality Research*, *11*, 101–169.

Kreitler, S., and Kreitler, H. (1987a). Plans and planning: Their motivational and cognitive antecedents. In S. L. Friedman, E. K. Scholnick, and R. R. Cocking (Eds.). *Blueprints for thinking: The role of planning in cognitive development*. New York: Cambridge University Press, pp. 110–178.

Kreitler, S., and Kreitler, H. (1987b). The motivational and cognitive determinants of individual planning. *Genetic, Social and General Psychology Monographs*, 113, 81–107.

Kreitler, S., and Kreitler, H. (1988a). The cognitive approach to motivation in retarded individuals. In N. W. Bray (Ed.), *International Review of Research in Mental Retardation*, 15, 61–123. San Diego, CA: Academic Press.

Kreitler, S., and Kreitler, H. (1988b). Horizontal decalage: a problem and its resolution. *Cognitive Development*, 4, 89–119.

Kreitler, S., and Kreitler, H. (1990a). Psychosemantic foundations of creativity. In K. J. Gilhooly, M. Keane, R. Logie, and G. Erdos (Eds.), Lines of thought: Reflections on the psychology of thinking . Chichester, UK: Wiley, Vol. 2, pp. 191–201.

Kreitler, S., and Kreitler, H. (1990b). *The cognitive foundations of personality traits*. New York: Plenum.

Kreitler, S., and Kreitler, H. (1994). Motivational and cognitive determinants of exploration. In H. Keller, K. Schneider, and B. Henderson, (Eds.), Curiosity and exploration. New York: Springer-Verlag, pp. 259–284.

Krippendorf, K. (2004). Intrinsic motivation and human-centred design. *Theory Issues in Ergonomic Science*, 5, 1, 43-72.

Kröper, M., Fay, D., Lindberg, T. and Meinel, C. (2010). Interrelations between Motivation, Creativity and Emotions in Design Thinking Processes – An Empirical Study Based on Regulatory Focus Theory. *First International Conference on Design Creativity ICDC2010*, Kobe, pp. 97-104.

Lawson, B. (2005). Oracles, draughtsman, and agents: The nature of knowledge and creativity in design and the role of IT. *Automation in Construction*, *14*, 3, 383-391.

Lepper, M., Greene, D., and Nisbett, R. (1973). Understanding children's intrinsic interest with extrinsic rewards: A test of the "overjustification" hypothesis. *Journal of Personality and Social Psychology*, 28, 129–137.

Lindemann, U. (2010). Systematic Procedures Supporting Creativity – A Contradiction? *First International Conference on Design Creativity ICDC2010*. Taura T. and Nagai Y. (eds.), Kobe, pp. 23-28.

Margaliot, A. (2005). *A model for teaching the cognitive skill of melioration to pre-service science teachers in a college for teachers.* Unpublished doctoral dissertation, Bar-Ilan University, Ramat Gan, Israel.

Nagai, Y., Taura, T., and Sano, K. (2010). Research methodology for the internal observation of design thinking through the creative self-formation process. *First International Conference on Design Creativity ICDC2010.* Taura T. and Nagai Y. (eds.), Kobe, pp. 215-222.

Nagai, Y. and Taura, T. (2010). Discussion on direction of design creativity research (Part 2) – Research Issues and Methodologies: From the Viewpoint of Deep Feelings and Desirable Figure. *First International Conference on Design Creativity ICDC2010.* Taura T. and Nagai Y. (eds.), Kobe, pp. 9-14.

Naughton, J. (1986). What is 'technology' anyway? In A.Cross and B. McCormick (Eds.), *Technology in Schools,* Milton Keynes: Open University Press, 2-10.

Perkins, D. N. (1984). Creativity by design. *Educational Leadership, 42,* 1, 18-25.

Ralph, P. and Wand, Y. (2009). A proposal for a formal definition of the design concept. In Lyytinen, K., Loucopoulos, P., Mylopoulos, J., and Robinson, W., (Eds.), *Design Requirements Workshop (LNBIP 14).* New York: Springer-Verlag, pp. 103-136.

Runco, M. A. (2004). Creativity as an extracognitive phenomenon. In L. V. Shavinina and M. Ferrari (Eds.), *Beyond knowledge: extracognitive aspects of developing high ability.* Mahwah, NJ: Lawrence Erlbaum Associates Publishers, pp. 17–25.

Runco, M. A. (2005). Motivation, competence, and creativity. In A. J. Elliot and C. S. Dweck (Eds.), *Handbook of competence and motivation New York: Guilford,* pp. 609–623.

Rubenson, D.L., and Runco, M.A. (1992). The psychoeconomic approach to creativity. *New Ideas in Psychology, 10,* 131–147.

Schmitt, G.. (1993). Case-based design and creativity. *Automation in Construction, 2,* 1, 11-19.

Simon, H. (1981). *The sciences of the artificial.* Cambridge, MA: MIT Press.

Stokes, A. (1963). Painting and the inner world. London: Tavistock.

Suwa, M., Gero, J., and Purcell, T. (1999). Unexpected discoveries and s-invention of design requirements: Important vehicles for a design process. *Design Studies, 21,* 6, 539-567.

Tegano, D. (1990). Relationship of tolerance of ambiguity and playfulness to creativity. *Psychological Reports, 66,* 1047 - 1056.

Vattam, S., Wiltgen, B., Helms, M., Goel, A. K., and Yen, J. (2010). DANE: fostering creativity in and through biologically inspired design. *First International Conference on Design Creativity ICDC2010.* Taura T. and Nagai Y. (Eds.). Kobe, pp. 115-122.

Verner, I. M, and Maor, S. (2001). Integrating design problems in mathematics curriculum: an architecture college case study. *International Journal of Mathematics Education Science Technology,* 32, 6, 817-828.

Waks, S. and Merdler, M. 2003. Creative thinking of practical engineering students during a design project. *Research in Science and Technological Education,* 21, 1, 101-121.

Zha, P., Walczyk, J. J., Griffith-Ross, D. A., Tobacyk, J. J., and Walczyk, D. F. (2006). The impact of culture and individualism–collectivism on the creative potential and achievement of American and Chinese adults. *Creativity Research Journal, 18,* 3, 355-366.

In: Handbook on Psychology of Motivation
Editors: J. N. Franco and A. E. Svensgaard

ISBN: 978-1-62100-755-5
© 2012 Nova Science Publishers, Inc.

Chapter 6

INFLUENCES OF MOTIVATIONAL FACTORS ON EDUCATIONAL OUTCOMES: CULTURE AND GENDER ISSUES

Alexander Seeshing Yeung[*] *and Gurvinder Kaur*
University of Western Sydney, Australia

ABSTRACT

Motivation research has shown significant relations of self-concept and value of schooling to educational outcomes, but has not simultaneously scrutinized the relative influences of different constructs on various educational outcomes. In the present investigation, a sample of Australian students from 6 primary schools in Western Sydney ($N = 730$) completed a multidimensional self-concept scale that measured components of self-concept (competence and affect) for each scale and a motivational construct (value of schooling). They were also asked to rate their sense of identity. Their achievement scores were obtained by conducting both a reading and a numeracy test. Structural equation modeling (SEM) was applied to relate the motivational constructs (competence, affect, and value) to the outcomes (achievement and identity). Multivariate analysis of variance was also conducted to test cultural and gender differences in the motivational constructs. Results showed that students' sense of competence was the strongest predictor of achievement whereas value of schooling, was a strong predictor of both achievement and sense of identity. Australian students with an Asian ethnicity tended to be higher in their self-concepts (both competence and affect) compared to their Anglo peers. Girls were also slightly higher than boys in affect to learning. There were small ethnicity x gender interaction effects showing that the difference between the Asian and Anglo Australian students in self-concept (both competence and affect) was predominant for boys. Given that a sense of competence was found to be a strong predictor of achievement, it seems that educators should pay more attention to enhancing Anglo students' development of their sense of competence so as to maximize their potential. In addition, as value of schooling was also a strong predictor of both outcomes (achievement and identity), it is important to maintain the students' high level of value of school so that they can enjoy both short-term and long-term benefits of education.

---

[*] Phone: +61 (2) 9772 6264, Fax: +61 (2) 9772 6432, email: a.yeung@uws.edu.au

Keywords: Motivation; self-concept; primary; structural equation modeling

INTRODUCTION

The present study examined the unique contribution of each of three motivational constructs (perceived value of schooling, sense of competence, and affect to learning) in predicting educational outcomes. The outcomes considered in this investigation included student identity (i.e., a long-term educational outcome for an individual's lifelong wellbeing) and achievement (which is often the major concern for educators and researchers). The sample was primary school students from six schools in Western Sydney, Australia. With an increasing influx of new migrants of Asian origins, the study also examined potential cultural differences between Asian-Australians and Anglo-Australians to elucidate similarities and differences between cultures. Furthermore, the issue of potential culture x gender interaction effects on student motivation is particularly interesting as it has not been fully elucidated in the literature.

Academic Motivation Constructs

Students' academic behavior and achievement are known to be closely associated with their academic motivation (e.g., McInerney & Ali, 2006; Smith, Duda, Allen, & Hall, 2002). Of the various motivational constructs examined in recent research, self-beliefs and perceived value of schooling have been found to have significant impacts on a variety of outcomes. For example, research has demonstrated that students' self-beliefs tend to have significant influence on essential academic outcomes (e.g., McInerney, Yeung, & McInerney, 2001; Smith et al., 2002). Perceived value of schooling has also been shown to have significant influence on performance and other educational outcomes (Wigfield & Eccles, 2000). However, although the existent literature has provided us with knowledge about the significant roles the various motivational constructs may play, there has been almost no vigorous test of the relative influences of these constructs on various short-term and long-term educational outcomes. Our purpose in this investigation is to consider three well documented factors (value, competence, and affect) and scrutinize the positive impacts of each factor on short-term and long-term outcomes.

Value of Schooling

Students' value of schooling is an important construct in achievement motivation (Martin, 2007). Value of schooling deals with the extent students believe what they learn at school is useful, important and relevant (Martin, 2007; Pintrich, Smith, Garcia, & McKeachie, 1991). Students who value school consider schoolwork and therefore find interest in and enjoyment of school and learning (Martin, 2003). Hence valuing of a learning task by a student contributes significantly to motivation and active engagement (Wigfield & Eccles, 2000). That is, higher valuing of task along with higher expectations predicts higher motivation and engagement (Wigfield, 1994; Wigfield & Eccles, 2000). In contrast, negative valuing of education is a significant negative predictor of achievement results. That is why students who value education are often better achievers than those who do not (Suliman & McInerney, 2006). Besides, culture helps to shape an individual's value beliefs (Markus & Kitayama, 1991). As such, sociocultural context has an important role to play in boys' and girls' development in their value beliefs regarding schooling (McInerney, 2008). Hence whereas researchers have emphasized the importance of students' valuing of school, it is also important to explore related cultural and gender issues.

Competence

For competence, it may be conceptualized as the cognitive component of self-concept (i.e., how good is a student in learning), which can be separated from the affective component (i.e., how much a student likes to learn)(Marsh, Craven, & Debus, 1999). Marsh and colleagues have demonstrated the causal relationship between this cognitive component of academic self-concept and achievement outcomes (e.g., Marsh & Craven, 2006). In essence, sense of competence in academic work is a strong predictor of academic performance and it is often found to be even a stronger predictor than students' actual ability in the specific task (Pajares & Schunk, 2002). Hence researchers have emphasized the enhancement of students' sense of competence as a vital goal in many education settings (Craven, Marsh, & Burnett, 2003; Marsh & Craven, 2006). It has also been demonstrated that a high self-perception of competence promotes goals, expectancies, coping mechanisms, and behaviors that facilitate productive achievement and work experiences in the long-term (e.g., Sommer & Baumeister, 2002).

Affect

Affect is another important component of self-concept (Marsh et al., 1999). Affect to learning is an important construct in educational settings because students tend to have a stronger tendency to learn when they find themselves interested in learning (Ryan & Deci, 2000). When students are interested in the academic context, they will attend to learning activities, hold positive attitudes, engage themselves in academic work, and persist in learning (Linnenbrink-Garcia, Durik, Conley, Barron, Tauer, Karabenick, & Harackiewicz, 2010; Trautwein & Lüdtke, 2009; Van Damme, De Fraine, Van Landeghem, Opdenakker, & Onghena, 2010). However, the influence of affect on academic outcomes may not be as clear as the influence of a sense of competence. Yeung (2005) argues that the extent to which students like school and enjoy engaging in schoolwork and learning activities would have important long-term benefits to learners of all ages, although immediate benefits may not be apparent. Nevertheless, there has been evidence showing that students' positive affect to learning does have positive influences on achievement (Singh, Granville, & Dika, 2002; Williams, Williams, Kastberg, & Jocelyn, 2005).

Educational Outcomes

To predict the invaluable outcomes of motivational constructs is one of the main issues of educational research. With education, students link content to context and imbibe knowledge and develop skills to meet self and social needs. These transform into self-concept and values which subsequently lead to important educational outcomes. Outcomes of motivation may be academic or social. This study focused on one long-term social outcome (identity) and one short-term academic outcome (achievement).

Identity

Hinkley, Marsh, & McInerney (2002) have suggested that one's identity is multidimensional. It may be personal (e.g., locus of control), cultural (e.g., individualism and collectivism), and social (inter-group behaviors and attitudes). Western societies are mostly individualistic-oriented and emphasize independence of the self from others whereas non-western societies are often collectivistic-oriented and emphasize interdependence (Markus & Kitayama, 1991; Triandis, 1994). Taking into consideration the western and non-western backgrounds of the students in the chosen schools, this study focused on a general identity construct that encompasses both personal and social identities. An individual's personal and social identities are shaped by culture; and as such, the socio-cultural dynamics of school life have significant influences on students' identity development. Personal and social identities provide motives for engagement in schoolwork, which shape students' self-perceptions and dispositions (Kaplan & Flum, 2009). People's self-perceptions further reinforce the formation of their personal and social identities because they give them a meaning both for themselves and for the interpretation of the social world around them (Eccles, 2009). Furthermore, McCaslin (2009) has argued that identity is formed as a continuous process in school which is regulated not only by personal and social influences but also cultural influences.

Achievement

Researchers have suggested that student achievement is related to their motivation and self-concept (Craven, et al., 2003; Marsh & Craven, 2006; McInerney & Ali, 2006). Studies have demonstrated that students' motivation and self-concept could have significant influence on essential academic outcomes including achievement scores (e.g., Craven et al., 2003; McInerney et al., 2001). Academic self-concept has been demonstrated to have mutual cause and effect relationships with academic achievement (Marsh & Craven, 2006). That is, an increase in academic self-concept leads to an increase in academic achievement and vice versa. Furthermore, academic self-concept has a mediating effect on other educational outcomes. Therefore, it is important to enhance both academic self-concept and academic achievement to obtain long-lasting desirable outcomes as both are mutually reinforcing (Marsh & Martin, 2011). Considering the cognitive and affective components of self-concept, children's competence beliefs (i.e., the cognitive component) seem to have particularly strong influence on different aspects of performance (WigField, 1994), and are a particularly strong predictor of achievement (Pajares & Schunk, 2002). Affect has also been found to influence achievement. Willams et al. (2005) have demonstrated the motivational influences of affect on achievement in their study across different national settings. That is, students who hold positive affect to learning are more likely to achieve better. Value of schooling also has an important role to play in predicting achievement outcomes (Suliman & McInerney, 2006). That is, students who value learning are usually good achievers. However, it is unclear which of these motivational constructs (competence, affect, and value) is a stronger predictor of achievement.

Cultural Issues

In academic motivation research, researchers have stressed the importance of culture in shaping the achievement goals of students (Markus & Kitayama, 1991). Researchers have suggested that societal values are linked to academic achievement goals across a number of societies (Decker & Fischer, 2008; Hau & Salili, 1991; Stevenson & Stigler, 1992). In the more egalitarian cultures (i.e., where individuals are expected to care and show a strong concern for others as moral equals), mastery goals are often perceived to be more important whereas in the more embedded societies (i.e., where individuals are socialized to conform to group norms and duties), more emphasis may be placed on performance goals (Decker & Fischer, 2008). In western cultures, learning ability is valued whereas Asian learners endorse effort more (Hau & Salili, 1991; Stevenson & Stigler, 1992). As Li (2002) puts it, the learning models are complex and they tend to differ between cultures and that children begin developing them early in life. That is, western students attribute high achievement to high ability, and this is primarily an individualistic perspective typical of western cultures, as opposed to a collectivistic perspective in many eastern cultures (Markus & Kitayama, 1991). Stevenson and Stigler (1992) suggest that such cultural differences may be the reason for Asian students, who emphasize effort, to obtain high achievement scores compared to western students, who emphasize ability.

A major difference between these emphases is that an individual's ability brings about immediate outcomes whereas effort takes time to yield desirable outcomes. As such, western students are more likely to expect immediate results whereas non-western students are more willing to invest their effort for more distal goals. In terms of motivating students in different cultures, westerners probably benefit more from a proximal value manipulation (such as competence beliefs) whereas non-western students would benefit from a more distal (e.g., effort) value manipulation (Shecter, Durik, Miyamoto, & Harackiewicz, 2011). Consistent with these suggestions, studies have shown that Australian, Canadian, and English students have higher competence beliefs than those from eastern regions (Eaton & Dambo, 1997; Zusho & Pintrich, 2003) whereas Asian students have higher effort orientations (Markus & Kitayama, 1991; Yeung, 2005). Furthermore, Asian students were found to not only value school more than many other students (McInerney, 2008), but also tend to perform better in a range of achievement measures (Stevenson & Lee, 1990). Studies have also revealed that non-Anglo students are relatively more positive about school experience (Sturman, 1997).

Culture also has strong influences on identity formation. Individuals' interpretation of race and culture serves as a resource for negotiating identity across context and time (Chatman, Eccles, & Malanchuk, 2005). For example, Anglos were found to generally view their gender and ethnic identities less important as compared to Asians and Hispanics (Garza & Herringer, 2001), probably because of their different beliefs. In this sense, we may expect cultural differences between Asian- and Anglo-Australians in the relationship between their motivation beliefs and identity formation.

Gender Issues

Research on motivation has indicated that there may be gender differences on some motivational constructs (Yeung, Lau, & Nie, 2011). Studies have revealed that girls' and boys' motivation related beliefs and behaviors are often influenced by gender role stereotypes (Meece, Glienke, & Burg, 2006). Boys tend to be more motivated in science and math subjects and tend to have higher ability perceptions in these curriculum areas than girls even though they may not achieve any higher than the girls in their class (Klapp Lekholm & Cliffordson, 2009; Marsh & Yeung, 1998). Such findings are also supported by Marsh (1993) who reported that girls had higher self-concepts in English as opposed to boys who had higher self-concepts in mathematics and science. In general, for students' sense of competence, boys tend to overestimate their abilities whereas girls often underestimate their abilities (Metalidou & Vlachou, 2007). Competence beliefs start to emerge in early elementary school (Eccles Wigfield, Harold, & Blumenfield, 1993), and therefore gender differences may be observable at an early age. Meece et al. (2006), for example, have shown that gender differences in reading and athletic abilities emerge early and persist over the school years. Furthermore, gender differences in competence beliefs may also be domain specific. For example, boys have more positive competence beliefs about sports and mathematics whereas girls have more positive competence beliefs about instrumental music than boys (Eccles et al., 1993). Although girls tend to have greater self-competence than boys in verbal areas (Kurtz-Costes, Rowley, Harris-Britt, & Woods, 2008), overall, boys tend to have a higher sense of competence than girls (Midgley, Kaplan, & Middleton, 2001).

Like competence beliefs, gender differences are evident also in value beliefs. They are again generally consistent with gender norms and stereotypes. Boys tend to place higher value on sports activities and girls place higher values on musical and reading activities (Eccles et al., 1993). For both competence beliefs and value of learning, however, they do not always match students' actual achievement. Lai (2010) found that for Chinese and American students, girls did better than boys in achievement. However, a more significant female dominance in achievement was found for Chinese than for Americans, even though boys gradually caught up during middle school, especially in math and science. That is, Chinese girls performed better than boys throughout primary and middle school. As well, girls reported a more positive school experience than boys. Hence cultural differences in school motivation may also exist. For example, contrary to findings with gifted American students, Dai (2001) found that gifted Chinese adolescent females reported higher academic self-concept than males. For lower achievers, the association between math self-concept and math achievement was found to be stronger for boys, and for students in countries that were wealthier, more egalitarian, or more tolerant of uncertainty (Chui & Klassen, 2010). In addition to these studies, some studies have also shown that gender differences on self-perceptions and beliefs do not generalize across cultures (Akande, 2009). Overall, cultural differences are mostly unclear and are worth further exploration.

The Present Investigation

In the present study, we surveyed a diverse sample of primary school students in Australia and examined self-beliefs and perceived value of schooling, and their influences on learning outcomes. The multicultural student population in Western Sydney provided an interesting context for the study of cultural and gender similarities and differences in these constructs. Particularly from the literature suggesting differences between Asian and western students' pattern of motivation and self-perceptions, we may expect some interesting differences between western students and students with an Asian origin (e.g., Shen & Tam, 2008). Therefore, there may be some distinct differences between Anglo-Australian students and students with an Asian origin within the same Australian schools. By comparing and contrasting the constructs for these students, it may be possible to scrutinize the generalizability of motivational patterns found in studies with predominantly western samples and elucidate the best strategies to maximize the potential of both Anglo- and Asian-Australian samples. Findings for any potential culture x gender interaction effects, which few researchers have explored, may also have important implications for curriculum design and pedagogical processes.

METHOD

Participants

Australian students from six primary schools in Western Sydney ($N = 730$) participated in this study. Students came from grades 3, 4, 5 and 6 (353 boys, 377 girls). Typical of students in public schools of the Western Sydney Region, they were multicultural and were mostly from families of relatively lower socio-economic status compared to other regions in Sydney. In this sample, about 88 different languages were reported, and most families spoke a variety of languages, with less than 35% of the students from monolingual English-speaking families. The present study focused on Anglo-Australian students ($n = 446$: 221 boys and 225 girls) and Asian-Australian students ($n = 284$: 132 boys and 152 girls), categorized on the basis of the ethnic background of the students' fathers. 'Asian' ethnicities in the sample refer to students whose father was born in an Asian country, and in the current Asian subsample ($n = 284$), they were Cambodia, Indonesia, Malaysia (2.1%), Indian, Sri Lanka, Bangladesh (71.8%), Korea, Japan (1.1%), Lebanon, Iraq (6.7%), Vietnam, China (8.5%), and other Asian and middle-east countries (9.9%).

Materials

In a survey, the students were asked to rate themselves on four factors (value, competence, affect, and identity). Background variables included age, gender, ethnicity, and language background. For the four factors, there were a total of 19 items with four to five items in each factor (see Appendix). They were:

Value of Schooling
Perceived value of schooling was adapted from Martin's (2003) Student Motivation and Engagement Scale. An example is: "What I learn at school will be useful one day."

Competence
This is the cognitive component of self-concept adapted from Marsh (1993) Academic Self-Description Questionnaire II (SDQII). An example is: "I am good at all school subjects."

Affect

This is the affective component of self-concept which was also adapted from Marsh's (1993) SDQII (also see Yeung et al., 2004). An example is: "I am interested in all school subjects."

Identity

This scale was adapted from Linnakyla's (1996) Quality of School Life Scale. An example is: "I learn to get along with other people."

In addition to these four constructs, we also collected achievement data from the students. These included a test on reading and a test on numeracy.

Achievement Scores

Reading and numeracy test materials were provided by the Department of Education and Communities (DEC) Western Sydney Region, New South Wales, Australia. The materials were designed for mid primary and upper primary students. The students were asked to answer 20 multiple-choice questions for reading and numeracy respectively for middle primary, and 24 respectively for upper primary students. Each correct answer was scored as one, incorrect as zero. A total achievement score was computed by adding up all the correct answers on the reading and the numeracy tests. The analysis used achievement scores in percentages.

Procedure

The schools were randomly selected and the principals of the schools were invited to participate. Data collection was conducted in the second half of the school year. Due to the large sample size, the whole data collection process took about 2 months. Procedures of the research followed university guidelines to ensure confidentiality and approval was obtained from the university's ethics committee. Informed consent was obtained from the school and the parents of the students before data collection. The survey was piloted at the beginning of the year and the scales and items were refined after preliminary analysis. The survey was administered in groups by a research assistant, and in some schools the class teacher also assisted to ensure students who needed help would be supported. The students responded to the survey items in a random order on a 5-point scale (1 = false to 5 = true).

Statistical Analysis

The students' responses to the survey items were coded such that higher scores reflected more favorable responses. In preliminary analysis, we examined the Cronbach's alpha estimate of internal consistency of each *a priori* scale. Then we conducted confirmatory factor analysis (CFA) with the statistical package of Mplus, Version 6.0 (Muthén & Muthén, 1998-2010). Although the amount of missing data was very small (about 1%), we used the full information maximum likelihood (FIML) estimator for imputation of missing values.

The procedures for conducting CFA have been described elsewhere (e.g., Byrne, 1998; Jöreskog & Sörbom, 2005) and are not further detailed here. The goodness of fit of the CFA models was evaluated based on suggestions of Marsh, Balla, and McDonald (1988) and Marsh, Balla, and Hau (1996), with an emphasis on the Tucker-Lewis index (TLI, also known as the non-normed fit index) as the primary goodness-of-fit index. However, the chi-square test statistic and root mean square error of approximation (RMSEA) and the comparative fit index (CFI), are also reported. In general, for an acceptable model fit, the values of TLI and CFI should be equal to or greater than .90 for an acceptable fit and .95 for an excellent fit to the data. For RMSEA, according to Browne and Cudeck (1993), a value of .05 indicates a close fit, values near .08 indicate a fair fit, and values above .10 indicate a poor fit.

Specifically, based on commonly accepted criteria (Browne & Cudeck, 1993; Jöreskog & Sörbom, 2005; Marsh, Balla, & Hau, 1996; Marsh, Balla, & McDonald, 1988), support for an acceptable model requires (a) acceptable reliability for each scale (i.e., alpha = .70 or above), (b) an acceptable model fit (i.e., TLI and RNI = .90 or above and RMSEA < .08), (c) acceptable factor loadings for the items loading on the respective factors (> .30), and (d) acceptable correlations among the latent factors such that they would be distinguishable from each other ($r < .90$).

We started by testing a measurement model (Model 1) with three motivation factors (Value, Competence, and Affect). Then, another CFA model (Model 2) was tested with these three motivation factors together with two outcomes (Achievement and Identity). Based on the established measurement of Model 2, a structural equation model (SEM) tested the relative predictive strength of each of the three predictors on each of the two outcomes (Model 3).

To examine cultural and gender differences in the students' value and beliefs in regards to schooling, a 2 (culture: Anglo vs. Asian) x 2 (gender: boys vs. girls) multivariate analysis of variance (MANOVA) was conducted with value, competence, and affect as dependent variables. Based on previous research, we hypothesized that: (1) CFA Model 2 with three motivation factors and two outcomes would provide a good fit, (2) Asian-Australian students would score higher on value and affect and lower on competence than Anglo-Australians, and (3) girls would score higher on value and affect and lower on competence than boys. However, because we did not have sufficient evidence from the literature to hypothesize the differential effects of the motivation factors on achievement and identity outcomes, we attempted to answer a research question: Which motivation factors would display stronger paths to achievement (a more immediate outcome) and to identity (a more distal outcome)?

RESULTS

CFA

The alpha reliability of each scale was acceptable ($\alpha > .70$), providing preliminary support for the *a priori* scales. The lowest alpha value was .75 for Value in the primary sample and the highest alpha was .89 for the Affect construct (Appendix). All CFA models resulted in a proper solution (Table 1). Model 1 (TLI = .94, CFI = .95, RMSEA = .065), and Models 2 and 3 (TLI = .92, CFI = .94, RMSEA = .060) provided a good fit to the data. Table

2 presents the standardized solution of Model 2. The factor loadings were acceptable (all > .5). The factor correlations ranged from .22 to .78. The highest correlation was between the Competence and Affect constructs, which was logical. Although the correlation was high ($r = .78$), they were clearly distinguishable from each other. In sum, Model 2 provided reasonable support for the measurement, which formed the basis for subsequent examination of paths from predictors to outcomes.

An inspection of the factor correlations (Table 2) found that Achievement was positively correlated with all three motivation factors (rs = .36, .38, and .28, respectively with Value, Competence, and Affect) whereas Identity was even more strongly correlated with these factors (rs = .76, .61, and .64, respectively with Value, Competence, and Affect). The correlation between Achievement and Identity was moderate ($r = .22$), indicating a clear distinction between the short-term and long-term outcomes. Overall, Model 2 provided support for the integrity of the motivation factors as well as the outcome variables to be examined in the current study.

SEM

Model 3 tested the paths from three motivation predictors to two learning outcomes (Figure 1). The results showed that all the paths were statistically significant ($p < .05$). Firstly, the path from Value to Achievement ($\beta = .27$) and Identity ($\beta = .57$) were both positive but the path to Identity was much stronger. For Competence, again both paths were positive but the path to Achievement was stronger ($\beta = .37$) than that to Identity ($\beta = .19$). For affect, interestingly, whereas the path to Identity was positive ($\beta = .15$), the path to Achievement was significantly negative ($\beta = -.17$) even though the correlation between Affect and Achievement was positive ($r = .28$). In sum, all three motivation factors had positive influences on Identity. However, the influences of Value and Competence were stronger than Affect on Achievement.

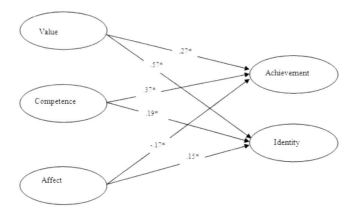

Note: * $p < .05$.

Figure 1. SEM: Paths from 3 motivation variables to 2 outcomes.

Table 1. Goodness-of-fit Summary for Models

Model	Items	χ^2	df	TLI	CFI	RMSEA
1. 3 predictors	14	301.59	74	.94	.95	.065
2. 3 predictors + 2 outcomes	21	642.69	179	.92	.94	.060
3. Path model	21	642.69	179	.92	.94	.060

Note: N = 730. CFI= Comparative Fit index. TLI= Tucker-Lewis index. RMSEA = Root mean square error of approximation.

Table 2. Solution of CFA (Model 2)

Variable	Value	Competence	Affect	Achievement	Identity	Uniqueness
Mean	4.50	3.89	3.78	73.95	4.16	
SD	0.69	0.76	1.05	18.83	0.82	
Factor Loadings						
value1	.65*	--	--	--	--	.56*
value2	.69*	--	--	--	--	.52*
value3	.60*	--	--	--	--	.64*
value4	.72*	--	--	--	--	.49*
compet1	--	.62*	--	--	--	.62*
compet2	--	.73*	--	--	--	.46*
compet3	--	.67*	--	--	--	.55*
compet4	--	.49*	--	--	--	.76*
compet5	--	.82*	--	--	--	.33*
affect1	--	--	.79*	--	--	.38*
affect2	--	--	.54*	--	--	.71*
affect3	--	--	.83*	--	--	.31*
affect4	--	--	.89*	--	--	.21*
affect5	--	--	.88*	--	--	.22*
readpc	--	--	--	.75*	--	.43*
numpc	--	--	--	.90*	--	.20*
Identity1	--	--	--	--	.65*	.58*
Identity2	--	--	--	--	.72*	.49*
Identity3	--	--	--	--	.74*	.46*
Identity4	--	--	--	--	.71*	.49*
Identity5	--	--	--	--	.60*	.64*
Factor Correlations						
value	--					
compet	.54*	--				
affect	.61*	.78*	--			
achieve	.36*	.38*	.28*	--		
Identity	.76*	.61*	.64*	.22*	--	

Note: N = 730. Parameters estimates are completely standardized. * $p < .05$.

Table 3. Means and (Standard Deviations) by Group

Variable	Anglo-Australians (N = 446)		Asian-Australians (N = 284)	
	Boys	Girls	Boys	Girls
N	221	225	132	152
Value	4.29 (0.87)	4.54 (0.58)	4.67 (0.57)	4.59 (0.58)
Competence	3.68 (0.88)	3.85 (0.74)	4.15 (0.62)	4.02 (0.59)
Affect	3.26 (1.16)	3.69 (0.98)	4.31 (0.78)	4.20 (0.74)

Group Comparisons

The scores of items for each scale were averaged to obtain a scale score. The means and standard deviations for boys and girls in two cultural groups (Anglo-Australians and Asian-Australians) are presented in Table 3. The results showed that for each of the three motivational constructs, all the students tended to have a high mean score (all $Ms > .3$ on a 5-point scale). For the Anglo-Australian students, girls tended to score higher than boys in all three motivational constructs (Ms = 4.54, 3.85, and 3.69 for girls compared to Ms = 4.29, 3.68, 3.26, respectively for Value, Competence, and Affect). For Asian-Australian students, gender differences are not so clear (Table 3). Furthermore, there was a clear pattern showing that Asian-Australians scored higher than Anglo-Australians for all three constructs (Table 3).

MANOVA was conducted using the three motivation factors as dependent variables (Value, Competence, and Affect) and culture and gender as independent variables. The analysis found statistically significant effects of culture, but gender differences seemed to be small.

Culture

Cultural difference was statistically significant for Value, $F(1, 729) = 32.09$, $MSN = 0.55$, $p < .001$, $\eta^2 = .04$, indicating that the Asian-Australian students had higher perceived value of schooling than their Anglo-Australian peers. For Competence, cultural difference was also statistically significant, $F(1, 729) = 112.76$, $MSN = 0.55$, $p < .001$, $\eta^2 = .13$, indicating that the Asian-Australian students had a higher sense of competence. For Affect, cultural difference was again statistically significant, $F(1, 729) = 17.28$, $MSN = 0.55$, $p < .001$, $\eta^2 = .04$, indicating that the Asian-Australian students had more positive affect to school than Anglo-Australian students.

Gender

Gender difference was not statistically significant for Value, $F(1, 729) = 0.10$, $MSN = 0.93$, $p > .05$; neither was it significant for Affect $F(1, 729) = 2.78$, $MSN = 0.93$, $p > .05$. For

Competence, gender difference was statistically significant, $F(1, 729) = 4.93$, $MSN = 0.93$, $p < .05$, but the effect was small ($\eta^2 < .01$).

Culture X Gender Interaction

The interactions between culture and gender were found to be significant for all three motivational constructs, $F(1, 729) = 6.82$, $MSN = 0.46$, $p < .05$, $\eta^2 = .01$ for Value, $F(1, 729) = 13.64$, $MSN = 0.46$, $p < .001$, $\eta^2 = .02$ for Competence, and $F(1, 729) = 10.90$, $MSN = 0.46$, $p < .001$, $\eta^2 = .02$ for Affect. Consistent across the three constructs, cultural differences were primarily due to differences in boys. Specifically, the differences between Asian-Australian boys in Value, Competence, and Affect (Ms = 4.67, 4.15, and 4.31, respectively) and Anglo-Australian boys (Ms = 4.29, 3.68, and 3.26, respectively) were greater than the differences between Asian-Australian girls (Ms = 4.59, 4.02, and 4.20, respectively) and Anglo-Australian girls (Ms = 4.54, 3.85, and 3.69, respectively) (Table 3).

DISCUSSION

In the present study, we sought to investigate the differences in motivation types between Asian and Anglo students of Australia. We also examined what motivational constructs predicted short- and long-term outcomes of education. Before we examined group differences and tested paths from motivation factors to outcome variables, we attempted to establish the validity of the measurement. In this regard, hypothesis 1 was supported. That is, the CFA model with three motivation factors and two outcomes provided a reasonable fit to the data.

Cultural Differences

Hypothesis 2 tested cultural differences. One major finding from this study was that Asian students indicated significantly higher motivation scores for the three motivation types considered here (value of schooling, competence and affect) than Anglo students. This result may lead to a meaningful discussion of the influence of different cultures on learner motivation. The finding is in agreement with McInerney, Maehr, and Dowson (2004) who propose that motivation may be conceptualized very differently by different cultural groups. The differences found in the two groups of students in our study could be because of the different ways education is perceived by the two cultures. Education is emphasized not only for the proximal goal of good academic achievement but also for distal goals of getting a good career and being successful in life in Asian cultures (Shecter et al., 2011). Asian parents expect their children to achieve high levels of academic achievement and professional success (Fuligni, 2001). An inability to attain good achievement scores may lead to feelings of inadequacy amongst Asian children and their parents.

The Asian students' significantly higher mean scores for value of schooling and affect can be explained from the perspective that Asian students are more oriented toward effort attributions and performance goals, and have a stronger tendency toward a control of their own learning processes (Markus & Kitayama, 1991; Stevenson, Lee, & Stigler, 1986; Yeung, 2005). However, the Asian students' significantly higher mean score for competence was inconsistent with previous studies that showed higher competence beliefs for western than for eastern cultures (Eaton & Dambo, 1997; Shen & Pedulla, 2000; Zusho & Pintrich, 2003). That is, hypothesis 2 was only partially supported. Earlier studies had primarily compared across-nation cohorts where the curriculum is different for each nation. The more positive perceptions of students found in previous research in western cultures may be due to the relatively undemanding educational system of these western countries (Kawanda, Stigler, & Hiebert, 1999). However, our data show that when students from different cultures in a western context are compared, Asian students' self-perceptions are higher. This may be due to the fact that curriculum task demands are lower, and probably much lower than their expectations. Combined with their parents' expectation of high academic achievement and professional success in future based on high school performance (Fuligni, 2001), it is possible for Asian students in a western country such as Australia to report a higher sense of competence. Perhaps the Asian students find it easier to achieve academically and to satisfy their parents' expectations in a western school system than in an eastern context. However, this speculation needs further research to confirm.

Gender Differences

For hypothesis 3, gender differences were tested. There were no significant differences for Value and Affect between boys and girls, and even though some gender differences were found for Competence, the small effect size ($\eta^2 = .01$) indicate that the difference may not be practically meaningful. That is, there were more cultural differences than gender differences for this sample. However, the means in Table 3 indicate that whereas Asian-Australian boys were higher than their Anglo-Australian peers in all three constructs (Ms = 4.67, 4.15, and 4.31 vs. 4.29, 3.68, and 3.26, respectively for Value, Competence, and Affect), girls were very similar between the Asian and Anglo subsamples. As such, the culture x gender interaction effects were statistically significant, favoring Asian boys for each construct.

The strikingly consistent pattern of results for culture and gender differences is noteworthy. For all three motivational constructs, the greatest differences were primarily found between boys. Between Asian boys and girls, the findings are partly consistent with the recent findings of Yeung, Lau, and Nie (2011) who reported that Asian boys were lower in motivation and sense of competence than girls in primary schools. However, this pattern favoring girls was found only in our Anglo subsample. That is, whereas Yeung et al. (2011) found that boys tended to be lower in motivation and competence beliefs in an Asian context, the Asian boys in our Australian context did not seem to suffer from such lowered scores.

The reason for this reversed pattern is unclear. Studies have revealed that cultural values tend to moderate the links between gender and motivation. In more masculine countries (where there are more rigidly-defined gender roles favoring males), girls were found to have lower reading achievement compared to girls in other countries (Chiu & Chow, 2010). Also, Pajares and Valiante (2001) have argued that gender differences in motivation and achievement of students may be more "a function of gender orientation rather than gender". This is in agreement with studies revealing that students' achievement-related perceptions may be shaped by the gender stereotypes they hold for a specific academic domain under consideration (Eccles, 1987; Meece & Courtney, 1992). However, the motivational constructs considered in our study were in more general terms; therefore, it was unclear how gender stereotypes would affect students' perceptions in such a consistent way. Hence whereas the reason for the contrasting scores of boys and girls on motivational constructs between the two cultures considered here may be somewhat due to the more rigid gender roles and beliefs of the Asian culture than the Anglo culture, it was unclear why the Asians in an Asian country and those in the Australian context can be so different.

Relations between Motivation and Outcomes

Although all three motivational constructs were found to be positively associated with identity (as can be seen in the positive correlations), surprisingly, affect ($r = .28$ with achievement) was found to display a negative path to achievement ($\beta = -.17$) when considered together with competence and value as predictors (Figure 1). By applying a structural equation modeling approach to examining the paths from each motivation factor to each of two outcome constructs, we were able to delineate the relative strength of each predictor on each outcome. Hence the negative path indicates that affect, although positively associated with both achievement and identity, was not as strong a predictor as were a sense of competence and value of schooling, which were so strong that the relative effect of affect became even negative. Other than this negative path, all the other paths were positive and significant (Figure 1). For identity as an outcome, the path from affect was significantly positive ($\beta = .15$). That is, after accounting for the strong effects of the other predictors (value and competence), affect to learning positively influences students' identity development. In other words, affect may not have strong influences on more direct and immediate outcomes such as achievement. However, it does have strong positive influences on more long-term outcomes such as identity development, even when the influences of value and competence are also taken into account.

Value of schooling was found to have relatively strong influences on both achievement and identity but there seemed to be a stronger positive association with identity ($\beta = .57$) than with achievement ($\beta = .27$). The results suggest that students who value school may have both the benefits of obtaining better achievement and forming a desirable identity (Figure 1). This means that value of schooling not only predicts achievement but is also a significant predictor of more long-term gains such as students' identity. Ideally, because of the strong links between this motivator and outcomes, teachers and schools need to implement strategies to maintain this motivation at a high level through the primary school years.

In contrast, competence had a relatively stronger influence on achievement ($\beta = .37$) than on identity ($\beta = .19$). This indicates that an increase in students' sense of competence would probably lead to better achievement results (Figure 1). This is consistent with previous research that demonstrated the causal relationship between the cognitive component of academic self-concept and achievement outcomes (e.g., Marsh & Craven, 2006; Marsh, et al., 1999) and the salience of a sense of competence in academic work in predicting academic performance (Pajares & Schunk, 2002). Further to these findings, our data also show that students' sense of competence may also foster the development of identity. This has important implications as healthy identity development is an important dimension for successful living in the growing multicultural environment of schools and the workplace in an Australian context. Nevertheless, this pattern needs to be investigated further as the association between self-concept and identity development as a long-term outcome has not been thoroughly explored and should warrant further research.

It is important to note that the results showed significant correlations between all three motivation factors and the two outcome factors (all rs were positive and statistically significant), demonstrating that all three school motivational constructs were positively related to both the short-term and long-term outcomes when considered separately. It is therefore important to note that the purpose of the path model (Figure 1) was to provide a more stringent explication of the relative strength of each predictor in predicting each outcome variable. The advantage of using this structural equation modeling approach is to be able to answer the research question of which predictor best predicts which outcome when there are multiple predictors and multiple outcomes to be tested simultaneously.

The consistently positive correlations of identity with the three motivation factors (rs = .76, .61, and .64 respectively with value, competence, and affect) and positive paths from these motivation variables (β = .57, .19, and .15, respectively) indicate that all these motivational constructs are important for student' development of identity. As such, they may also be important predictors of other distal goals of education. This gives support to the suggestion that students conceive education for their distal wellbeing as well as their proximal goal of doing well academically (Miller & Brickman, 2004). The findings also provide support to Kaplan and Flum's (2009) suggestion that students' motivation in school and identity styles are potentially related; and therefore engagement in schoolwork may have an important role to play in shaping students' identity. Nevertheless, future research should also attempt to investigate how these motivational constructs may be related to other long-term goals such as self-efficacy, optimism, and psychological wellbeing.

This study has some limitations which can be addressed in future research. First, students sampled in this study were not fully representative of all cultures. There is a need to study cultural differences in motivation and educational outcomes across a variety of cultural settings. Second, future studies can address longitudinal design, placing special emphasis on developmental changes on motivation and educational outcomes across cultures. Even within the cultural group, there is a need to study cultural capital, cultural values and their differential influences on motivation. Another direction for future research is to examine how gender differences in motivation differ by culture. There is a dearth of studies showing how culture and its influences combine with gender to form students' social identities that may further influence learning.

CONCLUSION

Our results show that students' sense of competence was a predictor of achievement and affect was a predictor of identity, whereas value of schooling was a strong predictor of both. These motivational predictors were found to be higher for Asian-Australian boys than for Anglo-Australian boys while gender differences were mostly negligible. Our findings have important implications for theory and practice. It seems that educators should pay attention to enhancing all three motivational factors so that students can enjoy both short-term and long-term benefits of education. However, it is important that researchers and educators keep in mind the cultural specificity of students' ethnic background when designing strategies to maximize students' potentials.

AUTHOR'S NOTE

The research was funded by the Australian Research Council and the New South Wales Department of Education and Communities, Australia. Enquiries concerning this paper should be directed to Alexander S. Yeung, Educational Excellence & Equity (E³) Research Program, University of Western Sydney, Bankstown Campus, Locked Bag 1797, Penrith, NSW 2751, Australia.

REFERENCES

Akande, A. (2009). The self-perception and cultural dimensions: cross-cultural comparison. *Educational Studies, 35*, 81-92.

Browne, M. W., & Cudeck, R. (1993). Alternative ways of assessing model fit. In K. A. Bollen, & J. S. Long (Eds.), *Testing structural equation models* (pp. 136-162). Newbury Park, CA: Sage.

Byrne, B. M. (1998). *Structural equation modeling with LISREL, PRELIS, and SIMPLIS: Basic concepts, applications, and programming*. Mahwah, NJ: Erlbaum.

Chatman, C. M., Eccles, J. S., & Malanchuk, O. (2005). Identity negotiation in everyday settings. In G. Downey, J.S. Eccles, & C.M. Chatman (Eds.), *Navigating the future: Social identity, coping and life tasks* (pp.116-139). New York: Russell Sage Foundation.

Chiu, M. M., & Chow, B. W. Y. (2010). Culture, motivation and reading achievement, high school students in 41 countries. *Learning and Individual Differences, 20*, 579-592.

Chiu, M. M., & Klassen, R. M. (2010). Relations of mathematics self-concept and its ca bration with mathematics achievement: Cultural differences among fifteen year olds in 34 countries. *Learning and motivation, 20*, 2-17.

Craven, R. G., Marsh, H. W., & Burnett, P. C. (2003). Cracking the self-concept enhancement conundrum: A call and blueprint for the next generation of self-concept enhancement research. In H. W. Marsh, R. G. Craven & D. M. McInerney (Eds.), *International advances in self research: Speaking to the future* (pp. 67-90). Greenwich, CT: Information Age.

Dai, D. Y. (2001). A comparison of gender differences in academic self-concept and motivation between high-ability and average Chinese adolescents. *Journal of Secondary Gifted Education, 13*, 22-32.

Eaton, M. J., & Dembo, M. H. (1997). Differences in the motivational beliefs of Asian American and non-Asian students. *Journal of Educational Psychology, 89*, 433-440.

Eccles, J. S. (1987). Gender roles and women's achievement-related decisions. *Psychology of Women Quarterly, 11*, 135–172.

Eccles, J.S. (2009). Who am I and what am I going to do with my life? Personal and collective identities as motivators of action. *Educational Psychologist, 44*, 78-89.

Eccles, J.S., Wigfield, A., Harold, R.D., & Blumenfield, P. (1993). Age and gender differences in children's self and task perceptions during elementary school. *Child Development, 64,* 830-847.

Dekker, S., & Fischer, R. (2008). Cultural differences in academic motivation goals: A meta-analysis across 13 societies. *The Journal of Educational Research, 102,* 99-110.

Fuligni, A. J. (2001). Family obligation and the academic motivation of adolescents from Asian, Latin American, and European backgrounds. *New Directions for Child and Adolescent Development, 94,* 61-75.

Garzer, R.T., & Herringer, L.G. (2001). Social identity: A multidimensional approach. *Journal of Social Psychology, 127,* 299-308.

Hau, K. T., & Salili, F. (1991). Structure and semantic differential placement of specific cases: Academic causal attributions by Chinese students in Hong Kong. *International Journal of Psychology, 26,* 175–193.

Hinkley, J. W., Marsh, H. W., & McInerney, D. M (2002). Social identity and Navajo high school students: Is a strong social identity important in the school context? In W. J. Lonner, D. L. Dinnel, S. A. Hayes, & D. N. Sattler (Eds.), *Online readings in psychology and culture* (Unit 3, Chapter 5), (http://www.wwu.edu/~culture), Center for Cross-Cultural Research, Western Washington University, Bellingham, Washington USA.

Jöreskog, K. G., & Sörbom, D. (2005). *LISREL 8.72: Structural equation modeling with SIMPLIS command language.* Chicago: Scientific Software International.

Kaplan, A., & Flum, H. (2009). Motivation and identity: The relations of action and development in educational contexts-An introduction to the special issue. *Educational Psychologist, 44,* 73–77.

Kawanaka, T., Stigler, J. W., & Hiebert, J. (1999). Studying mathematics classrooms in Germany, Japan, and the United States: Lessons from the TIMSS videotape study. In G. Kaiser, E. Luna, & I. Huntley (Eds.), *International comparisons in mathematics education* (pp. 86-103). Bristol, PA: Falmer Press.

Klapp Lekholm, A., & Cliffordson, C. (2009). Effects of student characteristics on grades in compulsory school. *Educational Research and Evaluation, 15,* 1-23.

Kurtz-Costes, B., Rowley, S., Harris-Britt, A., & Woods, T. A. (2008). Gender stereotypes about mathematics and science and self-perceptions of ability in late childhood and early adolescence. *Merrill-Palmer Quarterly, 54,* 386-409.

Lai, F. (2010). Are boys left behind? The evolution of the gender achievement gap in Beijing's middle schools. *Economics of Education Review, 29,* 383-399

Li, J. (2002). Learning models in different cultures. *New directions for Child and Adolescent Development, 96,* 45-63.

Linnakyla, P. (1996). Quality of school life in the Finnish comprehensive school: A comprarative view. *Scandinavian Journal of Educational Research, 40,* 69- 85.

Linnenbrink-Garcia, L., Durik, A. M., Conley, A. M. M., Barron, K. E., Tauer, J. M., Karabenick, S. A., & Harackiewicz, J. M. (2010). Measuring situational interest in academic domains. *Educational and Psychological Measurement, 70,* 647-671.

Markus, H. R., & Kitayama, S. (1991). Culture and the self: Implications for cognition, emotion, and motivation. *Psychological Review, 98,* 224-253.

Marsh, H.W. (1993). The multidimensional structure of academic self-concept: Invariance over gender and age. *American Educational Research Journal, 30,* 841-860.

Marsh, H. W., Balla, J. R., & Hau, K. T. (1996). An evaluation of incremental fit indices: A clarification of mathematical and empirical processes. In G. A. Marcoulides, & R. E. Schumacker (Eds.), *Advanced structural equation modeling techniques* (pp. 315-353). Hillsdale NJ: Erlbaum.

Marsh, H. W., Balla, J. R., & McDonald, R. P. (1988). Goodness-of-fit indices in confirmatory factor analyses: The effect of sample size. *Psychological Bulletin, 103*, 391-410.

Marsh, H. W., & Craven, R. G. (2006). Reciprocal effects of self-concept and performance from a multidimensional perspective: Beyond seductive pleasure and unidimensional perspectives. *Perspectives on Psychological Science, 1*, 133-163.

Marsh, H. W., Craven, R. G., & Debus, R. (1999). Separation of competency and affect components of multiple dimensions of academic self-concept: A developmental perspective. *Merrill-Palmer Quarterly, 45*, 567-601.

Marsh, H. W., & Martin, A. J. (2011). Academic self-concept and academic achievement: Relations and causal ordering. *British Journal of Educational Psychology ,81*, 59-77.

Marsh, H. W., & Yeung, A. S. (1998). Longitudinal structural equation models of academic self-concept and achievement: Gender differences in the development of Math and English constructs. *American Educational Research Journal, 35*, 705-738.

Martin, A. J. (2003). Boys and motivation. *Australian Educational Researcher, 30*, 43-65.

Martin, A. J. (2007). Examining a multidimensional model of student motivation and engagement using a construct validation approach. *British Journal of Educational Psychology, 77*, 413-440.

McCaslin, M. (2009). Coregulation of student motivation and emergent identity. *Educational Psychologist, 44*, 137-146.

McInerney, D. M. (2008). Personal investment, culture and learning: Insights into school achievement across Anglo, Aboriginal, Asian and Lebanese students in Australia. *International Journal of Psychology, 43,* 870–879.

McInerney, D. M., & Ali, J. (2006). Multidimensional and hierarchical assessment of school motivation: Cross-cultural validation. *Educational Psychology, 26*, 717-734.

McInerney, D. M., Maehr, M. L., & Dowson, M. (2004). Motivation and culture. *Encyclopedia of Applied Psychology, 2,* 631-639.

McInerney, D. M., Yeung, A. S., & McInerney, V. (2001). Cross-cultural validation of the Inventory of School Motivation (ISM): Motivation orientations of Navajo and Anglo students. *Journal of Applied Measurement, 2*, 135-153.

Meece, J. L., Glienke, B. B., & Burg, S. (2006). Gender and motivation. *Journal of School Psychology, 44,* 351-373.

Meece, J. L., & Courtney, D. P. (1992). Gender differences in students' perceptions: Consequences for achievement-related choices. In D. L. Schunk & J. L. Meece (Ed.), *Students perceptions in the classroom* (pp. 209–228). Hillsdale, NJ: Erlbaum.

Metallidou , P., & Vlachou, A. (2007). Motivational beliefs, cognitive engagement, and achievement in language and mathematics in elementary school children. *International Journal of Psychology, 42*, 2-15.

Midgley, C., Kaplan, A., & Middleton, M. (2001). Performance-approach goals: Good for what, for whom, under what circumstances, and at what cost? *Journal of Educational Psychology, 93*, 77-86.

Miller, R. B., & Brickman, S. J. (2004). A model of future-oriented motivation and self-regulation. *Educational Psychology Review, 16*, 9-33.

Muthén, L. K., & Muthén, B. O. (1998 –2010). *Mplus user's guide* (5th ed.). Los Angeles, CA: Muthén & Muthén.

Pajares, F., & Schunk, D. H. (2002). Self and self-belief in psychology and education: A historical perspective. In J. Aronson (Ed.), *Improving academic achievement: Impact of psychological factors on education* (pp. 3-21). San Diego, CA: Academic Press.

Pajares, F., & Valiante, G. (2001). Gender differences in writing motivation and achievement of middle school students: A function of gender orientation? *Contemporary Educational Psychology, 26*, 366-381.

Pintrich, P. R., Smith, D. A. E., Garcia, T., & McKeachie, W. J. (1991). *A manual for the use of the Motivated Strategies for Learning Questionnaire (MSLQ)*. Ann Arbor, MI; National Center for Research to Improve Postsecondary Teaching and Learning.

Ryan, R., & Deci, E. (2000). Self-determination theory and the facilitation of intrinsic motivation, social development, and well-being. *American Psychologist, 55*, 68-78.

Shechter, O. G., Durik, A. M., Miyamoto, Y., & Harackiewicz, J. M. (2011).The role of utility value in achievement behavior: The importance of culture. *Personality and Social Psychology Bulletin, 37*, 303–317.

Shen, C., & Tam, H. P. (2008). The paradoxical relationship between student achievement and self-perceptions: A cross-national analysis based on three waves of TIMSS data. *Educational Research and Evaluation, 14*, 87-100.

Shen, C., & Pedulla, J. J. (2000). The relationship between students' achievement and their self-perception of competence and rigor of Mathematics and Science: A cross-national analysis. *Assessment in Education, 7*, 237–253.

Singh, K., Granville, M., & Dika, S. (2002). Mathematics and science achievement: Effects of motivation, interest, and academic engagement. *Journal of Educational Research, 95*, 323-332.

Smith, M., Duda, J., Allen, J., & Hall, H. (2002). Contemporary measures of approach and avoidance orientations: Similarities and differences. *British Journal of Educational Psychology, 72*, 155-190.

Sommer, K. & Baumeister, R. F. (2002). Self-evaluation, persistence, and performance following implicit rejection: The role of trait self-esteem. *Personality and Social Psychology Bulletin, 28*, 926-938.

Stevenson, H. W., & Lee, S. Y. (1990). Contexts of achievement: A study of American, Chinese, and Japanese Children. *Monographs of the Society for Research in Child Development, 55*, 2-21.

Stevenson, H. W., Lee, S., & Stigler, J. W. (1986).Mathematics achievement of Chinese, Japanese, and American children. *Science, 231*, 693–699.

Stevenson, H. W., & Stigler, J. W. (1992). *The learning gap: Why our schools are failing and what we can learn from Japanese and Chinese education*. New York: Simon & Schuster.

Suliman, R. & McInerney, D. M. (2006). Motivational goals and school achievement: Lebanese-background students in south-western Sydney. *Australian Journal of Education, 50*, 242–264.

Triandis, H. C. (1994). *Culture and social behavior*. New York: McGraw-Hill.

Trautwein, U., & Lüdtke, O. (2009). Predicting homework motivation and homework effort in six school subjects: The role of person and family characteristics, classroom factors, and school track. *Learning and Instruction, 19*, 243-258.

Van Damme, J., De Fraine, B., Van Landeghem, G., Opdenakker, M-C., & Onghena, P. (2010). A new study on educational effectiveness in secondary schools in Flanders: An introduction. *School Effectiveness and School Improvement, 13*, 383-397.

WigField, A. (1994). Expectancy-value theory of achievement motivation: A developmental perspective. *Educational Psychological Review, 6*, 49-78.

Wigfield, A., & Eccles, J. S. (2000). Expectancy-value theory of achievement motivation. *Contemporary Educational Psychology, 25*, 68-81.

Wigfield, A., Tonks, S., & Eccles, J. S. (2004). Expectancy-value theory in cross-cultural perspective. *Research on Sociocultural Influences on Motivation and Learning, 4*, 165-198.

Williams, T., Williams, K., Kastberg, D., & Jocelyn, L. (2005). Achievement and affect in OECD nations. *Oxford Review of Education, 31*, 517–545.

Yeung, A. S. (2005). Reconsidering the measurement of student self-concept: Use and misuse in a Chinese context. In H. W. Marsh (Ed.), *The new frontiers of self research* (pp. 233-257). Sydney: Information Age.

Yeung, A. S., Chow, A. P. Y., Chow, P. C. W., Luk, F., & Wong, E. K. P. (2004). Academic self-concept of gifted students: When the big fish becomes small. *Gifted and Talented International, 19*, 91–97.

Yeung, A. S., Lau, S., & Nie, Y. (2011). Primary and secondary students' motivation in learning English: Grade and gender differences. *Contemporary Educational Psychology, 36*, 246-256.

Yeung, A. S., & McInerney, D. M. (2005). Students' school motivation and aspiration over high school years. *Educational Psychology, 25*, 537-554.

Zusho, A., & Pintrich, P. R. (2003). A process-oriented approach to culture: Theoretical and methodological issues in the study of culture and motivation. In F. Salili & R. Hoosain (Eds.), *Teaching, learning, and motivation in a multicultural context* (pp. 33-65). Greenwich, CT: Information Age.

APPENDIX

Variables Used in the Study

Factor/Example Items	Alphas Total
Value (4 items)	.75
What I learn at school will be useful one day	
Learning at school is important	
Competence (5 items)	.80
Work in all school subjects is easy for me	
I am good at all school subjects	
Affect (5 items)	.89

(Continued)

I enjoy doing work in all school subjects	
I look forward to all school subjects	
Achievement	.85
Reading test score (%)	
Numeracy test score (%)	
Identity (5 items)	.82
I learn a lot about myself	
I have learnt to accept other people as they are	

In: Handbook on Psychology of Motivation
Editors: J. N. Franco and A. E. Svensgaard
ISBN: 978-1-62100-755-5
© 2012 Nova Science Publishers, Inc.

Chapter 7

BEHAVIORAL CONSEQUENCES OF COUNTERFACTUAL THINKING: A SELF-EVALUATION MODEL

Maurissa P. Tyser[*] and Sean M. McCrea
University of Wyoming, Laramie, WY, US

ABSTRACT

Upward counterfactual thoughts identify how a prior performance could have been better. For example, after receiving a low grade on an important test, a student might think to him or herself "I should have studied more for the test." Such thoughts have been linked to increased intentions to improve in the future and better subsequent performance. One would therefore expect the student in this example to increase his or her study effort in the future. Of course, people do not always act out of such conscientious motives. Individuals often attempt to shift the blame for their failure elsewhere rather than seek to improve, and in other cases persist only out of a reluctance to admit failure. We propose a new theoretical model integrating theories of self-regulation and self-evaluation to explain the consequences of counterfactual thinking for motivation and performance. We suggest the effects of upward counterfactual thoughts crucially depend upon their implications for self-evaluation. Currently active self-evaluation motives determine whether upward counterfactuals are used to excuse poor performance, motivate additional effort, or justify prior decisions. Moreover, counterfactuals that suggest personal responsibility for prior outcomes appear to accentuate the behavioral consequences of these thoughts.

BEHAVIORAL CONSEQUENCES OF COUNTERFACTUAL THINKING: A SELF-EVALUATION MODEL

Counterfactual thinking is a common yet powerful process by which individuals consider past behavior and events. These thoughts indicate how a past outcome could have turned out

---

[*] Address for correspondence:Sean McCrea, Department of Psychology, University of Wyoming Dept. 3415, 1000 E. University Ave.Laramie, WY 82070 USA , Tel.: (307) 766-6149, Fax: (307) 766-2926

differently (Kahneman and Miller, 1986; Roese, 1997). Upward counterfactual thoughts indicate how a past outcome could have been better (e.g., "If I had studied more, I could have done better on the exam") and are therefore of particular interest to understanding how individuals respond to failure. Indeed, upward counterfactual thoughts are strongly evoked by difficulties that arise during goal pursuit and have important consequences for persistence and performance on subsequent tasks (Epstude and Roese, 2008). Upward counterfactuals also provide causal explanations for past outcomes (Roese and Olson, 1996; Wells and Gavanski, 1989), and thus should influence how individuals evaluate the self and how they respond to failure. In the example above, the student may be upset with herself, but intend to study more in the future in order to avoid another poor test result. Alternatively, failure may be so threatening to her self-worth that she uses this thought to excuse her poor performance. From this perspective, self-evaluation motives are likely to influence the way that individuals generate and interpret upward counterfactual thoughts. In this chapter, we propose a model that seeks to explain the impact that self-evaluation motives have on the behavioral consequences of upward counterfactual thoughts.

Motivational Models of Counterfactual Thinking

Early studies of counterfactual thinking provided evidence that upward counterfactual thoughts serve a preparative function (Roese, 1997). They were found to enhance persistence and improve performance on subsequent tasks, albeit at a cost of heightened negative affect (Markman, Gavanski, Sherman, and McMullen, 1993; Roese, 1994). A variety of explanations for this finding have been offered. Epstude and Roese (2008) characterize these explanations as postulating either a content-neutral or a content-specific pathway to performance. The content-specific pathway involves the identification of corrective actions that can be taken in the future (Smallman and Roese, 2009). Because upward counterfactuals suggest why a better performance did not occur, individuals can convert these thoughts into behavioral intentions. For example, the thought, "If I had studied more, I could have done better on the exam," can be easily translated into the strategy to study more for the next exam. These behavioral intentions are then likely to influence subsequent behavior (Ajzen, 1991; Gollwitzer, 1999).

The content-neutral pathway involves benefits of counterfactual thinking for performance, independent of any behavior mentioned in the thought (Epstude and Roese, 2008). For example, upward counterfactuals have been shown to increase self-efficacy (Tal-Or, Boninger, and Gleicher, 2004), increase perceptions of control (Nasco and Marsh, 1999), improve creative and flexible thinking (Galinsky and Moskowitz, 2000), and increase effort mobilization and persistence (Markman, McMullen, and Elizaga, 2008; Roese, 1994). Markman and McMullen's (2003) Reflection-Evaluation Model (REM) proposes that affect resulting from counterfactual thinking influences judgments of whether one has met one's goal for the task. In other words, individuals assess their progress towards the goal based upon how they are feeling at the moment. This proposition is consistent with past work demonstrating that individuals use their current mood as input for a variety of evaluative judgments, so long as no objective information is available and they believe their current feelings did not originate from an unrelated source (Martin, Ward, Achee, and Wyer, 1993; Schwarz, 1990). According to the REM, generating counterfactuals that increase negative affect causes individuals to judge that their progress toward a salient goal has thus far been inadequate. As a result, they should increase task effort and perform better. In contrast, generating counterfactuals that increase positive affect causes individuals to judge their goal progress as adequate. As a result, they should maintain or reduce their effort and performance. Other models of motivation similarly emphasize the importance of evaluating prior performance in determining subsequent action. For example, Control Theory (Carver and Scheier, 1999) and Social Cognitive Theory (Bandura and Cervone, 1983; Bandura and Locke, 2003) both hold that goal-directed effort is increased on subsequent tasks only when the person perceives a discrepancy between the goal and the performance outcome. Markman, McMullen, and Elizaga (2008) found evidence for these predictions, demonstrating that benefits of counterfactual thinking for task persistence and performance were mediated by affect. Thus, counterfactual thinking seems to involve a trade-off of negative affect in the present for improved performance in the future.

Taking a Self-Evaluation Perspective to Counterfactual Thinking

Self-evaluation is the process by which individuals make judgments about and modify the self-concept (Sedikides and Strube, 1997), and has been identified as a critical aspect of self-regulation (Taylor, Neter, and Wayment, 1995). Primary self-evaluation motives include self-improvement, self-protection, and self-justification. Self-improvement refers to the desire to accurately judge one's performance and ability in order to improve in the future (Crocker and Park, 2004; Sedikides and Strube, 1997; Taylor et al., 1995; Trope, 1986). Self-protection refers to the desire to positively judge one's performance and ability in order to maintain or increase self-esteem (Crocker and Park, 2004; Greenwald, 1980; Sedikides and Strube, 1997; Taylor et al., 1995). Self-justification refers to the desire to avoid admitting that one has made a mistake and to hold beliefs and attitudes that are consistent with one's past behavior (Brehm, 1956; Brockner, 1992; Festinger and Carlsmith, 1959; McGuire and McGuire, 1991).

The existence of these motives has been demonstrated in a wide-range of contexts, including social comparison (Taylor et al., 1995), task choice (Trope, 1986), information search (Butler, 1993; Trope, Ferguson, and Raghunathan, 2001), task persistence (Henderson, Gollwitzer, and Oettingen, 2007), choice satisfaction (Brehm, 1956; Kahneman, Knetsch, and Thaler, 1990), and causal attribution (Zuckerman, 1979). Which motive an individual pursues in a given situation depends on a number of factors. For example, when ability in a domain is perceived as malleable (Dunning, 1995; Dweck and Leggett, 1988), when the task is less ego-threatening (Butler, 1993), or when self-protection concerns have already been addressed (D. K. Sherman and Cohen, 2006; Trope et al., 2001), long-term self-improvement motivations are stronger than more short-term self-protection motivations. When individuals feel personally responsible for an unwanted outcome or have acted in a hypocritical fashion (Cooper and Fazio, 1984; Festinger and Carlsmith, 1959; Stone, Wiegand, Cooper, and Aronson, 1997), revisit past decisions (Brehm, 1956; Kahneman et al., 1990), or invest considerable resources in a failing course of action (Henderson et al., 2007; Staw, 1976), the desire to rationalize behavior can overwhelm long-term self-improvement goals.

Multiple self-evaluation motives can arise in a given situation and create behavioral conflicts (Taylor et al., 1995), particularly between actions that serve self-improvement and those that serve to protect self-esteem or justify one's past behavior. For example, self-justification concerns might lead one to discount or ignore potentially useful negative feedback (Staw, 1976), forego opportunities to learn about alternative options (Kahneman et al., 1990), or fail to switch to more effective strategies (Henderson et al., 2007), whereas self-improvement concerns might require attention to information that could be damaging to mood and self-esteem (Campbell and Sedikides, 1999; Zuckerman, 1979). The pursuit of self-esteem can have negative implications for performance and self-regulation (Baumeister, Campbell, Krueger, and Vohs, 2003; Crocker and Park, 2004), and attempts to cope with controllable events solely through the regulation of emotion are less effective than more problem-focused approaches (Lazarus and Folkman, 1984). Thus, self-protection and self-justification concerns can undermine effective self-regulation.

Counterfactuals are likely to be highly relevant to evaluating the self because they tend to be generated at the same phase of goal pursuit in which evaluation of past action is required. According to the model of action phases (Heckhausen, 2003; Heckhausen and Gollwitzer, 1987), goal-pursuit occurs in four phases: a pre-decisional phase in which individuals deliberate whether to pursue a goal, a post-decisional phase in which individuals plan how to implement their decision, an action phase in which the goal is actively pursued, and a post-actional phase in which progress towards the goal is evaluated. This final phase is said to involve an evaluative mindset, in that individuals must decide whether they have successfully completed the goal, and if not, whether and how to continue. In the case of a failure to achieve a goal, individuals engage in causal attribution to determine the cause. Attribution processes suggest corrective actions that can be taken should another opportunity to pursue the goal arise, or degenerate into negative self-evaluation (Beckmann and Heckhausen, 1988; Heckhausen, 2003). Because they occur in the post-actional phase (see also Epstude and Roese, 2008), upward counterfactuals are particularly likely to inform judgments concerning the adequacy of goal progress, guide judgments of causality, and thereby influence self-evaluation and future behavior.

To date, research examining the role of self-evaluation in counterfactual thinking has concerned the influence of these motivations on counterfactual thought content. For example, individuals have been shown to generate counterfactuals that are biased towards the self and ingroups (Goerke, Möller, Schulz-Hardt, Napiersky, and Frey, 2004; McCrea, 2007; Roese and Olson, 1993a), that serve to defend existing attitudes and beliefs (Crawford and McCrea, 2004; Tetlock, 1998), and that guide subsequent improvement (Roese and Olson, 1993b; Sanna, Chang, and Meier, 2001). However, there has been less attention paid to the role of self-evaluation motives in determining the behavioral consequences of counterfactual thoughts.

As in many previous models of the motivational consequences of counterfactual thinking (Epstude and Roese, 2008; Markman and McMullen, 2003), we assume that these thoughts affect behavior by influencing judgments of goal progress (Markman et al., 2008; McMullen and Markman, 2000) and perceived controllability of the performance outcome (Markman, Gavanski, Sherman, and McMullen, 1995; Nasco and Marsh, 1999; Tal-Or et al., 2004). However, we argue that the meaning of these judgments differs across motivational contexts. This is because the same thought can have different implications for each self-evaluation motive. Consider the example of a student who thinks to herself "If I had studied more, I could have done better on the test." Without additional information, we do not know whether she is making an excuse for her poor performance in order to protect self-esteem, searching for a way to improve on a subsequent test, or justifying her decision to major in chemistry rather than music. Taken a step further, we would need to know the reasons why she generated this thought in order to predict whether she is likely to be content with her performance, change her study habits, or change her major.

Similar arguments can be found in the literature examining causal attribution. Attributing failure to a lack of effort has been shown to protect mood and self-esteem (Covington and Omelich, 1979; Jones and Berglas, 1978; Weiner, 1985). With regard to self-improvement, attributions of failure to a lack of effort lead to increased persistence and maintain expectations of success (Bandura, 1977; Weiner, 1985). With regard to self-justification, both rationalization of past behavior (Cooper and Fazio, 1984) and persisting in failing courses of action (Staw, 1976) are heightened by feelings of personal responsibility. Thus, the same causal attribution (i.e., one's past behavior) can have quite different consequences for behavior depending on the motivational context in which they occur. Because upward counterfactual thoughts are used to evaluate goal progress (Epstude and Roese, 2008; Markman and McMullen, 2003) and are closely linked to causal judgments (Mandel and Lehman, 1996; Wells and Gavanski, 1989), we expect self-evaluation motives will moderate the consequences of these thoughts for behavior in a similar manner.

We propose a self-evaluation model of the behavioral consequences of counterfactual thinking. The model has two critical implications for understanding how counterfactual thoughts impact subsequent behavior. First, the model holds that dominant self-evaluation motives will moderate the consequences of counterfactual thinking for subsequent behavior. Namely, we expect that upward counterfactuals will 1) maintain self-esteem but undermine subsequent motivation to improve when individuals are concerned with self-protection, 2) undermine mood but enhance motivation to improve when individuals are concerned with self-improvement, and 3) increase commitment to a failing course of action when individuals are concerned with self-justification. Second, we argue that the effects of goal progress on subsequent behavior will be accentuated when counterfactuals suggest that performance outcomes are controllable. We next present data from several lines of research that provide support for each of these predictions.

Counterfactual Thinking under a Self-Protection vs. Self-Improvement Motive

We first consider evidence that counterfactual thoughts can serve self-improvement or self-protection functions for the individual. Considerable past research has documented benefits of upward counterfactual thinking for performance and persistence, consistent with self-improvement motives (Nasco and Marsh, 1999; Roese, 1994; Sanna et al., 2001). More recently, our research has examined whether upward counterfactual thoughts can serve to protect self-esteem by identifying excuses for a poor performance, particularly in the context of self-handicapping. Self-handicapping involves creating or claiming an obstacle prior to a performance in order to protect self-esteem in the event of failure (Berglas and Jones, 1978; McCrea and Hirt, 2001). In this case, one can point to the self-handicap as having prevented a better outcome. For example, one might study inadequately for an exam and blame subsequent failure on this lack of study effort. McCrea (2008) conducted several studies examining the role of upward counterfactual thinking in self-handicapping behavior. First, it was shown that the presence of a self-handicap (i.e., insufficient practice effort) increased the generation of upward counterfactuals concerning this handicap. Second, exposure to upward counterfactuals concerning a handicap protected self-esteem following failure, but reduced future preparation and performance, compared to control thoughts. In one study (McCrea, 2008, Study 4), participants were induced to listen to distracting noises during a math exam. After receiving failure feedback, participants were assigned to consider a thought about this handicap ("I would have performed better had I listened to the neutral noises"), a thought about their ability ("I would have performed better if I was better at math"), or a control thought ("The test was interesting"). They then completed a measure of state self-esteem and could choose which type of noise they would listen to during a subsequent math test, using a seven-point scale (1 = *very distracting* to 7 = *very helpful*). Self-esteem was higher when the counterfactual concerned the noise handicap, but individuals in this condition also elected to listen to less helpful noise for the subsequent test (see Table 1). These results are consistent with the notion that upward counterfactuals can serve to protect self-worth, but at the expense of self-improvement.

A final study (McCrea, 2008, Study 5) demonstrated that upward counterfactuals concerning a self-handicap undermine subsequent persistence and performance. Participants were induced to insufficiently practice for a math exam and received failure feedback. They considered an upward counterfactual concerning lack of practice or a control thought, and then completed a second math exam, correctly answering as many items as they could in a four minute period. Supporting our view that upward counterfactuals serving to protect self-worth undermine motivation to improve, persistence and performance on the subsequent test were lower in the counterfactual condition than in the control condition, see Table 2.

Although these findings are consistent with the notion that counterfactuals can serve different self-evaluation motives, it is not clear under which conditions a given counterfactual will benefit or undermine efforts to improve. Tyser, McCrea, and Knüpfer (2011) more directly tested whether the prevailing self-evaluation motive moderates the behavioral consequences of upward counterfactual thinking. In Study 1, we examined the consequences of upward counterfactual thinking for persistence when individuals were pursuing different self-evaluation motives. Prior research suggests that individuals are more likely adopt a self-improvement motive if default self-protection concerns have been previously addressed. For example, individuals are less reluctant to examine negative feedback if they have previously had a positive experience or are currently experiencing a more positive mood (Trope et al., 2001).

Table 1. Self-esteem and subsequent behavior by counterfactual condition (McCrea, 2008; Study 4)

Measure	Handicap	Ability	Control
Post-exam self-esteem	37.17$_a$	35.33$_{ab}$	34.80$_b$
Noise choice	5.00$_a$	6.33$_b$	5.50$_{ab}$

Notes. Means with different subscripts differ at $p < .05$. Higher scores on the self-esteem measure reflect more positive views of the self. Higher scores on the noise choice measure reflect the selection of less distracting noise.

Table 2. Persistence and performance by counterfactual condition (McCrea, 2008; Study 5)

Condition	Number of items attempted	Number correct	Percent correct
Handicap	8.85	5.62	62.1%
Control	11.20*	8.20*	74.3%*

* $p < .05$.

Likewise, affirming the overall integrity of the self reduces a variety of self-protective behaviors, including downward social comparison (Tesser and Cornell, 1991), rejecting threatening feedback (D. K. Sherman, Nelson, and Steele, 2000), and self-handicapping (McCrea and Hirt, 2011; Siegel, Scillitoe, and Parks-Yancy, 2005).

Based on these findings, we expected that the prior satisfaction of self-protection concerns via self-affirmation would result in the adoption of a self-improvement motive. We therefore predicted that, within the affirmation condition, counterfactuals would increase persistence compared to a control thought. Conversely, those facing an ego-threatening task who had not previously affirmed the self were expected to pursue a self-protection motive. We therefore predicted that, within the no affirmation condition, counterfactuals would not increase (and potentially reduce) persistence compared to the control thought. Thus, we expected the exact same counterfactual thought would have different consequences for preparatory effort, depending on the prevailing self-evaluation motive. Participants were assigned to either a self-affirmation condition in which they wrote about a value that most exemplified their character (e.g., sense of humor, relationships with family and friends), or a control condition in which they listed everything they had had to eat in the past 48 hours.

Next, the participants were introduced to an ego-threatening memory test and informed that practice had been shown to have a significant effect on performance on the memory test. They were also told that a computer error had occurred and were asked if they would not mind being in the "no practice" condition. This ensured that participants knew that the choice to not practice was their own. Participants then completed an initial memory test and received failure feedback that they were among the bottom 40% of participants. They were then asked to consider either an upward counterfactual statement (i.e., "If I had practiced more, I would have done better") or a neutral statement (i.e., "The test items were similar to each other"). Following the presentation of these statements, participants were told that they would be tested on their memory for the translations of 20 Swahili words (actually nonwords). They learned the word-translation pairings by guessing the correct translation from four possible answers and receiving feedback. They could repeat this process as many times as they wanted until they felt they knew the correct translations for all of the words. Time spent learning the words was recorded. Results revealed a significant Self-affirmation x Thought interaction on the learning time measure, see Figure 1.

Within the self-affirmation condition, exposure to counterfactual thoughts increased preparative effort relative to the control thought. Thus, self-affirmation appeared to free participants to pursue self-improvement motives.

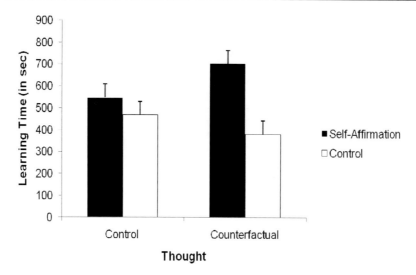

Figure 1. Self-affirmation x Thought interaction on Swahili task learning time (Tyser, McCrea, and Knüpfer, 2011; Study 1).

As a result, upward counterfactuals were processed in a manner that facilitated improvement. However, within the no-affirmation control condition, preparative effort was non-significantly lower in the counterfactual condition than in the control condition. Without a chance to affirm the self, the threatening nature of the task induced a self-protective motivation among participants. As a result, upward counterfactuals were processed in a manner that excused poor performance and eliminated any concern with improvement. These results demonstrate how the operation of different self-improvement motives explains the apparent discrepancy between work showing preparatory benefits of upward counterfactual thoughts (e.g., Roese, 1994) and work showing that the same thoughts can undermine subsequent task effort (McCrea, 2008).

In a second study, we (Tyser et al., 2011, Study 2) sought to replicate these findings using a different manipulation of self-evaluation motive. In addition, we wished to demonstrate that these effects would hold for task performance as well as persistence. The self-evaluation motive in this study was manipulated by focusing on mastery and performance achievement goals. Mastery goals are those in which an individual's past performance serves as a gauge for evaluating success or failure, whereas performance goals are those in which the evaluation of one's competence is based on a comparison to the performance of others (Elliot and McGregor, 2001). Whereas mastery (particularly mastery-approach) goals lead to a self-improvement motive, performance goals (particularly performance-avoidance goals) are associated with more defensive and negative behaviors (Elliot, 1999; Elliot and McGregor, 2001). We predicted that when individuals pursue a mastery-approach goal (and thus a self-improvement motive), upward counterfactual thoughts will increase preparatory effort and performance on a subsequent task, compared to a control thought. In contrast, when individuals pursue a performance-avoidance goal (and thus a self-protection motive), the same upward counterfactual thought should reduce preparatory effort and performance on a subsequent task, compared to a control thought.

Participants were informed that they would be taking two memory tests and that performance on the memory tests predicts academic abilities and future career success.

Participants in the mastery-approach goal condition were then given the goal to try their best to improve their performance on the two memory tests, whereas those in the performance-avoidance goal condition were given the goal to demonstrate that they do not lack memory ability relative to other students. As in the first study, participants were induced not to practice for the memory test, received failure feedback following the test, and were then asked to consider either an upward counterfactual statement (i.e., "If I had asked to practice the memory test, I would have done better.") or a neutral statement (i.e., "The test items were pretty similar to each other."). The second memory test involved learning a series of 15 pictures that had to be serially recalled at the end of the task. Participants were instructed to try to learn the picture sequence during a practice session. They were instructed to review the sequence until they felt they had memorized it and could recall the pictures in the correct order. The study concluded when participants quit the practice session and completed the memory test. Results revealed significant Goal x Thought interactions on both practice effort (see Figure 2) and memory performance (see Figure 3).

Within the performance-avoid goal condition, those exposed to the upward counterfactual practiced significantly less than did those in the control condition. Within the mastery goal condition, there was no effect of thought condition. With regard to performance, participants in the mastery-approach goal condition who were exposed to the upward counterfactual performed better than did those in the control condition. Within the performance-avoid goal condition, this effect was not significant.

Taken together, our findings show that self-evaluation concerns influence both the generation of counterfactuals (e.g., McCrea, 2007) and the consequences of a given thought for affect, self-esteem, and subsequent behavior.

When individuals pursue a self-improvement motive, thoughts about how a past performance could have been better are likely to be used as an assessment of goal progress. These thoughts indicate that performance was inadequate, suggest that improvement is possible, and provide strategies for corrective action. On the other hand, when individuals pursue a self-protection motive, individuals are likely to be more concerned with maintaining the view that they are capable and intelligent. In this context, upward counterfactuals point to excuses for failure. As a result, dissatisfaction is reduced and the motivation to improve is undermined.

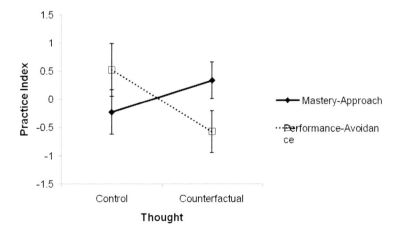

Figure 2. Goal x Thought interaction on practice index (Tyser, McCrea, and Knüpfer, 2011; Study 2).

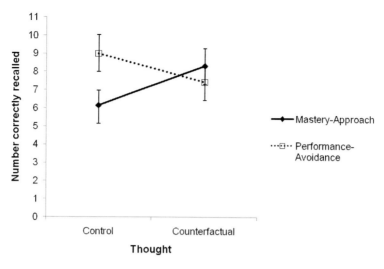

Figure 3. Goal x Thought interaction on memory performance (Tyser, McCrea, and Knüpfer, 2011; Study 2).

Counterfactual Thinking under a Self-Justification vs. Self-Improvement Motive

Thus far, we have focused exclusively on tasks for which increased persistence leads to better outcomes. What about situations in which performance is unrelated to effort expenditure? In such cases, it is more functional to disengage from the task in order to save psychological and physical resources (Arkes and Blumer, 1985; Henderson et al., 2007). Escalation of commitment occurs when individuals persist on tasks that have little to no chance of success in order to justify prior investment decisions (Arkes and Blumer, 1985; Staw, 1976). Escalation effects are particularly likely when the individual is responsible for the initial decision to pursue a particular course of action and has already invested significant amounts of effort or resources into the task (Brockner, 1992). Escalation of commitment is typically explained in the context of yet another self-evaluation motive: self-justification. Research in the cognitive dissonance tradition provides many examples of the various ways in which individuals attempt to justify prior purchase decisions (Brehm, 1956) and behaviors (Festinger and Carlsmith, 1959; Stone et al., 1997). In the case of escalation of commitment, self-justification motives encourage persistence despite evidence that success is unlikely (Brockner, 1992). Conversely, self-improvement motives would require a change in strategy in order to more effectively allocate one's resources (Henderson et al., 2007).

Our model suggests that the consequences of counterfactual thinking for persistence should likewise be moderated by the strength of a self-justification motive, relative to a self-improvement motive. Specifically, heightened self-justification motives should increase the likelihood that counterfactuals result in the escalation of commitment (see also S. J. Sherman and McConnell, 1995). Escalation effects are heightened by personal responsibility for negative outcomes, particularly when large sunk costs are involved (Brockner, 1992; Staw, 1976). We therefore reasoned that large sunk costs should be experienced as threatening and increase the adoption of a self-justification motive. As a result, upward counterfactuals should increase escalation effects. In contrast, losing a small initial investment is relatively non-threatening and will allow a self-improvement motive to dominate. As a result, upward counterfactuals should encourage changing strategies or disengaging from a poor investment decision.

Participants in two studies (McCrea and Tyser, 2011) were told they would be playing a game called "Venture Capitalist." Players could choose to invest funds in one of three companies. Each company was seeking to develop a new product, but needed to purchase five new pieces of equipment and hire five specialists in order to develop this product. Players stood to profit or lose part of their investment, dependent on the success of the company and the amount invested. Specifically, the more funds one risked by investing, the greater the likelihood that the company would be successful in acquiring the necessary equipment and specialists. In actuality, the outcomes were fixed such that the company was never successful and participants incurred losses throughout the game. The dependent measure was how much participants would invest in the company after each round of negative feedback.

Consistent with past work on escalation of commitment (Arkes and Blumer, 1985; Staw, 1976), we manipulated the amount participants lost on an initial investment. Because individuals are more motivated to recover large losses, escalation is more likely when individuals have previously invested a greater amount of resources (Brockner, 1992). All participants were told to imagine they had $1 million of funds to invest. Those assigned to the small loss condition were told they had to invest $100,000 on one of the three companies to begin the game. Those assigned to the large loss condition were told they had to invest $500,000 on one of the three companies to begin the game. Participants in both conditions were told they lost half of their investment (i.e., small $50,000; large $250,000).

Counterfactual generation was manipulated by varying how close the company was to succeeding. Psychologically close outcomes have been shown to increase the generation of counterfactual thoughts (Kahneman and Varey, 1990) and signal the possibility of improvement when additional performance opportunities exist (McMullen and Markman, 2002). When an outcome "almost" occurs, it is easier to generate counterfactuals indicating how it could have come about. Participants assigned to the control outcome condition were told that the company was only able to acquire three of five pieces of equipment and hire two of five specialists required to develop the product. Participants assigned to the close outcome condition were told that the company was able to acquire all five pieces of equipment but only to hire four of five specialists. Thus, it was easier to imagine that the company could have been successful, and return a profit, had this one specialist been hired. Participants were then given the opportunity to invest as much of their remaining funds as they wished in three subsequent rounds of the game. However, the company never made any subsequent progress and participants continued to lose a portion of their investment (15%, 35%, and 25% respectively).

Average amount invested across the three rounds is presented in Figure 4. Consistent with our predictions, escalation effects were highest when participants had previously lost a large sum and the outcome was psychologically close. In contrast, escalation effects were lowest when participants had previously lost only a small sum and the outcome was psychologically close.

In a second study, counterfactual thought was more directly manipulated, and participants were given actual money to invest. They were told they could keep any profits they made in the game, but also risked losing it all if the company failed.

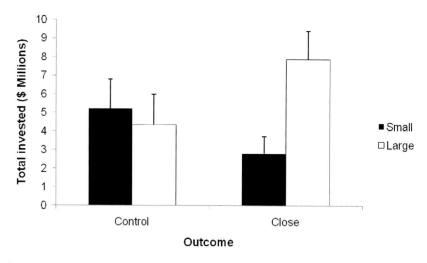

Figure 4. Outcome closeness x Initial investment (McCrea and Tyser, 2011; Study 1).

Those assigned to the small initial loss condition were told they had $5.00 to invest, and that they lost $0.10 in the first round as a result of a failure to hire the needed specialists. Those assigned to the large initial loss condition were told they had $6.00 to invest, and that they lost $1.10 in the first round as a result of a failure to hire the needed specialists. Participants were then randomly assigned to thought condition.

Those in the counterfactual condition were asked to write a thought indicating how the outcome of their investment could have turned out better. Those in the control condition were asked to indicate how much they had lost in the first round. All participants then played three rounds of the investment game, consistently losing as in Study 1. Average amount invested across the three rounds is presented in Figure 5. Consistent with our predictions and replicating Study 1, counterfactuals increased escalation effects when participants had initially lost a large sum. In contrast, counterfactuals tended to reduce escalation effects when participants had initially lost only a small sum.

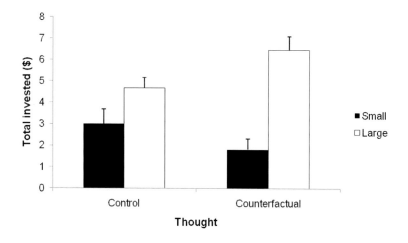

Figure 5. Thought x Initial investment (McCrea and Tyser, 2011; Study 2).

In summary, the availability of upward counterfactual thoughts increased dysfunctional persistence when participants were motivated to recover previous costs. In contrast, when previous costs were low, upward counterfactuals were used to more critically evaluate goal progress and facilitate disengagement from the task. Thus, whether upward counterfactuals result in better self-regulation or increase commitment to a failing course of action is moderated by the motivational context in which these thoughts occur.

Accentuating Counterfactual Consequences

The second principle of the self-evaluation model holds that the behavioral consequences of goal progress will be stronger to the extent that a counterfactual thought suggests that performance outcomes are controllable. Classic models of motivation suggest that effort is mobilized to the greatest extent when individuals perceive that goal progress has been insufficient, but that effort is maintained or reduced when goal progress is adequate. According to Control Theory (Carver and Scheier, 1999), individuals increase effort when goal progress is low, but maintain or reduce effort when progress towards the goal is high. Similarly, Social Cognitive Theory (Bandura and Cervone, 1983; Bandura and Locke, 2003) suggests that goal-directed effort is highest when a goal is not yet complete. Lewin and colleagues (Lewin, 1951; Lewin, Dembo, Festinger, and Sears, 1944) also suggested that action results from a tension between current and desired states. As we have shown, upward counterfactuals can result in judgments that goal progress is sufficient or insufficient depending on how the thought is interpreted by the individual. Thus, an important moderator of the behavioral consequences of a counterfactual thought is the individual's current affective state (see also Markman and McMullen, 2003).

These models of motivation also hold that effort will be expended only when the performance is controllable. For example, Social Cognitive Theory (Bandura and Cervone, 1983; Bandura and Locke, 2003) argues that individuals will exert more effort and perform better when they experience high self-efficacy. According to expected-value models of motivation, goal-directed effort will be greatest when both desirability of the goal and expectations of success are high (Heckhausen and Gollwitzer, 1987; Vroom, 1964). Attribution theory similarly suggests that persistence will be greatest when failure is attributed to relatively unstable causes such as a lack of effort (Weiner, 1985). As discussed earlier, upward counterfactual thoughts affect causal judgments (Mandel and Lehman, 1996; Wells and Gavanski, 1989), perceptions of control (Nasco and Marsh, 1999) and self-efficacy (Tal-Or et al., 2004). Thus, the content of the counterfactual should be an additional moderator of the behavioral consequences of the thought.

Taken together, theories of motivation suggest that self-improvement efforts should be heightened when an upward counterfactual implies that goal progress is insufficient and that performance on the task is controllable. In contrast, when the counterfactual implies that goal progress has thus far been sufficient, there is little reason to increase effort. Particularly when the counterfactual indicates that progress on the task is due to one's (successful) actions, there is even less reason to increase one's effort or to alter one's behavior. In this case, individuals may instead shift resources to other tasks or "coast," thereby reducing task-directed effort (Carver and Scheier, 1999).

To test these predictions, McCrea and Tessa (2011, Study 1) conducted a study examining the effects of goal progress and counterfactual controllability on subsequent persistence and performance. Participants were told they would be completing two versions of a verbal task, and that their goal was to be among the best 30% of participants. The task required them to complete ten word fragments. Each item was an eight-letter word with all but two letters missing. A category label was provided to aid in solving the items, and each correct answer received six points. In addition, participants could "purchase" one letter per item at a cost of two points each, choose to skip over difficult items and return to them at a later time, or quit the task altogether. Importantly, one set of items was considerably more difficult than the other set. Half of participants completed the difficult items first, and the other half completed the easier items first. After completing the first word completion task, participants received feedback that they were in the top 33% of participants. We assumed that those who completed the difficult task and received this feedback would interpret their goal progress as insufficient, because it would presumably be challenging to improve upon this performance. In contrast, we assumed that those who completed the easy task and received this feedback would interpret their goal progress as sufficient, as it would be a relatively simple matter to improve upon this performance.

Next, participants were randomly assigned to one of three thought conditions. Those assigned to the behavior condition were asked to consider the thought "If I had only used more clues, then I would have reached my goal." Those assigned to the ability condition were asked to consider the thought "If only I was better at verbal tasks, then I would have reached my goal." The former counterfactual suggests the outcome was controllable, whereas the latter suggests the outcome was not controllable. Finally, those assigned to the control condition were asked to consider the thought "I wonder what would have happened if my friends had also participated in the test." All participants were asked to write the statement three times and to relate this statement to their own performance on the task.

They then completed the second block of ten word fragments. Results are presented in Table 3. When initial goal progress was likely to be viewed as insufficient (i.e., participants completed the more difficult set first), the behavior counterfactual led to greater use of clues and a higher number of items correctly solved, relative to the control condition. The ability counterfactual did not differ from the control thought on these measures.

Table 3. Task performance by thought and initial goal progress conditions (McCrea and Tessa, 2011, Study 1)

	Thought Condition		
	Behavior	Ability	Control
Items Solved			
Insufficient	0.44_a	0.27_{ab}	-0.31_b
Sufficient	-0.44_a	-0.27_{ab}	0.65_b
Clues Selected			
Insufficient	0.63_a	0.14_{ab}	-0.26_b
Sufficient	-0.34_a	-0.03_a	0.32_a

Note. Means in each row with different subscripts differ at $p < .05$.

In contrast, when initial goal progress was likely to be viewed as sufficient (i.e., participants completed the easier set first), the behavior counterfactual led to significantly fewer items correctly solved, and a tendency to use fewer clues, relative to the control condition. The ability counterfactual did not differ from the control thought on these measures.

Thus, individuals only instituted efforts to take corrective actions when they were likely to be disappointed with their goal progress and believed that the performance was due to their own controllable actions. These efforts extended beyond using the strategy implied by the thought (i.e., using more clues). In contrast, when participants were satisfied with their performance they had little reason to seek improvement. Particularly when the counterfactual suggested a controllable action was responsible for the performance, efforts to improve were actually lower.

To replicate this finding and demonstrate the mediating role of personal responsibility in determining the behavioral consequences of counterfactual thoughts, we conducted another study (McCrea and Tessa, 2011, Study 2). Participants were presented with a set of twelve pictures, and learned that each picture had a corresponding point value. Each trial involved the presentation of a pair of pictures drawn from this set. Participants' task was to, as quickly as possible, select the picture from the pair that was associated with the higher point value. They received points for correct responses, with a deduction for longer reaction times. Importantly, a picture of a basil plant was associated with the highest point value, and thus was the correct answer regardless of the picture with which it was paired. Participants were given the goal to perform among the top 30% of participants. They reported to what extent they felt responsible for their performance, and completed an initial block of 132 trials. They received accurate feedback concerning their average reaction time, number correct, and score. As in Study 1, they were told they narrowly missed being among the top 30% of participants.

Participants were then assigned to one of three thought conditions. Those assigned to the behavior counterfactual thought condition considered the thought "If I had pressed the corresponding key as soon as I saw the basil, then I could have been among the best 30% of participants." Those assigned to the ability counterfactual thought condition considered the thought "If I was better at this type of task, then I could have been among the best 30% of participants." Finally, those assigned to the control condition considered the thought "I wonder what I could have done differently yesterday." Participants were asked to write the thought three times and consider how it related to their own performance.

They then were asked to rate how responsible they felt for their performance, rated their current mood, and completed a second block of 132 trials of the reaction time task.

Results revealed a Negative mood x Counterfactual condition interaction on performance improvement from the first to the second block of trials, see Figure 6. Participants who reported higher negative mood following the first block and who had considered the behavior counterfactual improved more than any other group. The behavior counterfactual was also found to increase post-feedback responsibility, relative to the pre-task baseline. Moreover, change in perceived responsibility was found to mediate the effects of counterfactual condition. Those in a more negative mood and who felt more responsible improved their performance to a greater extent than did other groups, see Figure 7. In contrast, those in a less negative mood and who felt more responsible showed no improvement whatsoever.

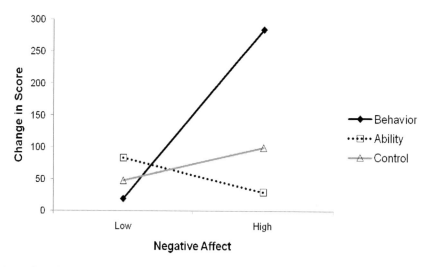

Figure 6. Negative affect x Counterfactual condition interaction on performance (McCrea and Tessa, 2011; Study 2).

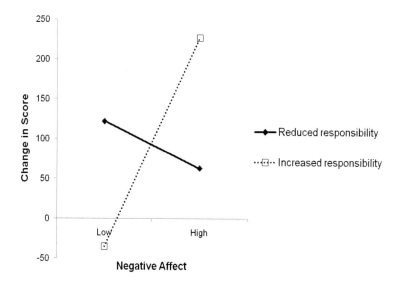

Figure 7. Negative affect x Change in perceived responsibility interaction on performance (McCrea and Tessa, 2011; Study 2).

Thus, upward counterfactuals appear to improve performance to the extent that the individual is dissatisfied with prior outcomes and the thought suggests that improvement is within one's control. Thoughts concerning relatively stable factors, such as low ability, are unlikely to motivate efforts at improvement. Conversely, responsibility for a relatively satisfactory outcome suggests that progress towards the goal is sufficient and so there is little reason to increase subsequent effort.

AUTHOR'S NOTE

Maurissa P. Tyser, Sean M. McCrea, Department of Psychology, University of Wyoming, Laramie, WY, 82071, USA. This research was supported by a grant to the second author from the German Science Foundation (DFG MC68/2-1).

CONCLUSION

Upward counterfactuals identify how a prior performance could have been better. They occur in the post-actional phase of goal pursuit and therefore have important consequences for self-evaluation and self-regulation. Drawing on these perspectives, we have sought to provide an integrative model of the consequences of counterfactual thoughts for subsequent behavior. Specifically, we have demonstrated that the same counterfactual thought can have varying effects on subsequent behavior, depending on the currently active self-evaluation motive. If the goal is self-protection, upward counterfactual thoughts protect self-esteem but undermine performance improvement. When individuals pursue a self-improvement goal, upward counterfactuals lead to dissatisfaction and higher subsequent performance. Finally, upward counterfactuals can result in persistence in failing courses of action when individuals are motivated by self-justification motives. Researchers interested in counterfactual thought should therefore consider not only the content of counterfactuals thoughts but also the motivational context in which they occur.

Second, the impact of a counterfactual thought on subsequent behavior is magnified to the extent that it refers to a controllable aspect of one's past behavior. Counterfactualizing past controllable behavior facilitates forming intentions to take corrective action and heighten self-efficacy, particularly when goal progress is insufficient. At the same time, these thoughts can serve to shift blame for failure to a self-handicap and thereby excuse poor performance. Resulting judgments that goal progress has been sufficient are likely to lead to coasting or a reduction in task effort. Finally, counterfactuals that suggest that personal responsibility for negative outcomes can heighten commitment to failing courses of action.

In conclusion, upward counterfactual thoughts can be helpful or harmful, depending on the circumstances under which they are employed. Our research suggests that there are benefits of upward counterfactual thought for self-regulation when individuals are motivated by self-improvement. With the right structure and content, counterfactuals have the ability to assist individuals in reaching their goals. However, counterfactuals can also undermine effective self-regulation when individuals pursue self-protection or self-justification.

REFERENCES

Ajzen, I. (1991). The theory of planned behavior. *Organizational Behavior and Human Decision Processes, 50*, 179-211.

Arkes, H. R., and Blumer, C. (1985). The psychology of sunk cost. *Organizational Behavior and Human Decision Processes, 35*, 124-140.

Bandura, A. (1977). Self-efficacy: Toward a unifying theory of behavioral change. *Psychological Review, 54*, 191-215.

Bandura, A., and Cervone, D. (1983). Self-evaluative and self-efficacy mechanisms governing the motivational effects of goal systems. *Journal of Personality and Social Psychology, 45*, 1017-1028.

Bandura, A., and Locke, E. A. (2003). Negative self-efficacy and goal effects revisited. *Journal of Applied Psychology, 88*, 87-99.

Baumeister, R. F., Campbell, J. D., Krueger, J. I., and Vohs, K. D. (2003). Does high self-esteem cause better performance, interpersonal success, happiness, or healthier lifestyles? *Psychological Science in the Public Interest, 4*, 1-44.

Beckmann, J., and Heckhausen, H. (1988). Handlungsbewertung und Aufmerksamskeitsumschaltung. *Jahrbuch 1988 der Max-Plank-Gesselschaft*. Munich, Germany: Vandenhoeck and Rupprecht.

Berglas, S., and Jones, E. E. (1978). Drug choice as a self-handicapping strategy in response to noncontingent success. *Journal of Personality and Social Psychology, 36*, 405-417.

Brehm, J. W. (1956). Post-decision changes in the desirability of choice alternatives. *Journal of Abnormal and Social Psychology, 52*, 384-389.

Brockner, J. (1992). The escalation of commitment to a failing course of action: Toward theoretical progress. *Academy of Management Review, 17*, 39-61.

Butler, R. (1993). Effects of task- and ego-achievement goals on information seeking during task engagement. *Journal of Personality and Social Psychology, 65*, 18-31.

Campbell, W. K., and Sedikides, C. (1999). Self-threat magnifies the self-serving bias: A meta-analytic integration. *Review of General Psychology, 3*, 23-43.

Carver, C. S., and Scheier, M. F. (1999). Themes and issues in the self-regulation of behavior. In R. S. Wyer (Ed.), *Perspectives on behavioral self-regulation* (pp. 1-105). Mahweh, NJ: Lawrence Erlbaum.

Cooper, J., and Fazio, R. H. (1984). A new look at dissonance theory. *Advances in Experimental Social Psychology, 17*, 229-266.

Covington, M. V., and Omelich, C. L. (1979). Effort: The double-edged sword in school achievement. *Journal of Educational Psychology, 71*, 169-182.

Crawford, M. T., and McCrea, S. M. (2004). When mutations meet motivations: Attitude biases in counterfactual thought. *Journal of Experimental Social Psychology, 40*, 65-74.

Crocker, J., and Park, L. E. (2004). The costly pursuit of self-esteem. *Psychological Bulletin, 130*, 392-414.

Dunning, D. (1995). Trait importance and modifiability as factors influencing self-assessment and self-enahcement motives. *Personality and Social Psychology Bulletin, 21*, 1297-1306.

Dweck, C. S., and Leggett, E. L. (1988). A social cognitive approach to motivation and personality. *Psychological Review, 95*, 256-273.

Elliot, A. J. (1999). Approach and avoidance motivation and achievement goals. *Educational Psychologist, 34*, 169-189.

Elliot, A. J., and McGregor, H. A. (2001). A 2 x 2 achievement goal framework. *Journal of Personality and Social Psychology, 80*, 501-519.

Epstude, K., and Roese, N. J. (2008). The functional theory of counterfactual thinking. *Personality and Social Psychology Review, 12*, 168-192.

Festinger, L., and Carlsmith, J. M. (1959). Cognitive consequences of forced compliance. *Journal of Abnormal and Social Psychology, 58*, 203-210.

Galinsky, A. D., and Moskowitz, G. B. (2000). Counterfactuals as behavioral primes: Priming the simulation heuristic and consideration of alternatives. *Journal of Experimental Social Psychology, 36*, 384-409.

Goerke, M., Möller, J., Schulz-Hardt, S., Napiersky, U., and Frey, D. (2004). "It's not my fault - but only I can change it": Counterfactual and prefactual thoughts of managers. *Journal of Applied Psychology, 89*, 279-292.

Gollwitzer, P. M. (1999). Implementation intentions and effective goal pursuit: Strong effects of simple plans. *American Psychologist, 54*, 493-503.

Greenwald, A. G. (1980). The totalitarian ego: Fabrication and revision of personal history. *American Psychologist, 35*, 603-618.

Heckhausen, H. (2003). *Motivation und handeln* (2nd ed.). Berlin: Springer.

Heckhausen, H., and Gollwitzer, P. M. (1987). Thought contents and cognitive functioning in motivational versus volitional states of mind. *Motivation and Emotion, 11*, 101-120.

Henderson, M. D., Gollwitzer, P. M., and Oettingen, G. (2007). Implementation intentions and disengagement from a failing course of action. *Journal of Behavioral Decision Making, 20*, 81-102.

Jones, E. E., and Berglas, S. (1978). Control of attributions about the self through self-handicapping strategies: The appeal of alcohol and the role of underachievement. *Personality and Social Psychology Bulletin, 4*, 200-206.

Kahneman, D., Knetsch, J. L., and Thaler, R. H. (1990). Experimental tests of the endowment effect and the Coase Theorem. *Journal of Political Economy, 98*, 1325-1348.

Kahneman, D., and Miller, D. T. (1986). Norm theory: Comparing reality to its alternatives. *Psychological Review, 93*, 136-153.

Kahneman, D., and Varey, C. A. (1990). Propensities and counterfactuals: The loser that almost won. *Journal of Personality and Social Psychology, 59*, 1101-1110.

Lazarus, R. S., and Folkman, S. (1984). *Stress, appraisal, and coping*. New York: Springer.

Lewin, K. (1951). *Field theory in social science*. New York: Harper.

Lewin, K., Dembo, T., Festinger, L. A., and Sears, P. S. (1944). Level of aspiration. In J. M. Hunt (Ed.), *Personality and the behavior disorders* (pp. 333-378). New York: Ronald Press.

Mandel, D. R., and Lehman, D. R. (1996). Counterfactual thinking and ascriptions of cause and preventability. *Journal of Personality and Social Psychology, 71*, 450-463.

Markman, K. D., Gavanski, I., Sherman, S. J., and McMullen, M. N. (1993). The mental simulation of better and worse possible worlds. *Journal of Experimental Social Psychology, 29*, 87-109.

Markman, K. D., Gavanski, I., Sherman, S. J., and McMullen, M. N. (1995). The impact of perceived control on the imagination of better and worse possible worlds. *Personality and Social Psychology Bulletin, 21*, 588-595.

Markman, K. D., and McMullen, M. N. (2003). A reflection and evaluation model of comparative thinking. *Personality and Social Psychology Review, 7*, 244-267.

Markman, K. D., McMullen, M. N., and Elizaga, R. A. (2008). Counterfactual thinking, persistence, and performance: A test of the Reflection and Evaluation Model. *Journal of Experimental Social Psychology, 44*, 421-428.

Martin, L. L., Ward, D. W., Achee, J. W., and Wyer, R. S. (1993). Mood as input: People have to interpret the motivational implications of their moods. *Journal of Personality and Social Psychology, 64*, 317-326.

McCrea, S. M. (2007). Counterfactual thinking following negative outcomes: Evidence for group and self-protective biases. *European Journal of Social Psychology, 37*, 1256-1271.

McCrea, S. M. (2008). Self-handicapping, excuse-making, and counterfactual thinking: Consequences for self-esteem and future motivation. *Journal of Personality and Social Psychology, 95*, 274-292.

McCrea, S. M., and Hirt, E. R. (2001). The role of ability judgments in self-handicapping. *Personality and Social Psychology Bulletin, 27*, 1378-1389.

McCrea, S. M., and Hirt, E. R. (2011). Limitations on the substitutability of self-protective processes: Self-handicapping is not reduced by related-domain self-affirmations. *Social Psychology, 42*, 9-18.

McCrea, S. M., and Tessa, E. (2011). *Counterfactual controllability and perceptions of goal progress: Corrective action or Coasting?* Unpublished manuscript. Laramie, WY.

McCrea, S. M., and Tyser, M. P. (2011). *Counterfactual thoughts and the escalation of commitment*. Unpublished manuscript. Laramie, WY.

McGuire, W. J., and McGuire, C. V. (1991). The content, structure, and operation of thought systems. In R. S. Wyer and T. K. Srull (Eds.), *The content, structure, and operation of thought systems. Advances in social cognition* (Vol. 4). Hillsdale, NJ: Lawrence Erlbaum Associates.

McMullen, M. N., and Markman, K. D. (2000). Downward counterfactuals and motivation: The wake-up call and the Pangloss effect. *Personality and Social Psychology Bulletin, 26*, 575-584.

McMullen, M. N., and Markman, K. D. (2002). Affective impact of close counterfactuals: Implications of possible futures for possible pasts. *Journal of Experimental Social Psychology, 38*, 64-70.

Nasco, S. A., and Marsh, K. L. (1999). Gaining control through counterfactual thinking. *Personality and Social Psychology Bulletin, 25*, 556-568.

Roese, N. J. (1994). The functional basis of counterfactual thinking. *Journal of Personality and Social Psychology, 66*, 805-818.

Roese, N. J. (1997). Counterfactual thinking. *Psychological Bulletin, 121*, 133-148.

Roese, N. J., and Olson, J. M. (1993a). Self-esteem and counterfactual thinking. *Journal of Personality and Social Psychology, 65*, 199-206.

Roese, N. J., and Olson, J. M. (1993b). The structure of counterfactual thought. *Personality and Social Psychology Bulletin, 19*, 312-319.

Roese, N. J., and Olson, J. M. (1996). Counterfactuals, causal attributions, and the hindsight bias: A conceptual integration. *Journal of Experimental Social Psychology, 32*, 197-227.

Sanna, L. J., Chang, E. C., and Meier, S. (2001). Counterfactual thinking and self-motives. *Personality and Social Psychology Bulletin, 27*, 1023-1034.

Schwarz, N. (1990). Feelings as information: Informational and motivational functions of affective states. In E. T. Higgins and R. M. Sorrentino (Eds.), *Handbook of motivation and cognition: Foundations of social behavior* (Vol. 2, pp. 527-561). New York: Guilford.

Sedikides, C., and Strube, M. J. (1997). Self-evaluation: To thine own self be good, to thine own self be sure, to thine own self be true, and to thy own self be better. In M. P. Zanna (Ed.), *Advances in experimental social psychology* (Vol. 29, pp. 209-269). New York: Academic Press.

Sherman, D. K., and Cohen, G. L. (2006). The psychology of self-defense: Self-affirmation theory. In M. P. Zanna (Ed.), *Advances in experimental social psychology* (Vol. 38, pp. 183-242). San Diego, CA: Elsevier Academic Press.

Sherman, D. K., Nelson, L. D., and Steele, C. M. (2000). Do messages about health risks threaten the self: Increasing the acceptance of threatening health messages via self-affirmation. *Personality and Social Psychology Bulletin, 26*, 1046-1058.

Sherman, S. J., and McConnell, A. R. (1995). Dysfunctional implications of counterfactual thinking: When alternatives to reality fail us. In N. J. Roese and J. M. Olson (Eds.), *What might have been: The social psychology of counterfactual thinking* (pp. 199-231). Hillsdale, NJ, England: Lawrence Erlbaum Associates, Inc.

Siegel, P. A., Scillitoe, J., and Parks-Yancy, R. (2005). Reducing the tendency to self-handicap: The effect of self-affirmation. *Journal of Experimental Social Psychology, 41*, 589-597.

Smallman, R., and Roese, N. J. (2009). Counterfactual thinking facilitates the formation of intentions: Evidence for a content-specific pathway in behavioral regulation. *Journal of Experimental Social Psychology, 45*, 845-852.

Staw, B. M. (1976). Knee-deep in the big muddy: A study of escalating commitment to a chosen course of action. *Organizational Behavior and Human Performance, 16*, 27-44.

Stone, J., Wiegand, A. W., Cooper, J., and Aronson, E. (1997). When exemplification fails: Hypocrisy and the motive for self-integrity. *Journal of Personality and Social Psychology, 72*, 54-65.

Tal-Or, N., Boninger, D. S., and Gleicher, F. (2004). On becoming what we might have been: Counterfactual thinking and self-efficacy. *Self and Identity, 3*, 5-26.

Taylor, S. E., Neter, E., and Wayment, H. A. (1995). Self-evaluation processes. *Personality and Social Psychology Bulletin, 21*, 1278-1287.

Tesser, A., and Cornell, D. P. (1991). On the confluence of self-processes. *Journal of Experimental Social Psychology, 27*, 501-526.

Tetlock, P. E. (1998). Close-call counterfactuals and belief-system defenses: I was not almost wrong but I was almost right. *Journal of Personality and Social Psychology, 75*, 639-652.

Trope, Y. (1986). Self-enhancement and self-assessment in achievement behavior. In R. M. Sorrentino and E. T. Higgins (Eds.), *Handbook of motivation and cognition: Foundations of social behavior* (pp. 350-378). New York: Guilford Press.

Trope, Y., Ferguson, M., and Raghunathan, R. (2001). Mood as a resource in processing self-relevant information. In J. P. Forgas (Ed.), *Handbook of affect and social cognition.* (pp. 256-274). Mahwah, NJ: Lawrence Erlbaum Associates Publishers.

Tyser, M. P., McCrea, S. M., and Knüpfer, K. (2011). *Pursuing perfection or pursuing protection?: Self-evaluation motives moderate the behavioral consequences of counterfactual thoughts.* Manuscript submitted for publication. Laramie, WY.

Vroom, V. H. (1964). *Work and motivation.* New York: Wiley.

Weiner, B. (1985). An attributional theory of achievement motivation and emotion. *Psychological Review, 92*, 548-573.

Wells, G. L., and Gavanski, I. (1989). Mental simulation of causality. *Journal of Personality and Social Psychology, 56*, 161-169.

Zuckerman, M. (1979). Attribution of success and failure revisited: or The motivational bias is alive and well in attribution theory. *Journal of Personality, 47*, 245-287.

In: Handbook on Psychology of Motivation
Editors: J. N. Franco and A. E. Svensgaard

ISBN: 978-1-62100-755-5
© 2012 Nova Science Publishers, Inc.

Chapter 8

A Trans-Contextual Model of Motivation in Physical Education

Vassilis Barkoukis[1] and Martin S. Hagger[2]

[1] Aristotle University of Thessaloniki, Greece
[2] Curtin University, Australia

Abstract

The trans-contextual model of motivation has been developed to describe and explain the motivational processes by which motivation from one context can be transferred to another. The model comprises an integration of self-determination theory, the hierarchical model of intrinsic and extrinsic motivation, and the theory of planned behaviour. This chapter reviews the rationale for integrating these theories into the trans-contextual model and outlines recent developments in research using the model. Empirical data from the application of the trans-contextual model in the context of physical education are presented. These data provide support for the model's assumptions and highlight the efficacy of the model to describe the mechanisms by which support for autonomous motivation and motivational regulations in educational contexts (e.g., physical education) can lead to motivation in other contexts (e.g., leisure time physical activity). Finally, avenues for future research on the conceptual and methodological aspects of the model are outlined.

A Trans-Contextual Model of Motivation in Physical Education

Social environment is an important factor affecting human behaviour. In educational contexts, theory and research has highlighted that an environment fostering autonomous motivation will lead to greater behavioural persistence with key tasks, such as solving challenging problems, and more adaptive outcomes such as better grades (Deci and Ryan, 1985, 2002; Reeve, 2002; Vallerand, 2007). Social environment can be defined as behaviours exhibited by agents and significant others in the social context that provide support for learning. Several theories of motivation in social psychology, such as self-determination theory (Deci and Ryan, 1985), include social environment as a central variable and these theories have been adopted to examine the effects of the social environment on motivation and behaviour in educational contexts (e.g., Deci, Spiegel, Ryan, Koestner, and Kauffman, 1982; Reeve, Bolt, and Cai, 1999; Meece, Blumenfeld, and Hoyle, 1988). The present review aims to provide a thorough description of the tenets of a trans-contextual model of motivation (TCM; Hagger, Chatzisarantis, Culverhouse, and Biddle, 2003), an integrated model investigating the role of the motivational environment in an educational context (e.g., a physical education class) that supports children's motivation on motivation for activities outside the school (e.g., physical activity participation in a leisure-time context). An additional aim of this review is to describe the empirical evidence examining the application of TCM in physical education and discuss future directions based on the development of the model's component theories.

The Trans-Contextual Model of Motivation: Component Theories

The Trans-Contextual Model of motivation (TCM) is a theoretical model of motivation that integrates components of self-determination theory (Deci and Ryan, 1985, 2002), the hierarchical model of intrinsic and extrinsic motivation (Vallerand, 1997, 2007; Vallerand and Ratelle, 2002), and theory of planned behaviour (Ajzen, 1985, 1991, 2002). The basic aim of the model is to describe and explain the mechanisms by which motivational climate in one context (e.g., school physical education lessons) can affect motivation in another different but related context (e.g., out-of-school leisure-time physical activity; Hagger et al., 2003). We will provide a brief description of these approaches highlighting some of their fundamental premises and how they are incorporated into the TCM.

Central to self-determination theory is the distinction between two main forms of motivation; intrinsic and extrinsic motivation. Intrinsic motivation corresponds to engagement in behaviour for the pleasure and satisfaction derived from participation and, most importantly, for no external contingency or reinforcement. Extrinsic motivation reflects behaviours that are driven by external contingencies such as gaining rewards or avoiding punishment (Deci and Ryan, 2002; Vallerand, et al., 1992). Ryan and Connell (1989) contended also that extrinsic motivation encompasses the more specific motives of external, introjected, and identified regulations. External regulation, the prototypical form of extrinsic motivation, corresponds to engagement in an activity to gain rewards or avoid punishment, introjected regulation reflects extrinsically motivated behaviours performed out of feelings of guilt or shame and identified regulation reflects behaviours which are performed out of choice, as individuals acknowledge and value their outcomes. Yet, participation in these behaviours is not motivated by involvement in the behavior for its own sake.

According to self-determination theory, intrinsic motivation and identified regulation constitute autonomous forms of motivation, whereas external and introjected regulations represent controlling forms of motivation (Deci and Ryan, 1985, 2002, 2008). The engagement in an activity due to autonomous motivation is out of the individual's choice as he/she has an inherent interest and/or personally value the activity itself. On the other hand, the engagement in an activity due to controlling motivation is directed by external demands (e.g., gaining contingent outcomes such as rewards, praise, or feedback, or avoiding negative reinforcements such as punishment) and internal pressures (e.g., guilt or shame; Ryan and Deci, 2006). Empirical evidence has shown that autonomous motivation is associated with adaptive responses in terms of activity involvement and persistence, whereas controlling motivation was related to lower levels of satisfaction and enjoyment, and persistence with the activity (Deci and Ryan, 2008).

Fundamental to the theory is the tenet that an environment supporting autonomy will increase autonomous motivation, which in turn, will result to an adaptive pattern of responses (Deci and Ryan, 2002; Reeve, 2002). Social agents can foster an autonomy-supportive environment "by taking their [students] perspective, encouraging initiation, supporting a sense of choice, and being responsive to their thoughts, questions, and initiatives" (Deci and Ryan, 2008, p. 18).

Vallerand (1997) adopted several aspects of the self-determination theory and developed a hierarchical model of intrinsic and extrinsic motivation. This model focuses on different levels of abstraction or generality of the environmental factors from SDT and the effects of these levels on the outcomes of motivated behaviour (Vallerand and Ratelle, 2002). Vallerand (2007) suggested that autonomous and controlling forms of motivation exist at three levels of generality: global, contextual, and situational levels. Motivation at the contextual level is the most important level of motivation in the TCM. It represents motivation in specific contexts, such as the academic, social, and physical contexts. These motives can be influenced by external factors (social and environmental). An important corollary of the model corresponds to the interplay between different contexts (Vallerand and Ratelle, 2002). For example, autonomous motives in an academic context (i.e., physical education) could be transferred to another, alternative context and promote autonomous motives in a social or sport context (i.e., leisure-time physical activity). Consistent with self-determination theory, motives at the contextual level are affected by the social environment at the context level. Autonomy-support by social agents in a specific context is thought to promote autonomous motivation in the respective context, which in turn is considered to have a positive effect on autonomous motivation in a similar and relevant setting (Vallerand, 2007; Vallerand and Ratelle, 2002).

The theory of planned behaviour is an important social-cognitive theory that aims to explain the volitional antecedents of intentional behaviour (Ajzen, 1985). A key concept of the theory is that actions are preceded by effortful thinking and premeditation. A key variable in the theory is behavioural intention, which is conceptualized as the immediate antecedent of behaviour, and reflects a person's commitment and determination to enact this behaviour (Armitage and Conner, 2001; Conner and Armitage, 1998). Intentions are shaped by one's attitudes, subjective norms, and perceived behavioural control. Attitudes represent the combination of outcome expectancies (i.e., a behaviour will lead to specific, desired outcomes) and the valences attached to these outcomes (Ajzen, 2002; Sparks, Shepherd, and Frewer, 1995). Subjective norms reflect perceived social pressures from significant others to perform the behaviour and an individual's motivation to comply with those significant others. Perceived behavioural control (PBC) denotes a person's belief in perceived ability to perform the target behaviour and the importance attached to those ability beliefs (Ajzen, 2002; Sheeran, Trafimow, and Armitage, 2003).

Recently there is increased evidence linking self determination and planned behaviour theories. Deci and Ryan (1985) and Vallerand (1997) argued that self-determination theory can offer explanations for the development of the social cognitive beliefs predicting intentions. Deci and Ryan (1985) outlined that individuals may form beliefs about activities performed out of inherent interest for the activity (e.g., physical activity participation due to the pleasant feelings experienced during exercise) or out of sense of obligation or duty (e.g., physical activity participation due to doctor's prescription due to an illness such as diabetes). According to Fishbein and Ajzen (2010) the variables of the theory of planned behaviour are hypothesised to be the result of beliefs about outcomes and that it is these beliefs that are likely to be influenced by motivation-related variables, such as those described in self-determination theory. They argued that motivation is a predecessor of such social cognitive beliefs leading to intention towards behaviour. Hagger, Chatzisarantis and Harris (2006) indicated that autonomous motivation act as distal predictor of attitudes and PBC, which in turn lead to the formation of intentions towards health-related behaviour. More recently, Hagger and Chatzisarantis' (2009) meta-analysis of 36 integrated studies providing 45 tests of effects between self determination and planned behaviour theories' variables provided support for the theoretical integration of self-determination and planned behaviour theories.

Integration of the Component Theories

There is a growing body of research suggesting that self-determination and planned behaviour theories can be integrated to provide complementary explanations of the processes that underlie motivated behaviour (Standage, Duda, and Ntoumanis, 2003; Wilson and Rodgers, 2004). Hagger and Chatzisarantis (2009) argued that self-determined motivation is linked to the belief systems that underpin attitudes, subjective norms, and PBC from the theory of planned behaviour which, in turn, form behavioural intentions. The hierarchical model serves as a unifying framework providing the basis for the trans-contextual components of the model. Hagger and his associates (Hagger and Chatzisarantis, 2007; Hagger, Chatzisarantis, Barkoukis, Wang, and Baranowski, 2005; Hagger et al., 2003) provided four premises for the integration of these theories: (1) Whether the behaviour is autonomous or controlled as outlined in self determination theory leads to the formation of differential social cognitive judgments in the theory of planned behaviour; (2) The motivational regulations identified in SDT reflect the belief-systems that underpin social cognitive judgement and, thus, act as distal influences on these variables; (3) The motivational regulations at the contextual level affect the theory of planned behaviour's variables which reflect situational-level social cognitive (e.g., attitudes, PBC) and motivational constructs (e.g., intention); and (4) Measures of motivation from self determination theory focus on current contextual reasons whereas the theory of planned behaviour's constructs typically measure anticipated future behavioural expectations.

With respect to the first premise, autonomous motivation acts as the impetus in the formation of judgments and expectations regarding future behavioural engagement (Deci and Ryan, 1985, 2002). Deci and Ryan (1985) argued that social-cognitive theories, such as the theory of planned behaviour, identify the immediate psychological antecedents of behaviour, but neglect the origins of such antecedents, while Ajzen (1991) and Fishbein and Ajzen (2010) complemented this premise in stating that the formation of the constructs from the theory of planned behaviour is based on dispositional constructs like personality as well as beliefs regarding the behaviour.

Regarding the second premise for integration, the theory of planned behaviour does not explicitly specify the autonomous and controlled reasons for which each behaviour is pursued

(Deci and Ryan, 1985). Individuals might harbor beliefs that a certain behaviour is performed for either autonomous or controlled reasons (McLachlan and Hagger, 2010). Hence, self determination theory offers an interpretation of these beliefs. In addition, Fishbein and Ajzen (2010) proposed that the theory of planned behaviour constructs will mediate the effects of motivation-related variables on intentions and behaviour. Hagger and Chatzisarantis' (2009) meta-analysis confirmed the proposed link between self determination and planned behaviour theories.

In the third premise for integration, Vallerand (2007) proposed the cross-contextual interplay between motivation at the contextual level suggesting the possibility of transferring motivation from one context (i.e., physical education) to another (i.e., leisure-time). In addition, an important corollary of Vallerand's (1997, 2007) model corresponds to the top-down effect between different levels of generality. Autonomous motivation reflects motivation at the contextual level, whereas the theory of planned behaviour constructs are more akin to the situational level in Vallerand's model (Hagger and Chatzisarantis, in press).

The fourth premise for integration refers to the measurement of the TCM constructs. Autonomous motivation is typically measured as an individual's cited reasons for acting in the relevant context. On the other hand, measures of the theory of planned behaviour constructs reflect expectations for acting in the future. The constructs, therefore, differ in terms of their focus (current contextual reasons vs. anticipated future engagement) and that is why it is thought that they offer complimentary explanations of the processes that lead to intentional behaviour (see Hagger and Chatzisarantis, in press for a more thorough description of the premises of integration).

Overall, each of these theories contributes to the formation of the TCM (Hagger, 2009). Self-determination theory (Deci and Ryan, 1985) offers information on the effect of social environment (i.e., motivational climate) on motivational tendencies in specific contexts. Vallerand's (1997, 2007) hierarchical model contributed the interaction of contextual motives between different contexts. The theory of planned behaviour (Ajzen, 1985) provided the decision making process through which individual plans lead to actual behaviour.

Research Evidence in Physical Education

Empirical tests of the model. With regard to the context of school physical education, the TCM proposes that autonomy support in an educational context like physical education will lead to autonomous motivation within this context, which, in turn, will be transferred into autonomous motivation toward activities in other contexts related to the educational context (e.g., physical activity in a leisure-time context). Furthermore, perceptions of autonomous motivation toward activities in leisure-time affect behaviour in this context through the influence of the constructs from the theory of planned behaviour. So far there is substantial research evidence to support these premises in physical education contexts. In the article introducing the TCM, Hagger et al. (2003) investigated the core TCM hypotheses; a) perceived autonomy support from physical education teachers will have a significant effect on physical education students' autonomous motivation in a physical education context b) autonomous motivation toward leisure-time physical activity will be determined by autonomous motivation in physical education, c) perceived autonomy support from physical education teachers will have a significant indirect effect on autonomous motivation for leisure-time physical activity, mediated by physical education autonomous motivation, d) leisure-time physical activity autonomous motivation will have a significant indirect effect on intentions to engage in physical activity in the future, mediated by attitudes and PBC, e) intentions will be the only direct predictor of leisure-time physical activity behaviour and will mediate the effects of attitudes, subjective norms and PBC on behaviour, f) the effects in the model will be independent of the effects of past physical activity behaviour.

A typical three-wave prospective design was introduced to test the model. In wave one measures of autonomy support and physical education autonomous motivation were taken, in wave two measures of leisure-time physical activity autonomous motivation and variables from the theory of planned behaviour were taken, and in wave three self-reports of physical activity behaviour were taken. The results of the study supported all the hypotheses of the model indicating that autonomy support in physical education had a positive and direct effect on autonomous motivational regulations, namely, intrinsic and identified motivational regulations in physical education. In addition the motivational regulations in physical education positively influenced the respective motivational regulations from self-determination theory in the leisure-time physical activity context. Intrinsic motivation in physical education was found to have a significant and positive effect on identified regulation in the leisure-time physical activity context. The next set of analyses demonstrated that intrinsic motivation in the leisure-time physical activity context had a positive effect on attitudes and perceived behavioural control, while identified regulation was a positive predictor of attitudes. Finally, in accordance with the model's hypotheses, attitudes and perceived behavioural control completely mediated the effect of intrinsic motivation and identified regulation on intention. This study integrated contemporary theoretical approaches and prior empirical evidence and offered a mechanism to describe and explain the process by which social agents in school physical education can contribute to the development of leisure-time physical activity behaviour.

Shen, McCaughtry and Martin (2007) also examined the possible integration of self determination theory and the theory of planned behaviour by testing the effect of autonomy support in school physical education on leisure-time physical activity behaviour and whether this effect was mediated by the variables of the theory of planned behaviour in a sample of African-American students. The study's findings offered further evidence for the theoretical integration proliferated by the TCM as the theory of planned behaviour's variables mediated the effect of autonomy support on leisure-time physical activity. Furthermore, Shen, McCaughtry and Martin (2008) replicated the research design and hypotheses and tested for gender invariance. The results of the analyses indicated that, although gender-specific characteristics influence the effect of school physical education on leisure-time physical activity, gender did not moderate the overall contribution of the TCM for the prediction of intentions and actual physical activity participation.

Cross-cultural invariance of the model. Given the converging evidence that supports the universality of the hypotheses of self-determination theory across cultures (Deci and Ryan, 2002; Sheldon, Elliot, Kim, and Kasser, 2001), Hagger, et al. (2005) investigated the cross-cultural invariance of the TCM in four nations: Great Britain, Greece, Poland and Singapore. Although some idiosyncratic differences emerged among the countries, the findings generally supported the hypothesized pattern of effects proposed in the TCM and confirmed the replicability and cross-cultural invariance of model in four nations with different cultural backgrounds. More specifically, besides Poland, autonomy support in physical education enhanced the students' motives for an out-of-school activity. Importantly, these findings imply that the motivational process leading from participation in the physical education context to participation in the leisure-time context is similar in both individualistic and collectivistic countries.

Hagger et al. (2009) extended the study of the cross-cultural invariance and replicability of the TCM by including three other nations with collectivistic cultural norms. In this study, perceptions of students from Finland, Estonia and Hungary were compared to those of British students to test the replicability of the TCM. Overall, the results of this study indicated that the pattern of effects was consistent across samples from collectivistic cultural norms and the British one. Similar to the Hagger et al. (2005) study there were some minor culture-specific variations in relationships that were relatively few compared to the overall pattern of effects. The most important hypotheses of the model, i.e. the effects of a) physical education teachers' autonomy support on autonomous motivation in physical education, b) physical education autonomous motivation on leisure-time physical activity autonomous motivation, c) leisure-time physical activity autonomous motivation on attitudes and d) intention on behaviour, were significant across all samples. These findings corroborate the motivational sequence proposed in the TCM and suggest that this sequence is universal across nations with different cultural backgrounds.

In this vein, Barkoukis and Hagger (2009) further investigated the TCM hypotheses in the Greek culture. Results lend further support to the hypothesized motivational sequence. Autonomy support in physical education influenced autonomous motivational regulations in a leisure time context. In addition, they affected intentions, through the mediating effect of attitudes and perceived behavioural control. Finally, intentions predicted leisure-time physical activity behaviour and mediated the effect of attitudes and perceived behavioural control. Only two of the model's hypotheses were not supported; the effect of autonomous motivational regulations in physical education on the respective regulations in leisure-time and the effect of subjective norms on intention. Overall, the model explained a substantial proportion of the variance in leisure-time physical activity behaviour and the proposed motivational sequence was generally supported, thus providing evidence for the cross-cultural replicability of the model.

Extensions of the model. Following the investigation of the main hypotheses of the model, Hagger and his associates expanded several aspects of the model. A key hypothesis of the model was that students' perceptions of autonomy support in an educational context (e.g., physical education) will influence autonomous motivational regulations in that context. However, as Hagger and Chatzisarantis (2007) pointed out, prior research with the TCM did not take into account the effect of other sources of autonomy support. Obviously, autonomy support from physical education teachers is not the sole source of autonomy support for adolescents, especially regarding the development of leisure-time physical activity-related variables such as motives, attitudes and intentions. Baker, Little, and Brownell (2003) proposed that autonomy support from peers and parents might have a proportionally greater influence on young people's perceptions and decisions regarding leisure-time physical activity compared to physical education teachers', whose influence occurs in a different, more distal, context. Towards this end, Hagger et al. (2009) investigated the effect of parents' and peers' autonomy support on leisure time autonomous motivation, complementary to that of physical education teachers. They assumed that if the effect of physical education teachers' autonomy support on leisure-time physical activity autonomous motivation remained after the inclusion of autonomy support from other sources, this would further support the hypothesis of the TCM that autonomy support in physical education will have a unique effect on motivation for leisure-time physical activity behaviour. Results indicated a strong indirect effect of autonomy support in physical education on autonomous motivation in a leisure-time physical activity context. The latter was influenced by autonomy support from parents and peers but these effects were weak. Importantly, the indirect effect of physical education teachers' autonomy support on autonomous motivation in a leisure-time physical activity context was independent of the effect of autonomy support from peers and parents. These findings provided further support to the motivational sequence proposed in TCM and highlighted the important role of motivation in school physical education in the development of leisure-time physical activity behaviour.

Another study by Barkoukis, Hagger, Lambropoulos, and Tsorbatzoudis (2010) investigated the role of psychological need satisfaction within the TCM premises. The effect of role of psychological needs in the development of autonomous motivational regulations was implied in the original formulation of the TCM but not formally stated or tested empirically (Hagger et al., 2003). Barkoukis et al. assumed, based on self determination theory, that need satisfaction would mediate the effect of autonomy support on physical education autonomous motivational regulations. In addition they hypothesized that need satisfaction in physical education would have both direct and indirect effects on the leisure-time physical activity autonomous motivational regulations. The results of the study partially confirmed these hypotheses. Competence and autonomy need satisfaction mediated the effect of autonomy support on physical education autonomous motivational regulations. In addition competence need satisfaction showed a direct effect on leisure-time physical activity autonomous motivational regulations and an indirect one, through the effect of physical education autonomous motivation. These findings demonstrated some unique mechanisms in the model concerning the role of psychological need satisfaction.

In a similar vein, Pihu, Hein, Koka, and Hagger (2008) investigated the effect of specific components of physical education teachers' autonomy support (i.e., perceptions of use of learning strategies and positive general feedback) on physical education and leisure-time physical activity autonomous motivation. Koka and Hein (2005) indicated that students' perceptions of teachers' positive general feedback is positively associated with physical education autonomous motivation. In addition, Hein and Muur (2004) suggested that the use of learning strategies was among the most important mediators of the relationship between motivational climate and leisure-time physical activity intentions. Based on this evidence, Pihu et al. (2008) argued that students using learning strategies and receiving more positive general feedback are likely to feel more autonomous in their actions. Thus, they assumed that these constructs could influence PE autonomous motivation and possibly affect autonomous motivation in a leisure-time physical activity context. Results supported the hypothesis that use of learning strategies and positive general feedback were significant predictors of physical education autonomous motivation. In addition, a significant indirect effect of learning strategies and positive general feedback on autonomous motivation in a leisure-time physical activity context was found. Physical education autonomous motivation fully mediated the effect of use of learning strategies and positive general feedback on autonomous motivation in a leisure-time physical activity context. Importantly, the model with the specific components of autonomy support explained a greater amount of variance in leisure-time physical activity behaviour compared to the models where the autonomy support was not differentiated (Hagger et al., 2003; Hagger et al., 2005). These findings imply that a more detailed investigation of teacher-initiated motivational climate in the future could provide a more comprehensive understanding of how school physical education can lead to increased leisure-time physical activity behaviour.

Overall, prior research has generally supported the hypotheses of TCM in physical education and leisure-time physical activity contexts. Autonomy support in a physical education context has consistently been found to be a significant predictor of autonomous motivation in PE which in turn influences the formation of autonomous motivation in a leisure-time physical activity context (Hagger and Chatzisarantis, 2007). The latter had a significant effect on behavioural intention and physical activity behaviour through the variables of the theory of planned behaviour (i.e., attitudes and PBC) (Barkoukis and Hagger, 2009; Hagger and Chatzisarantis, 2007; Hagger et al., 2003; Hagger et al., 2005; Shen, et al., 2007, 2008).

Practical Implications of the Model

The support of the model's premises has offered some important practical implications for physical education teachers and policy-makers. First, physical education teachers would benefit from the adoption of autonomy-supportive behaviours (Barkoukis and Hagger 2009; Barkoukis et al., 2010). Such behaviours include the use of questioning and skill-based approaches to learning new tasks, the provision of several activities and opportunities for students to choose among them, the provision of a clear rationale for the activities included in the lesson, acknowledging conflict in decision-making regarding doing physical tasks, providing informational feedback, encouraging exploratory behaviour, and empowering students in lessons and fostering goal setting with an emphasis on personally-relevant goals (Reeve, 2002; Reeve and Jang, 2006). In addition, students should be encouraged to participate in decision making during the lessons. For instance, they should be allowed to select their own teammates, the location and order of tasks, the starting time of the task, the pace and rhythm of the task, the stopping time of the task, and the interval between tasks (Barkoukis, Tsorbatzoudis and Grouios, 2008).

Second, Pihu et al. (2008) suggested that providing positive general feedback to students during physical education lessons and teaching them how to use learning strategies was among the most important autonomy-supportive techniques that should be provided by teachers for their students. Both behaviours influenced significantly autonomous motivation in physical education and leisure-time physical activity contexts. Hence, physical education teachers should adopt them in order to foster leisure-time physical activity behaviour. They further suggested that some autonomy-supportive behaviours, such as positive feedback, might be more effective compared to others in facilitating students' motivation in both physical education and leisure time and enhance leisure-time physical activity. Perhaps different autonomy-supportive behaviours are effective for different students in terms of cultural, educational and socioeconomic level and personality. Clearly, teachers should employ a wide range of autonomy-supportive behaviours to capture a wide range of students and identify the most effective ones for their students.

Third, as Hagger et al. (2009) pointed out, parents have a significant influence on young people's intentions to engage in leisure-time physical activity behaviours. Parents could, therefore, assist in the development of positive attitudes and intentions towards such behaviours. Autonomy-supportive styles to promote children's leisure-time physical activity behaviour would be more appropriate in order to foster their intentions to engage in future physical activity. Clearly, a joint effect of an autonomy-supportive environment in school and family would have the strongest effect on the development of intentions towards leisure-time physical activity.

Theoretical Developments and Future Directions

Thus far we have outlined the theoretical bases of the TCM, the premises for integrating these theoretical approaches and the studies testing the TCM premises in physical education and leisure-time physical activity contexts. There is a growing empirical support for the TCM and the premise that autonomous motivation in one context can form motivation in another one (Hagger and Chatzisarantis, 2007). Hagger and Chatzisarantis (2011) commented on two possible venues of future research with the TCM: a) testing the premises of the model using experimental and intervention designs, and b) applying the model in more diverse educational contexts. In this review we will focus on extending the TCM by including aspects and recent developments of the theories formatting TCM and discuss why they are important to further understanding of the trans-contextual motivational process.

Social environment. To date, social environment has been investigated through the lens of self determination theory and included a unidimensional measurement of autonomy support. Recent extensions in the TCM indicated that the study of more specific components of autonomy support (Pihu et al., 2008) would offer a more comprehensive view on the role of the social environment. The measurement of specific components of the class social environment could target specific aspects of the contextual motivation to a greater extent compared to a global measure of autonomy support. Thus, they might help in increasing the predictive ability of the model.

Furthermore, different instructional styles in physical education might differentially affect the formation of physical education autonomous motivation. Reeve and Jang (2006) found eight instructional styles to provide autonomy support to students, while other six thwarted it. The investigation of how each instructional style influences physical education autonomous motivation and, either directly or indirectly, autonomous motivation in a leisure-time physical activity context would provide useful information on the most effective way to promote physical education and autonomous motivation in a leisure-time physical activity context and, subsequently, leisure-time physical activity behaviour.

Besides self determination theory, achievement goal theory (Ames 1992; Nicholls, 1989) has offered a comprehensive framework to study the effect of social environment in educational contexts such as the classroom (i.e., motivational climate) on motivation and motivational-related variables. According to achievement goal theory there are two main perceptions of social environment, mastery- and performance-oriented environments. Mastery-oriented individuals focus on personal improvement and mastery of tasks and define success based on self-referenced criteria, whereas performance-oriented individuals define success using normative criteria or through comparison with others (Ames, 1992). Mastery-oriented motivational climate is associated with a more adaptive pattern of motivational, cognitive, affective and behavioural responses in physical education compared to performance-oriented climate (Ntoumanis and Biddle, 1999). Recent research in physical education has suggested that the integration of these approaches in the investigation of perceptions of motivational climate would provide a more thorough understanding on the role of social environment (Liukkonen, Barkoukis, Watt and Jaakkola, 2010; Ntoumanis, 2001; Ommundsen and Kvalø, 2007). Indeed, preliminary research towards this end indicated that mastery-oriented climate was a significant predictor of both physical education and leisure-time physical activity autonomous motivation and mediated the effect of autonomy support on physical education autonomous motivation, while performance-oriented climate showed no significant effect on physical education and leisure-time physical activity autonomous motivation (Barkoukis and Hagger, in press).

Psychological need satisfaction. Another important avenue for future research involves the study of psychological need satisfaction within the TCM. Barkoukis et al. (2010) provided some preliminary evidence in support of the role of psychological need satisfaction as a mediator of the effect of autonomy support on motivation in physical education and leisure-time physical activity contexts. Psychological need satisfaction showed a direct effect on physical education and leisure-time physical activity autonomous motivation and mediated the effect of autonomy support on physical education autonomous motivation. Hence, the investigation of the mediating role of basic psychological need satisfaction to all these motivational climate dimensions could provide further information on the process by which physical education teachers contribute to the development of physical education and leisure-time physical activity autonomous motivation.

Furthermore, besides the mediating effect on the motivational climate-autonomous motivation relationship in physical education, psychological need satisfaction could provide an important process in the model. Harris and Hagger (2007) suggested that psychological need satisfaction moderated the effects of subjective norms on intention. Individuals with high psychological need satisfaction at the global level form their intentions based on subjective norms to a greater extent compared to those with lower psychological need satisfaction. These findings imply that psychological need satisfaction can have a strong effect to variables in other and distal levels and contexts. Therefore, it seems that psychological need satisfaction could play an important role in several steps of the motivational process described by TCM and they should further be examined in relation to the different contexts included in the model and their interplay.

Trans-contextual effect. A central premise of the TCM is the trans-contextual effect of motivation, i.e., the effect of motivation at one context on the respective form of motivation in a different but related context. This proposition was based on the notion that each context represents schemas in which the relevant motivational representation and information are stored. This representation and information is then transferred to the motivation of the other related context. An important venue for future research would involve the investigation of how these schemas are developed. A sound hypothesis would be that the positive affective consequences of motivation in one context could result in the formation of these schemas. For instance, prior research evidence indicated that autonomously motivated students experience higher levels of interest, enjoyment, positive affect, and lower levels of anxiety during physical education classes (Liukkonen, et al., 2010; Mouratidis, Vansteenkiste, Sideridis and Lens, 2011; Standage, Duda and Ntoumanis, 2005). It is possible that these positive affective experiences lead to the development of a positive schema for physical activity behaviours, including physical education, organized competitive sports and recreational physical activity participation, which help to the transfer of motivation from one context to another.

In a similar vein, cognitive parameters of the participation in physical education lessons could influence the effect on autonomous motivation in a physical education context on autonomous motivation in a leisure-time physical activity context. Efklides (2011) and Volet, Vauras, and Salonen (2009) argued that motivation and affect interact with meta-cognitive skills. Motivational-related variables are thought to be antecedents of self-regulated learning, because exercising control requires cognitive effort, which, in turn, draws on motivation resources. Prior research has indicated that students experiencing adaptive motivational states displayed higher levels of self-regulation (Ommundsen, 2003). If this is the case, self-regulation might consist of an important mechanism explaining the transfer of motivation from one context to another relevant one.

Decision making process. There is substantial evidence in the TCM tradition that the effect of autonomous motivation in a leisure-time physical activity context on intentions and actual leisure-time physical activity behaviour was mediated by the theory of planned behaviour variables, mainly attitudes and perceived behavioural control (Barkoukis and Hagger, 2009; Hagger et al., 2003; Hagger et al., 2005). The results pertaining to subjective norms were not consistent. Yet, the need to encounter the effect of social norms and normative beliefs is still apparent (Hagger et al., 2009). Recent developments in the theory of planned behaviour have indicated that the addition of nornative beliefs (i.e., individual's beliefs about what is actually happening; Cialdini, Reno, & Kallgren, 1990). Lazuras, Barkoukis, Rodafinos and Tsorbarzoudis (2010) investigated among others the effect of normative beliefs on intentions to use prohibited substances in sport and reported that they were important determinants of doping-related cognitions. Similarly, there is evidence that perceived behavioural control is an important mediator of the leisure-time physical activity autonomous motivation - intentions relationship (Hagger & Chatzisarantis, 2009). Yet, PBC is thought to be multidimensional, incorporating both internal control (e.g., a person's abilities and skills to perform the target behaviour), as well as external control mechanisms (e.g., efficacy to resist social pressures to act in a certain way, or efficacy to perform the behaviour when given the opportunity) (Armitage and Conner, 2001). External control mechanisms are usually assessed through situational temptation, i.e., people's eagerness to endorse behaviours under specific circumstances (e.g., coercion, internal pressures; Maddock, Laforge, and Rossi, 2000; Plummer et al., 2001). Lazuras et al. (2010) found situational temptation to be an important determinant of intentions to use doping in the future. These constructs have not yet been tested in leisure-time behaviour. Their inclusion to the TCM could potentially improve the predictive ability of the model and offer a new mechanism describing the role of normative beliefs in the autonomous motivation-intentions relationship.

Criticisms of the Model

There are numerous criticisms of the TCM. A prominent criticism is that the factors encompassed by the situational decision-making components of the variables from the theory of planned behaviour are already encompassed by self determination theory, particularly in Deci and Ryan's (1985) proposal that autonomous and controlling forms of motivation provide the impetus for the origins of social cognitive constructs in many theories and models. The satisfaction of basic psychological needs for autonomy and competence, in particular, are likely to be involved in the formation of autonomous and control-related perceptions regarding future behavioural engagement as well as intentions to perform need-satisfying behaviour in future. This claim is accurate and the TCM is explicit in using this as a basis for integration. However, it must be stressed that Deci and Ryan's claims linking the social cognitive factors that affect behaviours in cognitive theories like the theory of planned behaviour with the motivational components from self determination theory have, until the advent of the TCM, been untested. Therefore, the TCM provides confirmatory support for the premises of self determination theory and also demonstrates how the TCM can add to knowledge on the origins of the social cognitive constructs in the theory of planned behaviour.

A further criticism of the TCM is that the links between the motivational components from self determination theory (e.g., motivational regulations in leisure time) and the theory of planned behaviour's constructs are not explicitly articulated and that it is not made explicit exactly why, for example, autonomous motives should have a significant and positively-valenced effect on attitudes. In our promulgation of the theory, we have been clear on this matter. We have indicated that the link between autonomous motivation and attitudes, for example, reflects the extent to which beliefs about engaging in the behaviour in the future are congruent with autonomous motivational regulations and reflect a desire to pursue behaviours that are consistent with psychological needs. The mechanism for this, as proposed in a recent paper (Hagger and Chatzisarantis, 2009), was through the effect of the autonomous motives on the belief systems underpinning the direct measures of attitude (and the other directly-measured constructs – subjective norms and PBC) in the theory of planned behaviour. However, until recently, this was theorized but not tested empirically. A recent study demonstrated that people clearly make the distinction between autonomous and controlled beliefs (McLachlan and Hagger, 2011). We demonstrated that people are clearly able to distinguish between beliefs about future behaviour that are autonomous and those that are controlling in nature. We have also demonstrated that the pursuit of outcomes, which is an important component of attitudes, that are appearance-related versus those that are consistent with more personal goals is significantly related to global measures of autonomous motivation (McLachlan and Hagger, 2010). These findings provide the basis for the link between global autonomous motivation and the directly-measured belief-based constructs from the theory of planned behaviour within the TCM.

EPILOGUE

There is a trend in national physical education curricula to promote students' out of school participation in physical activities (Klein and Hardman, 2007). School can be an agency that can convey health-related messages, such as physical activity participation, to adolescents. Towards this end, the TCM is an interesting theoretical approach aiming to explain and describe the mechanism through which teacher behaviour in physical education lessons influences out of school physical activity participation. Importantly, the premises of the TCM in the physical education setting have been supported in several studies and have been found to be invariant across different cultures. Hence, it seems that the proposed sequence adequately describes the link between physical education lessons and leisure-time physical activity.

The appeal of the TCM in understanding the school physical education-leisure time physical activity relationship and in offering information for curriculum development provided the basis for this review. The present review extends that of Hagger and Chatzisarantis (2007) by incorporating the most recent research evidence examining TCM in the context of physical education. Also, in contrast to Hagger and Chatzisarantis' (2011) review that aimed to describe the application of TCM in general educational contexts, the present review focused only on the application of the model in context of physical education. Further, the theoretical developments and future directions discussed in the present review are focused on the physical education context aiming to promote research in this setting and offer information that might be used in future curriculum development in this context.

REFERENCES

Ajzen, I. (1985). From intentions to actions: A theory of planned behavior. In J. Kuhl and J. Beckmann (Eds.), *Action-control: From cognition to behavior* (pp. 11-39). Heidelberg: Springer.

Ajzen, I. (1991). The theory of planned behaviour. *Organizational Behaviour and Human Decision Processes, 50,* 179-211.

Ajzen, I. (2002). Residual effects of past on later behaviour: Habituation and reasoned action perspectives. *Personality and Social Psychology Review, 6,* 107-122.

Ames, C. (1992). The relationship of achievement goals to student motivation in classroom settings. In G. Roberts (Ed.) *Motivation in sport and exercise* (pp. 161-176). Champaign, IL: Human Kinetics.

Armitage, C. J., and Conner, M. (2001). Efficacy of the theory of planned behaviour: A meta-analytic review. *British Journal of Social Psychology, 40,* 471-499.

Baker, C. W., Little, T. D., and Brownell, K. D. (2003). Predicting adolescent eating and activity behaviors: The role of social norms and personal agency. *Health Psychology, 22,* 189–198.

Barkoukis, V., and Hagger, M. S. (in press). The trans-contextual model: Perceived learning and performance motivational climates as analogues of perceived autonomy support. *European Journal of Psychology of Education.*

Barkoukis V. and Hagger, M. S. (2009). A test of the trans-contextual model of motivation in Greek high school pupils. *Journal of Sport Behavior, 32,* 1-23.

Barkoukis, V., Hagger, M. S., Lambropoulos, G., Tsorbatzoudis, H. (2010). Extending the trans-contextual model in physical education and leisure-time contexts: Examining the role of basic psychological need satisfaction. *British Journal of Educational Psychology, 80,* 647-670.

Barkoukis, V., Tsorbatzoudis, H., and Grouios, G. (2008). Manipulation of motivational climate in physical education: Effects of a 7-month intervention. *European Physical Education Review, 14,* 376-387.

Cialdini, R. B., Reno, R. R., and Kallgren, C. A. (1990). A focus theory of normative conduct: Recycling the concept of norms to reduce littering in public places. *Journal of Personality and Social Psychology, 58,* 1015-1026.

Conner, M., and Armitage, C. A. (1998). Extending the theory of planned behavior: A review and avenues for further research. *Journal of Applied Social Psychology, 28,* 1429-1464.

Deci, E. L., and Ryan, R. M. (1985). *Intrinsic motivation and self-determination in human behavior.* Plenum Press. New York.

Deci, E. L., and Ryan, R. M. (2002). *Handbook of self-determination research.* Rochester, NY: University of Rochester Press.

Deci, E. L., and Ryan, R. M. (2008). Facilitating optimal motivation and psychological well-being across life's domains. *Canadian Psychology, 49,* 14-23.

Deci, E. L., Spiegel, N. H., Ryan, R. M., Koestner, R., and Kauffman, M. (1982). The effects of performance standards on teaching styles: The behavior of controlling teachers. *Journal of Educational Psychology, 74,* 852-859.

Efklides, A. (2011). Interactions of metacognition with motivation and affect in self-regulated learning: The MASRL model. *Educational Psychologist, 46,* 1, 6-25.

Hagger, M. S. (2009). Theoretical integration in health psychology: Unifying ideas and complimentary explanations. *British Journal of Health Psychology, 14,* 189-194.

Hagger, M.S., and Chatzisarantis, N.L.D. (2007). The trans-contextual model of motivation. In M.S. Hagger and N.L.D. Chatzisarantis (Eds.), *Intrinsic Motivation and Self-determination in Exercise and Sport,* (pp. 53-70). Champaign, IL: Human Kinetics.

Hagger, M. S., and Chatzisarantis, N. L. D. (2009). Integrating the theory of planned behaviour and self-determination theory in health behaviour: A meta-analysis. *British Journal of Health Psychology, 14,* 275-302.

Hagger, M. S., & Chatzisarantis, N. L. D. (2011). Transferring motivation from educational to extramural contexts: A review of the trans-contextual model. *European Journal of Psychology of Motivation.* Advance online publication. doi: 10.1007/s10212-011-0082-5

Hagger, M. S., Chatzisarantis, N. L. D., Barkoukis, V., Wang, C. K. J., and Baranowski, J. (2005). Perceived autonomy support in physical education and leisure-time physical activity: A cross-cultural evaluation of the trans-contextual model. *Journal of Educational Psychology, 97,* 376-390.

Hagger, M. S., Chatzisarantis, N. L. D., Culverhouse, T., and Biddle, S. J. H. (2003). The processes by which perceived autonomy support in physical education promotes leisure-time physical activity intentions and behavior: A trans-contextual model. *Journal of Educational Psychology, 95,* 784–795.

Hagger, M. S. and Chatzisarantis, N. L. D. (in press). Transferring motivation across educational contexts: The trans-contextual model of motivation. *European Journal of Psychology of Education.*

Hagger, M. S., Chatzisarantis, N. L. D., and Harris, J. (2006). The process by which relative autonomous motivation affects intentional behavior: Comparing effects across dieting and exercise behaviors. *Motivation and Emotion, 30,* 306-320.

Hagger, M. S., Chatzisarantis, N. L. D., Hein, V., Pihu, M., Soós, I., Karsai, I., Lintunen, T., and Leemans, S. (2009). Teacher, peer, and parent autonomy support in physical education and leisure-time physical activity: A trans-contextual model of motivation in four nations. *Psychology and Health, 24,* 689-711.

Harris, J., and Hagger, M. S. (2007). Do basic psychological needs moderate relationships within the theory of planned behavior? *Journal of Applied Biobehavioral Research, 12,* 43-64.

Hein, V., and Muur, M. (2004). The mediating role of cognitive variables between learning oriented climate and physical activity intention. *International Journal of Sport Psychology, 35,* 60 - 76.

Fishbein, M. and Ajzen, I. (2010). *Predicting and changing behaviour: The reasoned action approach.* New York, NY: Psychology Press.

Klein G., and Hardman, K. (2007). *Physical Education and Sport Education in the European Union.* Paris: Editions Revue EP.S.

Koka, A., and Hein, V. (2005). The effect of perceived teacher feedback on intrinsic motivation in physical education. *International Journal of Sport Psychology, 36,* 91-106.

Lazuras, L., Barkoukis, V., Rodafinos, A., and Tsorbatzoudis, H. (2010). Predictors of doping intentions in elite level athletes: A social cognition approach. *Journal of Sport and Exercise Psychology, 32,* 694-710.

Liukkonen, J., Barkoukis, V., Watt, A., and Jaakola, T. (2010). The relationship between motivational climate and students' emotional experiences and effort in school physical education. *Journal of Educational Research, 103,* 1-14.

Maddock, J. E., Laforge, R. G. and Rossi, J. S. (2000). Short form of a Situational Temptation Scale for heavy episodic drinking. *Journal of Substance Abuse, 11,* 281-288.

McLachlan, S., and Hagger, M. S. (2010). Associations between motivational orientations and chronically accessible outcomes in leisure-time physical activity: Are appearance-related outcomes controlling in nature? *Research Quarterly for Exercise and Sport, 81,* 102-107.

McLachlan, S., and Hagger, M. S. (2011). The influence of chronically accessible autonomous and controlling motives on physical activity within an extended theory of planned behavior. *Journal of Applied Social Psychology, 41*(2), 445-470.

Meece, J., Blumenfeld, P. C., and Hoyle, R. (1988). Students' goal orientations and cognitive engagement in classroom activities. *Journal of Educational Psychology, 80,* 514-523.

Mouratidis, A. A., Vansteenkiste, M., Lens, W. and Sideridis, G. (2011). Vitality and interest–enjoyment as a function of class-to-class variation in need-supportive teaching and pupils' autonomous motivation. Journal of Educational Psychology, 103, 353-366.

Nicholls, J. (1989). *The competitive ethos and democratic education.* London: Harvard University Press.

Ntoumanis, N. (2001). A self-determination approach to the understanding of motivation in physical education. *British Journal of Educational Psychology, 71,* 225–242.

Ntoumanis, N., and Biddle, S.J.H. (1999). A review of motivational climate in physical activity. *Journal of Sport Sciences, 17,* 643-665.

Ommundsen, Y. (2003). Implicit theories of ability and self-regulation strategies in physical education classes. *Educational Psychology, 23,* 141-157.

Ommundsen, Y., and Kvalø, S. (2007). Autonomy-mastery, supportive or performance focused? Different teacher behaviours and pupils' outcomes in physical education. *Scandinavian Journal of Educational Research, 51,* 385-413.

Pihu, M., Hein, V., Koka, A., and Hagger, M. S. (2008). How students' perceptions of teachers' autonomy-supportive behaviours affect physical activity behaviour: An application of trans-contextual model. *European Journal of Sport Science, 8,* 193-204.

Plummer, B. A., Velicer, W. F., Redding, C. A., Prochaska, J. O., Rossi, J. S., Pallonen, U. E., and Meier, K. (2001). Stage of change, decisional balance, and temptations for smoking: measurement and validation in a large, school-based population of adolescents. *Addictive Behaviors, 26*, 551-571.

Reeve, J. (2002). Self-determination theory applied to educational setting. In E.L. Deci, and R.M. Ryan (Eds.), *Handbook of self-determination research* (pp. 183-203). Rochester, New York: University of Rochester Press.

Reeve, J., Bolt, E., and Cai, Y. (1999). Autonomy-supportive teachers: How they teach and motivate students. *Journal of Educational Psychology, 91*, 537–548.

Reeve, J., and Jang, H. (2006). What teachers say and do to support students' autonomy during a learning activity. *Journal of Educational Psychology, 98*, 209-218.

Ryan, R. M., and Connell, J. P. (1989). Perceived locus of causality and internalization: Examining reasons for acting in two domains. *Journal of Personality and Social Psychology, 57*, 749–761.

Ryan, R. M., and Deci, E. L. (2006). Self-regulation and the problem of human autonomy: Does psychology need choice, self-determiniation, and will? *Journal of Personality, 74*, 1557-1586.

Sheeran, P., Trafimow, D., and Armitage, C. J. (2003). Predicting behaviour from perceived behavioural control: Tests of the accuracy assumption of the theory of planned behaviour. British Journal of Social Psychology, 42, 393-410.

Sheldon, K. M., Elliot, A. J., Kim, Y., and Kasser, T. (2001). What's satisfying about satisfying events? Comparing ten candidate psychological needs. *Journal of Personality and Social Psychology, 80*, 325-339.

Shen, B., McCaughtry, N., and Martin, J. (2007). The influence of self-determination in physical education on leisure-time physical activity behaviour. *Research Quarterly for Exercise and Sport, 78*(4), 328-338.

Shen, B., McCaughtry, N., and Martin, J. (2008). Urban adolescents' exercise intentions and behaviors: An exploratory study of a trans-contextual model. *Contemporary Educational Psychology, 33*(4), 841-858.

Sparks, P., Shepherd, R. and Frewer, L. J. (1995). Assessing and structuring attitudes toward the use of gene technology in food production: The role of perceived ethical obligation. *Basic and Applied Social Psychology, 16*(4), 267-285.

Standage, M., Duda, J. L., and Ntoumanis, N. (2003). A model of contextual motivation in physical education: Using constructs from self-determination and achievement goal theories to predict physical activity intentions. *Journal of Educational Psychology, 95*, 97-110.

Standage, M., Duda, J. L, and Ntoumanis, N. (2005). A test of self-determination theory in school physical education. *British Journal of Educational Psychology*, 75, 411-433.

Vallerand, R. J. (1997). Toward a hierarchical model of intrinsic and extrinsic motivation. In: M. Zanna (Ed.), *Advances in Experimental Social Psychology,* Vol. 29(pp. 271-360). Toronto: Academic Press.

Vallerand, R.J. (2007). A hierarchical model of intrinsic and extrinsic motivation for sport and physical activity. In M.S. Hagger and N.L.D. Chatzisarantis (Eds.), *Intrinsic Motivation and Self-Determination in Exercise and Sport* (pp. 255-279). Champaign, IL: Human Kinetics.

Vallerand, R. J. and Ratelle, C. F. (2002). Intrinsic and extrinsic motivation: A hierarchical model. In E.L Deci and R.M. Ryan (Eds.). *Handbook of self-determination research.* Rochester, New York: University of Rochester Press.

Vallerand, R. J., Pelletier, L. G., Blais, M. R., Briere, N. M., Senecal, C., and Vallieres, E. F. (1992). The Academic Motivation Scale: A measure of intrinsic, extrinsic and amotivation in education. *Educational and Psychological Measurement, 52,* 1003-1017.

Volet, S., Vauras, M., and Salonen, P. (2009). Psychological and social nature of self- and co-regulation in learning contexts: An integrative perspective. *Educational Psychologist, 44,* 1-12.

Wilson, P. M., and Rodgers, W. M. (2004). The relationship between perceived autonomy support, exercise regulations and behavioral intentions in women. *Psychology of Sport and Exercise, 5,* 229-242.

In: Handbook on Psychology of Motivation
Editors: J. N. Franco and A. E. Svensgaard

ISBN: 978-1-62100-755-5
© 2012 Nova Science Publishers, Inc.

Chapter 9

COGNITIVE AND MOTIVATIONAL FACTORS FOR READING: THE NEED FOR A DOMAIN SPECIFIC APPROACH TO MOTIVATION

Emma Medford and Sarah P McGeown[*]
Psychology Department, University of Hull, UK

ABSTRACT

This study examined the importance of both cognitive and motivational factors for children's reading attainment. Furthermore, the nature of motivation that contributes to children's reading attainment was examined: whether domain specific (reading motivation) or general (school motivation). One hundred and five children (44 boys, aged 8 - 9) completed assessments of reading skill, cognitive ability (verbal IQ, phonological decoding and memory) and questionnaires examining their motivation and competency beliefs for reading (domain specific) and school (general). It was found that both cognitive and motivational factors contributed unique variance to children's reading attainment; however only children's intrinsic reading motivation and reading competency beliefs explained variance in their reading skills; extrinsic reading motivation, school motivations and school competency beliefs did not. The importance of considering both cognitive and specific motivational factors for reading instruction and intervention are discussed.

INTRODUCTION

Reading is an essential skill that children must possess in order to be successful academically, as most school subjects rely to some extent on reading ability. Reading skills have been found to predict children's general school achievement and choice of further education (Savolainen, Ahonery, Aro, Tolvanen and Halopainen, 2008), as well as achievement in specific school subjects such as mathematics (Grimm, 2008). Therefore, it is

---

[*] Corresponding author's email address: S.P.McGeown@hull.ac.uk.

not surprising that there is a significant body of research which has investigated the cognitive skills that support reading development and which may explain individual differences in reading skill. However, this focus on cognitive skills has often been at the expense of understanding the role of motivational factors. This chapter explores the relative importance of both cognitive and motivational factors in children's reading, and examines whether general levels of school motivation contribute to reading skill or whether domain specific motivation (i.e., reading motivation) better explains variation in children's reading skills.

READING AND COGNITIVE ABILITIES

There is a considerable field of research which has investigated solely the cognitive skills that support children's reading. Reading skills can be measured at the word recognition level (i.e., by examining whether a child can read individual words presented out of context, e.g., 'cat' or 'sandwich') or alternatively children's reading comprehension skills can be assessed (i.e., by examining children's ability to read and understand text). As the main goal of reading is to understand and gain information (rather than recognise individual words), reading comprehension is typically considered to be the more important skill and is the type discussed and investigated in the current study. It is often argued that reading comprehension is underpinned by two main cognitive components: decoding skill and verbal ability. This idea stems from the simple view of reading (Hoover and Gough, 1990) where it is argued that in order to understand a text, a child must be able to read the individual words (phonological decoding skill) and understand the meaning (verbal ability). This model is often cited and studies have consistently shown that both skills are crucial for children's reading comprehension. For example, Kendeous, Van den Broek, White and Lynch (2009) found that both oral language skills and decoding skills each independently predicted children's reading comprehension, illustrating that both were important contributors. Similarly, many other studies have shown that decoding skill (Nation and Snowling, 2004; Share, 1995) and verbal abilities (Nation and Snowling, 2004; Ouellette, 2006; Ricketts, Nation and Bishop, 2007) support children's reading comprehension.

However, the simple view of reading has been criticized for being overly simplistic and in addition to decoding and verbal ability, working memory has been found to explain additional variance in reading comprehension after controlling for these cognitive abilities (Cain, Oakhill and Bryant, 2004). In addition, children with reading comprehension deficiencies have been found to perform poorly on verbal working memory tasks (Swanson and Berninger, 1995). Within school, working memory skills have been found to predict subsequent learning outcomes (Alloway and Alloway, 2010) and are closely related to children's attainment on national curriculum assessments (Gathercole, Pickering, Knight et. al., 2004). Whilst not exhaustive, it is generally considered that these three abilities (decoding, verbal IQ and working memory) are the main cognitive skills that support children's reading comprehension.

MOTIVATION

Increasingly however, researchers are examining the influence that motivation may have on children's reading and academic success. Motivation is generally considered to be a multi-dimensional construct that determines the extent to which an individual will choose to engage or persevere with a given activity. There are many different conceptualisations of motivation; however the theory which is most commonly used within reading research (e.g. Wang and Guthrie, 2004; Wigfield and Guthrie, 1997), and which will be focused on in the following study is that of intrinsic and extrinsic motivation (Ryan and Deci, 2000). According to this theory, an individual is intrinsically motivated when they choose to engage in an activity because it is inherently interesting or enjoyable, and extrinsically motivated when they choose to engage in an activity because it leads to a separable outcome, such as gaining a reward or avoiding a punishment. Ryan and Deci (2000) suggest therefore that these dimensions of motivation provide different explanations as to why an individual will choose to engage in or avoid specific activities. It is suggested that intrinsically motivated individuals typically show greater persistence at a task than those who are extrinsically motivated who may be engaging in a task with disinterest or though coercion (Ryan and Deci, 2000). Interestingly, research shows that whilst intrinsic motivation is generally positively associated with academic achievement, extrinsic motivation is generally negatively associated with academic achievement (Lepper, Henderlong-Corpus and Iyengar, 2005). These dimensions of intrinsic and extrinsic motivation can be further divided into more specific dimensions of motivation, based on more precise reasons as to why an individual will to choose to engage in or persist with an activity. The current study will focus on the intrinsic-extrinsic model of reading motivation proposed by Wang and Guthrie (2004), in which three dimensions of intrinsic motivation (curiosity, involvement and challenge) and five dimensions of extrinsic motivation (recognition, grades, competition, social and compliance) are examined. These dimensions take into account children's achievement goals, performance goals and social reasons for reading, and have a strong theoretical basis as well as empirical support (Guthrie, Wigfield, Metsala et. al., 1999; Baker and Wigfield, 1999; Wang and Guthrie, 2004; Wigfield and Guthrie, 1997).

MOTIVATION: A DOMAIN SPECIFIC APPROACH

Researchers have argued that a domain specific approach to motivation is crucial as children's motivation across domains will vary (Wigfield, 1997). Indeed, there is research to suggest that children's academic motivation is school subject-specific, with children reporting distinct levels of motivation for different school subjects (Guay, et. al., 2010). For example, a child who enjoys reading may be motivated during class reading activities but they may not necessarily be motivated during maths lessons. Further support for between-subject differentiation of motivation comes from correlational data showing that children's motivation towards a specific school discipline (e.g. reading) is more closely associated with other motivational constructs (e.g. self-concept) corresponding to the same discipline than to other disciplines (Gottfried, 1985; Guay et. al., 2010). Furthermore, Gottfried (1985) found that children's subject-specific intrinsic motivation is more closely associated with other corresponding subject-specific measures of motivation than with a measure of general academic motivation. In addition, subject-specific measures of motivation have been found to be more strongly related to measures of children's class participation and educational aspirations within the same subject area than within different subject areas (Green, Martin and Marsh, 2007). This suggests that it is important to consider children's motivation towards specific school subjects or disciplines when investigating the influences of motivation on educational attainment.

The majority of studies that have examined the relationship between reading motivation and reading attainment have focused on children's reading motivation specifically, rather than general school or academic motivation. However, Gottfried (1985) examined the relationships between reading motivation, general academic motivation and reading attainment. Results showed that both reading motivation and general academic motivation were associated with reading attainment, with general academic motivation showing slightly more consistent links with reading achievement across three studies. Similarly, Logan and Medford (2011) found that children's intrinsic school motivation was slightly more closely correlated with their reading attainment than their intrinsic reading motivation. As academic motivation has been found to be domain specific (Gottfried, 1985; Guay et. al., 2010) it may be predicted that motivation relating to a particular domain would best predict attainment in that domain. However, with conflicting results in this area, there is a need for further research to examine this.

READING MOTIVATION AND READING ATTAINMENT

In the reading research literature, many studies have investigated the association between children's reading motivation and reading attainment and have consistently found that these are significantly associated (Baker and Wigfield, 1999; Morgan and Fuchs, 2007; Wang and Guthrie, 2004). Furthermore, Wang and Guthrie (2004) found that whilst children's intrinsic reading motivation was positively correlated with their reading skill, their extrinsic reading motivation was negatively correlated with their reading skill. It was suggested that extrinsically motivated readers, who may be reading with disinterest or through coercion, use more surface level reading strategies for reading comprehension, such as guessing or memorisation of the text, rather than more deeper level strategies that result in better understanding of the text. Other studies have also highlighted the positive relationship between intrinsic reading motivation and reading attainment and the negative relationship between extrinsic reading motivation and reading (Becker, McElvany and Kortenbruck, 2010; Mucherah and Yoder, 2008). However extrinsic motivation may not necessarily be detrimental to children's reading attainment. Logan and Meford (2011) found no relationship between extrinsic reading motivation and reading skill. In addition, Park (2011) found that extrinsic reading motivation was only detrimental to reading attainment if the student had low levels of intrinsic motivation. Furthermore, a moderate level of extrinsic reading motivation was actually found to benefit reading skill if coupled with a moderate level of intrinsic reading motivation. Nevertheless, the results of these studies clearly stress the importance of intrinsic reading motivation for children's reading success.

The direction of the relationship between reading motivation and reading attainment is yet to be fully established, although research suggests that the relationship is bidirectional (Morgan and Fuchs, 2007). It is likely that children who are more intrinsically motivated to read spend more time reading and put more effort into learning to read, and thus become better readers. Similarly, it is likely that children who are better readers are more intrinsically motivated to read because they find reading to be easier and are thus more likely to enjoy reading. Some studies indicate that the link between reading motivation and reading attainment may be mediated by children's reading frequency and amount of reading. Reading motivation has been found to predict the amount of reading that children engage in (Guthrie et al, 1999; Wigfield and Guthrie, 1997), which in turn has been found to predict reading comprehension (Guthrie et al., 1999). It may be that children who are more motivated to read engage in reading activities more, which thereby facilitates the development of their reading comprehension skills. Indeed, research has shown that children and adolescents who engage more often in reading activities have better literacy skills (Anderson, Wilson and Fielding, 1988; Cunningham and Stanovich, 1997; Guthrie et. al., 1999).

COMPETENCY BELIEFS AND READING ATTAINMENT

In addition to motivation, children's competency beliefs have also been found to be closely associated with their reading attainment (Aunola, Leskinen, Onatsu-Anilommi and Nurmi, 2002; Chapman and Tunmer, 1995; 1997; Katzir, Lesaux and Kim, 2009; Logan and Johnston, 2009; Logan and Medford, 2011). Competency beliefs refer to children's beliefs or self-estimates about how competent they are at a given activity, and have been found to be evident in children from a young age (Chapman, Tunmer and Prochnow, 2000). Children's competency beliefs are subject-specific, with children reporting distinct competency beliefs in different academic domains (Eccles, Wigfield, Harold and Blumenfled, 1993). In addition, the relationship between competency beliefs and reading attainment also appears to be domain specific, as children's competency beliefs in reading have been found to be more closely associated with their reading skill than their competency beliefs in school (Logan and Medford, 2011).

Children's reading self-concept has been found to predict variance in their reading comprehension skill after controlling for word reading and verbal ability (Katzir et. al., 2009) suggesting an important role for this factor after accounting for cognitive abilities. In addition, students' competency beliefs in reading have been found to be associated with their reading attainment even after controlling for other dimensions of intrinsic motivation (Boufford, Marcoux, Vezeau et.al., 2003). Interestingly, Chapman et. al. (2000) found that young children who were poorer readers had more negative self-concepts of their general academic ability, suggesting that self-concepts of skills such as reading may influence the development of more general academic competency beliefs.

COGNITIVE AND MOTIVATIONAL INFLUENCES ON READING

Recently there have been several studies that have examined the relative importance of both cognitive and motivational factors in children's reading. For example, Taboada, Tonks, Wigfield and Guthrie (2009) found that both cognitive factors (background knowledge and student questioning) and intrinsic motivation explained independent variance in children's reading comprehension skill and reading growth, suggesting that both were important contributors. Taboada et al., (2009) suggested that rather than acting separately from cognitive skills, intrinsic motivation acts as an energiser that enables students to engage their cognitive resources and strategies, leading to improved reading comprehension. Unfortunately Taboada et. al. (2009) did not include the cognitive skills typically found to support reading (verbal IQ, decoding and working memory); however the inclusion of both cognitive and motivational variables illustrated that both were important. Similarly, Anmarkrud and Braten (2009) found that reading task value (measuring the usefulness, importance and intrinsic interestingness of reading comprehension) predicted reading comprehension ability after variance explained by gender, reading achievement, topic knowledge and strategy use were controlled for. In addition, as stated earlier, Katzir et. al. (2009) found that children's reading self-concept explained additional variance in reading comprehension after controlling for word reading skills and verbal ability.

However, research suggests that there may be individual differences in the importance of children's reading motivation for their reading comprehension skills. Logan, Medford and Hughes (2011) found that after controlling for verbal IQ and decoding skill, intrinsic reading motivation did not explain additional variance in the reading comprehension skill of all readers. However, when children were identified as either high or low ability readers, it was found that motivation predicted significant variance in reading performance and growth in reading skills in the low ability group (after controlling for cognitive ability). It was suggested that poor readers have a more difficult task when presented with the same reading assessment as their more able peers. Poor readers will be challenged more by the texts which will be slower and harder to read, which may then lead to greater levels of disengagement. It was suggested therefore that motivation may be particularly important for these children, as they will need to persevere more with difficult reading material.

AIMS AND PREDICTIONS

As highlighted, studies have begun to consider the role of both cognitive and motivational factors for children's reading development; albeit using different measures of cognitive ability and motivation. In the current study, the cognitive skills commonly associated with reading (verbal IQ, decoding and memory) were examined, in addition to children's motivation and competency beliefs (in both reading and school). As stated, previous studies have often included cognitive skills less commonly associated with reading (e.g., Anmarkrud and Braten, 2009; Taboada et. al., 2009), therefore the current study included those skills which have been shown to explain the most variance in children's reading. If children's motivation or competency beliefs were found to predict additional variance in their reading after accounting for these skills, it would provide stronger evidence that these were important factors contributing to children's reading skill. Therefore, the first aim of the study was to examine whether children's motivation or competency beliefs would predict additional variance in their reading skill after accounting for the cognitive skills commonly associated with reading.

In addition, previous studies which have investigated the associations between reading skill, motivation and competency beliefs have generally focused on subject specific motivation and competency beliefs (Chapman and Tunmer, 1997; Wang and Guthrie, 2004). Research studies examining the relationship between reading skill and general school motivation and competency beliefs have produced conflicting results (Gottfried, 1985; Logan and Medford, 2011). Therefore a further aim of the study was to examine whether general levels of school motivation contribute to children's reading skill or whether reading motivation better explains variation in children's reading.

METHOD

Participants

One hundred and five children (44 boys, 61 girls), with an average age of 8 years and 8 months (.28 *SD*) took part in this study. The children came from two cohorts of Year 4 classes within one large school (there were two classes in each cohort). All children included in the study had English as their first language. Percentage of free school meals was taken as an index of social deprivation: 47.4% of children were entitled to free school meals (national average is approximately 18%). The children came from a low achieving school as in the most recent review (2009), only 65% of children were achieving a Key Stage 2 Assessment Level of 4 or above (the national average that year was 80%).

Materials

Reading Comprehension
All children completed a group administered test measuring reading comprehension ability (Group Reading Test II, Macmillan Test Unit, 2000). Reading comprehension was measured using a 45 item sentence completion task, in which children were required to select appropriate words to complete a series of sentences (e.g., "The _____ was filled with hay", options: play, idea, barn, horse, table). Forms C and D of the test were given to children alternately based on where they were seated to prevent copying. The examiner read through the practice items with the children beforehand to ensure they understood the test. The assessment was completed in approximately 25 minutes, although no time restriction was imposed for completion. Children's standardised scores were used for the purposes of analysis.

Verbal IQ
Verbal ability was assessed using the British Ability Scales II (Elliot, Smith and McCulloch, 1997) verbal similarities and word definition tests, a combination of which

provides a measure of a child's verbal IQ. For the verbal similarities task, the child was required to state how three things were similar (e.g. *peas, cabbage* and *carrots* are all vegetables), and for the word definitions task, the child was required to explain the meanings of individual words (e.g. an *assistant* is someone who helps or works for someone else). These assessments were administered in accordance with manual guidelines and standardised scores were used for the analysis.

Phonological Decoding

Phonological decoding ability was assessed using a nonword reading task, which requires children to use phonics rules (i.e., application of letter-sound correspondences) in order to read nonsense words. The list of nonwords used in the assessment were: hast, kisp, mosp, drant, prab, sted, gromp, trolb, snid, twesk, tegwop, balras, molsmit, nolcrid, twamket, stansert, hinshink, chamgalp, kipthirm, sloskon, hognelkrag, bisgakdip, joklentos, shodrinmert, lomcrenkin, yimterbesfich, ronbikculgan, foyminlantos, basrelwathrin, wosraltsenbith. The first twenty nonwords were taken from Snowling, Stothard and Mclean (1996) Graded Nonword reading Test and a further ten words were added to remove the chance of ceiling effects. The children read five practice nonwords beforehand and were informed of any mispronunciations by the examiner. The percentage of nonwords read correctly was used for the analysis.

Memory Span

Children's memory span was assessed using the British Ability Scales II (Elliot et al., 1997) recall of digits forward and recall of digits backward tasks. The recall of digits forward task is an assessment of children's short term memory span, and requires the child to repeat sequences of digits of increasing length presented orally by the examiner. The recall of digits backward task is a measure of children's working memory span, and requires the child to repeat sequences of digits presented orally in reverse order. Children's scores on both tasks were converted to standardised scores and summed to form a composite measure of memory span. These tasks were administered in accordance with manual guidelines and standardised scores were used for the analysis.

Reading and School Motivation Questionnaire

All children completed a group administered 40 item questionnaire measuring motivation and competency beliefs for reading and school (see Appendix). Children's motivation was measured using a multi-dimensional approach, with dimensions proposed by Wang and Guthrie (2004). This questionnaire identifies three dimensions of intrinsic motivation: challenge (desire to work with/master complex materials), curiosity (desire to learn more/new things) and involvement (child's level of engagement/involvement) and five dimensions of extrinsic motivation: competition (desire to outperform others), recognition (desire for achievements to be recognised by others), grades (desire to achieve good marks), compliance (conformity to an external requirement) and social (social interactions involving books/school). These dimensions have a strong theoretical basis as well as empirical support (Wang and Guthrie, 2004; Wigfield and Guthrie, 1997). The motivation items were created so that they referred to either reading (16 items) or school (16 items). Competency beliefs were measured by asking children to report their perceived level of reading skill (4 items for reading) or general academic ability (4 items for school). Children answered each statement using a 4 point Likert scale (definitely disagree, probably disagree, probably agree, definitely agree). Half of the items were positively worded and half were negatively worded in order to prevent children from circling the same option without considering the question. In addition, three practice questions were given beforehand to ensure children understood the nature of the assessment. This questionnaire had been used in a previous study with a larger sample of pupils (Logan and Medford, 2011) and has shown high internal consistency using Cronbach's alpha: competency beliefs for reading (four items, $\alpha = 0.69$), competency beliefs for school (four items, $\alpha = 0.73$), motivation for reading (16 items, $\alpha = 0.79$) and motivation for school (16 items, $\alpha = 0.74$).

Procedure

Assessments were carried out in the third month of the children's fifth school year. All children completed the questionnaire and reading comprehension assessment within their classroom. This took approximately one hour. Following this, all children completed individual assessments (verbal IQ, phonological decoding and memory span) in a quiet room close to their classroom. Each individual assessment session lasted approximately 30 minutes.

RESULTS

The results are split into three sections: 1) Correlations between reading skill, cognitive abilities and reading and school motivation; 2) Predicting reading skill using cognitive skills and reading motivation and 3) Predicting reading skill using cognitive skills and school motivation.

Correlations between Reading Skill, Cognitive Abilities and Reading and School Motivation

Correlations were carried out to examine the strength of association between reading attainment, cognitive skills (verbal IQ, decoding, memory) and motivational factors for reading and school (motivation (intrinsic/extrinsic), competency beliefs).

Table 1. Associations between reading skill, cognitive and motivational factors

	1	2	3	4	5	6	7	8	9	10	11
Reading attainment	.56**	.60**	.52**	.21	.27*	.10	.27*	.30**	.14	.47**	.20

Note: 1 = Verbal IQ, 2 = Decoding skill, 3 = Memory, 4 = Motivation Reading (composite), 5 = Motivation Reading (Intrinsic), 6 = Motivation Reading (Extrinsic), 7 = Motivation School (Composite), 8 = Motivation School (Intrinsic), 9 = Motivation School (Extrinsic), 10 = Competency Beliefs (Reading), 11 = Competency Beliefs (School). *$p < .05$, **$p < .001$.

Children's cognitive skills correlated significantly and closely with their reading attainment (see Table 1). Whilst children's school motivation correlated significantly with their reading attainment, their reading motivation did not (however, this difference was not large). When examining intrinsic and extrinsic motivation, children's intrinsic motivation (for both reading and school) correlated significantly with their reading skill, whilst their extrinsic motivation did not. In addition, children's reading competency beliefs correlated significantly with their reading skill, whilst their school competency beliefs did not. Generally, children's cognitive abilities correlated significantly more closely with their reading attainment that their motivation and competency beliefs.

Predicting Reading Skill Using Cognitive Skills and Reading Motivation

Table 2. Predicting reading skill using cognitive abilities and reading motivation (composite measure of intrinsic and extrinsic motivation)

Enter	Variable Added	R^2	p	Final β
Reading Skill				
1	Verbal IQ	.296	.000	.376
2	Decoding	.422	.005	.274
3	Memory	.490	.007	.257
4	Reading Motivation (composite)	.522	.031	.182

Table 3. Predicting reading skill using cognitive abilities and reading motivation (intrinsic)

Enter	Variable Added	R^2	p	Final β
Reading Skill				
1	Verbal IQ	.292	.000	.346
2	Decoding	.433	.001	.310
3	Memory	.479	.011	.224
4	Reading Motivation (intrinsic)	.520	.010	.205

Table 4. Predicting reading skill using cognitive abilities and reading motivation (extrinsic)

Enter	Variable Added	R^2	p	Final β
Reading Skill				
1	Verbal IQ	.307	.000	.373
2	Decoding	.434	.005	.269
3	Memory	.505	.003	.285
4	Reading Motivation (extrinsic)	.518	.167	.115

Table 5. Predicting reading skill using cognitive abilities and reading competency beliefs

Enter	Variable Added	R²	p	Final β
Reading Skill				
1	Verbal IQ	.311	.000	.333
2	Decoding	.449	.001	.278
3	Memory	.496	.034	.180
4	Reading Competency Beliefs	.568	.000	.287

Hierarchical regression analyses were carried out to examine the variance in reading comprehension skill explained by cognitive abilities and motivation, with separate analyses conducted for motivation (composite, intrinsic, extrinsic) and competency beliefs for both reading and school.

Children's reading competency beliefs and motivation (composite measure) both made significant and independent contributions to their reading attainment after controlling for verbal IQ, decoding skill and memory. When dimensions of motivation were analysed separately, only intrinsic motivation explained additional variance in children's reading skill, extrinsic motivation did not. In addition, each of the cognitive abilities made a significant and independent contribution to children's performance on the reading assessment. In general, children's reading competency beliefs explained more variance than their reading motivation.

Table 6. Predicting reading skill using cognitive abilities and school motivation (composite measure of intrinsic and extrinsic motivation)

Enter	Variable Added	R²	p	Final β
Reading Skill				
1	Verbal IQ	.340	.001	.343
2	Decoding	.452	.002	.302
3	Memory	.505	.011	.244
4	School Motivation (composite)	.525	.091	.150

Table 7. Predicting reading skill using cognitive abilities and school motivation (intrinsic)

Enter	Variable Added	R²	p	Final β
Reading Skill				
1	Verbal IQ	.312	.001	.317
2	Decoding	.433	.001	.311
3	Memory	.488	.010	.244
4	School Motivation (intrinsic)	.504	.125	.136

Table 8. Predicting reading skill using cognitive abilities and school motivation (extrinsic)

Enter	Variable Added	R^2	p	Final β
Reading Skill				
1	Verbal IQ	.336	.000	.358
2	Decoding	.462	.001	.325
3	Memory	.512	.008	.247
4	School Motivation (extrinsic)	.527	.130	.125

Table 9. Predicting reading skill using cognitive abilities and school competency beliefs

Enter	Variable Added	R^2	p	Final β
Reading Skill				
1	Verbal IQ	.311	.000	.341
2	Decoding	.433	.003	.291
3	Memory	.493	.006	.262
4	School Competency Beliefs	.502	.261	.094

Predicting Reading Skill Using Cognitive Skills and School Motivation

Finally, hierarchical regression analyses were carried out to examine the variance in reading comprehension skill explained by cognitive abilities and school motivation.

In contrast to reading motivation and competency beliefs, children's school motivation and competency beliefs did not make independent contributions to their reading attainment after controlling for verbal IQ, decoding skill and memory. In addition, when analysed separately, neither intrinsic nor extrinsic motivation explained significant variance.

DISCUSSION

The aim of this study was to examine whether children's motivation and competency beliefs for reading or school would predict variance in their reading skills after accounting for the cognitive abilities commonly associated with reading (verbal IQ, decoding and memory). It was found that children's reading motivation and competency beliefs did explain significant variance in their reading comprehension after accounting for these cognitive skills. However, when intrinsic and extrinsic dimensions of reading motivation were analyzed separately, only intrinsic reading motivation explained additional variance, extrinsic did not. Finally, children's school motivation and competency beliefs did not explain additional variance in reading comprehension skill after accounting for cognitive skills. By including the cognitive skills known to be the best predictors of children's reading, this study provided a thorough test of whether motivation is an important factor contributing to children's reading attainment. The results suggest that it is and highlight the importance of considering both cognitive and motivational factors for children's reading; but also emphasize that some aspects of motivation will be more important than others.

As stated earlier, in contrast to the wealth of research examining solely the cognitive skills supporting reading, there is little research that has examined the contribution of both cognitive and motivational factors in children's reading. Those that have, have often used cognitive skills less commonly associated with reading comprehension skill (e.g., background knowledge and student questioning, Taboada et. al., 2009). With regard to cognitive abilities, in accordance with previous research (Gough and Tunmer, 1986; Kendeous et. al., 2009; Nation and Snowling, 2004; Ouellette, 2006; Ricketts et. al., 2007; Share, 1995) both verbal ability and decoding skill explained independent and significant variance in children's reading skill. Indeed these two cognitive abilities explained the largest amount of variance in children's reading attainment. This is unsurprising, as in order to understand a text, a child must be able to both decode (to read unfamiliar words) and understand the meanings of words and sentences within text. However, children's memory capacity explained additional variance in reading comprehension ability after accounting for these skills, suggesting that the simple view of reading (Hoover and Gough, 1990) is too restrictive.

In this study, children's reading motivation and competency beliefs explained additional variance in reading comprehension skill after accounting for the variance explained by verbal ability, decoding skill, and memory capacity. These findings are consistent with previous research which has demonstrated the importance of both cognitive and motivational factors in reading (Anmarkrud and Braten, 2009; Katzir et. al., 2009; Taboada et. al., 2009) and are also in accordance with other studies which suggest that reading motivation and competency beliefs are related to reading skill (Aunola et. al., 2002; Baker and Wigfield, 1999; Chapman and Tunmer, 1995; 1997, Katzir et al, 2009; Logan and Medford, 2011; Morgan and Fuchs, 2007; Wang and Guthrie, 2004). However, the results of this study can be further understood in terms of a multi-dimensional approach to motivation. Whilst children's intrinsic reading motivation explained additional variance, their extrinsic reading motivation did not. Similarly, it was only children's reading motivation that predicted variance in their reading skill; their general school motivation did not. These differences in the relationship between intrinsic and extrinsic motivation and ability have been previously highlighted and the results regarding intrinsic motivation are consistent with previous research (Becker et. al., 2010; Logan and Medford, 2011; Mucherah and Yoder, 2008; Wang and Guthrie, 2004). However, in this study, extrinsic motivation was not associated with reading attainment. This is consistent with Logan and Medford (2011), who also found no relationship between extrinsic motivation and reading attainment, but inconsistent with other studies (e.g. Becker et. al., 2010; Lepper et. al., 2005), which have suggested a negative association between the two. Indeed, research examining the association between extrinsic motivation and attainment is often mixed (e.g., Park, 2011). Therefore further research should be carried out to better understand the role of extrinsic motivation in children's attainment.

In terms of interpreting the results of this study, it may be that children who are more motivated to read and have higher reading competency beliefs put more cognitive effort into understanding texts, decoding unfamiliar words, and may process information more deeply. Indeed, motivation and competency beliefs may exert their effect on reading attainment by acting as energisers (Taboada et a., 2009) that enable children to engage their cognitive abilities during reading, leading to improved reading attainment. Although conclusions regarding causality cannot be warranted based on the correlational nature of this study, it is likely that reading motivation and reading competency beliefs share a reciprocal relationship with reading attainment. Indeed, in a review of studies examining the relationship between reading motivation and attainment, it was suggested that this relationship is bi-directional (Morgan and Fuchs, 2007). Children who are more motivated to read and believe that they are more competent readers are likely to engage in reading activities more, and put more effort into reading activities, which in turn will develop their reading comprehension abilities. Conversely, children who are less motivated to read and who believe they are incompetent readers are less likely to engage in reading activities and put effort into reading, and thus their reading abilities are less likely to improve. Therefore, whilst it is clear that motivation is important, it is currently not as clear why motivation is important; whether it improves children's engagement and perseverance in reading activities leading to higher levels of attainment or whether motivation leads to greater levels of reading frequency which therefore develops children's reading skills. It is therefore important that future research consider whether motivation directly influences reading attainment or influences reading attainment via a mediating factor (e.g., reading frequency).

Children's motivation and competency beliefs regarding school work in general did not predict significant additional variance in reading comprehension ability after accounting for the variance explained by cognitive skills. This suggests that motivation should be studied at the domain specific level (Wigfield, 1997). However, it is important to note that a close association was found between children's school motivation and reading attainment, which is consistent with previous research (Logan and Medford, 2011; Gottfried, 1985). Due to the importance of reading for academic attainment, children's reading skills are likely to be closely correlated with their overall academic ability. It may be that as children progress through school, their reading skill affects their motivation towards school because of positive or negative academic experiences. For example, if a child increasingly has difficulty with reading which consistently affects their performance at school, they may begin to become de-motivated towards school in general. Interestingly, research has shown that the strength of association between reading skill and school motivation grows stronger with age (Logan and Medford, 2011), suggesting that motivation may become more important as children get older. This is despite the fact that longitudinal and cross-sectional research studies illustrate that children's motivation generally decreases with age (Lepper et al., 2005; Unrau and Schlackman, 2006).

Educational Implications

The results of this study have some important educational implications. Firstly, the results highlight that children's reading motivation and beliefs in reading skills may be important contributors to their reading attainment. Therefore reading instruction in school should not only focus on developing cognitive abilities (e.g., phonics and language skills), but also instil an enjoyment of reading so that children have the desire to read and engage with reading activities. This is consistent with previous suggestions (Guthrie, McKae and Klauda, 2007). A reading curriculum focused on developing both cognitive skills and motivational factors should arguably be in place from the earliest stages of reading instruction and continue throughout children's primary school education. Furthermore, as the importance of motivation and competency beliefs appear to be domain specific, reading instruction should focus on fostering greater levels of reading motivation (rather than general motivation) to be most effective. In addition, fostering greater levels of intrinsic reading motivation may be particularly important. Intrinsic reading motivation may be fostered by providing children with access to reading materials that are interesting and engaging for them and allowing them time throughout the school day to read books of their choice. Alternatively, methods fostering extrinsic motivation are more likely to involve using a grade or level system within school for children to chart their reading progress or providing recognition to children for their reading skills.

The focus on fostering greater levels of intrinsic motivation rather than extrinsic motivation is consistent with Souvignier and Mokhlesgerami (2006) who found that framing young adolescent's learning around intrinsic goals resulted in better understanding of learning material than framing their learning around extrinsic goals. Similarly, Guthrie et. al. (2006) found that intrinsic reading motivation and reading comprehension performance could be increased by fostering children's situational interest in texts by using stimulating tasks related to the topic of interest. It is crucial that teachers are aware of the importance of motivation in children's education and have the knowledge and resources available to identify ways to improve children's motivation within the classroom. Indeed, research by Guthrie et. al. (2004) showed that children who received reading instruction combining both cognitive strategy instruction and motivational support had better reading comprehension ability than children who were only taught cognitive strategy instruction or who were taught with a traditional approach that placed little emphasis on reading motivation. Nevertheless, whilst teachers often receive information and training about developing cognitive skills within the classroom (e.g., phonics, language skills etc), there are very few resources available for teachers to develop children's motivation and interest. It may be beneficial to provide more resources for teachers that enable their ability to do this.

Limitations and Suggestions for Future Research

Firstly, it is important to note that a single age group was included in this study, therefore further research is necessary to examine the importance of both reading and school motivation as children progress through school. As stated earlier, there is evidence that the association between motivation and attainment becomes stronger with age, but that children's level of motivation generally decreases with age, therefore future research should examine the role of both cognitive and motivational factors among different age groups. An understanding of this would allow teachers to identify at which stages they should focus more on motivational factors for reading. In addition, the school in which this data was collected was a relatively low attaining school; therefore the sample is not necessarily representative of the typical school population. Furthermore, as Logan et al. (2011) found that motivation was particularly important for poor readers' reading skills, it may be the case that among higher attaining schools, motivation is less important. However, knowledge of the factors that contribute to reading skills in low attaining schools is particularly important as there is considerable interest and focus on helping children from less privileged backgrounds improve their reading skills (Duncan and Seymour, 2000). Nevertheless, additional research in a number of different schools with different attainment levels would test whether these results can be generalised.

In the current study, the assessment used to measure reading was a group administered test (which is similar to the group administered tests that are given in schools as part of national assessments). However, group assessments rely on children completing the task themselves, with no encouragement from someone to continue when it gets difficult. This is in contrast to individually administered assessments where children might be encouraged by the assessor to continue. Future research should consider the extent to which motivation is important for reading skill in individually versus group administered tests. Given the use of group administered assessments within national tests, an understanding of this is clearly important. Finally, it would be interesting to investigate whether the domain specific link between children's motivation and competency beliefs regarding reading and reading attainment is also found across other academic subjects (e.g., mathematics).

CONCLUSION

To conclude, this study provided a thorough test of the importance of motivation for reading by including the cognitive skills most commonly associated with reading. The results highlight the importance of considering both cognitive and motivational factors in reading instruction and when identifying ways to improve children's reading skills. However, rather than fostering greater levels of academic motivation, a focus on increasing reading motivation is likely to provide the greatest gains for children's reading skills.

REFERENCES

Alloway, T. P. and Alloway, R. G. (2010). Investigating the predictive roles of working memory and IQ in academic attainment. *Journal of Experimental Child Psychology, 106,* 20-29. doi: 10.1016/j.jecp.2009.11.003

Anderson, R. C., Wilson, P. T., and Fielding, L. G. (1988). Growth in reading and how children spend their time outside of school. *Reading Research Quarterly, 23,*(3) 285-303. doi: 10.1598/RRQ.23.3.2

Anmarkrud, O. and Braten, I. (2009). Motivation for Reading Comprehension. *Learning and Individual Differences, 19,* 252-256. doi: 10.1016/j.lindif.2008.09.002

Aunola, K., Leskinen, E., Onatsu-Anilommi, T., and Nurmi, J. (2002). Three methods for studying developmental change: a case of reading skills and self-concept. *British Journal of Educational Psychology, 72,* 343-364. doi:10.1348/000709902320634447

Baker, L. and Wigfield, A. (1999). Dimensions of children's motivation for reading and their relations to reading activity and reading achievement. *Reading Research Quarterly, 34*(4), 452-477. doi: 10.1598/RRQ.34.4.4

Becker, M., McElvany, N., Kortenbruck, M. (2010). Intrinsic and extrinsic motivation as predictors of reading literacy: A longitudinal study. *Journal of Educational Psychology, 102*(4), 773-785. doi: 10.1037/a0020084

Bouffard, T., Marcoux, M., Vezeau, C., and Bordeleau, L. (2003). Changes in self-perceptions of competence and intrinsic motivation among elementary school children. *British Journal of Educational Psychology, 73,* 171-186. doi: 10.1348/00070990360626921

Cain, K., Oakhill., and Bryant, P. (2004). Children's reading comprehension ability: concurrent prediction by working memory, verbal ability, and component skills. *Journal of Experimental Psychology, 96*(1), 31-42. doi: 10.1037/0022-0663.96.1.31

Chapman, J. W. and Tunmer, W. E. (1995). Development of young children's reading self-concepts: An examination of emerging subcomponents and their relationship with reading achievement. *Journal of Educational Psychology, 87*(1), 154-167. doi: 10.1037/0022-0663.87.1.154

Chapman, J. W. and Tunmer, W. E. (1997). A longitudinal study of beginning reading achievement and reading self-concept. *British Journal of Educational Psychology, 67,* 279-291.

Chapman, J. W., Tunmer, W. E., and Prochnow, J. E. (2000). Early reading-related skills and performance, reading self-concept, and the development of academic self-concept: A longitudinal study. *Journal of Educational Psychology, 92*(4), 703-708. doi: 10.1037/0022-0663.92.4.703

Cunningham, A. E. and Stanovich, K. E. (1997). Early reading acquisition and its relation to reading experience and ability 10 years later. *Developmental Psychology, 33*(6), 934-945. doi: 10.1037/0012-1649.33.6.934

Duncan, L. G., and Seymour, P. H. K. (2000). Socio-economic differences in foundation-level literacy. *British Journal of Psychology, 91*(2), 145-167. doi: 10.1348/000712600161736

Eccles, J. S., Wigfield, A., Harold, R., and Blumenfeld, P. B. (1993). Age and gender differences in children's self and task perceptions during elementary school. *Child Development, 64,* 830-847. doi: 10.2307/1131221

Elliott, C. D., Smith, P., and McCulloch, K. (1997). British Ability Scales: Second ed. Windsor, Berkshire: NFER-Nelson.

Gathercole, S. E., Pickering, S. J., Knight, C., and Stegmann, Z. (2004) Working memory skills and educational attainment: evidence from national curriculum assessments at 7 and 14 years of age. *Applied Cognitive Psychology, 18,* 1-16. doi: 10.1002/acp.934

Gottfried (1985). Academic intrinsic motivation in elementary and junior high school students. *Journal of Educational Psychology, 77*(6), 631-645. doi: 10.1037/0022-0663.77.6.631

Green, J., Martin, A. J., Marsh, H. W. (2007). Motivation and engagement in English, mathematics and science high school subjects: towards and understanding of multidimensional domain specificity. *Learning and Individual Differences, 17,* 269-279. doi: 10.1016/j.lindif.2006.12.003

Grimm, K. J. (2008). Longitudinal associations between reading and mathematics achievement. *Developmental Neuropsychology, 33*(3), 410-426. doi: 10.1080/87565640801982486

Guay, F,. Chanal, J., Ratelle, C. F., Marsh, H. W., Larose, S., and Boivin, M. (2010). Intrinsic, identified, and controlled types of motivation for school subjects in young elementary school children. *British Journal of Educational Psychology, 80,* 711-735. doi: 10.1348/000709910X499084

Guthrie, J. T., Mckae, A., and Klauda, S. L. (2007). Contributions of concept-oriented reading instruction to knowledge about interventions for motivations in reading. *Educational Psychologist, 42*(4), 237-250.

Guthrie, J.T., Wigfield, A., Barbosa, P., Perencevich, K. C., Taboada, A., Davis, M.H., Scafiddi, N.T., and Tonks, S. (2004) Increasing reading comprehension and engagement through concept-oriented reading instruction. *Journal of Educational Psychology, 96*(3), 403-423. doi: 10.1037/0022-0663.96.3.403

Guthrie, J. T., Wigfield, A., Humenick, N. M., Perencevich, K.C., Taboada, A., and Barbosa, P. (2006). Influences of stimulating tasks on reading motivation and comprehension. *Journal of Educational Research, 99*(4), 232-245. doi: 10.3200/JOER.99.4.232-246

Guthrie, J. T., Wigfield, A., Metsala, J. L., and Cox, K. E. (1999). Motivational and cognitive predictors of text comprehension and reading amount. *Scientific Studies of Reading, 3*(3), 231-256. doi: 10.1207/s1532799xssr0303_3

Hoover, W. A. and Gough, P. B. (1990). The simple view of reading. *Reading and Writing: An Interdisciplinary Journal, 2,* 127-160. doi: 10.1007/BF00401799

Katzir, T., Lesaux, N. K., and Kim, Y. (2009). The role of reading self-concept and home literacy practices in fourth grade reading comprehension. *Reading and Writing, 22,* 262-276. doi: 10.1007/s11145-007-9112-8

Kendeous, P., Van den Broek, P., White, M. J., and Lynch, J. S. (2009). Predicting reading comprehension in early elementary school: the independent contributions of oral language and decoding skills. *Journal of Educational Psychology, 101*(4), 765-778. doi: 10.1037/a0015956

Lepper, M.R., Henderlong-Corpus, J.H., and Iyengar, S.S. (2005). Intrinsic and extrinsic motivational orientations in the classroom: age differences and academic correlates. *Journal of Educational Psychology, 97*(2), 184-196. doi: 10.1037/0022- 0663.97.2.184

Logan, S. and Johnston, R. (2009) Gender differences in reading ability and attitudes: examining where these differences lie. *Journal of Research in Reading, 32*(2), 199-214. doi: 10.1111/j.1467-9817.2008.01389.x

Logan, S. and Medford, E. (2011). Gender differences in the strength of association between motivation, competency beliefs and reading skill. *Educational Research, 53*(1), 85- 94. doi: 10.1080/00131881.2011.552242

Logan, S., Medford, E., and Hughes, N. (2011). The importance of intrinsic motivation for high and low ability readers' reading comprehension performance. *Learning and Individual Differences, 21,* 124-128. doi: 10.1016/j.lindif.2010.09.011

Macmillan Test Unit. (2000). Group reading test II 6–14. nferNelson, Windsor.

Morgan, P. L. and Fuchs, D. (2007). Is there a bidirectional relationship between children's reading skills and reading motivation? *Exceptional Children, 73*(2), 165-183

Mucherah, W. and Yoder, A. (2008) Motivation for reading and middle school students' performance on standardised testing in reading. *Reading Psychology, 29,* 214-235. doi: 10.1080/02702710801982159

Mueller, C. M., and Dweck, C. S. (1998). Praise for intelligence can undermine children's motivation and performance. *Journal of Personality and Social Psychology, 75*(1), 33-52.

Nation, K. and Snowling, M. J. (2004). Beyond phonological skills: broader language skills contribute to the development of reading. *Journal of Research in Reading, 27*(4), 342-356. doi: 10.1111/j.1467-9817.2004.00238.x

Ouellette, G. P. (2006). What's meaning got to do with it: the role of vocabulary in word reading and reading comprehension. *Journal of Educational Psychology, 98*(3), 554-566. doi: 10.1037/0022-0663.98.3.554

Park, Y. (2011). How motivational constructs interact to predict elementary student's reading performance: Examples from attitudes and self-concept in reading. *Learning and Individual Differences,* doi: 10.1016/j/lindif.2011.02.009

Ricketts, J., Nation, K., Bishop, D. V. M. (2007). Vocabulary is important for some, but not all reading skills. *Scientific Studies of Reading, 11*(3), 235-257.

Ryan, R. M. and Deci, E. L. (2000). Intrinsic and extrinsic motivations: classic definitions and new directions. *Contemporary Educational Psychology, 25,* 54-67. doi: 10.1006/ceps.1999.1020

Savolainen, H., Ahonery, T., Aro, M., Tolvanen, A., Halopainen, L. (2008) Reading comprehension, word reading and spelling as predictors of school achievement and choice of secondary education. *Learning and Instruction, 18,* 201-210. doi: 10.1016/j.learninstruc.2007.09.017

Share, D.L. (1995). Phonological recoding and self-teaching: sine qua non of reading acquisition. *Cognition, 55*(2), 151-218. doi: 10.1016/0010-0277(94)00645-2

Snowling, M. J., Stothard, S. E., and McLean, J. (1996). Graded nonword reading test. England: Harcourt Assessment.

Souvignier, E. and Moklesgerami, J. (2006). Using self-regulation as a framework for implementing strategy instruction to foster reading comprehension. *Learning and Instruction, 16*(1), 57-71. doi: 10.1016/j.learninstruc.2005.12.006

Swanson, H. L and Berninger, V. (1995). The role of working memory in skilled and less skilled readers' comprehension. *Intelligence, 21,* 83-108. doi: 10.1016/0160-2896(95) 90040-3

Taboada, A., Tonks, S. M., Wigfield, A., and Guthrie, J. T. (2009). Effects of motivational and cognitive variables on reading comprehension. *Reading and Writing, 22,* 85-106. doi: 10.1007/s11145-008-9133-y

Unrau, N. and Schlackman, J. (2006). Motivation and its relationship with reading achievement in an urban middle school. *The Journal of Educational Research, 100*(2). doi: 10.3200/JOER.100.2.81-101

Wang, J. H. and Guthrie, J. T. (2004). Modelling the effects of intrinsic motivation, extrinsic motivation, amount of reading, and past reading achievement on text comprehension between U.S. and Chinese students. *Reading Research Quarterly, 39*(2), 162-186. doi: 10.1598/RRQ.39.2.2

Wigfield, A. (1997). Reading motivation: A domain specific approach to motivation. *Educational Psychologist, 32*(2), 59-68. doi: 10.1207/s15326985ep3202_1

Wigfield, A. and Guthrie, J. T. (1997) Relations of children's motivation for reading to the amount and breadth of their reading. *Journal of Experimental Psychology, 89*(3), 420-432. doi: 10.1037/0022-0663.89.3.420

APPENDIX

Reading and School Motivation Questionnaire
Note: R = Negatively worded item (Likert Scale score is reversed).

Part 1: Competency Beliefs
Reading
- I am a good reader.
- I am good at working out hard words myself.
- I find it difficult to understand the stories we read in class. (R)
- I make a lot of mistakes when I'm reading. (R)

School
- I am good at doing school work.
- I find school work easy.
- The work I do in class is often too hard for me. (R)
- I make lots of mistakes in my school work. (R)

Part 2: School Motivation
Intrinsic
-Challenge
- I like it when the teacher gives us hard, challenging work.
- If something is difficult, I just give up. (R)
-Curiosity
- If the teacher discusses something interesting, I like to find out more.
- I am not interested in learning about new things. (R)
-Involvement
- I often get really involved in the work I am doing in class.
- I don't like to be involved in group and class discussions. (R)

Extrinsic
-Recognition
- It is important to me that my parents notice when I do good work.
- I don't care whether the teacher notices when I do good work. (R)
-Grades
- I work hard in class to get a good grade.
- I don't care what my final grade is at the end of the year. (R)
-Compliance
- I don't listen to the teacher when I'm told to get on with my work.
- I finish my work on time so that I don't get into trouble. (R)
-Social
- I help my friends with their school work.
- I don't talk about school with my family. (R)
-Competition

- I try to get more answers right than my friends.
- I don't care if my friends get better grades than me. (R)

Part 3: Reading Motivation

Intrinsic

-Challenge
- I like it when the teacher gives us a hard, challenging book to read.
- I don't like it when I have to work out difficult words in stories. (R)

-Curiosity
- I think reading is a good way to learn more about things.
- I am not interested in learning new things from books. (R)

-Involvement
- I often imagine how things would look in the stories I read.
- I am never very interested in the stories I read. (R)

Extrinsic

-Recognition
- I like it when the teacher says I have read well.
- I don't care about getting compliments for my reading. (R)

-Grades
- I read to improve my grades.
- I don't think it is important to get a good reading grade. (R)

-Compliance
- I read in class so that I won't get into trouble.
- I don't listen to the teacher when I'm told to do my reading. (R)

-Social
- I talk about books with my friends.
- I never read at home with my family. (R)

-Competition
- I like to finish my reading before everyone else in the class.
- I don't care if my friends are better readers than me. (R)

In: Handbook on Psychology of Motivation
Editors: J. N. Franco and A. E. Svensgaard

ISBN: 978-1-62100-755-5
© 2012 Nova Science Publishers, Inc.

Chapter 10

MOTIVATION TO LEARN, SELF-REGULATION AND ACADEMIC ACHIEVEMENT: HOW EFFECTIVE ARE STUDY SKILLS PROGRAMMES?

Marcus Henning[1] and Emmanuel Manalo[2]
[1]Centre for Medical and Health Sciences Education,
University of Auckland, Auckland, New Zealand
[2]Centre for English Language Education,
Faculty of Science and Engineering, Waseda University,
Shinjuku-ku, Tokyo, Japan

ABSTRACT

Background: There is an established body of research that links various forms of motivation to academic achievement. It has further been documented that students' engagement in educational activities is moderated by motivation and self-regulatory processes, and levels of the latter processes have been shown to be associated with outcome measures of effort, persistence, choice, and achievement. Because of these apparent connections, study skills courses are often provided in universities and other tertiary institutions to ameliorate student problems in motivation, self-regulation, and achievement. However, the effectiveness of such courses, as well as the mechanisms by which they may work, have not been sufficiently examined in research.

Purpose: The purpose of this study was to assess the impact of a study skills course on students' levels of motivation and self regulation, and ultimately their academic achievement. The main research questions were: (1) Do students who attend study skills courses differ from those who do not in their levels of motivation and self regulation? (2) Do students who participate in such courses evidence change in their levels of motivation and self regulation? (3) Does completion of study skills courses contribute to better academic outcomes?

Method: Three hundred and seventeen students (241 female, 76 male), predominantly from social science and education disciplines, volunteered to participate in this study. The students were asked to complete a demographic survey and the Learning and Study Skills Strategies Inventory (LASSI) at the beginning and at the end of an academic semester. A study skills course was offered to all these students, and comparisons were subsequently made between those who participated in the course and those who did not. In addition, with their permission, academic grades were obtained for all the students.

Results: Statistical analyses incorporating a hierarchical regression procedure revealed a number of significant findings. With regard to attendance of the study skills course, significant correlations were found with the students' scores on the LASSI attitude (ATT) scale and their age. With regard to the academic grades obtained by the students, significant correlations were found with attendance of the course, the students' age, and changes in the LASSI ATT and motivation (MOT) scales. Older students who attended the course evidenced improvements in the LASSI information processing (INP), selecting main ideas (SMI), and use of study aids (STA) scales. A comparison of the students according to their attendance of the course also revealed that those who did not attend subsequently evidenced increases in their scores on the LASSI anxiety (ANX) scale and decreases in their scores on the STA and self testing (SFT) scales.

Discussion and Conclusion: The findings indicate that students who possessed better attitudes and interest in academic success, and those who were older, were more likely to attend the study skills course. In turn, students who attended the course, and those who were older, achieved better grades. Better grade achievement could therefore be partly explained by the better attitudes that attendees bring to their studies, as well as possibly the experience and maturity in outlook of the older students leading them to apply more of the study techniques advised in the course. Finally, indications of some deterioration in anxiety and application of study techniques among those who did not attend the study skills course – not observed among those who attended the course – suggest a more stable management of the demands of tertiary education among the latter group. In conclusion therefore, the findings of this research suggest that both the attitude and maturity that students bring to their studies, as well as input from study skills courses, have significant impact on grade achievement.

MOTIVATION TO LEARN, SELF-REGULATION AND ACADEMIC ACHIEVEMENT: HOW EFFECTIVE ARE STUDY SKILLS PROGRAMMES?

Over the past four decades, a global trend in providing more comprehensive academic advising services for tertiary-level students has brought with it the development of support mechanisms for those who are considered at risk of attrition (Beatty, 1991; Van Rij-Heyligers, 2005). The support mechanisms have included study skills programs. These programs share a common objective of promoting effective academic learning and performance skills in students by addressing key achievement-related factors such as motivation and self-regulation (Henning, 2009; Huijser, Kimmins, and Galligan, 2008; Polson, 2003).

Research studies that have been reported in the academic literature provide strong support for the notion that study skills programs elevate academic achievement (Fraser and Hendren, 2002; Manalo, Wong-Toi, and Henning, 1996; Onwuegbuzie, Slate, and Schwartz, 2001; Trotter and Roberts, 2006; Tuckman, 2003; Wai-yung and Lai-ling, 1984). Tuckman (2003), for example, pointed out that academic performance in higher education settings could be enhanced when students participate in programs designed to teach them cognitive and motivation strategies: results from his study, showing significantly higher grade point averages for students attending a study skills program than for those not attending, back up this claim. In addition, Knox (2005) found that a generic transition program incorporating study skills instruction enhanced students' perceived sense of self-confidence and self-efficacy. Her findings have been corroborated by a similar study (Durkin and Main, 2002) showing that students were more confident about their writing skills after attending an eight-week discipline-based study skills workshop. Following a meta-analysis of 51 research studies, Hattie, Biggs, and Purdie (1996) observed that the best achievement results appeared when study skill programs focused on metacognitive strategy development alongside motivational and contextual relevance, suggesting an important connection between the core teaching and assessment context and study skills courses.

Motivation and self-regulation are generally considered to be integral to the development of effective learning and study strategies (Boekaerts, 2004; Covington, 2000; Eccles and Wigfield, 2002; Pintrich, 2003; Zimmerman, Bandura, and Martinez-Pons, 1992). Learning and study strategies is a term used to convey the acquisition, understanding and transfer of knowledge and skills (Weinstein, Husman, and Dierking, 2000). This model of learning is congruent with a four-phase self-regulation process model that has been developed to explain the cyclical interactions between the concepts of fore-thought, monitoring, control, and reflection (Pintrich and Zusho, 2007; Zimmerman, 2000). Fore-thought is linked to planning and goal setting after careful consideration of the learning context. Monitoring occurs through the engagement process of learning to ensure task activation is optimally achieved. Control is required to ensure that the process of learning is in line with the learning goals. Finally, reflection occurs after task completion and involves appraisals of success and failure.

In an earlier paper, Weinstein and Meyer (1991) deliberated over some of the key strategies that students need to develop in order to be effective in their study. They felt that incorporation of appropriate strategies would be instrumental to achieving academic goals and that self realization in terms of strategy use would enable students to become more competent learners. They proposed that to be effective learners students need to have awareness about how they can memorize information at both short and long term levels and to have insight into how they can organize acquired information in order to facilitate effective use. Cano (2006) further suggested that students' awareness of the applications of affective and metacognitive elements of learning is important in the development of learning strategies. It was from this basis that Weinstein and her colleagues developed an instrument that could be used to enhance students' levels of awareness about their own learning (Weinstein and Palmer, 2002; Weinstein, Palmer, and Schulte, 1987; Weinstein, Palmer, and Shulte, 2002).

This instrument, the Learning and Study Skills Inventory (LASSI), was developed as a pragmatic tool that could be mapped onto a study skills training program (Entwistle and McCune, 2004). The instrument appraises key aspects of the learner's perceptions in relation to a comprehensive range of study skills required for effective learning and, thus, provides feedback about corresponding skills, attitudes, motivations, and beliefs (Weinstein and Palmer, 2002). The areas of learning are broken down into three components of strategic learning, namely: skill, will, and self-regulation. Each component is represented by a composite score computed from a selection of 10 scale measures. Given its pragmatic nature and inclusive coverage of pertinent skills in academic study, the LASSI was selected as the measurement instrument for the investigation described in this paper. Independent psychometric examinations of the LASSI have also returned largely favourable verdicts: for example, Cano (2006) reported acceptable psychometric properties, a three-factor model consistent with the LASSI's supposed structure, and positive links of two of those factors to student academic performance.

Two dominant theories found in the contemporary literature of achievement motivation in education are the achievement goal theory (Cano and Berbén, 2009) and the expectancy-value theory (Pintrich and Zusho, 2007; Wigfield and Cambria, 2010). Cano and Berbén (2009) summarized some of the developments in the achievement goal theory and noted that its main tenets relate to four main concepts: mastery-approach, mastery-avoidance, performance-approach, and performance-avoidance. Wigfield and Cambria (2010) presented a model that incorporates the main features of the expectancy-value theory: according to this model, expectancies for success and subjective task values interact to influence achievement-related choices and performance. Several factors affect these expectancies and values, such as students' goals, their perceptions of task difficulty and competence, and their prior learning experiences. Behind the individual student are complex societal and cultural values and norms that inevitably influence the individual's choices. It is also probable that students who are highly motivated would more likely attend study skills workshops, and study skills programs would more likely impact on highly motivated students than those with lower levels of motivation (Hirsch, 2001).

Even though there are instruments like the LASSI that can be used to assess students' awareness about and use of study strategies, few studies have actually examined data about such awareness and use in relation to student participation in tertiary level study skills programs. Likewise, although there are viable models that propose possible links between student motivation, participation in study skills programs, and subsequent achievement, the present authors are not aware of any previous studies that have empirically examined those relationships. Thus, the objective of the present study was to better understand the effects of study skills programs on student achievement – taking into consideration their awareness and use of study strategies prior and subsequent to participation in such programs. More specifically, the study set out to address the following main questions:

1. Do students who attend study skills courses differ from those who do not in their levels of motivation and self regulation?
2. Do students who participate in such courses evidence change in their levels of motivation and self regulation?
3. Does completion of study skills courses contribute to better academic outcomes?

METHOD

Participants

Three hundred and seventeen self-selected students (241 female, 76 male) voluntarily participated in the study which was conducted at a university in Auckland, New Zealand. The average age of the sample was 24.76 years ($SD = 9.24$). Most of the students in the sample came from the faculties of social sciences and education.

Procedure

Data for this investigation was collected over a three semester period. At the beginning of each of the three semesters, students were asked to complete a demographic survey and the LASSI. This first administration of the LASSI constituted the students' "pre-LASSI" measures (i.e., their LASSI scores prior to possible attendance of study skills courses on offer during that semester). The students were requested to complete the questionnaires in regular classroom environments during class time. Students were also asked for informed consent to allow the researchers to have access to their academic records so that their grades could be factored in the study. The "post-LASSI" measures (i.e., the students' LASSI scores later in the semester after they had had opportunities to attend skills courses on offer) were obtained by sending the instrument to the students via conventional mail in week 10 of the semester, which was prior to the high stakes examinations in weeks 12 and 13. Ethics approval for the collection and use of data was obtained from the institution's ethics committee.

Measures

Three main measures were incorporated into the study design, namely self-report scores from the LASSI (pre-, and post-), enrolment in and completion of a study skills course (completion, or non-enrolment), and grade average computations.

The LASSI (Weinstein and Palmer, 2002; Weinstein et al., 2002) has 80 items; the instrument appraises students' self-perceptions about their use of learning and study strategies in relation to 10 scales and three components. Each LASSI item measures responses on a five-point counterbalanced response format ranging from "Not at all typical of me" to "Very much typical of me". The 10 scales pertain to measurements of anxiety, attitude, concentration, information processing, motivation, self-testing, selecting main ideas, study aids, time management, and test strategies. These 10 scales can be represented as three components of "will" (anxiety, attitude, and motivation), "skill" (information processing, selecting main ideas, and test strategies) and "self-regulation" (concentration, self-testing, study aids, and time management).

The students' successful completion – or otherwise – of a generic study skills course was also used as a variable (completion; non-enrolment). The students could enrol in these courses voluntarily; the courses were free of charge, and various means were employed to ensure that the students were fully aware of them. These means included provision of details about the courses via the enrolment packs sent to the students and through infomercials, as well as through direct communication from key people that the students were in regular or semi-regular contact with (i.e., student mentors, the students' lecturers, and other faculty personnel). These courses aimed to develop the students learning and study strategies, including their motivation and self-regulation strategies, by teaching them methods for enhancing memory, taking useful notes, planning assignments, developing effective referencing, engaging in writing practice, practicing test and examination skills, and so on (AUT University, 2007).

To compute the students' grade averages, letter grades, derived from the students' end of semester cumulative summative mark, were converted to a numerical value, which is common practice for this type of analysis (Edwards, 2005). The conversion scale used was as follows: A+ = 11, A = 10, A- = 9, B+ = 8, B = 7, B- = 6, C+ = 5, C = 4, C- = 3, D = 2, and E = 1. Students who did not complete their courses were excluded from the analyses as there were far too many possible reasons for such attrition apart from academic performance, including personal, health, and financial problems.

Of the demographic information provided by the participants, a review of the literature pertinent to this topic area suggested that age and gender in particular were important variables that could impact on the results (Heckhausen and Dweck, 1998; Hoskins and Hooff, 2005). Thus, the students' age and gender details were factored in the analyses conducted.

Data Analysis

First, a binary regression analysis was utilized to ascertain whether engagement in a study skills course could be explained by LASSI measures taken before the study skills courses were made available. Second, the data were split in terms of completion of a study skills course (completion; non-enrolment) and then a series of t-tests were conducted for each pre- and post-LASSI measure. Third, a multiple regression approach was carried out to investigate whether the change scores could be used to explain the students' grade averages.

RESULTS

Research question 1: Do students who attend study skills courses differ from those who do not in their levels of motivation and self regulation?

Table 1. Binary Logistic Regression Statistics: Study skills attendance as a function of the 10 pre-LASSI measures, gender and age

Variable	β	S.E.	Wald χ^2	df	Sig	$Exp(\beta)$
age	-.028	.014	4.176	1	.041	.972[*]
gender	.481	.299	2.592	1	.107	1.618
Anxiety	.120	.207	.336	1	.562	1.127
Attitude	-.618	.279	4.914	1	.027	.539[*]
Concentration	-.106	.298	.125	1	.724	.900
Information processing	.404	.253	2.540	1	.111	1.498
Motivation	-.259	.292	.786	1	.375	.772
Self testing	-.283	.257	1.214	1	.271	.754
Selecting main ideas	.317	.313	1.024	1	.311	1.373
Study aids	-.228	.266	.735	1	.391	.796
Time management	.273	.325	.706	1	.401	1.314
Test strategies	-.199	.333	.359	1	.549	.819

[*] $p < .05$.

Table 2. Means (and standard deviations) for each of the pre- and post-LASSI scale scores

Attendance at a study skills course	LASSI scale	Pre-LASSI measures M	SD	Post-LASSI measures M	SD
Completed a course	Anxiety	2.998	.877	3.177	.841
	Attitude	4.049	.531	4.021	.642
	Concentration	3.440	.702	3.445	.686
	Information processing	3.568	.718	3.636	.582
	Motivation	3.828	.689	3.906	.668
	Self-testing	3.246	.679	3.177	.733
	Selecting main ideas	3.233	.723	3.318	.730
	Study aids	3.440	.600	3.342	.603
	Time management	3.179	.574	3.225	.620
	Test strategies	3.327	.731	3.408	.714
Did not enrol in a course ($n = 74$)	Anxiety	3.015	.802	3.191	.818
	Attitude	3.838	.594	3.824	.628
	Concentration	3.194	.702	3.225	.703
	Information processing	3.564	.695	3.435	.659
	Motivation	3.554	.619	3.627	.681
	Self-testing	3.137	.682	2.943	.686
	Selecting main ideas	3.253	.648	3.361	.612
	Study aids	3.374	.577	3.077	.550
	Time management	2.990	.594	2.925	.591
	Test strategies	3.309	.640	3.379	.668

According to a binary logistic regression that was carried out, the model including 10 pre-LASSI measures, gender and age were significant predictors of attendance at the study skills workshop ($\chi^2 = 21.339$, $df = 12$, $p = .046$, Nagelkerke $R^2 = .092$). More specifically, the results depicted in Table 1, show significant associations for the model components of age ($\beta = -.028$, $p < .05$) and the pre-LASSI measure of attitude ($\beta = -.618$, $p < .05$) in predicting attendance (and completion) of a study skills course. A negative Beta coefficient (study skills completion = 0; non-enrolment = 1) between attitude and attendance of a study skills course suggests that students with higher levels of positive study attitude will be more likely to complete study skills courses. A similar result for age suggests that older students will more likely attend (and complete) a study skills course than younger students. A post hoc Pearson correlation between age and attitude indicated no interaction between these two variables ($r = -.01$, $p = .83$).

Research question 2: Do students who participate in study skills courses evidence change in their levels of motivation and self regulation?

The data was first split so that students who completed a study skills course could be compared with those students who did not enrol in any of the courses. Means and standard deviations are presented in Table 2 for each of the pre- and post-LASSI scale scores.

Paired sample *t*-tests were computed to determine whether the changes between the pre- and post-LASSI measures were significant. No significant changes were found for students who completed a study skills course. However, the analysis revealed three significant changes for students who did not enrol in a course (see Table 3). These changes were as follows:

1. Their LASSI 'anxiety' scores were significantly higher at the post stage ($M = 3.015$, $SD = .802$) than at the pre stage ($M = 3.191$, $SD = .818$), $t(73) = -2.444$, $p < .05$, $d = -.176$. It should be noted, however, that the actual magnitude of difference was very similar to that of the students who completed a study skills course, so the significant difference obtained for the students who did not enrol in a study skills course must have been due to a greater number of them consistently showing deterioration in their anxiety scores.
2. Their LASSI 'self-testing' scores were significantly lower at the post stage ($M = 2.943$, $SD = .686$) than at the pre stage ($M = 3.137$, $SD = .682$), $t(73) = 2.650$, $p < .05$, $d = .194$. The magnitude of the difference here is quite different from that of the students who completed a study skills course.
3. Their LASSI 'study aids' scores were significantly lower at the post stage ($M = 3.077$, $SD = .550$) than at the pre stage ($M = 3.374$, $SD = .577$), $t(73) = 4.924$, $p < .01$, $d = .297$. Again, the magnitude of the difference here is quite different from that of the students who completed a study skills course.

Table 3. Pre- and post-LASSI scale scores comparison for students who attended and did not attend a study skills course

Attendance at a study skills course	LASSI scale	Mean difference (pre-post)	SD	t	Sig. (2 tailed)
Completed a course	Anxiety	-.179	.796	-1.924	.058
	Attitude	.028	.534	.445	.658
	Concentration	-.005	.513	-.090	.929
	Information processing	-.068	.671	-.865	.390
	Motivation	-.078	.522	-1.275	.206
	Self-testing	.069	.759	.777	.439
	Selecting main ideas	-.085	.652	-1.116	.268
	Study aids	.097	.564	1.478	.144
	Time management	-.046	.546	-.717	.476
	Test strategies	-.080	.602	-1.140	.258
Did not enrol in a course	Anxiety	-.176	.620	-2.444	.017[*]
	Attitude	.014	.731	.162	.872
	Concentration	-.031	.616	-.431	.668
	Information processing	.129	.591	1.879	.064
	Motivation	-.073	.622	-1.006	.318
	Self-testing	.194	.631	2.650	.010[*]
	Selecting main ideas	-.108	.508	-1.829	.071
	Study aids	.297	.519	4.924	.000[**]
	Time management	.064	.510	1.087	.280
	Test strategies	-.070	.545	-1.103	.274

[*] $p < .05$, [**] $p < .01$.

Table 4. Results of a 3-step model showing the grade average score predictive ability of the variables investigated

Variable	b	SE b	β
Constant	5.555	.708	
Age	.046	.021	.186*
Gender	.190	.451	.034
Study skills workshop	-1.282	.397	-.266**
Change in anxiety	-.095	.334	-.028
Change in attitude	1.048	.409	.267*
Change in concentration	.098	.421	.023
Change in information processing	-.022	.417	-.006
Change in motivation	-1.092	.441	-.258*
Change in self-testing	.629	.339	.182
Change in selecting main ideas	.106	.410	.025
Change in study aids	-.086	.415	-.020
Change in time management	.244	.418	.054
Change in test strategies	-.161	.426	-.038

note: for the 3-Step model: $R^2 = .199$, *$p < .05$, **$p < .01$.

Research question 3: Does completion of study skills courses contribute to better academic outcomes?

The result of a preliminary analysis of the participants' pre-LASSI scores showed that these predicted grade average: $β = .20$, $t(286) = 2.89$, $p < .01$. To provide a more comprehensive answer to the research question, however, a three step hierarchical process was carried out whereby the initial demographics variables were considered, then attendance or otherwise of a study skills course, and finally the resulting change indicated by the differences between the pre- and post-LASSI measures. Table 4 shows that several variables in the *3-Step* model significantly predicted grade average scores. More specifically:

1. The result for the 'Age' variable indicates that older students yielded higher grade averages than younger students: $β = .186$, $t(130) = 2.166$, $p < .05$.
2. The result for the 'Study skills workshop' variable indicates that students who completed a study skills course gained higher grade averages: $β = -.266$, $t(130) = -3.233$, $p < .01$.
3. The result for the 'Change in attitude' variable indicates that students who evidenced improvements in their attitude scores received higher grade averages: $β = .267$, $t(130) = 2.563$, $p < .05$.
4. The result for the 'Change in motivation' variable indicates that students who evidenced improvements in their motivation scores received lower grade averages: $β = -.258$, $t(130) = -2.477$, $p < .05$.

To identify the possible cause of the anomalous results for the change in attitude and change in motivation variables, two further regressions were conducted: one for participants who completed a study skills course and another for those who did not. Non-significant results were obtained for the dataset of students who completed a study skills course, and one significant result was obtained for the students who did not enrol in a course. Essentially, lower scores of motivation predicted higher grades for students who did not complete a study course: $\beta = -.356$, $t(59) = -2.445$, $p < .05$. For the non-enrolled data set, a marginally significant results was observed for change in attitude: $\beta = .317$, $t(59) = 1.995$, $p = .051$. Therefore, it can be concluded that the source of the anomalous result (i.e., that students who improved in their study motivation gaining lower grade averages) lies with the data set of those who did not attend a study skills course. The additional regression that was carried out showed no presence of this anomalous finding in the data set of the students who completed a study skills course.

DISCUSSION

This discussion will focus on the practical implications of the findings: more specifically, it will consider what the results of this study suggest about the usefulness of tertiary level study skills courses in relation to student motivation, self-regulation, and achievement. Three main issues will be examined. The first concerns students' attitudes and motivations in enrolling in and completing optional study skills courses. The second is about the question of how such courses might in turn impact on students' attitudes, motivations, and study self-regulation. The final issue is the nature of the relationship between such courses and students' academic achievement.

Students Who Participate in Study Skills Courses: Older and Possessing better Attitudes

Two significant findings were obtained in relation to the first research question of whether students who participate in study skills courses differ from those who do not in their levels of motivation and self-regulation. More specifically, the findings indicate that older students, and students with higher scores indicative of a positive study attitude, were more likely to complete a study skills course. Interestingly, no significant differences were found in the students' actual motivation and self-regulation scores at the start of the semesters – contrary to assumptions that some educators and researchers have made that higher levels of motivation may distinguish students who choose to participate in study skills courses (see, e.g., Lipsky and Ender, 1990; Mealey, 1990).

Wigfield and Cambria (2010), in their review of motivation in children, commented that instrumentality will likely change with age. Upon reaching the various stages of adulthood, it is also likely that people's views about the instrumentality of activities and resource options that are available to them will change (Heckhausen and Dweck, 1998). It is therefore possible that the more mature students in the present study perceived higher levels of instrumentality in the activity of study skills course participation – prompting more of them to enrol in such courses. There is, therefore, a likely interplay between expectancy and perceived value in the way older students choose to engage with academic support services that are available in tertiary education environments. Future research will need to verify the existence of such perceptions among more mature students and any causal links to uptake of services.

Additionally, Pintrich and Zusho (2007) observed that students become more adept with the implementation of self-regulation strategies as they grow older, noting that age is likely to be a moderator between maintaining motivation and cultivating self-regulation strategies. Again, future research will need to examine such connections: perhaps through the use of a more longitudinal design it may be possible to elucidate the mechanisms by which age might impact on student decision making, particularly in regard to using academic and other support services.

In addition to the finding that older students were more proactive in selecting study skills courses, students with higher LASSI attitude scores were also found to more likely participate in such courses. However, it is important to note that older students did not necessary score higher in the attitude scale indicating that these two factors were independent. Weinstein and Palmer (2002) described the LASSI attitude scale as being related to students' levels of motivation and predispositions toward engagement in educational activities. It is also likely linked to better determined life goals and higher levels of self-responsibility in promoting self-regulation. As with age, attitude is one of the key components in the expectancy-value model of motivation (Pintrich and Zusho, 2007; Wigfield and Cambria, 2010) as it aptly connects with students' perceptions of subjective task value and is likely related to their previous learning experiences and successes. The notion that students with strong attitudinal beliefs seek out study skills courses also resonates with self-determination theory whereby students will likely engage in activities because they are viewed as important and clearly linked to goal attainment (Wigfield and Cambria, 2010).

In direct answer to the first research question, therefore, the students who chose to participate in study skills courses were found not to differ in their levels of motivation and self-regulation. However, they were found to be older and in possession of more positive attitudes toward their studies. Apart from being predictors of participation in study skills courses, the research literature pertaining to age and study attitude suggests that they are potential influences on students' academic achievment. Thus, they need to at least be considered as possible moderator variables in any claims made about better academic achievement that study skills courses facilitate.

Promotion of Stability in Levels of Anxiety and Perceptions of Performance Management

In answer to the second research question, the findings of this study suggest that students who participate in study skills courses evidence more stable self-perceptions about their use of learning and study straegies over time compared to students who do not participate in such courses. Students who completed study skills courses did not manifest changes in their LASSI motivation and self-regulation strategies, but students who did not complete such courses subsequently manifested higher LASSI anxiety scores and lower LASSI scores in self-testing and use of study aids.

It is important to note that when the second administration of the LASSI (post-LASSI) was carried out in week 10 of the semesters, the students were only a few weeks away from high stakes final examinations which occur at the end of each semester. The students therefore would likely have been experiencing considerable exam-related stress. Furthermore, as it was the latter end of the semester, students would have already experienced the demanding nature of their courses of study and, for many, such experiences might have highlighted the inadequacy of techniques they had been using for study management. The post-LASSI score in anxiety, self-testing, and study aids of students who did not participate in study skills courses suggest such an outcome – of a deterioration in self-perception about their study approaches and levels of anxiety. In contrast, those who completed study skills courses evidenced stability in the same measures, suggesting a possible beneficial outcome of such participation. In other words, the study skills courses could have promoted the students abilities to deal with the demands of their studies, resulting in more stable levels of anxiety and perceptions about their own competence in self-testing and study aid use.

The notion of stability has been used in many guises, but stable expectancies about study performance are more likely to result from experiences of success: as such, they may be a good predictor of future academic achievement (Pintrich and Zusho, 2007). The observed LASSI scores stability among the students who completed a study skills course may also be an indicator that they had formulated achievement goals as a consequence of that course completion, thus influencing their processes of goal implementation and regulation (Fryer and Elliot, 2007). Moreover, the goals adopted by the study skills participants might have been facilitative of the establishment of a cognitive framework for the self-regulation strategies of self-testing and study aid use: if so, the participants would have in effect developed *mastery goals* (i.e., goals that are "focused on attaining task-based or intrapersonal competence", (Fryer and Elliot, 2007).

There is a possible link between the affective measure of test anxiety and the self-regulatory measures of self-testing and use of study aids, which were seen to deteriorate in non-participant students. It is likely that students who engage in self-testing and use of study aids are promoting approach strategies to learning which will likely have a moderating effect on anxiety (Covington, 2000). The presence of increased anxiety is also likely to be evidence of a lack of preparation for the forthcoming examinations. This line of argument supports the previous suggestion that stability is often brought about by a history of sustained successes leading to an increased likelihood of future success and increased expectations about future academic achievement (Covington, 2000; Pintrich and Zusho, 2007). If these assumptions are correct, it would provide a useful, viable explanation for the benefits of attending study skills courses. That explanation would be that: acquisition of the skills taught in such courses are effective for managing learning and assessment demands, thus stabilizing levels of anxiety and perceptions relating to one's own study management performance. Such stability in turn promotes more stable performance expectations, leading to better academic achievement.

Factors that Predict Academic Achievement

The findings in this study suggest that several of the variables investigated can predict academic achievement as measured by the students' GPAs. These variables were the maturity in age of the students, their initial attitude to their studies, and their attendance of a study skills course. Furthermore, changes in the students' attitude and motivation levels were able to predict subsequent GPAs – although, for the latter, it was in a way contrary to expectation.

The idea of mature aged students being motivated by different goals compared to their younger peers is not a new concept. Knowles (1990), for example, developed a set of assumptions about adult learners, proposing that they need to know the reasons behind studying information, are more self-directed and responsible, have more life experiences which can be used as a rich resource for learning, have a greater readiness for learning, and are thus more motivated to learn. Therefore, it was not surprising to find in the present study that they were more inclined to take study skills courses in the first place and, as a consequence, likely accumulated even more self-regulatory strategies that could be added to their already richer life and educational experiences (Pintrich and Zusho, 2007). The resulting combination of old and new educational experiences and skills would likely have contributed to their better academic achievement.

The results of this study also lend support to claims in previous research studies of a link between study skills course participation and better academic performance (Manalo, et al., 1996; Trotter and Roberts, 2006; Tuckman, 2003). The results, however, were not all congruent with original expectations. As previously reported: (1) students – irrespective of study skills course participation – who evidenced improvements in their LASSI attitude scores achieved better academic outcomes; (2) students who participated in study skills courses evidenced no significant changes in their LASSI scores across the semesters; and (3) students who did not participate in such courses showed deterioration in their LASSI anxiety, self-testing, and use of study aids scores, and those who obtained lower LASSI motivation scores achieved higher GPAs.

The first of these results is perhaps understandable: students' attitude scores at the start of the semesters also proved to be a significant predictor of academic achievement, suggesting that it is very important for students to possess – or develop – a positive attitude to their studies if they want to do well. This finding is in line with Cano's (2006) report that the LASSI 'affective strategies' construct – which includes the attitude scale – is positively linked to academic performance. This finding also suggests that for study skills courses to be effective, one of their objectives ought to be the promotion of improved study attitudes among participants.

The second result has been discussed in the previous subsection as indicative of a stabilizing effect that study skills courses facilitate in student participants. As the non-participants evidenced deterioration in some of their LASSI scores, this explanation may well be adequate. However, if academic-related skills are significantly linked to academic outcomes (see, e.g., Robbins, Lauver, Le, Davis, Langley, and Carlstrom, 2004), and study skills courses are intended to promote the development of those academic skills, a more desirable result would have been to find evidence of improvements in the participants' scores in at least some of the LASSI's affective and goal strategies (cf. Cano, 2006). It is possible that the study skills courses that were offered to the students in the present study were simply limited in their effectiveness and that more effective courses could have promoted such improvements. For example, it may be that, as some authors have suggested, study skills courses that are embedded within subject disciplines (see, e.g., Baik and Greig, 2009; Hattie et al., 1996) or those that are offered in the context of specific subject disciplines (e.g., Manalo and Leader, 2007) would produce better outcomes. Alternatively, as Manalo (2006) explained, study skills courses that are generic in nature can be effective if instructors ensure that student participants fully understand and can competently apply the strategies taught to the requirements of their own courses of study. Both generic and embedded (or subject contextualized) study skills courses have been reported as effective (see, e.g., Manalo, Marshall, and Fraser, 2010), so it may not be the embedded or generic nature of these courses that matters. In light of the present study's findings and these other considerations, it would appear useful in future investigations to distinguish qualities of effective and not-so-effective study skills courses – in terms of both the content and pedagogical approaches used in the courses, and the changes in perceptions and skills they may faciliate in student participants.

The finding that students who did not take part in study skills courses deteriorated in their anxiety, self-testing, and use of study aid scores had been discussed earlier and can perhaps be considered understandable in the context of when the post-LASSI assessments were administered (i.e., toward the end of the semesters, just a few weeks prior to final examinations). However, the finding that among these students, those who scored lower in motivation subsequently gained higher GPAs was unexpected and probably warrants more careful examinaton in future research. It is possible that this finding is simply an anomaly specific to the cohort of students who participated in the present study: for example, that there might have been sufficient numbers among them who were academically competent but poorly motivated, and who nevertheless achieved well in their final examinations. It is also possible that, despite previously reported links between motivation and academic achievement (e.g., Cano, 2006; Weinstein et al., 2002), motivation on its own – without the necessary skills for executing target tasks – is insufficient for influencing the desired performance outcomes. As the students did not participate in study skills courses, it is possibe to assume that fewer among them would have been adequately knowledgeable about academic-related skills and, even if they possessed high levels of motivation, they might not have been able to approach their learning and exam preparation in ways that would have led to successful outcomes.

CONCLUSION

This study found evidence to support the notion that study skills courses promote academic achievement among students who participate in them. However, this conclusion requires qualification in that, although no differences at the start of the semesters were found in motivation and self-regulation scores of students who participated in study skills courses as compared to to those who did not, differences were found in age and attitude to study. Consequently, it cannot be ruled out that the better academic achivement of students who participate in study skills courses may be due to greater proportions of them being more mature in age and/or possessing better attitudes toward their studies. Further investigations will therefore need be carried out to tease out the relative contributions of participation, maturity in age, and possession of positive study attitudes on academic achievement. The finding that students who participated in study skills courses did not evidence improvements in the LASSI measurements suggests – as one possibility – that such courses promote stability among participants in their academic-related perceptions and study management skills – especially in light of the additional finding that non-participants evidenced deterioration in their LASSI anxiety, self-testing and study aid scores. However, this finding also raises a question about variability in quality and effectiveness of study skills courses that are offered to students at the tertiary level: in other words, whether no improvements were observed in students who participated in the study skills courses because of limitations of those particular courses in facilitating such improvements. Thus, a more pertinent objective in future research may not be to determine whether study skills courses promote academic achievement, but to identify the characteristics of study skills courses that effectively promote academic achievement in students.

REFERENCES

Beatty, J. D. (1991). The national academic advising association: A brief history. *NACADA Journal, 11*(1), 5-25.

Boekaerts, M. (2004). Motivation, learning and instruction. In N. J. Smelser (Ed.), *International encyclopedia of social and behavioral sciences* (pp. 10112-10117). New York: Elsevier.

Cano, F. (2006). An in-depth analysis of the Learning and Study Strategies Inventory (LASSI). *Educational and Psychological Measurement,, 66*(6), 1023-1038.

Cano, F., and Berbén, A. (2009). University students' achievement goals and approaches to learning in mathematics. *British Journal of Educational Psychology, 79*(1), 131-153. doi: 10.1348/000709908X314928

Covington, M. V. (2000). Goal theory, motivation, and school achievement: An integrative review. *Annual Review of Psychology, 51*(171-200).

Durkin, K., and Main, A. (2002). Discipline-based study skills support for first-year undergraduate students. *Active Learning in Higher Education, 3*(1), 24-39.

Eccles, J., and Wigfield, A. (2002). Motivational beliefs, values, and goals. *Annual Review of Psychology, 53*, 109-133.

Edwards, P. A. (2005). Impact of technology on the content and nature of teaching and learning. *Nursing Education Perspectives, 26*(6), 344-347.

Entwistle, N., and McCune, V. (2004). The conceptual bases of study strategy inventories. *Educational Psychology Review, 16*(4), 325-345.

Fraser, C., and Hendren, G. (2002). Revisiting agendas: Confirming the value of transitional study skills programmes Retrieved March 20, 2006, from http://www.ecu.edu.au/conferences/herdsa/main/papers/nonref/pdf/CathFraser.pdf

Fryer, J. W., and Elliot, A. J. (2007). Stability and change in achievement goals. *Journal of Educational Psychology, 99*(4), 700-714. doi: 10.1037/0022-0663.99.4.700

Hattie, J., Biggs, J., and Purdie, N. (1996). Effects of learning skills interventions on student learning: A meta-analysis. *Review of Educational Research, 66*(2), 99-136.

Heckhausen, J., and Dweck, C. S. (1998). Introduction. In J. Heckhausen and C. S. Dweck (Eds.), *Motivation and self-regulation across the life span* (pp. 1-14). New York: Cambridge University Press.

Henning, M. (2009). Students' motivation to access academic advisory services. *NACADA Journal, 29*(1), 22-30.

Hirsch, G. (2001). *Helping college students succeed: A model for effective intervention.* Mineapolis: Brunner-Routledge.

Hoskins, S. L., and Hooff, J. C. V. (2005). Motivation and ability: Which students use online learning and what influence does it have on their achievement? *British Journal of Educational Technology, 36*(2), 177-192.

Huijser, H., Kimmins, L., and Galligan, L. (2008). Evaluating individual teaching on the road to embedding academic skills. *Journal of Academic Language and Learning, 2*(1), A23-A38.

Knowles, M. S. (1990). *The Adult Learner: A neglected species* (4th ed.). Houston: Gulf Publishing.

Knox, H. (2005). Making the transition from further to higher education: the impact of a preparatory module on retention, progression and performance. *Journal of Further and Higher Education, 29*(2), 103 - 110.

Lipsky, S. A., and Ender, S. C. I. (1990). Impact of a study skills course on probationary students. *Journal of the freshman year experience, 2*(1), 7-15.

Manalo, E. (2006). The usefulness of an intensive preparatory course for EAL thesis writers. *Journal of research in international education, 5*(2), 215-230.

Manalo, E., and Leader, D. (2007). Learning center and statistics department collaboration in improving student performance in introductory statistics. *College Student Journal, 41*(2), 454-459.

Manalo, E., Marshall, J., and Fraser, C. (2010). *Student learning support programmes that demonstrate tangible impact on retention, pass rates, and completion.* (ERIC Document Reproduction Service No. ED 516 139). Auckland: Ako Aotearoa (New Zealand National Centre for Tertiary Teaching Excellence) from members of the Association of Tertiary Learning Advisors Aotearoa New Zealand (ATLAANZ).

Manalo, E., Wong-Toi, G., and Henning, M. (1996). Effectiveness of an intensive learning skills workshop for university students on restricted enrolment. *Higher Education Research and Development, 15*(2), 189-199.

Mealey, D. L. (1990). Understanding the motivation problems of at-risk college students. *Journal of reading, 33*(8), 598-601.

Onwuegbuzie, A. J., Slate, J. R., and Schwartz, R. A. (2001). Role of study skills in graduate-level educational research courses. *Journal of Educational Research, 94*(4), 238-246.

Pintrich, P. R. (2003). A motivational science perspective on the role of student motivation in learning and teaching contexts. *Journal of Educational Psychology, 95*(4), 667–686.

Pintrich, P. R., and Zusho, A. (2007). Student motivation and self-regulated learning in the college classroom. In R. P. Perry and J. C. Smart (Eds.), *Scholarship of teaching and learning in higher education: An evidence-based perspective* (pp. 731-810). Dordrecht, The Netherlands: Springer.

Polson, C. J. (2003). Adult graduate students challenge institutions to change. *New Directions for Student Services, 2003*(102), 59-68.

Trotter, E., and Roberts, C. A. (2006). Enhancing the early student experience. *Higher Education Research and Development, 25*(4), 371 - 386.

Tuckman, B. (2003). The effect of learning and motivation strategies training on college students' achievement. *Journal of College Student Development, 44*(3), 430-437.

Van Rij-Heyligers, J. (2005). *Globalisation and pluri-scalar orchestrations in higher education : Locating the University of Auckland's Student Learning Centre historically and globally.* Degree of Doctor of Education, University of Auckland, Auckland, New Zealand.

Wai-yung, E. M. F., and Lai-ling, B. Y. L. (1984). The effects of a study skills programme on academic achievement. *CUHK Education Journal, 12*(1), 96-105.

Weinstein, C. E., Husman, J., and Dierking, D. R. (2000). Self-regulation interventions with a focus on learning strategies. In P. R. Pintrich and M. Boekaerts (Eds.), *Handbook on self-regulation* (pp. 728–744). New York: Academic Press.

Weinstein, C. E., and Meyer, D. K. (1991). Cognitive learning strategies and college teaching. *New directions for teaching and learning, 1991*(45), 15-26. doi: 10.1002/tl.37219914505

Weinstein, C. E., and Palmer, D. R. (2002). *LASSI user's manual for those administering the Learning and Study Strategies Inventory* (2nd ed.). Clearwater, FL: H and H Publishing Company, Inc.

Weinstein, C. E., Palmer, D. R., and Schulte, A. (1987). *Learning and Study Strategies Inventory (LASSI)*. Clearwater, FL: HandH Publishing Company, Inc.

Weinstein, C. E., Palmer, D. R., and Shulte, A. C. (2002). LASSI: The Learning and Study Strategies Inventory (2nd ed.). Clearwater, FL: H and H Publishing Company, Inc.

Wigfield, A., and Cambria, J. (2010). Expectancy-value theory: retrospective and prospective. In T. C. Urdan and S. A. Karabenick (Eds.), *The decade ahead: Theoretical perspectives on motivation and achievement* (Vol. 16, pp. 35-70). Bingley, UK: Emerald Group Publishing Limited.

Zimmerman, B. J. (2000). Attaining self-regulation. In M. Boekaerts, P. R. Pintrich and M. Zeidner (Eds.), *Handbook of self-regulation* (pp. 13-39). San Diego: Academic Press.

Zimmerman, B. J., Bandura, A., and Martinez-Pons, M. (1992). Self-motivation for academic attainment: The role of self-efficacy beliefs and personal goal setting. *American Educational Research Journal, 29*(3), 663-676.

In: Handbook on Psychology of Motivation
Editors: J. N. Franco and A. E. Svensgaard
ISBN: 978-1-62100-755-5
© 2012 Nova Science Publishers, Inc.

Chapter 11

THEORETICAL CONTENT OF PHYSICAL ACTIVITY WEBSITES FOR PERSONS WITH DEPRESSION

Paul D. Saville, Jennifer R. Tomasone, Desmond McEwan and Kathleen A. Martin Ginis
McMaster University, ON, Canada

ABSTRACT

Because physical activity (PA) messages based on behavior change theories have been found to enhance intentions, motivation, and PA behavior, efforts need to be directed toward making such information available to sedentary individuals (Doshi, Patrick, Sallis, & Calfas, 2003; Fisbein & Cappella, 2006). Previous research has identified a lack of theory-based information in PA websites aimed at increasing PA among the general population (Bonnar-Kidd, Black, Mattson, & Coster, 2009; Doshi et al., 2003); however, with the exception of the spinal cord injury population (Jetha, Faulkner, Gorczynski, Arbour-Nicitopoulos, & Martin Ginis, 2010), the content of PA websites directed toward populations with chronic health conditions remain largely unexplored. Because research has identified PA as an effective means for preventing and treating depression (Craft & Landers, 1998; Fox, 1999; Mutrie, 2000), this study was designed to extend scientific knowledge by evaluating the theoretical content of PA websites specifically designed for people with depression.

Findings indicated that approximately two-thirds of messages on PA websites targeting people with depression were theory-based. The majority of messages concerned individuals' outcome expectations, while relatively few messages were devoted to self-regulation or self-efficacy messages. This is disconcerting because both self-efficacy and self-regulation are important theoreical constructs (Bandura, 1997) that can enhance the influence of PA information on readers' PA beliefs and behavior (Latimer, Brawley, & Bassett, 2010). Moreover, messages based on self-efficacy and self-regulation have been shown to be particularly useful for influencing behavior in people with depression (Biddle & Mutrie, 2001). Therefore, PA websites aimed at people with depression would benefit from including additional theory-based messages that embody an equal distribution of all the theoretical constructs.

Because the Internet has become a primary source of health-related information for many individuals looking to get physically active (Bonnar-Kidd, Black, Mattson, &

Coster, 2009), the current study identifies a specific need to improve the content of websites designed to increase PA among individuals with depression. Therefore, future investigations should be directed toward analyzing the content of PA websites intended for other populations with chronic health conditions that may also be seeking to increase their PA levels for both mental and physical health benefits.

INTRODUCTION

Engaging in regular physical activity (PA) is associated with several physical and psychological health benefits including reducing the risk for chronic metabolic conditions and improving mental well-being (Warburton, Nicol, & Bredin, 2006). However, over half of North American adults perform less than the minimum recommended amount of daily PA (CFLRI, 2005; CDC, 2005). Unfortunately, efforts to promote PA seem to be a constant challenge. For example, physicans, a prominent source of health information (Lewis & Lynch, 1993), admit that they are not adequately prepared to prescribe appropriate PA information (Andersen, Blair, Cheskin, & Bartlet, 1997). This may cause sedentary individuals to seek out such information from other sources including books, pamphlets, and most commonly, the Internet (Statistics Canada, 2009; Andersson, Bergstrom, Hollandare, Carlbring, Kaldo, & Ekselius, 2005).

Since the introduction of the Internet, people have begun to change the way they interact, manage their lives, and exchange information. With approximately 80% of North Americans admitting to using the Internet for personal endeavours (Statistics Canada, 2009; Internet World Stats, 2010), it is clear that websites and other forms of online resources are often considered to be an efficient means for obtaining information. In fact, Bonnar-Kidd, Black, Mattson, and Coster (2009) found that half of Internet users consult the Internet for health-related purposes including health promotion and PA information. Therefore, PA websites may act as a prime source of information for individuals looking to become more physically active. However, the accuracy and quality of information typically provided on PA websites can vary (Bonnar-Kidd et al., 2009; Doshi, Patrick, Sallis, & Calfas, 2003; Jetha, Faulkner, Gorczynski, Arbour-Nicitopoulos, & Martin Ginis, 2010). For example, a keyword search using a popular Internet search engine (i.e., Google and Yahoo) will yield a list of websites that are ranked according to their relevance to the search criteria. Berland and colleagues (2001) found that less than 25% of those top-ranked websites provided information that is up-to-date and consistent with accepted recommendations. Although the accuracy of online information is undoubtedly problematic, some studies have suggested that the poor *theoretical quality* of online information (Bonnar-Kidd et al., 2009; Jetha et al., 2010), as well as the way such information is framed (Latimer, Brawley, & Bassett, 2010), may be of even greater concern.

Theory is an integral part of the behavior change process and has been shown to facilitate the development of effective interventions in many health behaviors including PA (Kahn et al., 2002). Michie, Johnston, Francis, Hardeman, and Eccles (2008) emphasize three primary advantages of using theory to guide evidence-based research: (1) allows one to target causal determinants specifically identified to influence change in a particular behavior; (2) allows one to continually evaluate and develop the theory via interventions; and (3) allows one to apply the theory to various contexts, populations, and behaviors. Each of these characteristics add to the value of evidence-based research and, when incorporated into PA messages, have been shown to increase PA intentions, motivation, and behavior (Brawley & Latimer, 2007; Doshi et al., 2003).

Although there is no ideal theory for predicting PA behavior, complimentary constructs from multiple theories may be combined to offer a more complete understanding of the factors that drive health behavior change and that are commonly used in the evaluation of PA information (Brawley, 1993). Two previous studies have identified a lack of theory-based information in PA websites aimed at increasing PA among the able-bodied population. An initial study, conducted by Doshi et al., (2003), evaluated 26 PA websites and found that the majority of information was of low theoretical quailty. Likewise, a subsequent study by Bonnar-Kidd et al. (2009) found that 78% of 41 PA websites achieved a low quality rating. Jetha and colleagues (2010) were the first to explore PA information on websites targeting a population with a chornic health condition (i.e., spinal cord injury). Results were comparable to those of websites directed at the able-bodied population in that a low level of theory-driven information was presented (Jetha et al., 2010). Moreover, message content on these PA websites primarily relied on the description of benefits and barriers to PA while utilizing a very limited number of cognitive/behavioral strategies to promote PA. Consequently, the utility of the information is obscured, which compromises its potential impact on readers' PA beliefs and subsequent behavior (Bonnar-Kidd et al., 2009; Doshi et al., 2003; Jetha et al., 2010).

Although each of these studies confirm that theoretical information is rarely integrated into PA websites, no previous studies have evaluated the content of PA websites aimed at people with mood disorders, specifically depression. Therefore, the purpose of this study was to evaluate the theoretical content of PA websites specifically aimed toward people with depression.

Making the Connection: Depression and Physical Activity

Depression is a psychological disorder characterized by altered mood and a loss of interest or pleasure in activities (USDHHS, 1999). Symptoms can include: sustained feelings of sadness or elation; feelings of guilt or worthlessness; disturbances in sleep patterns/appetite; psychomotor agitation; lack of energy; and difficulty concentrating, all of which can potentially lead to suicidal thoughts and even death (Strawbridge, Deleger, Roberts, & Kaplan, 2002; USDHHS, 1999). Traditional treatments for depression include a combination of anti-depressant medication and behavioral therapy that are typically accompanied by numerous negative side effects (Fox, 1999; Mutrie, 2000). However, research has shown that regular PA (both aerobic and restistance exercise) can be equally as effective at alleviating depressive symptoms, creating a positive mood, and improving mental well-being without the associated costs and social stigmatism that accompany traditional treatments (Craft & Landers, 1998; Fox, 1999; Mutrie, 2000). Biddle & Mutrie (2001) suggest that the benefits of PA extend beyond the general population and have been shown to produce specific advantages for people with depression. Moreover, PA has been show to help reduce the risk of developing clinical depression and can also evoke feelings of accomplishment that may be directly and indirectly related to increasing PA behavior in people with depression. Research by Andersson et al. (2005) suggests that people with depression are also avid Internet users and are comfortable sharing depression related information online. To the best of our knowledge, there is no supporting evidence to suggest that people with depression interpret online health information any differently than those without depression; therefore, an evaluation of the amount and persuasiveness of theoretical content on PA websites targeting people with depression was warranted.

Maximizing Message Influence

A Theoretical Collaboration

The most effective health promotion information stems from messages targeting multiple constructs rooted in several behavior change theories (Brawley, 1993) including: Social Cognitive Theory (SCT; Bandura, 1977), Theory of Planned Behavior (TPB; Ajzen, 1991), and Health Action Process Approach Model (HAPA; Schwarzer, 2008). SCT posits that human motivation and behavior is largely influenced by peoples' belief in their capabilities, anticipated outcomes, and external pressures (Bandura, 1977). This theory includes self-efficacy (i.e., one's belief in their ability to successfully perform a desired course of action; Bandura, 1977), which has been proven to be a strong and consistent predictor of PA behavior, along with outcome expectancies (i.e., perceptions of outcomes resulting from a behavior) and socio-cultural factors (i.e., social pressures that either facilitate or impede performance of the desired behavior; Hagger, Chatzisarantis, & Biddle, 2002; Luszczynska & Schwarzer, 2005; McAuley, Jerome, Elavsky, Marquez, & Ramsey, 2003; Rovniak, Anderson, Winett, & Stephens, 2002). McAuley et al. (2003) found that self-efficacy and outcome expectancies explained 36% of the variance in both short and long-term maintenance of PA in older adults. When testing the SCT, in its entirety, Rovniak et al. (2002) found that self-efficacy had both direct and indirect effects on PA behavior and was able to explain 55% of the variance in PA. However, the majority of this effect was attributable to the use of self-regulatory strategies such as goal setting, self-monitoring, planning, and problem solving. Self-regulatory strategies are prevalent in highly self-efficacious individuals and are theorized to contribute to a more persistent pursuit of desired behaviors, particularly when facing adverse situations (Bandura, 1997, Luszczynska & Schwarzer; 2005; Rovniak et al., 2002). Consequently, the direct effect of self-efficacy on PA was reduced after accounting for the effect of self-regulation, thus identifying self-regulation as both a mediator in the self-efficacy-PA relationship and as a critical theoretical construct in explaining the complex behavior of PA (Rovniak et al., 2002). Therefore self-efficacy, self-regulation, and outcome expectancies are each regarded as key constructs of SCT that help explain PA behavior.

Another leading theoretical perspective in health behavior change is the TPB (Armitage & Conner, 2001). In this theory, behavioral intentions (i.e., a person's decision or self-instruction to perform a behavior) represent the most proximal antecedent of PA behavior and are predicted by attitude, perceived behavioral control (PBC), and subjective norms (Conner & Sparks, 2005). TPB contains many parallel constructs to Bandura's SCT. For example, outcome expectancies are manifested within behavioral beliefs and contribute to the formation of a person's attitude, defined as one's overall evaluation of a desired behavior (Conner & Sparks, 2005). Also, PBC displays conceptual similarities with Bandura's construct of self-efficacy and is defined as a person's belief that performing a behavior is within his/her control and typically refers to external influences (i.e., time, facility availability, and required resources; Conner & Sparks, 2005). Subjective norm is the third construct that contributes to the formation of behavioral intention in TPB and is defined as the degree to which one feels obligated and motivated to comply with one's own perceptions as well as others' expectations (Conner & Sparks, 2005). Of the three cognitive antecedents of intentions (attitudes, subjective norms, and PBC), PBC has been shown to be the strongest predictor of intention (Hagger et al., 2002). Together, these constructs are responsible for explaining considerable variance in intentions to perform PA and, to a lesser extent, variance in actual PA behavior (Hagger et al., 2002). A meta-analytic review of studies using the TPB showed that the TPB was able to account for an average of 27% of the variance in PA, thus making it another reputable theory that utilizes similar constructs to SCT (Hagger et al., 2002).

The HAPA model is different from both SCT and TPB in that it distinguishes two different phases of behavior change: a *motivational* (or pre-intentional) phase, and a *volitional* (or self-regulatory or action) phase (Schwarzer, 2008). Self-efficacy is also a key construct in this model and takes on three phase-specific roles: task self-efficacy in the motivational phase, and both recovery and maintenance self-efficacy in the volitional phase. In the motivational phase, task self-efficacy, outcome expectancies and risk awareness operate as key social cognitive predictors of PA intentions. Once an individual forms an intention, one progresses into the volitional phase where key constructs —action and coping planning (i.e., self-regulatory strategies), and maintenance and recovery self-efficacy—are used to effectively translate one's intentions into action and to foster prolonged maintenance of the behavior. Sniehotta, Scholz & Schwarzer (2003) tested several variations of the HAPA model and found that task self-efficacy, outcome expectancies and risk awareness alone were able to explain 65% of the variance in PA intentions and just 11% of the variance in PA itself. However, when the model included action/coping planning, the amount of explained variance in PA behavior increased to 32%, thus highlighting the advantage of combining key theoretical constructs to explain additional variance in PA (Brawley, 1993). A more recent study by Arbour-Nicitopoulos, Martin Ginis, and Latimer (2009) showed that a combination of action and coping plans were also able to increase leisure-time PA in people with spinal cord injury. These self-regulation skills were also found to be associated with an increase in an individual's confidence to conquer foreseen barriers (i.e., barrier self-efficacy) to PA, which reaffirms the benefit of using theory-based constructs to explain a complex behavior like PA (Arbour-Nicitopoulos et al., 2009). Once again, incorporating these theoretical constructs into PA messages could greatly enhance their influence on readers' PA beliefs and behavior.

Overall, the value of behavior change theory is monumental in identifying constructs that may lead to a change in PA behavior (Fishbein & Cappella, 2006). Although past research has not identified the relevance of these constructs explicitly to people with depression, self-efficacy, outcome expectancies, and self-regulation are each considered essential constructs that have been subjected to empirical scrutiny and have shown to be critical components of developing effective PA messages (Latimer et al., 2010). Failure to incorporate a sufficient number of messages representing each of these key constructs into a PA website could limit its potential to influence change in PA beliefs and subsequent PA behavior in targeted users looking to become more physically active.

Message Framing Effects

Health behavior messages are communicated in one of two ways: gain- or loss-framed. Gain-framed messages are defined as messages that emphasize the benefits attained or costs avoided from participating in a specific behavior, whereas loss-framed messages emphasize the costs or missed benefits from failing to participate in a specific behavior (Brawley & Latimer, 2007). Gain-framed messages have been shown to have a greater likelihood of motivating an individual to become active than loss-framed messages (Brawley & Latimer, 2007; Latimer et al., 2010). Moreover, Latimer et al. (2010) found similar findings when messages were considered to be from a credible source (i.e., websites that provided references for their content), which amplifies the effect that outcome expectancy messages can have on behavior change. Therefore, failure to provide a sufficient number of gain-framed messages may also reduce the influence of PA messages.

THE CURRENT STUDY

Objectives and Hypothesis

The purpose of this study was to evaluate the use of behavior change theory and the appropriate use of message framing techniques in websites that provide information about PA for people with depression. More specifically, key behavioural change constructs including self-efficacy, outcome expectations, and self-regulation as well as the prevalance of gain versus loss-framed outcome expectancy messages were assessed within the theoretical content of websites promoting the use of PA as a treatment for depression.

It was hypothesized that the theoretical content of PA websites targeting people with depression would be low, which is consistent with previous research that has assessed the content of other PA websites (Bonnar-Kidd et al., 2009; Doshi et al., 2003; Jetha et al., 2010). Because this was one of the first studies to evaluate online messages targeting this specific population, no a priori hypothesis were made regarding the prevalence of gain or loss-framed messages on PA websites targeting people with depression.

METHOD

Latimer et al. (2010) found that PA messages were more persusasive when they came from reputable sources. Therefore, PA websites used in the current analysis were identified by searching the Internet for credible websites created by government or community health organizations, as well as those that contained academic references. Four keyword searches were performed in the following order: "exercise depression .org", "exercise depression .gov", "physical activity depression .org", and "physical activity depression .gov". The keywords ".gov" and ".org" were included to increase the chance that credible websites (i.e., created by the government or community health organizations) would be found.. Each string of keywords was entered into Google, the most commonly used search engine in Canada (Nielson Company, 2010).

Inclusion Criteria

Websites were included if they: (1) targeted PA for people with depression with no other comorbid diseases (i.e., anxiety disorders, diabetes, cancer); (2) were from a credible source (i.e., provincial or federal government, organizations); (3) had academic references listed within the website's entirety (i.e., although not necessarily on the page that was listed in the search results); (4) directly targeted individuals with depression as opposed to a parent or caregiver; (5) were found within the first four pages of the search results; and (6) gave information within two mouse-clicks of the original search results page. All inclusion criteria were based on typical Internet search patterns and had been used to guide the collection of websites in previous content analysis research (Bonnar-Kidd et al., 2009; Bhatnagar & Ghose, 2004; Eysenbach & Kohler, 2004; Jetha et al., 2010). The search was also limited to four pages of search results to stay consistent with previous research methodology, which suggests that most users are likely to discontinue their search within the first four pages of results (Jetha et al., 2010).

The Coding Manual

A modified version of the Content Analysis Approach to Theory-Specified Persuasive Educational Communication (CAATSPEC), which has been used in previous research to evaluate the content of PA brochures (Gainforth, Barg, Latimer, Schmid, O-Malley, & Salovey, 2011a) and alcohol-education leaflets (Abraham, Southby, Quandte, Krahe, & van der Sluijs, 2007;) was also used in the current study. The coding manual produced by Gainforth, Barg, Latimer, Schmid, O-Malley, & Salovey (2011b) was developed using a combination of the leading behavior change theories (i.e., SCT, TPB, and HAPA) and categorizes messages into five mutually exclusive groups: three of which distinguish theoretical messages (i.e., outcome expectancies, self-regulation, and self-efficacy) and two of which capture non-theoretical messages (i.e., general knowledge-based information, and non-theoretical information. Two subcategories within the outcome expectantcy category were explicitly used to assess the prevalence of gain- and loss-framed messages (i.e., positive outcomes of exercising and negative outcomes of not exercising, respectively) on PA websites targeting people with depression. This codebook has shown to produce acceptable inter-rater reliability when used to code messages and was found to be an appropriate measure for the purpose of the current study (Gainforth et al., 2011a).

A brief description of each category and its corresponding subcategories is provided next. A more comprehensive description of the categories can be found by consulting the coding manual directly (Gainforth et al., 2011b).

Outcome Expectancies

Three subcategories were used to code messages associated with why people may or may not choose to engage in PA. These subcategories included messages that provided the benefits of being physically active (i.e., gain-framed or positive outcome expectancies), risks associated with physical inactivity (i.e., loss-framed or negative outcome expectancies), and messages concerned with other general risks associated with PA (e.g., injury or fatigue) (Gainforth et al., 2011b).

Self-Regulation

Four subcategories were used to code messages that encouraged the use of strategies to overcome challenges associated with maintaining regular PA participation including: active monitoring (e.g., recording of PA progress in a log), setting goals, structured planning, and other strategies to manage time or barriers (Gainforth et al., 2011b).

Self-Efficacy

Three subcategories were used to code messages that used strategies to increase the readers' confidence in their ability to become more physically active. Sources of self-efficacy used within this category included: learning from the success of others (i.e., modeling), persuasive statements, and general instructions used to carryout PA (Gainforth et al., 2011b).

General Knowledge-Based Information

This category used five subcategories to code messages that provide an overall understanding of the basic principles of PA including definitions of PA and intensity levels, as well as potential barriers that may prevent the adoption of PA without specifically suggesting a strategy to overcome it. Statistics and medical information regarding when to seek a doctor's approval upon beginning PA were also included in this category (Gainforth et al., 2011b). Although such information is not tied to a specific behavior change theory, it may still be considered useful for people initiating or maintaining regular PA.

Non-Theoretical Information

This category was reserved for messages that failed to provide information pertaining to any of the preceding categories (Gainforth et al., 2011b). Messages in this category typically referred to population-specific information including: definitions, symptoms, and treatments of depression without reference to PA.

Because only three of the five categories from the coding manual (i.e., outcome expectancies, self-regulation, and self-efficacy) delineate theoretical information from the websites, messages coded within these categories will remain the primary focus for the duration of this chapter.

Table 1. Means and Standard Deviations of Messages by Category Across All Websites

	M	SD
GEN	7	3.96
OE	12	3.58
SR	3	3.97
SE	4	1.52
NON	3	1.48

Note: These results are reported with respect to total messages from all websites. The five categories used to analyze messages included: general knowledge-based information (GEN), outcome expectancies (OE), self-regulation (SR), self-efficacy (SE), non theoretical (NON).

CODING PROCEDURES

Website content was divided into dicrete messages according to guidelines from the Gainforth et al. (2011b) codebook. Two raters continued to follow these strict guidelines to appropriately code messages from each website. The raters proceeded to code each website independently and were in agreement 66% (20/30 for website four) to 88% (15/17 for website one) of the time. Any discrepancies in assigning codes were discussed by the two raters until agreement was reached.

ANALYSIS

To determine the nature of the content displayed on PA websites targeting people with depression, a percentage score for each of the five categories, within each website, was calculated by dividing the frequency of each coding category by the total number of website messages. Likewise, a percentage score for each of the given categories for all websites was calculated by summing the frequency of each coding category from each website and dividing by the total number of coded messages.

RESULTS

A total of 145 messages, across five eligible websites, were coded. There was considerable variability in message content across the five websites (see Table 1). In total, 64% of PA messages targeting people with depression were theory-based while the remaining 36% were non-theory based. Of the theory-based content, 40% of messages described outcome expectancies, 12% described self-regulation, and 12% described self-efficacy. Of the non-theory based content, 25% of messages described general knowledge-based information and 11% described non-theoretical information and is presented in Figure 1.

Table 2. Frequency and Percentage of Website Content by Subcategory

Website	1	2	3	4	5	Total	
Category	f	f	f	f	f	f (%)	(% of all messages)
I. Knowledge-based information:						**36 (100)**	**(24.83)**
Definitions of physical activity	4	5	7	6	14	0 (0)	
Statistics and similar facts	0	0	0	0	0	2 (5.5)	
Medical information (i.e., when to see doctor)	1	0	1	0	0	11 (30.6)	
Suggestions and examples of different types of exercise	0	2	4	2	3	11 (30.6)	
Barriers frequently encountered (without strategies to overcome barriers)	2	3	1	3	2	12 (33.3)	
	1	0	1	1	9		
II. Outcome expectancies:						**58 (100)**	**(40.00)**
Negative outcomes of not exercising	9	17	8	11	13	1 (1.7)	
Positive outcomes of exercising	1	0	0	0	0	55 (94.8)	
Other outcomes: Risks associated with exercising	8	17	8	9	13	2 (3.4)	
	0	0	0	2	0		
III. Self-regulation:						**17 (100)**	**(11.72)**
Encourage self-monitoring	1	0	2	4	10	1 (5.8)	
Encourage goal setting	0	0	0	0	1	2 (11.8)	
Encourage planning	0	0	0	1	1	2 (11.8)	
Other strategies to manage time and overcome barriers	0	0	0	1	1	12 (70.6)	
	1	0	2	2	7		

Table 2. (Continued)

	2	3	4	6	3	
IV. Self-efficacy:						**18 (100)** (12.41)
Modeling	0	0	1	0	0	1 (5.5)
Persuasion	0	0	0	1	1	2 (11)
General "how to" information	2	3	3	5	2	15 (83.3)
V. Other (non theoretically-based) statements	**1**	**3**	**5**	**3**	**4**	**16 (100)** (11.03)
Total Messages	17	28	26	30	44	145 (100) (100)

Note. f= frequency of messages. Percentages are in parentheses. Bold-face text indicates frequency and percentage of messages for each main category.

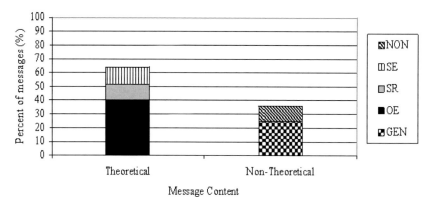

Note. Non-theoretical categories include general knowledge-based information (GEN) and non-theoretical messages (NON). Theoretical categories include: self-efficacy messages (SE), self-regulation strategies (SR), and outcome expectancy messages (OE).

Figure 1. Percent of Messages by Content Category.

A more detailed description of the message content, by subcategories, can also be found in Table 2. Subcategories within the main category of outcome exectancies also found that approximately 95% of outcome expectancy messages emphaiszed the benefit of engaging in PA (i.e., gain-framed outcome expectancies) as opposed to the costs associated with abstaining from PA (i.e., loss-framed outcome expectancies).

The overall percentage of message content is grouped by category (theoretical versus non-theoretical) and subcategories in order to describe the degree to which content from physical activity websites targeting persons with depression are represented.

DISCUSSION

The current study investigated the theoretical content of physical activity (PA) websites targeting people with depression using quantitative content analysis rooted in three behavior change theories: Social Cognitive Theory (SCT), the Theory of Planned Behavior (TPB), and the Health Action Process Approach (HAPA; Gainforth et al., 2011b). Our results indicated that approximately two-thirds of website content was, in fact, theory-based and included the constructs of outcome expectancies, self-regulation, and self-efficacy.

In comparison to PA website content aimed at the spinal cord injury population (Jetha et al., 2010), results revealed a higher level of theoretical content within PA websites for people with depression; however, an uneven representation of theoretical categories was reported. Outcome expectancies accounted for the highest proportion of messages representing 40% of all messages based on behavior change theories, while self-efficacy and self-regulation messages were far less prevalent, each representing a mere 12% of message content.

Outcome expectancy messages were the most prominent type of theoretically-based messages in PA websites targeting people with depression and predominantly emphasized the benefits of engaging in PA (i.e., gain-framed messages). A possible explanation for the large percentage of outcome expectancy messages is that the website authors may have recognized the importance of making an individual aware of the consequences associated with performing a behavior. Outcome expectancy messages enhance the persuasiveness of messages by altering people's attitudes towards PA, contributing to the formation of stronger intentions (Brawley & Latimer, 2007; Latimer et al., 2010). The impact of outcome expectancy messages is even greater when the information is delivered by a credible source (Latimer et al., 2010). Because this study used reputable websites that provided references for their content, the websites can be considered credible, further amplifying the effect that outcome expectancy messages can have on behavior change. However, only providing information about the benefits of PA is not the most effective method for promoting initial or prolonged PA behavior change; thus, outcome expectancy messages need to be accompanied by additional messages that integrate other essential behavior change constructs, namely self-efficacy and self-regulation (Brawley & Latimer, 2007). Moreover, a lack of these other types of theoretical content displayed on PA websites may obscure the utility of the information and reduce its impact on readers' PA beliefs and subsequent behavior (Bonnar-Kidd et al., 2009; Doshi et al., 2003; Jetha et al., 2010).

Self-regulation and self-efficacy messages were considerably underrepresented in PA websites targeting people with depression and, as a result, the websites' ability to influence PA beliefs and behavior of their readers is limited. In fact, Rhodes and Pfaeffli (2010) suggest that self-regulatory strategies and self-efficacy beliefs have the most potential as targets for increasing PA. A study by Rovniak et al. (2002), which used SCT to predict PA, found that self-efficacy had the greatest effect on PA behavior. However, this effect was found to be largely mediated by the use of self-regulatory strategies. In other words, people with high self-efficacy were, in fact, more likely to become physically active; however, their use of self-regulation strategies (i.e., goal-setting, self-monitoring, planning and problem solving) were predominantly responsible for their persistent behavior (Luszczynska & Schwarzer, 2005). This demonstrates the value of self-regulation strategies in the pursuit of PA and may be particularly advantageous to include in online PA information. However, despite the benefits of such messages, self-regulation strategies were found to be relatively sparse in PAwebsites targeting people with depression. Therefore, the incorporation of additional self-regulation strategies would enhance the utility of the information by allowing individuals to understand the important steps required to plan and monitor their progress toward adopting and maintaining sufficient PA to help remedy their depressive symptoms.

Messages regarding self-efficacy were also scarce in PA websites targeting people with depression despite the fact that they may be the most influential in terms of developing PA beliefs and behavior in people with depression. More specifically, Biddle & Mutrie (2001) suggest that incorporating various types of self-efficacy messages (e.g., past mastery experiences, modeling, and/or verbal persuasion; Bandura, 1977) may evoke feelings of self-worth and a sense of control over one's environment, thus enabling people with depression to cope with their symptoms in a more productive manner. This suggests that self-efficacy is a key construct to target when providing PA messages for people with depression.

A large proportion of the total website messages focused on providing knowledge-based information about PA. Information provision messages may be useful for influencing change in one's attitude towards the behavior, which has previously been described to be a strong predictor of one's intention to change their behavior (Hagger et al., 2002). However, as demonstrated above, intention alone is not the ideal predictor of behavior (Sniehotta et al., 2005). Simply providing information about the frequency, duration and intensity at which one should exercise will not necessarily motivate individuals to initiate, and more importantly adhere to, a PA program; thus, information provision messages should be kept to a minimum in websites targeting PA for people with depression.

LIMITATIONS

The process used in this study can be applied to evaluate websites that target PA for other chronic physical and mental health conditions, such as diabetes, cancer, and anxiety disorders. However, the current study has several limitations. First, websites are continually being updated and new websites are constantly becoming available, so this study only represents a snapshot in time. Moreover, if this study were to be replicated in the future, the content of the five websites may be altered or updated. Therefore, website updates may impact the percentage of messages that are theory-based, thus changing the current analysis. Second, because the present analysis included strict credibility criteria (i.e., websites created by government or community organizations and containing academic references), it is plausible that these websites may not have been the most frequently accessed websites by all users. Third, although research suggests that theoretically based PA messages may be more effective in terms of changing beliefs and behaviour, this study did not directly measure PA behaviour change in people with depression; however, this may be a promising direction for future research. Lastly, the primary goal of this study was strictly to assess the theoretical content within the websites. Other website characteristics such as overall presentation, understandability and user-friendliness may also influence whether an individual chooses to attend to the messages beyond the title of a website. These characteristics were not assessed in the present study. Therefore, future research may benefit from including such website characteristics in their content analysis as they could have a prominent role in website usability and may also contribute to the website's capacity to influence change in its readers.

CONCLUSION AND FUTURE DIRECTIONS

Overall, the amount of theoretically-derived messages on PA websites targeting people with depression was greater than that found in previous research targeting both the able-bodied and spinal cord injury populations (Bonnar-kidd et al. 2009; Jetha et al. 2010). However, an even higher percentage of theoretical messages would certainly add to the value of such online information. To maximize impact on cognitive determinants of behavior change, websites targeting PA should continue to use gain-framed messages when delivering outcome expectancy messages, as suggested by previous researchers (e.g., Latimer et al., 2010). Moreover, updates to existing websites or the creation of new websites should increase the percentage of theory-based messages, especially self-efficacy and self-regulatory messages, and decrease the percentage of non-theory based messages. The notion of self-efficacy is particularly important for individuals with depression (Rhodes & Pfaeffli, 2010) and should be a focus when delivering PA messages to this population. Improving PA messages on the Internet may lead to a greater number of people with depression engaging in PA so that they may enjoy the physical and mental health benefits of an active lifestyle.

ACKNOWLEDGMENT

External Reviewer: Amy Latimer, Queen's University.

REFERENCES

Abraham, C., Southby, L, Quandte, S., Krahé, B., & van der Sluijs, W. (2007). What's in a leaflet? Identifying research-based persuasive messages in European alcohol-education leaflets. *Psychology and Health, 22*, 31-60.

Ajzen, I. (1991). The theory of planned behavior. *Organizational Behavior and Human Decision Processes, 50*, 179-211.

Andersson, G., Bergrstrom, J., Hollandare, G., Carlbring, P., Kaldo, V., & Ekselius, L. (2005). Internet-based self-help for depression: Randomised controlled trial. *The Bristish Journal of Psychiatry, 187*, 456-461.

Andersen, R. E., Blair, S. N., Cheskin, L. J., & Bartlet, S. J. (1997). Encouraging patients to become more physically active: The physician's role. *American College of Physicians, 127*, 395-400.

Arbour-Nicitopoulos, K. P., Martin Ginis, K. A., & Latimer, A. E. (2009). Planning, leisure-time physical activity, and coping self-efficacy in persons with spinal cord injury: A randomized controlled trial. *Archives of Physical Medicine and Rehabilitation, 90*, 2003-2011.

Armitage, C. J., & Conner, M. (2001). Efficacy of the theory of planned behavior: A meta-analytic review. *British Journal of Social Psychology, 40*, 471-499.

Bandura, A. (1977). Self-efficacy: Toward a unifying theory of behavioral change. *Psychological Review, 84*, 191-215.

Bandura, A. (1997). *Self-efficacy: The exercise of control*. New York: Freeman.

Berland, G. K., Elliott, M. N., Morales, L. S., Algazy, J. I., Kravitz, R. L., Broder, M. S.,... McGlynn, E. A. (2001). Health information on the Internet: Accessibility, quality and readability in English and Spanish. *Journal of the American Medical Association, 285*, 2612-2621.

Bhatnagar, A., & Ghose, S. (2004). Online information search termination patterns across product categories and consumer demographics. *Journal of Retailing, 60*, 221-228.

Biddle, S. J. H., & Mutrie, N. (2001). Depression and other mental illnesses. In S. Biddle & N. Mutrie. (Eds.). *Psychology of physical activity: Determinants, well-being and interventions* (pp. 202-235). London: Routledge.

Bonnar-Kidd, K. K., Black, D. R., Mattson, M., & Coster, D. (2009). Online physical activity information: Will typical users find quality information? *Health Communication, 24*, 165-175.

Brawley, L. R. (1993). The practicality of using social psychology theories for exercise and health research and intervention. *Journal of Applied Sport Psychology, 5*, 99-115.

Brawley, L., & Latimer, A. (2007). Physical activity guides for Canadians: Messaging strategies, realistic expectations for change, and evaluation. *Applied Physiology, Nutrition, & Metabolism, 32*, S170-S184.

Canadian Fitness Lifestyle Reseach Institute (2005). Physical Activity Among Canadians: The Current Situation. Ontario, Canada.

Centers for Disease Control and Prevention. U.S. Physical Activity Statistics (2005). Department of Health and Human Services: Washington, DC.

Conner, M., & Sparks, P. (2005). Theory of planned behavior. In M. Conner & P. Norman (Eds.), *Predicting health behavior* (2nd ed) (pp. 170-222). Berkshire, UK: Open University Press.

Craft, L. L, &Landers, D. M. (1998). The effect of exercise on clinical depression and depression resulting from mental illness: A meta analysis. *Journal of Sport and Exercise Psychology, 20*, 339–357.

Doshi, A., Patrick, K., Sallis, J. F., & Calfas, K. (2003). Evaluation of physical activity web sites for use of behavior change theories. *Annals of Behavioral Medicine, 25*, 105-111.

Eysenbach, G., & Kohler, C. (2004). Health-related searches on the Internet. *Journal of the American Medical Association, 291*, 2946.

Fishbein, M., & Cappella, J. N. (2006). The role of theory in developing effective health communications. *Journal of Communication, 56*, S1-S17.

Fox, K. R. (1999). The influence of physical activity on mental well-being. *Public Health Nutrition, 2*, 411-418.

Gainforth, H., Barg, C., Latimer, A. E., Schmid, K., O'Malley, D., & Salovey, P. (2011a). An investigation of the theoretical content of physical activity brochures. *Psychology of Sport & Exercise, 12*, 615-620.

Gainforth, H., Barg, C., Latimer, A. E., Schmid, K., O'Malley, D., & Salovey, P. (2011b). Coding manual for content analysis of physical activity leaflets. Manusciript submitted for publication.

Hagger, M. S., Chatzisarantis, N. L. D., & Biddle, S. J. H. (2002). A meta-analytic review of the theories of reasoned action and planned behavior in physical activity: Predictive validity and the contribution of additional variables. *Journal of Sport and Exercise Psychology, 24*, 3-32.

Internet World Stats (2010). The big picture: World internet users and population stats. Retrieved November 12, 2010 from http://www.internetworldstats.com/stats.htm

Jetha, A., Faulkner, G., Gorczynski, P., Arbour-Nicitopoulos, K., & Martin Ginis, K. (2010). Physical activity and individuals with spinal cord injury: Accuracy and quality of information on the Internet. *Disability and Health Journal, 4*, 112-120.

Kahn, E. B., Ramsey, L. T., Brownson, R. C., Heath, G. W., Howze, E. H., Powell, K. E.,...Corso, P. (2002). The effectiveness of interventions to increase physical activity: A systematic review. *American Journal of Preventative Medicine, 22*, 73-107.

Latimer, A. E., Brawley, L. R., & Bassett, R.L. (2010). A systematic review of three approached for constructing physical activity messages: What messages work and what improvements are needed? *International Journal of Behavioral Nutrition and Physical Activity, 7*, 36.

Lewis, B. S., & Lynch, W. D. (1993). The effects of physician advice on exercise behavior. *Preventive Medicine, 22*, 110-121.

Lox, C. L., Martin Ginis, K. A., & Petruzzello, S. J. (2010). Depression and exercise. In, *The psychology of exercise: Integrating theory and practice.* (pp. 313-343). Scottsdale, Arizona: Holcomb Hathaway.

Luszczynska, A., & Schwarzer, R. (2005). Social cognitive theory. In M. Conner & P. Norman (Eds.), *Predicting health behavior* (2nd ed) (pp. 127-169). Berkshire, UK: Open University Press.

McAuley, E., Jerome, G. J., Elavsky, S., Marquez, D. X., & Ramsey, S. N. (2003). Predicting long-term maintenance of physical activity in older adults. *Preventive Medicine, 37,* 110-118.

Michie, S., Johnston, M., Francis, J., Hardeman, W., & Eccles, M. (2008). From theory to intervention: Mapping theoretically derived behavioral determinants to behavior change techniques. *Applied Psychology, 57,* 660-680.

Mutrie, N. (2000). The relationship between physical activity and clinically defined depression. In S. Biddle, K. Fox, & S. Boutcher (Eds.), *Physical activity and psychological well-being* (pp. 46-62). London: Routledge.

Nielson Company. (2010). Internet rankings: Top 5 U.S. search providers, home & work. Retrieved November 3, 2010 from http://enus.nielsen.com/content/nielsen/en_us/insights/rankings/internet.html

Rhodes, R. E., & Pfaeffli, L. A. (2010). Mediators of physical activity behavior change among adult non-clinical populations: A review update. *International Journal of Behavioral Nutrition and Physical Activity, 7,* 37.

Rovniak, L. S., Anderson, E. S., Winett, R. A., & Stephens, R. S. (2002). Social cognitive determinants of physical activity in young adults: A prospective structural equation analysis. *Annals of Behavioral Medicine, 24,* 149-156.

Schwarzer, R. (2008). Modeling health behavior change: How to predict and modify the adoption and maintenance of health behaviors. *Applied Psychology: An International Review, 57,* 1-29.

Sniehotta, F. F., Scholz, U., & Schwarzer, R. (2005). Bridging the intention-behavior gap: Planning, self-efficacy and action control in the adoption and maintenance of physical exercise. *Psychology and Health, 20,* 143-160.

Statistics Canada. (2010). Internet use by individuals, by type of activity (Internet users at home). Retrieved November 9, 2010 from http://www40.statcan.gc.ca/l01/cst01/comm29a-eng.htm.

Strawbridge, W. J., Deleger, S., Roberts, E. R., & Kaplan, G. A. (2002). Physical activity reduces the risk of subsequent depression for older adults. *American Journal of Epidemiology, 156,* 328-334.

U.S. Department of Health and Human Services. (1999). *Mental health: A report of the Surgeon General.* Rockville, MD: U.S. Department of Health and Human Services, Substance Abuse and Mental Health Services Administration, Center for Mental Health Services, National Institutes of Health, National Institute of Mental Health.

Warburton, D.E., Nicol, C. W., & Bredin, S. S. (2006). Health benefits of physical activity: The evidence. *Canadian Medical Association Journal, 174,* 801-809.

APPENDIX A

Websites Included in the Analysis

Beyond Blue. Beyond Blue Website. 2007. "Depression and exercise". http://www.beyondblue.org.au/index.aspx?link_id=9.697. Accessed November 5, 2010.

British United Provident Association. British United Provident Association Website. 2005. "Exercise beats the blues." http://www.bupa.co.uk/health_information/ html/health_news/060405exercise_blues.html Accessed November 5, 2010.

Mental Health Foundation. Mental Health Foundation Website. 2005. "Up and running! How exercise can help beat depression." http://www.mentalhealth.org.uk/ campaigns/exercise/how-exercise-can-beat-depression/ Accessed November 5, 2010.

WebMD. WebMD Website. 2010. "Exercise and depression." http://www.webmd.com/depression/guide/exercise-depression Accessed November 5, 2010.

Mayo Clinic. Mayo Clinic Website. 2009. "Depression: Exercise eases symptoms." http://www.mayoclinic.com/ health/depression-and-exercise/MH00043 Accessed November 5, 2010.

In: Handbook on Psychology of Motivation
Editors: J. N. Franco and A. E. Svensgaard
ISBN: 978-1-62100-755-5
© 2012 Nova Science Publishers, Inc.

Chapter 12

INTRINSIC AND EXTRINSIC MOTIVATION AMONG JAPANESE ELEMENTARY SCHOOL STUDENTS

Junko Matsuzaki Carreira
Tokyo Future University, Tokyo, Japan

ABSTRACT

To elucidate development and gender differences in motivation between 20 years ago and now in Japanese elementary school, this study investigated intrinsic and extrinsic motivation using a questionnaire developed by Sakurai and Takano (1985). Third, fourth, fifth, and sixth graders in two elementary schools, located in a suburb of Tokyo, were selected to participate in the present study. The total number of participants in this research was 485. This study revealed that there is more of a developmental decline in intrinsic motivation among elementary school pupils, compared to those 20 years ago; gender differences are almost similar to 20 years ago.

INTORODUCTION

In Japan, a relaxed education policy has been introduced into the school education system since the mid-1980s (Nozaki, 2006). In 1997, the program for educational reform was released by Monbusho (Ministry of Education, Science, Sports and Culture, now Monbukagakusho or Ministry of Education, Culture, Sports, Science, and Technology [MEXT]), aiming to change the teaching methods resulting in students' passive learning to one encouraging their autonomous learning (Ministry of Education, Science, Sports and Culture, 1997). In 1998, Monbusho released the National Curriculum Standards Reform, with the aim of helping children (a) cultivate rich humanity, sociality and identity as a Japanese living in the international community, (b) develop the ability to learn and think independently, and (c) acquire basic abilities and skills and be able to develop themselves (Ministry of Education, Science, Sports and Culture, 1998). Further, MEXT (2001) drew up the Education Reform Plan for the 21st Century, which urges teachers to make classes more enjoyable, free of worry, and easy to understand. Then, the comprehensive five-day school week system started in April 2002, aiming at letting children spend more time free from pressure at home and in the community, and engage in socially beneficial activities in order to foster "Ikiru Chikara" (the zest for living), including the abilities to learn and think on their own (MEXT, n.d.). School education has been shifting from cramming and competition to creativity and a more relaxed approach for the last 20 years.

Then, how has pupils' *motivation,* "the process whereby goal-directed activity is instigated and sustained" (Pintrich and Schunk, 2002, p. 5), changed during the last 20 years? This paper focuses on *intrinsic motivation*, referring to "motivation to engage in an activity for its own sake" (Pintrich and Schunk, 2002, p. 245) and *extrinsic motivation*, referring to "motivation to engage in an activity as a means to an end" (Pintrich and Schunk, 2002, p. 245). Several researchers (e.g., Harter, 1981; Lepper, Sethi, Dialdin, and Drake, 1997) have investigated pupils' intrinsic and extrinsic motivation for learning. They found that elementary school pupils decreased in intrinsic motivation with age, although with slight differences among them. In Japan, Sakurai and Takano (1985) examined the developmental trend in intrinsic motivation among Japanese elementary school pupils.

To elucidate development and gender differences in motivation between 20 years ago and now in Japanese elementary school, this study investigated intrinsic and extrinsic motivation using a questionnaire developed by Sakurai and Takano (1985). Thus, the purpose of the present study is to compare (a) elementary school pupils' developmental trends and (b) their gender differences between 20 years ago and now. It is hoped that this study will lead to a number of implications for elementary school education in Japan and expand its scope.

DEFINITION OF INTRINSIC AND EXTRINSIC MOTIVATION

There have been mainly two types of definitions of intrinsic and extrinsic motivation in psychology. First, Kruglanski (1975) introduced *endogenous-exogenous* attribution, which refers to means-goal categories. That is, endogenous action means an end in itself. For example, persons who have endogenous attribution enjoy learning English without special reasons (Carreira, 2006). Their goal is only to learn English. Exogenous action refers to "a means that mediates a further goal, one exogenous to it" (Kruglanski, 1975, p. 390). For example, individuals who have exogenous attribution study English for external reasons such as entrance examinations and careers (Carreira, 2006). Kruglanski stated that endogenous action is linked with intrinsic motivation.

Secondly, Heider (1958) introduced *perceived locus of causality* (PLOC), referring to actions or outcomes which can be perceived as personally caused or as a result of impersonal causes. *Personal causality* refers to "instances in which P causes x intentionally" (Heider, 1958, p. 100). For example, individuals who have personal causality do it on their own (Carreira, 2006). *Impersonal causality* refers to instances in which "P may cause x unintentionally merely because his physical or social being exerts some influence on the environment" (Heider, 1958, p. 100). For example, individuals who have impersonal causality do something with unconscious motivations (Carreira, 2006).

Moreover, deCharms (1968/1983) expanded Heider's concept and proposed *origin* and *pawn*. "An Origin is a person who perceives his behavior as determined by his own choosing; a Pawn is a person who perceives his behavior as determined by external forces beyond his control" (deCharms, 1968/1983, p. 273). An origin is intrinsically motivated, whereas a pawn is extrinsically motivated (deCharm, 1968/1983).

DEVELOPMENTAL TRENDS OF INTRINSIC AND EXTRINSIC MOTIVATION

Several researchers (e.g., Harter, 1981; Lepper et al., 1997; Sakurai and Takano, 1985) found that pupils' intrinsic motivation decreases with age. Harter (1981) conducted research on intrinsic and extrinsic motivation in Connecticut, New York, Colorado, and California. Over 3,000 pupils (third through ninth graders) participated in her study (Harter, 1981). Harter investigated five subscales: challenge, curiosity, mastery, judgment, and criteria. She (1981) defined them as follows:

> Five separate dimensions are defined by an intrinsic and an extrinsic pole: preference for challenge versus preference for easy work, curiosity/interest versus teacher approval, independent mastery attempts versus dependence on the teacher, independent judgment versus reliance on the teacher's judgment, and internal versus external criteria for success/ failure. (p. 300)

Harter's questionnaire forced children to decide which of the options was truest for them. There were two sentences in one item: one was based on intrinsic motivation and the other on extrinsic motivation. Children were asked to decide which kind of child was like them and then asked whether this description was only partially true or completely true for them. Each item was scaled ranging from 1 to 4. Scale 1 indicated the maximum extrinsic motivation and 4 indicated the maximum intrinsic motivation (Harter, 1981). The challenge, curiosity and mastery subscales changed from intrinsic to extrinsic motivation with age (Harter, 1981). In contrast, there was a shift from extrinsic to intrinsic motivation on the judgment and criteria subscales (Harter, 1981).

In Japan, Sakurai and Takano (1985) developed a questionnaire, Scale of Intrinsic versus Extrinsic Motivation (SIEM), based on Harter (1981). The participants in Sakurai and Takano were 486, second (7 or 8 years old) through seventh (12 or 13 years old) graders, who lived in Nagano, located in central Japan. There were 240 boys and 246 girls. Sakurai and Takano changed some items, including perceived locus of causality, endogenous-exogenous attributions, and enjoyment as well as curiosity, challenge, and mastery which were used by Harter. Six factors were extracted as follows: curiosity, causality, enjoyment, mastery, challenge and attribution. Sakurai and Takano found three types of developmental trends. First, the curiosity, causality, and enjoyment subscales declined gradually from second through fifth grades, but increased in sixth grade and decreased in seventh grade again. Secondly, the mastery and challenge subscales decreased with age. Thirdly, the attribution subscale increased with age.

Regarding gender differences, Sakurai and Takano (1985) revealed that the curiosity and causality scores of girls were significantly higher than those of boys in all the grades except sixth grade. The enjoyment scores of girls were significantly higher than those of boys only in second grade. The challenge scores of boys were significantly higher than those of girls in sixth and seventh grades.

PRESENT STUDY

Purpose

As has been shown above, Japanese school education has been shifting from cramming to a more relaxed approach for the last 20 years. It can be predicted that the intrinsic and extrinsic motivation of elementary school pupils now will be different from 20 years ago. Thus, this study employed the SIEM developed by Sakurai and Takano (1985) and attempted to explore differences in (a) developmental trends and (b) gender of intrinsic and extrinsic motivation of Japanese elementary school pupils between 20 years ago and now.

Research Questions

The present study has addressed the three following research questions:

1. Are there any differences in developmental trends in intrinsic motivation of Japanese elementary school pupils between 20 years ago and now?
2. Are there any gender differences in intrinsic motivation of Japanese elementary school pupils between 20 years ago and now?

METHOD

Participants

Third (8 to 9 years old), fourth (9 to 10 years old), fifth (10 to 11 years old), and sixth (11 to 12 years old) graders in two elementary schools, located in a suburb of Tokyo, were selected to participate in the present study. The total number of participants in this research was 485: 119 third, 132 fourth, 125 fifth and 109 sixth graders; 264 boys and 221 girls, respectively. Their parents are relatively eager for their children to study. Some of the students take entrance examinations in order to attend other prestigious private junior high schools.

Instruments

SIEM measures (adapted from Sakurai and Takano, 1985). The SIEM, based on Harter (1981), was created by Sakurai and Takano (1985). The following 6 variables were assessed using the SIEM. The SIEM had 30 items meant to assess intrinsic and extrinsic motivation: curiosity, causality, mastery, attribution, challenge, and enjoyment. Each subscale contains five items. There were two sentences in each item: one was based on intrinsic motivation and the other on extrinsic motivation. Children were asked to decide which kind of child was like them. Each item was scaled as 0 and 1. Scale 0 indicated extrinsic motivation and 1 indicated intrinsic motivation. In October 2004, the SIEM was piloted to determine whether the items were suitable, readable, and comprehensive to contemporary elementary school pupils. For each of the following measures, the Cronbah's alpha reliability coefficients are presented in parentheses.

Descriptions and a sample item from each scale are as follows (see Appendix A):

1. Curiosity ($\alpha = .69$). A high score indicates that students study for the sheer pleasure that they experience while learning something new. Sample: "I always want to know as much as possible" as intrinsic choice versus "I do not want to know many things" as extrinsic choice.
2. Causality ($\alpha = .76$). A high score represents that individuals study voluntarily. Sample: "I study because I want to" as intrinsic choice versus "I study because my parents tell me to do" as extrinsic choice.
3. Mastery ($\alpha = .69$). A high score indicates higher desire to work independently. Sample: "I try to solve difficult problems by myself" as intrinsic choice versus "I ask a teacher soon when a problem is difficult" as extrinsic choice.
4. Attribution ($\alpha = .62$). Endogenous-exogenous attribution was introduced by Kruglanski (1975) as described above. A high score reflects that individuals study because they feel studying is fun. A low score indicates that persons study for external reasons, such as for careers and entrance examinations. Sample: "I study because studying is fun" as intrinsic choice versus "I study in order to get a good grade" as extrinsic choice.
5. Challenge ($\alpha = .85$). A high score indicates that individuals have more desire to engage in challenging schoolwork. Sample: "I like to solve more difficult problems" as intrinsic choice versus "I like to solve easier problems" as extrinsic choice.
6. Enjoyment ($\alpha = .75$). A high score indicates that respondents enjoy schoolwork. Sample: "Schoolwork is fun" as intrinsic choice versus "Schoolwork is not fun" as extrinsic choice.

Procedures

The data was collected in October 2005. To reduce environmental bias that could be created in different schools, a tape recorded by the researcher was used to give instructions during the data collection sessions. In the present study, the informed consent statement was received from the pupils' teachers in each school. In the informed consent statement, each participant was assured of anonymity and confidentiality. After the questionnaires were distributed to the subjects by the teachers, the pupils listened to the tape. The total administration of each questionnaire lasted between 10-15 minutes. The returned questionnaires were coded. The collected data was analyzed using the Statistical Package for the Social Sciences (SPSS) computer program. A multivariate analysis of variance (MANOVA) was conducted to detect the effects of grade and gender on the SIEM. When necessary, post-hoc tests were conducted to determine the precise contrasts in which the observed significance occurred.

RESULTS

MANOVA was performed to examine the effects of grade and gender on the six variables extracted from the SIEM. Results of the multivariate tests revealed a significant effect of grade and gender, but no significant effect of grade by gender interaction (see Table 1). At the multivariate level, significant main effects of grade, Pillai's Trace = .13, $F(18, 1422) = 3.54$, $p < .01$, partial eta squared = .043 and gender, Pillai's Trace = .11, $F(6, 472) = 9.20$, $p < .01$, partial eta squared = .105, were observed.

As a result, the six scales could be analyzed individually using univariate F-tests. Grade had significant effect on, curiosity, $F(3, 477) = 4.42$, $p < .01$, partial eta squared = .027, mastery, $F(3, 477) = 6.60$, $p < .01$, partial eta squared = .040, and challenge $F(3, 477) = 7.67$, $p < .01$, partial eta squared = .046.

Table 1. Multivariate and Univariate Analyses of Variances F Ratios for Grade × Gender Effects for SIEM

Variable	MANOVA $F(6, 472)$	ANOVA Curiosity $F(1,477)$	Causality $F(1,477)$	Mastery $F(1,477)$	Attribution $F(1,477)$	Challenge $F(1,477)$	Enjoyment $F(1,477)$
Grade	3.54**	4.42**	2.71	6.60**	2.38	7.67**	2.57
Gender	9.20**	13.38**	29.29**	.57	8.51**	1.10	8.16**
Grade × Gender	.67	1.72	1.05	.17	.36	1.05	.22

Note. F ratios are Pillai's Trace's approximation of Fs. MANOVA = multivariate analysis of variance; ANOVA = univarite analysis of variance.
**$p < .01$.

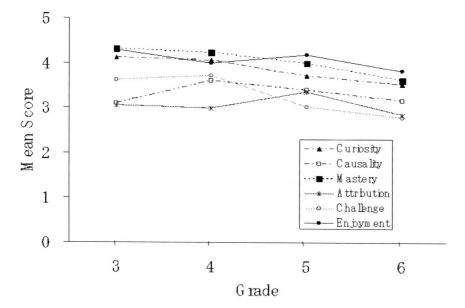

Figure 1. Mean scores for third grade (n = 119), fourth grade (n = 132), fifth grade (n = 125), and sixth grade (n = 109) in the six subscales of SIEM.

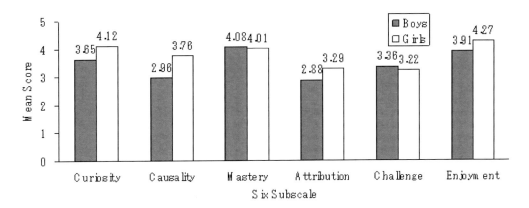

Figure 2. Mean scores for boys (n = 264) and girls (n = 221) in the six subscales of SIEM.

In the case of significant grade main effects, Tukey's post hoc test was performed to identify statistical differences. Figure 1 shows mean scores for grade and six measures of SIEM. Curiosity scores decreased during grades 3-6, and then showed statistically significant differences between third and sixth grades. Mastery scores decreased during grades 3-6, and then revealed statistically significant differences between third and sixth grades and between fourth and sixth grades. Challenge scores increased slightly (NS) in fourth grade, but decreased during grades 4-6, showing statistically significant differences between third and sixth grades and between fourth and sixth grades.

Gender had significant effect on curiosity, $F(1, 477) = 13.38$, $p < .01$, partial eta squared = .027, causality, $F(1, 477) = 29.29$, $p < .01$, partial eta squared = .058, attribution, $F(1, 477) = 8.51$, $p < .01$, partial eta squared = .018, and enjoyment, $F(1, 477) = 8.16$, $p < .01$, partial eta squared = .017 (see Table 1). As shown in Figure 2, girls had higher scores in the four subscales.

DISCUSSION

Research Question 1

Are there any differences in developmental trends in intrinsic motivation of Japanese elementary school pupils between 20 years ago and now?

Grade had significant effect on challenge, curiosity, and mastery. Figure 1 shows that curiosity and mastery scores decrease through grades 3-6 and challenge scores increase slightly (NS) in the fourth grade and decrease through grades 4-6. Therefore, it can be generally concluded that intrinsic motivation decreases during grades 3-6.

Next, I discuss differences in developmental trends of intrinsic and extrinsic motivation of Japanese elementary school pupils between 20 years ago and now. Sakurai and Takano (1985) found that the mastery and challenge subscales decreased with age. The present study also found that the two variables generally decreased with age. Further, enjoyment and curiosity in Sakurai and Takano decreased gradually from second through fifth grades, but temporarily increased in the sixth grade. In this study, such an increase was not observed. It might be said that the students 20 years ago had higher expectations for entering junior high school than contemporary elementary school pupils. According to Sakurai and Takano, the attribution subscale increased with age. This study, however, does not show such an increase. Thus, it can be said that elementary school pupils 20 years ago were more intrinsically and autonomously motivated to learn than contemporary pupils.

In sum, there are rather differences in the developmental trends of motivation between 20 years ago and now. The students 20 years ago temporarily increased curiosity, causality, and enjoyment in sixth grade, but such an increase cannot be found in this study. Although Sakurai and Takano (1985) found the attribution subscale increased with age, this study does not show such an increase. That is, this study has shown that contemporary elementary school pupils have a greater developmental decline in intrinsic motivation than those of 20 years ago. Then, what causes these differences?

As has been said above, the Japanese school education system has been shifting from a highly competitive to a more relaxed approach for the last 20 years, which might have influenced contemporary pupils' intrinsic motivation. Contrary to our expectations, the more relaxed approach might not be doing well in enhancing the intrinsic motivation of elementary school pupils, especially, in the case of higher graders.

Moreover, it is often said that contemporary elementary school students tend to play computer games indoors and not to play outdoors. Since the mid-1900s, many researchers (e.g., Anderson and Dill, 2000; Dill and Dill, 1998; Sakamoto, 2005; Sakamoto, Ozaki, Mori, Takahira, and Ibe, 1998) have discussed the bad effects of video and computer game. For example, Sakamoto explored the relationship between video game use and children's psychological development. It might be said that such changes in play styles affect pupils' intrinsic motivation.

Then, what can be done about the developmental decline in intrinsic motivation? A first approach for combating the developmental decline in motivation involves promoting perceptions of autonomy (Lepper and Henderlong, 2000). Intrinsic motivation derives from students feeling a sense of control over their learning environments and activities (Lepper and Hodell, 1989). It is important to create an autonomous climate in the classroom. One of the ways to enhance perception of autonomy is to provide opportunities for pupils to control and choose different activities within a range of activities that fit into the curriculum.

A second potential response to the developmental decrease in motivation is to encourage pupils to have clear and specific goals in the classroom. According to Csikszentmihalyi and Rathunde (1993), flow experience, referring to a subjective state of being completely involved in something, forgetting time, fatigue and everything else but the activity itself, usually happens when there are clear goals one can reach. According to Pintrich and Schunk (2002), clear and specific goals promote motivation better than vague general goals such as "Do your best". Pintrich and Schunk also said that proximal or close-at-hand goals enhance motivation better than distant goals, because individuals can judge progress toward the former.

A third potential response to the developmental decrease in motivation is to provide activities that are challenging but reasonable in terms of students' capabilities (Lepper and Henderlong, 2000). According to Deci and Ryan (1985), pupils should be given activities that are difficult and challenging, but not outside their range of competence. Lepper and Hodell (1989) said that optimally challenging activities are ones in which goals are of intermediate difficulty and attainment is uncertain. Csikszentmihalyi and Rathunde (1993) also state flow experience happens when an appropriate balance between skills and challenges is achieved.

Research Question 2

Are there any gender differences in intrinsic motivation of Japanese elementary school pupils between 20 years ago and now?

Sakurai and Takano (1985) found the curiosity and causality scores of girls were significantly higher than those of boys in all the grades except the sixth grade. The present study also shows that girls have higher scores than boys in the four subscales: causality, enjoyment, curiosity, and attribution. Thus, it can be said that gender differences are almost similar to 20 years ago.

LIMITATIONS AND CONCLUSION

A few more limitations of the study and suggestions for future study need to be addressed. First, the data was collected only by means of a questionnaire. Qualitative research, including interviews with students and teachers and classroom observations, would provide significant further layers of analysis.

Secondly, data collection was cross-sectional. A cross-sectional study is less effective in identifying individual variations in growth or to establish causal relationships (Cohen, Manion, and Morrison, 2000). Longitudinal studies are particularly appropriate in research on human growth and development (Cohen et al., 2000). To investigate the change in motivation with age more precisely, longitudinal data collection should be conducted.

Thirdly, whereas the participants in this study lived in the suburbs of Tokyo, those in Sakurai and Takano (1985) lived in the Japanese countryside. These contextual differences may affect the results. To compare more precisely motivation of elementary school pupils between 20 years ago and now, research should be done in Nagano as conducted by Sakurai and Takano. Moreover, inferences drawn from the results of this study are limited by the nature of the particular sample used, which consisted solely of students who live in the suburbs of Tokyo. These results may be specific to one group and not generalizable to Japanese elementary school pupils as a whole. As with all studies, then it is essential to replicate this study to determine the applicability of the results to other contexts.

Notwithstanding its limitations, this study does make a contribution towards revealing and understanding the motivation of Japanese elementary pupils. This study reveals that there is a developmental decline in intrinsic motivation among today's Japanese elementary school pupils, compared to pupils 20 years ago. This study narrows its focus down to motivational studies and this is obviously just one aspect of the picture representing elementary school pupils. Thus, other areas like cognitive development and socio-cultural factors will have to be investigated in the future.

REFERENCES

Anderson, C. A., and Dill, K. E. (2000). Video games and aggressive thoughts, feelings, and behavior in the laboratory and in life. *Journal of Personality and Social Psychology, 78,* 772-790.

Carreira, M.J. (2006). Motivation for learning English as a foreign language in Japanese elementary schools, *JALT Journal, 28, 135-157.*

Cohen, L, Manion, L, and Morrison, K. (2000). *Research methods in education* (5th ed.). London: Routledge Falmer.

Csikszentmihalyi, M., and Rathunde, K. (1993). The measurement of flow in everyday life: Toward a theory of emergent motivation. In J. E. Jacobs (Ed.), *Developmental perspectives on motivation* (pp. 57-97).Lincoln: University of Nebraska Press.

deCharms, R. (1968/1983). *Personal causation: The internal affective determinants of behavior.* New York: Academic Press.

Deci, E. D. and Ryan, R. M. (1985). *Intrinsic motivation and self-determination in human behavior.* New York: Plenum Press.

Dill, K. E.and Dill, J. C. (1998). Video game violence: A review of the empirical literature. *Aggression and Violent Behavior, 3,* 407–428.

Harter, S. (1981) A new self-report scales of intrinsic versus extrinsic orientation in the classroom: Motivational and informational components. *Developmental Psychology, 17,* 300-312.

Heider, F. (1958). *The psychology of interpersonal relations.* New York: John Wiley.

Kruglanski, A. W. (1975). The endogenous-exogenous partition in attribution theory. *Psychological Review, 82,* 387-406.

Lepper, M. R. and Henderlong, J. (2000). Turning "Play" into "Work" and "Work" into "Play": 25 years of research on intrinsic versus extrinsic motivation. In C. Sansone and J. M. Harackiewicz (Eds.), *Intrinsic and extrinsic motivation: The search for optimal motivation and performance* (pp. 257-372). San Diego: Academic Press.

Lepper, M.R., and Hodell, M. (1989). Intrinsic motivation in the classroom. In C. Ames and R. Ames (Eds.). *Research on motivation in education* (Vol.3, pp.73-105).San Diego: Academic Press.

Lepper, M.R., Sethi, S., Dialdin, D.,and Drake, M. (1997). Intrinsic and extrinsic motivation: A developmental perspective. In S. S. Luthar, J. A. Burack, D. Cicchetti and J. R. Weisz (Eds.), *Developmental psychology: Perspectives on adjustment, risk, and disorder* (pp. 23-50). New York: Cambridge University Press.

Ministry of Education, Science, Sports and Culture. (1997) *Program for educational reform.* Retrieved December 21, 2006, from http://www.mext.go.jp/english/news/1997/10/971002.htm

Ministry of Education, Science, Sports and Culture. (1998). *National curriculum standards reform for kindergarten, elementary school, lower and upper secondary school and schools for the visually disabled, the hearing impaired and the otherwise disabled: Synopsis of the report.* Retrieved October 21, 2006, from: http://www.mext.go.jp/english/news/1998/07/980712.htm

Ministry of Education, Culture, Sports, Science and Technology (2001). *The education reform plan for the 21st century: The rainbow plan, the seven priority strategies.*

Retrieved December 21, 2006, from http://www.mext.go.jp/english/topics/21plan/010301.htm

Ministry of Education, Culture, Sports, Science and Technology. (n.d.). *Educational reform: Education reform plan for the 21st century.* Retrieved December 21, 2006, from http://www.mext.go.jp/english/org/reform/07.htm

Nozaki, Y. (2006). The historical transition of the courses of study and people's attitudes toward education, *The Bulletin of Kokugakuin Junior College, 23*, 151-171.

Pintrich, P. R., and Schunk, D.H. (2002) *Motivation in education: Theory, research, and application* (2nd ed.). New Jersey: Merrill Prentice Hall.

Sakamoto, A. (2005). Video games and the psychological development of Japanese children. In I. Sigel (Series Ed.), D. W. Shwalb, J. Nakazawa, and B. J. Shwalb (Vol. Eds.), *Advances in applied developmental psychology: Theory, practice, and research from Japan* (pp.3-21). Greenwich, CT: Information Age Pub Inc.

Sakamoto, A., Ozaki, M., Mori,T., Takahira, M., and Ibe, N. (1998). Video games and Human Violence: Impacts of Interactivity in Media. *Interaction' 98*, Retrieved December 26, 2006, from http://www.interaction-ipsj.org/archives/paper1998/pdf1998/paper98-109.pdf

Sakurai, S.,and Takano, S. (1985). Naihatsuteki gaihatsuteki doukizuke sokutei no kaihatsu [A new self-report scale of intrinsic versus extrinsic motivation toward learning in children]. *Tsukuba Psychological Research, 7*, 43-54.

APPENDIX A

Items for Scale of Intrinsic versus Extrinsic Motivation (SIEM) (The original version was written in Japanese, adapted from Sakurai and Takano, 1985)

1. "I want to study various things voluntarily" as intrinsic choice versus "I think I should study only what my teachers teach" as extrinsic choice.
2. "I study because I want to" as intrinsic choice versus "I study because my parents tell me to" as extrinsic choice.
3. "I try to solve difficult problems by myself" as intrinsic choice versus "I ask a teacher soon when a problem is difficult" as extrinsic choice.
4. "I study because I can learn what I like" as intrinsic choice versus "I study in order to get a good grade" as extrinsic choice.
5. "I like difficult problems" as intrinsic choice versus "I like easier problems" as extrinsic choice.
6. "I enjoy lessons at school" as intrinsic choice versus "I don't enjoy lessons at school" as extrinsic choice.
7. "I want to study as much as possible" as intrinsic choice versus "I want to study only what I learn at school" as extrinsic choice.
8. "I do excises because I want to know how to solve various problems" as intrinsic choice versus "I do excises because I am told to" as extrinsic choice.
9. "When I make a mistake, I try to find an answer" as intrinsic choice versus "When I make a mistake, I try to ask a teacher for the answer" as extrinsic choice.

10. "I study because studying is fun" as intrinsic choice versus "I study in order to get a good grade" as extrinsic choice.
11. "I like difficult problems" as intrinsic choice versus "I don't like difficult problems" as extrinsic choice.
12. "Schoolwork is fun" as intrinsic choice versus "Schoolwork is not fun" as extrinsic choice".
13. "I want to read various types of books" as intrinsic choice versus "I don't want to read books except comics" as extrinsic choice.
14. "I do homework voluntarily" as intrinsic choice versus "I do homework because my parents tell me to do" as extrinsic choice.
15. "I try to solve problems by myself even if I cannot solve them" as intrinsic choice versus "I ask teachers soon when I cannot solve problems" as extrinsic choice.
16. "I do not study only because I want to receive praise from my parents" as intrinsic choice versus " I study because I want to receive praise from my parents" as extrinsic choice..
17. "I like difficult problems" as intrinsic choice versus "I like easy problems" as extrinsic choice.
18. "I feel happy when I can solve difficult problems" as intrinsic choice versus " I do not feel happy even if I can solve difficult problems" as extrinsic choice.
19. "I study not only homework but also what I think is interesting" as intrinsic choice versus "I study only homework" as extrinsic choice.
20. "I study even if teachers and parents do not tell me to study" as intrinsic choice versus "I don't study until teachers and parents tell me to study" as extrinsic choice.
21. "I solve problems by myself" as intrinsic choice versus "My teachers teach me how to solve problems" as extrinsic choice.
22. "I study because I like to" as intrinsic choice versus "I study because I want to get better grades than my friends" as extrinsic choice.
23. "I like to solve more difficult problems" as intrinsic choice versus "I like to solve easier problems" as extrinsic choice.
24. "There are many days when I enjoy studying at school" as intrinsic choice versus "There are hardly any days when I enjoy studying at school" as extrinsic choice.
25. "I always want to know as much as possible" as intrinsic choice versus "I do not want to know many things" as extrinsic choice.
26. "I study voluntarily before my parents tell me" as intrinsic choice versus "I study reluctantly because my parents tell me" as extrinsic choice.
27. "I try to solve difficult problems by myself" as intrinsic choice versus "I ask my friends when problems are difficult" as extrinsic choice.
28. "I study because studying is fun" as intrinsic choice versus "I study because I do not want to be scolded by my parents" as extrinsic choice.
29. "In selecting one of two problems, I select the more difficult one" as intrinsic choice versus "In selecting one of two problems, I select the easier one" as extrinsic choice.
30. "To study new things is fun" as intrinsic choice versus "To study new things is not fun" as extrinsic choice.

In: Handbook on Psychology of Motivation
Editors: J. N. Franco and A. E. Svensgaard

ISBN: 978-1-62100-755-5
© 2012 Nova Science Publishers, Inc.

Chapter 13

INCENTIVE DESIGN UTILIZING INTRINSIC MOTIVATION

Ryohei Matsumura[1] *and Norimasa Kobayashi*[2]

[1]Faculty of Business Administration, Toyo University, Tokyo, Japan
[2]Department of Value and Decision Science,
Graduate School of Decision Science and Technology,
Tokyo Institute of Technology, Tokyo, Japan

ABSTRACT

In this article, we introduce a mathematical model in economics called principal agent model. We then present our work that extends a standard principal agent model by referring to the literature in psychology.

Principal agent model is used for the design of a contract regarding a two-person relationship called agency relationship. In an agency relationship, the principal hires the agent to work for her. Due to the private information the agent possesses, it is impossible for the principal to specify the work in detail. Instead, the model suggests the contract that controls the effort level of the agent indirectly by providing adequate outcome-based incentives.

Standard principal agent models in economics consider only extrinsic incentives. However, the literature in psychology shows that intrinsic motivation is also important. We thus extended the standard model by introducing intrinsic motivation.

1. INTRODUCTION

In this article, we introduce the generalization of a mathematical model in economics called *principal agent* model via incorporation of intrinsic motivation. Principal agent model is used for the design of a contract regarding a two-person relationship called *agency relationship*. In an agency relationship, the agent works for the principal and the principal pays the reward for the work. Due to factors such as private information or expertise, it is impossible for the principal to monitor the actual effort made by the agent. The core of principal agent model has thus been to suggest a type of contract that controls the effort level of the agent *indirectly* by providing adequate performance-based incentives.

Designing incentives requires the understanding of the agent's utility regarding work. The standard principal agent model has assumed that the intrinsic utility brought about by work to the agent is only stress (disutility) related. Hence without extrinsic incentives, the agent would try to minimize the effort. This is known as *moral hazard* and the key strategy of principal agent model has been to avoid moral hazard via performance based incentives.

The huge literature in social psychology shows however that intrinsic motivation is also important. Moreover intrinsic motivation may be influenced by extrinsic incentives, the effect of which is known as motivation crowding. It thus feels natural that principal agent models should also incorporate factors related to intrinsic motivation. Though still very little, such models have started to appear in the literature.

The article proceeds as follows. In the next section, we present a simple formal principal agent model and describe its implications. Section 3 is devoted to a brief survey on the literature discussing the effect of intrinsic motivation under the context of agency relationship. Section 4 and 5 are devoted to our own works (Matsumura and Kobayashi, 2008, 2006, and Matsumura, 2007). In section 4, we study a setting in which the principal can take explicit measures to increase the agent's intrinsic motivation by designing the environment of work or work itself. In section 5, we study a setting in which the principal utilizes the intrinsic motivation of the agent by sharing *information* with the agent. We conclude the article by proposing a possible collaboration between psychology and economics.

2. A STANDARD PRINCIPAL AGENT MODEL

In this section, we introduce the standard principal agent model. For a thorough generic treatment of principal agent models in standard economics, the reader should refer to Mas-Colell et al. (1995) for instance.

As was stated in the introduction, the most generic component of a principal agent model is the indirect control of effort through incentive design. The incentive design is formalized in the following constrained optimization problem.

$$\begin{aligned}&\max_{s,f} \quad P(s, f; e_{opt}) \\ &s.t. \quad A_{s,f}(e_{opt}) \geq B \\ &\qquad e_{opt} \in \arg\max_{e} A_{s,f}(e)\end{aligned} \quad (1)$$

e : the agent's level of effort,

f : the fixed wage,

s $(0 < s < 1)$: the share,

$P(s, f; e)$: the principal's utility,

$A_{s,f}(e)$: the agent's utility,

B : the reservation utility – the agent accepts the job offer only if the value of $A(e)$ is larger than B. The reservation utility is determined by the labor market. If the agent cannot expect a utility above B, he will seek opportunities elsewhere in the market.

The incentive design depends on the specification of $A(e)$. Notice here that the standard model introduced above does not consider intrinsic incentives.

For purpose of the generalizations introduced in section 4, we confine our focus on a simple model based on Spremann (1987) in the subsequent analysis. We have added the parameters characterizing productivity and disutility from work.

All variables and parameters are real numbers. Random variable θ and fixed wage f can have both, positive and negative values. Empirically, fixed wage f has a positive value in most cases in which the agent is an ordinary employee. However, if the agent is a franchisee, for example, the franchise fee or space fee corresponds to a fixed wage and may, therefore, be negative. All other variables take positive values.

The output is assumed to depend both on the effort level of the agent and the environmental uncertainty.

$pe + \theta$: output

p : productivity

θ : environmental risk, which varies according to a normal distribution with a mean of 0 and a variance of σ^2. Large σ^2 implies large environmental uncertainty. Output is assumed to be constant in return with respect to e.

$spe + f - rs^2\sigma^2/2$: the agent's monetary utility

$spe + f$: the expected value of the monetary income of the agent

$rs^2\sigma^2/2$: risk premium

The agent is assumed to be risk averse with respect to monetary income. The monetary utility is assumed to take the form used in mean-variance approach.

ce^2 : the agent's cost function

c : cost sensitivity of the agent.

The cost of work consists of opportunity cost, and physical and mental exhaustion. Predominantly, time becomes extremely precious as free time decreases. Thus, we assume that the marginal cost of work increases with respect to the effort level of the agent. For purpose of simplicity, we adopt the functional form ce^2.

$$A(e) = (spe + f) - r(s^2\sigma^2)/2 - ce^2 \qquad (2)$$

The principal is interested in monetary gain only and is assumed to be risk neutral. The monetary gain of the principal is output minus wages.

Thus the principal's utility is

$$P(s, f) = (1-s)pe - f \qquad (3)$$

Substituting the concrete functional form (2) and (3) into the generic constrained optimization problem (1), the optimal share level

$$s_{opt} = \frac{1}{1 + 2rc\sigma^2 / p^2}$$

is obtained. The following inequalities are fulfilled regardless of the parameter settings.

A: $\partial s_{opt} / \partial \sigma < 0$ The higher the uncertainty, the less effective the performance based wage.

B: $\partial s_{opt} / \partial p > 0$ The higher the productivity, the more effective the performance based wage.

C: $\partial s_{opt} / \partial c < 0$ The higher the cost of work, the less effective the performance based wage.

3. PRINCIPAL AGENT MODELS AND INTRINSIC MOTIVATION

Though still little, the literature relating intrinsic motivation to principal agent models is growing. Probably the most influential is the argument regarding *Motivation Crowding Effect (MCE)* (Frey and Jegen, 2001). According to Frey and Jegen (2001), "the Motivation Crowding Effect suggests that external intervention via monetary incentives or punishments may undermine, and under different identifiable conditions strengthen, intrinsic motivation." Namely, there may be motivation crowding *out* (MCO) or motivation crowding *in* depending upon the work setting. There is a huge literature regarding the MCE itself; the reader may refer to Ryan and Deci (2000) for instance.

Of the two MCE, social psychologists may feel more accustomed to MCO. The theoretical insight underlying MCO is attribution theory. Kreps (1997) eloquently illustrates the logic as follows. "Turning revealed preference on its head, the idea is that when a person performs some act, he looks for rationales that justify his actions. Specifically, if an employee undertakes some effort without the spur of some extrinsic incentive, he will rationalize his efforts as reflecting his enjoyment of the task. And since he enjoys it, he works at it. But if extrinsic incentives are put in place, he will attribute his efforts to those incentives, developing a distaste for the required effort."

Staw (1977) for instance claims that several necessary conditions must exist for MCO to be valid and that these conditions limit the applicability of MCO to industrial work organizations. These necessary conditions are: 1) the task is interesting; 2) the reward is remarkable; and, 3) the norm of rewarding does not exist beforehand. External rewards tend to strengthen intrinsic motivation when these conditions are not fulfilled. However, in many organizations, these conditions are not met.

Thus, in what particular way motivation crowding takes effect is not straightforward. James Jr. (2004) incorporates the insights obtained in social psychology into an actual utility functional form of the agent and classifies the conditions under which motivation crowding out or motivation crowding in takes effect. Benabou and Tirole (2003), instead of directly formalizing the recent literature of psychology into a mathematical model, models the attributions in the original way and shows how performance incentives offered by an informed principal can adversely impact an agent's perception of the task, or of his own abilities.

The relationship between the intrinsic motivation and principal agent models is not confined to MCE. Even when extrinsic incentives and intrinsic motivation are independent, it is meaningful to discuss intrinsic motivation in a principal agent model, so long as intrinsic motivation is controllable for the principal. Our work in the next section along with Murdock (2002) falls in this category. Murdock (2002) discusses an interesting setting like research and development in drug producing firms. The researchers are intrinsically motivated to develop drugs that are not profitable as well. He shows that it may be optimal for the firm to commit to produce drugs that are under the break-even point, in order to increase the intrinsic motivation of the researchers, which results in the higher productivity of profitable drugs. The argument does not require MCE and is still inspiring for the incentive design of research and development.

Furthermore, incentive system design even goes beyond the extrinsic / intrinsic motivation dichotomy. *Self-determination theory (SDT)* (Deci and Ryan, 1985) proposes that extrinsic motivation can vary greatly in the degree to which it is autonomous. There are several reasons why the more internal motivations are more desirable. First, it is often less costly for the principal to foster internal motivations than giving monetary incentives. Second, the more external an extrinsic incentive is, the more it is expected to crowd out the intrinsic motivation (Frey and Jegen, 2001). Third, autonomous motivations are expected to be more sustainable for a long term than external motivations. Finally, the more autonomously motivated an agent is, the more creative he is expected to be in achieving the task (Greenberg, 1992, Rejskind, 1982, and Sheldon, 1995).

4. INCREASING INTRINSIC MOTIVATION THROUGH PHYSICAL FACTORS

In this section, we generalize the standard principal agent model introduced in section 2 by assuming that intrinsic motivation of the agent is controllable by the principal. This makes a clear contrast with the standard literature in economics. Frey and Jegen (2001) states "Intrinsic motivation is assumed to be an exogenously given constant, and often it is completely disregarded. There is a good reason why much of economic theory neglects intrinsic motivation. In spite of the seemingly simple definition offered by Deci, it is difficult, if not impossible, to determine which parts of an employee's motivation to perform his or her job are intrinsic, and which not. Although intrinsic motivation may play an important role in many areas of the economy and society, it is difficult to influence or control, especially in comparison with the large array of readily available extrinsic motivators." However, this classical commonsense in economics may not necessarily be dominant in all sorts of works. We have already seen that Murdock (2002) takes the stance similar to ours. In his setting, the firm increases intrinsic motivation by committing to implement the projects that are not profitable as well, so long as the increase in motivation is also expected to have the positive effect on other profitable projects.

In our model, we take a much more direct approach and assume that the principal invests to improve intrinsic motivation of the agent. The means of improving intrinsic motivation includes work environment design, job assignment and job design for example.

The reader may possibly have the impression that work environment design is related to hygiene factors (Herzberg, 1966). However, such measures may indirectly increase the intrinsic satisfaction from work via the improvement of productivity. Moreover, the workers may gain the sense of autonomy and ability via better communication among the team members. For example, Deci, Connell, and Ryan (1989) show that when managers are more autonomy supportive, their subordinates become more trusting of the organization and display more positive work-related attitudes.

There is no doubt that individuals have a variety of tastes regarding work. "Although, in one sense, intrinsic motivation exists within individuals, in another sense intrinsic motivation exists in the relation between individuals and activities. People are intrinsically motivated for some activities and not others, and not everyone is intrinsically motivated for any particular task." (Ryan and Deci, 2000). Hence, it seems apparently effective to assign jobs to adequate individuals.

Jobs are often designed for purpose of improving productivity or cost efficiency. However, job design is also applicable for fostering intrinsic motivation. Hackman and Oldham (1980) argues that in order to increase internal work motivation, the jobs should be designed in such a way that they will (1) provide variety, involve completion of a whole, and have a positive impact on the lives of others; (2) afford considerable freedom and discretion to the employee (what action theorists refer to as decision latitude); and (3) provide meaningful performance feedback (Gagne and Deci, 2005).

Such direct measures for increasing the non-monetary motivations of the agent are not merely a theoretical construct. There exists a company in Japan called Link and Motivation Inc. (http://www.lmi.ne.jp/) . The company states that it is the first management consulting firm that specializes in what they call "motivation engineering". The company was founded in 2000 and is growing very fast with over 1,800 clients in 2009.

Next, we proceed to our formal model (Matsumura and Kobayashi, 2008). We omit the components explained in section 2 and present the newly introduced variables and parameters.

We first quantify the measures taken by the principal to increase the agent's motivation according to Hackman and Oldham (1980).

Motivating potential scale (MPS) = (Skill Variety + Task Identity + Task Significance) × Autonomy × Feedback

The meanings of the terms in this equation are given below:

Skill Variety: The degree to which a job requires a variety of activities in carrying out the work.

Task Identity: The degree to which a job requires completion of a whole and identifiable piece of work.

Task Significance: The degree to which a job has a substantial impact on the lives of other people.

Autonomy: The degree to which a job provides an individual substantial freedom, independence, and discretion in scheduling the work and in determining the procedures to be used in carrying it out.

Feedback: The degree to which carrying out the work activities required by the job results in the individual obtaining direct and clear information about the effectiveness of his or her performance.

Using the above defined motivation increasing variable m, the constrained optimization problem (1) is modified as follows:

$$\max_{s,f,m} \quad P(s,f,m;e_{opt})$$
$$s.t. \quad A_{s,f,m}(e_{opt}) \geq B$$
$$e_{opt} \in \arg\max_{e} A_{s,f,m}(e)$$

Modification of the concrete functional form of A are given below.

m^2 : motivating cost
a : the agent's sensitivity to improvements in the pleasure of work
mae : intrinsic utility

The intrinsic motivation variable m makes the work more attractive for the agent. We assume that the cost of work design is increasing in m and diminishing in marginal return. For purpose of simplicity, we use m^2 as the concrete functional form of cost required for job design and so forth.

We assume that the marginal intrinsic utility the agent receives from a unit amount of effort is constant and equals ma. Thus, when the effort level is e, the agent gains mae intrinsic utility level. Note that in some jobs, the agent may become bored as working hours increase. We classify boredom into the cost of work.

We do not assume MCE on the intrinsic motivation, thus the agent's utility is the sum of monetary and non-monetary utilities. Since different MCE are expected for different work conditions, we have started our analysis in the simplest setting. The model incorporating MCE in addition may be a candidate of the future research.

Thus, (2) and (3) (the utility functions of the principal and the agent) are redefined as follows.

$$A(e) = (spe + f) - r(s^2\sigma^2)/2 + mae - ce^2$$
$$P(s,f,m) = (1-s)pe - f - m^2$$

By substituting the redefined utility functions into (1)', the modified constrained optimization problem is obtained with the following interior solution, provided that the second-order condition $4c - a^2 > 0$ is met.

$$s_{opt} = \frac{1}{1 + 2rc\sigma^2/p^2}, \quad f_{opt} = B - \frac{(sp+ma)^2}{4c} + \frac{r}{2}(s^2\sigma^2), \quad m_{opt} = \frac{ap}{4c-a^2}$$

When the second-order condition is not satisfied, m and f diverge to infinity and minus infinity, respectively. The interpretation of the second order condition $4c - a^2 > 0$ is that work is not as enjoyable as a hobby. When this condition is not met, the agent is willing to pay as much of his wage as possible to make the job attractive for himself.

Regarding comparative static analyses of the solutions $s_{opt}, f_{opt}, m_{opt}$ with respect to parameters σ, a, p, c the following relationships hold, irrespective of the parameters' values:

A: $\partial s_{opt} / \partial \sigma < 0$

The higher the uncertainty, the less effective the performance based wage.

B: $\partial s_{opt} / \partial a = 0$

The performance-based wage was unaffected by the agent's intrinsic utility sensitivity.

C: $\partial s_{opt} / \partial p > 0$

The higher the productivity, the more effective the performance based wage.

D: $\partial s_{opt} / \partial c < 0$

The higher the cost of work, the less effective the performance-based wage.

E: $\partial f_{opt} / \partial a < 0$

The higher the intrinsic utility sensitivity, the less effective the fixed wage.
Using B and E, we can also put forward the next proposition;
F: The total wage payment decreases as the intrinsic utility sensitivity rises.

G: $\partial m_{opt} / \partial p > 0$

The higher the productivity, the more effective the investment in intrinsic motivation.

H: $\partial m_{opt} / \partial c < 0$

The higher the cost of work, the less effective the investment in intrinsic motivation.

Comparing (C,D) and (G,H), we can say that performance-based wage and motivating cost are positively correlated with respect to the change in the parameters p, c. In general, the tendency for both extrinsic incentives and the investment in intrinsic motivation to be effective when productivity is high is believed to be due to the fact that profit increases significantly if a productive worker works more. When cost sensitivity is higher, it may be more efficient to employ multiple agents rather than require a single effort-averse agent to work longer hours.

The comparative statics obtained above critically depends on the assumption that there is no MCE. Other types of work settings where we can observe MCE is a future research agenda.

5. MOTIVATING THE AGENT THROUGH AUTONOMY

In the previous section, we introduced a model in which a principal changes the physical work environment or job itself to increase the intrinsic motivation of an agent. In this section, we deal with a much more fundamentally mental approach, where we assume that tasks themselves and other physical components are fixed. There is a limit to the level at which tasks and other physical components can be modified to be attractive for the agent. When a principal has done all her best regarding the physical work environment or job itself to increase the intrinsic motivation of an agent, is there nothing left for the principal to do other than giving the agent monetary incentives? Ryan and Deci (2000) may be eloquent enough to state our generic problem setting under the context of education – "Frankly speaking, because many of the tasks that educators want their students to perform are not inherently interesting or enjoyable, knowing how to promote more active and volitional (versus passive and controlling) forms of extrinsic motivation becomes an essential strategy for successful teaching."

In this section, we thus propose an agency model, which we call *autonomous agency model*, that fully utilizes the notion of autonomy of the agent. In the model, instead of providing an agent with monetary rewards or ordering him, a principal motivates an agent by *convincing* him that the task is important for the agent himself.

There are a number of assumptions for effective conviction to take place: (i) the task is indeed important for the informed agent, (ii) it is difficult enough for the agent to find out the true *potential utility* of the task and (iii) the principal is more knowledgeable about the potential utility. We think the concept of potential utility plays an essential role in the context of conviction. Ryan and Deci (2000) also states that "a student could be motivated to learn a new set of skills because he or she understands their potential utility or value or because learning the skills will yield a good grade and the privileges a good grade affords". The parents are often more knowledgeable than a child about what the child can expect in the long-term future from studying seriously. The parents can therefore motivate the child effectively via communicating to him the correct potential utility.

There may be a variety of applications of autonomous agency model. In a highly sophisticated economy today, division of labor is indispensable. The causal relationship between each worker's work and final products may be enormously complex. It is no longer evident for each worker how his work may impact the final product, and in terms of division of labor, such understanding by each worker is not required. In traditional hierarchical organizations, the information concentrated at the management level. From the perspective of autonomy however, it looks essential that each worker is consciously aware of the implication of his work. It thus looks natural that excellent companies today often share corporate ideals with basically all the employees.

An interesting aspect of potential utility is that both in the context of complex causal relationships or of long-term decision making, it is difficult for an agent to examine the physical effect of his actions. Hence, even when an agent is autonomous and believes he is making rational choice, it in fact may be that he is making a seriously *incorrect* choice. Standard economics (Bayesian games) and decision analysis (expected utility maximization) of uninformed agents do not deal with such situations. Standard economics and decision analysis assume that the agent is aware of the incompleteness of information. We thus apply our own framework of *potential utility model*.

Autonomous agency model is formulated as follows.

$$\max_{c} \quad P(c; e^*, e_k)$$

$$s.t. \quad e^* \in \arg\max_{e} A(e)$$

$$e_k \in \arg\max_{e} A_k(e)$$

k : the perception of the agent regarding the decision situation before learning from the principal
e : the agent's level of effort
c : measures taken by the principal to convince the agent
P : the principal's utility
A : the agent's utility

The agent maximizes the utility A_k he perceives in his mind, and acts according to the optimal solution e_k. However, the actual true potential utility he physically obtains in the long run is $A(e_k)$. When the agent is well informed of the potential utility A, he acts according to the optimal solution e^* and physically obtains the potential utility $A(e^*)$.

The principal invests in the conviction of the agent. c represents the degree to which the agent is convinced. Though conviction is costly, the principal expects to gain from the change in the agent's action from e_k to e^* due to conviction.

In the previous section, the generalization was to introduce intrinsic motivation factor to a standard principal agent model, but other factors related to agency relationship were untouched. In this section, we continue to deal with a two-person constrained optimization problem of how a principal should motivate an agent, but we no longer confine our attention to agency contracts where the utility of the principal is profit. Thus the applications include the government convincing the citizens not to drive after drinking for example. Similar generalization is also possible in the settings of Section 4 as well.

Henceforth, we apply framework to a case of motivating people to stop driving after drinking (Matsumura, 2007). e represents the effort required for a person to switch from driving to other means of transportation. The risk of traffic accidents is decreasing in e. k represents the increase in the agent's gain caused by a unit increase in the effort of the agent. k is affected by the decrease in the probability of traffic accidents, the expected loss of social status due to an accident, the expected amount of compensation caused by an accident or the decrease in the probability of being caught by the police. k is larger if the agent is weak in alcohol for instance.

We assume that an uninformed agent subjectively estimates the value of k. Here, our approach makes a clear contrast with expected utility or Bayesian games. The value of k reflects agents' initial information, and k^* represents the true value.

ake : the positive utility obtained by agents

a : gain sensitivity

For instance, a sensitive agent may feel extremely guilty by hurting a person by accident, whereas an insensitive agent may not care strongly.

de^2 : the direct cost caused by the effort

d : cost sensitivity

de^2 represents the inconvenience caused by taking a train back home instead of driving back home, or the monetary cost of taking a taxi for example.

$A_k(e) = ake - de^2$:the utility of the agent during the decision-making process

This represents that the agent makes decision based on the subjective assessment of k.

$A(e) = A_{k^*}(e) = ak^*e - de^2$:the potential utility the agent will experience ex-post

Before the principal convinces the agent, the agent does not know the potential utility in general.

Here, we consider a benevolent principal like the parents that wishes to maximize the agentgeneral.e monetary co

$$P(c, e^*, e^k) = A(e^*) - A(e_L) - c^2/a \tag{4}$$

c^2/a : the cost required for conviction

The decision problem of the principal is how much she should invest to convince the incorrectly informed agent. Conviction entails various costs on the principal, the opportunity cost to say the least. The marginal cost of conviction is increasing in c and is decreasing in a since it is easier to convince more sensitive agents. Particularly, it is impossible to convince completely indifferent agent for whom $a = 0$.

The solution of the maximization of the principalentutility (4) is

$$c_{opt} = a^2(k - k^*)^2/8d$$

Comparative statics on the solution of the principal implies the following features.

A: $\partial c_{opt}/\partial a > 0$ The higher the gain sensitivity, the more effective conviction.

B: $\partial c_{opt}/\partial d < 0$ The higher the cost sensitivity, the less effective conviction.

C: $\partial c_{opt}/\partial (k - k^*) > 0$ The larger the difference between the information the agent has before and after the conviction, the more effective conviction.

Finally, we should note that giving the correct information does not necessarily motivate the agent to avoid driving less after drinking. Some agents may be overly risk averse towards traffic accidents, such that the subjective assessment leads to absolutely no driving after drinking, while the potential utility in fact may suggest that he can drive to some extent. If the principal absolutely no driving after drinking, while the potential utility in fact may suggest that he can drive to some rincipal hence may actually hide information from the agent in such a case.

CONCLUSION

In this article, we introduced a model of incentive design in economics called principal agent model, and explored how the insights obtained in psychology of motivation have been incorporated into the model.

On the one hand, we observe that psychology has contributed in establishing more realistic utility functions of the agent. We hope on the other hand that the pieces of research like ours may inspire psychologists to look for new research agenda.

REFERENCES

Benabou, R. and Tirole, J. , 2003, pIntrinsic and Extrinsic Motivations, *Review of Economic Studies*, 70, 3, pp.489-520.
Besley, T. and Ghatak, M., 2005, nCompetition and Incentives with Motivated Agentsc, *The American Economic Review*, 95, 3, pp.616-636.
Deci, E.L. and Ryan, R.M., 1985, oIntrinsic motivation and self-determination in human behaviorn, Springer.
Deci, E.L., Connell,J.P. and Ryan, R.M., 1989, huelf-determination in a work organization 19*Journal of Applied Psychology*, 74, pp.580-590.
Deci,E.L., 1975, d ntrinsic Motivationo, Plenum Press.
Frey, B.S. and Jegen, R., 2001, vMotivation crowding theory20 *Journal of Economic surveys*, 15, 5, pp.589-611.
Frey, B.S., 1997, 1Not just for the money An economic theory of personal motivations, Edward Elgar.
Gagnrd Elgar. he money An economi*Self-determination theory and work motivation, Journal of Organizational Behavior*, 26, 4, pp.331-362.
Greenberg, E., 1992, onal Behavior motivation, rsonal motivationstablishing more realistic utility functions of t*The Journal of Creative Behavior*, 26, 2, pp.75-80.
Hackman,J.R. and Oldham,G.R., 1976, otivation, rsonal motivationstablishing more realistic util*Organizational Behavior and Human Performance*, 16, pp.250-279.
Hackman,J.R. and Oldham,G.R., 1980, rformance, rsonal mdison-Wesley.
Herzberg, F., 1966, ham,G.R., 1980, rformance, rsonal md
Howard, R. A., 1980, am,G.R., 1980, rformance, rsonal mdiso*Operations Research*, 28, 1, pp. 4-27.
James Jr., H. S., 2005. GWhy did you do that? An economic examination of the effect of extrinsic compensation on intrinsic motivation and performancee h*Journal of Economic Psychology*, 26, 4, pp. 549-566
Kreps, D. M., 1997, PIntrinsic Motivation and Extrinsic Incentiveso, *The American Economic Review*, 87, 2, pp. 359-364.

Mas-Colell,A., and Whinston,M.D., 1995, tivesof the effect of extrinsic compensation on

Matsumura, R. and Kobayashi, N., 2005, ayashi, N. Whinston,M.D., 1995, tivesof the effect of extrinsic compensation ost World Congress of IFSR.

Matsumura, R., 2007, SR.ton,M.D., 1995, tivesof the effect of extrinsic compensation on intrinsic motivatist Annual Meeting of the ISSS.

Matsumura, R. and Kobayashi, N., 2008, bAre increased costs worth paying to raise non-monetary utility?: Analysis of intrinsic motivation and fringe benefits"ri*International Transactions in Operational Research,* 15, 6, pp. 705-715.

Murdock, K., 2002, .Intrinsic Motivation and Optimal Incentive Contractsr, *The RAND Journal of Economics*, 33, 4, pp. 650-671.

Rabin, Matthew, 1993, oIncorporating Fairness into Game Theory and Economicsy, *The American Economic Review*, 83, 5, pp1281-1302.

Rejskind, FG., 1982, ReviewGame Theory and Economicsy utili*The Journal of Creative Behavior*, 16, 1, pp.58-67.

Ryan, R.M. and Deci, E.L., 2000, TIntrinsic and Extrinsic Motivations: Classic Definitions and New Directionsf, *Contemporary Educational Psychology*, 25, 1, pp.54-67.

Sheldon, M., 1995, ional Psychology: Classic Definitions and New Direct*Creativity Research Journal*, 8, 1, pp.25-36.

Spremann,K., 1987, Journalychology: Classic DAgency Theory, Information, and Incentivesotivation and fring

Staw, B.M., 1977, Journalychology: Classic DAgency Theory, Information, and Incentivesotivation and fringe benefitsormancee hope on the other ha

In: Handbook on Psychology of Motivation
Editors: J. N. Franco and A. E. Svensgaard

Chapter 14

SECONDARY STUDENTS JOURNALYCHOLOGY: CLASSIC DAGENCY THEORY, INFORMATION, AND INCENTIVESOTIVATION AND FRINGE BENEFITSORMANCEE

Kee Ying Hwa, Wang C. K. John[*], Lim B. S. Coral and Liu Woon Chia*

Motivation in Educational Research Laboratory,
National Institute of Education, Singapore

ABSTRACT

The aim of this research is to profile secondary school students' motivated strategies for learning using Pintrich and De Groot's Motivated Strategies for Learning Questionnaire (MSLQ). The sample of the study consisted of 382 secondary students from Singapore. The students completed the MSLQ, Learning Climate Questionnaire, and Academic Self-Regulation Questionnaires. The results of the cluster analysis found four unique clusters with differing MSLQ profiles. Students with either high or average MSLQ, regardless of anxiety levels, seems to perform better in their academic performance. However, students with very low MSLQ scores performed badly for their tests. Having an autonomy-supportive learning climate and more autonomous regulations may be the keys to enhance students' motivation and learning strategies.

Keywords: self-determination, MSLQ, cluster analysis, self-regulated learning

INTRODUCTION

In classroom settings, it is expected that different students would approach learning tasks differently given their varied upbringing and prior experiences. While the way in which

---
[*] E-mail: john.wang@nie.edu.sg, Fax: (65) 6896 9260, Tel: (65) 67903690

students approach learning cannot be easily discerned, their academic grades may indicate who had been more motivated and more effective as a result of adaptive learning strategies. Some of the better known learning strategies which could predict academic grades include those outlined in the Pintrich and De Groot (1990)'s Motivation and Learning Strategies Profiles. They are self-regulation, elaboration, meta-cognition and rehearsal, to name a few. Understandably, a heightened motivation in using these learning strategies would facilitate deeper learning than if there was a lack of willingness to adopt them (Deci, Ryan, and Williams, 1996). However, the question remains as to why some students may be more motivated and are using these learning strategies more often compared to others. Upbringing and parental influence could have some effect on their learning behavior, but there is a need to look at how learning behavior may be changed by teachers in the classroom. We propose that constructs pertaining to psychological needs satisfaction outlined by the self-determination theory (Deci and Ryan, 1985) – specifically autonomy and autonomy-support – would be relevant for explaining students' adaptive learning behavior, and that teachers could work at imparting these qualities. In the present study, we adopted the cluster analytic approach to uncover differences in learning strategies among a sample of secondary school students in Singapore, and examined whether students with distinct learning strategies outlined by Pintrich and De Groot (1990) differed in their own levels of autonomous regulation, perceptions of being autonomously-supported by their teachers, and in terms of grades.

Learning strategies in the current context is essentially synonymous with self-regulated learning, and the latter can be understood as the application of regulatory strategies such as the use of various cognitive and metacognitive strategies, and the use of resource management strategies for controlling learning (Pintrich, 1999). Given this emphasis on regulation and resource management, it is no surprise that learner's motivation is one of two key factors in Pintrich's conceptualization of self-regulated learning. Under this framework, motivation can be inferred from beliefs about the value attached to the learning task, and self-efficacy related to competence of performing a learning task well (Pintrich, Smith, Gracia, and McKeachie, 1991, 1993; Duncan and McKeanie, 2005). When perceived value of the task and/or learner's self-efficacy is higher, there would be more willingness to engage in the learning activity using learning strategies that promote deeper learning. Learning strategies, the other factor in Pintrich's conceptualization of self-regulated learning includes specific cognitive learning strategies such as rehearsal, elaboration and organizational strategies, metacognitive and self-regulatory strategies (Pintrich, 1999). Taken together, the actual act of engaging in self-regulated learning involves use of various cognitive and self-regulatory strategies which demand more time and effort for students, and would need considerable motivation on the learner's part (Duncan and McKeanie, 2005). In short, motivation and learning strategies goes hand in hand in self-regulated learning.

Given that 'self-regulated learning is neither easy nor automatic' (Pintrich, 1999, p. 467), shaping students' adaptive learning behavior requires considerable efforts. Through a meta-analysis of studies on self-regulated learning training programmes conducted in primary schools, Dignath, Buettner, and Langfeldt (2008) found that interventions grounded on social-cognitive theory or a combination of social-cognitive and metacognitive theories were more effective than interventions which were based only on motivational theories. In essence, to help students shape self-regulated learning behavior, intervention should consider the impact of interaction of behaviour, cognition, personal and environmental factors (Dignath et al.,

2008). Learners should be viewed as active participants in the learning process who will thrive with adequate social support (Dignath et al., 2008).

Accordingly, the source of social support in the classroom that would most directly facilitate self-regulated learning would be from their teachers. Research on the promotion of self-regulated learning in classrooms were previously undertaken (e.g. Kistner et al. 2010), and teachers' behavior were frequently examined as a critical factor for promoting self-regulated learning. The focus placed on teacher behavior is understandable as teachers are in close contact with students and often play a major role in enhancing students' self-regulated learning most directly (Ames and Archer, 1988; Zimmerman and Martinez-Pons, 1986). However, the question remains whether support from teachers should come by way of directly promoting self-regulated learning skills in class or indirectly by nurturing students' psychological needs.

There are two ways of promoting learning strategies directly, either implicitly or explicitly (Kistner et al. 2010). Implicitly, teachers can induce certain learning behavior from their students without highlighting the significance of the learning activity undertaken. For example, the teacher can apply a particular learning strategy by verbalizing his thought processes while working on a problem in class (e.g., Collins, Brown, and Holum, 1991). With this approach, the teacher is providing a source of role-modeling implicitly for the students. Explicitly, teachers can tell their students that a particular activity undertaken in class facilitates a learning strategy which improves learning performance. The rationale can also be provided to the students. In comparing the two, the value of explicit promotion generally outweighs that of the implicit approach (e.g., Pintrich, 2002). In a study of teachers' natural classroom teaching behavior via video analysis, Kistner et al. (2010), however, observed that self-regulated learning were mostly promoted via implicit instructions, even though they found that explicit approach yielded the most benefit. Certainly much more can be done to promote self-regulated learning in the classroom, judging from the fact that self-regulated learning is hard to acquire and most teachers are not promoting it well yet.

Besides the direct approach, the indirect way of fostering self-regulated learning has also been identified. Kistner et al. (2010) noted that a supportive learning environment as a form of indirect approach grounded in constructivism and transfer of learning related strongly to students' improvement in mathematical knowledge and skill. Consistent with the advocacy of adopting the social-cognitive approach, providing a supportive learning environment encouraged learners to learn in a self-determined fashion (Kistner et al., 2010). To this end, the self-determination theory which posits that satisfaction of basic needs – specifically autonomy, competence and relatedness – could lead to increased self-determination (Deci and Ryan, 1985), and is thus appropriate for understanding the indirect fostering of self-regulated learning behavior. Recently, Sierens, Vansteenkiste, Goossens, Soenens, and Dochy (2010) noted that teachers should provide help, instructions, and expectations in an autonomy-supportive way to help their students adopt self-regulated learning behavior. Such evidence points to the usefulness of indirect approach in the shaping of self-regulated learning, and suggests that fostering self-regulated learning by satisfying basic psychological needs could be fruitful.

The type of environment provided by teachers seems important for shaping students' self-regulated learning behavior (Young, 2005). We propose that exploring the role of autonomy from the self-determination framework would be a useful approach as research shows that learners' autonomy could be promoted by teachers (e.g. Sierens et al., 2010), and is thus a controllable factor should it be related to self-regulated behavior. The present cross-sectional study seeks to examine the extent of autonomous regulation and autonomy-support experienced by the students in class, comparing them in relation to the differences in learning habits reported. We hope that this study may further inform researchers and educators of the factors promoting self-regulated learning. The cluster analytic approach is adopted in this study to uncover clusters of students with distinctive self-regulated learning profiles, and differences in terms of personal perception of self-determination, perceived autonomy-support by their teachers and in academic grades will be examined. The differences between the adaptive and maladaptive clusters will also be discussed.

METHOD

Participants and Procedure

A sample of 382 secondary school students from seven schools took part in the study. There were 177 boys and 166 girls ranging in age from 13 to 18 years old. The data were collected based on their perceptions towards either Math or Science subject in school. Ethical approval was given by the University Ethical Review Board. Participants were informed that there were no right or wrong answers, assured of the confidentiality of their responses, and encouraged to ask questions if necessary.

Measures

Motivated Strategies for Learning Questionnaire (MSLQ). We used a shortened version of the MSLQ adopted from Pintrich and De Groot (1990). The shortened version consisted of 28 items. The psychometric properties of the shortened version of the MSLQ were examined elsewhere (Wang, Kee, Liu, Lim, and Chua, 2011). There were six items measuring task value, five items each assessing student's self-efficacy and elaboration, four items each for test anxiety, rehearsal, and metacognitive self-regulation. Students responded on a 7-point scale ranging from 1 (not true at all) to 7 (very true of me).

Learning Climate Questionnaire (LCQ). We used the shortened form of the LCQ from Liu and her colleagues (Liu, Wang, Tan, Ee, and Koh, 2007). There were six items measuring perceived autonomy-support of the teachers. Example item for autonomy was 'I feel that my teacher provides me with choices and options in Maths'. Student indicated the extent to which they thought each item was true of them on a 7-point scale from 1 (not true at all) to 7 (very true).

Academic Self-Regulation Questionnaire (SRQ-A). The Academic Self-Regulation Questionnaire (SRQ-A) developed by Ryan and Connell (1989) was used to assess four types of behavioural regulation in the project work context. The scale was modified with a stem for all fourteen items 'My reasons for doing my work in Math / Science ...'. External regulation (e.g., 'because I'll get into trouble if I don't') and introjection (e.g., 'because I'll feel bad about myself if I didn't') were assessed through four items each. Identification (e.g., 'because I want to improve in Math / Science') and intrinsic motivation (e.g., 'because Math / Science work is fun') were measured through three items each. A 7-point scale was used (1= Not at all true, to 7 = Very true). An overall relative autonomy index (RAI) was calculated by weighting each subscale to indicate the level of autonomy in the following way: external regulation (-2) + introjection (-1) + identification (+1) + intrinsic regulation (+2) (see Goudas, Biddle, and Fox, 1994). A positive RAI score represents more autonomous regulation and a negative RAI score represents more controlled regulation.

Grades. The participants were asked to recall their most recent test score for Math / Science. However, only 95 students provided their test scores.

Data Analysis

A series of Confirmatory Factor Analyses (CFAs) were conducted to examine the validity of the main measures (MSLQ, LCQ, and SRQ-A) followed by internal consistency tests using EQS for Windows 6.1 (Bentler, 2006). Descriptive statistics and Pearson product-moment correlations of the main variables were computed. In the main analysis, cluster analysis was used to identify homogenous groupings of participants with distinct patterns of MSLQ using SPSS.

Following that, we examined the cluster differences in relation to autonomy-support, RAI and grades. Three one-way ANOVAs were conducted, followed by post-hoc tests using Tukey's HSD to examine the cluster differences.

RESULTS

Confirmatory Factor Analyses for the Measures

The fit indices of the three CFAs are presented in Table 1. The results showed that the measurement models of the MSLQ, LCQ, and SRQ-A were acceptable. The internal consistency coefficients (Rho) all the subscales were also satisfactorily (see Table 2).

Table 1. The Fit Indices for the Measurement Models

Fit Index	MSLQ	LCQ	SRQ-A
Scaled χ^2	520.90	19.64	110.84
df	326	9	56
χ^2/df	1.60	2.18	1.98
NNFI	.932	.971	.821
Robust CFI	.942	.984	.943
IFI	.943	.985	.944
RMSEA	.043	.069	.055
(Confidence Intervals)	(.036, .050)	(.031, .108)	(.040, .070)

Note. NNFI = Non-Normed Fit Index, Robust CFI = Robust Comparative Fit Index; RMSEA = Root Mean Square Error of Approximation.

Descriptive Statistics

The means, standard deviations, internal consistency and Pearson product-moment correlations coefficients of the main variables are presented in Table 2. The participants scored high in task value, elaboration, and rehearsal. Self-efficacy, metacognition and autonomy-supportive learning climate were at moderate levels. Task value positively correlated with self-efficacy, rehearsal, elaboration, metacognition, and autonomy-support. Self-efficacy was also positively associated with rehearsal, elaboration, metacognition, and autonomy-support. Autonomy-supportive learning climate was strongly related to all the motivated and strategies for learning, except anxiety.

Cluster Profiles of the Motivated Strategies for Learning

Hierarchical Cluster analysis using Ward's method was conducted using the standardized scores of the MSLQ measures. The dendrogram and agglomeration schedule both supported a four-cluster solution. The profile of the four clusters is shown in Figure 1. There are 77 students in Cluster 1 (22.1%). The unique cluster had very high MSLQ scores, including anxiety (see Table 3). There were 36 boys and 38 girls. In the second cluster, we had a group of student with moderately high task value and self-efficacy, but extremely low anxiety level. There were 37 boys and 37 girls. In the third cluster, we had 100 students (28.7%) with very low task value, self-efficacy, rehearsal, elaboration, and metacognition self-regulation with low anxiety as well. There were 58 boys and 38 girls in this cluster. The final cluster (Cluster 4) of 93 students (26.7%) had an average MSLQ profile but with a very high anxiety score. There were 42 boys and 51 girls.

The results of the first ANOVA showed that the four clusters differed significantly in their perceptions of self-determination, as indicated by RAI, $F(3, 344) = 9.98, p < .001, \eta^2 = .08$. Follow-up tests using Tukey's HSD showed that Clusters 3 and 4 had lower RAI than the other two clusters, and that Cluster 3 had significantly lower RAI than Cluster 4. In terms of their perceptions of the autonomy-supportive learning climate, the results found main effect on clusters, $F(3, 343) = 32.86, p < .001, \eta^2 = .22$. The post hoc tests showed that all pairwise comparisons were significant at $p < .05$ level (see Table 3). Finally, the four clusters also differed significantly in the grades achieved, $F(3, 112) = 8.33, p < .001, \eta^2 = .18$. Students from Clusters 3 scored worst test scores compared to the other three clusters.

Table 2. Means, Standard Deviations, Internal Consistency and Pearson Correlation of the Key Variables of the Overall Sample

Subscales	Mean	SD	Rho	1	2	3	4	5	6	7	8
1. Intrinsic Value	5.23	1.15	.89								
2. Anxiety	4.07	1.39	.73	.17**							
3. Self-Efficacy	4.60	1.17	.84	.77**	.08						
4. Rehearsal	4.84	1.22	.76	.58**	.24**	.50**					
5. Elaboration	4.96	1.15	.82	.68**	.19**	.66**	.75**				
6. Metacognition	4.55	1.22	.76	.63**	.22**	.59**	.74**	.77**			
7. Autonomy-Support	4.47	1.32	.89	.60**	.11*	.54**	.35**	.42**	.36**		
8. RAI	2.26	4.69	--	.29**	-.08	.25**	.19**	.22**	.25**	.22**	
9. Grades	61.70	12.35	--	.31**	-.09	.26**	.18**	.28**	.27**	.05	-.10

Note. ** $p < .001$, * $p < .05$.

Table 3. Descriptive Statistics of the Four Cluster (Z Scores in Parentheses)

Variable	Cluster 1 (N = 77) M (Z)	SD	Cluster 2 (N = 78) M (Z)	SD	Cluster 3 (N = 100) M (Z)	SD	Cluster 4 (N = 93) M (Z)	SD
1. Intrinsic Value	6.36 (.99)	.63	5.64 (.35)	.75	3.96 (-1.11)	.79	5.32 (.07)	.70
2. Anxiety	4.71 (.46)	1.59	2.75 (-.95)	.87	3.71 (-.26)	.98	5.03 (.69)	.81
3. Self-Efficacy	5.74 (.98)	.88	4.85 (.22)	.84	3.46 (-.98)	.76	4.64 (.04)	.83
4. Rehearsal	6.20 (1.12)	.60	4.65 (-.16)	.96	3.68 (-.95)	.90	5.11 (.22)	.76
5. Elaboration	6.33 (1.19)	.51	4.94 (-.01)	.82	3.75 (-1.05)	.78	5.10 (.13)	.60
6. Metacognition	6.01 (1.20)	.70	4.33 (-.18)	.92	3.45 (-.91)	.95	4.72 (.13)	.57
7. Auto-Support	5.33 (.65)a	1.38	4.77 (.22)b	1.18	3.64 (-.64)c	.95	4.42 (-.04)b	1.16
8. RAI	4.17 (.41)a	5.67	3.20 (.20)a	4.33	.83 (-.31)b	3.84	1.46 (-.17)c	4.28
9. Grades	66.09 (.35)a	9.18	667.23 (.45)a	11.08	54.00 (-.62)b	11.85	61.97 (.02)a	12.20

Note: Means in the same row with different subscripts differ significantly at $p<0.05$ in the Tukey's HSD comparison.

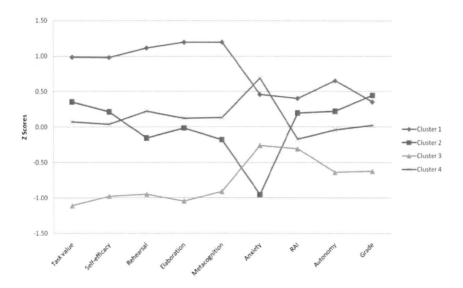

Figure 1. Graphical representation of the four cluster profiles.

DISCUSSION

Cluster analysis results show that self-regulated learning profiles differ between students. Clearly, cluster 1 is most adaptive while cluster 3 is most maladaptive among the clusters. In fact, Figure 1 shows that these two clusters have cluster profiles that are almost opposite of each other. Cluster 1 is characterised by high scores on task value, self-efficacy, rehearsal, elaboration, metacognition, and relatively lower score on anxiety compared to their other ratings. On the other hand, cluster 3 has higher anxiety score relative to their scores on other clustering variables. Although cluster 1 has higher anxiety score than cluster 3 in absolute term, in taking the cluster analytic approach we appreciate that overall profile of cluster 1 is more adaptive than the latter cluster as they have better task value, self-efficacy, rehearsal, elaboration, and metacognition. This speculation of clusters' adaptability can be tested by checking the differences in dependent variables. The two remaining clusters (2 and 4) share similar patterns in terms of task value, self-efficacy, rehearsal, elaboration and metacognition, but too differ in anxiety. In this case, cluster 2 is relatively more adaptive because it has the lowest anxiety level.

Taken together, these four clusters represent different degrees of self-regulated learning undertaken by a sample of secondary students in Singapore. The difference in clusters is evident in the academic grades, in that the most maladaptive clusters (cluster 3) scored the lowest grades among the clusters. This result concurs with previous observation that degrees of self-regulated learning are associated with superior grades (e.g., Lynch, 2010). Lower use of strategies such as rehearsal, elaboration and metacognition suggests weaker cognitive engagement during learning, and therefore weakens academic performance. Furthermore, students in cluster 3 also perceived lower task value and self-efficacy towards learning, which again signifies their lowered motivation toward learning. Lower motivation coupled with lesser use of learning strategies explains poorer academic performance in cluster 3. However, our current results on grades should be treated with caution as only 25% of the participants provided their grades.

The question remains whether students' sense of self-determination differs between clusters. Results show that the most adaptive cluster (cluster 1) reported significantly higher sense of self-determination compared to the most maladaptive cluster (cluster 3), supporting our differentiation of adaptive and maladaptive clusters of students. However, clusters 1 and 2 also differ significantly in terms of sense of self-determination from clusters 3 and 4. Anxiety towards testing might explain this observed difference. Figure 1 shows that ratings of anxiety by members of clusters 1 and 2 tended to be lower than their ratings of task value, self-efficacy, rehearsal, elaboration, and metacognition, while clusters 3 and 4 tended to rate anxiety higher than their rating of the rest of the clustering variables. One interpretation is that students who rated anxiety items relatively lower than their ratings on the rest of the items can be considered as having more adaptive profiles, and that their higher sense of self-determination supports this view. This finding is not surprising since the negative link between anxiety and autonomous regulation was previously suggested, as Ryan and Connell (1989) found that controlling regulation is associated with greater anxiety among students. From this study, we conclude that students' self-regulated learning and personal autonomous regulation may be associated with their ratings of anxiety towards assessment.

In terms of the impact of classroom teachers, the clusters also differed in their perceptions of autonomy-support provided by their teachers. Cluster 3 – characterised by lowest task value, self-efficacy, rehearsal, elaboration, and metacognition – perceived lowest autonomy support from their teachers. Perceived autonomy support is highest for cluster 1, where students rated these five clustering variables higher. Cluster 2 and 4 is characterised by moderate ratings of those five clustering variables, and their ratings of perceived autonomy support occupies mid-range of the scale. In short, the collective effect of these five clustering variables (ignoring test anxiety) appears to share a linear relation with autonomy-support. The higher their rating of these MSLQ subscales, the higher the perceived autonomy-support. Incidentally, the correlations between these five clustering variables and autonomy-support range from .35 to .60, supporting our suggestion that the providence of autonomy-support climate by teachers could influence the adoption of self-regulated learning positively. This concurs with findings by Sierens at al. (2010) which suggest that moderate to high autonomy-support facilitates the use of structure in promoting self-regulated learning.

In this study, the adoption of cluster analysis allowed us to study the intraindividual differences of self-regulated learning in the sample more closely. We discover that the current Singaporean sample's rating of test anxiety in relation to their ratings of other clustering variables tends to be higher when their perception of autonomous regulation is lower. This perhaps suggests that the development of one's autonomous regulation may have some roles in lowering test anxiety in the current sample. However, since autonomous regulation is more of a personal factor, we suggest that test anxiety may be better dealt with at the individual level rather than through the climate created by teachers. Perhaps test anxiety could be more effectively alleviated from outside the classroom, such as through changing parent's child rearing practices (e.g. Rapee, 1997). On the other hand, the remaining five of the self-regulated learning strategies seems to relate better with the availability of autonomy-supportive classroom climate. Since higher perceived autonomy-support is linked with higher ratings of task value, self-efficacy, rehearsal, elaboration, and metacognition, the role of autonomy supportive classroom structure cannot be underestimated. In summary, this study suggests that autonomy-support classroom structure may co-relate with motivation and use of self-regulated strategies, but does not necessarily have a reduced effect on test anxiety.

Overall, the results suggest that adaptive self-regulated learning profiles correspond with better academic grades, and these strategies may be associated with autonomy-supportive learning climate and more autonomous regulations. However, the idea of promoting self-regulation of learning through satisfaction of students' need for autonomy is not new. Deci and his colleagues (Deci et al., 1996) work, though did not include the MLSQ framework, advocates that students' needs satisfaction (including that of autonomy) is important for self-regulation in learning. The present study, adopting a cluster analytic approach, examined the profiles of learning strategies based on MSLQ more closely and further supports the value of providing autonomy-support and nurturing autonomous regulation for effective learning. This is in line with previous recommendation that self-regulated learning may be indirectly facilitated by way of providing classroom environment which promotes satisfaction of psychological needs, adopting the social-cognitive approach.

REFERENCES

Ames, C. and Archer, J. (1988). Achievement goals in the classroom: Students' learning strategies and motivation processes. *Journal of Educational Psychology, 80*, 260-267.

Bentler, P. M. (2006). *EQS 6 Structural Equations Program Manual*. Encino, CA: Multivariate Software, Inc.

Collins, A., Brown, J. S., and Holum, A. (1991). Cognitive apprenticeship: Making thinking visible. *American Educator, 6*(11), 38-46.

Deci, E. L., and Ryan, R. M. (1985). *Intrinsic motivation and self-determination in human behavior*. New York: Plenum.

Deci, E. L., Ryan, R. M. and Williams, G. C. (1996). Need satisfaction and the self-regulation of learning. *Learning and Individual Differences, 8*, 165-183.

Dignath, C., Buettner, G., and Langfeldt, H. (2008). How can primary school students learn self-regulated learning strategies most effectively? A meta-analysis on self-regulation training programmes. *Educational Research Review, 3*, 101-129.

Duncan, T. G., and McKeachie, W. J., (2005). The making of the Motivated Strategies for Learning Questionnaire. *Educational Psychologist, 40*, 117-128.

Goudas, M., Biddle, S., and Fox, K. (1994). Perceived locus of causality, goal orientations, and perceived competence in school physical education classes. *British Journal of Educational Psychology, 64*, 453-463.

Kistner, S., Rakoczy, K., Otto, B., Dignath-van Ewijk, C., Büttner, G. and Klieme, E. (2010). Promotion of self-regulated learning in classrooms: investigating frequency, quality, and consequences for student performance. *Metacognition and Learning, 5*, 157-171.

Liu, W. C., Tan, O. S., Wang, C. K. J., Koh, C., and Ee, J. (2007). Motivation in the context of project work: The self-determination perspective. In D. M. McInerney, S. Van Etten and M. Dowson (Eds.), *Research on Sociocultural Influences on Motivation and Learning: Standards in Education* (Vol. 7, pp. 189-213). Greenwich, CT: Information Age Publishing.

Lynch, D. J. (2010). Motivational beliefs and learning strategies as predictors of academic performance in college physics. *College Student Journal, 44*(4), 920-927.

Pintrich, P.R. (1999). The role of motivation in promoting and sustaining self-regulated learning. *International Journal of Educational Research, 31*(6), 459-470.

Pintrich, P.R. (2002). The role of metacognitive knowledge in learning, teaching, and assessing. *Theory into Practice, 41*(4), 219-225.

Pintrich, P.R., and De Groot, E. V. (1990). Motivational and self-regulated learning components of classroom academic performance. *Journal of Educational Psychology, 82*(1), 33-40.

Pintrich, P. R., D. A. Smith, T. Gracia., and W. J. McKeachie. (1993). Reliability and predictive validity of the motivated strategies for learning questionnaire (MSLQ). *Educational and Psychological Measurement, 53*, 801-813.

Pintrich, P. R., Smith, D. A., Gracia, T., and McKeachie, W. J. (1991*). A manual for the use of the Motivational Strategies for Learning Questionnaire (MSLQ).* University of Michigan: National Centre for Research to Improve Postsecondary Teaching and Learning.

Rapee, R. M. (1997). Potential role of childrearing practices in the development of anxiety and depression. *Clinical Psychology Review, 17*(1), 47-67.

Ryan, R.M., and Connell, J. P. (1989). Perceived locus of causality and internalization: Examining reasons for acting in two domains. *Journal of Personality and Social Psychology, 57*, 749-761.

Sierens, E., Vansteenkiste, M., Goossens, L., Soenens, B., and Dochy, R. (2009). The synergistic relationship of perceived autonomy support and structure in the prediction of self-regulated learning. *British Journal of Educational Psychology, 79*, 57-68.

Wang, C. K. J., Kee, Y. H., Liu, W. C., Lim, B. S. C., and Chua, L. L. (2011, Jan). *College students' motivation and learning strategies profiles and academic achievement: a self-determination theory approach.* Paper presented at The Hwa Chong-Nanyang Girls High Education Conference 2011, Singapore.

Young, M. (2005). The motivational effects of the classroom environment in facilitating self-regulated learning. *Journal of Marketing Education, 27*(1), 25-40.

Zimmerman, B. J., and Martinez-Pons, M. (1986). Development of a structured interview for assessing student use of self-regulated learning strategies. *American Educational Research Journal, 23*(4), 614-628.

In: Handbook on Psychology of Motivation
Editors: J. N. Franco and A. E. Svensgaard
ISBN: 978-1-62100-755-5
© 2012 Nova Science Publishers, Inc.

Chapter 15

IMPLICIT THEORIES OF INTELLIGENCE, EFFORT BELIEFS, AND ACHIEVEMENT GOALS AS ANTECEDENTS OF LEARNING MOTIVATION AND ENGAGEMENT

Dirk T. Tempelaar[1], Bart Rienties[2], Bas Giesbers[1] and Sybrand Schim van der Loeff[1]

[1]Maastricht University School of Business and Economics, the Netherlands
[2]Centre for Educational and Academic Development (CEAD), University of Surrey, England

ABSTRACT

This empirical chapter focuses on the analysis of the Motivation and Engagement Wheel, a framework for learning motivation designed to integrate several theoretical perspectives, whilst at the same time offering a use-inspired approach suitable for practitioners (Martin, 2009, 2008). The framework encompasses aspects of cognitive views on motivation as developed by Pintrich (2003), attributions and expectancy and valuing dimensions (Wigfield, Hoa, and Klauda, 2008), self-regulation, planning and task management (Zimmerman and Schunk, 2008), and self-efficacy (Pajares, 2008). The architecture of the framework consists of four higher order dimensions, being the adaptive cognitive, the adaptive behavioral, maladaptive cognitive or impeding, and maladaptive behavioral dimensions, shaped by 11 first-order dimensions. The suitability of this integrative motivation theory for practical purposes is based on the presumption of changeability of these dimensions: motivation is learnable. Using a sample of first year university students (N=2587) in a collaborative learning context based on problem-based learning, we investigate this aspect of malleability of motivations by developing a model that explains motivational factors from stable, individual difference antecedents. Implicit theories of intelligence and associated conceptions such as beliefs about the role of effort in learning (Dweck, 1999) and goal setting behavior serve the role of these stable antecedents. Implicit theories of intelligence refer to beliefs people develop about the nature of their intelligence, and contrast two opposite beliefs: that of the 'entity theorists', who view intelligence as being a fixed internal characteristic, and the 'incremental theorists', who believe that intelligence is fluid and can be cultivated by learning. Students endorsing an entity view are hypothesized to see effort as a negative characteristic, signaling lack of intelligence, whereas those with an incremental view develop a positive effort belief: exerting effort is the key to cultivating intelligence (Blackwell, Trzesniewski, and Dweck, 2007; Dweck, 1999). In turn, implicit theories and effort views determine students' goal setting behavior, especially whether students are stronger mastery or performance goal oriented. Relationships between these antecedents implicit theories, effort beliefs, and goal setting behavior, and the dimensions of the Motivation and Engagement Wheel, are investigated with structural equation models. Results indicate that implicit theories of intelligence are only indirectly impacting motivational factors, but that effort views play a crucial role in explaining both goal setting behavior and motivation and engagement.

INTRODUCTION

This empirical contribution focuses on the analysis of the Motivation and Engagement Wheel, a framework for learning motivation designed to integrate several theoretical perspectives, whilst at the same time offering a use-inspired approach suitable for practitioners (Martin, 2007, 2008, 2009, 2010). The framework encompasses aspects of cognitive views on motivation as developed by Pintrich (2003), attributions and expectancy and valuing dimensions (Wigfield, Hoa, and Klauda, 2008), self-regulation, planning and task management (Zimmerman and Schunk, 2008), and self-efficacy (Pajares, 2008). The architecture of the framework consists of four higher order dimensions, being the adaptive cognitive, the adaptive behavioral, maladaptive cognitive or impeding, and maladaptive behavioral dimensions, shaped by 11 first-order dimensions. The suitability of this integrative motivation theory for practical purposes is based on the presumption of changeability of these dimensions: motivation is learnable. Using a sample of first year university students (N=2587) in a collaborative learning context based on problem-based learning, we investigate this aspect of malleability of motivations by developing a model that explains motivational factors from stable, individual difference antecedents. Implicit theories of intelligence and associated conceptions, such as beliefs about the role of effort in learning (Dweck, 1999) and goal setting behavior, serve the role of being these stable antecedents. Implicit theories of intelligence refer to beliefs people develop about the nature of their intelligence, and contrasts *two opposite* beliefs: that of the 'entity theorists', who view intelligence as being a fixed internal characteristic, and the 'incremental theorists', who believe that intelligence is fluid and can be cultivated by learning. Students endorsing an entity view are hypothesized to see effort as a negative characteristic, signaling lack of intelligence, whereas those with an incremental view develop a positive effort belief: exerting effort is the key to cultivating intelligence (Blackwell, Trzesniewski, and Dweck, 2007; Dweck, 1999). In turn, implicit theories and effort views determine students' goal setting behavior, especially whether students are stronger mastery or performance goal oriented. Relationships between these antecedents' implicit theories, effort beliefs, goal setting behavior, and the dimensions of the Motivation and Engagement Wheel, are investigated with structural equation models. Results indicate that implicit theories of intelligence are only indirectly impacting motivational factors, but that effort views play a crucial role in explaining both goal setting behavior and motivation and engagement.

METHOD

Participants and educational context. This study is based on the investigation of three cohorts of about equal size of first year students of a Business and Economics School in the south of the Netherlands (academic years 08/09, 09/10 and 10/11). Programs offered by this school deviate from main stream European university education in two important ways: the student-centered learning approach of problem-based learning, and a strong international orientation: the programs are offered in the English language, and attract mainly international students. Amongst the 2587 students on which this study is based, 73.4% have an international background (mostly European, and somewhat more than 50% from German speaking countries in Europe), against 26.6% of Dutch students. Of the students 36.9% are female and 63.1% male. The average age of students was 20.12 years with a range of 17-31 years, with most students being in their teens: the median age was 19.82 years. All students are enrolled in a business and economics program. The students are learning in a problem-based learning setting of which the main principles of collaborative learning in small groups of students, steered by open-ended problems, are well documented in e.g. Gijselaers, Tempelaar, Keizer, Blommaert, Bernard, and Kasper (1995) and Wilkerson and Gijselaers (1996) within the context of business and economics education, and in Schmidt, Van der Molen, Te Winkel, and Wijnen (2009) reporting on effect analysis of problem-based learning referring to data of the medical school of the same university.

Materials. Implicit theories of intelligence. Measures of entity and incremental implicit theories of intelligence were adopted from Dweck's (1999) Theories of Intelligence Scale – Self Form for Adults. The scale consists of eight items: four *entity theory* statements (e.g., '*You have a certain amount of intelligence, and you can't really do much to change it*') and four *incremental theory* statements (e.g., '*You can always substantially change how intelligent you are*').

Effort beliefs. Measures of Effort beliefs have two different sources: Dweck (1999) and Blackwell (2002). In Dweck (1999), several sample statements are provided that portray effort as a negative thing, where exerting effort mirrors the view that one has low ability, and depict effort as a positive thing, where exerting effort is regarded as a way to activate and increase one's ability. Of both of these sets of statements (see Dweck, 1999, p. 40), the first ones are used as the first item of both subscales. These are for the *negative effort belief* subscale: '*If you have to work hard on some problems, you're probably not very good at them*', and for the *positive effort belief* subscale: '*When you're good at something, working hard allows you to really understand it*'. In addition, the full sets of Effort beliefs of Blackwell (2002) were used, containing five positive and five negative items (see also Blackwell et al., 2007). A sample item of viewing effort negatively related to ability is '*To tell the truth, when I work hard at my schoolwork, it makes me feel like I'm not very smart*', while the item '*The harder you work at something, the better you will be at it*' expresses the view that effort leads to positive outcomes.

Goal orientations. Goal setting is operationalized by the revised PALS: Midgley et al. (2000). It is a trichotomous instrument, distinguishing one type of mastery goal, and two types of performance goals: approach and avoidance. A mastery goal sample item is: '*It's important to me that I learn a lot of new concepts this year*', whereas sample items for approach and avoidance performance goals are '*It's important to me that other students in my class think I am good at my class work'* and *'One of my goals is to keep others from thinking I'm not smart in class'*.

Motivation and Engagement Scale. The MES-UC (Martin, 2007, 2008, 2009, 2010) measures university or college students' motivation and engagement. The MES-UC consists of four scales and eleven subscales subsumed under the four scales. The MES-UC scales and subscales as well as sample items are as follows. The adaptive cognition scale, reflecting students' positive attitudes and orientations to academic learning, is composed of the subscales self-belief, valuing school, and learning focus. Self-belief refers to the confidence to do well in university, e.g. *'If I try hard, I believe I can do my university work well'*. Valuing is the belief that what you learn at university is useful and important, e.g. *'Learning at university is important to me'*. Learning focus is being centered on learning, solving problems, and developing skills, e.g *'I feel very pleased with myself when I really understand what I'm taught at university'*. The second scale, adaptive behavior, reflecting students' positive behaviors and engagement in academic learning, contains the subscales persistence, planning, and study management. Persistence, e.g. *'If I can't understand my university work at first, I keep going over it until I do'*, signals how much students keep trying to work out an answer or to understand, even when the problem is difficult or challenging. Planning, e.g., *'Before I start an assignment, I plan out how I am going to do it'*, measures how much students plan their work and keep track of their progress. Study management, e.g. *'When I study, I usually study in places where I can concentrate'* covers the organization of the study time table, choosing and arranging where to study, and use of study time. Students' attitudes and orientations that inhibit academic learning are collected in the impeding or maladaptive cognition scale, including anxiety, failure avoidance, and uncertain control. Anxiety, e.g. *'When exams and assignments are coming up, I worry a lot'* is the extent to which students feel anxious when thinking about or doing university work. Failure avoidance is the motivation to do university work to avoid doing poorly, e.g. *'Often the main reason I work at university is because I don't want to disappoint others'*. Uncertain control echoes the extent to which students are uncertain about how to do well and how to avoid doing poorly, e.g. *'I'm often unsure how I can avoid doing poorly at university'*. The maladaptive behavior scale, reflecting students' problematic learning behaviors, includes self-handicapping and disengagement as subscales. Self-handicapping, e.g. *'I sometimes don't study very hard before exams so I have an excuse if I don't do as well as I hoped'* refers to doing things that reduce chances of success at university, so creating an excuse for not doing well. Lastly, disengagement stands for students' inclination to give up in their university work or university more generally, e.g. *'I often feel like giving up at university'*.

Procedure. In the first term of their first academic semester, students took two required, parallel eight week courses: an integrated course organizational theory and marketing, two subjects from the behavioral sciences domain, and an integrated course mathematics and statistics. In the first three weeks of the term, students filled in self-report questionnaires on implicit theories, motivation and engagement, and goal orientations, as part of a data-analysis directed student project for statistics. For reasons of consistency, all instruments apply a 7-point response Likert scale, ranging from 1 (strongly disagree) to 7 (strongly agree). Students consent that their data, in anonymous format, are used for educational and research purposes.

RESULTS

Descriptive statistics. Table 1 contains means, standard deviations, and Cronbach's alpha reliabilities for all scales and subscales. Since in other studies, as e.g. Martin (2007), gender differences in motivation and engagement were found, we add as the last column in Table 1 the test statistics of independent samples *t*-tests on gender differences, where a positive difference indicates that female students have higher scores than male students. Figure 1 depicts mean scale scores by gender.

Mean scores for adaptive cognitions and behaviors are all in the same order of magnitude, but slightly higher, than mean scores for high school students reported in Martin (2007). Mean scores of maladaptive cognitions and behaviors are slightly lower than those reported in Martin (2007) for high school students, with one notable exception: scores for *Anxiety* found in our sample are relatively high at about the neutral level of four. The circumstance that our sample of students possesses more positive motivation and engagement profiles than those of high school students reported in Martin (2007), is in line with the general finding reported in Martin (2009): university students reflect higher mean levels of motivation and engagement than do their high school counterparts.

Table 1. Descriptive statistics, reliabilities, and test statistics for gender difference tests

	Mean	SD	Cronbach's α	t –value gender difference
Implicit theories:				
Incremental Theory	4.57	1.14	0.83	2.46
Entity Theory	3.59	1.27	0.82	-1.50
Effort beliefs:				
Effort Positive	5.32	0.70	0.65	3.08
Effort Negative	2.94	0.86	0.68	-1.74
Goal orientation:				
Mastery Goal	5.96	0.75	0.87	6.40
Performance Approach Goal	3.66	1.19	0.88	0.78
Performance Avoid Goal	3.96	1.20	0.82	3.35
Adaptive cognitions:				
Self-belief	5.84	0.77	0.78	1.34
Valuing school	5.84	0.73	0.69	4.10
Learning focus	5.92	0.75	0.79	7.94
Adaptive behaviors:				
Planning	4.80	0.97	0.72	6.24
Study management	5.61	0.90	0.77	8.32
Persistence	5.28	0.94	0.82	5.61
Impeding cognitions:				
Anxiety	4.49	1.28	0.83	16.07
Failure avoidance	2.48	1.21	0.85	-0.65
Uncertain control	3.41	1.16	0.81	6.58
Maladaptive behaviors				
Self-handicapping	2.42	1.13	0.83	-4.20
Disengagement	2.02	1.00	0.78	-3.78

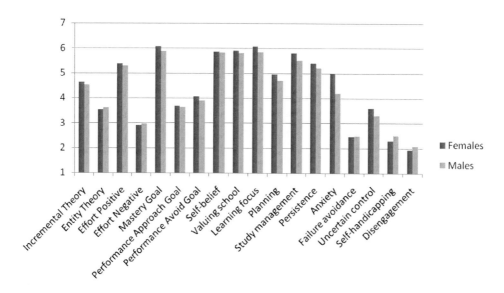

Figure 1. Scale means, by gender.

The high level of *Anxiety* scores we find might be understood in the context of the administration of the questionnaire: students in a social sciences program respond to the MES instrument whilst doing a mathematics and statistics course, a service course with the reputation to be difficult and a potential obstacle for first year study success.

We find substantial and meaningful gender differences in most of the scale means. Turning to MES scales first, we find significant differences in all scales but *Self-belief* and *Failure avoidance*. Gender differences in adaptive cognitions and behaviors all favor female students. With regard to the maladaptive aspects, an interesting pattern emerges.

Female students have higher levels of negative thoughts, maladaptive cognitions, most clearly expressed by the huge difference in *Anxiety*. However, these thoughts are not materialized: with regard to negative, impeding behavior, male students score higher than female students. Findings are again in line with Martin (2007), who concludes that differences in mean levels can still be compatible with invariant factor structures.

Gender differences in the antecedent scales confirm the general pattern of female students possessing more appropriate learning profiles than male students (and more study success in this sample, which is, however, beyond the scope of this chapter). Female students have more appropriate implicit theories, with significantly higher scores for *Incremental theory*. They have more appropriate effort beliefs, with significantly higher scores for *Effort positive*. And they possess higher levels of goal orientation, both with regard to *Mastery goal*, and *Performance avoid goal* (with the last outcome having a mixed impact on students' learning profiles). Correlations between all scales and subscales can be found in Table 2. Several values call attention.

First, although the two implicit theories *Incremental theory* and *Entity theory* are negatively correlated, that correlation (-.73) is not that strong as to make the combination of both subscales into one implicit theory scale an inevitable step, the standard modeling approach in most empirical studies into implicit theories (Blackwell et al., 2007; Plaks, Grant, and Dweck, 2005).

Table 2. Scale and subscale correlations

	01	02	03	04	05	06	07	08	09	10	11	12	13	14	15	16	17	18
01 Incremental Theory	1.00																	
02 Entity Theory	-.73	1.00																
03 Effort Positive	.31	-.21	1.00															
04 Effort Negative	-.25	.43	-.36	1.00														
05 Mastery Goal	.22	-.20	.48	-.30	1.00													
06 Performance Approach Goal	.01	.07	.05	.11	.02	1.00												
07 Performance Avoid Goal	.00	.09	.07	.12	.08	.81	1.00											
08 Self-belief	.16	-.15	.41	-.36	.60	.00	.01	1.00										
09 Valuing school	.17	-.14	.41	-.31	.67	.01	.05	.61	1.00									
10 Learning focus	.18	-.17	.46	-.29	.67	.01	.07	.60	.66	1.00								
11 Planning	.17	-.17	.33	-.19	.41	.11	.11	.33	.37	.39	1.00							
12 Study management	.18	-.14	.36	-.25	.48	.03	.06	.46	.47	.58	1.00							
13 Persistence	.18	-.17	.47	-.29	.54	.05	.05	.48	.50	.53	.49	1.00						
14 Anxiety	.04	.05	.03	.19	.07	.12	.19	.01	.11	.01	.09	-.02	1.00					
15 Failure avoidance	-.05	.15	-.12	.29	-.27	.42	.40	-.29	-.26	-.25	-.10	-.18	-.19	.27	1.00			
16 Uncertain control	-.07	.15	-.16	.34	-.19	.13	.17	-.35	-.24	-.16	-.15	-.14	-.25	.52	.40	1.00		
17 Self-handicapping	-.11	.15	-.28	.33	-.42	.20	.18	-.33	-.37	-.39	-.32	-.34	-.41	.10	.45	.32	1.00	
18 Disengagement	-.08	.16	-.27	.34	-.48	.15	.10	-.48	-.51	-.47	-.24	-.32	-.39	.09	.45	.35	.55	1.00

Nb. For the current sample size, correlations in absolute value larger than .05 are significant at 1% level, larger than .04 are significant at 5% level.

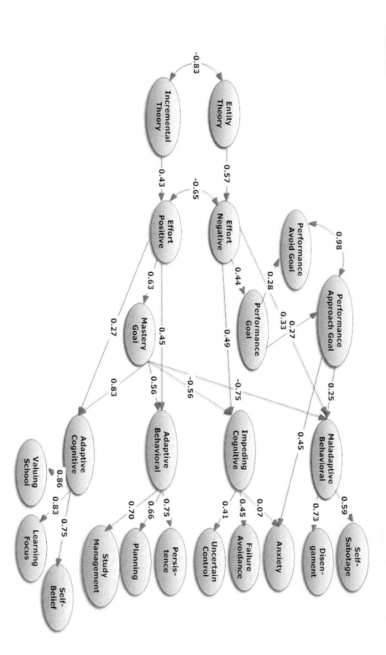

Figure 2. Structural component of the full structural equation model of the antecedents of motivation and engagement.

Second, the correlation between the two effort beliefs, *Positive* and *Negative Effort* belief, is even rather weak, and denies the logic of constructing one effort belief construct out of both subscales (the approach taken by Blackwell et al., 2007). Third, when looking at the correlations from the perspective of finding potential antecedents of motivation and engagement, the three candidates appear to be the two effort beliefs, and *Mastery goal* orientation. The bivariate relationships between effort views and all motivation and engagement subscales uniformly dominate the bivariate relationships between implicit theories and motivation and engagement subscales. That is a remarkable finding, since most empirical studies in the tradition of implicit theories specify implicit theories as direct antecedents of goal setting, achievement motivation or performance, rather than as distal antecedents, mediated by effort beliefs (see e.g. Dweck, Chiu, and Hong, 1995; Murphy, and Dweck, 2010). Fourth: performance goals are strongly interrelated, but only loosely connected with motivation and engagement, with the exception of *Failure avoidance*.

Structural models. On the basis of considerations related to the correlation matrix as discussed above, it was decided to design a full structural equation model with *Incremental theory* and *Entity theory* as separate latent constructs, the *Effort positive* and *Effort negative* positions as two separate latent constructs for effort beliefs, and to include a second order latent factor *Performance goal* as to absorb the strong correlation between the *Performance approach* and *Performance avoid* goals.

With regard to the motivation and engagement measurements, we follow the approach of Martin (2007, 2008, 2009, 2010) and specify four second order latent factors, *Adaptive cognitive*, *Adaptive behavioral*, *Impeding cognitive*, *Maladaptive behavioral*, based on eleven first order latent factors.

The first modeling step is the estimation of one, overall measurement model for implicit theories, effort beliefs, goal orientations, and motivation and engagement, using the 78 items of the four instruments as indicator variables. That model has satisfactory fit (χ^2=11514, df=2773, CFI=.98, RMSEA=.038, 90% CI RMSEA =.038-.039), indicating the adequacy of all four instruments. The second step comprises the introduction of structural paths, to arrive at a full structural model specifying the antecedent relationships between implicit theories, effort beliefs, goal orientations, and motivation and engagement. The final, best fitting model has appropriate fit (χ^2=10023, df=2867, CFI=.98, RMSEA=.034, 90% CI RMSEA =.033-.035) and is depicted in Figure 2. The figure contains all latent factors, both first and second order, and standardized estimates of all regression coefficients of structural paths, and three of the latent factor correlations: those between the implicit theories, between the effort beliefs, and the goal orientation latent factors. For reasons of readability, latent correlations amongst MES factors, both first and second order factors, are not included in the figure.

The structural paths confirm the findings reported in the discussion of the correlation matrix: implicit theories are adequately modeled by distinguishing *Incremental* and *Entity theory* constructs; effort beliefs are adequately modeled by distinguishing *Positive* and *Negative effort* belief constructs; and implicit theories impact motivation and engagement only indirectly through the mediating relationship of effort beliefs.

In the interplay between implicit theories and motivation and engagement constructs, three pivotal constructs are present: both types of effort beliefs, positive and negative, and the mastery goal orientation. In this interplay, the *Mastery goal* construct occupies a special position: it is the antecedent of both positive thoughts and behaviors, with a positive beta, and of negative thoughts and behaviors, with a negative beta. Beyond this double role of mastery orientation, the remainder of the structural part of the model can be fully decomposed in a positive and negative model component. That is: *Incremental theory* is antecedent for the *Effort positive* belief, which in turn is the antecedent of *Mastery goal* and the positive thoughts and behaviors: *Adaptive cognitions* and *Adaptive behavior*. And in parallel, *Entity theory* is antecedent for the *Effort negative* belief, which in turn is the antecedent of the negative thoughts and behaviors: *Impeding cognitions* and *Maladaptive behavior*. Beyond the role of mastery orientation, the latent factor correlations provide a coupling of these otherwise independent partial systems.

CONCLUSION

The estimated model of structural paths of antecedent relationships of motivation and engagement constructs is satisfactory not only in the sense of proper model fit, but also in the sense that paths between effort beliefs and mastery orientation contain strong betas. That is: a substantial part of individual differences in motivation and engagement is explained by individual differences in implicit theories, effort beliefs, and goal orientation. Context does certainly have an impact, as was visible from the unexpected high level of *Anxiety*. But its impact seems to shift general levels of constructs, rather than change individual differences. This outcome questions the validity of the hypothesis that motivation and engagement are strongly malleable and context specific constructs.

Other lessons to be learned from this modeling exercise is that implicit theories and effort beliefs are best conceptualized as separate incremental and entity theory constructs, and separate positive and negative effort belief constructs, that are indeed negatively related, but certainly not opposing poles of a single construct. And that the role of implicit theories is much better modeled as one of mediation through effort beliefs, than as a direct antecedent of motivation and engagement.

REFERENCES

Blackwell, L. S. (2002). Psychological mediators of student achievement during the transition to junior high school: The role of implicit theories. Unpublished doctoral dissertation, Columbia University, New York.

Blackwell, L., Trzesniewski, K., and Dweck, C. S. (2007). Implicit theories of intelligence predict achievement across an adolescent transition: A longitudinal study and an intervention. *Child Development*, 78, 246-263.

Dweck, C. S. (1999). *Self-theories: Their role in motivation, personality, and development.* Philadelphia: Psychology press.

Dweck, C. S., Chiu, C., and Hong, Y. (1995). Implicit theories and their role in judgments and reactions: A world from two perspectives. *Psychological Inquiry,* 6, 267-285.

Gijselaers, W. H., Tempelaar, D. T., Keizer, P. K., Blommaert, J. M., Bernard, E. M., and Kasper, H. (1995). *Educational innovation in economics and business education: The case of problem-based learning.* Dordrecht: Kluwer Academic Publishers.

Martin, A. J. (2007). Examining a multidimensional model of student motivation and engagement using a construct validation approach. *British Journal of Educational Psychology*, 77, 413-440.

Martin, A. (2008). Enhancing student motivation and engagement: The effects of a multidimensional intervention. *Contemporary Educational Psychology*, 33, 239–269.

Martin, A. (2009). Motivation and engagement across the academic lifespan: A developmental construct validity study of elementary school, high school, and university/college students. *Educational and Psychological Measurement*, 69, 794–824.

Martin, A. J. (2010). Building classroom success: *Eliminating academic fear and failure.* London: Continuum.

Midgley, C., Maehr, M. L., Hruda, L. Z., Anderman, E., Anderman, L., Freeman, K. E., et al. (2000). *Manual for the Patterns of Adaptive Learning Scales* (PALS). Ann Arbor: University of Michigan.

Murphy, M. C., and Dweck, C. S. (2010). A Culture of Genius: How an Organization's Lay Theory Shapes People's Cognition, Affect, and Behavior. *Personality and Social Psychology Bulletin*, 36, 283-296.

Pajares, F. (2008). Motivational role of self-efficacy beliefs in self-regulated learning. In D. H. Schunk and B. J. Zimmerman (Eds.), *Motivation and self-regulated learning*: *Theory, research, and applications* (pp. 111-139). Erlbaum.

Pintrich, P. R. (2003). A motivational science perspective on the role of student motivation in learning and teaching contexts. *Journal of Educational Psychology*, 95, 667-686.

Plaks, J. E., Grant, H., and Dweck, C. S. (2005). Violations of Implicit Theories and the Sense of Prediction and Control: Implications for Motivated Person Perception. *Journal of Personality and Social Psychology*, 88(2), 245-262.

Schmidt, H. G., Van der Molen, H. T., Te Winkel, W. W. R., and Wijnen, W. H. F. W. (2009). Constructivist, problem-based learning does work: A meta-analysis of curricular comparisons involving a single medical school. *Educational Psychologist*, 44: 227-249.

Wigfield, A., Hoa, L. W., and Klauda, S. L. (2008). The role of achievement values in the self-regulation of achievement behaviors. In D. H. Schunk and B. J. Zimmerman (Eds.), *Motivation and self-regulated learning: Theory, research, and applications* (pp. 169-195). Erlbaum.

Wilkerson, L., and Gijselaers, W. H. (1996). *Bringing problem-based learning to higher education: Theory and practice.* San Francisco: Jossey-Bass.

Zimmerman, B. J., and Schunk, D. H. (2008). Motivation: An essential dimension of self-regulated learning. In D. H. Schunk and B. J. Zimmerman (Eds.), *Motivation and self-regulated learning: Theory, research, and applications* (pp. 1-30). Erlbaum.

In: Handbook on Psychology of Motivation
Editors: J. N. Franco and A. E. Svensgaard

ISBN: 978-1-62100-755-5
© 2012 Nova Science Publishers, Inc.

Chapter 16

MOTIVATION: IMPLICATIONS FOR INTERVENING WITH ADOLESCENT SUBSTANCE ABUSERS

Ashley Austi and Brett Engle
Barry University School of Social Work, FL, US

ABSTRACT

Client motivation has emerged as an increasingly important topic for substance abuse treatment providers and researchers and has been implicated as one of the most important predictors of successful treatment engagement and outcome. There is a growing interest in identifying and understanding the specific factors that both enhance and inhibit motivation for substance use change among clients, particularly among specific subgroups of substance use clients including adolescent substance users. Because it is widely recognized that motivation for change plays a critical role in treatment response, it is increasingly expected that substance abuse treatment providers take an active role in enhancing client motivation for change. As adolescent substance users present with unique needs and challenges particular to their developmental stage (i.e., striving toward autonomy and individuation), substance use patterns (i.e., binge use vs. dependency) and reasons for entering treatment (i.e., mandated by parents, schools or courts), motivational interventions may be particularly appropriate. Motivational interviewing (MI) is a person-centered and increasingly evidence-based approach for addressing substance abuse among adolescents. Fundamental components that comprise the "spirit" of MI will be discussed particularly as they apply to work with high-risk adolescents. Evidence-based interventions targeting client motivation, such as MI, espouse a very different view of motivation as it relates to substance use and recovery. These interventions do not view motivation as an explanation for treatment failure and continued substance use problems but rather as the key to engaging clients in the behavior change process.

Keywords: motivation, motivational interviewing, adolescents, youth, substance abuse, alcohol abuse

MOTIVATION FOR ADOLESCENT SUBSTANCE USE CHANGE

The role of client motivation has emerged as an increasingly important topic for substance abuse treatment providers and researchers. Motivation for change has been described in the substance abuse literature as "an individual's concerns about or interest in the need for change, his or her goals and intentions, the need to take responsibility and make a commitment to change, and sustaining the behavior change and having adequate incentives to change" (DiClemente et al., 2008, p. 26). Research with adults has established that higher motivation for change predicts greater treatment engagement and retention (De Leon and Jainchill, 1986; De Leon, Melnick, and Hawke, 2000; Hiller, Knight, Leukefield, and Simpson, 2002), as well as better treatment outcomes (De Leon, Melnick, and Kressel, 1997; De Leon, Melnick, Kressel, and Jainchill, 1994). The importance of motivation for treatment in predicting treatment response has been demonstrated consistently across modalities including, outpatient methadone, outpatient drug free, and residential (Joe, Simpson, and Broome, 1998; 1999), as well as among adults in both community-based (Simpson and Joe, 1993) and criminal justice settings (Hiller et al., 2000).

Substance abuse treatment research has explored both motivation to change substance use and motivation to seek help with making substance use changes, which have been shown to be distinct, though positively correlated, constructs (Freyer et al., 2004; Lau et al., 2010). While research exploring motivation among adolescents lags behind research conducted with adults, there is an emerging base that points to its importance across multiple aspects of the treatment and recovery process.

For example, in a large multi-city study of adolescents (n=1,732) participating in treatment for substance misuse, authors found that treatment readiness (e.g., motivation to enter treatment as a means to address their substance use problems) was strongly associated with therapeutic engagement in outpatient, residential and short-term inpatient treatment (Broome, Joe and Simpson, 2001).

Additionally, adolescent motivation for substance use change has been linked to greater rates of treatment retention (Fickenscher, Novins, and Beals; 2006; Melnick, De Leon, Hawke, Jainchill, and Kressel, 1997).

Melnick and colleagues (1997) found that higher levels of motivation among adolescents (n > 1000) were positively associated with short term retention (45 days) in a therapeutic community setting. Moreover, a recent pilot study found that motivation for substance use change (measured through the treatment readiness scale) was positively associated with treatment completion for Native American substance abusing teens (n=89) participating in a residential treatment program (Fickenscher et al., 2006).

Finally, motivation is linked to better treatment outcomes and greater treatment success among adolescent substance users (Breda and Heflinger, 2007; Cady, Winters, Jordan, Solberg, and Stinchfield, 1996; Friedman, Granick, and Kreisher, 1994; King, Chung, and Maisto, 2009). For instance, King and colleagues (2009) examined (1) motivation to abstain and (2) perceived difficulty of abstaining among adolescents receiving treatment for marijuana problems, and found that these motivation to change constructs predicted changes in marijuana use.

Factors Influencing Motivation for Change

As illustrated, a growing body of evidence supports the important relation between adolescent motivation to change substance use and critical aspects of the treatment process. Unfortunately, among adolescents with substance use problems, denial of addiction problems and ambivalence (if not outright rejection) toward treatment participation are characteristic (Wagner, 2008). While these issues are present among substance abusing adults, adolescents with substance use problems appear to be significantly less motivated to change substance use than their adult counterparts (Melnick, De Leon, Hawke, Jainchill, and Kressel, 1997). Given their relatively brief history of substance use and normative developmental predisposition toward challenging authority (Wagner, 2008), it is no wonder that the great majority of teenagers with substance use problems are notably ambivalent about entering treatment and/or changing their substance use behaviors. Instead of viewing low motivation among adolescents as a barrier to treatment and recovery, it is increasingly argued that motivation be viewed as a developmentally appropriate target of intervention for substance use treatment with teens. Because it is now widely recognized that motivation for change plays such a critical role in substance abuse treatment, it is expected that treatment providers take an active role in enhancing client motivation for change (DiClemente, Garay, and Gemmell, 2008).

According to DiClemente and colleagues (2008) motivational considerations are often viewed as critical for initial engagement in treatment and subsequent substance use changes and motivational enhancement strategies are becoming an integral part of most outreach, detoxification, and treatment programs. Identifying the specific personal, familial and contextual (e.g., legal pressure) factors that impact an adolescent's level of motivation may be particularly beneficial to motivational enhancement efforts. There is speculation that a variety of psychosocial and contextual factors may influence adolescent motivation for change.

Individual Factors

Mental health problems among adolescents including diagnoses of internalizing and externalizing disorders likely have an influence on motivation. Battjes, Gordon, O'Grady, Kinlock, and Carswell (2003) explored the relationship between motivation ("internal recognition of the need to change") and measures of deviant behavior including a variety of conduct disorder symptoms, aggressive behavior, and days of illegal activities in the prior 90 days. One measure, number of days engaged in illegal activities was positively related to motivation to change. Austin, Wagner, Hospital and Morris (2010) found that among Hispanic and African American youth in substance abuse treatment, the presence of an externalizing disorder (e.g., Conduct Disorder, Oppositional Defiant Disorder, Attention Deficit Hyperactivity Disorder) was associated with lower motivation to change. Slesnick et al. (2009) found that among runaway adolescents with substance use problems, depressive symptomology and motivation for substance use change were positively associated. Another study examining the relation between depressive symptoms and motivation found that among adolescents being treated in the emergency department for an alcohol related issue, depressive symptoms were associated with a higher level of reported intention to change drinking, however not with actual substance use changes measured three months later (Barnett et al., 2002).

Substance use severity is another issue suspected to influence youths' motivation to change. A majority of research suggests that more severe substance abuse is associated with more motivation to change. For instance, in a study of substance using runaway youth, heavier substance use (i.e., percentage of days used) was positively correlated with motivation to change substance use (Slesnick, Bartle-Haring, Erdem, Budde, Letcher, Bantchevska, and Garren, 2009). Additionally, studies with college students found that young people indicating the greatest motivation to change substance use had higher levels of drinking (e.g. see Vik, Culbertson, and Sellers, 2000). A study conducted by Breda and Heflinger (2007) found that youth identified as more serious substance users are more likely to change at the outset of treatment and reduce substance use more quickly upon entering treatment. Finally, in a sample of Hispanic and African American youth in treatment for substance use problems, the greater the substance use reported by the adolescent, the more likely they were to endorse greater motivation to change (Austin et al., 2010). However, there are some contradictory research findings. Specifically, in a study examining motivation to change among adolescents being treated for an alcohol-related injury in the emergency department, higher levels of drinking and drinking problems at baseline were related to lower levels of motivation to change substance use (Barnett, Lebeau-Craven, O'Leary, et al., 2002). Moreover, in a study of 196 adolescents admitted to outpatient substance abuse treatment, Battjes and colleagues (2003) found that substance use severity was unrelated to motivation to change. While the influence of substance use severity on motivation to change substance use has received some research attention and appears to indicate a positive association between the two factors, the relation requires further elucidation.

Social and Familial Factors

In addition to individual factors such as substance use severity and mental health problems, there is a growing interest in the potential relation between social and familial factors and adolescent motivation to change substance use. Only recently have researchers begun to explore the potential relation between familial factors and teen motivation to change substance use (Broome et al., 2001). In the Broome et al. (2001) study, higher levels of social support from family and friends were associated with greater treatment motivation [readiness] to change substance use, while family substance use demonstrated no relation to motivation to change. Parental support and control have long been linked to dimensions of mental health and substance use among teens (Baumrind, 1991; Cohen and Rice, 1997; Weiss and Schwartz, 1996). Austin and colleagues (2010) found that the more adolescents perceived their parents to be supportive the greater their level of motivation to change; conversely, the more adolescents perceived their parents to be controlling, the less motivation to change they reported. Additionally, Barnett and colleagues (2002) found teen perceptions that parents will impose consequences for drinking were associated with greater motivation to change drinking behavior. Interestingly, in the Slesnick et al. (2010) study, family environment was not directly associated with motivation to change substance use among runaway youth. In sum, while it seems logical that social and familial factors contribute to youth motivation to reduce substance use, to date there is only minimal research addressing the nature and extent of these relationships.

Contextual Factors

As mentioned, research suggests that adolescents are less internally motivated to change substance use than adults and are more likely to enter substance abuse treatment as a result of extrinsic motivators including school, family or legal pressure (Cady et al., 1996; Melnick et al., 1997). Nevertheless, because teens' ambivalence about changing their substance use is widely recognized by parents, schools, lawmakers and treatment providers, a large proportion of adolescent substance abusers are legally mandated to attend substance abuse treatment each year, with over half (54%) of all youth substance abuse treatment admissions in 2002 coming from the criminal justice department referrals (Office of Applied Studies, 2004). While research on the role extrinsic motivation is limited for adolescent substance users, emerging findings suggest that the relationship between extrinsic motivators such as legal pressure and substance use change is complex but potentially important. Specifically, in their study of adolescents and adults receiving treatment in a therapeutic community study, Melnick and colleagues (1997) found that both intrinsic motivation (scores of internal motivation to change) and extrinsic motivation (legal referral) were predictive of short-term treatment retention (45 days). Interestingly, only extrinsic motivation (legal referral) was associated with long-term retention (one year) among adolescents while only intrinsic motivation was associated with long-term retention for adults in the study. Another study conducted by Bastien et al. (2003) examined the relation between several external consequences of substance use and motivation for change among adolescents. Findings were mixed whereby "having been in detention/jail" in the past 90 days was correlated with increased motivation for change, but the perception of "a lot of pressure to enter treatment" was associated with lower levels of motivation. Finally, Broome et al., (2001) found that involvement in the legal system was negatively associated with motivation among adolescents attending outpatient substance abuse treatment programs. While findings are inconsistent across studies, it is clear that external motivators such as legal mandates for treatment, jail time, and other external consequences of substance use: (1) are very common among adolescents with substance use problems and (2) serve the important function of getting substance abusing youth into treatment. However, it appears that external motivators are not sufficiently stimulating intrinsic motivation for change among adolescents. Once in treatment, additional steps need to be taken to enhance intrinsic motivation among adolescents.

Taken together existing research underscores the importance of focusing on motivation in efforts to engage, retain and successfully intervene with adolescents in need of treatment for substance use problems. Regardless of initial reasons for entering treatment or initial level of motivation, there is a need to implement strategies for building and sustaining motivational factors to promote substance use change among adolescents.

MOTIVATIONAL INTERVIEWING

Motivational interviewing (MI) is likely the most widely recognized motivationally based intervention approach for addressing adolescent substance abuse as well as a range of other health risk behaviors.

It has theoretical roots in social learning and cognitive-behavioral theory but is humanistic at its core. MI is defined as a "collaborative, person-centered form of guiding to elicit and strengthen motivation for change" (Miller and Rollnick, 2009, p. 137). MI has several components that characterize the "spirit" of the approach. The evidence-base of MI for addressing adolescent substance abuse and each component of the spirit of MI are described below.

Summary of MI Clinical Trials with AOD Abusing Adolescents

Featured in nearly 1000 peer reviewed articles and books and tested in approximately 200 clinical trials, the evidence-base for MI is growing rapidly. MI has strong empirical support for treating substance abuse disorders among adults. The literature on MI with adolescents is much more recent with the first published report targeting substance abuse with this age group being published in 1999 by Monti and colleagues. Since then, there have been a number of controlled studies.

In a recent review of these studies, Macgowan and Engle (2011) identified twelve adolescent substance abuse clinical trials testing MI. All were individualized interventions and the quality of the studies was generally strong. Most ($n = 5$) of the studies were in school settings, followed by three in primary medical care settings, and four for homeless and other "hard to reach" youth.

Most of the MI interventions were single session ($n = 8$), followed by two sessions ($n = 3$), and one of four sessions. Most of the studies involved youth with moderate to heavy use, and no studies targeted dually-diagnosed individuals, although some studies involved a majority with a substance use disorder. All of the studies reviewed by Macgowan and Engle (2011) reported reductions in at least one substance through follow-up.

In two studies, MI had superior outcomes to comparison conditions on all indicators through follow-ups. Five other studies reported significantly better outcomes than comparison conditions on some but not all outcome measures at follow-ups.

Jensen and colleagues (2011) conducted a meta-analysis on the use of MI for intervening in adolescent substance abuse including tobacco use. Like Macgowan and Engle (2011), Jensen and colleagues (2011) concluded that although the effects tend to be small and evidence of long term effects is lacking, the use of MI is promising and recommended particularly given how brief and therefore likely cost effective these interventions tend to be. Adolescents, even those with significant substance use problems, are not likely to seek treatment on their own. An estimated 85 percent of such youth do not receive appropriate treatment (Merikangas, et al., 2011). Thus, a greater percentage of these young people could be served by offering MI opportunistically in primary medical care, juvenile justice and school settings.

Using the Spirit of Motivational Interviewing to Engage Adolescents

MI specifically informs how to engage potentially reluctant teens in conversations about health behavior change. One of the components of the spirit of MI is that it is directive, meaning that there is a concerted purpose or direction to the work. Typically beginning with whatever brought the youth in to receive services, a "menu of options" is developed. In a primary care setting, substance abuse screening and brief MI intervention could focus on any health concerns. Potential goals for targeted behavior change would be explored within the context of presenting problems, general health and, for example, substance use patterns. The interviewer would seek to identify and prioritize health risk behaviors, such as the use of especially addictive and/or harmful drugs (e.g., methamphetamine, heroine, or glue) or dangerous use related behaviors (e.g., binge drinking, combining certain substances, or driving under the influence).

Once such a specific target behavior is identified the interviewer may ask the teen's permission to specifically discuss the target behavior (e.g., "Do you mind if we spend some time talking about when you combine drinking and prescription medications?"). Thus, using MI, the interviewer seeks to identify a specific behavior targeted for change and actively explores the adolescent's motivation to change the behavior.

A second component of the spirit of MI is an emphasis on supporting autonomy. Although MI was originally developed with adults, many argue that it is particularly well suited to the developmental stage of adolescence (e.g., Wagner, 2008). An important developmental task of adolescence is to strengthen their sense of autonomy and self-determination. Additionally, conflicts with authority figures often stem from adolescents' desire for increased independence. MI specifically informs how to build upon these developmental processes as strengths and avoid power struggles. In contrast to other more expert driven or authoritative approaches, MI fully accepts and openly acknowledges that any decision to change is wholly that of the adolescent. This principle builds upon well established studies, which have found that change is inversely associated with resistance and that the interviewer (e.g., therapist) has considerable and predictable influence on client resistance (Patterson and Forgatch, 1985). That is, the more the interviewer confronts or pushes for the change, the more the client "resists."

A third component of MI is evocation. The interviewer explores and elicits the client's own desire, ability (i.e., self-efficacy), reasons, and need (DARN) to make a change, which is expressed as what is referred to as *change talk*. MI primarily emphasizes the use of reflections and affirmations. However, certain questions are specifically worded to elicit change talk or the adolescent client's views in favor of change, rather than those views against change or *sustain talk*. Thus, the interviewer may ask: "Why would you want to make this change?" "What are the three best reasons to do so?" "On a scale of one to ten, how confident are you that you could make such a change?" and "Why are you not *lower* on that scale?" These questions stand in contrast to others grounded in decisional balance in which the interviewer may ask about the good things about substance use for example, or why a client is not higher on a confidence scale. Both of these latter questions inevitably elicit sustain talk.

A fourth component of MI is collaboration. The interviewer expresses a willingness to help in any way he or she can within the confines of his or her role. The interviewer is supportive and creative in problem solving and seeking ways to work together to pursue health behavior change. Confidence in the teen's own abilities to make good decisions is expressed, and the teen is encouraged to explore new ways of behaving, which typically relates back and stands in contrast to health risk behaviors. For example, an adolescent who has a particular career goal or who is an athlete is often able to recognize how heavy or other dangerous substance use can impede success.

Finally, empathy is considered to be the cornerstone of MI and its predecessor, the Rogerian person-centered approach. The interviewer works hard to feel what the client feels and express that feeling back to the client, again primarily through the use of reflections, which should be complex whenever possible. That is, the interviewer goes beyond the words the clients speaks and conveys some kind of change in meaning. For example, in response to a client who states: "You're nice and all but I am not quitting weed." The interviewer may say: "No one, including me, is going to be able to *make* you stop using." Such a statement not only emphasizes the adolescent client's autonomy, but also verbalizes the underlying meaning of the client's statement, or even fear, that the interviewer is going to try to make him or her do something he or she does not want or is not ready to do.

Empathy is integral to motivational and person-centered practice. A lack of understanding on the part of the interviewer creates an immediate disconnection and barrier to the other components of the MI spirit. Conversely, when the adolescent client feels understood and not judged, it has a freeing effect. Indeed the positive effects of empathy on client outcomes have been established for many years (Truax, 1970).

Furthermore, when clients are not threatened and feel understood their speech is very predictive of their future behavior. Drawing upon earlier linguistic concepts, Amrhein and colleagues (2003) found that under such "sincerity conditions" client DARN change talk constitutes *preparatory* language that predicts commitment. Commitment language then predicts future behavior. Amrhein et al. (2003) coded both the type and strength of client language and predicted substance use several months after a single motivational interview. Since then eliciting and strengthening change talk and ultimately commitment language as part of change planning has become integral to the MI theory of behavior change (Miller and Rose, 2009).

CONCLUSION

Lay people, the media, and even many recovering addicts and substance abuse counselors view individuals with substance use problems as lacking the motivation or will power to change. Moreover, failed treatment episodes were often blamed on the client's lack of motivation to change.

However, practice wisdom and research have converged to illustrate two points critical to substance use treatment: (1) ambivalence about making substance use changes (e.g., low or moderate motivation to change) is extremely common among individuals with substance use problems, particularly teens and (2) motivation to change substance use can be enhanced through effective intervention. As a result, many researchers and treatment providers espouse a very different view of motivation as it relates to substance use and recovery.

Motivation is no longer viewed as an excuse for continued substance use problems but rather as a primary target for intervention and the key to developing effective substance use change plans (Miller and Rollnick, 2009). It is increasingly expected that treatment providers take an active role in enhancing client motivation for change (DiClemente et al., 2008). Interventions embracing components consistent with the spirit of MI including: (1) directive, (2) supportive of autonomy, (3) focused on evocation, (4) collaborative, and (5) rooted in empathy have been widely and successfully used to enhance motivation and promote subsequent substance use changes among adolescent substance abusers, a particularly hard to reach subgroup who most often enter treatment with low motivation to change.

REFERENCES

Amrhein, P. C., Miller, W. R., Yahne, C. E., Palmer, M., and Fulcher, L. (2003). Client commitment language during motivational interviewing predicts drug use outcomes. *Journal of Consulting and Clinical Psychology,* 71, 862-878.

Austin, A., Hospital, M., Wagner, E. F. and Morris, S. L. (2010). Motivation for reducing substance use among minority adolescents: Targets for intervention. *Journal of Substance Abuse Treatment,* 39(4), 399-407.

Barnett, N. P., Lebeau-Craven, R., Wollard, R., Rohsenow, D. J., Spirito, A., and Monti, P. M. (2002). Predictors of motivation to change after medical treatment for drinking-related events in adolescents. *Psychology of Addictive Behaviors,* 16(2), 106-112.

Battjes, R. J., Gordon, M. S., O'Grady, K. E., Kinlock, T. W., and Carswell, M. A. (2003). Factors that predict adolescent motivation for substance abuse treatment. *Journal of Substance Abuse Treatment,* 24, 221-232.

Baumrind, D. (1991). The influence of parenting style on adolescent competence and substance use. *Journal of Early Adolescence,* 11(1) 56-95.

Breda, C. S. and Heflinger, C. A. (2007). The impact of motivation to change on substance use among adolescents in treatment. *Journal of Child and Adolescent Substance Abuse,* 16(3), 109-124.

Broome, K. M., Joe, G. W., and Simpson, D. D. (2001). Engagement models for adolescents in DATOS-A. *Journal of Adolescent Research,* 16, 608-623.

Cady, M. E., Winters, K. C., Jordan, D. A., Solberg, K. B., and Stinchfield, R. D. (1996). Motivation to change as a predictor of treatment outcome for adolescent substance abusers. *Journal of Child and Adolescent Substance Abuse,* 5, 73-91.

Cohen, D. A. and Rice, J. (1997). Parenting styles, adolescent substance use, and academic achievement. *Journal of Drug Education,* 27, 199-211.

De Leon, G. and Jainchill, N. (1986). Circumstance, motivation, readiness, and suitability as correlates of treatment tenure. *Journal of Psychoactive Drugs,* 18(3), 203-208.

De Leon, G., Melnick, G., and Hawke, J. (2000). The motivation-readiness factor in drug treatment: Implications for research and policy. In *Advances in medical sociology* (vol. 7, pp. 103-129). Greenwich, CT: JAI Press, Inc.

De Leon, G. Melnick, G. Kressel, and Jainchill, N. (1994).

DiClemente, C., Garay, M., and Gemmell, L. (2008). Motivational enhancement. In M. Galanter and H. D. Kleber (Eds.), *The American Psychiatric Publishing Textbook of Substance Abuse Treatment* (4th ed, pp. 361-372). American Psychiatric Publishing, Washington, DC, 366.

Fickenscher, A., Novins, D. K., and Beals, J. (2006). A pilot study of motivation and treatment completion among American Indian adolescents in substance abuse treatment. *Addictive Behaviors,* 31, 1402-1414.

Freyer, J., Tonigan, J.S., Keller, S., John, U., Rumpf, H.J., and Hapke, U. (2004). Readiness to change versus readiness to seek help for alcohol problems: The development of the Treatment Readiness Tool (TReaT). *Journal of Studies on Alcohol, 65*, 801–9.

Friedman, A. S., Granick, S., and Kreisher, C. (1994). Motivation of adolescent drug abusers for help and treatment. *Journal of Child and Adolescent Substance Abuse, 3*(1), 69–88.

Hiller, M. L., Knight, K. Leukefeld, C. and Simspon, D. D. (2002). Motivation as a predictor of therapeutic engagement in mandated residential substance abuse treatment. *Criminal Justice and Behavior, 29*(1), 56-75.

Jensen, C. D., Cushing, C. C., Aylward, B. S., Craig, J. T., Sorrell, D. M., and Steele, R. G. (2011). Effectiveness of motivational interventions for adolescent substance use behavior change: A meta-analytic review. *Journal of Consulting and Clinical Psychology,* 1-8.

Joe, G. W., Simpson, D. D., and Broome, K. M. (1998). Effects of readiness for drug abuse treatment on client retention and assessment of process. *Addiction, 93*, 1177-1190.

King, K.M., Chung, T., and Maisto, S.A. (2009). Adolescents' thoughts about abstinence curb the return of marijuana use during and after treatment. *Journal of Consulting and Clinical Psychology, 77*, 554–565.

Lau, K., Freyer-Adam, J., Gaertner, B., Rumpf, H.J., John, U., and Hapke, U. (2010). Motivation to change risky drinking and motivation to seek help for alcohol risk drinking among general hospital inpatients with problem drinking and alcohol-related diseases. *General Hospital Psychiatry, 32*, 86–93.

Macgowan, M. J., and Engle, B. C. (2010). Evidence for optimism: Behavior therapies and motivational interviewing in adolescent substance abuse treatment. *Child and Adolescent Psychiatric Clinics of North America*, 19, 527-545.

Melnick, G., De Leon, G., Hawke, J., Jainchill, N., and Kressel, D. (1997). Motivation and readiness for therapeutic community treatment among adolescents and adult substance abusers. *American Journal of Drug and Alcohol Abuse, 23*(4), 485-506.

Merikangas, K. R. et al. (2011). Service utilization for lifetime mental disorders in U.S. adolescents: Results from the National Comorbidity Survey Adolescent Supplement (NCS-A). *Journal of the American Academy of Child and Adolescent Psychiatry,* 1, 32-45.

Miller, W.R. and Rollnick, S. (2009). Ten things that motivational interviewing is not. *Behavioural and Cognitive Psychotherapy, 37*(02),129-140.

Miller, W. R., and Rose, G., S. (2009). Toward a theory of motivational interviewing. *American Psychologist* 64(6), 527–537.

Monti, P.M., et al., (1999). Brief intervention for harm reduction with alcohol-positive older adolescents in a hospital emergency department. *Journal of Consulting and Clinical Psychology, 67*(6), 989-994.

Office of Applied Studies. (2000). *National survey of substance abuse treatment services (N-SSATS).* Retrieved on February 17, 2003 from http://www.samsha.org.

Patterson, G. R., Forgatch, M. S. (1985) Therapist behavior as a determinant for client noncompliance: A paradox for the behavior modifier. *Journal of Consulting and Clinical Psychology*, 53(6), 846-851.

Simpson, D. D. and Joe, G. W. (1993). Motivation as a predictor of early dropout from drug abuse treatment. *Psychotherapy, 30*, 357-368.

Slesnick, N. Bartle-Haring, S., Erdem, G., Budde, H., Letcher, A., Bantchevska, D. and Garre, R. (2009). Troubled parents, motivated adolescents: Predicting motivation to change among runaways. *Addictive Behaviors, 34*(8), 675-684.

Truax, C. B. (1970) Length of therapist response, accurate empathy and patient improvement. *Journal of Clinical Psychology*, 26(4) 539-541

Vik, P. W., Culbertson, K. A. and Sellers, K. (2000). Readiness to change drinking among heavy-drinking college students. *Journal of Studies on Alcohol, 61*, 674-680.

Wagner, E.F. (2008). Developmentally informed research on the effectiveness of clinical trials: A primer for assessing how developmental issues may influence treatment responses among adolescents with alcohol use problems. *Pediatrics, 121*, S337-S347.

Weiss, L. H., and Schwarz, J. C. (1996). The relationship between parenting types and older adolescents' personality, academic achievement, adjustment, and substance use. *Child Development, 67*(5), 2101-2114.

In: Handbook on Psychology of Motivation
Editors: J. N. Franco and A. E. Svensgaard
ISBN: 978-1-62100-755-5
© 2012 Nova Science Publishers, Inc.

Chapter 17

MOTIVATION FOR LEARNING EFL AMONG JAPANESE UNIVERSITY STUDENTS

Junko Matsuzaki Carreira
Tokyo Future University, Japan

INTRODUCTION

In second language (L2) learning, we should pay attention to motivation, referring to "the process whereby goal-directed activity is instigated and sustained" (Pintrich & Schunk, 2002, p. 5) because "motivation can predict important academic outcomes like performance and persistence" (Ratelle, Guay, Larose, & Senécal, 2004, p.743). For several decades, motivation has long been considered one of the key factors that determine L2 achievement and attainment (Cheng & Dörnyei, 2007). "Due to its great importance, L2 motivation has been the subject of a considerable amount of research in recent decades, exploring the nature of this complex construct and how it affects the L2 learning process"(Cheng & Dörnyei, 2007, pp.153-154).

In order to reveal motivation that may be characteristic of Japanese EFL university students and reasons for language study that predict the greatest motivational strength, this study replicates Ely (1986). ELy revealed which reasons for language study predicted the greatest motivational strength. In addition to examining the type of learners' language learning motivation, it seems important to investigate the strength of motivation. Thus, firstly, this study reveals which types of motivation best predict the strength of motivation among university students in Japan.

METHOD

Materials

This study employed closed-ended questionnaires including the following two scales: strength of motivation items and motivation for learning EFL. All the questionnaires, on a 4-

point scale ranging from 1 (not at all true) to 4 (very true), were written in Japanese. A high score thus corresponded to a high degree of agreement with the proposed item.

Strength of Motivation Items

This scale, referring to Ely (1986), had seven items that measured strength of motivation (e.g., If possible, I would like to continue English study., I want to be able to use English in a wide variety of situations., Learning English well is really a high priority for me at this point.) According to Ely, the reliability was established via an alpha coefficient of intrinsic motivation (.86). The scores on the items were summed to show strength of motivation for learning EFL. A high mean score suggests a strong intention to study English.

Motivation for Learning EFL

As a measure of motivation for learning EFL, a questionnaire developed by Ely (1986) was used (e.g., Because I am interest in English culture, history or literature, and Because I want to use English when I travel to an English-speaking country, Because I think learning English is part of a well-rounded education). This 12 item scale assesses why the students study English.

Participants

A total of 118 Japanese university freshmen majoring in Economics at a private university in Japan participated in the present study. They enrolled in an English language course as a required subject. Their age ranged from 18 to 20. These students had broadly similar learning experience in that none of them had spent over six months in an English speaking country. The range of their TOEIC scores was between 250 and 450. The questionnaires which included the type of motivation scale and the strength of motivation scale were administered to the first-year students at the end of the second semester during course hours. The students were informed that the survey was not involved in the teacher's evaluation of them.

ANALYSIS

Firstly, an exploratory factor analysis was conducted to identify the underlying structures of each scale and establish construct validity. Any item that did not contribute appreciably to the solution (i.e., those with loadings < |.30| or that cross-loaded on other factors) was eliminated, and the correlation matrix was reanalyzed. Tests of internal consistency were also performed.

RESULTS AND DISCUSSION

Strength of Motivation Items

The scores of strength of motivation were totaled up to construct a strength of motivation scale. The scale was subjected to a reliability assessment. The cronbach alpha for the scale was found to be .86, which was very satisfactory.

Type of Motivation

An exploratory factor analysis using maximum likelihood estimation was conducted and promax rotation was used. By both examination of scree plots and factor selection based on eigenvalues greater than 1, evidence for only a three-factor solution was obtained. Item 15 was eliminated because its factor loadings were less than .40. The remaining 11 items were again factor analyzed. The three extracted factors accounted for 59.34%of the total variance.

Factor 1 obtained high loading from items such as "Because I am interest in English culture, history or literature" and "Because I want to use English when I travel to an English-speaking country", which seems to represent a dimension reflecting students' interests in English speaking countries and people. Thus, Factor 1 can be called Interests in English speaking countries and people. Factor 2 obtained high loadings from items such as "Because I feel English is an important language in the world" and "Because I think learning English is part of a well-rounded education". It seems to represent a dimension reflecting students' intellectual curiosity. Therefore, factor 2 can be called Intellectual curiosity. Factor 3 obtained high loadings from items such as: "Because I feel learning English may be helpful in my future career" and "Because learning English may make me a more qualified job candidate". It seems to represent utilitarian value. Thus, it can be called Utilitarian value. The scores for the items loading highest on each factor were added up to create the three subscales. The cronbach alpha index of internal consistency was acceptable for all subscales, varying between .83 and .69.

Relationships between Strength of Motivation Items and Motivation for Learning EFL

Multiple regression analysis was utilized to examine the association between strength of motivation and types of motivation. Strength of motivation was regressed on the three subscales using a simultaneous regression procedure. Multicollinearity was tested for each regression analysis and was found not to affect the regression model. The Interests in English speaking countries (beta = .58, $p < .01$) and people and Utilitarian value (beta = .23, $p < .01$) subscales had a significant effect on strength of motivation.

This report revealed that interest in foreign countries as well as utilitarian value influenced the strength of university's students' motivation for learning EFL. Therefore, we need to provide more techniques or support which can enhance learners' interest in foreign countries and instrumental motivation particularly when teaching lower level students who tend to lose desire to study English due to their poor English ability.

LIMITATIONS

This study has revealed important issues concerning motivation for learning EFL among Japanese university students, but there remain several issues to be examined in future research. Firstly, although this study revealed the relationship between motivation for learning EFL and the strength of motivation, it should be noted that the R square values were rather small on these regressions. There might be other factors which influence motivation for learning EFL. It is necessary to explore other potential factors in the future. Next, the data were collected only by means of questionnaires. Qualitative research, including interviews with students and teachers, assessments of actual performance, and classroom observations, may provide further layers of analysis.

REFERENCES

Cheng, H., & Dörnyei, Z. (2007). The use of motivational strategies in language instruction: The case of EFL teaching in Taiwan. *Innovation in Language Learning and Teaching, 1,* 153-174.

Ely, C. (1986a). Language learning motivation: A descriptive and causal analysis. *Modern Language Journal, 70,* 28-35.

Pintrich, P. R., & Schunk, D. H. (2002). *Motivation in education: Theory, research, and application (2nd ed.).* New Jersey: Merrill Prentice Hall.

Ratelle, C., Guay, F., Larose, S., & Senécal, C. (2004). Family correlates of trajectories of academic motivation during a school transition: A semiparametric group-based approach. *Journal of Educational Psychology, 96,* 743-754.

Chapter 18

THE ASSOCIATION BETWEEN DECEPTIVE MOTIVATIONS AND PERSONALITY DISORDERS IN MALE OFFENDERS

Alicia Spidel[1], Hugues Hervé[2,3] and John C. Yuille[2]
[1]University of British Columbia, Vancouver, BT, Canada
[2] The Forensic Alliance, Canada
[3]Simon Fraser University, Canada

ABSTRACT

The detection of deception is an integral part of any forensic assessment. Unfortunately, the motives underlying the use of deceptive strategies by offenders and how these may differ between different types of personality-disordered offenders are not well established. The aim of the present study was to identify different deception-related motivations in a sample of offenders and to examine the relationship between these motivations and personality pathology. Archived file and videotaped information for 103 Canadian federal offenders were reviewed in order to identify personality disorder pathology, as well as patterns of deceptive motivations (compulsive, secretive, avoiding punishment, avoiding negative evaluation, protective, to obtain a reward, to heighten self-presentation, altruistic, and careless). In general, as expected within a forensic context, offenders lied to avoid punishment. With respect to the other motivational categories investigated, personality pathology was found to significantly mediate the motivational patterns leading to offender-perpetrated deception. The relevance of these findings to credibility assessment and personality pathology is discussed.

ASSOCIATION BETWEEN DECEPTIVE MOTIVATIONS AND PERSONALITY DISORDERS IN MALE OFFENDERS

Deception is a frequent occurrence in everyday life (DePaulo and Kirkendol, 1989; Ekman, 1997; Spidel, Hervé, Greaves and Yuille, 2010), and its empirical study is of critical importance in the forensic context. The stakes for the individual and society are heightened when this group is involved, as their lies tend to have more significant consequences (e.g., influencing parole and sentencing decisions). Moreover some type of deception is typically an "essential prerequisite of most crimes" (Rogers and Cruise, 2000, p. 275). The present research was concerned with the motivations to deceive among adult male offenders. The central focus was on identifying different deceptive motivations and examining their relationship to the offenders' personality pathology.

Very little research has considered the relationship between personality disorders and deceptive motivations of offenders (Ekman 1997; Spidel et al., 2010), which is remarkable considering that lies reflect and influence offenders' experiences and interpersonal relationships. This is especially important given that an individual's personality style is delineated by behaviour patterns and characteristic responses to life events and specific stressors (Krueger and Tackett, 2003; Widiger and Samuel, 2005). To different degrees, personality disorders influence all facets of an individual including cognition, affect, behaviour, and interpersonal style (Widiger and Frances, 1988). This paper begins with a review of a current empirical foundation of deceptive motivations followed with an overview of the various categories of motivation. The pertinent personality disorders as well as related issues such as prevalence rates and relevance to credibility assessment and treatment are described. Finally, the current research is presented.

To date, several studies have explored the motivations for deception in non-forensic samples (Camden, Motley and Wilson 1984; Hample, 1980; Lippard, 1988; Turner, Edgley and Olmstead, 1975). Most of these studies have focused on white lies in an attempt to investigate social motivations. In one of the earlier studies to look at motivation for deception Turner et al. analyzed the motivations for lying and their relative frequencies and five motivations for deception were found: (1) to save face, (55.2%); (2) to avoid tension or conflict, (22.2%); (3) to guide social interactions (9.9%); (4) to influence interpersonal relationships, (9.6%); (5) and to achieve personal power, (3.2%). In a critique of this study and Hample's (1980) investigations Camden et al. (1984) reported that the aforementioned taxonomies were not adequately developed for the following reasons. Firstly, many white lies were not classifiable using either motivation taxonomy. Although Hample (1980) attempted to get around this by including a miscellaneous category, Camden et al. were of the opinion that this was insufficient as even in Hample's own study, 17% of the lies fell under this category. Secondly, they criticized the focus of the categories in each previous model. Turner et al.'s system is concerned with the nature of particular benefit to be gained by the deception and Hample's (1980) focus is on who benefits from the lie. Thirdly, Camden et al. posited that the categories were too broad to offer much in terms of explanation. To address these issues, Camden et al. adapted their research into a categorical system with four major reward categories, further delineated into sixteen subcategories. The four major categories are basic needs. affiliation. self-esteem, and other, which are further broken down (see Camden et al., 1984). Although Camden et al.'s categories improved upon previous models, they still only addressed deception that focused on white lies. In addition, they developed this model using only 20 subjects, therefore making it difficult to assign much weight to their findings.

Lippard (1988) attempted to test and refine Camden et al.'s (1984) model by increasing the sample size and including all forms of interpersonal deception. She investigated self-reported deception in everyday interpersonal interactions using undergraduates. Sixteen motivational categories emerged from her data, which she grouped into eight primary categories. The eight categories delineated included: resources (acquisition and request refusal), affiliation (increase interaction, leave-taking, and interaction avoidance), self-protection (social image and self-disclosure avoidance), conflict avoidance (request acceptance, lecture avoidance, fidelity), protection of other (avoid hurt feelings avoid worrying another, third party), manipulation of other, obligation of other, obligation-excuse, and joke. There are several advantages to this model including it being more expansive and therefore processing a finer distinction between the motivations that allows for an improved understanding of intention. In addition, it is more valid due to the increase in sample size. Another improvement of this model over previous is it's inclusion of all types of deception, not just white lies.

Two other researchers have empirically found different motives for lying (Ekman, 1997; Ford 1996). Ford (1996) focused more on pathologies associated with lying than on normal or social lies. Consequently, Ford (1996) described lying as a means to: avoid punishment, preserve autonomy, aid aggression, obtain power, put something over on someone, fulfill a wish, assist self-deception, manipulate behaviour in others, help another person, accommodate other's self-deception, avoid role conflict, maintain self-esteem, and/or to create a sense of identity.

The research reviewed above is not without flaws, particularly when researchers have attempted to generalize the findings to forensic populations. The participants used in most studies of this nature were undergraduates dissimulating about everyday situations (Camden et al., 1984; Hample, 1980; Lippard, 1988; Turner et al., 1975). As a result, the consequences of lying were typically minor and, for the most part, the liars were relatively unsophisticated (Lippard, 1988) compared with a forensic population. An exception to the minor consequences found in the previously discussed studies can be found in the Ekman and O'Sullivan (1991) studies with nurses. In those studies, informing the nurses that there was consequences (i.e., for their careers) if they were not able to lie effectively increased their motivation to lie. Ekman and O'Sullivan (1991) found that the more highly motivated the liars, the more accurate others were in detecting their deception. However, despite the fact that the liars were motivated, the liars only possessed one type of motivation and unlike the present study, the focus was on detection not ascertaining the target motivation. A further problem with the aforementioned studies is that the lies were repeatedly categorized as prosocial lies hence the motivations were generally social. Prosocial lies, more commonly known as white lies, are false statements that help keep social interactions smooth and positive (Ford, 1996; Spidel et al., 2010). Consequently, their impact on assessment of credibility, while important, is comparatively trivial with respect to lies revealed in a forensic population (Petitclerc and Hervé, 1999; Spidel et al., 2010). Lies can generally be categorized in motivational terms as aggressive, defensive, or as white lies (Ford et al., 1988) and by pathology as normal or abnormal (pathological) (Ford et al., 1988). The current investigation tends to focus on aggressive lies rather than white lies due to the population of focus. For example, a psychopath may be able to put on a good show for the parole board (Hare, Forth, and Hart, 1989) and thus achieve parole earlier than others (Hare et al., 1989). Another problem with the previous studies on motivation is that the studies were descriptive and relied on self report. When dealing with offenders, it is imperative not to solely rely on self-report; as they are unlikely to admit to the lies investigators are most interested in the lies with substantial consequences for the offender if detected, and for society if undetected. As such, it has been suggested by Hare et al. (2001) that caution should be taken when using self-report in prison populations to assess for deception.

Thus far, two studies have investigated motives for deception in forensic populations with adult samples (Petitclerc, Hervé, Spidel, and Hare, 2000; Rogers and Cruise, 2000). In addition one study looked at this relationship in adolescent populations (Spidel et al., 2010). Rogers and Cruise's (2000) evaluated differences in the deception-related motivations of psychopathic versus nonpsychopathic offenders, a goal similar to one of the present study. Rogers and Cruise analyzed an extensive data set based on previous studies of psychopathy (see Rogers and Cruise, 2000) and utilized a modified version of the Psychopathy Checklist Screening Version (PCL: SV; Hare, Cox, and Hart, 1989). They asked clinicians to rate the 58 subcriteria of the PCL:SV (17 were determined to address deception) in addition to the 12 criteria to assess deception. Of the 58 subcriteria, a principal axis factoring on the 17 subcriteria was performed and a three-factor model found which included: implausible presentation, characterized by an "unbelievable display with respect to statements and emotional expressions" (p.277), lies to con and manipulate the target, and lies to deny criminality, which refute criminal involvement and blame external sources. These motives are similar to ones found in models using non-forensic samples, with the exception of denying criminality. Implausible presentation is conceptually similar to lies to maintain self esteem (see Ford, 1996) and lies to win the admiration of others (see Ekman 1997). Conning and manipulate the target has parallels with lies to manipulate the behaviour of others (see Ford, 1996) and to obtain a reward (see Ekman, 1997). However, although this study employs a forensic sample, it does not address the motives for individual lie, rather its focus is on overall presentation of the offenders with specific application to psychopaths. Another study that addressed motives for deception in psychopaths was a pilot study performed by Petitclerc, Hervé, Spidel, and Hare (2000). In this study the 3 categories established in Rogers and Cruise's (2000) investigation (implausible presentation, lies to con and manipulate the target, and lies to deny criminality) were conceptually similar to motivations to heighten self-presentation, obtain a reward, and avoid punishment respectively [see Petitclerc and Hervé (1999) model below]. In the research with adolescent offenders (Spidel et al., 2010) significant differences were found on lies to obtain a reward; 2) to heighten self-presentation and 3) for duping delight between those that scored higher in psychopathic traits (above 20 on the PCL:YV) compared to those with lower scores (below 20 on the PCL:YV).

This research with forensic samples, although superior to the aforementioned non-forensic research, is still limited. To address issues associated with the heightened consequence of offenders' deceptive strategies, as well as facilitate the awareness of motivation for assessment of credibility, Petitclerc and Hervé's (1999) constructed a model describing motivations for deception in offenders. Petitclerc and Herve's model has advantages over previous frameworks in that it specifically focuses on lies of forensic interest. Given that lies provided in forensic contexts are of more diverse subject matter than typically associated with a sample of undergraduates, it is likely that they will have more variable motivations. Another advantage to this version is that it is based upon both clinical and research experience, as well as a review of the relevant literature, whereas previous types of motivation were specified from self-report, and were therefore descriptive. Petitclerc and Herve's model includes ten motivational categories. Briefly, they are as follows:

COMPULSIVE

These lies seem to be completely lacking a purpose. They are usually not self-serving and, in fact, may be self-destructive as the deception is random and likely to be discovered. Ford (1996) proposes that compulsive liars may focus more on the present and less on the past and/or future than other people may. This could explain their lack of concern about the possible consequences of their lies, as well as their naive belief that they will not be discovered (e.g., they do not realize that other people, using information from the past, can easily detect their lies). Compulsive lies are usually quite spontaneous (Ford, 1996). Those considered `pathological liars' are known for their compulsiveness (Ekman, 1997); that is, they cannot control telling them. The terms "compulsive liar" and "pathological liar" are often used in a sense that is broader than the one referred to here. Such expressions may refer to individuals who lie frequently, easily, and with no remorse. Several authors have suggested that psychopaths may fall into this category (Ekman, and Frank, 1993). Their lies, however, may be motivated by self-serving purposes, and therefore do not necessarily qualify for our "compulsive" category. In general, this form of lying may be based in an offender's lack of motivation to tell the truth.

SECRETIVE

A secretive lie is motivated by the offender's desire to keep some personal information concealed. The offender is reluctant to give the target personal information, regardless of the latter's desire or need to know the truth. The offender may believe that his or her right to privacy takes precedent in such circumstances. Ford (1996) talks about lying "to preserve a sense of autonomy" (p. 88). As adults, "people who react strongly to control or intrusiveness from others may resort to lying in an effort to maintain a sense of independence" (p. 88).

AVOID PUNISHMENT

Lies in this motivational category are by definition self-serving lies. They can take the form of a general deceptive statement to evade a punitive consequence, a fabricated excuse, as in an explanation for incomplete work assignments (Lippard, 1988), or as a lie to avoid a conflict, which is conceptualized by Petitclerc and Hervé's (1999) to be a form of punishment. Based upon his reviews of motivations discussed earlier, Ekman (1997) states that children and adults most often mention these lies in self-reports. For obvious reasons, these are also probably the most frequently encountered types of lies in the criminal justice system. The punishment referred to here can be legal or relational. Ford (1996), Kropp and Rogers (1993) propose that different types of individuals lie to avoid punishment due to various motivational pressures. Some individuals place their own needs and desires above the consequences of their lies, while others weigh the pros and cons of lying and telling the truth and reason that lying is the best way to cope with their present situation (Kropp and Rogers, 1993). In the first type of individual, the lies can be attributed to the liar's egocentricity, lack of empathy and irresponsibility (Cornell et al.,1996) and, therefore, are seen as egosyntonic.

Egosyntonic is defined as "consistent with the individuals ideals or with the individuals evaluation of himself" (Chaplin, 1985, p.149). In the second interpretation, the lies are attributed to the pressure from the situation (Cornell et al., 1996) and are seen as egodystonic. Egodystonic is defined as " unacceptable to the ego" (Chaplin, 1985, p.149). In the present study, lies in this category were judged as either egosyntonic or egodystonic, as previous research has indicated that different categories of offenders (i.e. psychopaths vs. non-psychopaths) behavior is driven by one or the other (Cornell et al., 1996).

AVOID NEGATIVE EVALUATION

This category includes lies concerning a topic that the offender is shameful or worried over being judged about. The offender deceives to avoid having the target make a negative evaluation of him. Such lies are said to occur when the offender is mindful of, and is concerned about, the target's opinion of him, or when he is generally careful about self-presentation (Petitclerc and Hervé 1999). People with low self-esteem may feel as though they are a failure when their talents and abilities fall short of their expectations (Ford, 1996). In an attempt to regulate the person may lie to close the gap (Ford, 1996) between their beliefs and reality. These lies however, are not included in the self-enhancing category, as they are not meant to make the offender look better than others, but rather not look bad. As such, these lies only serve to avoid feelings of shame by making the offender look normal rather than special or inflate another's opinion (Petitclerc and Hervé 1999).

PROTECTIVE

Lies in this category are used in order to avoid the physical retaliation of another person. The feared individual in question may or may not be the target of the lie. Classification of a deceptive statement in this category means that its purpose was not to avoid a legal or emotional punishment, but instead served to avoid serious physical injury or death to the liar (Petitclerc and Hervé 1999). Perceived threat of injury need not be completely rational in this case; instead, it is necessary that the offender believed deception was the only way to empathy and irresponsibility (Cornell et al.,1996) and, therefore, are seen as egosyntonic. Egosyntonic is defined as "consistent with the individuals ideals or with the individuals evaluation of himself" (Chaplin, 1985, p.149). In the second interpretation, the lies are attributed to the pressure from the situation (Cornell et al., 1996) and are seen as egodystonic. Egodystonic is defined as " unacceptable to the ego" (Chaplin, 1985, p.149). In the present study, lies in this category were judged as either egosyntonic or egodystonic, as previous research has indicated that different categories of offenders (i.e. psychopaths vs. non-psychopaths) behavior is driven by one or the other (Cornell et al., 1996).

AVOID NEGATIVE EVALUATION

This category includes lies concerning a topic that the offender is shameful or worried over being judged about. The offender deceives to avoid having the target make a negative evaluation of him. Such lies are said to occur when the offender is mindful of, and is concerned about, the target's opinion of him, or when he is generally careful about self-presentation (Petitclerc and Hervé 1999). People with low self-esteem may feel as though they are a failure when their talents and abilities fall short of their expectations (Ford, 1996). In an attempt to regulate the person may lie to close the gap (Ford, 1996) between their beliefs and reality. These lies however, are not included in the self-enhancing category, as they are not meant to make the offender look better than others, but rather not look bad. As such, these lies only serve to avoid feelings of shame by making the offender look normal rather than special or inflate another's opinion (Petitclerc and Hervé 1999).

PROTECTIVE

Lies in this category are used in order to avoid the physical retaliation of another person. The feared individual in question may or may not be the target of the lie. Classification of a deceptive statement in this category means that its purpose was not to avoid a legal or emotional punishment, but instead served to avoid serious physical injury or death to the liar (Petitclerc and Hervé 1999). Perceived threat of injury need not be completely rational in this case; instead, it is necessary that the offender believed deception was the only way to escape dire threats to physical integrity. This type of lie can be conceived of as being a special case of lies that serve to avoid punishment, where punishment in this case is defined as physical harm. Ekman (1997) also makes a separate category of this type of lie, but indicates that in this case the liar has done nothing wrong. In this study however, where the participants are offenders and frequently find themselves in situations where they have done something wrong. As a result, the absence of wrongdoing was not used as a criterion, but rather the threat of physical harm was employed.

OBTAIN A REWARD

Lying to obtain a reward can be regarded as going beyond lying to avoid punishment. Any gain from this lie is something undeserved, and would not have been obtained by the offender under other circumstances (Petitclerc and Hervé 1999). In this case, gains could be physical (e.g., obtaining sexual favors from a spouse), situational (e.g., early release from punishment), material (e.g., money), or internal, (e.g., attention). Ekman (1997) states that this is the second most often mentioned reason for lying, after lying to avoid punishment. DePaulo and Jordan (1982, cited in Stouthamer-Loeber, 1986) speculate that lying to obtain a reward comes at a latter stage of development than does lying to avoid punishment.

HEIGHTEN SELF-PRESENTATION

In contrast with lies to avoid a negative evaluation, lies to heighten self-presentation serve to present the perpetrator in a positive light (Petitclerc and Hervé 1999). This may be similar to a "faking good" strategy, defined as a tendency to deny symptoms. On the other hand, "faking bad" is defined as a strategy of endorsing symptoms (Hare et al., 1989). Although initially it may appear that the same argument could explain avoiding negative evaluation, this category serves to make the offender appear more normal, not good or bad. There is a large literature of faking good and bad (Austin, 1992; Bagby, Rogers, Buis, and Kalemba, 1994; Bagby, Rogers, and Buis, 1994; Paulhus, Bruce, and Trapnell, 1995). Many studies have looked at the association between psychopathy and these strategies (Hare et al., 1989). It appears when employing many measures (MMPI, EPQ, MCMI, and BIDR) that psychopathy is associated with a tendency to claim symptoms rather than deny them (Hare et al., 1989). In this category, the offender wants to gain respect from the target by trying to make a good impression with either simple, yet false, statements, or by launching into elaborate tales. This is distinct from duping delight, described later, as there is no pleasure derived from the deceit per say rather the pleasure comes from having the target think well of him or her (Petitclerc and Hervé 1999). The offender's motivation is to go beyond a good evaluation or him/herself, by making him/herself look better than normal.

ALTRUISTIC

Altruistic lies are motivated by the perpetrator's desire to protect another from some harm (Ford, 1996). Typically these lies take the form of lying to shield the feelings of the target, or to protect another from negative consequences. In the first case it may be argued that such lies are not truly altruistic, as they may defend the perpetrator from discomfort, shame, or conflict, more than they serve to protect the target (e.g., Ekman, 1985).

CARELESSNESS

Unlike compulsive lying, which may be due to an impulse control problem (Ford, 1996) and therefore beyond the offender's control, the careless liar is indeed in control of the lying behavior. Assessing the content of the lies, which is of secondary importance to the offender, can make the distinction. Here the offender simply does not care to give the target truthful information. Petitclerc and Hervé (1999) call these 'amotivational' lies because the offender has no motivation to comply with the target's desire to gain information.

DUPING DELIGHT

These lies are, quite simply, motivated by the pleasure of deceiving another. For this reason, Ekman (1985) coined the term 'duping delight'. Like the careless lie, the content is of secondary importance. What is primary is the offender's desire to prove his ability to deceive, and to take pleasure in outwitting and conning a target. The less gullible the target, the more challenging and exciting the successful deception will seem (Ekman and Frank, 1993). Lies in this category tend to be more elaborate and of longer duration than those in other categories. Some authors talk about lies that are motivated by a desire to obtain a sense of power (e.g., Ekman, 1997; Ford, 1996). The sense of power comes from possessing information that the other one does not have, or from misleading the other in order to cause him or her to make wrong decisions.

Petitclerc and Herve's (1999) ten motivational categories of deception were employed in the present study to investigate their associations to specific personality disorders. For the purposes of the present study, Ekman's (1997) definition of lies was adopted. This requires two criteria. First, deception must be deliberate. This serves to exclude misrepresentations of the truth that are unintentional, such as those due to delusions or memory failures. This element of intent is present in most definitions of lies used by deception researchers (see Miller and Stiff, 1993). Second, the target must not be warned (explicitly or implicitly) of the deception. Ekman's (1997) second criterion excludes prosocial lies, jokes, and secrets. Politeness and social conventions make these lies not only acceptable, but expected. Although it can be argued that prosocial lies can be altruistic, due to the nature of the information used in this study, namely a PCL-R (Hare, 1991) interview, it was unlikely to be the case as the topics of the interview were focused on criminal activity and the background of the offender. Humorous lies are also excluded from the current study since, by definition, the target is kept unaware of the deception for only a short period of time (Ford, 1996). According to Ekman (1997), a secret that is acknowledged by both parties does not qualify as a lie, because the other person is warned that the truth will be withheld.

Self-deception, although not explicitly outlined in Ekman's (1997) two criteria, is excluded from the definition of lies used for this study for a number of reasons. Ford (1996), for example, separates liars from self-deceivers as unlike a liar, the self-deceptive individual does not acknowledge something that would be considered truthful by others. This adds to Miller's definition (cited in Miller and Stiff, 1993) that a liar tries to make the target believe something that the liar himself or herself does not believe. This is accomplished by specifying that the liar does not believe in the false statement of which he is trying to convince others. The information available to the present study did not permit the collection of self-deceptive lies as defined. Therefore, unless the offender explicitly states that he lied about his opinions, or intentions, they can only be included as lies if the offender later reports having lied.

As discussed above, once a lie has been discovered using the previous criteria, the current study was concerned with distinguishing which deceptive motivations are found in various personality disorders. Motivations across personality disorders were the focus of investigation in this population for several reasons. One, there is a high prevalence rate of personality disorders in forensic populations. It has been found that personality disorders in general can be up to as high as 90% (Neighbours, 1987), making this an important area of focus. In terms of specific personality disorders of importance in a forensic sample, Coid (1998) examined the percentage of offenders in a sample of maximum-security hospitals and prisons in England following serious offending. He found a high percentage of borderline (69%), antisocial (55%), narcissistic (48%), paranoid (47%), passive-aggressive (31%), and histrionic (25%) personality disorders using the SCID II personality interview (Cold, 1988). These numbers are comparable to those found in many other studies with similar samples (Brink, Doherty, and Boer, 2001). Two, although personality disorders are common in offender populations (Hare, 1983, 1991, 2006), the disorders characterized by anger, impulsivity and behavioral instability (e.g., borderline, narcissistic, and histrionic) are associated with a heightened risk for criminal behaviour, violence and recidivism (Hare, 1991, 1999; Harris, Rice, and Quinsey, 1994). From these studies it can be determined that personality disorders, particularly the antisocial, borderline, narcissistic, and histrionic that form cluster B, are important to understand when doing research with offenders. Three, in addition to prevalence and risk for criminal behaviour, personality is an important determinant of lying style, and one's style of deception is an aspect of personality (Ford, 1996). Although lying is not associated with only one type of personality or characteristic, the antisocial, histrionic, borderline, and narcissistic personality disorders have conventionally been linked with deception (Ford et al., 1988). Hence, the current study attempted to understand motivations for lying across these personality disorders in a forensic population, by means of Petitclerc and Herve's (1999) categories, with the exception of APD.

In addition, psychopathy was included for reasons delineated below. The following sections briefly describe the disorders and delineate the rationale and hypotheses of the current investigation.

NARCISSISTIC PERSONALITY DISORDER (NPD)

The DSM- IV (APA, 2000) describes NPD as a pattern of grandiosity, need for admiration, and lack of empathy. It is also associated with vulnerable self-esteem, sensitivity, intense reactions of humiliation, emptiness, dislike for criticism, and vocational irregularities due to inability to tolerate criticism or competition. Feelings of shame, intense self-criticism, and withdrawal in social situations are also documented. As a result, narcissistic persons will rearrange the external world to correspond with their internal needs (Ford et al., 1988). Due to their desire for continuous approval from others, they will attempt to present themselves in a flattering light as they crave admiration and attention (Marin et al., 1990). Consequently, they tend to exaggerate many aspects of themselves, particularly in terms of accomplishments and abilities. It is this aspect; coupled with a sense of entitlement, which can result in lying and deception, as the narcissist is typically exploitive with little consideration for others. Bursten (1972) suggests that manipulation and narcissism are intertwined. He sees manipulation as deliberate deception paired with an exhilarating feeling of putting something over on the target, a definition similar to duping delight: motivation stemming from the pleasure of deceit. Through this feat, the narcissist's feelings of worthlessness are projected onto the target, increasing their fragile self-image. Accordingly, it was expected that the narcissistic individual would be motivated to lie to heighten self-presentation, and to a lesser extent would be motivated by duping delight as its own reward.

BORDERLINE PERSONALITY DISORDER (BPD)

Borderline personality disorder (BPD) is defined by the DSM- IV (APA, 2000) as the presence of five of the nine specified criteria including those that describe impulsivity (unstable relationships, self-damaging actions, inappropriate anger, or suicidal threats), and those that discuss emotional reactivity (affective instability, identity disturbance, emptiness or boredom, and frantic efforts to avoid abandonment). A third aspect of the disorder, added only in this latest addition of the DSM, addresses the cognitive or semi-psychotic aspect of the disorder (transient stress related paranoid ideation or severe dissociative symptoms).

The borderline's deception could have several motivations, including enhancement of self-esteem, projection of guilt, and need to achieve a sense of superiority over others (Snyder, 1986). In addition, lying in borderline personality disordered individuals may be the result of poor impulse control, which in extreme situations may be indistinguishable from delusions, as the borderline individual is often included in the deceived (Ford et al., 1988). Following Petitclerc and Herve's (1999) categories, it was expected that borderlines would lie compulsively due to their poor impulse control. Compulsive lies are usually told in a very spontaneous manner. Ford (1996) theorizes on the association between persistent lying and impulse control disorders, such as kleptomania (uncontrollable stealing), gambling, and compulsive shopping:

> "The lying that is frequently observed in persons with impulse control disorders appears to be more pervasive than just the need to cover up behaviours and avoid their consequences. Pathological (or compulsive) lying may itself be an impulse control problem, and thus its association with other difficulties in impulse control may reflect the underlying psychological or brain dysfunction problems common to several syndromes" (p. 142).

In addition, borderlines may be motivated to lie for duping delight as they are motivated by a desire to obtain a sense of power (e.g., Ekman, 1997; Ford, 1996) which comes from possessing information that the other does not have. Consequently, it was predicted that they might lie for duping delight and to a lesser extent compulsively. Moreover, it may be the case, considering their affective instability that they would lie to avoid a negative evaluation.

HISTRIONIC PERSONALITY DISORDER (HPD)

Several traits are considered to be at the core of histrionic personality disorder. They include egocentricity, seductiveness, theatrical emotionality, denial of anger and hostility, and a diffuse (or global) cognitive style (Phofl, 1991). Additional traits associated with this disorder are: gregariousness, manipulativeness, low frustration tolerance, pseudo-hypersexuality, suggestibility and somatizing tendencies (Millon and Davis, 1998). The DSM- IV (APA, 2000) criteria encompass the cognitive, affective and behavioral components. It is important to note that the histrionic may be extremely insecure and sensitive to rejection (Millon and Davis, 1998). As a result, their behaviour may be interpreted as manipulative or seductive in an attempt to obtain love, support and attention (Marin et al., 1990). For these individuals, self-esteem and self-worth depend on their ability to gain the attention of others as well as their ability to attract others (Marin et al.). Given this personality structure, it was expected that histrionic offenders would lie for two reasons: one, to heighten self- presentation and two, to obtain a reward, specifically attention. This is consistent with the finding that histrionics pay more attention to performance than accuracy of the story (Ford, 1996). Furthermore, they are frequently more concerned with creating a dramatic effect or influencing people to like them (Ford, 1996). It may be that the line between wishing and reality is easily blurred (Hollender, 1971) in that they desire the subject of the lie to be true so intensely that they lie to an unsuspecting target. This allows the perpetrator to feel as though the lie is true, as they have convinced others that it is the case. Moreover, histrionics have been shown to pay attention to their emotional state (Ford et al., 1988) more than others, a phenomenon called "affective truth". This is defined as truth that feels right at the moments (Ford et al., 1988).

PSYCHOPATHIC PERSONALITY DISORDER

For numerous reasons, the examination of antisocial personality disorder (APD; American Psychological Association, 2000 [APA]) was excluded from the current investigation. Although APD is important when looking at a civil psychiatric setting (Hart, 2001) as the presence of the pathology is lower and therefore has more discriminate ability, it is of little diagnostic significance in many forensic settings where virtually everyone has a record of arrest (APA, 2000). Hart (2001) suggests that professionals should avoid overestimating the significance of antisocial behaviours in the assessment of personality disorders in a forensic population. This is the case as 50-75% of offenders typically receive a diagnosis of APD (Hare, 1996, 2006).

A more forensically relevant personality disorder diagnosis is psychopathy (Hare, 1991, 2006) in that it serves to differentiate the more problematic offenders from those with APD. Since psychopaths make up only about 15-25% of the incarcerated criminal population (see Hare, 1991), but are responsible for a disproportionate amount of crime (Hemphill, Hare, and Wong, 1998), especially of an instrumental, violent, and interpersonal nature (e.g., Hemphill et al, 1998; Hervé, Petitclerc, and Hare 1999; Porter et al., 2000). Although PCL-R scores are significantly correlated with diagnoses of APD, the relationship is asymmetrical. That is, most psychopaths meet the criteria to receive a diagnosis of APD, however, most of the offenders who are diagnosed with APD are not psychopaths (Hare, 1996, 2006; Hare and Hart, 1989). For that reason, APD can be seen as synonymous with criminality. Therefore, psychopathy was considered substantially more relevant to the following analysis than APD.

Psychopathy is a clinical construct defined by a unique constellation of affective, interpersonal, and behavioral characteristics (Hare, 1991, 2006). These characteristics include pathological lying, egocentricity, manipulativenes, deceptiveness, callousness, grandiosity, impulsivity, shallow emotions, and lack of empathy, guilt, or remorse for repeatedly violating the rights of others (Cleckley, 1976; Hare, 1991, 1996, 2006). Given their talent and tendency to deceive, psychopaths may be viewed as natural liars or performers (Ekman, 1985; Ekman, 1997). Pathological lying, deception, and manipulation are key clinical features of the psychopath (Hare, Forth, et al., 1989), especially within interpersonal relationships where they are central elements (Rogers and Cruise, 2000). Due to their desire for continuous power and approval from others (Meloy, 1988), they will attempt to present themselves in a flattering light. Consequently, they tend to exaggerate many aspects of themselves, particularly in terms of accomplishments and abilities. It is this feature, coupled with a sense of entitlement that can result in deception. Having this pervasive sense of entitlement, they may also be motivated to lie across all subcategories specified previously. In many cases the goals of a lie are to obtain money, prestige and power (Hare et al., 1989). Although, the motivations for their lies are no doubt similar to those of ordinary people, psychopaths sometimes engage in deceptive behaviour that seems baffling and self-defeating (Hare et al., 1989). Additionally, due to the link between deception and crime, it is fairly certain that psychopaths are deceptive; the question remains whether they employ different deceptive strategies than other antisocial persons. Accordingly, it was expected that the psychopathic individual would be motivated to lie for five reasons: they would lie to heighten self-presentation; they would be motivated by duping delight to put something over on someone else; they would lie compulsively; to avoid punishment, specifically egosyntonic motivations; or they would lie to obtain a reward. No differences were predicted across the other categories. In addition, it was hypothesized that the psychopath would lie more frequently, compared with other offenders. These predictions were also made due to the results of the pilot study (Petitclerc, et al., 2000) mentioned previously. In this study, the model designed by Petitclerc and Hervé (1999) was used and psychopaths were found to lie significantly more than non-psychopaths for duping delight, to avoid punishment, to heighten self-presentation, and to obtain a reward. Although the results were of importance, the sample size was small (n = 40) and, therefore, they were able to draw only tentative conclusions regarding the types of motivations used by psychopaths. The current study uses the same paradigm (Petitclerc and Hervé, 1999) with a larger sample and expands the focus to include the cluster B personality disorders described previously.

Although the motivations of personality disordered offenders for many of their lies are likely similar to non-disordered offenders, they may use a unique rationale for lying. Therefore, an attempt was made to distinguish how narcissistic, borderline, histrionic and psychopathic offenders differ in their motivations of dissimulation by comparing these groups to offenders without personality disorders.

METHOD

Participants

Participants consisted of 103 Canadian adult male inmates who had participated in research conducted in federal prisons situated around Vancouver, British Columbia from the late 1960's to 1998. The present investigation utilized archived file and videotaped information randomly selected from a preexisting database of offenders that took part in a study to validated and access psychopathy. The subjects were selected to ensure equal groups of high and low psychopaths based on the Hare Psychopathy Checklist-Revised (PCL-R; Hare, 1991). The files contained reports from mental health professionals, case management officers, police, courts, and, at times, from victims, witnesses, parole officers, and prison officers. The videotaped interviews are based on the semi-structured interview protocol from the PCL-R (Hare, 1991). They contain information about the offender's childhood, school and work history, criminal career, alcohol and drug use, intimate relationships, and index (i.e., most recent) offence.

Measures

Assessment of Personality Disorders

Personality pathology was assessed from the archived information. Subjects with an Axis I diagnosis on file were excluded from the study. Files and videos were reviewed by trained research assistants and coded for DSM-IV (APA, 2000) Axis II pathology (see Hervé, Marxsen, Petitclerc, Spidel and Hare, 2001). To be considered reliable the raters were trained using training interviews and files until they made accurate diagnosis across all the personality disorders for ten cases consecutively. The original training files were coded by a senior clinical graduate student and double rated by a master's student. Each symptom for the DSM-IV personality disorders was coded on a three-point scale (i.e., Yes, Maybe, No) and the recommended diagnostic cut-offs (see APA, 2000) were employed. The prevalence rate of the personality disorders assessed in the current sample was 22 (21.3%) borderlines, 29 (28.2%) narcissistic individuals, 6 (5.8%) histrionics, and 81 (79%) APD. Two raters assessed the files for these personality disorders. The Spearman-Brown inter-class correlation co-efficient was .92, $p < .001$ for the personality coding.

Assessment of Psychopathy

Trained raters who had completed a PCL-R (Hare, 1991) training workshop demonstrated reliability before coding the files, viewed videotapes of semi-structured interviews and reviewed file information to rate the participant on the PCL-R. The PCL-R is a reliable and valid measure of psychopathy in adult forensic populations (see reviews by Fulero, 1995; Stone, 1995). It consists of 20 items that measure the interpersonal, affective and socially deviant/lifestyle features of psychopathy. Individual items are scored on a 3-point scale (0, 1, 2), and are summed to yield a total score that can range from 0 to 40. The total score represents the degree to which an individual resembles the prototypical psychopath. Although the PCL-R measures a unitary construct, factor analyses (e.g., Hare et al., 1990; Harpur, Hakstian and Hare, 1988) have revealed that the PCL-R items form two correlated but distinct factors, one describing interpersonal and affective features (Factor 1: 8 items) and the other marking socially deviant lifestyle features (Factor 2: 9 items).

The current study employed the PCL-R as a categorical measure of psychopathy. Ninety-two of the 103 offenders had PCL-R scores available. The sample was divided into High (H: n = 46), and Low (L: n = 46) PCL-R groups, using the adult version recommended cut-off of 30 for the High group and 20 for the Low group (see Hare, 1991, 2008). Two raters coded all the PCL-R's employed in the study. The Spearman-Brown inter-class correlation co-efficient was .97, $p < .001$ for a single measure and .99, $p < .000$ for the average of the two measures.

Procedure

Source of Deception

Offender-perpetrated deception was identified by file and interview review. An offender's statement was deemed to be a lie if it was found to be inconsistent across file information and/or the videotaped interview. There were several different ways in which lies were identified. Some lies were reported in the file by a third person. In other cases, the offender himself may have confessed to lying. The coders could also detect lies by finding contradictions between two different statements made by the offender, or contradictions between the offender's statement and file information from reliable sources. The sources were deemed reliable if mental health professionals, case management officers, police, or the courts made the statements. In some rare cases, the evidence for a lie came from the coder's own judgment, as when the offender's claim was so extreme that it was deemed virtually impossible. For example, an offender who claims that, after swimming for two years, he tried out for the Canadian swimming team for the Olympic Games, however, he is not able to recollect his best times. Trained research assistants, blind to personality disorder diagnosis, followed a strict protocol and identified motivations to deceive on a three-point scale (i.e., yes, maybe, no). Each lie was categorized into one of the 10 types of motivations. Subsequently, more general judgments were made on how characteristic or pervasive particular deceptive motivations were for each offender on a 3-point scale, with 0 being not at all characteristic, 1 being characteristic in some circumstances, and 2 being very characteristic. This is the summary motive rating for the offender. Two raters were trained until they reached reliability in terms of detecting the lies and categorizing their motives. Ten training tapes and files were used. To be considered reliable the raters were trained using training interviews and. files until they accurately detected the lies and categorized their motives for ten cases consecutively. Two senior graduate students coded the training files independently and the ones used for training were those for which they had perfect agreement as to the coding. Kappa coefficients were used to assess interrater reliability on the dichotomous scores for each pathway. The reliability of detection of individual lies comparing whether or not the raters detected the same lies was .932, $p. < .000$. Both raters identified the lies 94% of the time. The Spearman-Brown inter-class correlation co-efficient was .98, $p < .01$ for the reliability of the classification of individual lies into motives. The Spearman-Brown inter-class correlation co-efficient was .94, $p < .000$ for the summary deception coding.

RESULTS

Groups of narcissistic, histrionic, and borderline offenders were compared via two tailed t-tests for the summary motive ratings to offenders who did not possess these personality disorders. The summary motive ratings were used as the overall presentation of the offender was considered the most important measure in understanding their motives. As each personality disorder was compared across 10 motivational categories to subject without that personality disorder, the Bonferroni correction was used to control type I error. Therefore, to be considered significant, p had to be equal to or less than .005. For some t-tests, the assumption of homogeneity of variance was untenable, therefore Welch's t' was used instead.

Table 1. Means and Standard.Deviations (SD) for Borderline versus Non-borderline offenders across significant motivations

	Borderline		Non-borderline	
	Mean	SD	Mean	SD
Compulsive	1.67	.49	.02	.15

Table 2. Means and Standard Deviations (SD) for Narcissistic versus Non-narcissistic offenders across significant motivations

	Narcissistic		Non-narcissistic	
	Mean	SD	Mean	SD
Duping Delight	.57	.82	.05	.23
Heightened Self-Presentation	1.63	.56	.32	.58

Table 3. Means and Standard Deviations (SD) for Histrionic versus Non-histrionic offenders across significant motivations

	Histrionic		Non-histrionic	
	Mean	SD	Mean	SD
Obtain a Reward-Attention	1.33	1.03	.39	.67
Heighten Self-Presentation	1.83	.41	.63	.79

Table 4. Means and Standard Deviations (SD) for Psychopaths versus Non-psychopath offenders across significant motivations

	Non-psychopath		Psychopath	
	Mean	SD	Mean	SD
Avoid Punishment-Egosyntonic	.20	.40	1.07	.83
Obtain a Reward	.13	.40	.57	.81
Heighten Self-Presentation	.20	.50	.87	.86
Duping Delight	.00	.00	.24	.57

Table 5. Means and Standard Deviations (SD) for Psychopaths versus Non-psychopath offenders across total number of motivations

Non-psychopath		Psychopath	
Mean	SD	Mean	SD
4.04	4.83	8.54	4.51

Table 6. Means and Standard Deviations (SD) for Borderline offenders and offenders with no personality pathology across previously significant motivations

	Borderline		Non-disordered offenders	
	Mean	SD	Mean	SD
Compulsive	1.67	.49	0.00	0.00

Table 7. Means and Standard Deviations (SD) for Narcissistic offenders and offenders with no personality pathology across previously significant motivations

	Narcissistic		Non-disordered offenders	
	Mean	SD	Mean	SD
Duping Delight	.27	.64	.00	.00
Heightened Self-Presentation	1.63	.56	.11	.42

Table 8. Means and Standard Deviations (SD) for Histrionic offenders and offenders with no personality pathology across previously significant motivations

	Histrionic		Non-disordered offenders	
	Mean	SD	Mean	SD
Obtain a Reward-Attention	1.33	1.03	0.74	0.27
Heighten Self-Presentation	1.83	.41	0.11	.42

Narcissistic offenders lied significantly more than non-narcissistic offenders for both duping delight (t'(101) = 9.49, p < .002) and heightened self-presentation (t(101) = 10.603, p < .001). No significant differences were found across the other categories. In comparison to non-histrionics, the histrionic personality disordered men lied more often to heighten self-presentation (t'(101) = 6.495, p < .001) and to obtain a reward (specifically, attention) (t(101) = 3.257, p < .002). No significant differences were found across the other categories. The borderline groups lied more compulsively (t'(101) = 11.261, p <. 001) than the non-borderlines. No significant differences were found across the other categories. Psychopaths lied more often to obtain a reward (t(90) = 3.273, p <. 002), to heighten self-presentation (t(90) = 4.599, p <. 001), and for duping delight (t(90) = 2.907, p <. 005) compared to non-psychopaths. Moreover, psychopaths lied more than nonpsychopaths to avoid punishment when the motivation could be seen as egosyntonic (t(90) = 4.621, p <. 000). In addition, psychopaths lied more frequently than nonpsychopaths (t(64)= 2.526, p < .015), and their frequency of lying was associated more strongly with high factor one score (r = .422, p <. 000) than factor two (r = .151, p <.10), which was non-significant. No significant differences were found across the other categories.

In addition, groups of individuals who were narcissistic, histrionic, and borderline were compared via two-tailed t-tests for the summary motive ratings to offenders who did not possess any personality disorders including APD (n=22). The Bonferroni correction was used to control type I error therefore p had to be equal to or less than .005. For some t-tests, the assumption of homogeneity of variance was untenable, therefore Welch's t' was used instead. A similar pattern was found. Narcissistic offenders lied significantly more than non-narcissistic offenders for both duping delight (t'(55) = 2.283, p < .003) and heightened self-presentation (t'(55) = 11.691, p < .000). No significant differences were found across the other categories. In terms of histrionic personality disordered men lied more often to heighten self-presentation (t(31) = 9.059, p < .000) and to obtain a reward (specifically, attention) (t(31) = 5.795, p < .000). No significant differences were found across the other categories. The borderline groups lied more compulsively (t'(43) = 11.726, p <. 000) than the non-borderlines. No significant differences were found across the other categories.

Table 9. Means and Standard Deviations (SD) for Borderline offenders with comorbid psychopathy and without across previously significant motivations

	Borderline		Non-borderline	
	Mean	SD	Mean	SD
Compulsive	1.86	.38	1.40	.55

Table 10. Means and Standard Deviations (SD) for Narcissistic offenders with comorbid psychopathy and without across previously significant motivations

	Narcissistic		Non-narcissistic	
	Mean	SD	Mean	SD
Duping Delight	.54	.88	.59	.80
Heightened Self-Presentation	1.85	.38	1.47	.62

Table 11. Means and Standard Deviations (SD) for Histrionic offenders with comorbid psychopathy and without across previously significant motivations

	Histrionic		Non-histrionic	
	Mean	SD	Mean	SD
Obtain a Reward-Attention	1.50	1.00	1.00	1.41
Heighten Self-Presentation	2.00	.00	1.50	.71

Some personality disorders were comorbid with psychopathy (borderline = 32%; narcissistic = 45%; histrionic = 67%), meaning that they were diagnosed as borderline, narcissistic, or histrionic as well as having a PCL-R score over 30. Therefore, groups were also compared for presence of a personality disorder across psychopaths and non-psychopathy. As each personality disorder was compared across 10 motivational categories, the Bonferroni correction was used to control type I error. Therefore, to be considered significant, p had to be equal to or less than .005. No significant differences were found when the disorders were compared in this fashion. For histrionic offenders no significant differences existed when the offenders with dual diagnosis (histrionic and psychopathy) were compared to offenders who did not receive a diagnosis of psychopathy on either of the previously significant motivations, obtain a reward ($t(4) = .516, p > .60$) or heighten self-presentation ($t(4) = 1.63, p > .15$). Narcissistic offenders displayed no significant differences existed when the offenders with dual diagnosis (narcissism and psychopathy) were compared to offenders who did not receive a diagnosis of psychopathy on either of the previously significant motivations, duping delight ($t(28) = .163, p > .85$) or heighten self-presentation ($t(28) = 1.92, p > .05$). Finally, no significant differences were found when borderline offenders with dual diagnosis (borderline and psychopathy) were compared to offenders who did not receive a diagnosis of psychopathy on the previously significant motivations, compulsive ($t(21) = 1.72, p > .10$).

DISCUSSION

It was assumed that different personality structures would possess diverse motivations for lying given that each personality type tends to maintain a characteristic manner of dealing with the truth (Ford et al., 1988). The current study found significant evidence for summary motives including compulsive, duping delight, to heighten self-presentation, to avoid punishment, and to obtain a reward. All of these occurred significantly in the psychopathic participants except for compulsive. This may be accounted for in at least two ways. The present study found that psychopaths simply lie more often in general and this suggests that it may be here that their impulse control problem expresses itself. It appears they lie more often and over more categories compared to non-psychopaths, which may be due to poor impulse control. This makes sense, as two of the criteria for diagnosing psychopathy are impulsivity and poor behavioral controls (Hare, 1991,2008) The second possibility is that compulsive lies are generally not seen as self-serving. Therefore, it may be that psychopaths' lies are recognized to be motivated by direct benefit to themselves, which appears to be the case, as they lied more to obtain a reward and heighten self-presentation.

In the present study, psychopathic offenders were found to be the main perpetrators deception to obtain a reward. Their ability to read and to manipulate situations facilitates the use of these lies, as this deception requires slightly more sophisticated strategies than with social lies. Moreover, an understanding of social contexts is required to be executed successfully (Hart and Hare, 1989). Additionally, this conning and deceit to achieve personal objectives appears most related to factor one (Hare, 1991, 2008), even in the current study. This is expected as factor one encompasses the affective and interpersonal facets of psychopathy including the conning and manipulative items (Hare, 1991,2008).

The prevalence of psychopathic individuals who lied to avoid punishment, specifically egosyntonic, may be explained in two ways. One, the motivation to lie may have been due to the fact that they tend to blame others invariably for their crimes and to use unconvincing rationalization for their behavior (Harry, 1992a, 1992b as cited in Ford, 1996). In fact, one factor found to relate to PCL: Screening Version sub criteria in the Rogers and Cruise (2000) study was denial of criminality characterized by a disavowal of criminal involvement and an externalization of responsibility (Lilienfeld, 1996) that demonstrated their tendency to blame others. Two, there are different ways of interpreting lies to avoid punishment as present in conceptions of malingering. Rogers (e.g., Rogers, 1997) describes models of malingering, which include the criminological model and the adaptational model. Although both of the categories consider malingering as either goal-oriented, serving the purpose of avoiding punishment, or as obtaining a reward, Kropp and Rogers (1993) see the criminological mode adopted by the American Psychological Association (APA) in their diagnostic manual for mental disorders (DSM-III-R; APA 1987), as perceiving the malingerer's motivation as oppositional and the result of individual characteristics such as an antisocial personality, specifically psychopathy. In contrast, the adaptational model describes the malingerer as an individual who has weighed the costs and benefits of malingering, and chooses malingering.

This category focuses on the external circumstances instead of personality characteristics. Correspondingly, offenders who dissimulate to avoid punishment can be alleged to be placing their needs above the consequences of their lies. This can be viewed as egosyntonic: a strategy more prevalent in psychopaths than non-psychopaths in the current investigation. As a result, it was found that psychopaths are more likely than non-psychopaths to lie to avoid punishment when the source is due to placing their own needs and desires above the consequences of their lies. On the other hand, non-psychopaths may not lie to avoid punishment as they realize that they have been caught, assessed the situation, and choose to be more forthcoming (Petitclerc and Hervé, 1999).

The findings that psychopaths and narcissists deceived for sheer duping delight were expected. When these individuals are feeling powerless (or bored), they may find it thrilling to con another (Ford, 1996). Both personalities take great pains to appear superior and dominate others (Bursten, 1972; Ford, 1988; Hare et al., 1989). By lying for duping delight, they are reinforcing the fact that they are intellectually superior to peers by projecting a sense of worthlessness or inferiority onto the target of the lie while engaging in conscious manipulation (Ekman, 1997; Ford, 1996). Consequently, this deception may be regarded as an ego defence mechanism to bolster their low self-esteem (Ford, 1988). Moreover, as specific personality traits (e.g., conning, grandiosity, manipulation, pathological lying, Hare, 1991, 2006) are criteria in the assessment of psychopathy the fact that they have an increased propensity to deceive and an inflated view of their ability to do so, is not surprising. In addition, Hare et al. (1989) observed that psychopaths often engage in verbal behaviour that they seem to believe is consistent with the truth as they construct it, as they "seem to know the words but not the music" (Johns and Quay, 1962 as cited in Hare, 1991, p 57). As a result, it may appear that they are lying for no obvious motivation; however, their story is consistent with how they have manipulated the situation internally.

It is important to not here that the findings with psychopaths in this study were similar to those found in a similar study with adolescent offenders (Spidel et al., 2010). In that study Individuals with a higher psychopathy score were shown to be more likely to engage in deception for duping delight, in lies to heighten self-presentation and to obtain a reward, than were those with a lower psychopathy score. It would be interesting to see if these findings generalize to the other personality disorders that where studied here (i.e. borderline, narcissistic and histrionic). As such more research in this area would be of interest,

Histrionic offenders were more apt to lie to obtain a reward compared to non-histrionic offenders; nevertheless, attention was the only significant motivational category in which this result was present. This was in line with prediction for reward obtainment. Conclusions regarding histrionics must be made tentatively due to the low prevalence in the current investigation. Their relative absence may be due to diagnostic issues, as males who have histrionic tendencies likely possess antisocial ones as well, and therefore may frequently be labeled as antisocial as these traits subsume the antisocial ones (Hamburger, Lilienfeld and Hogben, 1996). Histrionic personality disorder is a diagnosis (correctly or incorrectly) primarily ascribed to women, and it has been suggested that histrionic and antisocial traits are two sides of the same coin - the difference determined by gender. As a result, men express the underlying disorder as APD (Hart and Hare, 1989). The pathology stems from socialization, causing them to externalize their behaviour and is therefore, interpreted as antisocial (Crawford, Cohen, and Brook, 2001). The histrionic women, however, internalize the pathology as the result of socialization giving a histrionic presentation (Crawford et al., 2001). Furthermore, it has been suggested that both disorders share a common etiology but their expression is due to gender and social expectations (Guze, Woodruff and Clayton, 1971). Therefore in the current investigation, the low prevalence of histrionics may be due to the subjects displaying the antisocial presentation. As a result, a next step in studying deceptive motivations and personality will be to replicate the present investigation across genders to determine if the findings hold. Additionally, increasing the sample size will allow more histrionic offenders to be assessed.

Borderline offenders only lied across one type of motivation in this analysis - they lied compulsively, without purpose more than non-borderline offenders. This may be related to their self-destructive nature and/or poor impulse control (Ford, 1996). As compulsive lies often leave the perpetrator open for discovery, it is likely the case that only offenders with substantive impulse control difficulties would lie in this fashion. Other offenders may be able to weigh the consequences of being detected more accurately. All personality-disordered offenders in this sample engaged in lies to heighten self-presentation, with the exception of borderlines. This may be due to the fact that Cluster B and psychopathic personality disordered offenders are more likely than those without these pathologies to take the lie one step further. That is, it may not be enough for them to lie to avoid negative evaluation, or to appear normal. Due to their criminal orientation or incarceration they may believe that others perceive them as having lower status. Accordingly, they may attempt to make themselves look better than they actually are to allow them to feel equal to the target of the lie.

In terms of the model utilized in the present investigation, this study found it to be reliable in terms of ability to accurately code between raters across lies and motivations, however some subtleties were unearthed that the model did not appear to accurately pick up on. For example with borderlines who were found to lie compulsively, there were instances when the lying appeared as more of an attempt to garner sympathy from others than to fit into the compulsive category. Although somewhat similar to lying to obtain a reward, namely attention, there was a different feel to these lies in that it was not attention that they craved but a desire to be given consideration. The current model failed to differentiate these lies in borderline offenders. As such, it can be concluded that although this model accurately assessed for the majority of lies found in the present investigation and was much more appropriate for use in a forensic sample, it still requires refinement. Therefore, it appears to be a good starting place for an exploratory study of this nature but more fine-tuning should be given to the model to account for these nuances.

None of the participants in the study engaged significantly in altruistic lies. This was not surprising, given the context and the offender sample that there would be little motivation on the part of an offender to protect well-being. With exception of psychopaths, as mentioned previously, none of the offenders differed across deception to avoid punishment. This is an obvious adaptive strategy in light of the offender's environment, as they may place their needs above others and therefore use strategies to avoid punishment (Kropp and Rogers, 1993). Further, self-preservation as a motivation persists across the personality disorders studied here, and can be viewed as a natural course of action to lie in order to avoid an unpleasant consequence (Petitclerc and Hervé, 1999).

Additionally of interest is the finding that although some of the offenders with narcissistic, borderline, and histrionic personality disorders also received a diagnosis of psychopathy, their motivations couldn't be explained by the comorbidity of psychopathy. That is, the personality disorders regardless of the presence of psychopathy still displayed the motivations found in the first analysis. Hence, these motivations can not be explained by the overlap with psychopathy. This is an important step as psychopaths in the study expressed the majority of the motivations, except compulsive. For that reason, without these findings it could be argued that the differences across these disorders were due to the comorbidity with psychopathy. However, to make these conclusions more solid, sample size would have to be increased.

Careless and secretive summary motivations were not significantly detected in this study. It may be the case that these types of motivations would not be present in cluster B personality disorders but more prevalent in cluster A. Cluster A consists of the schizoid, schizotypal, and the paranoid personality disorders (APA, 2000). Cluster A personality disorders is characterized by some social detachment and odd behaviour (Siever, Bernstein and Silverman, 1991). Schizotypal can be differentiated from the others by eccentricity and perceptual or cognitive distortion (Siever et al., 1991). Paranoid personality disorder can be distinguished as one displaying pervasive distrust and suspiciousness of others, such that their motives are interpreted as malevolent (Siever et al.). Finally schizoid personality disorders are characterized by a preference for solitary activities (Siever et al.). As careless lies are ones told by the offender who does not care to give the target truthful information, they may be likely in cluster A. They can be seen as 'amotivational' because the offender has no motivation to comply with the target's desire to gain information (Petitclerc and Hervé, 1999). The secretive lie is motivated by the offender's desire to keep some personal information concealed and to avoid undesired self-disclosure (Lippard, 1988). It would be expected that both these motivations would be exhibited by cluster A offenders; hence these categories should be studied further in future research.

In addition, future research should investigate the variability in deceptive motivations across various types of psychopaths. Theory and research suggests that psychopathy might best be understood in terms of subtypes (Arieti, 1967; Blackburn and Coid, 1999; Hervé, 2002; Karpman, 1955; Millon and Davis, 1998). Recent empirical work has identified three types of psychopaths - classic, macho, and manipulative, as well a subtype that appear to mimic psychopathy, most notably pseudopsychopaths (Nerve, 2002). It would be expected that as the classic and manipulative subtypes have similar interpersonal scores, they would therefore engage in deception for similar reasons. Although both are characteristically manipulative, the later is more likely to engage in deception than all other types, especially in regards to defrauding others. On the other hand, macho and pseudo have less interpersonal skills than the other two subtypes and may therefore be less likely to engage in certain types of deception that requires more verbal skills - the basis of manipulativeness. However, unlike idiopathic psychopaths, the pseudopsychopaths, presumably having some, although limited, emotional ties to others, are more likely to use deception to protect other people. As such it may be best when discussing types of deception to assess them across subtypes of psychopaths.

A study mentioned previously has further demonstrated (Rogers and Cruise, 2000) how subtypes are important to consider when investigating psychopathy. In the Rogers and Cruise (2000) study, it appears that in the three factor model of deception (implausible presentation, denial of criminality, and conning manipulative), these 3 factors were not highly intercorrelated and were similar to the motivations found in the current study. The authors concluded that some individuals with psychopathic traits might be limited to one or two types of deception, suggesting that there may be subtypes of deception that correspond to subtypes of psychopathy. Moreover, psychopaths were three times more likely to have high levels. of the three dimensions of deception than nonpsychopaths, with the largest difference being across implausible presentation, a similar category to heighten self-presentation in the current study.

As a result, they posit that the three types of deception found in their study should be examined separately when assessing offenders. This study indicates that a necessary future step in understanding deception and psychopathy would be to examine the deception across the subtypes. Although implausible presentation was present in 97.6% of psychopaths in Rogers and Cruise (2000) study, it may or may not be present in more than one subtype, as it appears to be a strategy utilized by most psychopaths. However, denial of criminal responsibility, similar to avoiding punishment in the current study, can be seen as situational and appears to be associated with antisocial perspectives and a tendency to blame others, both central to psychopathy (Hare, 1991, 2006). Therefore, denial of criminal responsibility may be present in all the subtypes espoused by Hervé and Hare unless egosyntonic and egodystonic are separated, as done in the current study. Conning and manipulation were seen in 3 out of 4 psychopaths in the Rogers and Cruise (2000) study. It would be predicted that this strategy, similar to obtain a reward and duping delight in the current study, would be present in the classic and manipulative psychopath for reasons previously suggested. With respect to the motivational categories, personality pathology was found to mediate significantly the motivational patterns leading to offender-perpetrated deception. However, there are several limitations of the current investigation, particularly in terms of the participant pool. For some offenders, file information was readily available while for others, it was substantially less expansive; a fact that necessarily impacts assessment, decreasing reliability and validity of the detection and categorization. Moreover, in cases where the information was limited, it was occasionally necessary to omit items when assessing personality. As a result, the prevalence of personality disorders in the sample was most likely underestimated. In addition, as this was a file-based study, with interviews used to assess for psychopathy, it was sometimes difficult to code accurately for a personality disorder. A semi-structured interview, such as the Structured Clinical Interview for DSM-IV Axis II Personality Disorders, (SCID-II; First, Gibbon, Spitzer, Williams and Benjamin, 1997) would be a more accurate means of making this diagnosis and a logical next step in validating these findings. Furthermore, the offenders were selected with diverse criminal histories, from all offending levels (robberies to murder), with some offenders (e.g., those facing longer sentences) having more motivation to lie than others (e.g. to gain early release).

This leads to another limitation of the current paradigm that is, lack of investigation into differences across situations or context. Previous research has found a substantial association of deception and context (Camden et al., 1984; Lippard, 1988; Turner et al.1975), with some subjects reporting certain situations where it seemed automatic to lie. These situations focused mostly on white lies however it would be of interest to investigate whether different types of lies were more apparent and strategies more frequently employed by offenders with specific personality disorders.

Another limitation of the current study is the issue surrounding personality disorders in general. According to Davis and Millon (1999) "no other area in the study of psychopathology is fraught with more controversy than personality disorders" (p. 485). Several issues are pertinent to this concern. First, there are difficulties concerning the diagnostic criteria associated with, and the overlap between, personality disorders. For example, impulsivity and poor temper are features in several disorders, but they exist within the separate disorders for different reasons. Specifically, impulsivity is present in both antisocial and borderline personality disorders, although it has dissimilar presentation in each. Davis and Millon (1999) posit that the very behaviors that justify the most intervention (e.g., impulsivity) are the ones that possess the greatest lack of specificity. In addition, there is debate as to whether the diagnostic criteria should be descriptions of the construct, exemplars, or some combination of these (Livesley and Jackson, 1992; Shea, 1992). Shea (1992) has proposed including inferences about motivation in diagnostic criteria might serve to decrease the overlap. Furthermore, she implies that failure to consider this variable may account to some degree for the high degree of comorbidity amongst personality disorders. It may be that understanding the motivation of specific behaviours that underlie specific personality disorders, as attempted in the current investigation, will facilitate a greater ability to differentiate the personality disorders and eliminate the overlap and comorbidity as troublesome in the assessment of personality disorders. Therefore, findings from this study showing different motivations associated with specific personality disorders strengthen this argument and make a necessary first step in the understanding of motivations of behaviour as a variant across personality disorders.

Second are concerns related to the boundaries between the personality disorders and the Axis I disorders (e.g., schizoid personality disorder and schizophrenia; borderline personality disorder and mood disorders; Davis and Millon, 1999). It has been suggested that it is of critical importance to separate offenders with an Axis I disorder, as it can substantially change or confound the offender's presentation (Hart, 2001; Widiger, 1989). This is of particular concern in a forensic population where personality disorders are frequently comorbid with Axis I disorders (Trestman, 2000). Therefore, researchers assume that when both are present simultaneously, the Axis I disorders should receive diagnostic primacy. Conversely, it is very important to consider how personality disorders influence Axis I disorders. Although participants possessing an Axis I pathology were excluded from this study, it is unclear as to whether personality disorders linked with Axis I are sub-clinical manifestations or predispositions to more severe Axis I disorders. There is considerable disagreement in the literature (see Livesley, Schroeder, Jackson and Jang, 1994) as to whether these Axes are distinct due to two etiologies or whether they possess similar etiologies with importance placed on both biogenetic and psychosocial. Therefore, the motivations for deception may be due to the influence of one Axis on the other or it may best be represented as two distinct etiologies. It is due to this confusion that participants with Axis I pathologies were excluded from the current study. However further studies may wish to assess whether the comorbidity of certain Axis I and Axis II disorders are distinct, or similar in terms of motivations to offenders with only Axis II pathologies, as investigated here. It has additionally been suggested (Hart, 2001) that individuals focusing on personality disorders should indicate the presence of Axis I and discuss how it influences the presentation of personality disorders.

The present findings suggest that what may separate the personality disorders are not the behaviours evidenced by each, but the underlying motivation a central and driving force behind the behaviours. Although similarities do exist between motivations across the four personality disorders considered in this study, there are also distinct and unique differences across the categories. For example, narcissistic offenders lied for duping delight compared with non-narcissistic offenders. Borderlines lied compulsively more than non-borderlines. On the other hand, cluster B personality disorders have several common traits. For instance, both narcissistic and histrionic offenders lied to heighten self-presentation. Nevertheless, their differences are determined by overt behaviors (Ford, 1996), although their underlying structures are similar (Kernberg, 1975). For example, borderlines may display impulsivity that is related to self-defeating behaviour, whereas antisocial or psychopaths may be impulsive in an outwardly destructive way towards others or society. Psychopathy proves to be the exception in this case as it is associated with the use of all motivations found in this study to a significant degree (with the exception of compulsive). This is not surprising as the PCL is expected to assess cluster B generally, but psychopathy specifically (Hart and Hare, 1989). As a result, findings that psychopaths display all of the motivations exhibited by other cluster B is expected as the criteria used to define the antisocial, borderline, narcissistic and histrionic personality disorders, are similar to those used in the diagnosis of psychopathy (Hart and Hare, 1989).

Notwithstanding the above limitations, the present findings have implications for assessing an offender's credibility, if the likely deceptive motivations of a particular type of offender are understood and known, as the interviewer can be on guard for these types of lies. Further investigation may give insight into which situations certain offenders are likely to lie. Assessment procedures can be tailored accordingly to facilitate an interviewer's ability to detect offender lies. For example, knowing that a narcissistic offender is likely to lie to heighten self-presentation in an interview can alert them to probe areas where he is describing situations that make him look better than normal. Therefore, it is important to be mindful of differing lie content when interviewing inmates with various Axis 11 diagnoses, knowing that the likelihood of certain lies arising varies as a function of personality disorder. Although understanding the motivations of deception may aid in assessing the credibility of statements made by the offenders in various situations, it may also raise new questions and controversies. On one hand, knowing that a psychopathic offender may lie to heighten their self-presentation or to dupe the target may cause the psychologist working with them to be more vigilant and wary of their claims of improvement (Kosson, Gacono and Bodholdt, 2000). This may be beneficial in that it will decrease the instances of parole granted on the report of a misled psychologist who incorrectly attests to the successful recovery of a manipulative psychopath (Hare, 1993). On the other hand, offenders who are assessed as psychopathic and who may benefit from therapy may be incorrectly assessed as not having profited due to being labeled psychopathic.

In addition to the issue of psychopaths and treatment, is the matter of treatment for all offenders. Although lying is a cultural normality and is a frequent occurrence in daily life, it becomes pathological when it is destructive to a person's everyday life (Ford et al. 1988) and may require intervention. Lying has many determinants including biological, development, and social (Ford, et al.) that necessarily impacts the method of treatment chosen by the therapist. Although lying is rarely the central reason for therapy, it can be of benefit to intervene when lying is determined to be pathological or to be interfering with the therapeutic process. With respect to treatment, lying may impede progress or cause the therapist to feel that substantiated gains have been made (Rogers and Cruise, 2000). In order to address lying in these individuals, one needs to individualize the intervention according to the symptoms it is accompanied by (Ford et al.). Although psychologists are in disagreement as whether to treat the deception before the other issues at hand (Kernberg, 1975), or whether-the lie must be seen in the context of the other needs of the client (Kohut, 1984), the necessity for individualized treatment is agreed upon. Therefore, empirical studies investigating deceptive motivations of personality-disordered offenders will facilitate a better understanding of their treatment needs so that they can be tailored to the individual client to address the underlying problems causing them to be motivated to lie. As certain personality disorders are associated with lying more frequently (Ford et al.), it is important to determine the types of lies typically seen in these individuals to avoid stagnation in therapy and enable the therapeutic process to evolve.

REFERENCES

American Psychiatric Association. (2000). Diagnostic and statistical manual of mental disorders (4th ed.) text-revision. Washington, D.C: APA.

American Psychiatric Association. (1987). Diagnostic and Statistical Manual of Mental Disorders, 3rd edition Revised (DSM-III-R). Washington, DC: American Psychiatric Press.

Arieti, S. (1967). The intrapsychic self.- Feelings, cognition, and creativity in the health and mental illness. New York, NY: Basic Books.

Austin, J. S.(1992). The detection of fake good and fake bad on the MMPI-2. *Educational and Psychological Measurement*, 52 (3), 669-674.

Bagby, R. M., Rogers, R., and Buis, T. (1994). Detecting malingered and defensive responding on the MMPI-2 in a forensic inpatient sample. *Journal of Personality Assessment*, 62, 191-203.

Bagby, R. M., Rogers, R., Buis, T., and Kalemba, V. (1994). Malingered and defensive response styles on the MMPI-2: An examination of validity scales. *Assessment*, 1 (1), 31-38.

Blackburn, R., and Coid, J. (1999). Empirical clusters of DSM-IV personality disorders in violent offenders. *Journal of Personality Disorders*, 13 (1), 18-34.

Bursten, B. (1972). The manipulative personality. Archive of General Psychiatry, 26, 318-321. Brink, J. H., Doherty, D., and Boer, A. (2001). Mental disorder in federal offenders: A Canadian prevalence study. *International Journal of Law and Psychiatry*, 24 (4-5), 339-356.

Camden, C., Motley, M. T., and Wilson, A. (1984). White lies in interpersonal communications: A taxonomy and preliminary investigation of social motivations. *Western Journal of Speech Communications*, 48, 309-325.

Chaplin, J. P. (1985). *Dictionary of Psychology* (2nd ed.). Dell: New York.

Cleckley, H. M. (1976). The Mask of Sanity (5`h ed.). St. Louis, MO: Mosby.

Coid, J. W. (1998). Axis II disorders and motivation for serious criminal behavior. In A. E. Skodol, (Ed.), Psychopathology and violent crime (pp. 53-97). Washington, DC, US: American Psychiatric Press, Inc.

Cornell, D. G., Warren, J., Hawk, G., Stafford E., Oran, G., and Pine, D. (1996). Psychopathy in instrumental and reactive violent offenders. *Journal of Consulting and Clinical Psychology*, 64, 783-790.

Crawford, T. N. Cohen, P., and Brook, J. S. (2001). Dramatic-erratic personality disorder symptoms: II. Developmental pathways from early adolescence to adulthood. *Journal of Personality Disorders*, 15 (4), 336-350.

Davis, R. D., and Millon, T. (1999). Models of personality and its disorders. In T. Millon, P. H. Blaney, and R. D. Davis (Eds.), Oxford textbook of psychopathology: Oxford textbooks in clinical psychology (4th ed., pp. 485-522). Oxford: Oxford University Press.

DePaulo, B., and Jordan, A. (1982). Age changes in deceiving and detecting deceit. In R.S. Feldman (Ed.), Development of nonverbal behavior in children (pp. 150-180). New York: Springer.

DePaulo, B. M., and Kirkendol, S. E. (1989). The motivational impairment effect in the communication of deception. In J. C. Yuille (Ed.), Credibility assessment (pp. 51-70). Boston: Kluwer Academic.

Ekman, P. (1985). Telling Lies: Clues to deceit in the marketplace, politics, and marriage. New York: WW Norton and Company.

Ekman, P. (1997). Deception, lying and demeanor. In D. F. Halpen and A. E. Voiskounsky (Eds.), States of mind: American and post-Soviet perspectives on contemporary issues in psychology (pp. 93-105). New York: Oxford University.

Ekman, P., and Frank, M. G. (1993). Lies that fail. In M. Lewis and C. Saarni (Eds.), Lying and deception in everyday life (pp. 184-200). New York: Guilford.

Ekman, P., and O'Sullivan, M. (1991). Who can catch a liar? *American Psychologist*, 46 (9), 913-920.

First, M.B., Gibbon, M., Spitzer, R.L., Williams, B.W., and Benjamin, L.S. (1997). Structured Clinical Interview for DSM-IV Axis-11 Personality Disorders. Washington, DC: American Psychiatric.

Ford, C.V. (1996). Lies! Lies!! Lies!!! The psychology of deceit. Washington, DC: American Psychiatric Press.

Ford, C.V., King, B.H., and Hollender, M.H. (1988). Lies and Liars: Psychiatric aspects of prevarication. *American Journal of Psychiatry*, 145 (5), 554-562.

Fulero, S. M. (1995). Review of the Hare Psychopathy Checklist- Revised. In J. C. Conoley and J. C. Impara (Eds.), Twelfth mental measurements yearbook (pp. 453-454). Lincoln, NE: Buros Institute.

Guze, S.B., Woodruff, R.A., and Clayton, P.J. (1971). Hysteria and antisocial behavior: Further evidence of an association. *American Journal of Psychiatry*, 127 (7), 957-960.

Hamburger, M. E., Lilienfeld, S. 0., and Hogben, M. (1996). Psychopathy, gender, and gender roles: Implications for antisocial and histrionic personality disorders. *Journal of Personality Disorders*, 10 (1), 41-55.

Hample, D. (1980). Purposes and effects of lying. *Southern Speech Communication Journal*, 46, 33-47.

Hare, R.D. (1983). Diagnosis of antisocial personality disorder in two prison populations. *American Journal of Psychiatry*, 140 (7), 887-890.

Hare, R.D. (1991). Manual for the Hare Psychopathy Checklist-Revised. Toronto, Ontario, Canada: Multi-Health Systems.

Hare, R.D. (1993). Without conscience: the disturbing world of the psychopaths among us. New York: Pocket Books.

Hare, R.D. (1996). Psychopathy: A clinical construct whose time has come. *Criminal Justice and Behavior*, 23 (1), 25-54.

Hare, R. D. (1999). Psychopathy as a risk factor for violence. Psychiatric Quarterly, 70(3), 181-197.

Hare, R. D. (2006). Psychopathy: A clinical and forensic overview. Psychiatric Clinics of North America, 29(3), 709-724.

Hare, R. D. (2008). Hare Psychopathy Checklist-Revised (2nd Edition) (PCL-R). In B. Cutler (Ed.), *Encyclopedia of psychology and law*. Thousand Oaks CA: Sage Publications.

Hare, R. D., Cox, D. N., and Hart, S. D. (1989). PCL:SV scoresheet. Unpublished measure, University of British Columbia, Vancouver, Canada.

Hare, R.D., Forth, A.E., and Hart, S.D. (1989). The psychopath as prototype for pathological lying and deception. In J.C.Yuille, (Ed.). Credibility assessment (pp. 25-49). Boston : Kluwer Academic.

Hare, R.D., Harpur, T.J., Hakstian, A.R., Forth, A.E., Hart, S.D., and Newman, J.P. (1990). The revised Psychopathy Checklist: Reliability and factor structure. *Psychological Assessment*, 2 (3), 338-341.

Harpur, T.J., Hakstian, A.R., and Hare, R.D. (1988). Factor structure of the Psychopathy Checklist. *Journal of Consulting and Clinical Psychology* 56 (5), 741-747.

Hart, S.D. (2001). Forensic Issues. In Livesley, W.J. (Ed.), Handbook of personality disorders: Theory, research, and treatment (pp. 555-569). New York: Guilford Press.

Hart, S.D., and Hare, R.D. (1989). Discriminant validity of the Psychopathy Checklist in a forensic psychiatric population. *Psychological Assessment*, 1 (3), 211-218.

Harris, G.T., Rice, M.E., and Quinsey, V. L. (1994). Psychopathy as a taxon: Evidence that psychopaths are a discrete class. *Journal of Consulting and Clinical Psychology*, 62, 387-397.

Harry, B. (1992a). Criminal's explanations of their criminal behaviour, I: the contribution of criminologic variables. *Journal of Forensic Science*, 37, 1327-1333.

Harry, B. (1992b). Criminal's explanations of their criminal behaviour, II: a possible role for psychopathy. *Journal of Forensic Science*, 37, 1334-1340.

Hemphill, J.F., Hare, R.D., and Wong, S. (1998). Psychopathy and recidivism: A review. *Legal and Criminological Psychology*, 3 (1), 139-170.

Hervé, H. F. (2002, June). Criminal Psychopathy and its subtypes: Implications for the assessment of risk as a function of psychopathy. In S. Porter (Chair), Investigations of aggression and violence as a function of psychopathy in both children and adults. Symposium conducted at the 62nd Annual Convention of the Canadian Psychology Association. Vancouver, British Columbia.

Hervé, H. F., Marxen, D., Petitclerc, A. M., Spidel, A. L., and Hare R. D. (2001). Crime Manual. Unpublished coding manual, University of British Columbia, Vancouver, Canada.

Hervé, H. F., Petitclerc, A. M., and Hare R. D. (1999, May). Violence-related motivations in psychopathic and non-psychopathic offenders: Egosyntonic versus egodystonic motivation. Poster session presented at the 60th Annual Convention of the Canadian Psychological Association, Halifax, Nova Scotia.

Hollender, M.H. (1971). Hysterical personality. *Comments on Contemporary Psychiatry*, 1 (1), 17-24.

Johns, J. H., and Quay, H.C. (1962). The effect of social reward on verbal conditioning in psychopathic and neurotic military offenders. *Journal of Consulting Psychology*, 26, 217-220.

Karpman, B. (1955). Criminal psychodynamics: A platform. *Archives of Criminal Psychodynamics*, 1, 3-100.

Kernberg, 0. (1975). Borderline conditions and pathological narcissism. New York: Jason Aronson.

Kohut, H. (1984). How does analysis cure? In Goldberg A. and Stepansky, P. (Eds.). University of Chicago Press (pp. 72-72).

Kosson, D.S., Gacono, C.B. and Bodholdt, R.H. (2000). Assessing psychopathy: Interpersonal aspects and clinical interviewing. In C.B. Gacono (Ed.). The clinical and forensic assessment-of psychopathy: A practitioner's guide. The LEA. series in personality and clinical psychology (pp. 203-229). Mahwah, N.J.: Lawrence Erlbaum Associates.

Kropp, P.R., and Rogers, R. (1993). Understanding malingering: motivation, method and detection. In M. Lewis and C. Saarni (Eds.), Lying and deception in everyday life (pp. 201-216). New York: Guilford.

Krueger, R. F., and Tackett, J. L. (2003). Personality and psychopathology: Working toward the bigger picture. *Journal of Personality Disorders*, 17, 109–128.

Lilienfeld, S. O. (1996). The MMPI-2 antisocial practices scale: Construct validity and comparison with the psychopathic deviate scale. Psychological Assessment, 8, 281-293.

Lippard, P.V. (1988). "Ask me no questions, I'll tell you no lies": Situational exigencies for interpersonal deception. *Western Journal of Speech Communication*, 52, 91-103.

Livesley, W. J., and Jackson, D. N. (1992). Guidelines for developing, evaluating, and revising the classification of personality disorders. *Journal of Nervous and Mental Disease*, 180, 609-618.

Livesley, W. J., Schroeder, M. L., Jackson, D. N., and Jang, K. L. (1994). Categorical distinctions in the study of personality disorders: Implications for classification. *Journal of Abnormal Psychology*, 103, 6-17.

Marin, D., Frances, A. J., and Widiger, T. A. (1990). Personality disorders. In A. Stoudemire (Ed.). Clinical psychiatry for medical students (pp. 137-156). Philadelphia: Lippincott.

Meloy, J. R. (1988). The psychopathic mind: Origins, dynamics, and treatment. Northvale, NJ, US: Jason Aronson, Inc.

Miller, G.R. (1983). Telling it like it isn't and not telling it like it is: Some thoughts on deceptive communication. In J.I. Sisco (Ed.), The Jensen lectures: Contemporary communication studies (pp. 91-116). Tampa: University of South Florida.

Miller, G.R., and Stiff, J.B. (1993). Deceptive communication. Newbury Park, CA.: Sage Publications.

Millon, T., and Davis, R. D. (1998). Ten subtypes of psychopathy. In T. Millon, E. Simonson, M. Burket-Smith, and R. Davis (Eds.), Psychopathy: antisocial, criminal. and violent behavior (pp. 161-170). New York: Guilford Press.

Neighbours, H. (1987). The prevalence of mental disorder in Michigan prisons. *DIS Newsletter*, 4, 8-11.

Paulhus, D. L., Bruce, M. N., and Trapnell, P. D. (1995). Effects of self-presentation strategies on personality profiles and their structure. *Personality and Social Psychology Bulletin*, 21 (2), 100-108.

Petitclerc, A. M., and Hervé H. F. (1999). Deceptive Motivations: Coding Instructions. Unpublished Manuscript, University of British Columbia, Vancouver, Canada.

Petitclerc, A.M., Hervé, H.F., Hare, R.D., and Spidel, A. (2000). Psychopaths'reasons to deceive. Poster session presented at the American Psychology-Law Society, Division 41 of the American Psychological Association, New Orleans.

Pfohl, B. (1991). Histrionic personality disorder: A review of available data and recommendations for DSM-IV. *Journal of Personality Disorders*, 5 (2), 150-166.

Pfohl, B., Coryell, W., Zimmerman, M., and Stangl, D. (1986). DSM-III personality disorders: Diagnostic overlap and internal consistency of individual DSM-III criteria. *Comprehensive Psychiatry*, 2 (1), 21-34.

Porter, S., Fairweather, D., Drugge, J., Hervé, H., Birt, A., and Boer, D.P. (2000). Profiles of psychopathy in incarcerated sexual offenders. *Criminal Justice and Behavior*, 27 (2), 216- 233.

Rogers, R. (1997). Clinical assessments of malingering and deception (2nd Ed.). New York: Guilford.

Rogers, R., and Cruise, K.R. (2000). Malingering and deception among psychopaths. In C.B. Gacono (Ed.). The clinical and forensic assessment of psychopathy: A practitioner's guide. The LEA series in personality and clinical psychology (pp. 269-284). Mahwah, N.J.: Lawrence Erlbaum Associates.

Shea, M. T. (1992). Some characteristics of the axis II criteria sets and their implications for the assessment of personality disorders. *Journal of Personality Disorders*, 6, 377-381.

Siegman, A.W., and Reynolds, M.A. (1983). Self-monitoring and speech in feigned and unfeigned lying. *Journal of Personality and Social Psychology*, 45 (6), 1325-1333.

Siever, L. J., Bernstein, D. P., and Silverman, J. M. (1991). Schizotypal Personality Disorder. *Journal of Personality Disorders*, 5 (2), 178-193.

Stone, G. L. (1995). Review of the Hare Psychopathy Checklist Revised. In J. C. Conoley and J. C. Impara (Eds.), Twelfth mental measurements yearbook (pp. 453-454). Lincoln, NE: Buros Institute.

Snyder, S. (1986). Pseudologia fantastica in the borderline patient. *American Journal of Psychiatry*, 143 (10), 1287-1289.

Stouthamer-Loeber, M. (1986). Lying as a problem behavior in children: a review. *Clinical Psychology Review*, 6, 267-289.

Trestman, R. L. (2000). Behind Bars: Personality Disorders. *Journal of the American Academy of Psychiatry and the Law*, 28, 232-235.

Turner, R.E., Edgley, C., and Olmstead, G. (1975). Information control in conversations: Honesty is not always the best policy. *Kansas Journal of Sociology*, 11, 69-89.

Widiger, T.A and Frances, A. (1988). Personality Disorders. In J.A.Talbott, R.E.Hales, S. Yudofsky, (Eds.), Textbook of Psychiatry (pp. 621-648). Washington, DC, American Psychiatric Press.

Widiger, T.A and Samuel, D. (2005). Diagnostic Categories or Dimensions? A Question for the Diagnostic and Statistical Manual of Mental Disorders—Fifth Edition. *Journal of Abnormal Psychology*. 2005, Vol. 114, No. 4, 494–504.

Widiger, T.A. (1989). The categorical distinction between personality and affective disorders. *Journal of Personality Disorders*, 5, 386-398.

INDEX

A

Abraham, 233, 241
abstraction, 171
abuse, xiii, 295, 296, 298, 299, 300
academic learning, 210, 286
academic motivation, 83, 126, 129, 142, 189, 190, 202, 310
academic performance, xii, 74, 127, 139, 210, 212, 214, 221, 271, 279, 282
academic success, xi, 83, 189, 210
academic tasks, 76
access, 24, 43, 93, 105, 201, 213, 223, 323
accommodation, 8, 20
accounting, 116, 139, 191, 192, 198, 199, 200, 230
acquaintance, 47
acquisition phase, 14
activism, 37
actuality, 157
adaptability, 279
adaptation, 17, 19
adjustment, 104, 254, 305
adolescent female, 130
adolescents, xiii, 104, 141, 142, 175, 181, 185, 191, 295, 296, 297, 298, 299, 300, 301, 303, 304, 305
adrenal gland, 2
adrenal glands, 2
adult obesity, 104
adulthood, 122, 218, 336
adults, viii, 46, 85, 86, 87, 89, 91, 95, 103, 124, 228, 230, 243, 296, 297, 299, 300, 301, 315, 338
advancement, 40, 112
advertisements, 33, 93
advocacy, 273
aesthetic, 5, 108
aesthetics, 115
affective disorder, 340
affective experience, 179

affirming, 153
African-American, 174
age, xi, 7, 12, 65, 87, 90, 91, 130, 131, 142, 191, 193, 200, 201, 203, 204, 210, 212, 214, 215, 218, 219, 220, 222, 246, 247, 251, 252, 253, 274, 285, 300, 308
agencies, 95, 101
aggression, 62, 313, 338
aggressive behavior, 297
AIDS, 40, 57
alcohol abuse, 295
alcohol problems, 304
alcohol use, 305
algorithm, 94
altruism, 36, 37, 39, 48
altruistic behavior, 35, 37, 38, 44
ambivalence, 297, 299, 302
American Educational Research Association, 81, 83
American Psychiatric Association, 336
American Psychological Association, 122, 322, 329, 339
anger, 320, 321
ANOVA, 250, 276
antisocial behavior, 337
antisocial personality, 322, 329, 337
anxiety, xi, xii, 179, 210, 213, 216, 217, 219, 220, 221, 222, 233, 240, 271, 276, 279, 280, 282, 286
anxiety disorder, 233, 240
APA, 320, 321, 322, 324, 329, 332, 336
appetite, 19, 229
appraisals, 211
ARC, viii, 61, 79
architect, 111, 114
architects, 113, 114, 115, 116, 121
arousal, 14
arrest, 322
arthritis, 91
aspiration, 145, 165

assessment, vii, viii, xiii, 2, 16, 18, 23, 24, 25, 76, 83, 100, 102, 103, 107, 110, 111, 113, 114, 115, 117, 119, 122, 143, 155, 192, 193, 194, 195, 197, 202, 211, 220, 267, 280, 304, 308, 311, 312, 313, 314, 322, 330, 333, 334, 337, 338, 339, 340
assets, 28, 83
assimilation, 88
asymptomatic, 90, 92
athletes, 184
Attention Deficit Hyperactivity Disorder, 297
attribution, 151, 167, 246, 247, 248, 249, 251, 252, 253, 254, 260
attribution theory, 167, 254, 260
authenticity, 112, 117
authority, 297, 301
autonomy, xii, xiii, 42, 171, 173, 174, 175, 176, 177, 178, 179, 181, 182, 183, 184, 185, 186, 252, 262, 265, 271, 272, 273, 274, 275, 276, 280, 281, 282, 295, 301, 302, 313, 315
autopsy, 2
aversion, 8
avoidance, 4, 144, 154, 155, 164, 212, 285, 286, 287, 288, 291, 313
awareness, 115, 117, 118, 211, 212, 231, 314

B

back pain, 91
Bangladesh, 131
barriers, 229, 231, 234, 236
base, 104, 233, 235, 238, 296, 300
basic needs, 273, 312
behavioral change, 90, 163, 241
behavioral dimension, xii, 283, 284
behavioral intentions, 148, 186, 230
behavioral sciences, 223, 286
behavioral theory, 300
behaviors, 35, 36, 37, 38, 41, 45, 47, 48, 86, 88, 89, 90, 94, 95, 99, 100, 101, 102, 104, 111, 112, 127, 128, 130, 153, 154, 156, 182, 183, 185, 228, 230, 243, 287, 288, 291, 293, 297, 299, 301, 333, 334
Beijing, 32, 142
belief systems, 172, 181
benefits, ix, xi, 8, 13, 18, 28, 36, 38, 39, 40, 41, 48, 92, 100, 125, 127, 139, 140, 148, 151, 154, 163, 220, 228, 229, 232, 233, 238, 239, 240, 243, 312, 329
bias, 75, 77, 101, 164, 166, 167, 249
Big Five traits, 47
binge drinking, 301
biological systems, 3
blame, ix, 147, 151, 163, 314, 329, 333
blood, viii, 2, 35, 36, 37, 39, 40, 42, 43, 45

blueprint, 141
BMI, 86, 87, 91
body dissatisfaction, 104
body weight, viii, 85, 86, 87, 89, 99, 103
bonding, 8
borderline personality disorder, 321, 333, 334
boredom, 27, 76, 263, 321
brain, 14, 47, 321
brand image, 27
Brazil, 32
break-even, 261
breast cancer, 47, 123
burnout, 48
business education, 292
businesses, 16, 17
bystander effect, 38

C

cabbage, 194
calculus, 109
caloric restriction, 89, 99
Cambodia, 131
campaigns, 244
cancer, 48, 233, 240
candidates, 291
cardiovascular disease, 91
career prospects, 43
career success, 154
case study, 30, 31, 33, 122, 124
cash, 42
categorization, 333
category a, 233, 315, 316, 317
category b, 235
causal attribution, 142, 149, 150, 151, 166
causal judgments, 151, 159
causal relationship, 25, 26, 127, 139, 253, 265
causality, 42, 101, 150, 167, 185, 200, 246, 247, 248, 251, 252, 253, 281, 282
causation, 254
CDC, 228
CFI, 68, 69, 70, 72, 133, 135, 275, 291
challenges, xiii, 12, 86, 101, 234, 253, 295
charitable organizations, 40, 50, 51
charities, viii, 35, 38, 40, 51
Chicago, 56, 142, 338
child rearing, 280
childhood, 142, 323
childrearing, 282
children, x, 2, 18, 22, 62, 63, 80, 83, 84, 123, 128, 129, 137, 142, 143, 144, 170, 178, 187, 188, 189, 190, 191, 192, 193, 194, 195, 196, 197, 198, 199,

200, 201, 202, 203, 204, 205, 218, 245, 247, 248, 252, 255, 315, 337, 338, 340
China, 131
chronic diseases, 91
citizens, 266
citizenship, 41, 48
classes, 7, 41, 65, 179, 184, 193, 245, 281
classification, 7, 10, 91, 103, 325, 339
classroom, 143, 145, 178, 182, 184, 195, 201, 204, 213, 224, 252, 253, 254, 271, 273, 280, 281, 282, 293, 310
classroom environment, 213, 281, 282
classroom settings, 182, 271
classroom teacher, 280
classroom teachers, 280
clients, xiii, 23, 262, 295, 302
climate, xii, 8, 17, 170, 173, 176, 178, 179, 182, 184, 252, 271, 276, 280, 281
climates, 182
clinical depression, 229, 242
clinical psychology, 336, 339, 340
clinical trials, 87, 103, 300, 305
cluster analysis, xii, 112, 271, 275, 280
clustering, 279, 280
clusters, xii, 19, 21, 28, 112, 271, 274, 276, 279, 280, 336
coding, 233, 234, 235, 324, 325, 338
coercion, 180, 189, 190
cognition, 84, 142, 166, 167, 182, 272, 286, 312, 336
cognitive abilities, 109, 114, 188, 191, 195, 196, 197, 198, 199, 200
cognitive ability, x, 187, 192
cognitive development, 123, 253
cognitive dissonance, 31, 156
cognitive effort, 180, 199
cognitive function, 165
cognitive models, 111
cognitive process, 4, 119
cognitive skills, 180, 188, 192, 195, 196, 198, 199, 200, 201, 202
cognitive style, 321
cognitive theory, 171, 243, 272
cognitive variables, 184, 205
collaboration, 61, 65, 110, 224, 258, 301
collectivism, 84, 118, 124, 128
college students, 223, 224, 286, 293, 298, 305
commercial, vii, 86, 87, 89, 90, 91, 93, 95, 99, 100, 101, 102, 104, 105
common law, 91
communication, 14, 16, 29, 30, 213, 262, 337, 339
communities, 62, 63, 65, 79, 80
community, 40, 41, 42, 45, 46, 64, 70, 71, 72, 73, 80, 83, 93, 103, 112, 232, 240, 245, 296

comorbidity, 331, 334
comparative advantage, viii, 2
Comparative Fit Index, 68, 275
compensation, 42, 266, 268, 269
competition, 39, 62, 74, 75, 189, 194, 246, 320
competitive sport, 180
competitiveness, 62, 74
complement, 45, 46
complexity, 121
compliance, 87, 164, 189, 194
complications, 87
composition, ix, 107, 118, 119
comprehension, 188, 191, 192, 193, 198, 199, 201, 204, 205
compulsory education, 62
computer, 153, 249, 252
computing, 92
conceptual model, 13, 14
conceptualization, 117, 118, 272
conditioning, 338
conduct disorder, 297
conference, 34
confidentiality, 132, 249, 274
configuration, 28
conflict, 45, 46, 51, 62, 177, 312, 313, 315, 318
conflict avoidance, 313
conformity, 94, 194
congruence, 28
conscious awareness, 120
consensus, 110
consent, 64, 93, 105, 132, 249, 286
conservation, 24, 25
construct validity, viii, 61, 65, 66, 68, 92, 293, 308
construction, 18, 32, 107, 109, 122
constructivism, 273
consulting, 233, 262
consumer loyalty, 26, 33
consumers, 8, 13, 16
consumption, vii, 1, 14, 16, 18, 44, 89, 90, 95
consumption patterns, 18
content analysis, 233, 238, 240, 242
contingency, 170
control condition, 105, 152, 153, 154, 155, 158, 160, 161
controlled studies, 300
controversies, 335
convention, vii, 2, 24, 26, 34
convergence, 7
conversations, 300, 340
conviction, 265, 266, 267
cooperation, 39, 44
correlation, 25, 105, 134, 215, 288, 291, 308, 324, 325

correlations, x, 37, 94, 97, 116, 133, 134, 140, 210, 275, 276, 280, 289, 291, 292
cost, 36, 38, 42, 65, 86, 143, 148, 160, 163, 259, 260, 262, 263, 264, 267, 300
cost of living, 42
creative potential, 124
creative process, 108
creative thinking, 108, 110
creativity, vii, viii, 107, 108, 109, 110, 111, 112, 113, 114, 115, 116, 117, 118, 119, 120, 121, 122, 123, 124, 246, 336
creativity training, ix, 107
crimes, 312, 329
criminal activity, 319
criminal behavior, 336
criminal justice system, 315
criminality, 314, 322, 329, 332
criticism, 180, 181, 320
Croatia, 121
cross-cultural comparison, 141
cross-sectional study, 253, 274
crowding out, 42, 43, 50, 260
cues, 119
cultural differences, 32, 81, 83, 126, 129, 130, 137, 138, 140
cultural heritage, 24
cultural influence, 128
cultural norms, 175
cultural values, 118, 138, 140, 212
culture, 6, 13, 21, 22, 62, 82, 84, 109, 118, 124, 126, 127, 128, 129, 131, 133, 136, 137, 138, 139, 140, 142, 143, 144, 145, 175, 308, 309
cure, 338
cures, 6
curricula, 181
curriculum, 79, 109, 121, 124, 130, 131, 138, 182, 188, 200, 203, 252, 254
curriculum development, 182
customers, 26
cycles, 2

D

data analysis, 103
data collection, 90, 93, 101, 132, 249, 253
data set, 218, 314
database, 323
deceivers, 319
decision-making process, 19, 22, 23, 267
decoding, x, 187, 188, 192, 194, 195, 197, 198, 199, 204
deduction, 161
deep learning, 76

defects, 39
defence, 330
deficiencies, 188
deficiency, 2, 3
degenerate, 150
delusions, 319, 321
demographic characteristics, vii, 1, 29
demographic data, 64
dendrogram, 276
denial, 297, 321, 329, 332, 333
Department of Education, 61, 65, 132, 141
Department of Health and Human Services, 242, 243
dependent variable, 133, 136, 279
depression, xi, 227, 228, 229, 231, 232, 233, 234, 235, 238, 239, 240, 241, 242, 243, 244, 282
depressive symptoms, 229, 239, 297
deprivation, 193
depth, 14, 111, 223
designers, 110
detachment, 332
detection, xiii, 123, 311, 313, 325, 333, 336, 339
detention, 299
detoxification, 297
developmental change, 140, 202
developmental process, 301
developmental psychology, 255
diabetes, 172, 233, 240
Diagnostic and Statistical Manual of Mental Disorders, 336, 340
diagnostic criteria, 333
dichotomy, 9, 11, 261
diet, 2, 90, 104
dietary intake, 89
dieting, viii, 85, 103, 183
dimensionality, vii, 2
direct cost, 267
direct measure, 104, 181, 262
directionality, 111, 112
disclosure, 313, 332
discomfort, 114, 318
discontinuity, 82
diseases, 233, 304
disorder, 229, 254, 297, 300, 321, 325, 328, 330, 332, 333, 334, 336
disposition, viii, 13, 107, 111, 112, 114, 119
dissatisfaction, 155, 163
dissonance, 6, 164
distress, 47
distribution, xi, 16, 95, 227
disutility, 258, 259
diversity, 29, 89, 111
division of labor, 265
dominance, 130

donations, viii, 35, 36, 37, 39, 40, 42, 43, 44, 45, 46, 47, 48, 50, 51
donors, 39, 40, 41, 42, 43, 44, 45, 46, 50, 51
doping, 180, 184
drawing, 71, 109
dream, 108
drug abuse, 304
drug abusers, 304
drug treatment, 303
drugs, 261, 301

E

eastern cultures, 129, 138
economic status, 131
economic theory, 261, 268
economics, vii, viii, xii, 35, 36, 37, 38, 39, 42, 43, 44, 45, 47, 50, 51, 257, 258, 261, 265, 268, 285, 292
education, viii, ix, x, 7, 10, 17, 21, 61, 62, 70, 79, 80, 82, 83, 90, 107, 108, 110, 120, 121, 125, 126, 127, 137, 140, 144, 169, 170, 173, 174, 175, 176, 177, 178, 179, 180, 181, 182, 184, 186, 187, 200, 201, 209, 212, 224, 233, 241, 245, 246, 248, 252, 254, 255, 265, 285, 308, 309, 310
education reform, 254
educational attainment, 190, 203
educational experience, 80, 221
educational institutions, 79, 80
educational opportunities, 80
educational research, 127, 224
educational settings, 79, 127
educational system, 138
educators, ix, 79, 125, 126, 140, 218, 265, 274
effort level, xii, 257, 258, 259, 263
elaboration, 77, 115, 272, 274, 276, 279, 280
elementary school, xii, 130, 142, 143, 203, 204, 245, 246, 248, 249, 251, 252, 253, 254, 293
elephants, 22
elucidation, 298
e-mail, 93, 94
emergency, 297, 298, 304
emotion, 4, 13, 142, 150, 167
emotional disorder, 8
emotional experience, 184
emotional stability, 47
emotional state, 322
emotionality, 321
empathy, 38, 302, 305, 315, 316, 320, 322
empirical studies, 11, 12, 288, 291, 335
employees, 41, 265
encouragement, 62, 202
energy, 50, 104, 113, 229

engineering, ix, 107, 108, 110, 113, 116, 117, 120, 122, 124, 262
England, 167, 205, 283, 319
English Language, 209
enrollment, 91
environment, 3, 4, 5, 10, 11, 18, 19, 21, 47, 50, 62, 107, 109, 111, 112, 113, 114, 116, 117, 118, 139, 169, 171, 178, 239, 246, 258, 265, 273, 331
environmental factors, 171, 272
environmental influences, 18
environmental variables, 13
equality, 63
equilibrium, 4, 20
equipment, 157
equity, 6
Estonia, 175
ethics, 132, 213
ethnic background, 131, 141
ethnicity, ix, 6, 90, 125, 131
etiology, 330
Europe, 56, 90, 285
European Union, 184
everyday life, 9, 22, 254, 311, 335, 337, 339
evidence, x, xiii, 4, 31, 34, 42, 44, 45, 46, 48, 49, 74, 78, 79, 86, 87, 88, 92, 94, 101, 113, 116, 127, 133, 148, 149, 151, 156, 170, 171, 173, 174, 175, 176, 179, 180, 182, 192, 201, 203, 209, 212, 215, 219, 220, 221, 222, 224, 228, 230, 243, 273, 295, 297, 300, 309, 325, 329, 337
evolution, 18, 122, 142
examinations, 211, 213, 219, 220, 222, 246, 248, 249
excess body weight, viii, 85, 86, 87, 101
exchange relationship, 38, 46, 47
exclusion, 43
exercise, 92, 103, 104, 105, 172, 182, 183, 185, 186, 229, 232, 236, 240, 241, 242, 243, 244, 292
exercise programs, 92
expectancy-value theory, 212
expertise, 12, 13, 120, 257
exposure, 10, 152, 153
external influences, 36, 39, 230
external locus of control, 42
external validity, 89, 90, 101
externalizing disorders, 297
extraversion, 47
extrinsic motivation, x, xii, 39, 41, 42, 43, 44, 45, 46, 48, 50, 82, 88, 104, 108, 109, 121, 169, 170, 171, 185, 186, 189, 190, 194, 196, 197, 198, 199, 201, 202, 204, 205, 245, 246, 247, 248, 251, 254, 255, 261, 265, 299
extrinsic rewards, 42, 43, 45, 46, 49, 51, 74, 123

F

Fabrication, 165
Facebook, 93
factor analysis, 68, 113, 132, 308, 309
families, viii, 61, 118, 131
family characteristics, 145
family environment, 298
family members, 10
family relationships, 10
family support, 15
fat, viii, 85, 87
fauna, 21, 22
fear, 8, 76, 293, 302
federal government, 233
feelings, 3, 8, 11, 13, 42, 77, 111, 115, 117, 137, 148, 151, 170, 172, 229, 239, 254, 313, 316, 317, 318, 320
fidelity, 313
financial, 27, 42, 43, 44, 214
financial incentives, 44
Finland, 175
fish, 145
fitness, 36, 93
flaws, 313
flexibility, 22, 109, 110, 113, 115, 121
flight, 12, 24
fluid, xiii, 284
food, 22, 49, 50, 93, 99, 101, 103, 185
food intake, 99
food production, 185
force, 14, 29, 108, 334
Ford, 313, 314, 315, 316, 317, 318, 319, 320, 321, 329, 330, 331, 334, 335, 337
foreign language, 254
forensic settings, 322
formation, 23, 28, 30, 32, 34, 110, 124, 128, 129, 167, 172, 173, 177, 178, 179, 181, 230, 239
formula, 91, 92, 105
foundations, 89, 123
fragments, 160
framing, 51, 201, 232
France, 121
franchise, 259
freedom, 68, 98, 114, 116, 117, 262
Freud, 4, 5, 108, 122
Freud, Sigmund, 122
friendship, 3, 12
fringe benefits, 269, 271
fruits, 87, 93
functional approach, 117
fundraising, 51
funds, 46, 48, 51, 157

G

gambling, 321
gender differences, ix, xii, 125, 129, 130, 133, 136, 138, 140, 141, 142, 145, 203, 245, 246, 247, 248, 253, 287, 288
gender orientation, 138, 144
gender role, 130, 138, 337
general education, 182
general knowledge, 233, 235, 238
generalizability, 89, 101, 131
Germany, 142, 164
gifted, 130, 145
glue, 301
goal attainment, 219
goal setting, xii, 177, 211, 225, 230, 236, 283, 284, 291
goal-setting, 239
goose, 122
grades, x, 63, 131, 142, 169, 189, 194, 207, 210, 213, 218, 247, 251, 253, 256, 272, 274, 275, 276, 279, 281
graduate students, 224, 325
Great Britain, 174
Greece, 169, 174
grouping, 112
growth, 2, 22, 41, 192, 253
guessing, 153, 190
guidance, 122
guidelines, 103, 132, 194, 235
guilt, 41, 88, 100, 170, 171, 229, 321, 322
guilty, 92, 267

H

happiness, 35, 164
harmony, 62
health, viii, xi, 7, 8, 15, 62, 85, 86, 87, 88, 89, 90, 91, 92, 95, 99, 100, 101, 102, 104, 167, 172, 181, 183, 214, 227, 228, 229, 230, 232, 241, 242, 243, 244, 297, 298, 299, 300, 301, 336
Health and Human Services, 243
health care, 86
health care system, 86
health condition, xi, 227, 228, 229
health effects, viii, 85
health information, 228, 230
health problems, 297
health promotion, 228, 230
health psychology, 183
health risks, 167
height, 8, 91
helping behavior, 35, 36, 38, 39

heterogeneity, 16, 30
hierarchy of needs, 12
high school, 65, 138, 141, 142, 145, 182, 203, 287, 293
higher education, 81, 84, 210, 224, 293
Hispanics, 129
history, 109, 220, 223, 297, 308, 309, 323
histrionic personality disorder, 321, 327, 331, 335, 337
hobby, 264
homeostasis, 2, 3
homes, 42, 63
homework, 145, 256
homogeneity, 325, 327
Hong Kong, 32, 34, 61, 142
hospitality, 24
host, 109
hostility, 321
hotel, 8, 50
House, 56, 58
housing, 62
human, 2, 4, 5, 18, 88, 90, 104, 109, 110, 123, 169, 183, 185, 230, 253, 254, 268, 281
human behavior, 90, 183, 254, 268, 281
human motivation, 4, 5, 88, 230
human nature, 104
Hungary, 175
Hunter, 62, 82
hygiene, 262
hypothesis, 24, 28, 100, 101, 115, 116, 123, 137, 138, 172, 175, 176, 179, 232, 292
hypothyroidism, 91

I

ideal, 109, 229, 239
ideals, 265, 316
identification, 15, 17, 19, 22, 24, 30, 148, 275
identity, ix, 7, 37, 44, 47, 88, 125, 126, 128, 129, 131, 133, 139, 140, 141, 142, 143, 245, 313, 321
ideology, 18
idiopathic, 332
idiosyncratic, 174
image, vii, 1, 16, 23, 27, 28, 29, 30, 31, 34, 40, 43
imagery, 122
images, 14, 30, 38
imagination, 12, 13, 112, 116, 165
improvements, xi, 210, 217, 221, 222, 242, 263
impulses, 4, 5, 23
impulsive, 335
impulsivity, 320, 322, 329, 333, 334
incarceration, 331
incidence, 28

income, 7, 40, 45, 84, 259
independence, 19, 22, 128, 262, 301, 315
independent variable, 136
indirect effect, 173, 176, 230
individual character, 40, 120, 329
individual characteristics, 40, 120, 329
individual differences, 37, 38, 41, 47, 51, 188, 192, 292
individualism, 118, 124, 128
individualistic values, 118
individuality, 62
individuation, xiii, 295
Indonesia, 131
industry, 34
inferences, 253, 334
inferiority, 330
inflation, 95
information processing, xi, 14, 210, 213, 217
information seeking, 164
informed consent, 64, 93, 213, 249
initiation, 171
injury, 234, 298, 316, 317
inmates, 323, 335
inner world, 112, 115, 116, 117, 124
institutions, viii, x, 2, 16, 43, 209, 224
instrumental music, 130
integration, x, 14, 88, 164, 166, 169, 172, 173, 174, 179, 181, 183
integrity, 134, 153, 167, 317
intellect, 122
intelligence, vii, xii, 204, 283, 284, 285, 292
interaction effect, ix, 125, 126, 131, 138
interaction effects, ix, 125, 126, 131, 138
interdependence, 128
interestingness, 192
interface, 93
internal consistency, 94, 96, 132, 195, 275, 276, 308, 309, 340
internalization, 185, 282
internalizing, 297
interpersonal communication, 336
interpersonal interactions, 312
interpersonal relations, 12, 46, 254, 312, 322
interpersonal relationships, 46, 312, 322
interpersonal skills, 332
interpretability, 93, 94
interrelations, 109
Intervals, 275
intervention, x, 82, 87, 104, 120, 178, 182, 187, 223, 241, 243, 260, 272, 292, 293, 297, 299, 301, 302, 303, 304, 333, 335
intrinsic motivation, xii, 41, 42, 43, 44, 45, 46, 50, 88, 89, 90, 94, 95, 99, 100, 102, 104, 108, 109,

110, 144, 170, 174, 184, 189, 190, 191, 192, 194, 196, 197, 199, 201, 203, 204, 205, 245, 246, 247, 248, 251, 252, 253, 257, 258, 260, 261, 262, 263, 264, 265, 266, 268, 269, 274, 299, 308
inventions, 121, 122
inventiveness, 122
investment, 82, 100, 112, 117, 143, 156, 157, 158, 264
Iraq, 131
isolation, 62, 79
Israel, 107, 124
issues, 16, 64, 80, 87, 88, 90, 92, 95, 102, 127, 145, 164, 218, 297, 305, 309, 312, 314, 330, 333, 335, 337
Italy, 8

J

Japan, 131, 142, 209, 245, 246, 247, 255, 257, 262, 307, 308
Jews, 56
job environment, 10
job performance, 48
Jordan, 296, 303, 317, 337
junior high school, 203, 248, 252, 292
justification, 149, 150, 151, 156, 163
juvenile justice, 300

K

Kenya, 22
Keynes, 124
kill, 191, 192, 197, 198, 199
kindergarten, 254
kinship, 10, 47
Korea, 32, 131
Kuwait, 30

L

labor market, 259
language skills, 188, 200, 201, 204
languages, 131
Latin America, 142
LEA, 339, 340
lead, x, 5, 7, 9, 108, 128, 137, 139, 150, 151, 154, 163, 169, 171, 172, 173, 177, 179, 192, 229, 231, 240, 246, 273
learned helplessness, 88
learners, 127, 129, 211, 220, 273, 307, 309
learning activity, 185, 272, 273

Learning and Study Skills Strategies Inventory (LASSI), x, 209
learning behavior, 272, 273, 286
learning environment, 252, 273
learning outcomes, 76, 130, 134, 188
learning process, xiii, 79, 137, 273, 307
learning skills, 223, 224, 273
learning task, 126, 271, 272
Lebanon, 131
leisure, viii, x, 9, 12, 13, 18, 24, 33, 85, 87, 92, 169, 170, 171, 173, 174, 175, 176, 177, 178, 179, 180, 181, 182, 183, 184, 185, 231, 241
leisure time, x, 92, 169, 175, 177, 181
leisure-time physical activity (LTPA), viii, 85, 87
lens, 178
liberty, 19
life course, 46
life expectancy, 86
life experiences, 221
lifestyle behaviors, viii, 85, 87, 89
lifetime, 304
light, vii, 2, 75, 80, 108, 221, 222, 318, 320, 322, 331
literacy, 191, 202, 203, 204
locus, 37, 42, 128, 185, 246, 247, 281, 282
logistics, 64
longitudinal study, 48, 81, 202, 203, 292
long-term retention, 299
love, 19, 321
loyalty, vii, 1, 2, 16, 17, 23, 26, 27, 30, 34
lying, 312, 313, 315, 317, 318, 320, 321, 322, 323, 325, 327, 329, 330, 331, 335, 337, 338, 340

M

magnetism, 28
magnitude, 81, 216, 287
majority, xi, 39, 115, 190, 227, 229, 230, 297, 298, 300, 331
Malaysia, 131
malingering, 329, 339, 340
man, 35
management, vii, xi, xii, 2, 14, 16, 29, 41, 87, 210, 213, 214, 215, 216, 217, 220, 222, 262, 265, 272, 283, 284, 286, 287, 323, 325
manipulation, 108, 129, 154, 313, 320, 322, 330, 333
MANOVA, 71, 75, 79, 133, 136, 249, 250
marijuana, 296, 304
marital status, 91
market segment, 16, 18, 32
marketing, viii, 7, 13, 14, 16, 17, 26, 35, 36, 37, 38, 39, 40, 43, 45, 49, 50, 51, 286
marketplace, 337
marriage, 337

mass, viii, 85
materials, 14, 74, 76, 114, 132, 194, 201
mathematical knowledge, 273
mathematical methods, 109
mathematics, 124, 130, 141, 142, 143, 187, 202, 203, 223, 286, 288
mathematics education, 142
matrix, 97, 112, 291, 308
matter, 119, 122, 160, 181, 314, 335
measurement, 28, 65, 70, 104, 133, 134, 137, 145, 173, 178, 185, 211, 254, 275, 291
measurements, 213, 222, 291, 337, 340
media, 30, 118, 302
median, 285
mediation, 292
medical, 2, 9, 40, 92, 234, 285, 293, 300, 303, 339
medical assistance, 92
medical care, 9, 300
medication, 229
memorizing, 76
memory, x, 153, 154, 156, 187, 188, 192, 194, 195, 197, 198, 199, 203, 213, 319
memory capacity, 199
memory performance, 155, 156
mental disorder, 304, 329, 336, 339
mental health, 6, 240, 298, 323, 325
mental health professionals, 323, 325
mental illness, 241, 242, 336
mental simulation, 165
mental state, 110
MES, 286, 288, 291
messages, xi, 49, 50, 51, 167, 181, 227, 229, 230, 231, 232, 233, 234, 235, 236, 237, 238, 239, 240, 241, 242
meta analysis, 242
meta-analysis, 83, 103, 142, 172, 173, 183, 211, 223, 272, 281, 293, 300
Metabolic, 103
metacognition, 183, 276, 279, 280
metacognitive knowledge, 282
methodology, 78, 110, 124, 233
migrants, 126
military, 338
Ministry of Education, 245, 254, 255
minority groups, 81
misuse, 145, 296
models, vii, xii, xiii, 2, 4, 6, 14, 22, 26, 62, 95, 98, 99, 108, 109, 111, 129, 133, 141, 142, 143, 149, 150, 159, 176, 181, 212, 257, 258, 260, 261, 275, 284, 291, 303, 312, 314, 329
moderates, 152
mood disorder, 229, 334
moral development, 37

moral hazard, 258
Motivated Strategies for Learning Questionnaire (MSLQ), xii, 144, 271, 274
motivation model, 10
MRI, 47
multidimensional, ix, 7, 16, 41, 45, 125, 128, 142, 143, 180, 203, 293
multiple factors, 7
multiple regression, 94, 214
multiple regression analyses, 94
multiple-choice questions, 132
multivariate analysis, 133, 249, 250
murder, 333
museums, 9, 19, 24, 25
music, 122, 151, 330
mutations, 164

N

naming, 21
narcissism, 320, 328, 338
narcissistic personality disorder, 320
national income, 45
National Institute of Mental Health, 243
National Institutes of Health, 243
national parks, 20
nationality, 11, 33
NCS, 304
negative consequences, 318
negative effects, 45, 46
negative emotions, 88, 100
negative experiences, 12
negative mood, 161
negative outcomes, 46, 156, 163, 166, 233
negative reinforcement, 171
negative relation, 190
neglect, 172
negotiating, 129
Netherlands, 224, 283, 285
neutral, 148, 152, 153, 155, 259, 287
New South Wales, 62, 83, 132, 141
New Zealand, 209, 212, 224
next generation, 102, 141
NNFI, 68, 69, 70, 72, 275
non-clinical population, 243
Non-Normed Fit Index, 68, 275
nonprofit organizations, viii, 35, 51
non-psychopathic offenders, 338
normal distribution, 259
North America, 228, 304, 337
Northern Territory (NT), viii, 61
Norway, 33
nostalgia, 15

O

obesity, 86, 103, 104
obstacles, 110
offenders, xiii, 311, 312, 313, 314, 316, 317, 319, 321, 322, 323, 324, 325, 326, 327, 328, 329, 330, 331, 332, 333, 334, 335, 336, 338, 340
OH, 35
online information, 228, 240
online learning, 223
openness, 112, 113, 116, 118
opportunities, 17, 43, 150, 157, 177, 213, 252, 259
Oppositional Defiant Disorder, 297
opt out, 45
optimism, 140, 304
optimization, 258, 260, 263, 266
organism, 3
organize, 211
organs, viii, 35, 36, 37, 40
original training, 324
originality, 110, 114
outreach, 297
overlap, 101, 331, 333, 340
overweight, 86, 87, 90, 91, 103
ox, 229

P

pain, 4
parallel, 230, 286, 292
paranoid personality disorder, 332
parental influence, 272
parenting, 303, 305
parents, xiii, 2, 64, 66, 132, 137, 138, 175, 177, 206, 248, 249, 255, 256, 265, 267, 295, 298, 299, 305
parole, 312, 313, 323, 335
parole board, 313
participants, xii, 38, 43, 44, 45, 49, 50, 63, 64, 65, 66, 71, 75, 78, 86, 90, 92, 93, 101, 102, 105, 113, 116, 152, 153, 154, 155, 157, 158, 159, 160, 161, 214, 217, 220, 221, 222, 245, 247, 248, 253, 273, 275, 276, 280, 313, 317, 329, 331, 334
partition, 254
passive-aggressive, 319
path model, 140
pathology, xiii, 311, 312, 313, 322, 324, 326, 327, 330, 333, 334
pathways, 336
patriotism, 7, 15
PCL-R, 319, 322, 323, 324, 328, 337
peace, 24
Pearson correlations, 97
peer group, 62

peer relationship, 82
peer review, 300
perceived control, 150, 165
perceptions of control, 148, 159
performers, 322
permission, x, 64, 210, 301
permit, 12, 17, 27, 30, 319
perpetrators, 329
perseverance, 77, 112, 117, 200
personal development, 18, 40
personal goals, 115, 118, 181
personal history, 4, 165
personal relations, 19, 74
personal relationship, 19, 74
personal responsibility, ix, 147, 151, 156, 161, 163
personal values, 22, 86
personality, xiii, 4, 17, 18, 37, 44, 47, 48, 50, 84, 109, 118, 122, 123, 164, 172, 177, 292, 305, 311, 312, 319, 320, 321, 322, 323, 324, 325, 326, 327, 328, 329, 330, 331, 332, 333, 334, 335, 336, 338, 339, 340
personality characteristics, 37, 329
personality differences, 37
personality disorder, xiii, 311, 312, 319, 320, 322, 323, 324, 325, 327, 328, 330, 331, 332, 333, 334, 335, 336, 338, 339, 340
personality traits, 37, 44, 47, 48, 50, 109, 118, 123, 330
personality type, 329
Philadelphia, 104, 292, 339
physical activity, viii, x, xi, 85, 87, 92, 95, 96, 97, 100, 103, 104, 169, 170, 171, 172, 173, 174, 175, 176, 177, 178, 179, 180, 181, 182, 183, 184, 185, 227, 228, 232, 236, 238, 241, 242, 243
physical activity (PA), xi, 227, 228, 238
Physical Activity Web, vi, 227
physical education, x, 169, 170, 171, 173, 174, 175, 176, 177, 178, 179, 180, 181, 182, 183, 184, 185, 281
physical exercise, 243
physical fitness, 92
physical health, xi, 6, 228
physical inactivity, 103, 234
physics, 282
Physiological, 6
physiology, 104
pilot study, 296, 303, 314, 323
PISA, 64, 69, 77, 78, 83
platform, 338
playing, 47, 157
pleasure, 4, 8, 13, 14, 19, 31, 32, 35, 91, 143, 170, 229, 249, 263, 318, 320
Poland, 174

police, 71, 72, 73, 266, 323, 325
policy, 16, 82, 177, 245, 303, 340
policymakers, 14
politics, 337
poor performance, ix, 147, 148, 150, 151, 154, 163
poor readers, 192, 201
population, xi, 46, 89, 130, 185, 201, 227, 229, 232, 234, 238, 240, 242, 313, 319, 322, 334, 338
Portugal, 32
positive attitudes, 49, 127, 178, 219, 286
positive behaviors, 286
positive correlation, 139, 140
positive feedback, 177
positive influences, 127, 134, 139
positive mood, 152, 229
positive relationship, 26, 190
potato, 2
poverty, 62
precedent, 315
predictive validity, 92, 93, 282
predictor variables, 98, 105
prejudice, 62
preparation, 152, 220, 222
preservation, 331
prestige, 3, 10, 28, 43, 44, 322
prevention, 49, 50, 87
primacy, 334
primary school, ix, 125, 126, 130, 131, 138, 139, 200, 272, 281
priming, 44
principles, 35, 37, 234, 285
prisons, 319, 323, 339
private information, xii, 257
probability, 14, 23, 27, 31, 98, 101, 113, 266
probe, 335
problem behavior, 340
problem drinking, 304
problem solving, 108, 110, 112, 114, 122, 230, 239, 301
problem-based learning, xii, 283, 284, 285, 292, 293
problem-solving, 108, 119
professionals, 86, 87, 92, 100, 101, 322
profit, 49, 157, 264, 266
profitability, 26
programming, 141
project, viii, 39, 61, 110, 124, 274, 281, 286
promax rotation, 309
proposition, 148, 179, 264
prosocial behavior, 35, 36, 41
protection, 149, 150, 151, 152, 153, 154, 155, 163, 167, 313
prototype, 338
psychiatry, 339

psychological development, 252, 255
psychological health, 228
psychological processes, 6
psychological variables, 63, 64
psychological well-being, 183, 243
psychologist, 335
psychology, vii, viii, xii, 7, 18, 35, 36, 37, 38, 39, 40, 42, 43, 45, 50, 51, 81, 83, 122, 123, 142, 144, 163, 167, 185, 243, 246, 254, 257, 258, 260, 268, 337
psychometric properties, 211, 274
psychopathic offenders, 323, 329
psychopathic personality disorder, 331
psychopathology, 333, 336, 339
psychopaths, 314, 315, 316, 322, 323, 327, 328, 329, 330, 331, 332, 333, 335, 337, 338, 340
psychopathy, 314, 318, 320, 322, 323, 324, 328, 329, 330, 331, 332, 333, 335, 338, 339, 340
Psychopathy Checklist Revised, 340
public goods, 38, 39, 44
public health, 86, 87, 103
public schools, 131
punishment, xiv, 43, 44, 45, 170, 171, 189, 311, 313, 314, 315, 316, 317, 323, 327, 329, 331, 333

Q

qualitative research, 80
quality of service, 16, 23, 28, 29
quantification, 18
query, 88
questioning, 177, 192, 199
questionnaire, viii, xii, 22, 64, 93, 107, 112, 116, 194, 195, 245, 246, 247, 249, 253, 282, 288, 308
questionnaire of creativity (COQ-CR), viii, 107

R

race, 17, 129
reaction time, 161
reactions, 292, 320
reactivity, 321
reading, vii, ix, x, 64, 65, 125, 130, 132, 138, 141, 187, 188, 189, 190, 191, 192, 193, 194, 195, 196, 197, 198, 199, 200, 201, 202, 203, 204, 205, 206, 207, 224
reading competency, x, 187, 196, 197, 199
reading comprehension, 188, 190, 191, 192, 193, 195, 197, 198, 199, 200, 201, 203, 204, 205
reading skills, x, 187, 188, 192, 198, 200, 201, 202, 204, 205
real numbers, 259
real time, 110

realism, 36
reality, 111, 119, 165, 167, 316, 317, 322
reasoning, 89, 90, 118
recall, 155, 194, 275
recidivism, 320, 338
reciprocity, 36, 39, 40
recognition, 6, 74, 189, 194, 201, 297
recommendations, 228, 339
reconciliation, 82
recovery, xiii, 20, 231, 295, 296, 297, 302, 335
recovery process, 296
recreation, 9, 12
recreational, 180
referees, 113
reform, 245, 254, 255
Reform, 245
regression, x, 10, 94, 95, 98, 99, 104, 105, 197, 198, 210, 214, 215, 218, 291, 309
regression analysis, 214, 309
regression model, 94, 95, 98, 99, 105, 309
regulations, x, xii, 88, 90, 92, 95, 98, 105, 112, 114, 117, 169, 170, 172, 174, 175, 176, 181, 186, 271, 281
reinforcement, 170
rejection, 8, 144, 297, 321
relatives, 11, 38
relaxation, 10, 11, 13, 19, 22, 24, 27, 28
relevance, xiv, 6, 64, 65, 79, 83, 211, 228, 231, 311, 312
reliability, viii, 61, 65, 66, 68, 78, 92, 94, 96, 133, 233, 249, 308, 324, 325, 333
relief, 6
REM, 148
remorse, 315, 322
remote schools, 63, 64, 65
replication, 116
reputation, 288
requirements, 5, 102, 108, 115, 116, 124, 221
researchers, viii, xiii, 9, 22, 28, 35, 36, 37, 38, 39, 40, 43, 44, 45, 46, 47, 49, 50, 51, 64, 126, 127, 129, 131, 140, 189, 213, 218, 240, 246, 247, 252, 261, 274, 295, 296, 298, 302, 313, 319, 334
reserves, 21, 22, 30
residuals, 95
resistance, 112, 301
resolution, 123
resource management, 272
resources, viii, 2, 16, 17, 29, 30, 38, 62, 99, 100, 109, 149, 156, 157, 159, 180, 192, 201, 228, 231, 312
response, xiii, 7, 13, 14, 23, 39, 42, 51, 64, 75, 77, 92, 94, 101, 105, 164, 213, 252, 286, 295, 296, 302, 305, 336
response format, 64, 92, 213

retaliation, 316, 317
retention rate, 62
rewards, 11, 42, 43, 51, 74, 118, 170, 260, 265
rhythm, 177
rights, 322
rings, 93
risk, xiii, 14, 30, 37, 91, 112, 117, 210, 224, 228, 229, 231, 243, 254, 259, 266, 267, 295, 299, 301, 304, 320, 337, 338
risks, 51, 233, 234
risk-taking, 37, 112, 117
RMSEA, 68, 69, 72, 133, 135, 275, 291
robberies, 333
role conflict, 313
root, 133
Root Mean Square Residual, 68
roots, 300
routines, 15, 20, 22
rules, 111, 112, 117, 194
rural areas, 31, 33
rural tourists, vii, 2, 24

S

sadness, 229
safety, 109, 122
schema, 179
schizoid personality disorder, 332, 334
schizophrenia, 334
Schizotypal Personality Disorder, 340
school achievement, 62, 81, 82, 143, 144, 164, 187, 205, 223
school work, 200, 206
schooling, ix, 62, 63, 64, 80, 83, 125, 126, 128, 130, 131, 133, 136, 137, 139, 140
science, x, 124, 130, 142, 144, 165, 203, 209, 224, 293
scientific knowledge, xi, 227
scientific progress, 122
scope, 37, 123, 246, 288
SCT, 230, 231, 233, 238, 239
second language, xiii, 63, 307
secondary education, viii, 61, 205
secondary school students, xii, 271, 272, 274
secondary schools, 145
secondary students, xii, 145, 271, 279
security, 5, 319
self esteem, 314
self-assessment, 164, 167
self-concept, ix, 82, 83, 125, 126, 127, 128, 130, 131, 132, 139, 141, 142, 143, 145, 149, 189, 191, 192, 202, 203, 204, 205
self-confidence, 211

Index

self-control, 87, 118
self-destructive behavior, 36
self-discovery, 6, 12
self-efficacy, xi, xii, 82, 140, 148, 159, 163, 164, 167, 211, 225, 227, 230, 231, 232, 233, 234, 235, 238, 239, 240, 241, 243, 272, 274, 276, 279, 280, 283, 284, 293, 301
self-enhancement, 41, 46
self-esteem, 6, 37, 40, 144, 149, 150, 151, 152, 155, 163, 164, 166, 312, 313, 316, 317, 320, 321, 330
self-image, 10, 320
self-improvement, 149, 151, 152, 153, 154, 155, 156, 159, 163
self-interest, 38, 42
self-monitoring, 230, 236, 239
self-perceptions, 128, 130, 138, 142, 144, 203, 213, 219
self-presentation, xiv, 311, 314, 316, 317, 318, 320, 323, 327, 328, 329, 330, 331, 332, 334, 335, 339
self-regulation, vii, ix, x, xi, xii, 77, 81, 84, 104, 144, 147, 149, 150, 159, 163, 164, 180, 184, 205, 209, 210, 211, 213, 218, 219, 220, 222, 223, 225, 227, 230, 231, 232, 233, 234, 235, 238, 239, 272, 274, 276, 281, 283, 284, 293
self-reports, 174, 315
self-worth, 88, 100, 148, 152, 239, 321
semi-structured interviews, 324
senior visitors, vii, 2
sensations, 29
sensitivity, 259, 263, 264, 267, 320
sentencing, 312
service quality, 26, 28
services, 8, 13, 25, 210, 218, 223, 301, 304
sex, 6
SFT, xi, 210
shame, 88, 100, 170, 171, 316, 317, 318, 320
shape, vii, 1, 2, 118, 127, 128, 272
short term memory, 194
showing, ix, 125, 127, 136, 140, 154, 189, 190, 210, 216, 217, 251, 334
shyness, 62
side effects, 229
signals, 286
silver, 8
simulation, 165, 167
Singapore, xii, 174, 271, 272, 279, 282
skills training, 211
smoking, 185
social acceptance, 43
social behavior, 144, 166, 167
social class, 17
social cognition, 166, 167, 184
social comparison, 149, 153

social context, 169, 329
social desirability, 101
social development, 144
social environment, 170, 171, 173, 178
social exchange, 30
social group, 18, 43, 44
social identity, 142
social image, 313
social influence, 51, 128
social influences, 51, 128
social interactions, 11, 46, 194, 312, 313
social justice, viii, 61
social learning, 300
social network, 51, 93
social norms, 44, 180, 182
social psychology, 30, 31, 33, 121, 166, 167, 170, 241, 258, 260
social relations, 6, 41
social relationships, 41
social rewards, 43, 45, 46, 51
social sciences, 212, 288
social situations, 320
social status, 6, 43, 44, 266
social support, 273, 298
socialization, 62, 63, 330
society, 19, 70, 112, 118, 119, 261, 311, 313, 335
sociology, 7, 303
solution, 122, 133, 263, 266, 267, 276, 308, 309
solution space, 122
South Africa, 84
Spain, 1, 8, 30, 33, 121
Spearman-Brown, 324, 325
specialists, 157, 158
species, 224
specifications, 107
speculation, 138, 279, 297
speech, 302, 340
spelling, 205
spinal cord, xi, 227, 229, 231, 238, 240, 241, 242
spinal cord injury, xi, 227, 229, 231, 238, 240, 241, 242
sports events, 19
Sri Lanka, 131
stability, 93, 116, 220, 222
standard deviation, 77, 136, 215, 276, 287
standard of living, 45
standpoint of consumption, vii, 1
state, 3, 4, 5, 7, 14, 49, 50, 88, 152, 159, 194, 252, 253, 265
states, 4, 9, 12, 111, 159, 165, 166, 180, 261, 262, 265, 302, 315, 317, 319
Statistical Package for the Social Sciences, 249
statistics, 70, 86, 94, 95, 96, 224, 275, 286, 287, 288

stereotypes, 130, 138, 142
stimulus, 4, 12, 13, 119
stomach, 5
strategic planning, 30
strategy use, 192, 211
stress, 6, 9, 12, 20, 21, 23, 27, 46, 190, 219, 258, 321
stressors, 312
structural equation modeling, 126, 139, 140, 143
structure, 5, 28, 83, 99, 102, 109, 111, 113, 116, 142, 163, 166, 212, 280, 282, 321, 338, 339
structuring, 185
student achievement, 128, 144, 212, 292
student motivation, 81, 83, 126, 143, 182, 212, 218, 224, 293
style, 7, 10, 62, 178, 303, 312, 320
Styles, 67, 68
subgroups, xiii, 295
substance abuse, xiii, 295, 296, 297, 298, 299, 300, 301, 302, 303, 304
substance use, xiii, 295, 296, 297, 298, 299, 300, 301, 302, 303, 304, 305
supervision, 102
support services, 218
survival, 3, 5, 45, 82
susceptibility, 87
Swahili, 153, 154
sweat, 92, 99
sympathy, 47, 331
symptomology, 297
symptoms, 234, 239, 244, 297, 318, 321, 335, 336

T

Taiwan, 310
talent, 114, 117, 322
target, 6, 14, 30, 51, 88, 89, 90, 171, 178, 180, 222, 228, 239, 240, 297, 301, 302, 313, 314, 315, 316, 317, 318, 319, 320, 322, 330, 331, 332, 335
target behavior, 88, 90, 301
target population, 89
target populations, 89
task demands, 138
task difficulty, 212
task performance, 154
taxonomy, 7, 41, 45, 312, 336
TDI, 28
teachers, 62, 63, 79, 110, 113, 120, 124, 139, 173, 175, 176, 177, 179, 183, 184, 185, 201, 245, 249, 253, 255, 256, 272, 273, 274, 280, 310
team members, 109, 262
teams, 109
techniques, xi, 101, 143, 177, 210, 220, 232, 243, 309

technology, 121, 122, 124, 185, 223
teens, 285, 296, 297, 298, 299, 300, 302
telephone, 93
tension, 4, 5, 6, 159, 312
tenure, 303
tertiary education, xi, 210, 218
test anxiety, 220, 274, 280
test items, 153, 155
test scores, 275, 276
test statistic, 133, 287
testing, xi, 36, 111, 115, 133, 174, 178, 204, 210, 213, 214, 215, 216, 217, 219, 220, 221, 222, 230, 280, 300
textbook, 336
textbooks, 336
theft, 2
theoretical approaches, 174, 178
theoretical support, 42, 43
therapeutic community, 296, 299, 304
therapeutic process, 335
therapist, 301, 305, 335
therapy, 229, 335
thoughts, ix, 77, 147, 148, 150, 151, 153, 154, 155, 157, 159, 161, 163, 165, 166, 167, 171, 229, 254, 288, 291, 304, 339
threats, 317, 320
tobacco, 300
tourism, vii, 1, 2, 3, 6, 7, 9, 11, 13, 14, 16, 17, 18, 19, 20, 22, 23, 24, 26, 27, 28, 29, 30, 31, 32, 33, 34
tourist sector, vii, 1, 2, 7
TPA, viii, 85, 87
trade, 45, 149
trade-off, 45, 149
traditions, 22
training, 9, 110, 119, 121, 201, 224, 272, 281, 324, 325
traits, 18, 36, 47, 48, 118, 314, 321, 330, 332, 334
translation, 153
transportation, 266
travel agency, 34
traveler behavior, vii, 1
treatment, xiii, 25, 29, 87, 232, 258, 295, 296, 297, 298, 299, 300, 302, 303, 304, 305, 312, 335, 338, 339
trial, 87, 104, 161, 241
turnover, 62

U

UK, 54, 104, 122, 123, 187, 225, 242, 243
understanding texts, 199
United Kingdom, 13, 87
United Nations, 7

universality, 174
universities, x, 50, 209
university education, 285
updating, 109
urban, 65, 66, 68, 70, 71, 73, 74, 75, 77, 79, 205
USA, 142, 147, 163

V

validation, 78, 81, 83, 101, 143, 185, 293
valuation, viii, 2, 24
variables, 7, 11, 18, 19, 20, 21, 22, 24, 26, 27, 28, 29, 31, 37, 38, 40, 46, 48, 63, 64, 75, 77, 79, 95, 98, 114, 115, 116, 131, 134, 137, 140, 172, 173, 174, 175, 177, 178, 179, 180, 192, 214, 215, 217, 219, 220, 242, 248, 250, 251, 259, 262, 275, 276, 279, 280, 291, 338
variations, 99, 175, 231, 253
vegetables, 87, 93, 194
vehicles, 124
vein, 24, 175, 176, 180
venue, 179
Verbal IQ, 193, 195, 196, 197, 198
verbal persuasion, 239
victims, 323
videos, 324
videotape, 142
Vietnam, 131
violence, 254, 320, 337, 338
violent behavior, 339
violent crime, 336
violent offenders, 336
visions, viii, 62
visual stimuli, 122
visualization, 122
vocabulary, 205
volunteer work, 48

W

Washington, 122, 142, 242, 303, 336, 337, 340
wealth, 8, 199
web, 94, 242
web sites, 242
websites, xi, 227, 228, 229, 230, 232, 233, 234, 235, 238, 239, 240
weight control, 86, 87, 89, 104
weight loss, 87, 103, 105
weight management, viii, 85
welfare, 36
well-being, 4, 15, 19, 49, 81, 82, 88, 90, 100, 102, 103, 144, 228, 229, 241, 242, 331
western culture, 129, 138
withdrawal, 320
witnesses, 323
word recognition, 188
work activities, 263
work environment, 9, 77, 262, 265
workers, 11, 262
working hours, 263
working memory, 188, 192, 194, 202, 203, 205
workplace, 139
worldview, 18
worldwide, 86, 94
worry, 245, 286
wrongdoing, 317

Y

yield, 100, 129, 228, 265, 324
young adults, 90, 92, 243
young people, viii, 61, 175, 177, 298, 300